SEVENTH EDITION

# Comparative Politics
## Notes and Readings

# Comparative Politics
## Notes and Readings

ROY C. MACRIDIS
Professor of Politics
*Brandeis University*

BERNARD E. BROWN
Professor of Political Science
*The City University of New York*
*(Graduate School)*

BROOKS/COLE PUBLISHING COMPANY
PACIFIC GROVE, CALIFORNIA

Brooks/Cole Publishing Company
A Division of Wadsworth, Inc.

© 1990 by Wadsworth, Inc., Belmont, California 94002.
© 1986, 1961, 1964, 1968, 1972, and 1977 by The Dorsey Press.

Printed in the United States of America

10  9  8  7  6  5  4  3  2

**Library of Congress Cataloging in Publication Data**

Comparative politics: notes and readings / edited by Roy C. Macridis
    and Bernard E. Brown. — 7th ed.
        p.    cm.
    Includes bibliographical references.
    ISBN 0-534-12636-7
    1. Comparative government.  I. Macridis, Roy C.  II. Brown,
Bernard Edward.
JF51.C617   1990
320.3—dc20                                            89-17308
                                                      CIP

Sponsoring Editor:  *Cynthia C. Stormer*
Marketing Representative:  *Jim Brace-Thompson*
Editorial Assistant:  *Mary Ann Zuzow*
Production Editor:  *Timothy A. Phillips*
Manuscript Editor:  *Alan R. Titche*
Permissions Editor:  *Carline Haga*
Interior Design:  *Vernon T. Boes*
Cover Design:  *Erin Mauterer, Bluewater A&D*
Art Coordinator:  *Lisa Torri*
Typesetting:  *Execustaff*
Cover Printing and Binding:  *Malloy Lithographing, Inc.*

# ABOUT THE EDITORS

ROY C. MACRIDIS is Wien Professor of International Cooperation in the Department of Politics at Brandeis University and has taught previously at Harvard, Northwestern, Washington University, and the State University of New York at Buffalo. He has served as a visiting professor at Harvard, Columbia, the Institute of Political Studies of the University of Paris, and at Nanterre University (France). After receiving his B.A. from Athens College in Athens, Greece, he studied law in the University of Paris and received his M.A. and Ph.D. in Government at Harvard University (1947). Dr. Macridis has written or edited numerous publications. Among them are: *Modern Political Systems: Europe* (1986); *Contemporary Political Regimes: Institutions and Patterns* (1986); *Contemporary Political Ideologies* (1985); *The De Gaulle Republic: Quest for Unity* (with Bernard E. Brown, 1976); *French Politics in Transition: The Years after De Gaulle* (1976); and *The Study of Comparative Politics* (1956).

BERNARD E. BROWN is Professor of Political Science at the City University of New York (Graduate School) and has served as visiting professor at the universities of Paris, Saigon, Delhi, Dakar, and at McGill University (Montreal). He has received research awards from the Fulbright Commission, the Rockefeller Foundation, and the National Endowment for the Humanities. Among his many books are: *Socialism of a Different Kind: Reshaping the Left in France* (1982); *Intellectuals and Other Traitors* (1980); *Eurocommunism and Eurosocialism: The Left Confronts Modernity* (coauthor and editor, 1978); *The De Gaulle Republic: Quest for Unity* (with Roy C. Macridis, 1976); *Protest in Paris: Anatomy of a Revolt* (1974); *New Directions in Comparative Politics* (1963); and *American Conservatives* (1951).

# PREFACE

It is with particular satisfaction that we have prepared the seventh edition of this book, which now enters its fourth decade. When the first edition appeared in 1961, our aim was to introduce students to major approaches in the field of comparative politics, especially those reflecting new theories and concepts. Since then the outpouring of literature in comparative politics has been torrential, as evidenced in part by the creation of two specialized journals. We have tried to keep successive editions up to date by selecting choice articles and essays from a wide range of professional journals and books. The extraordinary longevity of this book is a tribute to the creativity, vigor, and significance of the work being done by students of comparative politics and, we should like to think, a vindication of our original conception of the discipline.

As in the past we have sought to furnish the student with selections from recent literature without losing sight of classic statements. The readings provide both tools of analysis and substantive studies that illustrate their utility. In selecting materials we have sought to avoid bias in favor of any single school, theory, or concept, by instead offering a balanced overview of approaches.

More than half of the readings in this book are new to this edition. The section on comparative method has been reorganized so as to take into account the "rediscovery" of the state as a significant factor in political performance and evolution. Greater attention has also been given to changes in communist systems in the direction of political pluralism and recourse to a market economy; the transition from authoritarianism to democracy, especially in Southern Europe and Latin America; and the differing capacities of regimes to produce effective policies. We hope that this volume will encourage a new generation of readers to explore and analyze the major issues of our time in a comparative perspective.

Our thanks go to many friends and colleagues for their advice and support. We are especially grateful to Eric C. Browne, University of Wisconsin at Milwaukee; John Harbeson, The City University of New York; Barrett L. McCormick, Marquette University, Milwaukee, Wisconsin; Peter Regenstreif, University of Rochester; Gerard F. Rutan, Western Washington University, Bellingham, Washington; and Joel D. Wolfe, University of Cincinnati, for helpful suggestions. Our thanks go also to Brooks/Cole, the new publishers of this volume, and to Cynthia C. Stormer, the Political Science Editor, for making the transition arrangements so smoothly; also to Timothy A. Phillips for the speed and the efficiency with which he supervised the production of this new edition.

It remains difficult to do justice to all points of view within the confines of one volume, and responsibility for final choices is necessarily our own. We are also grateful, of course, to authors and publishers for granting their kind permission to reprint.

*Roy C. Macridis*
*Bernard E. Brown*

# LIST OF AUTHORS

GABRIEL A. ALMOND. Emeritus Professor of Political Science, Stanford University. Author, *The American People and Foreign Policy* (1950); *The Appeals of Communism* (1954); *Political Development, Essays in Heuristic Theory* (1970); *Progress and Its Discontents* (1982). Coauthor, *The Politics of Developing Areas* (1960); *The Civic Culture* (1963); *Comparative Politics: System, Process, and Policy* (rev. ed., 1978).

ARISTOTLE (384–322 B.C.). A good one-volume collection is the Modern Library edition, *Introduction to Aristotle* (1965), edited by Richard McKeon.

SAMUEL H. BEER. Emeritus Professor of Government, Harvard University. Author, *The City of Reason* (1949); *Treasury Control* (1956); *British Politics in the Collectivist Age* (1965, 1982); *Britain Against Itself* (1982).

CRANE BRINTON (1896–1968). Late Professor of Ancient and Modern History, Harvard University. Author, *The Jacobins* (1930); *Nietzsche* (1941); *The United States and Britain* (1948); *English Political Thought in the Nineteenth Century* (1949); *Ideas and Men* (1950); *The Americans and the French* (1968).

BERNARD E. BROWN. Professor of Political Science, City University of New York (Graduate School and University Center). Author, *American Conservatives* (1951); *New Directions in Comparative Politics* (1962); *Protest in Paris* (1974); *Intellectuals and Other Traitors* (1980); *Socialism of a Different Kind: Reshaping the Left in France* (1982). Coauthor, *The De Gaulle Republic* (1960, 1963); *Cases in Comparative Politics* (3rd ed., 1976);

*Eurocommunism and Eurosocialism: The Left Confronts Modernity* (1978).

RICHARD BUSH. Deputy Director of the Asia Society's China Council, Washington, D.C. Author, *The Politics of Cotton Textiles in Kuomantang China, 1927–1937* (1982); *China Briefing* (1982).

RALF DAHRENDORF. Warden, St. Anthony's College, University of Oxford, England. Formerly, Professor of Social Science, University of Konstantz, West Germany. Author, *Class and Class Conflict in Industrial Society* (1965); *Society and Democracy in Germany* (1967); *Essays in the Theory of Society* (1968); *Life Chances* (1979); *On Britain* (1982); and many works in German.

KARL W. DEUTSCH. Emeritus Stanfield Professor of International Peace, Harvard University, and Director of the International Institute for Comparative Research, Wissenschaftszentrum, Berlin, Germany. Author, *Nationalism and Social Communication* (1953); *The Nerves of Government* (1963); *Nationalism and Its Alternatives* (1969); *Politics and Government: How People Decide Their Fate* (1974); *Tides Among Nations* (1979). Coauthor, *Germany Rejoins the Powers* (1959); *Nation-Building* (1966).

MATTEI DOGAN. Scientific Director, Centre National de Recherche Scientifique (CNRS), Paris, France. Coauthor, *How to Compare Nations: Strategies in Comparative Politics* (1984). Editor, *The Mandarins of Europe* (1975). Author of many works in French.

THOMAS R. DYE. Foundation Professor of Government and Director of the Policy Sciences

Program, Florida State University. Author, *Who's Running America* (4th ed., 1986); *Understanding Public Policy* (6th ed., 1985). Coauthor, *The Irony of Democracy* (8th ed., 1990).

DAVID EASTON. Distinguished Professor of Political Science, University of California, Irvine. Author, *The Political System* (1953); *A Framework for Political Analysis* (1965); *A Systems Analysis of Political Life* (1965). Coauthor, *Children in the Political System* (1969).

HARRY ECKSTEIN. Distinguished Professor of Social Sciences, University of California, Irvine. Author, *Pressure Group Politics* (1960); *Division and Cohesion in a Democracy: A Study of Norway* (1966). Coauthor, *Patterns of Authority* (1975). Editor, *Comparative Politics* (1963); *Internal War* (1964).

JÜRGEN HABERMAS. Professor of Philosophy, University of Frankfurt, West Germany. Author, *Toward a Rational Society, Student Protest, Science, and Politics* (1970); *Knowledge and Human Interests* (1971); *Theory and Practice* (1973); *Legitimation Crisis* (1975); *Communication and the Evolution of Society* (1979); *Philosophical–Political Profiles* (1983); *The Theory of Communicative Action* (1984).

M. DONALD HANCOCK. Professor of Political Science, Vanderbilt University. Author, *Sweden, The Politics of Postindustrial Change* (1972); *West Germany: The Politics of Democratic Corporatism* (1989). Coauthor, *Politics in the Post-Welfare State* (1968).

SAMUEL P. HUNTINGTON. Eaton Professor of the Science of Government, Harvard University. Author, *The Soldier and the State* (1957); *The Common Defense* (1961); *Political Order in Changing Societies* (1968); *American Politics, the Promise of Disharmony* (1981). Coauthor, *Political Power, USA/USSR* (1965); *Authoritarian Politics in Modern Society* (1970); *The Crisis of Democracy* (1975); *No Easy Choice, Political Participation in Developing Countries* (1976).

RONALD INGLEHART. Professor of Political Science, University of Michigan. Author, *The Silent Revolution: Changing Values and Political Styles Among Western Publics* (1977).

PETER J. KATZENSTEIN. Walter S. Carpenter Professor of International Studies, Cornell University. Author, *Corporatism and Change: Austria, Switzerland and the Politics of Industry* (1984); *Small States in World Markets: Industrial Policy in Europe* (1985); *Policy and Politics in West Germany* (1987).

ROBERT O. KEOHANE. Professor of Government, Harvard University. Author, *After Hegemony: Cooperation and Discord in the World Political Economy* (1984); *Neorealism and Its Critics* (1986); *International Institutions and State Power* (1989).

NATHAN KEYFITZ. Andelot Professor of Demography and Sociology, Harvard University. Author, *Applied Mathematical Demography* (1977, 1985); *Population Change and Social Policy* (1982).

OTTO KIRCHHEIMER (1905–1965). Late Professor of Government, Columbia University. Author, *Political Justice* (1961); *Politics, Law, and Social Change: Selected Essays of Otto Kirchheimer* (1969), edited by F. S. Burin and K. L. Shell.

DAVID LANDES. Robert Walton Goelet Professor of French History, Harvard University. Author, *Bankers and Pashas* (1958); *The Unbound Prometheus* (1969); *History as Social Science* (1971); *Revolution in Time: Clocks and the Making of the Modern World* (1983).

SEYMOUR M. LIPSET. Professor of Political Science and Sociology, and Senior Fellow of the Hoover Institute, Stanford University. Author, *Agrarian Socialism* (1950); *The First New Nation* (1963); *Revolution and Counter-revolution* (1968); *Political Man* (rev. ed., 1981); *Consensus and Conflict* (1985). Coauthor, *Union Democracy* (1956); *The Politics of Unreason* (rev. ed., 1978); *Dialogues on American Politics* (1978); *The Confidence Gap* (1983).

JOHN LOGUE. Associate Professor of Political Science, Kent State University. Author, *Socialism and Abundance: Radical Socialism in the Danish Welfare State* (1982).

RICHARD LOWENTHAL. Emeritus Professor of Political Science, Free University of Berlin. Author, *World Communism: The Disintegration of a Secular Faith* (1966); *Model or Ally? The Communist Powers and the Developing Countries* (1977); and many works in German.

ROY C. MACRIDIS. Professor of Politics, Brandeis University. Author, *The Study of Comparative Government* (1955); *French Politics in Transition* (1975); *Contemporary Political Ideologies* (4th ed., 1989); *Modern Political Regimes* (1986). Coauthor, *The De Gaulle Republic* (1960, 1963); *Foreign Policy in World Politics* (6th ed., 1985); *France, Germany, and the Western Alliance* (1967); *Modern Political Systems: Europe* (1983).

MICHAEL MANN. Lecturer in Sociology, London School of Economics. Author, *Consciousness and Action Among the Western Working Class* (1973); *The Sources of Social Power* (1986). Editor, *The International Encyclopedia of Sociology* (1984).

JAMES C. MARCH. Professor of Political Science, Stanford University. Author, *Decisions and Organizations* (1988). Coauthor, *Organizations* (1958); *Ambiguity and Choice in Organizations* (1976). Editor, *Handbook of Organizations* (1965).

KARL MARX (1818–1883). Useful one-volume collections include *Marx and Engels: Basic Writings on Politics and Philosophy* (1959), edited by Lewis S. Feuer; and *The Marx-Engels Reader* (rev. ed., 1972), edited by Robert C. Tucker.

JOHN STUART MILL (1806–1873). Noted English philosopher and essayist. A convenient collection of his political writings is the Everyman edition of *Utilitarianism, Liberty, and Representative Government* (1940).

FRANZ L. NEUMANN (1900–1954). Late Professor of Government, Columbia University.

Author, *Behemoth: The Structure and Practice of National Socialism* (1944); *The Democratic and the Authoritarian State* (1957).

MICHEL OKSENBERG. Professor of Political Science and Research Associate of the Center for Chinese Studies, University of Michigan. Author, *China: The Convulsive Society* (1971); *China and America: Past and Future* (1977). Editor, *Dragon and Eagle* (1978).

JOHAN P. OLSEN. Professor of Political Science, University of Bergen, Norway. Author, *Organized Democracy, The Political Institutions of a Welfare State, The Case of Norway* (1983). Coauthor, *Ambiguity and Choice in Organizations* (1976).

RICHARD ROSE. Professor of Public Policy, University of Strathclyde, Glasgow, Scotland. *Governing Without Consensus: An Irish Perspective* (1971); *Understanding Big Government* (1984); *Do Parties Make a Difference?* (1984); *Politics in England* (1988).

JAMES P. SCANLAN. Professor of Philosophy and Director of the Center for Slavic and Eastern Studies, The Ohio State University. Author, *Marxism in the USSR* (1985).

PHILIPPE C. SCHMITTER. Professor of Political Science, Stanford University. Author, *Interest Conflict and Political Change in Brazil* (1971); *Corporatism and Public Policy in Authoritarian Portugal* (1975). Coauthor, *Transitions from Authoritarian Rule* (1987); *The Organization of Business Interests* (1988). Editor, *Patterns of Corporatist Policy-Making* (1982); *Private Interest Government* (1985).

RICHARD L. SKLAR. Professor of Political Science, University of California, Los Angeles. Author, *Nigerian Political Parties* (1963, 1983); *Corporate Power in an African State: The Political Impact of Multinational Mining Companies in Zambia* (1975).

THEDA SKOCPOL. Professor of Sociology, Harvard University. Author, *States and Social Revolution* (1979). Editor, *Bringing the State Back In* (1985).

S. FREDERICK STARR. President of Oberlin College, and Founding Secretary of the Kennan Institute for Advanced Russian Studies at the Woodrow Wilson International Center for Scholars. Author, *Decentralization and Self-Government in Russia, 1830–1870* (1972); *Melnikov: Solo Architect in a Mass Society* (1978); *Red and Hot: The Fate of Jazz in the Soviet Union* (1983). Coauthor, *Against Two Evils* (1981).

BRENT STEEL. Assistant Professor of Political Science, Oakland University (Michigan).

ALFRED STEPAN. Professor of Political Science, Columbia University. Author, *The Military in Politics: Changing Patterns in Brazil* (1974); *The State and Society: Peru in Comparative Perspective* (1978).

ALAIN TOURAINE. Director of Studies, Ecole des Hautes Etudes en Sciences Sociales, Paris, France. Author, *The May Movement* (1971); *The Post-Industrial Society* (1971); *The Self-Production of Society* (1977); *The Voice and the Eye* (1981); and many works in French.

TAKETSUGA TSURUTANI. Professor of Political Science, Washington State University. Author, *Politics and Government: A Brief Introduction* (1982). Coauthor, *Japanese Policy and East Asian Security* (1981).

ARTURO VALENZUELA. Professor of Political Science, Duke University. Author, *Political Brokers in Chile* (1977); *The Breakdown of Democracy in Chile* (1978). Coauthor, *Military Rule in Chile* (1986).

J. SAMUEL VALENZUELA. Professor of Sociology, University of Notre Dame. Coauthor, *Military Rule in Chile* (1986).

FREDERIC E. WAKEMAN, JR. President of the Social Science Research Council, New York. Author, *Strangers at the Gate: Social Disorder in South China, 1839–1861* (1966); *The Fall of Imperial China* (1975); *The Great Enterprise: The Manchu Reconstruction of the Imperial Order,* 2 vols. (1985).

IMMANUEL WALLERSTEIN. Distinguished Professor of Sociology and Director of the Fernand Braudel Center for the Study of Economics, Historical Systems and Civilization, State University of New York, Binghamton. Author, *Africa: The Politics of Unity* (1967); *The Capitalist World Economy* (1979); *The Modern World System,* 2 vols. (1980); *Historical Capitalism* (1983); *The Politics of the World Economy* (1984).

MAX WEBER (1864–1920). German sociologist and political scientist. Among his works in English translation are: *The Protestant Ethic and the Spirit of Capitalism* (1930); *The Theory of Social and Economic Organization* (1947); *From Max Weber: Essays in Sociology* (1946), edited by H. H. Gerth and C. W. Mills.

MYRON WEINER. Ford International Professor of Political Science, Massachusetts Institute of Technology. Author, *Party Politics in India* (1957); *The Politics of Scarcity: Public Pressure and Political Response in India* (1962); *Party Building in a New Nation: The Indian National Congress* (1967); *Sons of the Soil: Migration and Ethnic Conflict in India* (1978); *India at the Polls, 1980* (1981). Coauthor, *India's Preferential Policies* (1981).

HOWARD J. WIARDA. Professor of Political Science, University of Massachusetts, Amherst. Author, *The Dominican Republic: Nation in Transition* (1969); *Corporatism and National Development in Latin America* (1981); *Latin America at the Crossroads* (1987); *Foreign Policy Without Illusion* (1988). Editor, *New Directions in Comparative Politics* (1986); *Latin American Politics and Development* (1986).

AARON WILDAVSKY. Professor of Political Science, University of California, Berkeley.

Author, *The Revolt Against the Masses and Other Essays* (1971); *Speaking Truth to Power: The Art and Craft of Public Analysis* (1979); *The Nursing Father: Moses as a Political Leader* (1985); *The New Politics of the Budgetary Process* (1987). Coauthor, *Risk and Culture* (1982); *Implementation* (1984).

ALEKSANDR N. YAKOVLEV. Former social scientist and diplomat, now a member of the Politburo, and Secretary of the Central Committee of the Communist party of the Soviet Union. He is considered the leading theoretician of the Gorbachev reforms. Author, *Fundamentals of Political Science* (1975); and many works in Russian.

HARMON ZEIGLER. Philip M. Phibbs Professor, University of Puget Sound, and Affiliate Professor, University of Washington. Author, *The Political Life of American Teachers* (1967); *Pluralism, Corporatism, and Confucianism* (1988). Coauthor, *Interest Groups in American Society* (1972); *The Irony of Democracy* (8th ed., 1990).

# CONTENTS

SEVENTH EDITION

# Comparative Politics
## Notes and Readings

# PART ONE

# Comparative Analysis: Method and Concepts

The field of comparative politics remains in the state of flux described in the first edition of this volume over twenty-five years ago. There has been little theory building, cumulative empirical testing, and data collection since then. There also has been little agreement on concepts and definitions or on the scope and range of comparative analysis. The intellectual state of comparative analysis contrasts sharply with the broadening and revitalizing vision of the "comparatists" who launched their appeal for change more than thirty years ago. As Harry Eckstein pointed out, the circumstances for the development of comparative politics were then particularly propitious:

> First, the empirical range of the field has been greatly enlarged, primarily through the intensive study of non-Western systems; second, concerted attempts have been made to overcome the lack of rigor and system that characterized the field in the pre-war period to make it more scientific; third, there has been much greater emphasis upon the political role of social groups and upon political institutions that play an important role in molding political values and cognitions, loyalties, and identifications; finally, political systems have been analytically dissected and questions raised about them in terms of conceptual schemes largely imported from social sciences, above all in terms of structural-functional analysis.[1]

Two thoughtful students of comparative politics however, writing in 1970, list a set of caveats:

> Although it cannot be questioned that cross-cultural comparative research is indispensable to a developing science of politics, the problems that comparative politics specialists encounter are formidable. These range from the highly technical problems of indexing and sampling, to the more general problems of developing non-culture-bound categories, to the even more basic issues revolving around the rules of interpretation and the criteria for admissible explanation.... When this is done they will have a more solid intellectual base for developing more sophisticated conceptual schemes and more appropriate data processing routines.[2]

The road to the development of a solid base of theoretical conceptualization continues to be long and uncertain. In this introductory essay we shall trace the history of and trends in comparative politics, identify some of the major achievements, and indicate some of the continuing sources of discontent.

## GENERAL OBSERVATION OF TRENDS

After the Second World War, dissatisfaction with the state of comparative politics was widespread. One of the editors of this volume (Macridis) expressed the prevailing mood by pointing out some of the major shortcomings of the traditional approach:

1. It dealt primarily with a single-culture configuration, i.e., the Western world.
2. Within this cultural configuration, comparative study dealt mainly with representative democracies, until recently treating nondemocratic systems as aberrations from the democratic "norms."
3. This approach prevented the student from dealing systematically not only with nondemocratic Western political systems, but also

with colonial systems, other "backward" areas, and culturally distinct societies that superficially exhibit the characteristics of the representative process (e.g., India, Japan).

4. Research was founded on the study of isolated aspects of the governmental process within specific countries; hence it was comparative in name only.

The comparative study of politics was excessively formalistic in its approach to political institutions.

1. It focused analysis on the formal institutions of government, to the detriment of a sophisticated awareness of the informal arrangements of society and of their role in the formation of decisions and the exercise of power.

2. In neglecting such informal arrangements, it proved to be relatively insensitive to the nonpolitical determinants of political behavior and hence to the nonpolitical bases of governmental institutions.

3. Comparison was made in terms of the formal constitutional aspects of Western systems—that is, parliaments, chief executives, civil services, administrative law, and so on—which are not necessarily the most fruitful concepts for a truly comparative study.

The comparative study of politics was preponderantly descriptive rather than problem-solving, explanatory, or analytic in its method. Except for some studies of proportional representation, emergency legislation, and electoral systems, the field was insensitive to hypotheses and their verification. Even in the purely descriptive approach to political systems it was relatively insensitive to the methods of cultural anthropology, in which descriptions are fruitfully made in terms of general concepts or integrating hypotheses. Thus, description in comparative government did not readily lend itself to the testing of hypotheses, to the compilation of significant data regarding a single political phenomenon—or a class of such phenomena—in a large number of societies. Description without

systematic orientation obstructed the discovery of hypotheses regarding uniformities in political behavior and prevented the formulation, on a comparative basis, of a theory of political dynamics (i.e., change, revolution, conditions of stability).

How was one to counter these trends and develop a more sophisticated approach to comparative study? The prescription appeared simple at the time:

1. Comparison involves abstraction, and concrete situations or processes can never be compared as such. Every phenomenon is unique; every manifestation is unique; every process, every nation, like every individual, is in a sense unique. To compare them means to select certain types or concepts, and in so doing we have to "distort" the unique and the concrete.

2. Prior to any comparison it is necessary not only to establish categories and concepts but also to determine criteria of relevance of the particular components of a social and political situation to the problem under analysis (i.e., relevance of social stratification to the family system, or of sunspots to political instability).

3. It is necessary to establish criteria for the adequate representation of the particular components that enter into a general analysis or into the analysis of a problem.

4. It is necessary in attempting to develop a theory of politics to formulate hypotheses emerging either from the context of a conceptual scheme or from the formulation of a problem.

5. The formulation of hypothetical relations and their investigation against tested data can never lead to proof. A hypothesis or a series of hypothetical relations would be considered proven (i.e., verified) only as long as it withstands falsification.

6. Hypothetical series rather than single hypotheses should be formulated. In each case the connecting link between general hypothetical series and the particular social relations should be provided by the specification of conditions under

which any or all the possibilities enumerated in this series are expected to take place.

7. Comparative study, even if it falls short of providing a general theory of politics, can pave the way to the gradual and cumulative development of theory by (1) enriching our imaginative abilitiy to formulate hypotheses, in the same sense that any "outsidedness" enhances our ability to understand a social system; (2) providing a means for the testing of hypotheses; and (3) making us aware that something we have taken for granted requires explanation.

8. Finally, one of the greatest dangers in hypothesizing in connection with comparative study is the projection of possible relationships ad infinitum. This can be avoided by the orderly collection of data prior to hypothesizing. Such collection may in itself lead us to the recognition of irrelevant relations (climate and the electoral system, language and industrial technology, etc.). Such a recognition in itself makes for a more manageable study of data. *Hence some importance is attached to the development of some rough classificatory scheme prior to the formulation of hypotheses.*

In summary then, the major criticism of the traditional approach to the study of comparative politics was that it is centered upon the description of the formally established institutions of government—that it was in general singularly insensitive both to informal factors and processes (such as the various interest groups, the wielders of social and economic power, and at times even of political power operating outside of the formal governmental institutions) and to the more complex contextual forces that can be found in the ideological patterns and the social organization of the system. It lacked a systematic approach.

The very word "system" causes a number of people to raise their eyebrows. It has connotations of group research that suggest the suppression of the imagination and sensitivity of the observer for the sake of conceptually determined and rigidly adhered to categories. This is far

from being the case, however. A systematic approach simply involves the development of categories for the compilation of data and the identification of interrelationships within the data so compiled in the form of theories—that is, the suggestion of variable relationships.

The development of common categories establishes criteria of relevance. Once such categories are suggested, their relevance for the compilation of data should be determined through the study of problems in as many political systems as possible. For instance, if it is shown that the composition or recruitment of the elite in certain political systems accounts for the degree to which the system is susceptible to change, which in turn may lead us to certain general suppositions about political stability, then a systematic approach would require the examination of the same phenomenon in a number of politcal systems in the light of the same general categories. Although the traditional approach did not claim to be explanatory, a systematic approach claimed to be precisely this, for explanation simply means verification of hypothetical propositions. In the field of politics, given the lack of experimentation, only the testing of a hypothesis in as many systems as possible will provide us a moderate degree of assurance that we have an explanation.[3]

These general observations on the state of comparative politics appear in retrospect both modest and wistful: To develop a framework for comparison and to abandon the "country-by-country" approach in favor of either comparisons of problems, processes, and institutions or the comparative testing of hypotheses was not too much to ask. Nor was it too demanding to ask for a theory—vitually any theory—that spells out significant interrelationships in terms of crucial political phenomena that could be studied, compared, and evaluated. Nor was it extravagant to ask that the horizon of comparison in effect be broadened to include non-European countries. Finally, the hope that institutions—political institutions—would be studied in the context of the socioeconomic and ideological forces within which they operated was more than legitimate.

## MAJOR ACHIEVEMENTS AND
## NEW DIMENSIONS

Some significant contributions to the study of comparative politics were made in the 1950s and 1960s. Under the auspices of the Social Sciences Research Council, a committee on comparative politics was set up in 1954, and a number of publications appeared under its auspices, most of them dealing with problems of political development. However, with the exception of the first volume that attempted to suggest an overall theory of political development, these volumes were collections of essays on specific topics—political parties, bureaucracy, political culture, and so on—that lacked a common theoretical focus and comprehensive coverage. They resulted from separate conferences in which authors "did their thing." The undertaking displayed a synthetic quality, or rather an additive one. Having specialists on different countries address themselves to common topics is no assurance that comparability of any kind will emerge or that the comparative method will be tested (that is, will yield some meaningful generalizations).

Individual authors or authors working in combination with others have produced volumes that deal with significant problem areas, such as the political elite, socialization, political parties, interest groups, governmental structures, political development and its patterns of institutionalization, opposition, class cleavages and their reconciliation, electoral systems and their impact on representative government, totalitarian systems, constitutions, and constitutionalism and bureaucracies. Some of these studies are important contributions to our knowledge of individual countries, whereas others are seminal works of conceptualization and theoretical building. Among those dealing with countries are the work of Ralf Dahrendorf and Karl Bracher on the impact of the Nazi system upon German society; Samuel Beer on British political parties; Stanley Hoffmann on the French Republic; Merle Fainsod on the Soviet political system; Joseph LaPalombara on Italian interest groups; Robert Scalapino on the rise of political parties in Japan, and Eckstein on

Norway.[4] They have all enriched and deepened our understanding of individual political systems while raising significant theoretical questions.

The list is also impressive when it comes to theoretical works. New dimensions for comparative analysis are furnished by David Easton on system theory; Karl Deutsch on communication theory; Seymour Lipset on participation; Beer, Gabriel Almond, and Sidney Verba on political culture; Robert Dahl on the nature of political power and its various manifestations; William Kornhauser on mass society as it relates to democracy; Samuel Huntington on reevaluation of the role of political institutions in political change and development; Dahrendorf's reassessment of the role of class in contemporary politics; Barrington Moore, Jr., on totalitarianism and democracy; David Butler and Donald Stokes on the British voter; and Maurice Duverger on political parties.[5]

In general, the field of comparative politics has as a result shown remarkable progress in at least two ways: We look upon politics in one or more countries with far greater sophistication than in the past, and we approach it with a set of general concepts, even if they are not always agreed upon. We are no longer satisfied with institutional studies—either descriptive or legalistic—or with the study of constitutional provisions and the formal distribution of power they set up. We probe deeper into the political elite, the socioeconomic and ideological contextual forces within which they operate, political parties and interest groups, communication mechanisms between leaders and led, and the impact of economic and social change upon political participation and behavior. We search for the fundamentals, so to speak, of a political system: stability, legitimacy, authority (or, conversely, for the reasons for instability), nonperformance, and revolutions. This is no mean accomplishment.

But the authors and works cited here represent only an initial effort when compared to the hopes and expectations with which we began and the resources that have been made available. These works are the tip of the iceberg. There is no common theory, no generally accepted or acceptable proposition for further research, and no cumulative effort in the form of data collection, data sorting, and hypothesizing. There is no common body of theory and knowledge to which the student of comparative politics can be directed.

For a theory to be useful, a number of requirements must be fulfilled. The theory should be both comprehensive and parsimonious; it should be geared to the proper level of generality and abstraction to include the essentials for political analysis; it should be capable of generating hypotheses (fundamental "if-then" propositions that can be investigated empirically); it should allow the investigators enough freedom to choose from among the empirical data the particular phenomena and structures that relate to the general concepts embedded in the theory; and it should not prescribe one and only one research procedure but rather make it possible to use the procedure that is most likely to be feasible under the existing field situations. If, for instance, survey research is the *only procedure* prescribed, then it is obvious that only those countries where surveys are possible can be included; all others will have to be excluded.

Easton's theory of a political system meets many of these requirements despite the fact that his model is highly abstract.[6] The "system" is viewed as a decision-making mechanism operating within the framework of beliefs and attitudes held by the people about their regime (that is, about the basic form of their government). On the one side we have "demands" constantly pressing for satisfaction and "supports"—positive feelings of loyalty and attachment to the political system. On the other side we have "outputs"—decisions aimed at alleviating predicaments or meeting demands. The interplay between demands and decisions affects the level and the intensity of supports, which can range from very positive when the system is highly legitimate and stable to very negative when there is widespread disobedience. The role of "socialization" in creating supports is adequately stressed to involve not simply the education and induction of the young into the system

but also the responsiveness of the elite to new political groups and their openness to the participation of all groups in the decision-making process. "Exclusiveness" or "repression" will yield discontent and undermine the legitimacy of the system; prolonged ineffectiveness—the inability to translate demands into policy—will have the same consequences. "Revolution" in this sense is the only way for certain groups to make their "inputs." Generally speaking, the connecting links between inputs and the decision makers are the interest groups, other associations, and the political parties. They are transmission belts and as such they play a crucial role in keeping the system open and responsive. This is, in skeleton form, Easton's "system." It is not new—far from it. But it was formulated with great simplicity and could have generated a number of studies in comparative analysis. Its major difficulty was its very high level of generality and abstraction.

## INDICATIONS OF CONTINUING DISCONTENT

The most important reasons for our continuing discontent with the current state of comparative analysis lie, in our opinion, with the excessive and at times uncritical effort to apply the canons of the "behavioral revolution" to it.

Behavioralism provided a salutary emphasis upon political factors other than the governmental forms. Although the discovery of these factors was not entirely original, it opened up the study of what we may call the contextual factors within which political structures and forms develop and political roles flourish. Borrowing in great part from sociology and anthropology, behavioralism emphasized careful definitions of the empirical problems to be investigated and the formulation and testing of hypotheses. It sharpened the tools of our analysis by introducing new techniques—surveys, interviewing, the compilation of aggregate data—in an effort to provide correlations between various socioeconomic and psychological factors and political behavior. Weighing, measuring, and correlating are among the most positive aspects of the behavioral revolution in politics. When applied to a political scene, American or foreign, of which the observers had adequate knowledge, this emphasis was most beneficial. Students picked dark or shadowy areas and threw light upon them. Their findings, or at least their observations, added to the knowledge we had and helped us refine it.

Where the behavioral revolution went wrong was at its two extremes—in the efforts to build "grand theory" at the one extreme, and in the study of what may well be called political trivia at the other. In between the two lay a fertile field for study and exploration. But it was to the extremes that most of the work was directed, generally with disappointing results. This should become abundantly clear when we discuss the following points that exemplify the state of the discipline today: its failure to establish criteria of relevance and its gross neglect of the study of governmental structures and forms.

The search for relevance and the criteria of relevance has bedeviled political thought and inquiry. It is an issue that cannot be easily resolved. Society as an overall sytem (that is, as a set of interrelations, roles, and structures) consists of a number of subsystems for which no hard and fast boundaries can be drawn. In a sense, all that is social is also political and firmly rooted in history. What is social can be broken down analytically into subsystems; but again, the farther we go in identifying subsystems, the more difficult it becomes to set boundaries. Society is a "web."

Conceivably then, every manifestation, every attitude or relationship, every motivation or idea in society has a relevance to politics. They all may engender aspirations; may shape interests; may evoke demands; may call for decisions; may lead to conflicts about values and interests that necessitate arbitration. Child-rearing, the school curriculum, modes of entertainment, sex relations, to say nothing of economic interests and activities, are all *potentially* related to politics. Yet what is potential is not actual in empirical terms. In most cases and for most of the time, the great host of social, economic, and interpersonal relations has no actual relevance to politics and therefore to the discipline. Yet each and all *may*, at a given time and place and under a set of conditions that is impossible to foresee, assume a political revelance, only to subside again into the realm of the apolitical.

The dilemma is obvious. Should we study everything that is *potentially* political? Should we narrow our definition, and if so, how? Behavioralism provides the worst possible answer—study everything. It postulates that every aspect of political behavior relates to every aspect of social behavior; hence we may study manifestations and attitudes and relationships that have no discernible political relevance.

To be sure, there are no a priori grounds that justify discarding this holistic approach. The element of potentiality is ever present, and our inability to develop any rules about the intricate phenomenon that accounts for the actualization of what is potential makes it impossible to condemn potentiality as a criterion of relevance. Only two closely related grounds for its rejection can be suggested. The first is what Joseph LaPalombara has called the rule of parsimony, and the second is what we call the concern with focus. Parsimony suggests that we choose those categories and concepts about which we are as sure as we can be that what we are studying is politically relevant. Concern with focus simply suggest that we use the most direct way to examine politically relevant phenomena.

## The Fallacy of Inputism

Two terms that have gained wide use in the last decade are "input" and "output." The system converts demands into decisions. Through a feedback mechanism, output factors influence the input side. Emphasis is placed upon the input factors, but the state is given a degree of autonomy and independence, and through a process that is by no means clear it can influence supports and demands. The difficulty comes with the selection of the input factors (that is, with the same problem of relevance that we have discussed). Do we again study all societal manifestations on the assumption that they all make inputs? Do we consider attitudinal data, aggregate data, "hard" and "soft" data ranging from the number of hospital beds to child–father relations? Where and in what manner do we define the subject matter for study, and what is our cutoff point? Political scientists are often like thirsty people looking for water in a contextual Sahara, when more often than not it is right there fresh from the spring—or at least from a well-chlorinated reservoir. Their search in the contextual wasteland brings only further difficulties upon them, for there is no theory, no conceptual scheme that links—in any form that is testable— the amassed socioeconomic and psychological data with the political. In fact, emphasis upon the input factors very often not only neglects the political but sometimes explicitly avoids it.

We are inclined to define what we call "inputism" as the study of society by political scientists that lacks a political focus and very often lacks a political question. The job is enticingly easy: All that is needed is a questionnaire, interviewers, a pool of respondents, the *UN Statistical Yearbook,* and a countersorter (or even better, a computer). I wish to reemphasize the phrase "that lack a political focus and very often lack a political question." When the empirical political situation and empirical political phenomenon we are investigating make it necessary—as often happens—to study the socioeconomic or psychological factors on the input side, then such study is focused and relevant, for the input factors are analyzed to "explain" the situation we are investigating. We hypothesize that the attitude of the French military with regard to a series of political decisions or with regard to the process of decision making was, among other things, shaped by the education they received at the Jesuit schools. The linkage between the two, I believe, can be made. It will not fully explain the attitude of the military, but we think it may provide one of the first steps leading to explanation. We start with

the concrete political problem. Inputism would reverse the priorities, advocating the study of the socialization of the elite groups in the French educational system, with the unwarranted expectation that such study would clarify "politics" in general and help us explain political behavior. What behavior? With regard to what problem? At what time?

Inputism tends to lead to three fallacies: those of (1) determinism, (2) scientism, and (3) superficiality. All three fallacies are related.

According to determinism, input factors shape political action. The political phenomenon is almost invariably reduced either to a number of nonpolitical determinants, in which case we have a multiple kind of reductionism, or to one factor, in which case we have a single-factor reductionism. In either case, the state can play virtually no independent problem-solving or attitude-forming role. It is only through a process of feedback—not clearly understood and not easily demonstrated—that governmental action may influence the determinants that then in turn act upon the governmental decision-making process. Politics constantly remains a dependent variable. It is, to use Bentley's expression, the parallelogram of interest action and interaction—the parallelogram of all socioeconomic and psychological determinants that will shape the decision-making machinery and will determine its output. The famous "black box," as graduate students have come to know the government, is at its best a filter mechanism through which interests express themselves and at its worst a simple transmission mechanism. The role of the state is reduced to the narrow confines of an organization that channels, reflects, and expresses commands and instructions that come from "elsewhere." The hint to political scientists is obvious: Study everything but the machinery of the state and its organizational structures; study the "elsewhere."

Scientism constitutes the effort to measure as accurately as possible the weight, scope, and persistence of the input factors, on the purely gratuitous assumption that they are or can be linked causally to political phenomena. The assumption is gratuitous because we have failed as yet to establish any such causal links and because it is doubtful that we ever will. The assumption is confounded when the political phenomena with which the input factors are to be linked are not clearly stated. Sometimes system theory suggests the broadest possible relationship among "concepts," rather than such variables as consensus, stability, or performance; sometimes it offers a very narrow-gauge hypothesis linking some political manifestation to some nonpolitical variable (for example, voting with income or race). The first attempt obviously bogs down into an analytical exercise rather than empirical testing, whereas the second one will never attain the level of testability that concerns whatever higher-level propositions can be made. Even when system theory establishes clear-cut concepts linked to empirical phenomena from which testable propositions can emerge, it is impossible to move back from the propositions to the concepts and to the overall theory through a series of verifiable tests that exclude all alternative propositions, concepts, and theories. Scientism therefore leads us from hyperfactualism to hypertheorizing, which progressively becomes an exercise (often brilliant) in intellectual virtuosity. It lacks, however, the only thing that really counts—empirical relevance.

Because no theory as yet offered has shown its worth in causally linking determinants with political phenomena, our efforts very often end with the superficial juxtaposition of a given determinant with a given political phenomenon—that is to say, with correlations. Because no adequate theory has been offered, however, and because we therefore have no explanation, correlational findings are a somewhat more sophisticated version of the "sun spot" theory. Lipset's book *Political Man* is an illustration of this.[7] At the end of this excellent study, the reader is not sure whether open democratic societies are affluent because they are open and democratic or whether it is the other way around.

Determinism, scientism, and correlational studies that have a distinct trait of superficiality typify the state of a discipline that has consistently eschewed the hard and persistent empirical

phenomena that ought to concern it in the name of theory building and theory testing. Structures and processes and the manifestly political institutions through which decisions are made have been relegated to the level of epiphenomena. The examination and the evaluation of policies have been handed over to the journalists and politicians, and the formulation of a judgment *in the name of knowledge* is considered incompatible with the canons of a self-imposed scientific objectivity. It is these trends that account for the state of the discipline as a whole, and they affect particularly the study of comparative politics, or the comparative study of politics. The state of the discipline can be summed up in one phrase: the gradual disappearance of the political. To repeat, if government is viewed as the reflection of the parallelogram of socioeconomic and psychological and other determinants, the prescription for political science becomes a proscription of the study of government.

Yet the behavioral revolution has also had, as we have noted, beneficial effects. We shall never return exclusively to normative speculation, and we shall never be satisfied with judgments about political phenomena without the benefit of careful measurement. We shall continue to distinguish sharply between "facts" and "values," and we shall subject our postulates to a critical examination, demanding always clarity of definitions and terms. Whenever propositions about behavior can be tested, we shall test them under all the canons of controlled inquiry that the social sciences have developed. We shall continue to seek to build theory—a set of interrelated and interconnected propositions, each of which has direct empirical meaning and relevance—and we shall continue to develop narrow hypotheses that can be tested (that is, invariably falsified). We shall use the many tools of empirical inquiry available to us—survey opinion data, aggregate data—and in both the construction of our research and our search for the explanation of political phenomena we shall feel free to borrow, when the occasion demands, from the theoretical sophistication of many disciplines—sociology, anthropology, economics, and psychology—and, of course, to use the empirical data that history provides.

But the time has come to qualify and reconsider our quest for a science of politics in the full sense of the term. In the last analysis this may be a contradiction in terms. There can be no science where the element of human will and purpose predominates. Politics is a problem-solving mechanism; our study must deal with it and not with the laws surrounding behavior. The ultimate irony is that even if laws could be discovered, our discipline would be primarily concerned with an effort to explain why they are not obeyed—why the laws are really nonlaws. Natural sciences began by investigating empirical phenomena in order to understand them, explain them, and control them. The ultimate goal of the natural sciences has been to control nature. The higher the level of generalization that subsumes a number of measurable relationships, the higher the potentiality for control. It is the other way around with politics. The study of politics explicitly divorces knowledge from action and understanding from control. The laws that we constantly seek will tell us little about our political problems and what to do about them. Our concern becomes scholastic.

We therefore suggest that we reconcile ourselves to the fact that although we can have an understanding of some political phenomena —a history of politics and political movements, an understanding of the functioning of governmental forms and structures, a concern and indeed a focus on such major concepts as power, decision making, interest, organization, control, political norms and beliefs, obedience, equality, development, consensus, performance, and the like—we do not and cannot have a science of politics. We can have, at most, an art. Second, and this is the sign of the art, we may manage to arrive at some inductive generalizations based upon fragmentary empirical evidence. An inductive generalization is at best a statement about behavior. It can be derived from identical action and interaction under generally similar conditions over a long period of time in as many different contexts as possible. The behavior is

not explained, but the weight of evidence allows us to anticipate and often predict it. A series of solidly supported inductive generalizations may in the last analysis be the most fruitful way to move gradually to a scientific approach, as it provides us with a rudimentary form of behavioral patterns. Our knowledge of politics is then at most an understanding of our accumulated experience. It is in this area that comparative politics has an important role to play: By carefully identifying a given behavior or structure or movement and by attempting to study it in as many settings as possible and over as long a period of time as possible, we can provide generalizations backed by evidence.

If we view our discipline as an art and if we limit its goals to inductive generalizations about politics (that is, a well-ordered and catalogued table or listing of accumulated experience), then three imperatives for research emerge, providing focus and satisfying the need for parsimony. First, we must study the practitioners of the art, the political leaders who hold office and, more generally, the governing elite that aspire to or possess political power. Second, we must study the structures and organizations and mechanisms through which the elite gain political power and exercise it (that is, the parties and other political associations). Third, we must be concerned with governmental institutions through which demands are channeled or, just as often, by which they are generated. These imperatives do not exhaust our immediate task, but rather give us a starting point.

In studying the governmental elite and the institutions through which they gain and exercise power, we ought to consider the art of government as a problem-solving and goal-oriented activity. This kind of activity characterizes any art. The task of government is to identify problems (or to anticipate them) and provide solutions. Our study then is to ask ourselves constantly: How well is the art performed? Who within the government listens, who foresees, who advises and suggests policy? What are the skills of the practitioners, and what are their objective capabilities? Finally, what is the impact of a decision upon the problem or the predicament it was designed to alleviate or to remove? The practitioner is not strictly bound by determinants. Communal life suggests and often sets goals of performance and achievement that become more than normative goals. They become in a way the "operative goals" that give direction to political action. The governing elite play an independent role in seeking out the goals and in implementing them. In his book on planning Andrew Shonfield refers to the French planning as the result of an "elitist conspiracy."[8] More often than not decision making is an elitist conspiracy, the study and assessment of which would be far more rewarding than the survey and elaboration of all the input factors or the nonpolitical determinants involved.

But in the last analysis government is an act of will that can shuffle and reshuffle many of the determinants. Government involves choice, and the parameters are often wider than we are inclined to think. Any government will begin by surveying the conditions that appear to indicate the limits of freedom and choice; a government must always ask "what it has." But any government must also be in a position to assess what it wills. To say this is not to return to metaphysical speculation about the "will" of the state or the government; it is simply to reintroduce as integral parts of our discipline the state's performance and choices and the institutions through which they are implemented.

## Relevance and Focus: A Set of Priorities

First and above all, it is our obligation to study all those organized manifestations, attitudes, and movements that press directly for state action or oppose state action. No matter what terms we use—decision making, authoritative allocation of values, regulation, adjudication, enforcement—we are concerned with the same old thing: the state. What is it asked to do? And what is it that people in a community do not want to see it do? To deny this pervasive empirical phenomenon in the name of a given theory is to deny our art or,

for those who prefer, our science. The demand for state action or the demand that a given action cease is the very guts of politics. No science of politics—or for that matter, no science—can be built upon concepts and theories that disregard or avoid empirical phenomena. Why do French farmers throw their peaches in the river and their beets on the highway? Why did American students leave their comfortable homes to demonstrate in the streets? Why have American workers patterned their political demands in one way, but French workers in another? Obviously, to control, to influence, or to oppose state action.

Thus, our second priority also relates to what we have called the state, resurrecting what may appear to many graduate students to be an ancient term. We mean by it, of course, what we have always understood the term to mean, stripped of all its metaphysical trimmings. It means all the structures and organizations that make decisions and resolve conflicts with the expectation that their decisions will be obeyed—the civil service, the legislature, the executive, the judiciary, the host of public or semipublic corporations and organizations that are called upon to resolve differences and to make decisions. We include also the agencies whose function is to study facts, to deliberate about them, to identify areas of conflict, and to suggest policy decisions. The most relevant issue here is not the one that David Easton discusses, or rather suggests—a theory of likely problems and predicaments, especially when the theory is pitched at a very high level of generalization.[9] What is instead important is to study the preparedness of the state to discern predicaments or problems. Potential problems can be theorized about. The actual political phenomenon, however, is the existing machinery through which problems are perceived—the agencies, the research, the flow of information, the manner in which individual values and constituency considerations enter into the minds of the men and women who work for the state—and it ultimately includes that happy or fatal moment when the state copes with, ignores, or is simply unable to perceive the problem. The state can also, while perceiving the problem, either alleviate the predicament or suggest solutions utterly unrelated to it.

It is this second priority—the study of the state and all state agencies; of their organization and performance; of the scope of their decision making; of the attitudes of the men and women who perform within their structures the roles of informing, studying, consulting, and deciding; and of the major constituencies they serve—that has been so sadly neglected until very recently. Few are the studies that focus on the state as an agency of deliberation, problem identification, and problem solving. Few are the studies of the institutions of the state in the modern, developed systems. This is no accident at all. After the state was ostracized from the vocabulary of politics, we found it far more fashionable to study the systems in which there was no state—that is, the so-called developing, emerging, or new systems. The result was to eschew the urgent and nagging empirical situations in the modern and highly industrialized societies in which our fate is to be decided, in order to study political phenomena and especially political development in the societies in which there was no state. No wonder Huntington began to despair of studying the process of development in any terms other than "institutionalization"— that is, the building of institutions with authority and legitimacy, such as the state and the party.[10]

The third priority is the study of political attitudes—the "civic culture," as Almond puts it, or what Beer calls "the structure of norms and beliefs"[11] and what others have very loosely called ideology. But whatever name we give to them, the phenomena to be studied must point directly to peoples' beliefs, norms, and orientations about the state (its authority, scope of action, legitimacy, sense of participation, and involvement). If we are to remain strictly within the confines of relevance we must narrow our scope to those manifestations and attitudes that directly link the personal, economic, or psychological phenomena with the political. The linkage between "micro" and "macro" so well developed by Almond in his *Civic Culture* in order to identify meaningful political orientations needs to be carried a step forward. This can be done only when we reintroduce the state and its agencies and link them directly to political orientations. Unless we take this step, we shall remain at the "micro" level. We shall not link attitudes to structures and forms, to decisions and policies. The substance of governmental decisions and performance will elude us.

Finally, the fourth priority—which in a real sense is no priority at all—relates to the study of what may be called the infrastructure of the political world: attitudes and ideas; social, economic, and cultural institutions; norms and values that are prevalent in any given society, national or international. There is no reason why we shouldn't study child rearing, the patterns of socialization, the degree of concentration of economic power, the identification of personality types and traits, family life patterns, small groups and private associations, religious attitudes, and so on. All of these, as we indicated, *may* have a relevance to politics. In a number of cases—and they are the ones that count—the relevance is only too clear. It suggests itself by the very nature of the empirical phenomenon we are studying. It links a given organized political manifestation with a contextual factor that may explain it. It would be difficult to understand the role of the French military prior to the Dreyfus case without knowing something about the education its members received in Jesuit schools. But in this case we study education because we begin with the army as a political force operating within the government and the state. We go deeper into contextual factors in order to find an explanation for a manifest political phenomenon.

What we are trying to suggest by these priorities, then, is primarily a change of focus. Our concern is simply to pinpoint what is political. We begin with the political; we catch it, so to speak, in its most visible, open, and raw manifestation; we begin with the top of the iceberg before we go deep to search for its submerged base. We focus on the state and its agencies, on its types of action or inaction, and on all those organized manifestations that call for action or inaction on its part. We study the forms of decision making and analyze and evaluate its substance. We explore the reaction of groups, interests, and power elites within the system; we study in turn their reactions to state actions and their counterdemands as they are manifested through various media from political parties down to voting.

Therefore, the central focuses of politics, and of the study of comparative politics, are the governmental institutions and the political elite, their role, and their levels of performance and nonperformance. Stating this in such blunt terms appears to be utterly naive. Should we return then to the descriptive study of governmental institutions? Far from it. What we are suggesting is a starting point and a focus of investigation. Any such investigation, we know today, will inevitably lead us, as it should, far and wide in search of the contextual factors (rather than determinants) within the framework of which a government operates and to which its action, its performance, and its policies may often be attributed. We shall have to probe the infrastructure, but without losing sight of either our focus or the relevant question with which we began our investigation.

What accounts for a well-organized civil service? What is the impact of large-scale organizations—parties, bureaucracy, and so on—upon the citizen? Under what conditions does public opinion exercise its influence on the government? What accounts for political instability? Is an executive who is responsible to the people more restrained than one responsible to the legislature? How and under what conditions does representation degenerate into an expression of particular interests? Under what conditions do young people maintain political attitudes different from those of their parents, and at what point do they revolt? Under what conditions do ruling groups become responsive to popular demands?

We can multiply these questions, but they illustrate the point. None of them can lead to hard hypotheses and proof (or disproof). Some cannot be easily answered. But this is not too important

unless we are to accept that only those questions that can lead to testing in the rigorous—and therefore impossible—meaning of the term have the freedom of the market. In fact, the questions we suggest lead to a comparative survey, both historical and contemporaneous, of some of the most crucial political phenomena: responsiveness, performance, change, development, and a host of others. Such a survery will inevitably produce inductive generalizations, perhaps in the manner of Machiavelli, but with far more sophisticated tools and greater access to data than was ever the case before. It will inevitably help us to qualify our questions and to reformulate them as hypotheses that will suggest other qualifications—new variables, if you wish—and lead to further investigation—testing, if you wish—and to the reformulation of the questions—the gradual development of theory, if you like.

## RECENT CONTRIBUTIONS—"CLUSTERING"

The vitality of a discipline lies, let us repeat, in its capacity to project theories and concepts that help us familiarize ourselves with the outside world. Comparative politics is emerging as the most comprehensive and theoretical branch of political science. We do not use the term *familiarize* pejoratively. To familiarize means to identify and engage the facts in a dialogue that seeks explanations. To do so intelligently, however, one must know what questions to ask. Any dialogue must lead to intellectual processes whereby certain facts are discarded because they provide no answers while others are taken into account. In order to discard and to accept facts, one must have established certain "linkages" that make facts cluster together into patterns, so that sentences in the dialogue are meaningful. Like words, facts take on coherence and give at least a tentative answer to questions.

Nobody will deny that students of politics today are far more familiar with the empirical processes of politics than were students in the past. Familiarization has taken place in both horizontal and vertical terms. Horizontally, the world has indeed become our oyster. A mere perusal of articles on individual countries listed in the International Political Science Abstracts will show that the Eurocentric approach no longer prevails. Indeed, a committee of the Social Science Research Council has appealed for the revitalization of European studies, especially in politics.[12] We do not imply that with the world as our oyster, new pearls of wisdom have been found. We are simply pointing out that our laboratory for comparative study has been expanded as never before, so much so as to lead to some confusion and a pause.

Comparative politics has also been greatly enriched vertically: It has gained in depth. No other branch of political science has made so much effort to relate the state to society and to seek determinants of political phenomena in the larger socioeconomic matrix. Again the contrast between now and the past is marked. Fifty years ago the march toward democracy was considered irresistible and authoritarianism but an aberration. Textbooks on European governments were the indispensable fare. Institutional structures and procedures were minutely dissected and discussed, and comparison was little more than a cataloging of institutions. Carl J. Friedrich's *Constitutional Government and Democracy*[13] provided a more rewarding analysis. But, as Harry Eckstein pointed out, certain political trends were rejected as aberrant if they did not square with commonsense criteria that in the last analysis were defined by the author's notion of human nature. Comparative government textbooks were limited both horizontally (confined to Europe) and vertically (dealing only with formal governmental and legal structures).

We mentioned some of the factors that led to the expansion of the vertical dimension of comparative politics. They include the general behavioral revolution (the development of general system theories and borrowing from sociological and psychological theory) and a broadening of comparative political analysis (relating institutions to social factors such as class, status, personality, groups, culture,

socialization). Especially important has been the interest in modernization and its socioeconomic determinants or correlates. The dialogue has been refined. Institutions and their performance (or "outputs") are related to a multiplicity of inputs (perceptions, aspirations, outlooks, interests, claims). The enrichment of comparative politics literature has accounted, as noted, for an embarrassment of choices and perhaps a confusion of priorities.

At the scholarly level, the literature in comparative politics has led even the aficionados to distraction. There is a burgeoning subdivision of specializations—we call it clustering—not only by area or country as in the past, but by such subfields as developmentalism, public policy, neocorporatism, culturalism, institutionalism, and political economy. Most recent publications (1) compare political processes and a variety of political phenomena across a limited number of countries; (2) do so with regard to a coherent categorical concept—culture, interests, the elite, electoral processes, policy outputs, modernization, and so on; and (3) propose to give an explanation—that is, seek to identify the factors that account for a given political process or manifestation.

What we call *clustering* amounts, at least temporarily, to the abandonment of the search for a general theory that characterized our efforts in the 1960s. As Sidney Verba pointed out in a recent colloquium, "The absence of a single, unifying, integrating model and body of assumptions is clearly especially disappointing to graduate students and some young practitioners." He reported the general consensus of many comparatists that the field lacked clear focus, leadership, and an agreed-upon set of theoretical underpinnings.[14] Instead, clustering reflects a search for the development of middle-range theory capable of handling a limited number of variables applicable to a limited number of empirical situations. Typical topics include: the role of the military; the role of the military in modernization; the study of structures, including bureaucracy, in the formulation of social and public policy; the pervasive trend toward authoritarianism in developing nations; the impact of modernization on political stability and institution formation; the relationship between interests and the state in the making of public policy; electoral processes; the impact of international economic factors on public policy; and comparative assessment of policy outputs or performance of individual states.

In the last decade or so a number of clusters (often also referred to as "foci" or "islands") for comparative study have emerged. They have in common the development of middle-range theories that apply to limited phenomena or countries. One cluster is corporatism or, properly speaking, neocorporatism. It comprises the study of linkages between the state and its agencies with interest groups, including labor. The theories underlining it explore patterns of accommodation and decision making, regime stability or instability, and redistributive policies and outputs. A second cluster much in evidence since the publication of Charles Tilly's *Crises and Sequences*[15] is comparative history, either the study within one country or among many countries at different periods of time (dyachronic) or the study of specific events (like revolutions or democratization) in the same period in many countries (synchronic).

A third cluster is the focus on international economy, which posits that domestic behavior is constrained by international economic considerations. Fourth, there has been a growing interest in regime transitions—from authoritarian to democratic and from military to civilian. Most of these studies focus on the relationship between the state (and various forms of statism) and the civil society, seeking in society both the obstacles to authoritarianism and the seeds of its own ultimate demise. Finally, there is a wholesale return to what may be called "cultural history," which seeks in the interstices of tradition and crystallized forms of behavior, whether in law or in parliamentary practices and constitutional arrangements, the explanation of differing patterns of behavior. This approach links up to a tradition expressed in the works of British political philosophers such as A.V. Dicey or Walter Bagehot.

In the last few years the state has returned to prominence as a critically important variable. Viewed in traditional literature in legalistic and at times transcendental terms, it was downgraded by behavioral political scientists, especially in the United States. The state was considered by behaviorists and by orthodox Marxists alike as an entity that is dependent upon the sum total of societal interests—whether groups or the dominant class—and that lacks autonomy and independence. Today both neomarxists and many political scientists see in the state an agency that enjoys autonomy and independence, that weighs heavily in the initiation and making of policies, and that is capable of reacting against and even transforming the social forces that press upon it. In our previous editions we have insisted on the importance of the state in the study of comparative politics; and in this edition we have added a chapter to "welcome the state back."

Although comparative politics in its various approaches purports to describe and explain differences and similarities in political behavior, the student should not lose sight of the fact that the study of politics is and must be the study, in Aristotelian terms, of the "good life," of justice. "Kingdoms without justice how like they are robber bands," exclaimed St. Augustine. Such "kingdoms" without justice continue to be so, and their number is not getting smaller! How do regimes stack up qualitatively in terms of the basic ingredients of justice—equality and freedom? Students of comparative politics should always be prepared to move from the instrumental and the behavioral to the normative.

## Notes

1. Harry Eckstein and David Apter, eds., *Comparative Politics: A Reader* (New York: Free Press, 1963), p. 23.

2. Robert T. Holt and John E. Turner, eds., *The Methodology of Comparative Research* (New York: Free Press, 1970), p. 20.

3. For a fuller development, see Roy C. Macridis, *The Study of Comparative Government* (New York: Random House, 1955).

4. The works referred to are: Ralf Dahrendorf, *Society and Democracy in Germany* (Garden City, N.Y.: Doubleday Publishing, 1967); Karl Dietrich Bracher, *The German Dictatorship: The Origin, Structure and Effects of National Socialism* (New York: Praeger Publishers, 1970); Samuel H. Beer, *British Politics in the Collectivist Age* (New York: Alfred A. Knopf, 1966); Stanley Hoffmann, *Decline or Renewal? France since the 1930's* (New York: Viking Press, 1974); Merle Fainsod, *How Russia Is Ruled*, rev. ed. (Cambridge, Mass.: Harvard Univ. Press, 1963); Joseph LaPalombara, *Interest Groups in Italian Politics* (Princeton: Princeton University Press, 1964); Robert A. Scalapino, *Democracy and the Party Movement in Prewar Japan* (Berkeley: University of California Press, 1953); Harry Eckstein, *Division and Cohesion in a Democracy: A Study of Norway* (Princeton: Princeton University Press, 1966).

5. See: David Easton, *A Systems Analysis of Political Life* (New York: John Wiley & Sons, 1965); Karl Deutsch, *The Nerves of Government* (New York: Free Press, 1963); Seymour M. Lipset, *Political Man: The Social Bases of Politics*, rev. ed. (Baltimore: The Johns Hopkins Press, 1981); Samuel H. Beer, ed., *Patterns of Government*, 3d ed. (New York: Random House, 1973); Gabriel Almond and Sidney Verba, *The Civic Culture* (Princeton: Princeton University Press, 1963); Robert Dahl, *Polyarchy: Participation and Opposition* (New Haven: Yale University Press, 1971); William Kornhauser, *The Politics of Mass Society* (New York: Free Press, 1959); Samuel P. Huntington, *Political Order in Changing Societies* (New Haven: Yale University Press, 1968); Ralf Dahrendorf, *Class and Class Conflict in Industrial Society* (Stanford: Stanford University Press, 1959); Barrington Moore, Jr., *Social Origins of Dictatorship and Democracy* (Boston: Beacon Press, 1966); David Butler and Donald Stokes, *Political Change in Britain* (New York: St. Martin's Press, 1969); Maurice Duverger, *Political Parties*, 3d ed. (London: Methuen, 1969).

6. David Easton, "An Approach to the Analysis of Political Systems," *World Politics*, April 1957, pp. 383–400.

7. Lipset, *Political Man*, rev. ed. (Baltimore: The Johns Hopkins Press, 1981).

8. Andrew Shonfield, *Modern Capitalism* (London: Oxford University Press, 1965).

9. Easton, *A Systems Analysis*, esp. chapters 4, 14, and 15.

10. Samuel P. Huntington, "Political Development and Political Decay," *World Politics*, April 1965, pp. 383–430. See also his *Political Order in Changing Societies*.

11. Almond and Verba, *The Civic Culture*; and Samuel H. Beer, *Patterns of Government* (part I, chapter 3).

12. Suzanne Berger et al., "New Perspectives for the Study of Western Europe," Social Science Research Council *Items 29*, no. 3 (September 1975).

13. Carl J. Friedrich, *Constitutional Government and Democracy*, 4th ed. (Waltham, Mass.: Blaisdell, 1968).

14. Sidney Verba, from his unpublished paper, "Comparative Politics: Where We Have Been, Where Are We Going?" Center for International Affairs, Harvard University, 1982.

15. Charles Tilly, *Crises and Sequences* (Princeton: Princeton University Press, 1964).

# CHAPTER ONE

# Comparing Political Systems

## 1

## How We Compare

*John Stuart Mill*

There are two kinds of sociological inquiry. In the first kind, the question proposed is, what effect will follow from a given cause, a certain general condition of social circumstances being presupposed. As, for example, what would be the effect of. . .abolishing monarchy, or introducing universal suffrage, in the present condition of society and civilization in any European country, or under any other given supposition with regard to the circumstances of society in general: without reference to the changes which might take place, or which may already be in progress, in those circumstances. But there is also a second inquiry, namely, what are the laws which determine those general circumstances themselves. In this last the question is, not what will be the effect of a given cause in a certain state of society, but what are the causes which produce, and the phenomena which characterize, States of Society generally. In the solution of this question consists the general Science of Society; by which all the conclusions of the other and more special kind of inquiry must be limited and controlled.

In order to conceive correctly the scope of this general science, and distinguish it from the subordinate departments of sociological speculation, it is necessary to fix with precision the

SOURCE: John Stuart Mill, "Of the Inverse Deductive, or Historical Method," in *A System of Logic*, Book VI, chapter 10, (New York: Harper, 1846). Abridged by the editors.

ideas attached to the phrase, "A State of Society." What is called a state of society, is the simultaneous state of all the greater social facts, or phenomena. Such are, the degree of knowledge, and of intellectual and moral culture, existing in the community, and in every class of it; the state of industry, of wealth and its distribution; the habitual occupations of the community; their division into classes, and the relations of those classes to one another; the common beliefs which they entertain on all the subjects most important to mankind, and the degree of assurance with which those beliefs are held; their tastes, and the character and degree of their aesthetic development; their form of government, and the more important of their laws and customs. The condition of all these things, and of many more which will spontaneously suggest themselves, constitute the state of society or the state of civilization at any given time.

When states of society, and the causes which produce them, are spoken of as a subject of science, it is implied that there exists a natural correlation among these different elements; that not every variety of combination of these general social facts is possible, but only certain combinations; that, in short, there exist Uniformities of Coexistence between the states of the various social phenomena. And such is the truth: as is indeed a necessary consequence of the influence exercised by every one of those phenomena over every other. It is a fact implied in the *consensus* of the various parts of the social body.

States of society are like different constitutions or different ages in the physical frame; they are conditions not of one or a few organs or functions, but of the whole organism. Accordingly, the information which we possess respecting past ages, and respecting the various states of society now existing in different regions of the earth, does, when duly analyzed, exhibit such uniformities. It *is* found that when one of the features of society is in a particular state, a state of all the other features, more or less precisely determinate, always coexists with it. . . .

It is one of the characters, not absolutely peculiar to the sciences of human nature and society, but belonging to them in a peculiar degree, to be conversant with a subject matter whose properties are changeable. I do not mean changeable from day to day, but from age to age: so that not only the qualities of individuals vary, but those of the majority are not the same in one age as in another.

The principal cause of this peculiarity is the extensive and constant reaction of the effects upon their causes. The circumstances in which mankind are placed, operating according to their own laws and to the laws of human nature, form the characters of the men; but the men, in their turn, mould and shape the circumstances, for themselves and for those who come after them. From this reciprocal action there must necessarily result either a cycle or a progress. . . .

But, while it is an imperative rule never to introduce any generalizations from history into the social science unless sufficient grounds can be pointed out for it in human nature, I do not think any one will contend that it would have been possible, setting out from the principles of human nature and from the general circumstances of man's position in the universe, to determine a priori the order in which human development must take place, and to predict, consequently, the general facts of history up to the present time. The initial stages of human progress—when man, as yet unmodified by society, and characterized only by the instincts resulting directly from his organization, was acted upon by outward objects of a comparatively simple and universal character—might indeed, as M. Comte remarks, be deduced from the laws of human nature; which moreover is the only possible mode of ascertaining them, since of that form of human existence no direct memorials are preserved. . . .

If, therefore, the series of the effects themselves did not, when examined as a whole, manifest any regularity, we should in vain attempt to construct a general science of society. We must in that case have contented ourselves with that subordinate order of sociological speculation formerly noticed, namely, with endeavoring to ascertain what would be the effect of the introduction of any new cause, in a state of society supposed to be fixed; a knowledge sufficient for most of the ordinary exigencies of daily political practice, but liable to fail in all cases in which the progressive movement of society is one of the influencing elements; and therefore more precarious in proportion as the case is more important. But since both the natural varieties of mankind, and the original diversities of local circumstances, are much less considerable than the points of agreement, there will naturally be a certain degree of uniformity in the progressive development of man and of his works. . . . History accordingly does, when judiciously examined, afford Empirical Laws of Society. And the problem of general sociology is to ascertain these, and connect them with the laws of human nature by deductions showing that such were the derivative laws naturally to be expected as the consequences of those ultimate ones.

It is indeed, in most cases, hardly possible, even after history has suggested the derivative law, to demonstrate a priori that such was the only order of succession or of coexistence in which the effects could, consistently with the laws of human nature, have been produced. We can at most make out that there were strong a priori reasons for expecting it and that no other order of succession or coexistence would have been by any means so likely to result from the nature of man and his position upon earth. This, however—which, in the Inverse Deductive Method that we are now characterizing, is a real process of verification—is as indispensable (to be more so is impossible) as verification by specific experience has been shown to be where the conclusion is originally obtained by the direct way of deduction. The empirical laws must be the result of but a few instances, since few nations have ever attained at all, and still fewer by their own independent development, a high stage of social progress. If, therefore, even one or two of these few instances be insufficiently known or imperfectly analyzed into its elements, and therefore not adequately compared with other instances, nothing is more probable than that a wrong empirical law will result instead of the right one. Accordingly, the most erroneous generalizations are continually made from the course of history.... The only check or corrective is constant verification by psychological and ethological laws. We may add to this, that no one but a person competently skilled in those laws is capable of preparing the materials for historical generalization by analyzing the facts of history, or even by observing the social phenomena of his own time. No other will be aware of the comparative importance of different facts, nor consequently know what facts he is to look out for, or what to observe; still less will he be capable of estimating the evidence of those facts which, as is the case with most, cannot be observed directly, but must be inferred from marks.

The Empirical Laws of Society are of two kinds; some are uniformities of coexistence, some of succession....

In order to obtain better empirical laws, we must not rest satisfied with noting the progressive changes which manifest themselves in the separate elements of society, and in which nothing is indicated but the relation of the fragments of the effect to corresponding fragments of the cause. It is necessary to combine the statical view of social phenomena with the dynamical, considering not only the progressive changes of the different elements, but the contemporaneous condition of each; and thus obtain empirically the law of correspondence not only between the simultaneous states, but between the simultaneous changes, of those elements. This law of correspondence it is, which, after being duly verified a priori, will become the real scientific derivative law of the development of humanity and human affairs.

In the difficult process of observation and comparison which is here required, it would evidently be a very great assistance if it should happen to be the fact, that some one element in the complex existence of social man is preëminent over all others as the prime agent of the social movement. For we could then take the progress of that one element as the central chain, to each successive link of which, the corresponding links of all the other progressions being appended, the succession of the facts would by this alone be presented in a kind of spontaneous order, far more nearly approaching to the real order of their filiation than could be obtained by any other merely empirical process.

Now, the evidence of history and the evidence of human nature combine, by a most striking instance of consilience, to show that there is really one social element which is thus predominant, and almost paramount, among the agents of the social progression. This is, the state of the speculative faculties of mankind; including the nature of the speculative beliefs which by any means they have arrived at, concerning themselves and the world by which they are surrounded.

It would be a great error, and one very little likely to be committed, to assert that speculation, intellectual activity, the pursuit of truth, is among the more powerful propensities of human nature, or fills a large place in the lives of any, save decidedly exceptional individuals. But notwithstanding the relative weakness of this principle among other sociological agents, its influence is the main determining cause of the social progress; all the other dispositions of our nature which contribute to that progress, being dependent upon it for the means of accomplishing their share of the work. Thus (to take the most obvious case first), the impelling force to most of the improvements effected in the arts of life, is the desire of increased material comfort; but as we can only act upon external objects in proportion to our knowledge of them, the state of knowledge at any time is the impassable limit of the industrial improvements possible at that time; and the progress of industry must follow, and depend upon, the progress of knowledge. The same thing may be shown to be true, though it is not quite so obvious, of the progress of the fine arts. Further, as the strongest propensities of human nature (being the purely selfish ones, and those of a sympathetic character which partake most of the nature of selfishness) evidently tend in themselves to disunite mankind, not to unite them—to make them rivals, not confederates; social existence is only possible by a disciplining of those more powerful propensities, which consists in subordinating them to a common system of opinions. The degree of this subordination is the measure of the completeness of the social union, and the nature of the common opinions determines its kind. But in order that mankind should conform their actions to any set of opinions, these opinions must exist, must be believed by them. And thus, the state of the speculative faculties, the character of the propositions assented to by the intellect, essentially determines the moral and political state of the community, as we have already seen that it determines the physical.

These conclusions, deduced from the laws of human nature, are in entire accordance with the general facts of history. Every considerable change historically known to us in the condition of any portion of mankind, has been preceded by a change, of proportional extent, in the state of their knowledge, or in their prevalent beliefs. As between any given state of speculation, and the correlative state of everything else, it was almost always the former which first showed itself; though the effects, no doubt, reacted potently upon the cause. Every considerable advance in material civilization has been preceded by an advance in knowledge; and when any great social change has come to pass, a great change in the opinions and modes of thinking of society had taken place shortly before. Polytheism, Judaism, Christianity, Protestantism, the negative philosophy of modern Europe, and its positive science —each of these has been a primary agent in making society what it was at each successive period, while society was but secondarily instrumental in making *them*; each of them (so far as causes can be assigned for its existence) being mainly an emanation not from the practical life of the period, but from the state of belief and thought during some time previous. The weakness of the speculative propensity has not, therefore, prevented the progress of speculation from governing that of society at large; it has only, and too often,

prevented progress altogether, where the intellectual progression has come to an early stand for want of sufficiently favorable circumstances.

From this accumulated evidence, we are justified in concluding, that the order of human progression in all respects will be a corollary deducible from the order of progression in the intellectual convictions of mankind, that is, from the law of the successive transformation of religion and science. The question remains, whether this law can be determined, at first from history as an empirical law, then converted into a scientific theorem by deducing it a priori from the principles of human nature. As the progress of knowledge and the changes in the opinions of mankind are very slow, and manifest themselves in a well-defined manner only at long intervals; it cannot be expected that the general order of sequence should be discoverable from the examination of less than a very considerable part of the duration of the social progress. It is necessary to take into consideration the whole of past time, from the first recorded condition of the human race; and it is probable that all the terms of the series already past were indispensable to the operation; that the memorable phenomena of the last generation, and even those of the present, were necessary to manifest the law, and that consequently the Science of History has only become possible in our own time.

# 2

# Systems Theory and Comparative Analysis

*Karl Deutsch*

## THE PROCESS OF COMPARING

To compare two events or two things is always a process of matching. One matches either physical

SOURCE: Karl Deutsch, "The Systems Theory Approach as a Basis for Comparative Analysis," *International Social Science Journal*, vol. 37, no. 1 (1985), pp. 5–18. © Unesco 1985. Reproduced by permission of Unesco. Notes abridged by the editors.

events, such as the insertion of a key into a lock. It either fits or it does not. Or one could compare a map with a landscape, an aerial photograph, or a more symbolic representation, in each case it is an operation in which the results of the matching processes are monitored and noted.

To think is to compare. We begin by thinking of places, comparing locations in space and time. Where is something? And when did it happen? These are comparative judgements. Is it near or far from some other place? Did it happen earlier or later than something else? Words are also formed by comparison. We refer to classes of words. Nouns refer to classes of things; verbs refer to classes of processes.

No two events are alike in everything, but we compare them in those aspects that matter for the purpose at hand, or, in those that matter for a collection of purposes. We therefore also compare things which in other aspects are not comparable. Apples and planets are different in many ways, but the comparison by Newton of an apple and a planet was a success, since both are subject to gravitation.

The differences which we perceive in certain aspects of any two events, are perceived against a background of similarity with others, and so is the relative uniqueness of an event. We call an event unique if it is similar in very few aspects or dimensions, and different in very, very many from others. Without attempted comparison, how could we know that something was unique? If something were truly unique in every respect, how could we discuss it? We should have no words for it. We could only talk about it in negatives, calling it ineffable, unmeasurable and so on, and then we would be very close to magic or religion and well away from science.

Every object of comparison may be treated as a system with inner transactions and processes of covariance. Covariance means that if there is a change in $A$ then there is a change in $B$. The inner processes of covariance decline at the boundaries of systems, and that makes them inner processes. They may decline abruptly, similar to step-functions, or gradually, falling below some critical threshold. This distinguishes them from outer processes which do not necessarily decline at the

boundaries, and indeed may even be more frequent or more powerful outside the boundaries of the system than inside it.

## SOME CATEGORIES FOR COMPARING THE FUNCTIONS OF POLITICAL SYSTEMS

Systems have basic functions. I propose to keep identity, with, on the whole, very few people getting killed in the process. Similarly, the Japanese Meiji restoration changed Japan profoundly in many ways, yet preserved Japanese identity, and except for a minor military episode between the new government and the Satsuma and some other clans, there was little bloodshed. So much for the first six systems requirements or basic tasks or political functions. We could ask then, in comparing countries, how well they are doing with regard to these six basic functions.

### Eight Basic Political Needs of the Population

In the second set, eight political needs of the population are listed. The eight needs I refer to always come in pairs: one side dealing with tangibles and the other side dealing with intangibles.

Let us begin with the conservative or tangible investment pair, referring to the maintenance of physical equipment, such as machines, houses, fields and gardens and then the intangible side of the pair which refers to the habits and motivations to maintain both these physical things and the prestige and status order of the authority system of the society. Modern technologies and societies need much maintenance. Iron must be kept from rusting, homes must be dusted, floors and windows washed, roofs and cars repaired. Perhaps as much as 15 to 25 per cent of the cost of a new building goes into the yearly cost of cleaning and maintenance, if decay and shabbiness are to be avoided. Similarly, the maintenance of habits, practices and institutions of authority, rank and class privilege requires effort and resources.

The second pair involves the increase in physical capital, that is the savings functions, the investment function, the technologically innovative function, etc. Without increasing and improving the basic technological equipment, and also the physical capital of society, societies almost inevitably would become poorer, since some resources may deteriorate or become more expensive to exploit, while their populations grow. There is no way of getting around this needed increase in physical capital, to which some political parties and in mind three notions or catalogues of basic systems and functions which can be used for comparative research (each of these is plural).

## A Further Development of the Parsons Scheme

The first is the development of the four systems necessities or basic tasks that Talcott Parsons proposed in his time, and to which I have added two more, ultimately, I think, with Parsons' consent. Parsons wrote of every system having to *maintain* its own patterns, to *adapt* to its environment, to attain some *goals* and to *integrate* all these different tasks with each other.[1]

To these tasks of pattern maintenance, adaptation, goal attainment and integration, I propose to add, first, the task of goal change, particularly of states and political systems (we are very much aware that states and political systems very often do change their major goals, as in the Federal Republic of Germany in the 1950s, and it is not necessary to labour that point) and, second, self-transformation. A system may transform itself in many dimensions while retaining continuity in others so as not to lose its identity (by 'identity' I mean the applicability of memories). Examples are bloody revolutions, such as the English one in the seventeenth century, the French and American ones in the eighteenth, and the Russian and Chinese ones in the twentieth. Yet, after each of these revolutions, national and cultural identities largely persisted. The English remained recognizably English, the French recognizably French, the Americans remained American, or

even became more so. Benjamin Franklin in the 1750s, along with many of his countrymen, was already very American before the shooting started, and Richard Merritt has shown by analyses of colonial newspapers that the symbol 'American' became meaningful to them before the first shots were fired at Lexington.[2] In the twentieth century, following the Russian and Chinese revolutions, the Russians have remained very recognizably Russian, and the Chinese even more recognizably Chinese.

Self-transformations need not be bloody. The British industrial revolution profoundly transformed the country without destroying its movements or systems pay more attention, and some less. On the intangible side, there are the motives of achievement, of the work ethic, of thrift, of being diligent, successful, reliable, punctual, or what the Germans call *Leistungsethik*, or the ethics of performance, which implies very clearly the habits and preferences that are conducive to the building up of that physical and human capital.

The third pair relates to openness to the world. On the physical side, it involves transport and communications equipment, such as roads, railways, ships, airplanes, airports, telephones, telegraph lines, wireless telegraphy and television—in effect, all the physical equipment and organizations which belong to that openness to the world, including manpower. In regard to communications and transport, physical equipment and manpower and the interests in their use are inextricably linked, but curiosity, desire for travel, for reading foreign authors, for access to foreign goods, and for the mobility of persons, goods and capital all belong in this intangible category.

The above three sets tend to be of interest to conservative parties the world over. The first two, maintaining tangible things and social rank, is the old-line conservatism; by comparison, the increasing of capital goods, and progress, is closer to the modern type of conservatism. But whether it is Mrs Thatcher's Conservative Party or the Federal Republic of Germany's CDU or the Republicans in the United States, one will find a fairly close correlation between these orientations, and the programmes and activities of these parties.

There is, however, another psychic need and interest in the intangible things that can lead to tangible services, that is, interest in security and solidarity (by security, I mean social security within a country, and not the military 'security' of international power). Equality is also involved in this, and to some extent we shall call it internal mobility; the more unequal the society the less mobile are its members. For example, they cannot date the members of the opposite sex (or, nowadays, of the same sex) of another social stratum because they have no access, no contacts. This is one of the reasons why the cry for equality in many countries is also raised by the children of the privileged classes, since they, too, are denied mobility, barred and estranged from many human contacts. The typical parties demanding more solidarity and equality, full employment and social welfare are primarily the socialist and labour parties in all countries, for example the American Democrats, but also to a lesser but significant extent the Roman Catholic parties in many countries. Other parties, such as the Nazis, borrowed some of that appeal for its *Volksgenossen* [countrymen], at least for a time, before sending them out to the battlefields and turning their cities into the target areas of aerial bombardments.

The final two pairs are new and have been perceived as disturbing in the party landscapes of many countries. People want their physical and biological environment preserved. In West Berlin, for example, one could say that the ratio of trees to people is still very favourable, I believe there are at least ten trees to every person, but in colonial America there were at least 1,000 trees per person. The day may soon come in many countries when we no longer have very many trees per person. Environment, therefore, is a major issue, a major physical need. The physical environment must be preserved. Returning to the intangible side we find the need for spontaneity. The more dense the road traffic, the more we must teach our children to stop quickly at the edge of every pavement. The more tight an environment becomes, demographically, economically and

technologically, the less room is often left for spontaneity. We have therefore an environmental and a situational pressure against spontaneity, and since people frequently behave in proportion to marginal utility, they demand more of that which is in critically short supply. There have been also political demands for spontaneity, with slogans such as 'Life begins before death' or, 'There is a beach beneath the pavement', or, *'L'imagination au pouvoir.'*

Imagination, spontaneity, affection in small groups—all these are now urgent human needs. This need will not go away, and indeed, it may become even stronger, just as the need for protection of the environment gets stronger. As a result, political parties that concentrate on these two needs—environment and spontaneity will not disappear, but will remain in the political landscape, unless the major parties manage to integrate these two demands into other ones. But a trade union which wants discipline, or a bank which wants thrift, or an enterprise which wants improvements in capital, are not easily adapted to the provision of more affection and spontaneity. It is more likely that in a pluralistic democracy there will be separate movements and organizations catering to these differing basic needs. What seems likely is that, of these eight needs, or these four pairs, none will disappear, but all will become permanent parts of the landscape of pluralistic democracy to different extents. So far, this is a hypothesis. Comparative research on the twenty or thirty industrial democracies in the world could tell us whether this is in fact the case or not, and such research would be well worth the effort.

## A Set of Preferred State Functions and State Types

The third set of goals. . .are historical functions of the state, which can be observed in the course of history. Each state serves several functions, often to some extent all of them, but not in the same rank order of priorities nor with the same degree of urgency or the same proportion of means allocated to each of them.

The first state function is once again pattern-maintenance, to keep in power those who have power, and to keep those who are wealthy in possession of that wealth.

A second function stands foremost in states organized for conquest.[3] Such states are very often conservative in internal affairs, but seek to conquer foreign countries and populations. However, the operational necessities of organizing for conquest may then tend to interfere with pattern-maintenance. The results may show that the rulers a particular state had at the beginning of a war of conquest, such as the Tsars of Russia in 1914, turn out to be highly unsuited to the task. The overthrow in February 1917 of the Tsar by a government in favour of continuing the effort at military conquest, is one example. The head of the new regime, Alexander Kerenski, also wanted to conquer Istanbul for Russia, an enterprise no more promising than it had been for the Tsar, but at least the Kerenski Government imagined itself, and was for a time believed to be, more competent in pursuing that task. The resources of politics, society and culture may become so totally oriented to a conquest that a good part of the social fabric may be destroyed, but not all of it. The Hitler Government in Germany would be an example of this.

A third function is the pursuit of wealth. Governments, particularly since the sixteenth century, have usually been expected to make their peoples richer, not poorer. The mercantilist states, from the days of Colbert and onwards, tried to pursue wealth for the nation by careful government regulations. To this day, there are many states in the world that regulate their currencies and transactions and many other functions in the hope of defending or increasing national wealth by such means.

During the reign of Queen Victoria, states expected an increase in wealth from *laissez-faire* policies which became prominent. The peak of the *laissez-faire* ideology was probably between 1860 and 1870 about the time of the Cobden Treaty, when England and France agreed to a high degree of trade between their two countries.

Since the First World War, we also find states which try to promote national wealth by economic planning, usually centralized or indicative planning. A fourth function is the welfare state, based on two propositions: that it is less important whether a country is rich, and more important that no one in it should be intolerably poor; and that the pursuit of widely distributed welfare, health and education is quite compatible with economic and cultural progress. On the first point, a nation might prefer a moderately high plateau of wealth to a higher mathematical average of very high peaks and very deep abysses. As to the second point, it has often been argued that the welfare state interferes with economic growth. But Sweden has the most elaborate welfare state in the world, and also a higher per capita income than even the United States.

A fifth function may give rise to a fifth type of state: the mobilization state. Here we find states that mobilize mass efforts for some purpose, or for social transformation, as did the Soviet Union in the days of Lenin, and then of Stalin in the days of the first two Five-Year Plans. These are examples of mass mobilization which was used to change the country, to transform the society, and in these particular cases regardless of the cost. Similarly, Mao's China made huge transformation efforts at a vast cost in terms of human life and suffering. In both countries it has been argued that not to transform their societies so quickly would have implied even greater sacrifices in the long run. The worldwide debate about whether this was so has not yet ended. Earlier examples were the government of the French Revolution and the Jacobins in 1793, and the rule of Oliver Cromwell and the Puritans in the 1620s. After the American Revolution, Thomas Jefferson wrote that the United States should have a revolution every twenty-five years, but his countrymen were more cautious, and did quite well at a lower scale of cost.

When the great transformation and mobilization effort has achieved its main purposes, such regimes tend to become more conservative. States then return to pattern-maintenance, or return to the promotion of wealth through more or less efficient or inefficient forms of *laissez-faire*, or of economic planning.

Two further state goals are beginning to emerge. We find elements of them in certain periods of history, but these did not then become dominant. I would venture to predict on political grounds, however, that they will become of major importance, with the first occurring within the next half-century, and the second within the next 100 years.

The first function, which will become increasingly important, is adaptive learning. We have found some examples already, for example after the oil shock. Within ten years Europe managed to cut its oil imports by 25 per cent, which is a remarkable achievement. This is effective adaptive learning, and there will be more of this sort. As populations double at the end of the century, it will be discovered that the 6.1 billion people that the United Nations is now predicting for 2000 cannot be fed by the presently existing methods of agriculture, even with all-out production by today's grain-producing countries. When the population increases to 10 billion by the middle of the next century, not even American farming efficiency will be capable of doing the job. What will then happen? Will there be a transformation of agriculture—perhaps a worldwide shift to much more irrigation agriculture and to raising two crops per year? There may also be a shift from the historically inherited types of seed to the more high-yield types. New kinds of rice and wheat seed have already made India a food-surplus country in those two categories. But seeds of this type exhaust the soil, require vast quantities of water, and artificial fertilizer, which is largely based on petroleum. A huge adaptation will be necessary to develop 'miracle' beans, 'miracle' peanuts, 'miracle' peas—the legumes which enrich the soil instead of making it poorer. At the same time there wil be a need for more energy. If one does not have enough petroleum for artificial fertilizer, it may be necessary to fixate more nitrogen from the air, but this method is energy intensive.

All these shifts will, in turn, be capital intensive. Generally, adaptive learning by states will also involve a shift to higher levels of capital accumulation, and to some extent—present-day conservative politicians will be unhappy to hear—to some sort of guidance as to where the capital should be utilized. A good deal of capital nowadays goes into armaments which, at best, produce not much more than rust, and also into the production of luxury goods which do nothing to assist with the food, welfare and energy problems of the future. If catastrophe is to be avoided, much more capital will have to be diverted to the latter purposes.

There is no practical way of stopping population growth in the next twenty years. The 6 billion world of the year 2000 cannot be prevented, unless there is a major war. Practically all of the parents of the children who will be born by the year 2000 have been born already. They are here, at least 16 years old and able to start producing children; in the tropical countries they may even start somewhat earlier. Adaptive learning of new political and economic habits to cope with this 6 billion world will become increasingly necessary. It may well come to characterize the politics of the next half century, and early examples of its development—such as the learning of Danish peasants in the nineteenth century to adapt to a world market of cheap overseas grain—should become an important topic for political comparisons.

Another type of learning may become an important state function at a still later stage. This is initiative learning and it consists in the starting and sustaining of new activities of a scale that exceeds the capacities of individuals and small groups. Early examples occurred in the fifteenth-century decisions of Portugal under Prince Henry the Navigator to support the design and construction of ships capable of intercontinental voyages and the eventual opening of the sea route to India that followed; and in the decision of the Spanish state to support the voyage of Christopher Columbus and the conquest of large parts of the New World that followed. More recent examples include the Manhattan Project of the United States after 1939 and the space programmes of the United States and the Soviet Union from the 1950s onward. None of these activities were, in the main, adaptations to currently existing conditions. They were new initiatives, pointing beyond the economics and politics of their time, and they were understood as such by most of their initiators. Such initiative learning, still requiring the large resources that in all likelihood only states can marshal, may well become a major and perhaps the leading state function after the middle of the next century. Not only space transport, but also such fields as molecular biology, genetic engineering and artificial intelligence, now all in their beginnings, may come to offer increasing opportunities for such initiatives. The capacity of political systems, including both their state and non-state sectors, to develop and sustain such major initiatives should offer an increasingly important dimension of comparisons in political research.

## STRUCTURAL COMPARISONS: SOME USES OF SYSTEMS THEORY

Up to this point, we have considered mainly possible lists of functions of states and political systems. What about the structures of such systems, their contrasts and their changes? Here some of the concepts of general systems theory may be of help.

A system is a set of elements or components, which is distinguished from its environment, first of all, by a markedly higher degree of interdependence or covariance: if any component $m$ changes, some other component $n$ will also change, positively or negatively, in some predictable fashion. A system is further characterized by a markedly larger flow of transactions within it, relative to its size; by an easier transfer of information; by some system properties that differ from component properties; and usually by coherence, in the sense of a lower probability and higher cost of separation of its components. Most systems, relevant to our inquiry show all of these five characteristics; those that lack one or more of them form borderline cases. All these structural aspects and their possible changes may offer

opportunities for comparisons among political systems. Some or all of them have already been so used in comparative case-studies of political integration.

Usually, systems are organized hierarchically in system levels. Within the same political systems, a higher level differs from the next lower one by inclusion—it includes it as a component; by order of magnitude—it is usually larger by a factor of two to ten or more; and by a larger probability of prevailing in case of conflict; many well-developed nation-states tend to prevail over their provinces. Once again, exceptions form borderline cases.

Lower level systems are components or subsystems of higher level ones, which in turn form supra-systems for them. A system with several levels may be supra-system dominant, as are most nation states *vis-à-vis* the cities, regions and interest groups within them, or they may be subsystem dominant, as is the present-day international system.[4] So are also many weak nation-states where the armed forces repeatedly overthrow the government, or where strong economic interest groups may bring down the government by taking a part of their capital abroad or by ceasing to invest or by withholding needed goods or services.

All systems we know are embedded in supra-systems. Our planet is imbedded in the solar system, on which we depend such a great deal, and also in the larger environments beyond this, including cosmic rays and all that this entails. At the other end of the scale, there are the subsystems further and further down. For example, we draw energy from the splitting of atoms by reaching down into the subsystems beyond our normal bodily sizes. For comparative political studies, one could propose, very broadly, a formula: $i \pm 3$, $i$ meaning the system level, let us say the national government, and ask for the next three levels up: the international alliance system, the world political system and the global ecological system. In order to understand what can happen at the level $i$ we also may have to go at least three levels down, to the major regional units, or major regional classes and interest groups, the small groups, and even to some key individuals. Usually in such cases we have to look for cross-level effects. The Allende government in Chile in 1973 was overthrown from level $i - 1$ by the armed forces, aided by certain domestic interest groups, and in a context of pressure from level $i + 1$, that is the United States and its allies.

When we compare systems, we look for differences. Many of these differences are likely to be quantitative. Sometimes, we may try to present qualitative differences between different countries by giving the same general system model for a given set of twenty-five countries, but changing the quantitative parameters.... For example, in countries such as the Federal Republic of Germany and the United States employment in agriculture is very small by comparison with a country such as Indonesia where it is very large. We can see that by simply adjusting the quantitative parameters we can achieve a tolerable representation of the qualitative differences among the systems. What is equally, or even more important, we can then ask, in what directions are these parameters changing? Are they changing towards some critical threshold values, where some important side effects are changing rapidly?

Here it is useful to discuss some different ways of measuring quantitative changes. We often count quantitative changes in three ways which are relevant to the total activity under study. Thus, in studying comparative illiteracy we can show that the percentage of illiterates in a country is declining. Second, in terms of absolute numbers, as the population of that country increases faster than the percentage of illiterates declines, the illiterates increase in absolute numbers. Third, we may ask whether, or how far away an absolute number is, from critical mass or from a critical threshold. For example, young people are often unhappy at being ordered about by their elders. In past times, however, when the population was scattered around the countryside, when population was smaller, the masters and journeymen, parents and extended family kept them firmly under their respective control in the villages and artisans' workshops. Today, when the population is larger, the absolute number of people between the ages of 14 and 21 years of age has greatly increased and they are very often concentrated in large cities, we are reaching a critical mass. When a rock band comes to town, or there is a major soccer match, large numbers of young people may assemble at one place and get out of control, once critical mass is reached. Even though the child ratio per family is lower, these present-day children may then cause more trouble than the children of past generations ever did. Similarly, in some countries, the poor or the unemployed reach a critical mass and critical concentration, even though they may amount to only 20 per cent of the total population, or in the case of unemployment to between 8 and 10 per cent of the total labour force.

Another point to bear in mind is the reversal of proportions. When quantities change it is most important that we know whether what was originally a minority has now become a majority, as this will affect the outcome of many expectations.

We also need much more quantitative data for comparisons of time and speed. Time has been largely neglected in comparative political research, but more recently authors such as Jean Laponce have started to analyse this subject.[5] Similarly, there is a Unesco-supported publication edited by Alexander Szalai, Philip Converse and others, on time budgets.[6] It is a pioneering work in showing what one can learn by watching how people spend their time in seven countries. Much more research on the time dimension of politics is needed.

We also need to know more about what measures of political behaviour and economic behaviour are more or less culture-sensitive. By and large, armies in the First, Second and Third World, all using expensive modern fighter planes, show few differences if any, depending on their culture. Peru is as eager to buy supersonic fighter planes as are Arab states (whatever Islamic culture may indicate), and orders for fighter planes and Exocet rockets are as common to the Argentinians and the ayatollas, as to the Israelis. Other aspects such as the motivation to work, may be considerably more culture-sensitive. We also need careful investigations of the extent to which culture-sensitivity changes, or has been changing over time.

Related to this question of culture is the point which Richard Rose made, that it is important not only to distinguish countries and strata pro- grammes, but to find out what the differences are across programmes. Here we might begin by ask- ing what are the differences across programmes within the same country. Richard Rose tells us that it takes fewer bureaucrats to run the Treasury than it costs to run the income-maintenance pro- grammes, such as social security.[7] I would like to add also that this was the basic idea of Daniel Moynihan, who proposed that the poor should benefit from a negative income tax so that they would have some money, and his argument also covered the fact that one might not need any more bureaucrats to deal with the distribution of this income than would be needed to collect taxes from those whose income is larger. We could, in his view, save ourselves a huge apparatus of con- trollers and bureaucrats.[8]

In general, therefore, the administrative density of programmes, that is the number of bureaucrats one needs per million, within the budget, would be a very interesting figure to have access to. This could be achieved among pro- grammes within the same country, coupled with some research on the two famous competing theories: that of Max Weber who argued that bureaucracies are rational,[9] and that of Northcote Parkinson who maintained the exact opposite, namely that bureaucracies grow blindy and irra- tionally.[10] Which programmes in one country, and which country among several countries, are closer to the rationality model of Max Weber, and which are the ones closest to the Northcote Parkinson model of bureaucratic proliferation? And what of the mixed forms we might find in practice? We could, of course, compare the same programme among countries, as Richard Rose has suggested, and thereby make more specific comparisons of programme goals, in rationality of means, and in cost efficiency, implementation and time efficiency.

We have far too many comparisons as to what the programme costs in terms of money and far too few concerning what it costs in terms of time an upon whom the costs of delay are falling. Richard Rose has suggested that we do not need very many people to administer justice, because we tolerate the existing system which take two to three years to have a law case heard. Even the management of a grocery supermarket knows enough to open more check-outs when the queues get too long, but our judicial system has not yet reached this elementary degree of sen- sitivity. If we doubled the number of courts and justices, we could either halve the size of judicial districts, or else we could double the number of specialized courts for different functions. There are, of course, family and juvenile courts, but there could be special courts for traffic cases, for insurance claims, for commercial fraud and for the so-called white-collar crimes.

Here once again comparative research gets closer to policy research. Thus, if research on time efficiency discovers how the large costs of delay are incurred, one may ask: are costs of error higher than costs of delay and are error rates reduced significantly by long delays? If so, then one should choose delay over error, especially in cases of technical safety, or of trials for murder. The opposite may apply in automobile cases, where it is preferable to have 'no fault' automobile insurance because the cost of litigation and delay is higher than error in cases of this kind. We can begin with these points and learn how to make administration and government more effective than they are now.

Finally, we may compare the integrated per- formance of national political systems with regard to various values. Which integrated political system prevents the death of more children? Let us consider the following example: In 1975 General Pinochet's Chile and Fidel Castro's Cuba had similar per capita incomes, according to the World Bank (Chile $1,470, Cuba $1,270). Let us assume, for the moment, that the figures on both sides were not too distorted. The first-year child mortality rate in Cuba (27 per 1,000) was less than one-half of that in Chile (61 per 1,000), although the climate of Chile is no more unhealthy than that of Cuba.[11] The political system of Cuba performed well with regard to this particular dimension of public health.

We have to be careful, therefore, about what these systems provide, and about what they do not provide. We know that some Third World regimes are called "benevolent" dictatorships. With closer investigation it turns out that the decisive variable seems to be their benevolence to money. Their benevolence to people does not count nearly as much in allotting them this label in the financial and business section of many newspapers. If in a country foreign investments are safe, and child mortality is high, it would be considered more benevolent there than it would be if the reverse were true. We have, after all, special sections of newspapers which are devoted to business and while there may be reports in other parts of the same newspapers devoted to child deaths, these reports are usually briefer and rarer.

We could ask many other questions. For instance, is the world becoming more international or less? It appears that once again we have to return to the three dimensions of quantitative measurement: are international activities becoming a larger or a smaller portion of total activity in the world? And are international activities reaching levels which might have substantial side-effects, and perhaps threshold effects? Richard Merrit and I have discovered that the development of internationalism in the world is heterotropic[12] ('hetero' meaning different, and 'tropic' meaning going in some direction). In *Alice in Wonderland* there is someone who 'rode off furiously in several directions', and the world is, in effect, doing just that. Thus, the share of international trade in total in world economic activity is, in the long run, fairly stagnant. World trade today is no larger a proportion of world income than it was in 1913, which could be called a healthy world period, and considered to be a standard case of normality, but then look at what happened in 1914 and the years that followed. In other respects, such as communication and the diffusion of science, technology

and some patterns of mass culture, the world has become more unified than it used to be.

In absolute figures everything has increased. There are three times as many people as there were in 1913, and there is also a higher amount of economic activity than there was at that time. If one were to stress absolute figures, one could clearly prove that there is much more trade and many more international travellers. But if we were to look at the rates per million of the population, between 1950 and 1980, they would show how little has changed, how steady these proportions of the total population are. Take, on the one hand, the proportion of foreign students studying at universities in the Federal Republic of Germany and in the United States and, on the other, the proportion of students from these two countries studying abroad. Proportionately, there has been very little change in these figures. Of course, the Federal Republic of Germany now has four times as many students as it had in 1950 and, as was pointed out before, almost everything has increased. But one notices the great differences when one takes proportionate measures, as against absolute measures. Both of these are most important, and we ought to know much more about the political significance of each.

Certain types of internationalism are promoted by supra-system pressures. The world market requires a certain uniformity of performance, such as reliability of equipment, its cheapness, or its reliability of delivery and maintenance. The military balance puts pressure on the military of each country, which likes to think of itself as not falling behind other countries with regard to military power. We can think of two countries as being in a military balance if observers can state that one or the other has no predictably greater probability of winning in a dispute. This balance can be seen as a psychological concept of war, more so than a physical one. In so far as it rests on subjective perceptions, it may have no stable resting-point.

We may find that systems change in their sensitivity to distribution shifts. From time to time the distribution of status or income shifts among social groups. This can come partly from the pressure of world events, such as the oil shock of 1973 or the world depression of 1923–33. Or it may occur because of domestic events: the welfare state itself has brought about some of this type of shift. The crucial variable is whether the losing party is willing to adjust to this loss, or whether they prefer a civil war or a dictatorship. It may even come to pass that a loss in privileges for the middle classes, such as is resisted at the price of a civil war, as happened in Austria in 1930, is accepted at a later time, as it was in Austria in the late 1950s and 1960s without a civil war.

The ability of privileged groups to accept an adverse shift in status or income without trying to 'blow the place up' or starting to shoot, is quite important. On the whole, northwest European politics have been characterized by middle-class concessions to the welfare state, and until recently Mediterranean politics were characterized by the middle-class preferring military dictatorships to any major increase in the welfare state.

What are a system's propensities to promote economic growth and increases in productivity? The United Kingdom after 1960 may have been less prone to this than some other countries. And what of the plans for increasing arms competition or for disarmament? These two may be linked to each other. The world's model cases of economic growth, Japan, Singapore and Hong Kong, are remarkable for their low levels of military expenditure. But before we make a theory of it, let us note that the Republic of Korea spends a great deal more on military purposes and still grows.

And what of a national political system's propensity towards the proliferation of nuclear weapons? We have technological statements that country $X$ or $Y$ has the technical capacity to use nuclear weapons. There is, in fact, very little comparative research on which countries are likely to push towards national nuclear weapons, and conversely, on those countries not likely to do so. Are there any structural differences accounting for the differences? This could be very important to know.

What of shifts in legitimacy and stability of governments within nation states and what about probabilities of their supranational integration and secession? On what structural differences are they based?

Some of these examples clearly suggest that the distinction between structures and functions is always provisional. We call 'structure' a process that changes slowly, relatively to the time scale of the problem we are currently interested in; 'functions' is one of our names for a process that changes quickly, relatively to that same time scale, and that contributes to the maintenance of one or several major aspects of the system.

The older 'structural-functional' approach is gradually being replaced by the rise of models. A full model is a set of variables that are intended to resemble between them all those aspects of a system relevant for predicting the distribution of its outcomes, together with a set of parameters specifying the value of each variable at some initial stage, a set of coefficients stating how a change in one variable is correlated with changes in another, and a set of rules describing ways in which each variable can change. A partial or not fully specified model will lack some or many of these data.

In early writings I have tried to offer a sketch of a partial cybernetic model of this kind.[13] There is no need to repeat its basic categories here, but some of its basic features should lend themselves to comparisons among political systems. These might include external and internal feedback channels and processes, by which governments can find out about the consequences of their recent or current behaviour and adjust it appropriately to their goals. They might also include feedback processes by which the population of a country perceives and appraises the responsiveness of the government to some popular need or demand, with effects on changes in popular attitudes and actions toward that government or political system, and they might further be influenced by the memories of the system, and by those of the population, and by feedback channels and processes among them.

## SOME POSSIBLE APPLICATIONS

Even a good model of a country in many dimensions will never exhaust arguments. This also is why such a model could never give a prediction with any certainty, but it could tell us something about certain future probabilities—provided, of course, that no important variable was forgotten, and the importance of changes was not underrated.

Such a model could make political decisions, if not automatic or certain, a good deal more enlightened. Usually a great deal of time is wasted on polemics against world models or national models, insisting that they are not predictive. Of course they are not. What such models do, is tell us what to provide. One cannot predict on which farmer's field it will hail or on what date, but one could tell a farmer, in the absence of other information, what would be a reasonable amount of insurance to take out. This notion of provision, rather than prediction, of safety margins is very important in many other respects. In engineering and the natural sciences a well-established notion of safety margins, of operational reserves and of expectable or even acceptable margins of error often exists. But there is next to no research on the error frequency of governments, on the 'circular error probability' of foreign ministers, or generals, though there is a good deal of unorganized information on these subjects.

Engineers who know what the likelihood of failure of a bridge is also know how much extra strength they should allow for, and bankers who know just about how much money they should hold in reserve are not enemies of bridge-building or of banking. People who know how often governments commit errors or are misinformed are not enemies of government. Quite the contrary, they may be able to persuade governments to take out more insurance.

Finally, it might be desirable to obtain networks, of both types of models of countries, integrated world models and networks of sectoral world models, of which there are now quite a few.

Comparative political research is only at its beginning. Much has already been done, more is to be done; and if the world does not destroy itself, a great deal more will be done—and one hopes that some of it will be of wider usefulness and better quality.

## Notes

1. T. Parsons, *Politics and Social Structure* (New York: Free Press, 1969). T. Parsons and E. A. Shils, *Toward a General Theory of Action* (Cambridge, Mass.: Harvard University Press, 1952).

2. R. L. Merritt, *Symbols of American Community, 1735–1775* (New Haven: Yale University Press, 1966).

3. Compare here also the sociological approach of J. A. Schumpeter, *Imperialism and Social Classes* (New York: Kelley, 1954).

4. See Morton Kaplan, *System and Process in International Politics* (New York: Wiley, 1957).

5. Jean Laponce ed., 'Temps, espace et politique', *Social Science Information*, vol. 14, nos. 3–4, 1976, pp. 7–28.

6. Alexander Szalai et al., eds., *The Use of Time: Daily Activities of Urban and Suburban Populations in Twelve Countries* (The Hague: Mouton, 1972).

7. Richard Rose, 'Comparative Policy Analysis: The Programme Approach', paper presented at the Conference on Comparative Research on National Political Systems, West Berlin, 9–12 July 1984, organized by Wissenschaftszentrum Berlin.

8. Daniel Moynihan, *The Politics of a Guaranteed Income* (New York: Random House and Vintage Press, 1973).

9. Max Weber, *Theory of Social and Economic Organization* (New York: Free Press, 1947); and *Economy and Society: An Outline of Interpretive Sociology* (Berkeley: University of California Press, 1979).

10. Northcote Parkinson, *Parkinson's Law, and Other Studies in Administration* (Boston: Houghton Mifflin, 1957).

11. L. Taylor and D. Jodice, *World Handbook of Political and Social Indicators*, vol. I, pp. 111, 157 (New Haven: Yale University Press, 1983).

12. See K. W. Deutsch and R. L. Merritt, 'Transnational Communications and the International System,' *Annals of the American Academy of Political and Social Science,* vol. 442 (March 1979), pp. 84–97.

13. K. W. Deutsch, *The Nerves of Government* (New York: Free Press, 1963, 1966).

# 3

# Transnational and Comparative Research

*Frederic E. Wakeman, Jr.*

For some time now, social scientists have emphasized the need to address important issues that cut across basic assumptions concerning ways in which "national" and "international" studies are currently conceptualized and in which the nation-state is assigned a preeminent role as a unit of analysis.

This new emphasis is partly a result of the dramatic globalization of networks of all kinds that has taken place during the last decade. These global linkages range from international banking, trade and market networks, economic and military interdependencies, labor and political migrations, international standards and regulations, intellectual and information exchanges, multilateral treaties, multinational corporations, and energy and technology flows, to religious missionary movements, advertising media, and the cosmopolitanization of a middle-class consumer culture.

It is also partly a result of ecological and climatological impacts of considerable magnitude. World consumption of fossil fuels has gone from one billion tons per year in the 1920s and

SOURCE: Reprinted from *Items,* vol. 42, no. 4 (December 1988), pp. 85–89. By permission of the Social Science Research Council, 605 Third Avenue, New York, NY 10158. Article abridged by the editors.

1930s to six billion tons today. Exponential growth characterizes almost everything we see, implying an intensity and velocity of human interactions that increasingly force social scientists to work back and forth between area and international analysis in novel ways....

## CONTENDING CATEGORIES OF ANALYSIS

Time and again during meetings sponsored by the Social Science Research Council, social scientists insist that we cannot claim to understand the contemporary world conceptually as long as we presume that all one needs to know are the internal dynamics of particular states and the international relations among them. In the same breath, however, these scholars repeatedly express their dissatisfaction with the explanatory weakness of their own analytical models. Even the most positive-minded formulators of abstract schemes of international organization, for example, conceded that "neorealists" in international relations cannot explain the dynamics of phenomena such as institutionalized cooperation.[1] And while international relations scholars divided themselves into specialists in systems-level theory and those who would disaggregate the state, international economics specialists tended to think of themselves as being either macromodelers or business and trade experts.

Area studies scholars were also visibly divided, being strongly associated with either one of two distinct subtraditions. The first is associated with economics, politics, and international relations, and is often described as the "regional" perspective. The second tradition, more usually associated with humanistic scholarship, stresses history, language, and civilizational perspectives. Anthropology and sociology tend to mediate between these two area traditions in most non-Western contexts. Nevertheless, in many contemporary area studies domains, despite the common focus on a particular nation or region of the world, there is a continuing conflict between those who are primarily interested in international trade and foreign policy and those who are primarily interested in culture. The former criticize the latter for their scholastic fussiness and idiographic particularism while the latter fault the former for lacking linguistic, cultural, and historical sensitivity.

There is of course a certain fit between area studies specialists, concerned with international trade and foreign policy, and international relations scholars who have been, for some time, interested in disaggregating the state. The latter are eager consumers of country-specific knowledge because the logic of their enterprise requires the understanding of domestic-specific foreign policy studies. But while there is already much interaction between these two groups, there has been very little dialogue in the past between area studies scholars who specialize in cultural research and international relations experts interested in systems-level theory, the nature of the international system, and the applications of realist paradigms. Even though systematic comparativists are heavily dependent upon the people, ideas, and scholarship being generated in and by the area studies traditions (with their particularly close links to counterpart scholars overseas), it is sometimes difficult to find common ground—as might occur, for instance, when a rational choice theorist looks at village decision-making processes. In this particular dyad, the argument has to do with the connection between two different kinds of knowledge with, for example, culture-focused people arguing that there is no way to conduct an effective decision-making study without knowledge of the cultural setting.

## CONCEPTUAL CONTENTION AND CONFUSION

The analytical categories for all of these approaches are suspect, and there is a kind of consensus not to agree on fundamentals. In the disciplines, many social scientists have agreed to disagree about some of the core concepts of their fields: power for political scientists, capital for economists, status for sociologists, and culture for anthropologists. Paradigms are fuzzy, and although the most positivistically inclined among us might express a certain tough-minded impatience with such irresolve, many of our most thoughtful social scientists express considerable unease about the intellectual categories with which they work.

Rational choice theory, for example, is undermined by the problem of norms and the role of historically determined preferences. Some social scientists stress culture, and know that norms are important, but there are no clear rules for connecting this awareness with effective models. Political economists, on the other hand, have a very clear way of setting up analyses of economic actors and the international contexts of their action. But they do not have appropriate categories for many emergent properties of contemporary society such as worldwide entertainment habits, which have an overwhelming effect on mass perceptions and consequent patterns of conflict and control. The American movie industry has come to dominate European theaters, but Japanese films have had no comparable impact. Why? The most frequent answer seems to be that the Japanese are culturally different. But this explanation, which employs cultural analysis in a residual fashion, is only a bogus answer, providing yet another instance in which we lack appropriate analytical categories.

The truth is, of course, that most of us tend to answer questions like the ones raised above with the conventional response that "the world is getting more and more complex." But this way of thinking about the world lacks clarity and often fails to help us understand it, especially since the labels which we attach to its complexity have changed so dramatically in the last decade. One East Asian historian remarked that when he was in graduate school he was taught that capitalism did not develop in China and Korea because of Confucian values that militated against entrepreneurial rationality. The same specialists now argue that it is aggressive Confucianism that accounts for the economic transformation of these countries. And what once were viewed as revolutionary states, China and North Korea, are now seen as essentially conservative regimes, with the radical states being the "newly industrializing countries" (NICs) that are adopting capitalism with all of the great waves of change that Joseph A. Schumpeter once observed.

One important reason why categories are labile is that the world itself is undergoing a rapid "delocalization," and historians have begun to speak of a "retrocolonization" of the West. Clear categories seem to have accompanied imperial world structures. Periods such as the late 19th century or the 1950s and 1960s, in which we have had clear conceptualizations of what the social sciences ought to be doing, have been periods in which the world itself appeared to be much clearer, at least in terms of architechtonic world structures. As these structures lose their clarity, so do the categories of social science lose their limpidity and rigor. We are in a period today, both conceptually and structurally, that is characterized by imprecision and amorphousness.

## THE NEW PROBLEM ORIENTATION

One powerful response to this conceptual cloudiness is a substantive, problem-oriented approach to international and area studies. As one political scientist succinctly pointed out in our meetings, when you attack a real problem, especially one that speaks to anomalies in existing paradigms, you find yourself learning what you have to know. And at the same time that you find yourself bedeviled by theories that do not work, you also see their irrelevance to the task at hand and are forced to improvise new modes of analysis. This is particularly the case when dealing with problems that have to do with policy.

Although some of the most outstanding work in the social sciences is now institutional,

retrospective, and comparative in focus, our research strategies in international and area studies are ordered in such a way as to permit important problem-oriented issues to slip through our analytical nets. Such issues as the global emergence of an underclass, the spread of English and the access to power associated with speaking English, and differences among nations in how they use the same technologies, do not accord with ordinary discipline- or area-oriented committee agendas. Yet, although there is no neat theoretical framework for transnational research, certain common qualities are readily apparent. One common quality is, paradoxically, comparative coherence.

## TRANSNATIONAL APPROACHES

The study of regional sytems—norms, institutions, processes—provides a middle level of analysis where certain variables can more easily be held constant and which might provide better honed tools for global analysis. A good example is the question of industrial development and religious values, the so-called "Neo-Confucian issue." This is a transnational issue that lends itself to regional analysis across East Asia. Another example, more specifically historical, would be a comparative study of the impact of Japanese colonial rule on regional institutions in Southeast Asia.

Another characteristic has to do with international regimes, both in economic and cultural terms. The concept of "deterritorialization" applies not only to obvious examples like transnational corporations and money markets, but also to ethnic groups, sectarian allegiances, and political movements, which increasingly operate in ways that transcend specific territorial boundaries and identities. Deterritorialization has affected the loyalties of groups involved in complex diasporas, their manipulation of currencies and other forms of wealth and investment, and the strategies of states. The loosening of the bonds between people, wealth, and territories in turn has altered the basis of many significant global interactions, while simultaneously calling into question the traditional definition of the state.

The structural reach of the state has also been called into question by the increasingly international character of major threats to the environment, the growing interdependence of regional and global security systems, and the weakening of the power that many states have relative to the societies they theoretically govern. All of these developments challenge the traditional roles of states as providers of welfare for their citizens or elites and as mediators of transnational interactions and flows.

At the micro or substate level, there is the growing number and influence of political, developmental, and environmental "nongovernmental orgianizations" (NGOs), as well as a variety of ethnic and religious communities. At the macro level there are such formal institutions as the United Nations, the World Bank, the International Monetary Fund, and international regimes such as the General Agreement on Tariffs and Trade and the International Declaration of Human Rights, not to speak of multinational corporations and clandestine arms and narcotics networks. There are also more generalized globalwide processes or systems of international investment and labor markets, media, consumerization, and intellectual exchange. It appears to be the case that the presence, potency, and persistence of these relatively new and certainly more numerous substate and suprastate actors and processes account for much of the complaint that we have lost our ability to conceptualize, model, and systematically understand events in the world today.

Meanwhile, although many states are increasingly concerned with regulating some aspects of the traffic between their citizens and other polities, they have radically privatized and liberalized certain other transnational interactions. India's policies towards the United States, for example, encompass an often bewildering array of "poses," ranging from considerable suspicion on arms and security to relative openness on computers and industrial policy. This functional diversification of the

postures of states towards each other is a further incentive to disaggregate the state and not see it as a policy-making monolith.

At the same time, attention must be paid to cultural factors not in the state sphere that impinge upon the international sector. In intensifying the investigation of the relationship between politics and culture as an organizer of the traffic between states, it is crucial to remember that "culture" is itself no longer the sort of thing anthropologist once took it to be: homogeneous, local, well-bounded, and in clear one-to-one correspondence with distinct social units. Culture now leaks across national boundaries and this transnational flow is intimately tied not only to the many diasporas that characterize national populations, but also to the incredible force of media (movies, magazines, cassettes, videotapes, computers, and the like) which close the cultural distance (and accelerate the traffic) between overseas populations and their home societies. . . .

We therefore need to investigate carefully the relationship between those interactions which are the result of the "official" policies of states and elites, and those which emerge as the result of informal and nonofficial networks, movements, and exchanges between national populations. For example, the Taiwan reunification issue is badly misunderstood if we do not comprehend the effect of the "brain drain" from Taiwan to the United States and the ensuing changes in identity (including a new Sino-American biculturalism) of the island's elites.

Other examples of this sort of interaction include:

• *The transnational implications of labor flows.* Whether we are talking about Indians and Pakistanis in the middle East, Filipinos in the United States, Hispanics in the United States, Chinese in Malaysia, or Turks in Sweden, the nexus between immigration, the cultural reproduction of deterritorialized groupings, the security implications of all the variety of *Gastarbeiter* [Guest worker] concentrations, and other fiscal implications of transnational labor forces need to be explored. A single framework needs to be developed in which the fiscal, organizational, cultural, and political implications of transnational labor flows (whether of garbage collectors or of computer technicians) can be analyzed and understood.

• *Postwar global religious fundamentalism.* Although we are habituated to seeing Islamic fundamentalism as a complex transnational force, we have hardly investigated transnational Catholicism, Buddhism, or Hinduism with the same care. A controlled comparison of these various transnational religious forms would draw in more traditional area studies scholars, since one of the big issues here is the difference between contemporary global religious forms and their earlier translocal equivalents.

• *Cross-regional and cross-country sectoral analysis of capital development.* The Committee on States and Social Structures has already developed an extensive reseach design that examines the way in which the global evolution of selected industrial sectors intersects with the attempts of "newly industrializing countries" to transform the position of their own manufacturing industries within the international division of labor....

• *The paradox of Americanization.* Why is it that in so many parts of the non-Western world, state policies and certain aspects of popular sentiment are so profoundly anti-American, while other elite behaviors and popular sentiments (especially in the areas of leisure and life style) are so deeply influenced by American models? Is this divorce between the American government and American culture a function of some quirk of American self-presentation abroad, is it a feature of the political culture of the developing world, or is it both?

• *Media studies.* Although there has been a certain amount of research on transnational media and their effects, and on the controversies associated with "the new international information order," there is a paucity of work done on the relationship between producers and consumers of media images separated by cultural geography. The general matter of the reception of images

produced in one cultural milieu by audiences in a wholly different cultural milieu has barely been explored. For example, we know next to nothing about the cultural setting in which audiences in societies as diverse as Morocco, Vietnam, Nigeria, and Egypt consume commercial films produced in Bombay, which are in turn complicated transformations of Hollywood and European models. Since ideas about foreigners, about consumption, about crime, and about urban life are often transnationally formed through television and cinema, the reception of these seemingly alien images is not irrelevant to international relations, including peace and security studies. The methodologies for pursuing these links are at present extremely rudimentary.

• *The globalization of English and Arabic.* English has become the international language of science, commerce, and transportation, while Arabic is now taught in numerous non-Arabic speaking countries. What are implications of these developments for new forms of hegemony, the media, stratification, and transnational elite formation?

• *The revival of "national character" studies, and their relationship to the study of "political culture."* Though widely separated in space, Europe and East Asia are experiencing a revival of cultural nationalism. In Germany and France, a new form of historicism is being debated, while in Japan and China intellectual elites are increasingly focusing their primary attention upon the "question of Japaneseness," and the issue of Sinitic cultural identity vis-à-vis modernization. Specialists in the intellectual history of each of these countries are well aware of the dimensions of the debate in any particular case, but there has so far been no effort to bring together the individual phenomena in a consciously comparative way; and certainly no one has thought to ask whether the simultaneity of these nationally particularistic intellectual movements underlies a more universal global quality.

The need to link new analytical categories to area studies will undoubtedly be reinforced by collective global concerns during the last dozen years of this century.

## Notes

1. "Neorealism" is a doctrine of state interest and power. Realist theories, which are considered by individuals working within the security studies field to be the most parsimonious and powerful theories for explaining and predicting international behavior and outcomes, assume that states set goals and then harness the capabilities of their societies—military force, economic power, technological and natural resources, and geopolitical position—to attain these goals. While the "neorealists" acknowledge that changes in the international system play an important role in contextualizing state behavior, they nonetheless hold that states and state power, in combination with largely "immutable" factors such as geography and the self-interested nature of human behavior, lead to clashes of national interest and conflict and thus play a pivotal role in international and transnational relations.

# CHAPTER TWO

# The State and its Context

## 4

## What Is a State?

*Max Weber*

What do we understand by politics? The concept is extremely broad and comprises any kind of *independent* leadership in action. One speaks of the currency policy of the banks, of the discounting policy of the Reichsbank, of the strike policy of a trade union; one may speak of the educational policy of a municipality or a township, of the policy of the president of a voluntary association, and, finally, even of the policy of a prudent wife who seeks to guide her husband.... Our reflections are, of course, not based upon such a broad concept. We wish to understand by politics only the leadership, or the influencing of the leadership, of a *political* association, hence today, of a *state.*

But what is a 'political' association from the sociological point of view? What is a 'state'? Sociologically, the state cannot be defined in terms of its ends. There is scarcely any task that some political association has not taken in hand, and there in no task that one could say has always been exclusive and peculiar to those associations which are designated as political ones: today the state, or historically, those associations which have been the predecessors of the modern state. Ultimately, one can define the modern state sociologically only in terms of the specific *means*

SOURCE: Max Weber, "Politics as a Vocation," in *From Max Weber: Essays in Sociology,* edited and translated by H. H. Gerth and C. Wright Mills. © 1946 by Oxford University Press, Inc.; renewed 1973 by Hans H. Gerth. Reprinted by permission of the publisher.

peculiar to it, as to every political association, namely, the use of physical force.

'Every state is founded on force,' said Trotsky at Brest-Litovsk. That is indeed right. If no social institutions existed which knew the use of violence, then the concept of 'state' [the tribe] would be eliminated, and a condition would emerge that could be designated as 'anarchy,' in the specific sense of this word. Of course, force is certainly not the normal or the only means of the state—nobody says that—but force is a means specific to the state. Today the relation between the state and violence is an especially intimate one. In the past, the most varied institutions—beginning with the sib—have known the use of physical force as quite normal. Today, however, we have to say that a state is a human community that (successfully) claims the *monopoly of the legitimate use of physical force* within a given territory. Note that 'territory' is one of the characteristics of the state. Specifically, at the present time, the right to use physical force is ascribed to other institutions or to individuals only to the extent to which the state permits it. The state is considered the sole source of the 'right' to use violence. Hence, 'politics' for us means striving to share power or striving to influence the distribution of power, either among states or among groups within a state.

This corresponds essentially to ordinary usage. When a question is said to be a 'political' question, when a cabinet minister or an official is said to be a 'political' official, or when a decision is said to be 'politically' determined, what is always meant is that interests in the distribution, maintenance, or transfer of power are decisive for answering the questions and determining the decision or the official's sphere of activity. He who is active in politics strives for power either as a means in serving other aims, ideal or egoistic, or as 'power for power's sake,' that is, in order to enjoy the prestige-feeling that power gives.

Like the political institutions historically preceding it, the state is a relation of men dominating men, a relation supported by means of legitimate (i.e., considered to be legitimate) violence. If the state is to exist, the dominated must obey the authority claimed by the powers that be. When and why do men obey? Upon what inner justifications and upon what external means does this domination rest?

To begin with, in principle, there are three inner justifications, hence basic *legitimations* of domination.

First, the authority of the 'eternal yesterday,' i.e., of the mores sanctified through the unimaginably ancient recognition and habitual orientation to conform. This is 'traditional' domination exercised by the patriarch and the patrimonial prince of yore.

There is the authority of the extraordinary and personal *gift of grace* (charisma), the absolutely personal devotion and personal confidence in revelation, heroism, or other qualities of individual leadership. This is 'charismatic' domination, as exercised by the prophet or—in the field of politics—by the elected war lord, the plebiscitarian ruler, the great demagogue, or the political party leader.

Finally, there is domination by virtue of 'legality,' by virtue to the belief in the validity of legal statute and functional 'competence' based on rationally created *rules*. In this case, obedience is expected in discharging statutory obligations. This is domination as exercised by the modern 'servant of the state' and by all those bearers of power who in this respect resemble him.

It is understood that, in reality, obedience is determined by highly robust motives of fear and hope—fear of the vengeance of magical powers or of the power-holder, hope for reward in this world or in the beyond—and besides all this, by interests of the most varied sort. Of this we shall speak presently. However, in asking for the 'legitimations' of this obedience, one meets with these three 'pure' types: 'traditional,' 'charismatic,' and 'legal.'

These conceptions of legitimacy and their inner justifications are of very great significance for the structure of domination. To be sure, the pure types are rarely found in reality. But today we cannot deal with the highly complex variants, transitions, and combinations of these pure types, which problems belong to 'political science.' Here we are interested above all in the second of these types: domination by virtue of the devotion of those who obey the purely personal 'charisma' of the 'leader.' For this is the root of the idea of a *calling* in its highest expression.

Devotion to the charisma of the prophet, or the leader in war, or to the great demagogue in the *ecclesia* or in parliament, means that the leader is personally recognized as the innerly 'called' leader of men. Men do not obey him by virtue of tradition or statute, but because they believe in him. If he is more than a narrow and vain upstart of the moment, the leader lives for his cause and 'strives for his work.' The devotion of his disciples, his followers, his personal party friends is oriented to his person and to its qualities.

Charismatic leadership has emerged in all places and in all historical epochs. Most importantly in the past, it has emerged in the two figures of the magician and the prophet on the one hand, and in the elected war lord, the gang leader and *condotierre* on the other hand. Political leadership in the form of the free 'demagogue' who grew from the soil of the city state is of greater concern to us; like the city state, the demagogue is peculiar to the Occident and especially to Mediterranean culture. Furthermore, political leadership in the form of the parliamentary 'party leader' has grown on the soil of the constitutional state, which is also indigenous only to the Occident. . . . (pp. 77–80)

\* \* \*

We must be clear about the fact that all ethically oriented conduct may be guided by one of two fundamentally differing and irreconcilably opposed maxims: conduct can be oriented to an 'ethic of ultimate ends' or to an 'ethic of responsibility.' This is not to say that an ethic of ultimate ends is identical with irresponsibility, or that an ethic of responsibility is identical with unprincipled opportunism. Naturally nobody says that. However, there is an abysmal contrast between conduct that follows the maxim of an ethic of ultimate ends—that is, in religious terms, 'The Christian does rightly and leaves the results with the Lord'—and conduct that follows the maxim of an ethic of responsibility, in which case one has to give an account of the foreseeable results of one's action.

You may demonstrate to a convinced syndicalist, believing in an ethic of ultimate ends, that his action will result in increasing the opportunities of reaction, in increasing the oppression of his class, and obstructing its ascent—and you will not make the slightest impression upon him. If an action of good intent leads to bad results, then, in the actor's eyes, not he but the world, or the stupidity of other men, or God's will who made them thus, is responsible for the evil. However a man who believes in an ethic of responsibility takes account of precisely the average deficiences of people; as Fichte has correctly said, he does not even have the right to presuppose their goodness and perfection. He does not feel in a position to burden others with the results of his own actions so far as he was able to foresee them; he will say: these results are ascribed to my action. The believer in an ethic of ultimate ends feels 'responsible' only for seeing to it that the flame of pure intentions is not quelched: for example, the flame of protesting against the injustice of the social order. To rekindle the flame ever anew is the purpose of his quite irrational deeds, judged in view of their possible success. They are acts that can and shall have only exemplary value.

But even herewith the problem is not yet exhausted. No ethics in the world can dodge the fact that in numerous instances the attainment of 'good' ends is bound to the fact that one must be willing to pay the price of using morally dubious means or at least dangerous ones—and facing the possibility or even the probability of evil ramifications. From no ethics in the world can it be concluded when and to what extent the ethically good purpose 'justifies' the ethically dangerous means and ramifications. . . . (pp. 120–121)

\* \* \*

Whosoever contracts with violent means for whatever ends—and every politician does—is exposed to its specific consequences. This holds especially for the crusader, religious and revolutionary alike. Let us confidently take the present as an example. He who wants to establish absolute justice on earth by force requires a following, a human 'machine.' He must hold out the necessary internal and external premiums, heavenly or worldly reward, to this 'machine' or else the machine will not function. Under the conditions of the modern class struggle, the internal premiums consist of the satisfying of hatred and the craving for revenge; above all, resentment and the need for pseudo-ethical self-righteousness: the opponents must be slandered and accused of heresy. The external rewards are adventure, victory, booty, power, and spoils. The leader and his success are completely dependent upon the functioning of his machine and hence not on his own motives. Therefore he also depends upon whether or not the premiums can be *permanently* granted to the following, that is, to the Red Guard, the informers, the agitators, whom he needs. What he actually attains under the conditions of his work is therefore not in his hand, but is prescribed to him by the following's motives, which, if viewed ethically, are predominantly base. The following can be harnessed only so long as an honest belief in his person and his cause inspires at least part of the following, probably never on earth even the majority. This belief, even when subjectively sincere, is in a very great number of cases really no more than an ethical 'legitimation' of cravings for revenge, power, booty, and spoils. We shall not be deceived about this by verbiage; the materialist interpretation of history is no cab to be taken at will; it does not stop short of the promoters of revolutions. Emotional revolutionism is followed by the traditionalist routine of everyday life; the crusading leader and the faith itself fade away, or, what is even more effective, the faith becomes part of the conventional phraseology of political Philistines and banausic technicians. This development is especially rapid with struggles of faith because they are usually led or inspired by genuine leaders, that is, prophets of revolution. For here, as with every leader's machine, one of the conditions for success is the depersonalization and routinization, in short, the psychic proletarianization, in the interests of discipline. After coming to power the following of a crusader usually degenerates very easily into a quite common stratum of spoilsmen.

Whoever wants to engage in politics at all, and especially in politics as a vocation, has to realize these ethical paradoxes. He must know that he is responsible for what may become of himself under the impact of these paradoxes. I repeat, he lets himself in for the diabolic forces lurking in all violence. The great *virtuosi* of acosmic love of humanity and goodness, whether stemming from Nazareth or Assisi or from Indian royal castles, have not operated with the political means of violence. Their kingdom was 'not of this world' and yet they worked and still work in this world. The figures of Platon Karatajev and the saints of Dostoievski still remain their most adequate reconstructions. He who seeks the salvation of the soul, of his own and of others, should not seek it along the avenue of politics, for the quite different tasks of politics can only be solved by violence. The genius or demon of politics lives in an inner tension with the god of love, as well as with the Christian God as expressed by the church. This tension can at any time lead to an irreconcilable conflict. Men knew this even in the times of church rule. Time and again the papal interdict was placed upon Florence and at the time it meant a far more robust power for men and their salvation of soul than (to speak with Fichte) the 'cool approbation' of the Kantian ethical judgment. The burghers, however, fought the church-state. And it is with reference to such situations that Machiavelli in a beautiful passage, if I am not mistaken, of the *History of Florence*, has one of his heroes praise those citizens who deemed the greatness of their native city higher than the salvation of their souls.

If one says 'the future of socialism' or 'international peace,' instead of native city or 'fatherland' (which at present may be a dubious value to some), then you face the problem as it stands now. Everything that is striven for through political action operating with violent means and following an ethic of responsibility endangers the 'salvation of the soul.' If, however, one chases after the ultimate good in a war of beliefs, following a pure ethic of absolute ends, then the goals may be damaged and discredited for generations, because responsibility for *consequences* is lacking, and two diabolic forces which enter the play remain unknown to the actor. These are inexorable and produce consequences for his action and even for his inner self, to which he must helplessly submit, unless he perceives them. The sentence: 'The devil is old; grow old to understand him!' does not refer to age in terms of chronological years. I have never permitted myself to lose out in a discussion through a reference to a date registered on a birth certificate; but the mere fact that someone is twenty years of age and that I am over fifty is no cause for me to think that this alone is an achievement before which I am overawed. Age is not decisive; what is decisive is the trained relentlessness in viewing the realities of life, and the ability to face such realities and to measure up to them inwardly. . . . (pp. 124–127)

# 5

# The Civic Culture Concept

*Gabriel A. Almond*

## EARLY NOTIONS

Something like a notion of political culture has been around as long as men have spoken and

SOURCE: Gabriel A. Almond, "The Intellectual History of the Civic Culture Concept," in Gabriel A. Almond and Sidney Verba, eds., *The Civic Culture Revisited* (Boston: Little, Brown & Co., 1980), pp. 1–36. Essay and Notes abridged by the editors. We wish to thank Professor Almond for his personal permission to reprint.

written about politics. The prophets in their oracles, exhortations, and anathemas impute different qualities and propensities to the Amalekites, the Philistines, the Assyrians, and the Babylonians. The Greek and Roman historians, poets, and dramatists comment on the culture and character of the Ionians and Dorians, Spartans, Athenians, and Corinthians; the Rhaetians, Pannonians, Dacians, Parthians, and Caledonians.

The concepts and categories we use in the analysis of political culture—subculture, elite political culture, political socialization, and culture change—are also implied in ancient writings. . . .

Nowhere do we find a stronger affirmation of the importance of political culture than in Plato's *Republic* when he argues "that governments vary as the dispositions of men vary, and that there must be as many of the one as there are of the other. For we cannot suppose that States are made of 'oak and rock' and not out of the human natures which are in them." He speaks of aristocratic, timocratic, oligarchic, and democratic polities and men, deriving the structural and performance characteristics of the first from the vlues, attitudes, and socialization experiences of the second. In ways that surely would intrigue, if not embarrass, our contemporary psychohistorians he explains the qualities of the aristocratic, oligarchic, and democratic polity by the prevailing personal character types, which are in turn explained by typical family constellations with cultivated, glory-seeking, or money-grubbing fathers, dominant, compliant, or complaining mothers, and the like. And just as he stresses the importance of political culture, so does Plato in both *The Republic* and *The Laws* lay enormous weight on political socialization. ". . . [O]f all animals the boy is the most unmanageable, inasmuch as he has the fountain of reason in him not yet regulated; he is the most insidious, sharp witted, and insubordinate of animals. Wherefore he must be bound with many bridles. . . ."[1] Mothers and nurses, fathers, tutors, and political officials all have the obligation to guide and coerce the incorrigible animal

into the path of civic virtue. The last book of Aristotle's *Politics*, a fragment to be sure, was devoted to education. Plutarch reports how Lycurgus engineered the Spartan character from the moment of birth, so to speak, counseling the women to bathe their newborn sons in wine, rather than in water, in order to temper their bodies. The nurses used "no swaddling bands; the children grew up free and unconstrained in limb and form, and not dainty or fanciful about their food; not afraid in the dark, or of being left alone; and without peevishness, or ill-humour, or crying. . . ."[2]

Aristotle is a more modern and scientific political culturalist than Plato, since he not only imputes importance to political culture variables, but explicitly treats their relationship to social stratification variables on the one hand and to political structural and performance variables on the other. He argues that the best attainable form of government is the mixed form in a society in which the middle classes predominate. Mixed government is one organized on both oligarchic and democratic principles, hence giving some representation in governing to both the rich and the well born as well as to the poor and the base. Such a government is likely to arise and work best when wealth is widely distributed and when there is a large middle class which imparts its character to the state. He points out that the

> middle amount of all the good things of fortune is the best amount to possess. For this degree of wealth is the readiest to obey reason. . . . And the middle class are the least inclined to shun office and to covet office, and both of these tendencies are injurious to states. And in addition to these points, those who have an excess of fortune's goods, strength, wealth, friends and the like, are not willing to be governed and do not know how to be (and they have acquired this quality even in their boyhood from their homelife, which was so luxurious that they have not got used to submitting to authority even in schools) while those who are excessively in need of these things are too humble. . . .

A society in which the middle class is small produces a state "consisting of slaves and masters, not of free men, and of one class envious and another contemptuous of their fellows. This condition of affairs is very far removed from friendliness, and from political partnership...," which Aristotle believed to be the cultural basis of the best and most lasting form of government.[3]

Aristotle's conception of mixed government with a predominant middle class is related to what some of us in recent years have characterized as the civic culture in which there is a substantial consensus on the legitimacy of political institutions and the direction and content of public policy, a widespread tolerance of a plurality of interests and belief in their reconcilability, and a widely distributed sense of political competence and mutual trust in the citizenry....

## THE INFLUENCE OF EUROPEAN SOCIOLOGY

As the discipline of sociology developed in the course of the nineteenth century, the importance of subjective variables in the explanation of social and political phenomena was generally recognized. Henri de Saint-Simon attributed more importance to ideological-religious attitudes than economic ones in the maintenance of social stability and the attainment of social progress. Auguste Comte viewed society essentially as a system of common moral ideas. Marx viewed ideology as a significant weapon in the hands of the bourgeoisie in retarding revolutionary processes, and political consciousness in the working class as a necessary condition of proletarian revolution. Emile Durkheim based his conception of social solidarity on the "conscience collective," or the system of values, beliefs, and sentiments shared by the members of societies. And Pareto's concepts of logical and nonlogical action, of "residues" and "derivations," were parts of a substantially psychological theory of sociopolitical structure and social change.

But of all the European sociologists the most influential in the shaping of research on political culture was Max Weber. For Weber sociology had to be an "empathic" science, a *Verstehende*

*Soziologie* in which attitudes, feelings, and values were important explanatory variables. Perhaps Weber was the first truly modern social scientist. His concepts were empirically grounded; he was methodologically quite inventive and sophisticated. He himself had used questionnaires, developed a form of content analysis, and employed systematic field observation. Weber's work on the sociology of religion was a response to Marxian sociological theory, which stressed economic structure—the relations of production—as the basic formative influence on social institutions and ideas. Weber's comparative study of the economic ethos of the great world religions was intended to demonstrate that values and ideas can be the catalytic agents in changes in economic structure and in political institutions.

Weber's types of political authority—traditional, rational-legal, and charismatic—are subjective categories. They were the three ideal-typical reasons why leaders are obeyed by followers, the three ideal-typical bases of political legitimacy. Structural differences among political systems are treated as subordinate categories to these essentially subjective categories. Traditional orders are those in which the rulers are obeyed because they have been selected according to immemorial rules, and act in accordance with such rules. The main form of rational-legal order that Weber treats is *bureaucracy*, in which officialdom is obeyed because it is selected and acts according to written, rational, and enforceable rules. Charismatic authority is the extraordinary and transitional type of political order characterized by a belief in the superhuman or extra-human qualities of a leader.

Weber's typology of political parties again is based on the subjective reasons for membership and support. Class parties are those which recruit supporters on the basis of their appeal to class interest. Patronage parties are those which appeal to supporters on the basis of the promise of power, office, and other material advantages, while Weltanschauung (World-View) parties are based on an appeal to the ideals of political supporters. Finally, Weber's basic categories of types of social action—traditionality, affectuality, instrumental and value rationality— profoundly influenced theories of development and modernization which entered into political culture research.

Weber's principal interpreter in the United States was Talcott Parsons. His early theoretical work elaborated and specified some of the main Weberian categories. Thus, for example, Parsons's categories of orientation to action and his pattern variables[4] are quite clearly elaborations of the Weberian categories of types of social action. Parsons in his concept of orientation to social action speaks of cognitive, affective, and evaluative modes of orientation. Parsons's pattern variables—his pairs of contrasting modes of orientation to action—reflect the influence of both Weber and Durkheim; from the perspective of Weber, specificity, universalism, achievement motivation, and affective neutrality are properties of rational culture and structure, while diffuseness, particularism, ascriptiveness, and affectivity are aspects of traditionality. These Parsonian categories played an important role in studies of political modernization and in the research design of the *Civic Culture* study.

## THE INFLUENCE OF SOCIAL PSYCHOLOGY

A third intellectual stream entered into political culture conceptualization and research—that of social psychology. This discipline emerged in the first decades of the twentieth century largely out of efforts among sociologists and psychologists to understand and explain the social and political catastrophes of those years: the bloodshed and destruction of World War I, the Bolshevik Revolution, the Great Depression, the rise of Italian Fascism and German National Socialism, racial antagonisms, and the like. Social psychology represents an effort to understand and explain how and why the attitudes and behavior of individuals are conditioned and influenced by the presence and impact of other

individuals and social groupings. The units of analysis which social psychology has employed as building blocks of explanation are *instinct, habit, sentiment,* and *attitude.* Graham Wallas and Walter Lippmann were instinctivists, as were William McDougall, E. L. Thorndike, and John Dewey. Other early social psychologists stressed habit and sentiment as the basic units of analysis, but the mainstream of social psychology adopted attitude as its unit of analysis. The concept of attitude avoided the heredity or environment bias implied in such concepts as instinct and habit, and also avoided the stress on feeling implied in the concept of sentiment. As defined in social psychology, an attitude is a propensity in an individual to perceive, interpret, and act toward a particular object in particular ways. As the discipline became increasingly empirical, experimental, and rigorous in the 1940s and 1950s, it began to explore how particular social and political attitudes were formed and transformed, the effect of group structure and communication upon attitudes, the structure and interrelations of attitudes, and the like. . . .

## THE INFLUENCE OF PSYCHOANTHROPOLOGY

A fourth intellectual stream entering into political culture conceptualization and research was that of psychoanthropology, stemming from the work of Freud and his disciples and joining with anthropology in the 1930s in what later became known as the psychocultural approach. Freud himself commented on man's political fate but from a psychobiological point of view.[5] Neither he nor his students dealt with the special characteristics of nations and groups. It was the general fate of man limited by his instinctive endowments and psychological mechanisms that provided the themes for Freud and the early psychoanalytic theorists. The merger of psychoanalysis with the social sciences began in the 1920s and 1930s with the work of Bronislaw Malinowski, Ruth Benedict, Margaret Mead, and Harold Lasswell.[6]

Produced primarily by anthropologists and psychiatrists, this psychocultural literature sought to explain political culture propensities by childhood socialization patterns, unconscious motivation, and psychological mechanisms. During and immediately after World War II, efforts were made to characterize and explain the psychological propensities of the major nations at war—Germany, Russia, America, France, and Japan. But this effort to explain the politics and public policy of large and complex nations in the simple terms of libido theory and family authority and with the assumed homogeneity of the small village or tribal society aroused skepticism and gave way to the more sophisticated formulations of Abram Kardiner, Ralph Linton, Alex Inkeles, and Daniel Levinson.[7] Kardiner and Linton extended the scope of socialization beyond the earlier libidinal stages to the full life cycle, including adult experiences as factors influencing cultural propensities. They also introduced quasi-statistical notions such as "basic" or "modal" personality to correct the earlier assumption of culture-personality homogeneity. Linton was the first to deal directly with the heterogeneity of culture in large societies by introducing the concepts of subculture, role, and status culture. Inkeles and Levinson brought the psychocultural approach to a full statistical formulation, arguing that only rigorous sampling techniques with carefully formulated and tested questions could establish differences in the political culture of nations and the subgroups within them.

## THE DEVELOPMENT OF SURVEY RESEARCH METHODOLOGY

But as so often has happened in the history of scientific work, the invention of a new research technology was the catalytic agent in the political culture conceptualization and research that took place in the 1960s. . . .

This revolution in social science research technology had some four components: (1) the development of increasingly precise sampling methods, making it feasible to gather representative data on large populations; (2) the increasing sophistication of interviewing methods to assure greater reliability in the data derived by these methods; (3) the development of scoring and scaling techniques, making it possible to sort out and organize responses in homogeneous dimensions and relate them to theoretical variables; and (4) the increasing sophistication of methods of statistical analysis and inference, moving from simple descriptive statistics to bivariate, multivariate, regression, and causal-path analysis of the relations among contextual, attitudinal, and behavioral variables.

The development of survery research brought to bear on politics a set of precision tools enabling us to move from relatively loose and speculative inferences regarding psychological propensities from the content of communications, from clinical materials, or from behavioral tendencies. To be sure, the data yielded by survey research were created by the instruments and procedures of the researcher, by the questions asked of respondents, by his sampling decisions, and by his techniques of analysis and inference. As experience in voting studies, attitiude studies, and market research accumulated, these sources of error came under greater control, although, to be sure, they can never be fully eliminated.

## THE CIVIC CULTURE MODEL

The *Civic Culture* study drew on all these intellectual currents. From enlightenment and liberal political theory it drew the "rationality-activist model" of democratic citizenship, the model of a successful democracy that required that all citizens be involved and active in politics, and that their participation be informed, analytic, and rational. *The Civic Culture* argued that this rationality-activist model of democratic citizenship was *one* component of the civic culture, but not the sole one. Indeed, by itself this participant-rationalist model of citizenship could not logically sustain a *stable* democratic government. Only when combined in some sense with its opposites of passivity, trust, and deference to authority and competence was a viable, stable democracy possible. . . .

## POLITICAL CULTURE AND POLITICAL THEORY

Political culture is not a theory; it refers to a set of variables which may be used in the construction of theories. But insofar as it designates a set of variables and encourages their investigation, it imputes some explanatory power to the psychological or subjective dimension of politics, just as it implies that there are contextual and internal variables which may explain it. The explanatory power of political culture variables is an empirical question, open to hypothesis and testing.

As political culture research has developed in the last two decades, there has been a polemic of sorts organized around three questions: (1) differences of opinion as to definition and specification of the content of political culture; (2) controversy over the analytic separation of political culture from political structure and behavior; and (3) debate over its causal properties.

The various definitions of political culture are in most cases pretheoretic categorizations intended to affirm the importance of these cultural variables in the explanation of political phenomena, or preceding empirical investigations of some specific aspect or aspects of political culture. In an early formulation drawing on the work of Talcott Parsons, I defined political culture as consisting of cognitive, affective, and evaluative orientations to political phenomena, distributed in national populations or in subgroups, and then I proceeded to suggest some cultural hypotheses which might explain the differences in performance among Anglo-American, continental European, totalitarian, and preindustrial political systems.[8] In a formulation published around the same time, Samuel Beer, also drawing on Talcott Parsons, argued that a political culture orients a people toward a polity and its processes, providing it with a

system of beliefs (a cognitive map), a way of evaluating its operations, and a set of expressive symbols.[9]

In *The Civic Culture* the definition of the concept was adapted to the analysis of the cultural properties assumed to be associated with democratic stability. Consequently the elaboration of the concept stressed political knowledge and skill, and feelings and value orientations toward political objects and processes—toward the political system as a whole, toward the self as participant, toward political parties and elections, bureaucracy, and the like. Little or no stress was placed on attitudes toward public policy.

In a major collaborative investigation of varieties of political culture, Lucian Pye and Sidney Verba offered more comprehensive elaborations of the concept. Pye, focusing on political development themes, discussed the variety of ways the concept of political culture can help explain developmental problems and processes.[10] Verba defined the important dimensions of political culture as including the sense of national identity, attitudes toward oneself as participant, attitudes toward one's fellow citizens, attitudes and expectations regarding governmental output and performance, and knowledge about and attitudes toward the political processes of decision making.[11]

Dahl, in his study of political oppositions, discusses in detail several types of political orientation that have a bearing on patterns of political partisanship. The first of these is orientation toward the political system as a whole, which affects the extent and distribution of loyalty in a national society; attitudes toward cooperation and individuality and toward other people in general, which affect the formation of political groups and their interaction; and orientation toward problem solving (e.g., whether it is pragmatic or ideological), which affects the interactions of political parties. He then proceeds to show how these attitudes may affect the policies and tactics of political movements, drawing for illustrative purposes from case histories of the United States and a number of Western European democracies.[12]

In a recent formulation, Almond and Powell elaborate the concept of political culture in three directions: (1) substantive content, (2) varieties of orientation, and (3) the systemic relations among these components. An analysis of a nation's political culture would have to concern itself with all three. From the point of view of substantive content we may speak of "system" culture, "process" culture, and "policy" culture. The system culture of a nation would consist of the distributions of attitudes toward the national community, the regime, and the authorities, to use David Easton's formulation.[13] These would include the sense of national identity, attitudes toward the legitimacy of the regime and its various institutions, and attitudes toward the legitimacy and effectiveness of the incumbents of the various political roles.

The process culture of a nation would include attitudes toward the self in politics (e.g., parochial-subject-participant), and attitudes toward other political actors (e.g., trust, cooperative competence, hostility). The policy culture would consist of the distribution of preferences regarding the outputs and outcomes of politics, the ordering among different groupings in the population of such political values as welfare, security, and liberty.

Orientations toward these system, process and policy objects may be cognitive, consisting of beliefs, information, and analysis; affective, consisting of feelings of attachment, aversion, or indifference; or evaluative, consisting of moral judgments of one kind or another.

A third aspect of a political culture would be the relatedness or systemic character of its components. Philip Converse[14] suggested the concept of "constraint" to characterize situations in which attitudes toward political institutions and policies go together. Thus, in a given population, attitudes toward foreign policy, domestic economic policy, and racial segregation may be parts of a consistent ideology; for most individuals in this group, if one knew how they stood on foreign policy one could predict their views on taxation, on busing, and the like. In other groups these attitudes might be independent. Similarly, information, beliefs,

feelings, and moral judgments are interrelated. Generally speaking the political cultures of nations and groups may be distinguished and compared according to their internal constraint or consistency[15]. . . .

The criticism of *The Civic Culture* that it argues that political culture causes political structure is incorrect. Throughout the study the development of specific cultural patterns in particular countries is explained by reference to particular historical experiences, such as the sequence of Reform Acts in Britain, the American heritage of British institutions, the Mexican Revolution, and Nazism and defeat in World War II for Germany. It is quite clear that political culture is treated as both an independent and a dependent variable, as causing structure and as being caused by it.

The position taken in *The Civic Culture* that beliefs, feelings, and values significantly influence political behavior, and that these beliefs, feelings, and values are the product of socialization experiences is one that is sustained by much evidence. But *The Civic Culture* was one of the earliest studies to stress the importance of adult political socialization and experiences and to demonstrate the relative weakness of childhood socialization. These points are made unambiguously and are substantiated by evidence.

This relatively open conception of political culture, viewed as causing behavior and structure, as well as being caused by them, and including adult political learning and a rational cognitive component, is the special target of Ronald Rogowski, who rejects political culture theory as being too loosely and diffusely formulated to be acceptable as explanatory theory. He argues that there are clear-cut rational relationships between socioeconomic, ethnic, and religious interests and political structure, and that a rational individualist explanation of political structure is a more powerful and parsimonious theory than political culture theory.[16]

This polemic about the explanatory significance of political culture as defined in *The Civic Culture* can only be resolved by empirical research, and such research as has been done suggests that Rogowski's position is not sustainable by evidence. Much of human history stands in disproof of the argument that the structure of political institutions and their legitimacy can be explained by simple reference to rational self-interest. Surely the rational self-interest of social class and of ethnic and religious groups is a powerful dynamic illuminating political movements and conflicts, and contributing significantly to historical outcomes. But patriotism, community loyalty, religious values, and simple habit and tradition obviously enter into the explanation of political structure and legitimacy. . . .

## Notes

1. Plato, *The Works of Plato,* trans. Benjamin Jowett 1 vol. ed. (New York: Dial Press, n.d.), p. 445.

2. Plutarch, *The Lives of the Noble Grecians and Romans,* trans. John Dryden, rev. by Arthur Hugh Clough (New York: Random House, Modern Library, n.d.), p. 62.

3. Aristotle, *Politics,* trans. H. Rackham (London: Heinemann, 1932), pp. 285ff.

4. Talcott Parsons and E. A. Shils, *Toward a General Theory of Action* (Cambridge, Mass.: Harvard University Press, 1951).

5. See, for example, Sigmund Freud, *Civilization and Its Discontents (1930) in Complete Works,* vol. 22 (New York: Macmillan, 1962).

6. B. Malinowski, *Sex and Repression in Savage Society* (New York: Harcourt Brace Jovanovich 1927); Margaret Mead, *Coming of Age in Samoa* (New York: William Morrow, 1928); Ruth Benedict, *Patterns of Culture* (Boston: Houghton Mifflin, 1934); Harold Lasswell, *Psychopathology and Politics* (Chicago: University of Chicago Press, 1930).

7. Abram Kardiner, *The Psychological Frontiers of Society* (New York: Columbia University Press, 1945); Ralph Linton, *The Cultural Background of Personality* (New York: Appleton-Century-Crofts, 1945); Alex Inkeles and Daniel Levinson, "National Character: The Study of Modal Personality and Socio-Cultural Systems," in Lindzey and Aronson, *Handbook,* vol. 4; Alex Inkeles, "National Character and Modern Political Systems" in Franklin L. K. Hsu, ed., *Psychological Anthroplogy* (Belmont, Calif.: Wadsworth, 1961).

8. G. A. Almond, *Political Development* (Boston: Little, Brown, 1970), pp. 35ff.

9. Samuel Beer's most recent formulation, which elaborates his views first formulated in *Patterns of Government (1958),* is to be found in S. Beer and Adam Ulam, eds., *Patterns of Government,* 3rd ed., part 1 (New York: Random House, 1974).

10. Lucian Pye and Sidney Verba, *Political Culture and Political Development* (Princeton, N.J.: Princeton University Press, 1966), chap. 1.

11. Almond and Verba, *Civic Culture,* (Princeton, N.J.: Princeton University Press, 1963).

12. Robert A. Dahl, *Political Oppositions in Western Democracies* (New Haven: Yale University Press, 1966), pp. 352ff.

13. David Easton, *A System Analysis of Political Life* (New York: John Wiley and Sons, 1965).

14. Philip Converse, "The Nature of Mass Belief Systems," in David Apter, ed., *Ideology and Discontent* (New York: Free Press, 1964).

15. See also Donald Devine, *The Political Culture of the United States* (Boston: Little, Brown, 1972).

16. Ronald Rogowski, *A Rational Theory of Legitimacy* (Princeton, N.J.: Princeton University Press, 1976).

## 6

# The Analysis of Political Systems

*David Easton*

## I. SOME ATTRIBUTES OF POLITICAL SCIENCE

In an earlier work I have argued for the need to develop general, empirically oriented theory

SOURCE: David Easton, "An Approach to the Analysis of Political Systems," *World Politics* 9, no. 3 (April 1957), pp. 383–400. © 1957, 1985 renewed by Princeton University Press. Reprinted with permission of Princeton University Press. Article abridged by the editors.

as the most economical way in the long run to understand political life. Here I propose to indicate a point of view that, at the least, might serve as a springboard for discussion of alternative approaches and, at most, as a small step in the direction of a general political theory. I wish to stress that what I have to say is a mere orientation to the problem of theory; outside of economics and perhaps psychology, it would be presumptuous to call very much in social science "theory," in the strict sense of the term.

Furthermore, I shall offer only a Gestalt of my point of view, so that it will be possible to evaluate, in the light of the whole, those parts that I do stress. In doing this, I know I can run the definite risk that the meaning and implications of this point of view may be only superficially communicated; but it is a risk I shall have to undertake since I do not know how to avoid it sensibly.

The study of politics is concerned with understanding how authoritative decisions are made and executed for a society. We can try to understand political life by viewing each of its aspects piecemeal. We can examine the operation of such institutions as political parties, interest groups, government, and voting; we can study the nature and consequences of such political practices as manipulation, propaganda, and violence; we can seek to reveal the structure within which these practices occur. By combining the results we can obtain a rough picture of what happens in any self-contained political unit.

In combining these results, however, there is already implicit the notion that each part of the larger political canvas does not stand alone but is related to each other part; or, to put it positively, that the operation of no one part can be fully understood without reference to the way in which the whole itself operates. I have suggested in my book, *The Political System*,[1] that it is valuable to adopt this implicit assumption as an articulate premise for research and to view political life as a system of interrelated activities. These activities derive their relatedness or systemic ties from the fact that they all more or less influence the way in which authoritative

decisions are formulated and executed for a society.

Once we begin to speak of political life as a system of activity, certain consequences follow for the way in which we can undertake to analyze the working of a system. The very idea of a system suggests that we can separate political life from the rest of social activity, at least for analytical purposes, and examine it as though for the moment it were a self-contained entity surrounded by, but clearly distinguishable from, the environment or setting in which it operates. In much the same way, astronomers consider the solar system a complex of events isolated for certain purposes from the rest of the universe.

Furthermore, if we hold the system of political actions as a unit before our mind's eye, as it were, we can see that what keeps the system going are inputs of various kinds. These inputs are converted by the processes of the system into outputs and these, in turn, have consequences both for the system and for the environment in which the system exists. The formula here is very simple but, as I hope to show, also very illuminating: inputs—political system or processes—outputs. These relationships are shown diagrammatically in Figure 1. This diagram represents a very primitive "model"—to dignify it with a fashionable name —for approaching the study of political life.

Political systems have certain properties because they are systems. To present an overall view of the whole approach, let me identify the major attributes, say a little about each, and then treat one of these properties at somewhat greater length, even though still inadequately.

1. Properties of identification. To distinguish a political system from other social systems, we must be able to identify it by describing its fundamental units and establishing the boundaries that demarcate it from units outside the system.

a. Units of a political system. The units are the elements of which we say a system is composed. In the case of a political system, they are political actions. Normally it is useful to look

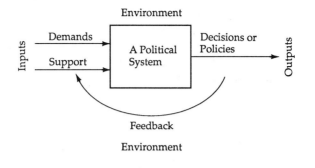

Environment

**FIGURE 1**

at these as they structure themselves in political roles and political groups.

b. Boundaries. Some of the most significant questions with regard to the operation of political systems can be answered only if we bear in mind the obvious fact that a system does not exist in a vacuum. It is always immersed in a specific setting or environment. The way in which a system works will be in part a function of its response to the total social, biological, and physical environment.

The special problem with which we are confronted is how to distinguish systematically between a political system and its setting. Does it even make sense to say that a political system has a boundary dividing it from its setting? If so, how are we to identify the line of demarcation?

Without pausing to argue the matter, I would suggest that it is useful to conceive of a political system as having a boundary in the same sense as a physical system. The boundary of a political system is defined by all those actions more or less directly related to the making of binding decisions for a society; every social action that does not partake of this characteristic will be excluded from the system and thereby will automatically be viewed as an external variable in the environment.

2. Inputs and outputs. Presumably, if we select political systems for special study, we do so because we believe that they have characteristically important consequences for society, namely, authoritative decisions. These consequences I shall call the outputs. If we judged that political systems did not have important outputs for society, we would probably not be interested in them.

Unless a system is approaching a state of entropy—and we can assume that this is not true of most political systems—it must have continuing inputs to keep it going. Without inputs the system can do no work; without outputs we cannot identify the work done by the system. The specific research tasks in this connection would be to identify the inputs and the forces that shape and change them, to trace the processes through which they are transformed into outputs, to describe the general conditions under which such processes can be maintained, and to establish the relationship between outputs and succeeding inputs of the system.

From this point of view, much light can be shed on the working of a political system if we take into account the fact that much of what happens within a system has its birth in the efforts of the members of the system to cope with the changing environment. We can appreciate this point if we consider a familiar biological system such as the human organism. It is subject to constant stress from its surroundings to which it must adapt in one way or another if it is not to be completely destroyed. In part, of course, the way in which the body works represents responses to needs that are generated by the very organization of its anatomy and functions; but in large part, in order to understand both the structure and the working of the body, we must also be very sensitive to the inputs from the environment.

In the same way, the behavior of every political system is to some degree imposed upon it by the kind of system it is, that is, by its own structure and internal needs. But its behavior also reflects the strains occasioned by the specific setting within which the system operates. It may be argued that most of the significant changes within a political system have their origin in shifts among the external variables. Since I shall be devoting the bulk of this article to examining some of the problems related to the exchange between political systems and their environments, I shall move on to a rapid description of other properties of political systems.

3. Differentiation within a system. As we shall see in a moment, from the environment come both energy to activate a system and information with regard to which the system uses this energy. In this way a system is able to do work. It has some sort of output that is different from the input that enters from the environment. We can take it as a useful hypothesis that if a political system is to perform some work for anything but a limited interval of time, a minimal amount of differentiation in its structure must occur. In fact, empirically it is impossible to find a significant political system in which the same units all perform the same activities at the same time. The members of a system engage in at least some minimal division of labor that provides a structure within which action takes place.

4. Integration of a system. This fact of differentiation opens up a major area of inquiry with regard to political systems. Structural differentiation sets in motion forces that are potentially disintegrative in their results for the system. If two or more units are performing different kinds of activity at the same time, how are these activities to be brought into the minimal degree of articulation necessary if the members of the system are not to end up in utter disorganization with regard to the production of the outputs of interest to us? We can hypothesize that if a structured system is to maintain itself, it must provide mechanisms whereby its members are integrated or induced to cooperate in some minimal degree so that they make authoritative decisions.

## II. INPUTS: DEMANDS

Now that I have mentioned some major attributes of political systems that I suggest require special attention if we are to develop a generalized approach, I want to consider in greater detail the way in which an examination of inputs and outputs will shed some light on the working of these systems.

Among inputs of a political system there are two basic kinds: demands and support. These inputs give a political system its dynamic character. They furnish it both with the raw material or information that the system is called upon to process and with the energy to keep it going.

The reason why a political system emerges in a society at all—that is, why men engage in political activity—is that demands are being made by persons or groups in the society that cannot all be fully satisfied. In all societies one fact dominates political life: scarcity prevails with regard to most of the valued things. Some of the claims for these relatively scarce things never find their way into the political system but are satisfied through the private negotiations of or settlements by the persons involved. Demands for prestige may find satisfaction through the status relations of society; claims for wealth are met in part through the economic system; aspirations for power find expression in educational, fraternal, labor, and similar private organizations. Only where wants require some special organized effort on the part of society to settle them authoritatively may we say that they have become inputs of the political system.

Systematic research would require us to address ourselves to several key questions with regard to these demands.

1. How do demands arise and assume their particular character in a society? In answer to this question, we can point out that demands

have their birth in two sectors of experience: either in the environment of a system or within the system itself. We shall call these the external and internal demands, respectively.

Let us look at the external demands first. I find it useful to see the environment not as an undifferentiated mass of events but rather as systems clearly distinguishable from one another and from the political system. In the environment we have such systems as the ecology, economy, culture, personality, social structure, and demography. Each of these constitutes a major set of variables in the setting that helps to shape the kind of demands entering a political system. For purposes of illustrating what I mean, I shall say a few words about culture.

The members of every society act within the framework of an ongoing culture that shapes their general goals, specific objectives, and the procedures that the members feel ought to be used. Every culture derives part of its unique quality from the fact that it emphasizes one or more special aspects of behavior and this strategic emphasis serves to differentiate it from other cultures with respect to the demands that it generates. As far as the mass of the people is concerned, some cultures, such as our own, are weighted heavily on the side of economic wants, success, privacy, leisure activity, and rational efficiency. Others, such as that of the Fox Indians, strive toward the maintenance of harmony, even if in the process the goals of efficiency and rationality may be sacrificed. Still others, such as the Kachins of highland Burma, stress the pursuit of power and prestige. The culture embodies the standards of value in a society and thereby marks out areas of potential conflict, if the valued things are in short supply relative to demand. The typical demands that will find their way into the political process will concern the matters in conflict that are labeled important by the culture. For this reason we cannot hope to understand the nature of the demands presenting themselves for political settlement unless we are ready to explore systematically and intensively their connection with the culture. And what I have said about

culture applies, with suitable modifications, to other parts of the setting of a political system.

But not all demands originate or have their major locus in the environment. Important types stem from situations occurring within a political system itself. Typically, in every ongoing system, demands may emerge for alterations in the political relationships of the members themselves, as the result of dissatisfaction stemming from these relationships. For example, in a political system based upon representation, in which equal representation is an important political norm, demands may arise for equalizing representation between urban and rural voting districts. Similarly, demands for changes in the process of recruitment of formal political leaders, for modifications of the way in which constitutions are amended, and the like may all be internally inspired demands.

I find it useful and necessary to distinguish these from external demands because they are, strictly speaking, not inputs of the system but something that we can call "withinputs," if we can tolerate a cumbersome neologism, and because their consequences for the character of a political system are more direct than in the case of external demands. Furthermore, if we were not aware of this difference in classes of demands, we might search in vain for an explanation of the emergence of a given set of internal demands if we turned only to the environment.

2. How are demands transformed into issues? What determines whether a demand becomes a matter for serious political discussion or remains something to be resolved privately among the members of society? The occurrence of a demand, whether internal or external, does not thereby automatically convert it into a political *issue*. Many demands die at birth or linger on with the support of an insignificant fraction of the society and are never raised to the level of possible political decision. Others become issues, an issue being a demand that the members of a political system are prepared to deal with as a significant item for discussion through the recognized channels in the system.

The distinction between demands and issues raises a number of questions about which we need data if we are to understand the processes through which claims typically become transformed into issues. For example, we would need to know something about the relationship between a demand and the location of its initiators or supporters in the power structures of the society, the importance of secrecy as compared with publicity in presenting demands, the matter of timing of demands, the possession of political skills or know-how, access to channels of communication, the attitudes and states of mind of possible publics, and the images held by the initiators of demands with regard to the way in which things get done in the particular political system. Answers to matters such as these would possibly yield a conversion index reflecting the probability of a set of demands being converted into live political issues.

If we assume that political science is primarily concerned with the way in which authoritative decisions are made for a society, demands require special attention as a major type of input of political systems. I have suggested that demands influence the behavior of a system in a number of ways. They constitute a significant part of the material upon which the system operates. They are also one of the sources of change in political systems, since as the environment fluctuates it generates new types of demand-inputs for the system. Accordingly, without this attention to the origin and determinants of demands we would be at a loss to be able to treat rigorously not only the operation of a system at a moment of time but also its change over a specified interval. Both the statics and historical dynamics of a political system depend upon a detailed understanding of demands, particularly of the impact of the setting on them.

## III. INPUTS: SUPPORT

Inputs of demands alone are not enough to keep a political system operating. They are only the raw material out of which finished products called decisions are manufactured. Energy in the form of actions or orientations promoting and resisting a political system, the demands arising in it, and the decisions issuing from it must also be put into the system to keep it running. This input I shall call support. Without support, demands could not be satisfied or conflicts in goals composed. If demands are to be acted upon, the members of a system undertaking to pilot the demands through to their transformation into binding decisions and those who seek to influence the relevant processes in any way must be able to count on support from others in the system. Just how must support, from how many and which members of a political system, are separate and important questions that I shall touch on shortly.

What do we mean by support? We can say that A supports B either when A acts on behalf of or when he orients himself favorably toward B's goals, interests, and actions. Supportive behavior may thus be of two kinds. It may consist of actions promoting the goals, interests, and actions of another person. We may vote for a political candidate, or defend a decision by the highest court of the land. In these cases, support manifests itself through overt action.

On the other hand, supportive behavior may involve not external observable acts, but those internal forms of behavior we call orientations or states of mind. As I use the phrase, a supportive state of mind is a deep-seated set of attitudes or predispositions, or a readiness to act on behalf of some other person. It exists when we say that a man is loyal to his party, attached to democracy, or infused with patriotism. What such phrases as these have in common is the fact that they refer to a state of feelings on the part of a person. No overt action is involved at this level of description, although the implication is that the individual will pursue a course of action consistent with his attitudes. Where the anticipated action does not flow from our perception of the state of mind, we assume that we have not penetrated deeply enough into the true feelings of the person but have merely skimmed off his surface attitudes.

Supportive states of mind are vital inputs for the operation and maintenance of a political system. For example, it is often said that the struggle in the international sphere concerns mastery over men's minds. To a certain extent this is true. If the members of a political system are deeply attached to a system or its ideals, the likelihood of their participating in either domestic or foreign politics in such a way as to undermine the system is reduced by a large factor. Presumably, even in the face of considerable provocation, ingrained supportive feelings of loyalty may be expected to prevail.

We shall need to identify the typical mechanisms through which supportive attitudes are inculcated and continuously reinforced within a political system. But our prior task is to specify and examine the political objects in relation to which support is extended.

## 1. The Domain of Support

Support is fed into the political system in relation to three objects: the community, the regime, and the government. There must be convergence of attitude and opinion as well as some willingness to act with regard to each of these objects. Let us examine each in turn.

*1. The political community.* No political system can continue to operate unless its members are willing to support the existence of a group that seeks to settle differences or promote decisions through peaceful action in common. The point is so obvious—being dealt with usually under the heading of the growth of national unity—that it may well be overlooked; and yet it is a premise upon which the continuation of any political system depends. To refer to this phenomenon we can speak of the political community. At this level of support we are not concerned with whether a government exists or whether there is loyalty to a constitutional order. For the moment we only ask whether the members of the group that we are examining are sufficiently oriented toward each other to want to contribute their collective energies toward pacific settlement of their varying demands. . . .

*2. The regime.* Support for a second major part of a political system helps to supply the energy to keep the system running. This aspect of the system I shall call the regime. It consists of all those arrangements that regulate the way in which the demands put into the system are settled and the way in which decisions are put into effect. They are the so-called rules of the game, in the light of which actions by members of the system are legitimated and accepted by the bulk of the members as authoritative. Unless there is a minimum convergence of attitudes in support of these fundamental rules—the constitutional principles, as we call them in Western society— there would be insufficient harmony in the actions of the members of a system to meet the problems generated by their support of a political community. The fact of trying to settle demands in common means that there must be known principles governing the way in which resolutions of differences of claims are to take place.

*3. The government.* If a political system is going to be able to handle the conflicting demands put into it, not only must the members of the system be prepared to support the settlement of these conflicts in common and possess some consensus with regard to the rules governing the mode of settlement; they must also be ready to support a government as it undertakes the concrete tasks involved in negotiating such settlements. When we come to the outputs of a system, we shall see the rewards that are available to a government for mobilizing support. At this point, I just wish to draw attention to this need on the part of a government for support if it is going to be able to make decisions with regard to demands. Of course, a government may elicit support in many ways: through persuasion, consent, or manipulation. It may also impose unsupported settlements of demands through threats of force. But it is a familiar axiom of political science that a government based upon force alone is not long for this world; it must buttress its position by inducing a favorable state of mind in its subjects through fair or foul means.

The fact that support directed to a political system can be broken down conceptually into three elements—support for the community, regime, and government—does not mean, of course, that in the concrete case support for each of these three objects is independent. In fact we might and normally do find all three kinds of support very closely intertwined, so that the presence of one is a function of the presence of one or both of the other types. . . .

## 2. Quantity and Scope of Support

How much support need to be put into a system and how many of its members needs to contribute such support if the system is to be able to do the job of converting demands to decisions? No ready answer can be offered. The actual situation in each case would determine the amount and scope required. We can, however, visualize a number of situations that will be helpful in directing our attention to possible generalizations.

Under certain circumstnces very few members need to support a system at any level. The members might be dull and apathetic, indifferent to the general operations of the system, its progress or decisions. In a loosely connected system such as India has had, this might well be the state of mind of by far the largest segment of the membership. Either in fact they have not been affected by national decisions or they have not perceived that they were so affected. They may have little sense of identification with the present regime and government and yet, with regard to the input of demands, the system may be able to act on the basis of the support offered by the known 3 percent of the Western-oriented politicians and intellectuals who are politically active. In other words, we can have a small minority putting in quantitatively sufficient supportive energy to keep the system going. However, we can venture the hypothesis that where members of a system are putting in numerous demands, there is a strong probability that they will actively offer support or hostility at one of the three levels of the system, depending upon the degree to which these demands are being met through appropriate decisions.

Alternatively, we may find that all the members of a system are putting in support, but the amount may be so low as to place one or all aspects of the system in jeopardy. Modern France is perhaps a classic illustration. The input of support at the level of the political community is probably adequte for the maintenance of France as a national political unit. But for a variety of historical and contemporary reasons, there is considerable doubt as to whether the members of the French political system are putting in anything but a low order of support to the regime or any particular government. This low amount of support, even though spread over a relatively large segment of the population, leaves the French political system on somewhat less secure foundations than is the case with India. There support is less widespread but more active—that is, quantitatively greater—on the part of a minority. As this illustration indicates, the amount of support is not necessarily proportional to its scope.

It may seem from the above discussion as though the members of a political system either put in support or withhold it—that is, demonstrate hostility or apathy. In fact, members may and normally do simultaneously engage in supportive and hostile behavior. What we must be interested in is the net balance of support.

## IV. MECHANISMS OF SUPPORT

To this point I have suggested that no political system can yield the important outputs we call authoritative decisions unless, in addition to demands, support finds its way into the system. I have discussed the possible object to which support may be directed, and some problems with regard to the domain, quantity, and scope of support. We are now ready to turn to the main question raised by our attention to support as a crucial input: how do systems typically manage to maintain a steady flow of support? Without it a system will not absorb sufficient energy from its members to be able to convert demands to decisions.

In theory, there might be an infinite variety of means through which members could be induced to support a system; in practice, certain well-established classes of mechanisms are used. Research in this area needs to be directed to exploring the precise way in which a particular system utilizes these mechanisms and to refining our understanding of the way in which they contribute to the making of authoritative policy.

A society generates support for a political system in two ways: through outputs that meet the demands of the members of society; and through the processes of politicization. Let us look at outputs first.

## 1. Outputs as a Mechanism of Support

An output of a political system, it will be recalled, is a political decision or policy. One of the major ways of strengthening the ties of the members to their system is through providing decisions that tend to satisfy the day-to-day demands of these members. Fundamentally this is the truth that lies in the aphorism that one can fool some of the people some of the time but not all of them all of the time. Without some minimal satisfaction of demands, the ardor of all but the most fanatical patriot is sure to cool. The outputs, consisting of political decisions, constitute a body of specific inducements for the members of a system to support that system.

Inducements of this kind may be positive or negative. Where negative, they threaten the members of the system with various kinds of sanctions ranging from a small monetary fine to physical detention, ostracism, or loss of life, as in our own system with regard to the case of legally defined treason. In every system support stems in part from fear of sanctions or compulsion; in autocratic systems the proportion of coerced support is at a maximum. For want of

space I shall confine myself to those cases where positive incentives loom largest.

Since the specific outputs of a system are policy decisions, it is upon the government that the final responsibility falls for matching or balancing outputs of decisions against input of demand. But it is clear that to obtain the support of the members of a system through positive incentives, a government need not meet all the demands of even its most influential and ardent supporters. Most governments, or groups such as political parties that seek to control governments, succeed in building up a reserve of support. This reserve will carry the government along even though it offends its followers, so long as over the extended short runs these followers perceive the particular government as one that is in general favorable to their interests. One form that this reserve support takes in Western society is that of party loyalty, since the party is the typical instrument in a mass industrialized society for mobilizing and maintaining support for a government. However, continuous lack of specific rewards through policy decisions ultimately leads to the danger that even the deepest party loyalty may be shaken....

Thus a system need not meet *all the demands* of its members so long as it has stored up a reserve of support over the years. Nor need it satisfy even *some of the demands* of all its members. Just whose demands a system must seek to meet, how much of their demands, at what time, and under what conditions are questions for special research. We can say in advance that at least the demands of the most influential members require satisfaction. But this tells us little unless we know how to discover the influentials in a political system and how new sets of members rise to positions of influence.

The critical significance of the decisions of governments for the support of the other two aspects of a system—namely, the political community and the regime—is clear from what I have said above. Not all withdrawal of support from a government has consequences for the success or failure of a regime or community. But persistent inability of a government to produce satisfactory outputs for the members of a system may well lead to demands for changing of the regime or for dissolution of the political community. It is for this reason that the input-output balance is a vital mechanism in the life of a political system.

## 2. Politicization as a Mechanism of Support

It would be wrong to consider that the level of support available to a system is a function exclusively of the outputs in the form of either sanctions or rewards. If we did so conclude, we could scarcely account for the maintenance of numerous political systems in which satisfaction of demands has been manifestly low, in which public coercion is limited, and yet which have endured for epochs. Alternately, it might be difficult to explain how political systems could endure and yet manage to flout or thwart urgent demands, failing thereby to render sufficient *quid pro quo* for the input of support. The fact is that whatever reserve of support has been accumulated through past decisions is increased and reinforced by a complicated method for steadily manufacturing support through what I shall call the process of politicization. It is an awkward term, but nevertheless an appropriately descriptive one.

As each person grows up in a society, through a network of rewards and punishments the other members of society communicate to and instill in him the various institutionalized goals and norms of that society. This is well known in social research as the process of socialization. Through its operation a person learns to play his various social roles. Part of these goals and norms relate to what the society considers desirable in political life. The ways in which these political patterns are learned by the members of society constitute what I call the process of politicization. Through it a person learns to play his political roles, which include the absorption of the proper political attitudes.

Let us examine a little more closely something of what happens during the process

of politicization. As members of a society mature, they must absorb the various orientations toward political matters that one is expected to have in that society. If the expectations of the members of society with regard to the way each should behave in specific political situations diverged beyond a certain range, it would be impossible to get common action with regard to the making of binding decisions. It is essential for the viability of an orderly political system that the members of the system have some common basic expectations with regard to the standards that are to be used in making political evaluations, to the way people will feel about various political matters, and to the way members of the system will perceive and interpret political phenomena.

The mechanism through which this learning takes place is of considerable significance in understanding how a political system generates and accumulates a strong reserve of support. Although we cannot pursue the details, we can mention a few of the relevant dimensions. In the first place, of course, the learning or politicization process does not stop at any particular period for the individual; it starts with the child and, in the light of our knowledge of learning, may have its deepest impact through the teen age....

In the second place, the actual process of politicization at its most general level brings into operation a complex network of rewards and punishments. For adopting the correct political attitudes and performing the right political acts, for conforming to the generally accepted interpretations of political goals, and for undertaking the institutionalized obligations of a member of the given system, we are variously rewarded or punished. For conforming we are made to feel worthy, wanted, and respected and often obtain material advantages such as wealth, influence, improved opportunities. For deviating beyond the permissible range, we are made to feel unworthy, rejected, dishonored, and often suffer material losses....

In the third place, the means used for communicating the goals and norms to others tend to be repetitive in all societies. The various political myths, doctrines, and philosophies transmit to each generation a particular interpretation of the goals and norms. The decisive links in this chain of transmission are parents, siblings, peers, teachers, organizations, and social leaders, as well as physical symbols such as flags or totems, ceremonies, and rituals freighted with political meaning.

These processes through which attachments to a political system become built into the maturing member of a society I have lumped together under the rubric of politicization. . . .

When the basic political attachments become deeply rooted or institutionalized, we say that the system has become accepted as legitimate. Politicization therefore effectively sums up the way in which legitimacy is created and transmitted in a political system. And it is an empirical observation that in those instances where political systems have survived the longest, support has been nourished by an ingrained belief in the legitimacy of the relevant governments and regimes.

What I am suggesting here is that support resting on a sense of the legitimacy of a government and regime provides a necessary reserve if the system is to weather those frequent storms when the more obvious outputs of the system seem to impose greater hardships than rewards. Answers to questions concerning the formation, maintenance, transmission, and change of standards of legitimacy will contribute generously to an understanding of the way in which support is sufficiently institutionalized so that a system may regularly and without excessive expenditure of effort transform inputs of demand into outputs of decision.

That there is a need for general theory in the study of political life is apparent. The only question is how best to proceed. There is no one royal road that can be said to be either the correct one or the best. It is only a matter of what appears as the given level of available knowledge to be the most useful. At this stage it appears that system theory, with its sensitivity to the input-output exchange between a system and its setting offers a fruitful approach. It is an economical way of organizing presently disconnected political data and promises interesting dividends.

## Notes

1. David Easton, *The Political System* (New York: Alfred A. Knopf, 1953).

## 7

# Bringing the State Back In

*Theda Skocpol*

The explanatory importance of "the state" has been highlighted during the last decade in a variety of comparative and historical studies by social scientists from several disciplines and geographical area specialties. The topics of these studies have ranged from the roles of Latin American states in instituting comprehensive reforms from above to the activities of states in the advanced industrial democracies of Europe, the United States, and Japan in developing social programs and managing economic problems. No explicitly shared research agenda or general theory has tied such diverse studies together, yet they have arrived at complementary arguments and strategies of analysis.

States, or parts of states, have been identified in these studies as taking weighty, autonomous initiatives—going beyond the demands or interests of social groups—to promote social change, manage economic crises, or develop innovative public policies. The administrative and coercive organizations that form the core of any modern state have been identified as the likely generators of autonomous state initiatives and varying organizational structures and

SOURCE: Reprinted from *Items*, vol. 36, nos. 1/2 (June 1982), pp. 1–8. By permission of the Social Science Research Council, 605 Third Avenue, New York, NY 10158.

resources of states have been probed in order to explain why and when states pursue their own strategies and goals. Finally, much interest has centered on the differing abilities of states to realize policy goals and a number of concepts and research strategies have been developed to address this issue through case studies and cross-national comparisons focused on state efforts to implement goals in particular policy areas.

The value of recent studies converging on common concerns about states as both actors and organizational structures can best be demonstrated by concrete illustrations from the literature. But, first, it makes sense to underline the paradigmatic reorientation embodied in the phrase "bringing the state back in."

## SOCIETY-CENTERED THEORIES OF POLITICS AND GOVERNMENT

Not long ago, the dominant theories and research agendas of the social sciences spoke of anything and everything but "the state." This was true even—indeed especially—when politics was at issue. Cultural values, socialized personalities, clashing interest groups, conflicting or allying classes, and differentiating social systems—these were supposed to provide sufficient keys both to the political process and to political conflicts. "The state" was an old-fashioned concept, associated with dry and dusty legal-formalist studies of nationally particular constitutional principles. The real dynamics of political life could only be discerned by social scientists willing to look at societies and economies, sites of the processes or structures believed to be universally basic to politics and social change. In place of the state, social scientists conceived of "government" as simply the *arena* in which social classes, or economic interest groups, or normative social movements contended or allied with one another to influence the making of public policy decisions. Interest centered on the societal "inputs" to government, and on the socioeconomic effects of governmental "outputs." Government itself

was not considered to be an independent actor, and variations in governmental structures were deemed less significant than general functions shared by the political systems of all societies.

Society-centered ways of explaining politics and governmental activities were especially characteristic of the pluralist and structural-functional theories predominant in political science and sociology in the United States during the 1950s and 1960s.[1] Yet even when rebellious "neo-Marxists" began to theorize about "the capitalist state," they too emphasized the social functions of the state as an arena for class struggles and as an instrument of class rule.[2] Indeed, the reluctance of pluralists and structural-functionalists to speak of states, and the near-unwillingness of even most neo-Marxists to grant autonomous substance to states, resonates with proclivities present from the start in the modern social sciences. These sciences emerged along with the industrial and democratic revolutions of Western Europe in the 18th and 19th centuries. Their founding theorists quite understandably perceived the locus of societal dynamics to be located not in outmoded monarchical and aristocratic states but in civil society, variously understood as "the market," "the industrial division of labor," or "class relations." Founding theorists as politically opposed as Herbert Spencer and Karl Marx (who now, not entirely inappropriately, lie just across a lane from one another in Highgate Cemetery, London) agreed that industrial capitalism was triumphing over the military and territorial rivalries of states. For both of these theorists, 19th century British socioeconomic developments presaged the future for all countries—and for the world as a whole.

## FOCUSING ON BRITAIN AND THE UNITED STATES

As world history moved—via colonial conquests, two world wars, and various state-building revolutions and anticolonial movements—from the Pax Britannica of the 19th century to the Pax

Americana of the period after World War II, the Western social sciences managed to keep their eyes averted from the explanatory centrality of states as potent and autonomous organizational actors. It was not that such phenomena as political authoritarianism or totalitarianism were ignored—just that the preferred theoretical explanations were always in terms of economic backwardness or the unfortunate persistence of non-Western "traditional" values. As long as capitalist and liberal Britain, and then capitalist and liberal America, could plausibly be seen as the unchallengeable "lead societies," the Western social sciences could manage the feat of downplaying the explanatory centrality of states in their major theoretical paradigms. For the dominant social science paradigms were riveted on understanding modernization—its causes and direction. And in Britain and America—the "most modern" societies—industrialization seemed to be spontaneous, socioeconomic and cultural processes appeared to be the primary loci of change, and the decisions of governmental legislative bodies were apparently the basic stuff of politics.

But by the 1970s, both Britain and the United States were unmistakably becoming beleaguered industrial economies in a world of competitive national states. It is probably not surprising that, at this juncture, it became theoretically fashionable to begin to speak of "the state" as an actor and as a society-shaping institutional structure. Indeed, social scientists are now willing to offer state-centered arguments about Britain and the United States themselves. Fittingly, many of these new arguments stress ways in which state actions and structures have distinctively shaped British and American national economic development and international economic policies. And some of them also ponder how the British and American states might fetter or facilitate current efforts at industrial regeneration in these countries.[3] In short, especially now that Britain and the United States seem much more like particular state-societies in an uncertain, competitive, and interdependent world of many such entities, a paradigmatic shift seems to be under way in the social sciences, a shift that involves a fundamental rethinking of the role of states in relation to societies and economies.

## REVIVAL OF A CONTINENTAL EUROPEAN PERSPECTIVE

In the 19th century, social theorists oriented to the realities of social change on the European Continent refused to accept the deemphasis of the state characteristic of those founders of the modern social sciences who centered their thinking on Britain. German scholars, especially, insisted upon the institutional reality of the state and its continuing impact upon and within civil society. Now that comparative social scientists are similarly reemphasizing the importance of states, it is perhaps not surprising that there is renewed reliance upon the basic understanding of "the state" passed down to contemporary scholarship through the widely known writings of such major German scholars as Max Weber and Otto Hintze.[4]

Max Weber argued that states are compulsory associations claiming control over territories and the people within them. Administrative, legal, and coercive organizations are the core of any state. These organizations are variably structured in different countries, and they may be embedded in one sort or another of a constitutional–representative system of parliamentary decision making and electoral contests for key executive and legislative posts. Nevertheless, as Alfred Stepan nicely puts it in a formulation that captures the biting edge of the Weberian perspective: "The state must be considered as more than the 'government.' It is the continuous administrative, legal, bureaucratic and coercive systems that attempt not only to structure relationships *between* civil society and public authority in a polity but also to structure many crucial relationships within civil society as well."[5] Moreover, as Otto Hintze demonstrated, thinking of states as organizations controlling territories leads us away from positing basic features common to all polities and leads us toward consideration of the varying ways in which state structures and actions are conditioned by historically changing transnational environments. These environments impinge upon individual states through geopolitical patterns of interstate domination and competition, through the communication of ideas and models of public policy, and through world-economic patterns of trade, division of productive activities, investment flows, and international finance. States necessarily stand at the intersections between domestic sociopolitical orders and the transnational structures within which they must maneuver for survival or advantage in relation to other states. The modern state as we know it, and as Weber and Hintze conceptualized it, has always been, since its birth in European history, part of a system of competing states.

## STATES AS AUTONOMOUS ACTORS

States conceived as organizations controlling territories and people may formulate and pursue goals that are not simply reflective of the demands or interests of social groups, classes, or society. This is what is usually meant by "state autonomy." Unless such independent goal formulation can be demonstrated and explained, there is little need to talk about states as important actors. In recent comparative-historical scholarship on different kinds of topics in separate parts of the world, collectivities of state officials are shown formulating and pursuing their own goals. Their efforts, moreover, are related to the order-keeping concerns of states, and to the linkages of states into international systems of communication and competition.

## REFORMIST MILITARY COUPS IN LATIN AMERICA

An unusually comprehensive kind of autonomous state action is analyzed in Alfred Stepan's book, *The State and Society: Peru in Comparative*

*Perspective*, which offers a causal explanation of attempts by state elites in Latin America to install "inclusionary" or "exclusionary" corporatist regimes.[6] A key element in Stepan's explanation is the formation of a strategically located cadre of officials holding great power inside and through existing state organizations, and also enjoying a unified sense of ideological purpose about the desirability of using state intervention to ensure political order and promote national economic development. To account for Brazil's "exclusionary" corporatist coup in 1964 and for Peru's "inclusionary" corporatist coup in 1968, Stepan stresses the prior socialization of what he calls "new military professionals." These were career military officers who, together, passed through training schools that taught techniques and ideas of national economic planning and counterinsurgency, along with "traditional" military skills. Such new military professionals then installed corporatist regimes in response to perceived crises of political order and of national economic development. The military professionals used state power to stave off or deflect threats to national order from subordinate classes and groups. They also used state power to implement socioeconomic reforms or plans for further national industrialization—something they saw as a basic requisite for their country's improved international standing.

## CIVIL BUREAUCRATS AND EUROPEAN SOCIAL POLICIES

If Stepan deals with extraordinary instances of state autonomy, in which nonconstitutionally-ruling strategic elites have used the state as a whole to redirect and restructure society and politics, other scholars have teased out more circumscribed instances of state autonomy in the histories of public policy making in liberal-democratic, constitutionalist polities. For example, Hugh Heclo's *Modern Social Politics in Britain and Sweden* provides an intricate comparative-historical account of the long-term development of unemployment insurance and policies of old-age assistance in these two nations.[7] Without being explicitly presented as such, Heclo's book is about autonomous state contributions to social policy making. The autonomous state actions Heclo highlights are not all acts of coercion or domination; they are, instead, the intellectual activities of civil service administrators engaged in diagnosing societal problems and framing policy alternatives to deal with them. According to Heclo, civil service administrators in both Britain and Sweden have consistently and substantively made more important contributions to social policy development than have political parties or interest groups. Socioeconomic conditions, especially crises, have stimulated only sporadic demands from parties and interest groups, he argues. It has been civil servants, drawing upon "administrative resources of information, analysis, and expertise," who have framed the terms of new policy elaborations as "corrective(s) less to social conditions as such and more to the perceived failings of previous policy" in terms of "the government bureaucracy's own conception of what it has been doing."[8] Heclo's evidence also reveals that the autonomous bureaucratic shaping of social policy has been greater in Sweden than in Britain. Sweden's premodern, centralized bureaucratic state was, from the start of industrialization and prior to the full liberalization and democratization of national politics, in a position to take the initiative in diagnosing social problems and proposing universalistic solutions.

Heclo says much less than he might about the influences shaping the timing and content of distinctive state initiatives. But he does present evidence of the sensitivity of civil administrators to the requisites for maintaining social and political order in the face of cycles of industrial unemployment. And he also points to the constant awareness of administrators of foreign precedents and models of social policy. Heclo demonstrates, above all, that well-institutionalized collectivities of administrative officials can have pervasive direct and indirect effects on the content and development of major government policies. He shows how to locate and analyze autonomous state contributions to "normal" politics.

## CAN STATES ACHIEVE THEIR GOALS?

Some comparative-historical scholars have not only investigated the underpinnings of autonomous state actions but have also tackled the still more challenging task of explaining the varying *capacities* of states to implement their policies. Of course, the explanation of such capacities is not entirely separable from the explanation of autonomous goal formulation by states, because state officials are most likely to try to do things that plausibly seem feasible. Nevertheless, not infrequently states pursue goals (whether their own, or those pressed upon them by powerful social groups) that are beyond their reach. Thus, the capacities of states to implement strategies and policies deserve close analysis.

A stable administrative–military control of a given territory is a precondition for any state's ability to implement policies. Beyond this, loyal and skilled officials and plentiful financial resources are basic factors relevant to state effectiveness in attaining all sorts of goals. Not surprisingly, histories of state building zero in on exactly these universal sinews of state power.[9] It is clear that certain of these resources come to be rooted in institutional relationships that are slow to change and relatively impervious to short-term manipulations. For example: Do state offices attract and retain career-oriented incumbents with a wide array of skills and keen motivation? The answer may well depend upon historically evolved relationships among elite educational institutions, state organizations, and private enterprises that compete with the state for educated personnel. The best situation for the state may be a regular flow of elite university graduates—including many with sophisticated technical training—into official careers that are of such high status as to keep the most ambitious and successful from moving on to posts outside the state. But if this situation has not been historically established by the start of the industrial era, it is difficult indeed to undo alternative patterns that are less favorable to the state.

## FINANCES AS "THE NERVES OF THE STATE"

Factors determining a state's financial resources may sometimes be more manipulable over time. The amounts and forms of revenues and credit available to a state grow out of institutionally conditioned, yet historically shifting, political balances and bargains among states and between a state and social classes. Basic sets of facts to sort out in any study of state capacities involve the sources and amounts of state revenues and the degree of flexibility possible in their collection and deployment. Domestic institutional arrangements and international situations set difficult-to-change limits within which state elites must maneuver to extract taxes and obtain credit. Does a state depend on export taxes (e.g., from a scarce national resource, or from products vulnerable to sudden world-market fluctuations)? Does a nonhegemonic state's geopolitical position allow it to reap the state-building benefits of military aid, or must it rely on international bankers or aid agencies which insist upon favoring private investments and restrict the domestic political options of the borrower state? What established authority does a state have to collect taxes, borrow, and invest in potentially profitable public enterprises; and how much "room" is there in the existing constitutional–political system to change patterns of revenue collection unfavorable to the state? Finally, what authority and organizational means does a state have to deploy whatever financial resources it does enjoy? Are particular kinds of revenues rigidly "earmarked" for special uses that cannot easily be altered by official decision makers?[10] Can the state channel (and manipulate) flows of credit to particular enterprises and industrial sectors, or do established constitutional–political practices favor only aggregate categorical expenditures? All of these

*sorts* of questions need to be asked in any study of state capacities; the answers to them, taken together, provide the best possible general insight into the direct or indirect leverage a state is likely to have for realizing any sort of goal it may pursue. For a state's means of raising and deploying financial resources tell us more than could any other single factor about its existing (and immediately potential) capacities to create or strengthen state organizations, to employ personnel, to coopt political support, to subsidize economic enterprises, and to fund social programs. "Financial means," are indeed, as the 16th century French jurist Jean Bodin said, "the nerves of the state."

## POLICY INSTRUMENTS FOR SPECIFIC KINDS OF STATE EFFORTS

Basic questions about a state's territorial integrity, financial means, and staffing may be the place to start in any investigation of its capacities to realize goals, yet the most fruitful studies of state capacities tend to focus on particular policy areas. As Stephen Krasner puts it: "There is no reason to assume a priori that the pattern of strengths and weaknesses will be the same for all policies. One state may be unable to alter the structure of its medical system but be able to construct an efficient transportation network, while another can deal relatively easily with getting its citizens around but cannot get their illnesses cured."[11] Many studies of the abilities of states to realize particular kinds of goals use the concept of "policy instrument" to refer to the relevant means that a state may have at its disposal. The nature and range of institutional mechanisms that state officials may conceivably be able to bring to bear on a given kind of problem must be specified through cross-national comparative research.

For example, Susan and Norman Fainstein compare the urban policies of northwest European nations to those of the United States. Accordingly, they are able to conclude that the U.S. national state lacks certain policy instruments for dealing with urban crises that are available to European states—intruments such as central planning agencies, state-controlled pools of investment capital, and directly administered national social welfare programs.[12] Analogously, Peter Katzenstein brings together a set of related studies of how six advanced-industrial capitalist countries manage the international trade, investment, and monetary involvements of their economies.[13] Katzenstein is able to draw fairly clear distinctions between the strategies open to states such as the Japanese and the French, which have policy instruments that enable them to intervene at the level of particular industrial sectors, and other states, such as Britain and the United States, which must rely upon aggregate macroeconomic manipulations. Once again, as in the Fainstein study, it is the juxtaposition of different nations' approaches to a given policy area that allows relevant policy intruments to be highlighted. Neither study, however, treats such "instruments" as the deliberate short-term creations of state officials. Both studies move out toward macrohistorical explorations of the broad institutional patterns of divergent national developments that determine why various countries now have—or do not have—policy instruments for dealing with particular problems or crises.

## STATES IN RELATION TO SOCIETAL ACTORS

Fully specified studies of state capacities not only entail examinations of the resources and instruments states may have for dealing with particular sorts of problems; they also necessarily look at more than states as such. They examine states *in relation* to particular kinds of socioeconomic and political environments, populated by actors with given interests and resources. One obvious use of a relational perspective is to investigate the power of states over domestic or transnational nonstate actors and structures, especially economically dominant ones. What capacities do states have to change the behavior or oppose the demands of such actors, or to transform recalcitrant structures? Answers lie

not only in features of states themselves, but also in the balances of states' resources and situational advantages compared to those of nonstate actors.

This sort of relational approach is used by Stephen Krasner in his exploration of the efforts of U.S. officials to implement foreign raw-materials policy in interactions with large corporations, whose preferences and established practices frequently ran counter to the state's definition of the "national interest."[14] This is also the sort of approach used by Alfred Stepan to analyze Peruvian military leaders' relative successes and failures in using state power to change the patterns of foreign capital investments in their dependent country.[15] Stepan does a brilliant job of developing a consistent set of causal hypotheses to explain the diverse outcomes across industrial sectors—i.e., sugar, oil, and manufacturing. For each sector, he examines regime characteristics—degree of commitment to clear policy goals, technical capacities, monitoring abilities, state-controlled investment resources, and the state's international position. He also examines the characteristics of existing investments and markets as they impinge upon the advantages to Peru and to foreign multinationals of any given further investments. The entire argument is too complex to reproduce here, but its significance extends well beyond the foreign investment issue area and the Peruvian case. By taking a self-consciously relational approach to the balances of resources that states and multinational corporations may bring to bear in their partially symbiotic and partially conflictual dealings with one another, Stepan has provided an important model for further studies of state capacities in many policy areas.

Another relational approach to the study of state capacities appears in Peter Katzenstein's *Between Power and Plenty,* where (as was indicated above) the object of explanation is ultimately not state power over nonstate actors, but nations' strategies for managing "interdependence" within the world capitalist economy. One notion centrally invoked in the Katzenstein collection is that of a "policy network" embodying a patterned interrelationship between state and society within each domestic national structure. The idea is that the definition and implementation of foreign economic policies grows out of the nexus of state and society. Both state goals and the interests of powerful classes may influence policy orientations. And the implementation of policies is shaped not only by the policy instruments available to the state but also by the organized support it receives from key societal groups. Thus, national policies—for example, industrial reorganization—may be efficaciously implemented because a strong central state controls credit and can intervene within industrial sectors. Yet it may be of equal importance that industries are organized into disciplined associations willing to cooperate with the state. In short, a complete analysis requires examinations of the organization and interests of the state, of the organization and interests of socioeconomic groups, and of the complementary as well as the conflicting relationships of state and societal actors. This is the sort of approach consistently used by the contributors to *Power and Plenty* to explain the foreign economic objectives of Britain, France, Germany, Italy, Japan, and the United States, as well as to explain the capacities of their domestic political systems to implement existing or conceivable alternative policies.

## AGENDAS FOR FUTURE COMPARATIVE RESEARCH

Now that states are back at the center of attention in macroscopic studies of societal change and public policy making, there are new needs and possibilities for comparative research and theory. Since it is clear from existing studies that the organizational structures of states underpin the initiatives they take and their capacities to achieve policy goals, we need to know much more about the long-term development of states themselves. How are states built and reconstructed? What roles have been played by wars or major economic and political crises; and how do state agencies and activities develop in more normal times? What social, economic, and political factors influence patterns of official

recruitment, the acquisition and deployment of state financial resources, and the establishment and use of specific policy instruments to address given kinds of problems faced by states and societies? We also need to know much more about the changing patterns of state–society relationships. How do states and socioeconomic groups affect one another's organization and goals? And how do conflicts and alliances between organized social or economic actors and state agencies affect the formulation and implementation of various kinds of public policies?

Answers to questions such as these will necessarily develop through analytically sharply-focused comparative and historical studies. And it seems very likely that some of the most strategic findings will arise from the juxtaposition of research findings about very different geographical areas and historical time periods. On issues of state building or the state's role in industrial development, for example, scholars looking at the contemporary Third World might have much to learn from, and say to, students of earlier eras in European and U.S. history. On other issues, such as the state's management of relationships to the world economy, contemporary comparisons of, say, very small or very large countries the world over may yield refreshing insights. And on matters such as the rise and development (and demise?) of Keynesian economic strategies, comparisons of European nations with the United States might be most appropriate. Exact comparative strategies are bound to depend upon the specific issues addressed. But it is clear that further scholarly dialogue will need to transcend parochial specialties based on time and geography in order to explain the processes by which states develop, formulate policies, and seek to implement them in domestic and international contexts.

Comparative, state-centered research along the above-suggested lines will have policy implications—but not of the short-term, how-to-do-it sort. Other sorts of social scientific research are better tailored to helping public officials decide what to do on a month-to-month basis.

Yet given the fact that states are so obviously and inextricably involved in the economic development, social change, and politics of all contemporary nations, social scientists also need to address the broader and longer-term determinants of the state's role. The limits and the possibilities of public policy are profoundly influenced by historically developed state organizations and their structured relationships to domestic and international environments. Citizens, public officials, and social scientists alike therefore share an interest in better understanding states themselves both as actors and as organizational structures.

## Notes

1. See, for example, David B. Truman, *The Governmental Process*, 2nd ed. (New York: Knopf, 1971; originally 1951); and the series of books on political development written under the auspices of the Council's Committee on Comparative Politics (1954–1972), published by the Princeton University Press.

2. For some examples of recent neo-Marxist theorizing on the capitalist state, see Nicos Poulantzas, *Political Power and Social Classes*, translated by Timothy O'Hagen (London: New Left Books, 1973); Claus Offe, "Structural Problems of the Capitalist State," *German Political Studies*, volume 1 (1974); Göran Therborn, *What Does the Ruling Class Do When It Rules?* (London: New Left Books, 1978); and Erik Olin Wright, *Class, Crisis, and the State* (London: New Left Books, 1978).

3. For some suggestive brief treatments, see the articles by Stephen Krasner and Stephen Blank in Peter Katzenstein (editor), *Between Power and Plenty: Foreign Economic Policies of Advanced Industrial States* (Madison: University of Wisconsin Press, 1978); Andrew Martin, "Political Constraints on Economic Strategies in Advanced Industrial Societies," *Comparative Political Studies* 10:3 (October 1977), pp. 323–354; and Paul M. Sacks, "State Structure and the Asymmetrical Society: An Approach to Public Policy in Britain," *Comparative Politics* 12:3 (April 1980), pp. 349–376.

4. See Max Weber, *Economy and Society*, edited by Guenther Roth and Claus Wittich (New York: Bedminister Press, 1968, originally 1922) Volume 2, Chapter 9, and Volume 3, Chapters 10–13; and *The Historical Essays of Otto Hintze*, edited by Felix Gilbert (New York: Oxford University Press, 1975, originally 1897–1932).

5. Alfred Stepan, *The State and Society: Peru in Comparative Perspective* (Princeton, N.J.: Princeton University Press, 1978), page xii.

6. Ibid., Chapters 3–4. See also Alfred Stepan, "The New Professionalism of Internal Warfare and Military Role Expansion," pp. 47–65 in Alfred Stepan (editor), *Authoritarian Brazil* (New Haven: Yale University Press, 1973).

7. Hugh Heclo, *Modern Social Politics in Britain and Sweden* (New Haven: Yale University Press, 1974).

8. Ibid., pp. 305–306, 303.

9. See, for examples: Charles Tilly (editor), *The Formation of National States in Western Europe* (Princeton, N.J.: Princeton University Press, 1975); Michael Mann, "State and Society, 1130–1815: An Analysis of English State Finances," in Maurice Zeitlin (editor), *Political Power and Social Theory* (A Research Annual), Volume 1 (Greenwich, Conn.: JAI Press, 1980), pp. 165–208; and Stephen Skowronek, *Building a New American State: The Expansion of National Administrative Capacities, 1877–1920* (Cambridge and New York: Cambridge University Press, 1982).

10. See John A. Dunn, Jr., "The Importance of Being Earmarked: Transport Policy and Highway Finance in Great Britain and the United States," *Comparative Studies in Society and History* 20:1 (January 1978), pp. 29–53.

11. Stephen D. Krasner, *Defending the National Interest: Raw Materials Investments and U.S. Foreign Policy* (Princeton, N.J.: Princeton University Press, 1978), p. 58.

12. Susan S. and Norman I. Fainstein, "National Policy and Urban Development," *Social Problems* 26:2 (December 1978), pp. 125–146. See especially pp. 140–141.

13. Peter J. Katzenstein (editor), *Between Power and Plenty: Foreign Economic Policies of*

*Advanced Industrial States* (Madison: University of Wisconsin Press, 1978).

14. Krasner, *National Interest*, especially Parts Two and Three.

15. Stepan, *State and Society*, Chapter 7.

# 8

# The Autonomous Power of the State

*Michael Mann*

This essay tries to specify the origins, mechanisms and results of the autonomous power which the state possesses in relation to the major power groupings of 'civil society'. . . . At the moment, my generalisations are bolder about agrarian societies; concerning industrial societies I will be more tentative. I define the state and then pursue the implications of that definition. I discuss two essential parts of the definition, centrality and territoriality, in relation to two types of state power, termed here *despotic* and *infrastructural* power. I argue that state autonomy, of both despotic and infrastructural forms, flows principally from the state's unique ability to provide a *territorially-centralised* form of organization. . . .

I will argue in this paper that the state *is* merely and essentially an arena, a *place*, and yet *this* is the very source of its autonomy.

## I. DEFINING THE STATE

The state is undeniably a messy concept. The main problem is the most definitions contain two different levels of analysis, the 'institutional'

SOURCE: *Archives Européennes de Sociologie*, vol. XXV, no. 1 (1985), pp. 185–213. Reproduced by permission of the *Archives Européennes de Sociologie* and the author. Article and references abridged by the editors.

and the 'functional'. That is, the state can be defined in terms of what it looks like, institutionally, or what it does, its functions. Predominant is a mixed, but largely institutional, view put forward originally by Weber. In this the state contains four main elements, being:

a) a *differentiated* set of institutions and personnel embodying

b) *centrality* in the sense that political relations radiate outward from a centre to cover

c) a *territorially-demarcated area*, over which it exercises

d) a monopoly of *authoritative binding rule-making*, backed-up by a monopoly of the means of physical violence. . . .

## Two Meanings of State Power

What do we mean by the 'the power of the state'? As soon as we begin to think about this commonplace phrase, we encounter two quite different senses in which states and their elites might be considered powerful. We must disentangle them. The first sense concerns what we might term the *despotic power* of the state elite, the range of actions which the elite is empowered to undertake without routine, institutionalised negotiation with civil society groups. The historical variations in such powers have been so enormous that we can safely leave on one side the ticklish problem of how we precisely measure them. The despotic powers of many historical states have been virtually unlimited. The Chinese Emperor, as the Son of Heaven, 'owned' the whole of China and could do as he wished with any individual or group within his domain. The Roman Emperor, only a minor god, acquired powers which were also in principle unlimited outside of a restricted area of affairs nominally controlled by the Senate. Some monarchs of early modern Europe also claimed divinely-derived, absolute powers (though they were not themselves divine). The contemporary Soviet state/party elite, as 'trustees' of the interests of the masses, also possess considerable despotic (though sometimes strictly unconstitutional) power. Great despotic power can be 'measured' most vividly in the ability of all these Red Queens to shout 'off with his head' and have their whim gratified without further ado—provided the person is at hand. Despotic power is also usually what is meant in the literature by 'autonomy of power.'

But there is a second sense in which people talk of 'the power of the state,' especially in today's capitalist democracies. We might term this *infrastructural power,* the capacity of the state to actually penetrate civil society, and to implement logistically political decisions throughout the realm. This was comparatively weak in the historical societies just mentioned—once you were out of sight of the Red Queen, she had difficulty in getting at you. But it is powerfully developed in all industrial societies. When people in the West today complain of the growing power of the state, they cannot be referring sensibly to the despotic powers of the state elite itself, for if anything these are still declining. It is, after all, only forty years since universal suffrage was fully established in several of the advanced capitalist states, and the basic political rights of groups such as ethnic minorities and women are still increasing. But the complaint is more justly levelled against the state's infrastructural encroachments. These powers are now immense. The state can assess and tax our income and wealth at source, without our consent or that of our neightbours or kin (which states before about 1850 were *never* able to do); it stores and can recall immediately a massive amount of information about all of us; it can enforce its will within the day almost anywhere in its domains; its influence on the overall economy is enormous; it even directly provides the subsistence of most of us (in state employment, in pensions, in family allowances, etc.). The state penetrates everyday life more than did any historical state. Its infrastructural power has increased enormously. If there were a Red Queen, we would all quail at her words—from Alaska to Florida, from the Shetlands to Cornwall there is no hiding place from the infrastructural reach of the modern state. . . .

## II. ORIGINS OF STATE POWER

## 1. The Necessity of the State

The only stateless societies have been primitive. There are no complex, civilized societies without any centre of binding rule-making authority, however limited its scope. If we consider the weak feudal cases we find that even they tend to arise from a more state-centred history whose norms linger on to reinforce the new weak states. Feudal states tend to emerge either as a check to the further disintegration of a once-unified larger state (as in China and Japan) or as a post-conquest division of the spoils among the victorious, and obviously united, conquerors. . . . Western European feudalism embodies both these histories, though in varying mixtures in different regions. The laws of the feudal states in Europe were reinforced by rules descending from Roman law (especially property law), Christian codes of conduct, and Germanic notions of loyalty and honour. This is a further glimpse of a process to which I will return later: a perpetual dialectic of movement between state and civil society.

Thus societies with states have had superior survival value to those without them. We have no examples of stateless societies long enduring past a primitive level of development, and many examples of state societies absorbing or eliminating stateless ones. Where stateless societies conquer ones with states, they either themselves develop a state or they induce social regress in the conquered society. There are good sociological reasons for this. Only three alternative bases for order exist, force, exchange and custom, and none of these are sufficient in the long-run. At some point new exigencies arise for which custom is inadequate; at some point to bargain about everything in exchange relations is inefficient and disintegrating; while force alone, as Parsons emphasized, will soon 'deflate.' In the long-run normally taken for granted, but enforceable, rules are necessary to bind together strangers or semi-strangers. It is not requisite that all these rules are set by a single monopolistic state. Indeed, though the feudal example is extreme, most states exist in a multi-state civilization which also provides certain normative rules of conduct. Nevertheless most societies seem to have required that some rules, be set monopolistically, and this has been the province of the state.

From this necessity, autonomous state power ultimately derives. The activities of the state personnel are necessary to society as a whole and/or to the various groups that benefit from the existing structure of rules which the state enforces. From this functionality derive the potentiality for exploitation, a lever for the achievement of private state interests. Whether the lever is used depends on other conditions, for—after all—we have not even established the existence of a permanent state cadre which might have identifiable interests. But necessity is the mother of state power.

## 2. The Multiplicity of State Functions

Despite the assertions of reductionists, most states have not in practice devoted themselves to the pursuit of a single function. 'Binding rule-making' is merely an umbrella term. The rules and functions have been extremely varied. As the two-dimensional models recognize, we may distinguish domestic and international or economic, ideological and military functions. But there are many types of activity and each tends to be functional for differing 'constituencies' in society. I illustrate this with reference to what have been probably the four most persistent types of state activities.

a) *The maintenance of internal order.* This may benefit all, or all law-abiding, subjects of the state. It may also protect the majority from arbitrary usurpations by socially and economically powerful groups, other than those allied to the state. But probably the main benefit is to protect existing property relations from the mass of the property-less. This function probably best serves a dominant economic class constituency.

b) *Military defence/aggression,* directed against foreign foes. 'War parties' are rarely coterminous with either the whole society or with one particular class within it. Defence may be genuinely collective; aggression usually has

more specific interests behind it. Those interests may be quite widely shared by all 'younger sons' without inheritance rights or all those expansively-minded; or they might comprise only a class fraction of an aristocracy, merchants or capitalists. In multi-state systems war usually involves alliance with other states, some of whom may share the same religion, ethnicity, or political philosophy as some domestic constituency. These are rarely reducible to economic class. Hence war and peace constituencies are usually somewhat idiosyncratic.

c) *The maintenance of communications infrastructures*: roads, rivers, message systems, coinages, weights and measures, marketing arrangements. Though few states have monopolized all of these, all states have provided some, because they have a territorial basis which is often most efficiently organized from a centre. The principal constituencies here are a 'general interest' and more particular trade-centred groups.

d) *Economic redistribution*: the authoritative distribution of scarce material resources between different ecological niches, age-groups, sexes, regions, classes, etc. There is a strongly collective element in this function, more so than in the case of the others. Nevertheless, many of the redistributions involve rather particular groups, especially the economically inactive whose subsistence is thus protected by the state. And economic redistribution also has an international dimension, for the state normally regulates trade relations and currency exchanges across its boundaries, sometimes unilaterally, sometimes in alliance with other states. This also gives the state a particular constituency among merchants and other international agents—who, however, are rarely in agreement about desirable trade policy.

These four tasks are necessary, either to society as a whole or to interest groups within it. They are undertaken most efficiently by the personnel of a central state who become indispensable. And they bring the state into functional relations with diverse, sometimes cross-cutting groups between whom there is room to manoeuvre. The room can be exploited. Any state involved in a multiplicity of power relations can play off interest groups against each other.

It is worth noting that one example of this 'divide-and-rule' strategy has been a staple of sociological analysis. This is the case of a 'transitional state,' living amid profound economic transformations from one mode of production to another. No single dominant economic class exists, and the state may play off traditional power groups against emergent ones. Such situations were discussed by both the classic stratification theorists. Marx analysed and satirised Louis Bonaparte's attempts to play off the factions of industrial and finance capital, petite bourgeoisie, peasantry and proletariat to enhance his own independent power.... Weber was struck by the ability of the Prussian State to use a declining economic class, the agrarian landlord Junkers, to hold on to autocratic power in the vacuum created by the political timidity of the rising bourgeois and proletarian classes.... All the various groups in both examples needed the state, but none could capture it. Another example is the development of absolutism in early modern Europe. Monarchs played off against each other (or were unable to choose between) feudal and bourgeois, land and urban, groups. In particular, military functions and functions performed in relation to dominant economic classes were different. States used war as a means of attempting to reduce their dependence on classes....

These are familiar examples of the state balancing between what are predominantly classes or class factions. But the balancing possibilities are much more numerous if the state involved in a multiplicity of relations with groups which may on some issues be narrower than classes and on others wider. Because most states are pursuing multiple functions, they can perform multiple manoeuvres. The 'Bonapartist balancing act' is skill acquired by most states. This manoeuvring space is the birthplace of state power.

And this is about as far as the insights contained within current two-dimensional theory can be expanded. It is progress, but not enough.

It does not really capture the *distinctiveness* of the state as a social organization. After all, necessity plus multiplicity of function, and the balancing-act, are also the power-source and stock-in-trade of any ruthless committee chairperson. Is the state only a chair writ large? No, as we will now see.

## 3. The Territorial Centrality of the State

The definition of the state concentrates upon its institutional, territorial, centralised nature. This is the third, and most important, precondition of state power. As noted, the state does not possess a distinctive *means* of power independent of, and analogous to, economic, military and ideological power. The means used by states are only a combination of these, which are also the means of power used in all social relationships. However, the power of the state is irreducible in quite a different *socio-spatial* and *organizational* sense. Only the state is inherently centralised over a delimited territory over which it has authoritative power. Unlike economic, ideological or military groups in civil society, the state elite's resources radiate authoritatively outwards from a centre but stop at defined territorial boundaries. The state is, indeed, a *place*—both a central place and a unified territorial reach. As the principal forms of state autonomous power will flow from this distinctive attribute of the state, it is important that I first prove that the state does so differ socio-spatially and organizationally from the major power groupings of civil society.

*Economic* power groupings—classes, corporations, merchant houses, manors, plantations, the *oikos*, etc.—normally exist in decentred, competitive or conflictual relations with one another. True, the internal arrangements of some of them (e.g. the modern corporation, or the household and manor of the great feudal lord) might be relatively centralised. But, first, they are oriented outwards to further opportunities for economic advantage which are not territorially confined nor subject to authoritative rules governing expansion (except by states). Economic power expansion is not authoritative, commanded—it is 'diffused,' informally. Second, the scope of modern and some historic economic institutions is not territorial. They do not exercise general control of a specific territory, they control a specialised function and seek to extend it 'transnationally' wherever that function is demanded and exploitable. General Motors does not rule the territory around Detroit, it rules the assembly of automobiles and some aspects of the economic life-chances of its employees, stockholders and consumers. Third, in those cases where economic institutions have been authoritative, centralised and territorial (as in the feudal household/manor of historic nobilities) they have either been subject to a higher level of territorial, central control by the (imperial) state, or they have acquired political function (administering justice, raising military levies, etc.) from a weak (feudal) state and so become themselves 'mini-states.' Thus states cannot be the simple instrument of classes, for they have a different territorial scope.

Analogous points can be made about ideological power movements like religions. Ideologies (unless state-led) normally spread even more diffusely than economic relations. They move diffusely and 'interstitially' inside state territories, spreading through communication networks among segments of a state's population (like classes, age-cohorts, genders, urban/rural inhabitants, etc.); they often also move transnationally right through state boundaries. Ideologies may develop central, authoritative, Church-like institutions, but these are usually functionally, more than territorially, organised: they deal with the sacred rather than the secular, for example. There is a socio-spatial, as well as a spiritual, 'transcendence' about ideological movements, which is really the opposite of the territorial bounds of the state.

It is true, however, that military power overlaps considerably with the state, especially in modern states who usually monopolise the means of organised violence. Nevertheless, it is helpful to treat the two as distinct sources of power. . . . Let me instead make two simple points. First, not all warfare is most efficiently organized territorially-centrally—guerillas, military feudalism and warrior bands are all examples of relatively decentred military organisations effective at many historical periods. Second, the effective scope of military power does not cover a single, unitary territory. In fact, it has two rather different territorial radii of effective control.

Militaristic control of everyday behaviour requires such a high level of organised coercion, logistical back-up and surplus extraction that it is practical only within close communications to the armed forces in areas of high surplus availability. It does not spread evenly over entire state territories. It remains concentrated in pockets and along communications routes. It is relatively ineffective at penetrating peasant agriculture, for example.

The second radius enables, not everyday control, but the setting of broad limits of outward compliance over far greater areas. In this case, failure to comply with broad parameters such as the handing over of tribute, the performance of ritual acts of submission, occasional military support (or at least non-rebellion), could result in a punitive expedition, and so is avoided. This radius of military striking power has normally been far greater than that of state political control, as Owen Lattimore (1962) brilliantly argued. This is obviously so in the world today, given the capabilities of modern armaments. It is also true of the Superpowers in a more subtle sense: they can impose 'friendly' regimes and de-stabilize the unfriendly through client military elites and their own covert para-military organisations, but they cannot get those regimes to conform closely to their political dictates. A more traditional example would be Britain's punitive expedition to the Falklands, capable of defeating and so de-legitimising the Argentine regime, and remaining capable of repeating the punishment, but quite incapable of providing a political future for the Islands. The logistics of 'concentrated coercion'— that is, of military power—differ from those of the territorial centralised state. Thus we should distinguish the two as power organizations. The militarist theory of the state is false, and one reason is that the state's organization is not coterminous with military organization.

The organizational autonomy of the state is only partial—indeed, in many particular cases it may be rather small. General Motors and the capitalist class in general, or the Catholic Church, or the feudal lords and knights, or the U.S. military, are or were quite capable of keeping watch on states they have propped up. Yet they could not do the states' jobs themselves unless they changed their own socio-spatial and organizational structure. A state autonomous power ensues from this difference. Even if a particular state is set up or intensified merely to institutionalise the relations between given social groups, this is done by concentrating resources and infrastructures in the hands of an institution that has different socio-spatial and organizational contours to those groups. Flexibility and speed of response entail concentration of decision-making and a tendency towards permanence of personnel. The decentred nonterritorial interest-groups that set up the state in the first place are thus less able to control it. Territorial-centralization provides the state with a potentially independent basis of power mobilization being necessary to social development and uniquely in the possession of the state itself.

If we add together the necessity, multiplicity and territorial-centrality of the state, we can in principle explain its autonomous power. By these means the state elite possesses an independence from civil society which, though not absolute, is no less absolute in principle than the power of any other major group. Its power cannot be reduced to their power either directly or 'ultimately' or 'in the last instance.' The state is not merely a locus of class struggle, an instrument of class rule, the factor of social cohesion, the expression of core values, the centre of social allocation processes, the institutionalization of military force (as in the various reductionist theories)—it is a different socio-spatial organization. As a consequence we can treat states as *actors*, in the person of state elites, with a will to power and we can engage in the kind of 'rational action' theory of state interests. . . .

# III. RESULTS: INFRASTRUCTURAL POWER

. . .When capitalism emerged as dominant, it took the form of a series of territorial segments—many systems of production and exchange, each to a large (though not total) extent bounded by a state and its overseas sphere of influence. The nation-state system of our own era was not a product of capitalism (or, indeed, of feudalism) considered as pure modes of production. It is in that sense 'autonomous.' But it resulted from the way expansive, emergent, capitalist relations were given regulative boundaries by pre-existing states. The states were the initially weak (in both despotism and in infrastructure) states of feudal Europe. In the twelfth century even the strongest absorbed less than 2% of GNP (if we could measure it), they called out highly decentralized military levies of at most 10 to 20,000 men sometimes only for 30 days in the campaigning system, they couldn't tax in any regular way, they regulated only a small proportion of total social disputes— they were, in fact, marginal to the social lives of most Europeans. And yet these puny states became of decisive importance in structuring the world we live in today. The need for territorial centralisation led to the restructuring of first European, then world society. The balance of nuclear terror lies between the successor states of these puny Europeans.

In the international economic system today, nation-states appear as collective economic actors. Across the pages of most works of political economy today stride actors like 'The United States,' 'Japan,' or 'The United Kingdom.' This does not necessarily mean that there is a common 'national interest,' merely that on the international plane there are a series of collectively organised power actors, nation-states. There is no doubting the economic role of the nation-state: the existence of a domestic market segregated to a degree from the international market, the value of the state's currency, the level of its tariffs and import quotas, its support for its indigenous capital and labour, indeed, its whole political economy is permeated with the notion that 'civil society' is its territorial domain. The territoriality of the state has created social forces with a life of their own.

In this example, increasing territoriality has not increased despotic power. Western states were despotically weak in the twelfth century, and they remain so today. Yet the increase in infrastructural penetration has increased dramatically territorial boundedness. This seems a general characteristic of social development: increases in state infrastructural powers also increase the territorial boundedness of social interaction. We may also postulate the same tendency for despotic power, though it is far weaker. A despotic state without strong infrastructural supports will only claim territoriality. Like Rome and China it may build walls, as much to keep its subjects in as to keep 'barbarians' out. But its success is limited and precarious. So, again we might elaborate a historical dialectic. Increases in state infrastructural power will territorialise social relations. If the state then loses control of its resources they diffuse into civil society, decentering and deterritorialising it. Whether this is, indeed, beginning to happen in the contemporary capitalist world, with the rise of multi-national corporations outliving the decline of two successively hegemonic states, Great Britain and the United States, is one of the most hotly-debated issues in contemporary political economy. Here I must leave it as an open issue.

\* \* \*

In this essay I have argued that the state is essentially an arena, a place—just as reductionist theories have argued—and yet this is precisely the origin and mechanism of its autonomous powers. The state, unlike the principal power actors of civil society, is territorially bounded and centralised. Societies need some of their activities to be regulated over a centralised territory. So do dominant economic classes, Churches and other ideological power movements, and military elites. They, therefore, entrust power resources to state elites which they are incapable of fully recovering, precisely because their own socio-spatial basis of organisation is not centralised and territorial.

Such state power resources, and the autonomy to which they lead, may not amount to much. If, however, the state's use of the conferred resources generates further power resources— as was, indeed, intended by the civil society groups themselves—these will normally flow through the state's hands, and thus lead to a significant degree of power autonomy. Therefore, *autonomous state power is the product of the usefulness of enhanced territorial-centralisation to social life in general*. This has varied considerably through the history of societies, and so consequently have the power of states.

...Most sociologists—indeed, most people anywhere who use this term—mean by 'society' the territory of a state. Thus 'American society,' 'British society,' 'Roman society,' etc. The same is true of synonyms like 'social formation' and (to a lesser extent) 'social system.' Yet the relevance of state boundaries to what we mean by societies is always partial and has varied enormously. Medievalists do not generally characterise 'society' in their time-period as state-defined; much more likely is a broader, transnational designation like 'Christendom' or 'European society.' Yet this change between medieval and modern times is one of the most decisive aspects of the great modernizing transformations; just as the current relationship between nation states and 'the world system' is crucial to our understanding of late twentieth-century society. How territorialised and centralised are societies? This is the most significant theoretical issue on which we find states exercising a massive force over social life, *not* the more traditional terrain of dispute, the despotic power of state elites over classes or other elites. States are central to our understanding of what a society is. Where states are strong, societies are relatively territorialised and centralised. That is the most general statement we can make about the autonomous power of the state.

## Bibliography

BENDIX, R. *Kings or People.* Berkeley: University of California Press, 1978.

CLASTRES, P. *Society against the State.* Oxford: Blackwell, 1977.

EISENSTADT, S. N. *The Political Systems of Empires*. New York: Free Press, 1969.

FINER, S. "State and nation-building in Europe: the role of the military." In *The Formation of National States in Western Europe*, edited by Charles Tilly. Princeton, N.J.: Princeton University Press, 1975.

GELLNER, E. *Nations and Nationalism*. Oxford: Blackwell, 1983.

GERSCHENKRON, A. *Economic Backwardness in Historical Perspective*. Cambridge, Mass.: Belknap Press, 1962.

KAUTSKY, J. H. *The Politics of Aristocratic Empires*. Chapel Hill: University of North Carolina Press, 1982.

LACHMAN, L. *The Legacy of Max Weber*. London: Heinemann, 1970.

LATTIMORE, O. "Feudalism in history: a review essay." *Past and Present* (1957), no. 12, pp. 47–57.

LATTIMORE, O. *Studies in Frontier History*. London: Oxford University Press, 1962.

LEVI, M. "The predatory theory of rule." *Politics and Society*. X (1981), pp. 431–465.

MACIVER, R. M. *The Modern State*. Oxford: Clarendon Press, 1926.

MANN, M. "States, ancient and modern." *Archives Européennes de Sociologie*. XVIII (1977), pp. 262–298.

MANN, M. "State and society, 1130–1815: an analysis of English state finances." In *Political Power and Social Theory*, edited by M. Zritlin, vol. 1. Greenwich, Conn.: JAI Press, 1980.

OPPENHEIMER, F. *The State*. New York: Free Life Editions, 1975 edition.

PEREZ-DIAZ, V. *State, Bureaucracy and Civil Society: A critical discussion of the political theory of Karl Marx*. London: Macmillan, 1979.

POULANTZAS, N. *Pouvoir politique et classes sociales*. Paris: Maspero, 1972.

RUSTOW, A. *Freedom and Domination: a historical critique of civilization*. Princeton, N.J.: Princeton University Press, 1982.

SERVICE, E. *Origins of the State and Civilization*. New York: Norton, 1975.

SKOCPOL, T. *States and Social Revolutions*. Cambridge: Cambridge University Press, 1979.

TILLY, CH. *The Formation of National States in Western Europe*. Princeton, N.J.: Princeton University Press, 1975.

TILLY, CH. *As Sociology Meets History*. New York: Academic Press, 1981.

TRIMBERGER, E. *Revolution From Above: military bureaucrats and development in Japan, Turkey, Egypt and Puru*. New Brunswick, N.J.: Transaction Books, 1978.

WEBER, M. *Economy and Society*. New York: Bedminster Press, 1968.

# PART TWO

# Contemporary Political Regimes

This volume is prepared on the basis of a general conception: A political system is, above all, a mechanism for the making of decisions. It is endowed with legitimacy; that is, the decisions made by the various organs of government are expected to be widely obeyed.

Decisions involve compromises among many conflicting points of view held by social groups, parties, associations, and interest organizations across regions. On the one hand, we have the governmental organs that make decisions—the legislature, the executive, the courts, and the bureaucracy. On the other hand, there are the social and economic forces and groupings, and the beliefs and values held by the members of the society about their political systems. This suggests a threefold distinction: (1) the government; (2) the "social and cultural configuration"—that is, social classes, economic groups, ethnic groups, regions, interest groups, and their modes of action; and (3) the pattern of values and ideologies relating specifically to political authority, permissive areas of governmental action, and the role and position of individuals and associations.

It is the interplay among social configuration, ideology, and the governmental organs that constitutes the dynamics of politics—the making of decisions. Social and economic groups, molded and patterned in accordance with the ideas people hold, press their claims upon the government. Interest groups and political parties function as conveyor belts between interest claims and governmental decisions. Political leadership sifts these claims, often provides for compromise, and articulates them in the form of pledges or decisions. It is not impossible, especially when conflicts assume a high level of

intensity and when opposing sides are evenly balanced, for a political system to find itself in a situation in which no decision can be made. The system is at a state of stalemate.

The efficiency of a political system can be gauged in terms of its ability to make decisions that are widely accepted. An efficient system maintains a balance between change and stability. Change is the result of constant claims that arise from the social groups because of evolving technical and economic conditions. Emerging social groups inevitably put forward demands as they gain access to positions of influence and power. Throughout the nineteenth century, for instance, the general theme of political change was associated with the claims of the lower middle classes and the workers (in some cases the slaves and serfs) for suffrage and political participation. As societies industrialize, these same groups organize in order to facilitate the translation of their newly acquired political influence into immediate socioeconomic benefits. Efficiency therefore depends on the nature of governmental response to the demands from groups. If existing institutions prove incapable of meeting these demands, the new groups may attempt to gain power by revolutionary means, which has disruptive effects upon the whole system.

The most persistent challenges to a political system derive from economic and technological modernization. In underdeveloped countries modernization involves literally the restructuring of society—the inculcation of new norms of behavior, the training of skilled bureaucrats, and drastic action on the basis of newly established goals. Modernization at the political level involves the identification of the masses of the people with these goals. Disciplined effort is indispensable because of the lack of available resources. These societies must rely upon their most plentiful and therefore cheapest commodity—human labor—the effective utilization of which requires sacrifice and unremitting toil. Max Weber has suggested that in Western Europe the Protestant religion provided the philosophy that broke down the barriers of feudal and medieval society, secularized human motivation, and supplied incentive that made possible the Industrial Revolution. Ideologies and values in the underdeveloped societies are now undergoing similar transformations. Will these nations follow the European pattern of economic individualism, or the Communist type of collective effort with emphasis on coercion and indoctrination? Their choice will largely determine the nature of their emerging political institutions.

Problems of modernization are naturally different for the societies that have already attained a high level of industrialization. The crucial problems in economically advanced systems are to maintain a constant rate of economic growth, to develop technology rapidly and effectively in order to increase the productivity of labor, and to make the benefits of increased productivity available to all in the form of better living conditions and welfare. The government is compelled to provide a wide range of services and to enforce social justice by means of income distribution.

To summarize: We have suggested that in a political system conflicting claims and demands are translated into accepted decisions. The claims are made by social groups. The manner in which conflicts are expressed depends to a great degree on the nature of ideologies and values concerning political authority. The links between the social structure and the governmental organs are political parties, interest groups, and other associations. It is the role of political leadership to articulate interests and conflicts, achieve a synthesis in the form of policy, and carry it out through the governmental organs. An efficient government is able to provide for change in a stable fashion—that is, without resort to violence on the part of important

groups. It must also be able to survive as a system in the midst of competing nation-states.

An examination of all these propositions calls for comparative analysis and study.

## THE COMPARATIVE APPROACH

A systematic approach requires an overall view or theory of politics. Political science has therefore borrowed extensively from sociological theory. For example, politics has been viewed by some analysts as a system of interaction between actors (individuals and groups) for the purpose of realizing specific goals. A political system must perform certain indispensable (or requisite) functions in order to survive. Certain institutions are also indispensable (or requisite) structures for the performance of these functions. Structures differ from one system to another and undergo profound modifications under the impact of diverse factors—war, industrialization, economic changes, new aspirations, and new demands.

The study of politics (as for Aristotle) becomes the study of a "system" linked organically with social structure, traditions and ideologies, culture, and the environment within which it operates. It may then be possible to discern significant similarities and differences that mere description of the legal forms of a state does not suggest. The discovery of *correlations* between political, economic, cultural, and social phenomena provides a perspective in terms of which the dynamics of change may be understood and broad generalizations made. In essence, this is the application of scientific method to the study of political phenomena. Hypotheses and theories about the political process are elaborated into a rational system and then examined critically in the light of available evidence.

The analytical approach, then, seeks to formulate a definition of a political system, identifies the most important structures through which a system functions, and studies differences and similarities. It purports to establish general propositions about political behavior. As in natural science, generalizations are stated in the form of hypotheses involving a series of conditions. For instance, it could be posited that if there are no serious ideological conflicts in a society and if there is a majority electoral system, then two parties will develop. It can be posited that industrialization and prosperity will, all other conditions being held in check, lead to a decrease in conflict about issues and to the development of a political system concerned with the solution of concrete problems. It may be posited that economic policies endangering the status of certain social groups will provoke a strong movement of protest on the part of the threatened groups, who will seek to protect themselves even by violence—or that groups denied participation in the political system will, all other things being equal, seek to gain status and influence, also by violence.

These hypotheses can be tested against reality and accordingly qualified, modified, or rejected. Field work and empirical observation are therefore indispensable for comparative study, as they are for all forms of scientific inquiry. This kind of analysis will add to our knowledge of the conditioning factors, the presence or absence of which accounts for the validation or the rejection of our hypothesis. For instance, if we propose that wherever there is *A* (for example, a majority electoral system) then *B* (a two-party system) will follow, and if we find that in one system this obtains but in another it does not, then we must seek the reasons for this disparity. We do so by finding a series of other factors ($X$, $X_1$, $X_2$, $X_3$, $X_4$, $X_5$, and so on). Our hypothesis then will be qualified to read *B* will follow *A* provided factors $X_2$ (religious differences), $X_3$ (regionalism), $X_4$ (ethnic groups), or others (depending upon field observation), obtain. In this manner a comprehensive explanation accounting for the differences between two systems may be given.

It is at this point that comparative analysis becomes both challenging and frustrating for the student. Rarely if ever can we provide a coherent and satisfactory generalization explaining the differences among systems. Historical and other factors give nations characteristics that are unique, that is to say, that cannot be duplicated. In fact we shall find it virtually impossible to verify any hypothesis or to develop any generalization that is valid for *all* political systems. It is necessary to lengthen the chain of conditioning factors ($Xs$) for each political system in order to take into account individual and idiosyncratic factors. The proposal to develop general laws seems to bog down in a never-ending explanation for unique situations. Some observers contend that there are no universally valid laws. In despair they conclude that the indeterminacy and uniqueness of political behavior do not permit generalization.

It would be a serious mistake to accept this point of view. Comparative analysis can at the very least identify and perhaps explain uniqueness, which is of crucial importance. Unless we start with general concepts and hypotheses, we are not able even to draw distinctions, let alone account for them. How can we tell what is unique without knowing what is general? Power, for instance, is manifested in many ways and contains many elements—religion, property, birth, administration, and so on. But these different manifestations can be distinguished, related, and understood only in terms of some general concept of power.

## The Range of Comparison

The range of comparison between the functioning of political systems as such will usually be determined by the theoretical scheme, by the formulation of a *problem* or the study of a *given area*. In all cases two crucial questions must be confronted: How do we compare? What do we compare?

Comparison may be attempted between segments of the political process in various systems, or between certain institutions, or between political systems as such, in order to clarify issues that preoccupy us. Let us take the multiparty system in France. The historian of French political institutions will describe the origin, development, ideologies, and characteristics of the French multiparty system. The student of comparative politics faced with the same problem would ask rather: What are the conditions for the existence of a multiparty system? Are they institutional?—social?—sectional?—ideological? Once the conditions have been identified, then comparison with other multiparty systems will show the relevance of some but not others; that is, comparative study may disprove the relationship between certain conditions and multipartism. We may find, for instance, that analogous sectional conditions in the United States have not produced a multiparty system—or that similar electoral systems exist in both two-party and multiparty systems.

Through comparison it is possible to explain the nature of a phenomenon like a multiparty system in the light of a chain of conditioning factors, such as sectionalism, proportional representation, the cabinet's inability to dissolve parliament, and so on. The chain of conditioning factors that we find in France cannot be reproduced historically or experimentally in any other country. But this in no way lessens the need for suggesting relationships among conditioning factors for the purpose of analysis and empirical investigation. Nor does it mean that because France and country X or Y are unique, they cannot be the subject of comparison. France is indeed unique, but in an analytical sense the conditions of multipartism are general categories permitting comparison of France with other political systems. Every suicide is unique, but as Emile Durkheim demonstrated, the conditions under which people commit suicide can be analytically identified in terms of a number of broad categories.

We compare, therefore, in order to discover the conditions under which certain phenomena take place. Conditions, or more precisely, a series of conditions, are hypothetically related to the phenomenon we study. The task of empirical observation is to test the validity of such hypothetical formulations. By so doing we enrich our knowledge of the factors that account for a given phenomenon until we are able to generalize about them. The presence or absence of some or others will enable us to make tentative judgments about political developments and occurrences.

Comparison may be either *static* or *dynamic*. In the first instance, we study anatomy, so to speak, of political systems. Structures are described and related. In this connection classificatory tables are useful in that they suggest analogies and differences. Structures, however, must be identified in terms of the particular function they perform in a system. This is much more difficult than it may seem to be. It is essential to discern the *overt* from the *covert* and the *manifest* from the *latent* functions. For instance, though there are striking structural analogies between the electoral system of the Soviet Union and that of the United States, their functions are wholly dissimilar. Elections in the United States are an integral part of the process of arriving at decisions over which the body politic is divided. In the Soviet Union, on the other hand, elections are used at least until recently, to express loyalty to the regime and to rally the people around their leaders.

*Dynamic* comparison is the study of the performance of various systems. We not only identify structures through which certain functions are performed but also account for the structural variations among systems. Ultimately an effort may be made to trace out consequences of alternative courses of action or to predict in the light of a chain of conditioning factors. This last stage is indeed the most significant, but at the same time it is the most difficult to reach.

## THE SEARCH FOR NEW DEFINITIONS

Awareness of the need for a more systematic approach to the study of politics, coupled with a new appreciation of the interrelationship between social and political structures, has played havoc with the old descriptive definitions and classifications. Traditionally, a state has been described as a community of people living in a given territory with a government. Wherever there is a stable relationship between governors and governed there is a state. Thus, both Ecuador and the United States are examples of "states." But the classic definition does not tell us what to look for and where to look in order to find out how and why these two states are different. The use of categories like ideology, social configuration, and government as a decision-making mechanism aids the student in understanding similarities and differences.

A profusion of new schemes for classifying governments was suggested after World War II. Many stem from Max Weber's distinction among three types of authority: traditional, rational, and charismatic. In his article "Comparative Political Systems," Gabriel Almond distinguishes among four major kinds of systems: consensual (primarily Anglo-American), fragmented (continental Europe), totalitarian (communist and fascist), and preindustrial. David Apter refers to political systems as dictatorial, indirectly and directly representational, and oligarchical. James Coleman refers to "terminal colonial democracy" and to "colonial or racial oligarchy." In addition, he describes "stable and unstable" systems and "underdeveloped and developing" societies. There are "transitional" societies; Daniel Lerner tells us that in them we must look for a cluster of interrelated phenomena—industrialization, urbanization, literacy, participation in mass media, role differentiation, and empathy. Karl W. Deutsch develops an impressive listing of variables for differentiating systems on the basis of diverse combinations.

The "boundaries" of the field of politics have become blurred. In identifying the component elements of a system, Gabriel Almond lists the following "input" (primarily political) functions: political socialization and recruitment, interest articulation, interest aggregation, and political communication. The "output" (or governmental) functions are more familiar, even if the terms appear to be new. They are rule making, rule application, and rule adjudication. Harold Lasswell goes a step further in describing the functions of a political system as follows: intelligence, recommendation, prescription, invocation, application, appraisal, and termination.

David Easton is, as we have seen, more parsimonious. He holds that the main aspects of a political system are demands, supports, and authoritative decisions; the latter determines the proper boundaries of politics. Samuel Beer discusses a political system with reference to its "political culture," the "pattern of power," the "pattern of interests," and the "pattern of policy."[1]

We are, therefore, as was said at the outset, in a state of flux. We are uncertain of the boundaries of political science in its relation to other social sciences, and we are in disagreement over the significant components of political systems. But a state of flux is not necessarily a state of confusion. It may rather be an indication of healthy curiosity and intellectual ferment. The discipline is maturing as it attempts to relate political and social factors, explain behavior, and clarify problems. Description of the institutions and policies of states continues to be of crucial importance, but they are properly viewed only as parts of the "political system."

# Notes

1. The works referred to include: Max Weber, *The Theory of Social and Economic Organization* (New York: Oxford University Press, 1947), pp. 324–391; Gabriel A. Almond, "Comparative Political Systems," *Journal of Politics,* August 1956; David Apter, "A Comparative Method for the Study of Politics," *American Journal of Sociology* (November 1958), pp. 221–237; Gabriel A. Almond and James S. Coleman, *The Politics of Developing Areas* (Princeton: Princeton University Press, 1960); Daniel Lerner, *The Passing of Traditional Society* (New York: Free Press, 1958); Karl W. Deutsch, "Towards an Inventory of Basic Trends and Patterns in Comparative and International Politics," *American Political Science Review,* March 1960; Harold D. Lasswell, *The Decision Process* (Bureau of Governmental Research, University of Maryland, 1956); David Easton, "An Approach to an Analysis of Political Systems," *World Politics,* April 1957 (see Reading 2); and Samuel Beer, *Patterns of Government* (New York: Random House, 1973), pp. 3–53.

# CHAPTER THREE

# Democracies

## 9

## Will More Countries Become Democratic?

*Samuel P. Huntington*

What are the prospects for the emergence of more democratic regimes in the world? This question has intellectual and policy relevance for the 1980s. During the 1950s and early 1960s, scholars concerned with this issue were generally optimistic that decolonization and economic development would lead to the multiplication of democratic regimes. The history of the next decade dealt roughly with these expectations, and people became more pessimistically preoccupied with the reasons for the breakdown of democratic systems. By the late 1970s and early 1980s, however, the prospects for democracy seemed to have brightened once again, and social scientists have responded accordingly. "Transitions to democracy" became the new focus of attention. The optimists of the 1950s were rather naively optimistic; those of the 1980s have been more cautiously optimistic, but the optimism and the hope are still there.... The purpose of this article is to use social science theory and comparative political analysis to see to what extent this new, more cautious optimism may be justified.

This issue is important for at least four reasons. First, the future of democracy is closely

SOURCE: Samuel P. Huntington, "Will More Countries Become Democratic?" *Political Science Quarterly* 99, no. 2 (Summer 1984), pp. 193–218. By permission. Notes abridged by the editors.

associated with the future of freedom in the world. Democracies can and have abused individual rights and liberties, and a well-regulated authoritarian state may provide a high degree of security and order for its citizens. Overall, however, the correlation between the existence of democracy and the existence of individual liberty is extremely high. Indeed, some measure of the latter is an essential component of the former. Conversely, the long-term effect of the operation of democratic politics is probably to broaden and deepen individual liberty. Liberty is, in a sense, the peculiar virtue of democracy; hence, if one is concerned with liberty as an ultimate social value, one should also be concerned with the fate of democracy.

Second, the future of democracy elsewhere in the world is of importance to the United States. The United States is the world's premier democratic country, and the greater the extent to which democracy prevails elsewhere in the world, the more congenial the world environment will be to American interests generally and the future of democracy in the United States in particular. Michael Doyle has argued quite persuasively that no two liberal societies have ever fought each other.[1] His concept of liberalism differs from the concept of democracy employed in this paper, but the point may well be true of democratic regimes as well as liberal ones. Other things being equal, nondemocratic regimes are likely to pose more serious challenges to American interests than democratic regimes.

Third, "a house divided against itself," Abraham Lincoln said, "cannot stand.... This government cannot endure permanently half-slave and half-free." At present the world is not a single house, but it is becoming more and more closely integrated. Interdependence is the trend of the times. How long can an increasingly interdependent world survive part-democratic and part-authoritarian and totalitarian? At what point does interdependence become incompatible with coexistence? For the Soviet bloc and the Western World, that point may still be some distance in the future, but tensions arising out of the growing interaction between totally different political systems are almost inevitably bound to increase. At some point, coexistence may require a slowing down or halting of the trends toward interdependence.

Fourth, the extension or decline of democracy has implications for other social values, such as economic growth, socioeconomic equity, political stability, social justice, and national independence. In societies at one level of development, progress toward one or more of these goals may be compatible with a high level of democracy. At another level of socioeconomic development, conflicts may exist. The question of the appropriateness of democracy for poor countries is, in this context, a central issue. But even highly developed societies may achieve their democracy at some sacrifice of other important values, such as national security.

In addition, if it is desirable to extend the scope of democracy in the world, obviously it is necessary to know what conditions favor that in the late 20th century. Empirical analysis is necessary to answer the question: What policies should governments, private institutions, and individuals espouse to encourage the spread of democracy? To what extent do efforts such as those of the Reagan administration have an impact, positive or negative, on the state of democracy in the world, and at what cost in terms of other social values and national goals?

The first step in evaluating the prospects for democracy is to define the dependent variable with which we are concerned. Definitions of democracy are legion. The term has been applied to areas and institutions far removed from politics. It has also been defined as an ideal impossible of human achievement. For Peter Bachrach, for instance, a democratic system of

government has for its paramount objective "maximization of the self-development of every individual." Robert Dahl says a democratic political system is one which is "completely or almost completely responsible to all its citizens."[2] Such definitions may be relevant to normative political theory, but they are not very useful for comparative empirical analysis. First, they are often so vague and general that it is virtually impossible to apply them in practice. How does one judge whether a political system is attempting to maximize the self-development of individuals or is completely responsive to all its citizens? Second, democracy may also be defined in such broad terms as to make it identical with almost all civic virtues, including social justice, equality, liberty, fulfillment, progress, and a variety of other good things. Hence it becomes difficult if not impossible to analyze the relationship between democracy and other social goals.

For comparative analysis a more empirical and institutional definition is desirable, and this paper follows in the tradition of Joseph A. Schumpeter. A political system is defined as democratic to the extent that its most powerful collective decision-makers are selected through periodic elections in which candidates freely compete for votes and in which virtually all the adult population is eligible to vote. So defined, a democracy thus involves the two dimensions —contestation and participation—that Dahl sees as critical to his realistic democracy or polyarchy.[3]

## THE RECORD OF DEMOCRATIC DEVELOPMENT

The historical emergence of modern democratic regimes falls into four phases. What could reasonably be called a democratic political system at the national level of government first appeared in the United States in the early 19th century. During the following century democratic regimes gradually emerged in northern and Western Europe, in the British dominions, and in a few countries in Latin America. This trend, which Alexis de Tocqueville had foreseen in 1835 and which James Bryce documented in 1920, appeared to be irreversible if not necessarily universal. Virtually all significant regime changes were from less democracy to more democracy. Writing at the end of this period, Bryce could well speculate as to whether this "trend toward democracy now widely visible, is a natural trend, due to a general law of social progress."[4]

The trend was reversing, however, even as he wrote. The year 1920 was in many aspects the peak of democratic development among the independent nations of the world.[5] During the following two decades, democracy or democratic trends were snuffed out in Germany, Italy, Austria, Poland, the Baltic states, Spain, Portugal, Greece, Argentina, Brazil, and Japan. The war fought to make the world safe for democracy seemed instead to have brought its progress to an abrupt halt and to have unleashed social movements from the Right and the Left intent on destroying it.

The aftermath of World War II, on the other hand, marked another dramatic, if brief, spurt in the multiplication of democratic regimes. With the support of its allies, the United States imposed democracy on West Germany, Austria, Italy, and Japan (where it took root), and attempted to do so in South Korea (where it did not). Coincidentally, the process of decolonization got underway with newly independent countries usually adopting at first the political forms of the imperial powers. In at least some cases, such as India, Israel, Ceylon, and the Philippines, the forms of democracy were accompanied by the substance also. Other countries, such as Turkey and some Latin American states, moved to emulate the political systems of the victorious Western powers. By the early 1950s, the proportion of democracies among the world's independent states had reached another high.

The fourth period in the evolution of democratic regimes, from the early 1950s to the 1980s, differs from the other three. In each of them, there was an overwhelmingly dominant trend, either toward the extension of democracy (1820–1920 and 1942–1953), or toward its reduction

(1920–1942). In each period there were very few, if any, significant regime shifts against the dominant trend. The thirty years from the early 1950s to the early 1980s, however, were not characterized by a strong move in either direction. The trends were mixed. As we have seen, the number of democratic regimes seemed to expand in the 1950s and early 1960s, to shrink in the middle-late 1960s and early 1970s, and then to expand again in the late 1970s and early 1980s. Overall, however, the net record of change in the state of democracy in the world was not very great. It would be difficult to argue that the world was more or less democratic in 1984 than it had been in 1954. Indicative of this relative stability, albeit for a much shorter period of time, are Freedom House's estimates of the proportion of the world's population living in "free" states. In the first such estimate, in January 1973, 32.0 percent of the world's population was found to live in "free" states. In the next year, the percentage increased to 36.0 percent. During the following 10 years, except for the 2 years India was under emergency rule (when it was 19.8 percent and 19.6 percent), the proportion of the world's population living in free states never went above 37.0 percent and never dropped below 35.0 percent. In January 1984 it was 36.0 percent, exactly where it had been 10 years earlier.[6]

The overall stability in the extent of democracy does, however, conceal some important developments in both directions. With a few notable exceptions, almost all colonies that achieved independence after World War II shifted from democratic to nondemocratic systems. In contrast, a few countries moved in the opposite direction. These include Spain, Portugal, Colombia, Venezuela, Greece, and the Dominican Republic. Several South American countries, including two with long-standing democractic systems (Chile, Uruguay) and two with less stable populist systems (Brazil, Argentina), became bureaucratic-authoritarian states, with military governments intent upon fairly sustained rule. By the end of 1983, however, Brazil had made substantial progress back towards a democratic system, and Argentina had a democratically elected government. Many other countries (including Peru, Ecuador, Ghana, Nigeria, and Turkey) seemed to oscillate back and forth between democratic and undemocratic systems, in a pattern traditionally characteristic of praetorian societies. In East Asia: Korea, Singapore, Indonesia, and the Philippines became less democratic, Taiwan remained undemocratic; the Indochinese states succumbed to a ruthless Vietnamese totalitarianism; and Thailand and Malaysia remained partially democratic. Finally, efforts to move Hungary, Czechoslovakia, and Poland toward more democratic politics were halted directly or indirectly by Soviet action.

Any estimate of the future of democracy in the world must be rooted in an explanation of why these mixed trends prevailed between the 1950s and the 1980s, and hence whether the overall stability in the prevalence of democratic regimes in the world will continue. Ancient and modern political analysts have many theories to explain the rise and fall of democratic regimes. To what extent do these various and conflicting theories explain what happened and did not happen after World War II and what could happen in the 1980s?

Thinking about the reasons for the emergence of democratic regimes has typically had two foci. One approach has focused on the preconditions in society that favor democratic development. A second approach has focused on the nature of the political processes by which that development has occurred. Each will be considered in turn.

## PRECONDITIONS OF DEMOCRATIZATION

In 1970, Dankwart Rustow published a penetrating article on "transitions to democracy," in which he criticized studies that focused on "preconditions" for democratization because they often tended to jump from the correlation between democracy and other factors to the conclusion that those other factors were responsible for democracy. They also tended, he argued,

to look for the causes of democracy primarily in economic, social, cultural, and psychological, but not political, factors.[7] Rustow's criticisms were well taken and helped to provide a more balanced view of the complexities of democratization. It would, however, be a mistake to swing entirely to the other extreme and ignore the environmental factors that may affect democratic development. In fact, plausible arguments can be and have been made for a wide variety of factors or preconditions that appear to be associated with the emergence of democratic regimes. To a large extent these factors can be grouped into four broad categories—economic, social, external, and cultural.

## Economic Wealth and Equality

In his critique, Rustow gave special attention to an influential article published by Seymour Martin Lipset a decade earlier. In that piece, Lipset highlighted the seeming correlation between high levels of economic development and the prevalence of democratic political systems among European, English-speaking, and Latin American nations. The "more well-to-do a nation," he postulated, "the greater the chances that it will sustain democracy."[8] His study stimulated a flood of further analyses that criticized, qualified, and refined his argument. Whatever the academic hairsplittings, however, his basic point seemed to make sense. "There is," as another scholar put it in 1960, "a positive correlation between economic development and political competitiveness."[9] A quarter century later, that correlation still seemed to exist. In 1981, for instance, a comparison of the World Bank's ratings of countries in terms of economic development with Freedom House's ratings of them in terms of liberty showed these results—2 of 36 low-income countries were classified "free" or democratic, 14 out of 60 middle-income countries were so classified, and 18 out of 24 countries with industrial economies were so classified.[10] As one moves up the economic ladder, the greater are the chances that a country will be democratic.

The correlation between wealth and democracy is thus fairly strong. How can it be explained? There are three possibilities. First, both democracy and wealth could be caused by a third factor. Protestantism has, for instance, been assigned by some a major role in the origins of capitalism, economic development, and democracy. Second, democracy could give rise to economic wealth. In fact, however, high levels of economic wealth require high rates of economic growth and high rates of economic growth do not correlate with the prevalence of democratic political systems.[11] Hence, it seems unlikely that wealth depends on democracy, and, if a connection exists, democracy must depend on wealth.

The probability of any causal connection running from wealth to democracy is enhanced by the arguments as to why this would be a plausible relationship. A wealthy economy, it is said, makes possible higher levels of literacy, education, and mass media exposure, all of which are conducive to democracy. A wealthy economy also moderates the tensions of political conflict; alternative opportunities are likely to exist for unsuccessful political leaders and greater economic resources generally facilitate accommodation and compromise. In addition, a highly developed, industrialized economy and the complex society it implies cannot be governed efficiently by authoritarian means. Decision-making is necessarily dispersed, and hence power is shared and rule must be based on consent. Finally, in a more highly developed economy, income and possibly wealth also tend to be more equally distributed than in a poorer economy. Since democracy means, in some measure, majority rule, democracy is only possible if the majority is a relatively satisfied middle class, and not an impoverished majority confronting an inordinately wealthy oligarchy. A substantial middle class, in turn, may be the product of the relatively equal distribution of land in agrarian societies that may otherwise be relatively poor, such as the early 19th century United States or 20th century Costa Rica. It may also be the result of a relatively high level of development, which produces greater income equality in industrial as compared to industrializing societies.

If these arguments are correct, economic development in the Communist world and the Third World should facilitate the emergence of democratic regimes. Yet one must be skeptical as to whether such an easy conclusion is warranted. In the first place, there is the question as to what level of economic development is required to make possible the transition to democracy. As Jonathan Sunshine has conclusively shown, the countries of Western Europe generally became democratic when their per capita gross domestic products were in the range of $300–$500 (in 1960 dollars). By 1981, perhaps two-thirds of the middle-income developing countries had reached or exceeded that level of development. Most of them, however, had not become democratic. If the economic theory holds, the level of economic development necessary to facilitate the transition to democracy must be higher in the late 20th century than it was in the century prior to 1950.[12] In addition, different countries may still transit to democracy at widely varying levels of development. Spain, after all, did grow extremely rapidly during the 1950s and 1960s and did become democratic after the death of Francisco Franco in the mid-1970s. Could this have happened without the industrialization, urbanization, and development of the middle class that were central to Spanish economic growth? Quite probably not. Lopez Rodo was at least partially right when he had earlier predicted that Spain would become democratic when its per capita income reached $2,000 per head.[13] But then what about Portugal? It made a simultaneous transition to democracy, without having experienced the massive economic development of Spain and while still at a much lower level of economic well-being.

In addition, what about the experience of the southern cone states of Latin America? They too went through major processes of economic development and yet turned away from democracy, a phenomenon that led Guillermo

O'Donnell to develop his theory of bureaucratic authoritarianism that posited just the opposite of the Lipset wealth-democracy theory. Instead, O'Donnell argued that economic development and particularly the strains produced by a heavy emphasis on import substitution led to the emergence of new, stronger, and more lasting forms of authoritarian rule.[14]

There is also the experience of the East Asian newly industrializing countries. In the 1960s and 1970s, these countries not only had the highest economic growth rates in the world, but they also achieved those rates while in most cases maintaining very equitable systems of income distribution. Yet none became more democratic and two of the most notable economic achievers, Korea and Singapore, became less so.

At the same time, the economic theory may still serve a purpose in terms of focusing attention on those countries where transitions to democratic or other types of modern political systems are most likely to occur. As countries develop economically, they can be conceived of moving into a zone of transition or choice, in which traditional forms of rule become increasingly difficult to maintain and new types of political institutions are required to aggregate the demands of an increasingly complex society and to implement public policies in such a society. In the 1981 World Bank ordering of countries by level of economic development, the zone of choice might be conceived as comprising the top one third of the middle-income countries, that is, those running from Number 77 (the Republic of Korea) up to Number 96 (Spain). To these should be added Taiwan, which in terms of per capita income fits in the middle of this group. Of these 21 countries:

- Seven were democracies, including four (Spain, Venezuela, Portugal, Greece) that transited to democracy after World War II, two that became democratic on independence (Israel, Trinidad and Tobago), and one that had sustained democracy for many years (Costa Rica).

- Four were the bureaucratic-authoritarian (B-A) states of the southern cone (Brazil, Chile, Argentina, Uruguay).
- Four were the newly industrializing countries (NICs) of East Asia (the Republic of Korea, Taiwan, Singapore, Hong Kong).
- Two were Communist (Rumania and Yugoslavia).
- The remaining four (Algeria, Mexico, Iran, and South Africa) were resource rich, ideologically diverse, and politically undemocratic.

Two years later, this group of countries, now labeled by the World Bank as "upper middle income countries" had been reduced by the graduation of Spain into the category of "industrial market economies," but had been enlarged by the movement upward of Malaysia, Lebanon, and Panama, and by the Bank's transfer into it of Iraq from the category of "high income oil exporters."[15]

If the wealth theory of democracy were valid, one would predict further movement toward democracy among the twenty-odd states in this group, perhaps particularly on the part of the East Asian NICs and the B-A states of South America. Experience suggests, however, that what is predictable for these countries in the transition zone is not the advent of democracy but rather the demise of previously existing political forms. Economic development compels the modification or abandonment of traditional political institutions; it does not determine what political system will replace them. That will be shaped by other factors, such as the underlying culture of the society, the values of the elites, and external influences.

In the late 1950s, for instance, both Cuba and Venezuela were reaching the level of economic development where the traditional sort of military despotism to which each had been subjected for years (Fulgencio y Batista Zaldivar, Marcos Pérez Jiménez) was no longer adequate for the needs of the society. These military despotisms came to their ends in 1958 and 1959. Batista collapsed in the face of an armed revolutionary movement that rapidly seized and consolidated power, nationalized private property, an installed a pervasive Marxist-Leninist dictatorship. The Pérez Jiménez regime collapsed as a result of the withdrawal of support by virtually all the major groups of Venezuelan society. That collapse was accompanied, however, by the negotiation of a series of pacts among Venezuelan leaders representing the major political and social groups that set the framework for a democratic political system. By the late 1950s, the days of traditional personalistic despotism in Cuba and Venezuela were numbered; what was not fixed was what would replace them. Fidel Castro chose to lead Cuba in one direction; Rómulo Betancourt chose to lead Venezuela in a very different one. Fifteen years later in somewhat comparable circumstances King Juan Carlos and Adolfo Suárez in Spain and António Ramalho Eanes in Portugal made similar choices on behalf of democracy. In another case, by the mid-1970s the rapid economic development of Iran had clearly undermined the basis for the shah's regime. The shah did not attempt to develop a broader, more participatory set of democratic institutions. His inaction, combined with the decision or lack of decision by the military leaders and the political skill of the mullahs, opened Iran to a religious revolution. Different and earlier decisions by Iranian leaders in the 1960s and 1970s might have moved Iran in a more democratic direction.

If the concept of a transition zone is valid, economic development produces a phase in a nation's history where political elites and the prevailing political values can shape choices that decisively determine the nation's future evolution. The range of choice may be limited. In 1981, for instance, all countries with per capita gross national products of $4,220 or more (aside from the small oil-exporting states and Singapore) were either democratic or Communist. Conceivably, transition zone countries could make other choices. Iran is obviously in the fanatic pursuit of a different course; possibly the East Asian NICs and the Latin American B-A regimes may find other alternatives. To date, however, those countries that have come through the transition zone have almost always emerged as either democracies or as Communist dictatorships.

## Social Structure

A second set of often-discussed preconditions for democracy involves the extent to which there is a widely differentiated and articulated social structure with relatively autonomous social classes, regional groups, occupational groups, and ethnic and religious groups. Such groups, it is argued, provide the basis for the limitation of state power, hence for the control of the state by society, and hence for democratic political institutions as the most effective means of exercising that control. Societies that lack autonomous intermediate groups are, on the other hand, much more likely to be dominated by a centralized power apparatus—an absolute monarchy, an oriental despotism, or an authoritarian or totalitarian dictatorship.[16] This argument can be made on behalf of groups and pluralism in general or on behalf of particular groups or types of pluralistic structure which are singled out as playing a decisive role in making democracy possible.

According to one line of argument, pluralism (even highly stratified pluralism) in traditional society enhances the probability of developing stable democracy in modern society. The caste system may be one reaon why India has been able to develop and to maintain stable democratic institutions.[17] More generally, the argument is made that societies with a highly developed feudalism, including an aristocracy capable of limiting the development of state power, are more likely to evolve into democracies than those that lack such social pluralism. The record of Western Europe versus Russia and of Japan versus China suggests that there may well be something to this theory. But the theory fails to account for differences between North America and South America. Tocqueville, Louis Hartz, and others attribute democracy in the former to the absence of feudalism. The failure of democracy in South America has, conversely, often been attributed precisely to its feudal heritage, although the feudalism that existed there was, to be sure, highly centralized.[18]

The theory that emphasizes traditional pluralism is, in a sense, the opposite of the one that emphasizes wealth as a precondition of democracy. The latter makes democracy dependent on how far the processes of economic development and modernization have gone. The traditional pluralism theory, in contrast, puts the emphasis on where the process started, on the nature of traditional society. Was it, in Gaetano Mosca's terms, primarily a "feudal" or a "bureaucratic" society? If pushed to the extreme, of course, this theory implies societal predestination: it is all determined in advance that some societies will become democratic and others will not.

The most significant manifestation of the social structure argument, however, concerns not the existence of a feudal aristocracy, but rather the existence of an autonomous bourgeoisie. Democracy, the Marxists argue, is bourgeois democracy, reflecting the interests of that particular social class. Barrington Moore has restated the proposition succinctly in a more limited formulation: "No bourgeois, no democracy."[19] This argument would seem to have much to commend it. The failure of democracy to develop in Third World countries despite their economic growth can, perhaps, be related to the nature of that growth. The leading roles have been played by the state and by multinational enterprises. As a result, economic development runs ahead of the development of a bourgeoisie. In those circumstances where a bourgeoisie has developed, however, the prospects for democracy have been greater. The move to democracy in Turkey in the 1940s coincided with the move away from the étatisme of Kemalism and the appearance of a group of independent businessmen. More significantly, the ability of a developing country to have an autonomous, indigenous bourgeoisie is likely to be related to its size. Countries with small internal markets are unlikely to be able to sustain such a class, but large ones can. This may be one factor explaining why India (with one short interlude) has sustained a democratic system, and why Brazil, which is also developing a vigorous indigenous bourgeoisie, steadily moved away from bureaucratic authoritarianism in the 1970s and early 1980s. In South Africa, businessmen have been among those most active in attempting to ameliorate apartheid and broaden democracy in that country.

The seemingly important role of an autonomous bourgeoisie for the development of democracy highlights the question of the relation between economic system and political system. Clearly political democracy is compatible with both a substantial role in the economy for state-owned enterprises and a substantial state welfare and social security system. Nonetheless, as Charles Lindblom has pointed out (in a volume that otherwise highlights the conflict between the business corporation and democracy), all political democracies have market-oriented economies, although quite clearly not all market-oriented economies are paired with democratic political systems.[20] Lindblom's message would seem to be like Moore's—a market-oriented economy, like a bourgeoisie, is a necessary but not sufficient condition for the existence of a democratic political system.

Why should this be the case? At least two reasons suggest themselves. Politically, a market economy requires a dispersion of economic power and in practice almost invariably some form of private property. The dispersion of economic power creates alternatives and counters to state power and enables those elites that control economic power to limit state power and to exploit democratic means to make it serve their interests. Economically, a market economy appears more likely to sustain economic growth than a command economy (although the latter may, as the Soviet and East European cases suggest, do so for a short period of time), and hence a market economy is more likely to give rise to the economic wealth and the resulting more equitable distribution of income that provide the infrastructure of democracy.

A third source of autonomous social pressure in a democratic direction may be provided by labor unions. Historically, unions played this role in Western Europe and the United States. In the contemporary world, unions have also had a role in the struggles against the racist oligarchy in South Africa, against military rule in the southern cone, and against the Communist dictatorship in Poland. At the same time, the experience of these cases also suggests the limits on the extent to which, in the absence of affiliated political parties, labor unions can affect political change.

Under some conditions, communal (that is, ethnic, racial, or religious) pluralism may be conducive to the development of at least limited forms of democracy. In most cases of communal pluralism, democracy can operate only on a consociational rather than a majoritarian basis.[21] And even when it is organized on a consociational basis, it will often break down as a result of social mobilization that undermines the power of elites or as a result of the intrusion of external political and military forces (as in Cyprus or Lebanon). Even in the best of circumstances, consociational democracy can often only remain stable by in effect becoming consociational oligarchy (as in Malaysia), that is, by sacrificing contestation in order to maintain representation.

## External Environment

External influences may be of decisive importance in influencing whether a society moves in a democratic or nondemocratic direction. To the extent that such influences are more important than indigenous factors, democratization is the result of diffusion rather than development. Conceivably, democracy in the world could stem from a single source. Clearly it does not. Yet it would be wrong to ignore the extent to which much of the democracy in the world does have a common origin. In 1984, Freedom House classified 52 countries (many of them extremely small) as "free."[22] In 33 of those 52 countries, the presence of democratic institutions could be ascribed in large part to British and American influence, either through settlement, colonial rule, defeat in war, or fairly direct imposition (such as in the Dominican Republic). Most of the other 19 "free" countries where democracy had other sources were either in Western Europe or in South America. The extension of democracy into the non-Western world, insofar as that has occurred, has thus been largely the product of Anglo-American efforts.

Ever since the French Revolution, armies have carried political ideologies with them. As we have indicated, where American armies went in World War II, democracy followed (in four cases enduringly, in one case temporarily). Where Soviet armies went, Communism followed. Military conquest is clearly one way of extending democracy and other political systems. Historically, however, Western colonialism has been the most important means of diffusing democratic ideas and institutions. The enduring results of such colonialism have, however, been rather limited. As of 1983, no former French, U.S., Dutch, Portuguese, or Belgian colony was rated "free" by Freedom House. Several former British colonies were. Myron Weiner has, indeed, emphasized that *"every single country in the third world that emerged from colonial rule since the second world war with a population of at least one million (and almost all the smaller countries as well) with a continuous democratic experience is a former British colony."*[23] British rule seemingly had a significantly different impact from that of other colonial powers. Only six countries meet Weiner's condition, however, and a much larger number of former British colonies have *not* sustained democracy. The question then becomes how to distinguish among former British colonies. One possibility is that the duration of democratic institutions after independence is a function of the duration of British rule before independence. The colonies where democratic institutions appear to have taken the firmest root are those such as India, Sri Lanka, and the West Indian Anglophone states, where British rule dates from the 18th century. The record of former British colonies in Africa, on the other hand, where British rule dates only from the late 19th century, is not all that different from that of the former African colonies of other European powers.

In large measure, the rise and decline of democracy on a global scale is a function of the rise and decline of the most powerful democratic states. The spread of democracy in the 19th century went hand in hand with the Pax Britannica. The extension of democracy after World War II reflected the global power of the United States. The decline of democracy in East Asia and Latin America in the 1970s was in part a reflection of the waning of American influence.[24] That influence is felt both directly, as a result of the efforts of the American government to affect political processes in other societies, and also indirectly by providing a powerful and successful model to be followed.

Regional external influences can also have a significant effect on political development within a society. The governments and political parties of the European Community (EC) helped to encourage the emergence of democratic institutions in Spain and Portugal, and the desire of those two countries plus Greece to join the community provided an additional incentive for them to become democratic. Even beyond the confines of the EC, Western Europe has generally become defined as a community of democratic nations, and any significant departure by one nation from the democratic norm would clearly create a major crisis in intra-European relations. In some measure, a similar development may be taking place among the countries of the Andean Pact. The departure from the Pact of Chile and the addition of Venezuela in the mid-1970s, plus the transitions to democracy in Ecuador and Peru, then laid the basis for identifying pact membership with the adherence to democratic government.

In some regions, but most notably in Latin America, regional trends may exist. By and large, Latin American governments moved in a democratic direction in the late 1950s and early 1960s, then in an authoritarian direction in the late 1960s and early 1970s, and then once again

in a democratic direction in the late 1970s and early 1980s. The reasons for these regional shifts are not entirely clear. They could be a result of four factors: simultaneous parallel socioeconomic development in Latin American societies; the triggering of a trend by the impact of one "pace-setting" Latin American society on its neighbors; the impact on Latin America of a common external influence (such as the United States); or some combination of these factors.

## Cultural Context

The political culture of a society has been defined by Sidney Verba as "the system of empirical beliefs, expressive symbols, and values which defines the situation in which political action takes place."[25] Political culture is, presumably, rooted in the broader culture of a society involving those beliefs and values, often religiously based, concerning the nature of humanity and society, the relations among human beings, and the relation of individuals to a transcendent being. Significant differences in their receptivity to democracy appear to exist among societies with different cultural traditions.

Historically, as many scholars have pointed out, a high correlation existed between Protestantism and democracy. In the contemporary world, virtually all countries with a European population and a Protestant majority (except East Germany) have democratic governments.[26] The case of Catholicism, particularly in Latin countries, on the other hand, is more ambivalent. Historically, it was often argued that a natural opposition existed between Catholicism and democracy. By and large, democratic institutions developed later and less surely in European Catholic countries than in Protestant ones. By and large, however, these countries also developed later economically than Protestant countries, and hence it is difficult to distinguish between the impact of economics and that of religion. Conceivably, the influence of the latter on politics could have been mediated through its impact on economic development and the rise of an entrepreneurial class. With economic development, however, the role of the church changed, and in most Catholic countries now the church is identified with support for democracy.

Islam, on the other hand, has not been hospitable to democracy. Of 36 countries with Moslem majorities, Freedom House in 1984 rated 21 as "not free," 15 as "partially free," none as "free." The one Islamic country that sustained even intermittent democracy after World War II was Turkey, which had, under Mustapha Kemal, explicitly rejected its Islamic tradition and defined itself as a secular republic. The one Arab country that sustained democracy, albeit of the consociational variety, for any time was Lebanon, 40 to 50 percent of whose population was Christian and whose democratic institutions collapsed when the Moslem majority asserted itself in the 1970s. Somewhat similarly, both Confucianism and Buddhism have been conducive to authoritarian rule, even in those cases where, as in Korea, Taiwan, and Singapore, economic preconditions for democracy have come into being. In India and Japan, on the other hand, the traditional Hindu and Shinto cultures at the very least did not prevent the development of democratic institutions and may well have encouraged it.

How can these differences be explained? Both doctrinal and structural aspects of the religions could play a role. At the most obvious level, those cultures that are consummatory in character—that is, where intermediate and ultimate ends are closely connected—seem to be less favorable to democracy. In Islam, for instance, no distinction exists between religion and politics or between the spiritual and the secular, and political participation was historically an alien concept.[27] Somewhat similarly, Confucianism in China was generally hostile to social bodies independent of the state, and the culture was conceived as a total entity, no part of which could be changed without threatening the whole. Instrumental cultures, in contrast, are "characterized by a large sector of intermediate ends separate from and independent of ultimate ends" and hence "ultimate ends do not color every concrete act."[28] The Hindu tradition, for example, is relatively tolerant of diversity. S.N.

Eisenstadt has written that "the basic religious and cultural orientations, the specific cultural identity of Indian civilization were not necessarily associated with any particular political or imperial framework. . . ."[29]

As a whole, consummatory culture is thus more resistant to change, and when change comes in one significant element of the culture, the entire culture is thrown into question or is displaced and destroyed. In the instrumental culture, on the other hand, change can come gradually and incrementally. Hence, less resistance exists to the adaptation of new political forms, such as democratic institutions, and the process of adaptation can be an extended one that in itself facilitates the development of stable democracy.

With respect to the more narrowly political culture of a society, it seems reasonable to expect that the prevalence of some values and beliefs will be more conducive to the emergence of democracy than others. A political culture that values highly hierarchical relationships and extreme deference to authority presumably is less fertile ground for democracy than one that does not. Similarly, a culture in which there is a high degree of mutual trust among members of the society is likely to be more favorable to democracy than one in which interpersonal relationships are more generally characterized by suspicion, hostility, and distrust. A willingness to tolerate diversity and conflict among groups and to recognize the legitimacy of compromise also should be helpful to democratic development. Societies in which great stress is put on the need to acquire power and little on the need to accommodate others are more likely to have authoritarian or totalitarian regimes. Social scientists have attempted to compare societies along these various dimensions, but the evidence remains fragmented and difficult to systematize.[30] In addition, of course, even if some beliefs and values are found to correlate with the presence of democratic institutions, the question still remains concerning the relationship among these in a developmental sense. To what extent does the development of a pro-democratic political culture have to precede the development of democratic institutions? Or do the two tend to develop more simultaneously with the successful operation of democratic institutions, possibly created for other reasons, generating adherence to democratic values and beliefs?[31]

# PROCESSES OF DEMOCRATIZATION

The classic model of democratization that has infused much discussion of the subject is that of Britain, with its stately progression from civic rights to political rights to social rights, gradual development of parliamentary supremacy and cabinet government, and incremental expansion of the suffrage over the course of a century. It is basically a linear model. Dankwart A. Rustow's model, based on Swedish experience —national unity, prolonged and inconclusive political struggle, a conscious decision to adopt democratic rules, habituation to the working of those rules—also involves a relatively simple linear progression. These "ingredients," he has argued, "must be assembled one at a time."[32] These linear models primarily reflect European experience during the century ending in 1920 and the experience of some Latin American countries (such as Argentina until 1930 and Chile until 1973).

Two other models have generally been more relevant than the linear model to the experience of Third World countries. One is the cyclical model of alternating despotism and democracy. In this case, key elites normally accept, at least superficially, the legitimacy of democratic forms. Elections are held from time to time, but rarely is there any sustained succession of governments coming to power through the electoral process. Governments are as often the product of military interventions as they are of elections. Such interventions tend to occur either when a radical party wins or appears about to win an election, when the government in power threatens or appears to threaten the prerogatives of the armed forces, or when the government

appears incapable of effectively guiding the economy and maintaining public order. Once a military junta takes over, it will normally promise to return power to civilian rule. In due course, it does so, if only to minimize divisiveness within the armed forces and to escape from its own inability to govern effectively. In a praetorian situation like this, neither authoritarian nor democratic institutions are effectively institutionalized. Once countries enter into this cyclical pattern, it appears to be extremely difficult for them to escape from it. In many respects, countries that have had relatively stable authoritarian rule (such as Spain and Portugal) are more likely to evolve into relatively stable democracies than countries that have regularly oscillated between despotism and democracy (such as Peru, Ecuador, Bolivia, Argentina, Ghana, Nigeria). In the latter, neither democratic nor authoritarian norms have deep roots among the relevant political elites, while in the former a broad consensus accepting of authoritarian norms is displaced by a broad consensus on or acceptance of democratic ones. In the one case, the alternation of democracy and despotism *is* the political system; in the other, the shift from a stable despotism to a stable democracy *is a change* in political systems.

A third model is neither linear nor cyclical but rather dialectical. In this case, the development of a middle class leads to increased pressures on the existing authoritarian regimes for expanded participation and contestation. At some point, there is then a sharp break, perhaps in the form of what I have elsewhere called the "urban breakthrough," the overthrow of the existing authoritarian regime, and the installation of a democratic one.[33] This regime, however, finds it difficult or impossible to govern effectively. A sharp reaction occurs with the overthrow of the democratic system and installation of a (usually right-wing) authoritarian regime. In due course, however, this regime collapses and a transition is made to a more stable, more balanced, and longer-lasting democratic system. This model is roughly applicable to the history of a number of countries, including Germany, Italy, Austria, Greece, and Spain.

Most theories of political development in general and of democratization in particular see these processes as involving a number of different elements. The sequence in which those components appear may have important implications for the overall results of the process. Several theorists have suggested, for instance, that the preferable overall process of development for a country is first to define its national identity, next to develop effective institutions of authority, and then to expand political participation. The "probabilities of a political system's development in a nonviolent, nonauthoritarian, and eventually democratically stable manner are maximized," Eric Nordlinger has argued, when this sequence occurs.[34] In somewhat parallel fashion, it has been argued that the development of broad-gauged political institutions for political participation, such as electoral and party systems, must coincide with or precede the expansion of political participation if instability and violence are to be avoided. Similarly, Robert A. Dahl emphasizes the greater probability of success in transitions to democracy (or polyarchy in his terms) if the expansion of contestation precedes the expansion of participation.[35]

All these theories thus emphasize the desirability for the eventual development of stable democracy of the expansion of political participation occurring relatively late in the sequence of change. However, given the widely accepted desirability of political participation (including in totalitarian regimes) and the major increases in social mobilization (such as urbanization, literacy, and media consumption) produced by economic development, the prevailing tendencies in the contemporary world are for participation to expand early in the process of development, and before or concurrently with contestation. This may be one reason why economic development in the Third World has not stimulated the emergence of more stable democratic regimes. At present, the one notable case where contestation has clearly developed in advance of participation is South Africa. Hence, according to the Dahl thesis, the prospects for democratic development should be greater in South Africa than elsewhere in Africa.

It is often assumed that since democracy, to a greater degree than other forms of government, involves rule by the people, the people therefore play a greater role in bringing it into existence than they do with other forms of government. In fact, however, democratic regimes that last have seldom, if ever, been instituted by mass popular action. Almost always, democracy has come as much from the top down as from the bottom up; it is as likely to be the product of oligarchy as of protest against oligarchy. The passionate dissidents from authoritarian rule and the crusaders for democratic principles, the Tom Paines of this world, do not create democratic institutions; that requires James Madisons. Those institutions come into existence through negotiations and compromises among political elites calculating their own interests and desires. They are produced when, as Rustow argued, political leaders decide "to accept the existence of diversity in unity and, to that end, to institutionalize some crucial aspect of democratic procedure." The political leaders may do this because they are convinced of the ethical and political superiority of democracy and hence view democracy as a desirable goal in itself. More likely, however, they will view democracy as a means to other goals, such as prolonging their own rule, achieving international legitimacy, minimizing domestic opposition, and reducing the likelihood of civil violence, from which they will probably suffer. Hence, whatever institutions are agreed on will, in Rustow's words, "seem second-best to all major parties involved."[36] One could paraphrase Reinhold Niebuhr: the ability of elites to compromise makes democracy possible; the inclination of elites to vengeance makes democracy desirable—for the elites.

In the decades after World War II, democratic regimes have usually been introduced in independent countries through one or some combination of two processes. *Replacement* occurs when an authoritarian regime collapses or is overthrown as a result of military defeat, economic disaster, or the withdrawal of support from it by substantial groups in the population.

Its leaders are killed, imprisoned, flee the country, or withdraw from politics. The leaders of the now-dominant groups, which had not been actively involved with the authoritarian regime, agree among themselves to institute a democratic system. This agreement may be reached very quickly because of previous experience with democracy and because its inauguration is seen as the "obvious" solution by the relevant political elites, as in Venezuela in 1958 and Greece in 1974. Or it may come about as a result of political struggle among elites with differing views as to the future of their country, out of which the leaders committed to democracy emerge successfully (as in Portugal in 1975–76). This process may involve, as it did in the case of Venezuela, a series of carefully negotiated pacts among the relevant groups that can cover economic policy and the role of institutions (such as the church and the army), as well as the procedures for choosing a government. One critical issue on which the constitutive elites must agree is how to treat those actively involved in the previous authoritarian regime.[37]

The alternative process for inaugurating a democratic regime might be termed *transformation*. In this case, the elites within an authoritarian system conclude that, for some reason or another, that system which they have led and presumably benefited from no longer meets their needs or those of their society. They hence take the lead in modifying the existing political system and transforming it into a democratic one. In this case, while there may well be a variety of internal and external pressures favoring change, the initiative for such change comes from the rulers. Transformation involves, as Juan Linz put is, "change through *reforma* rather than *ruptura*."[38] Notable examples include, of course, Britain in the 19th century and after World War II, Turkey in the 1940s, Spain in the 1970s, and Brazil in the 1970s and 1980s. The leaders of the transformation process typically confront all the problems of the political reformer, having to maneuver skillfully between the stand-patters opposed to any

democratization, on the one hand, and the committed dissident and opposition groups demanding the immediate dissolution of the authoritarian system, on the other. Essential to their success is that they be seen as keeping control, acting from a position of strength and not under duress, and dictating the pace of change.

The replacement process requires compromise and agreement among elites who have not been part of the authoritarian regime. The transformation process requires skilled leadership from and agreement among the elites who are part of that regime. In neither case is agreement necessarily required between elites who are within the regime and those opposing the regime. This situation makes replacement and transformation possible, since reaching an agreement between out-groups and in-groups is far more difficult than reaching an agreement among out-groups or among in-groups. Except for Costa Rica in 1948, it is hard to think of a case where a democratic system of any duration was inaugurated by explicit agreement between the leaders of a regime and the leaders of the armed opposition to that regime.

"As long as powerful vested interests oppose changes that lead toward a less oppressive world," Barrington Moore has argued, "no commitment to a free society can dispense with some conception of revolutionary coercion."[39] His thesis is that liberty and democracy can be inaugurated by bloody revolution and that such a course may well impose fewer costs than the alternative of gradual reform. When in world history, however, has violent revolution produced a stable democratic regime in an independent state? "Revolutionary coercion" may bring down an authoritarian regime, but, except again for Costa Rica in 1948, guerrilla insurgencies do not inaugurate democratic regimes. All revolutionary opponents of authoritarian regimes claim to be democrats; once they achieve power through violence, almost all turn out to be authoritarian themselves, often imposing an even more repressive regime than the one they overthrew. Most authoritarian regimes are thus replaced by new authoritarian regimes, and a democratic succession usually requires minimum violence. "In the future as in the past," as Dahl concluded his study of this issue, "stable polyarchies and near-polyarchies are more likely to result from rather slow evolutionary processes than from revolutionary overthrow of existing hegemonies.[40]

## THE PROSPECTS FOR DEMOCRACY

This brief and informal survey of the preconditions and processes conducive to the emergence of democratic regimes argues for caution in any effort to predict whether more countries will become democratic. It may, however, be useful to attempt to sum up the modest conclusions which seem to emerge from this review.

With respect to preconditions, the emergence of democracy in a society is helped by a number of factors: higher levels of economic well-being; the absence of extreme inequalities in wealth and income; greater social pluralism, including particularly a strong and autonomous bourgeoisie; a more market-oriented economy; greater influence vis-á-vis the society of existing democratic states; and a culture that is less monistic and more tolerant of diversity and compromise. No one of these preconditions is sufficient to lead to democratic development. With the possible exception of a market economy, no single precondition is necessary to produce such development. Some combination of some of these preconditions is required for a democratic regime to emerge, but the nature of that combination can vary greatly from one case to another. It is also necessary, however, to look not only at what preconditions must be present but also at the negative strength of any precondition that may be absent. The powerful absence of one favorable condition, or, conversely, the presence of a powerful negative condition, that overrides the presence of otherwise favorable conditions, may prevent democratic development. In terms of cultural tradition, economic development, and social structure, Czechoslovakia would certainly be a

democracy today (and probably Hungary and Poland also) if it were not for the overriding veto of the Soviet presence. In similar fashion, extreme poverty, extreme economic inequalities, or deeply ingrained Islamic and Confucian cultural traditions could have comparable effect in Africa, Central America, or the Middle East and East Asia.

With respect to the processes necessary to bring about democratic development, a central requirement would appear to be that either the established elites within an authoritarian system or the successor elites after an authoritarian system collapses see their interests served by the introduction of democratic institutions. The probability of stable democracy emerging will be enhanced to the extent that the transition can be a gradual one, that the introduction of contestation precedes the expansion of political participation, and that the role of violence in the transition is minimized. The probability of democratization decreases sharply to the extent that political life in a society becomes highly polarized and involves violent conflict between social forces.

### Possibility of Regime Changes

In terms of these generalizations, prospects for democratic development in the 1980s are probably greatest in the bureaucratic-authoritarian states of South America. Cultural traditions, levels of economic development, previous democratic experience, social pluralism (albeit with weak bourgeoisies outside Brazil), and elite desires to emulate European and North American models all favor movement toward democracy in these countries. On the other hand, the polarization and violence that has occurred (particularly in Argentina and Chile) could make such movement difficult. The prospects for a relatively stable democratic system should be greatest in Brazil. Beginning in the early 1970s, the leadership of the Brazilian regime began a process of distensão, gradually relaxing the authoritarian controls that had been imposed in the 1960s. By the early 1980s, Brazil had acquired many of the characteristics of a democratic system. The principal deficiency was the absence of popular elections for the chief executive, but those were generally viewed as certain to come sometime in the 1980s. The gradualness of the Brazilian process, the relative low level of violence that accompanied it, and the general recognition among elite groups of the importance of not disrupting it in any way, all seemed to enhance the prospects for democracy.

In Argentina, the economic and military failures of the authoritarian regime led to a much more dramatic and rapid transit to democracy in 1983. The probabilities of this replacement being sustained would seem to depend on three factors: the ability of the Alfonsin government to deal with the economic problems it confronted; the extent to which Peronista, as well as Radical, elites were willing to abide by democratic rules; and the extent to which military leadershp was effectively excluded from power or came to identify its interests with the maintenance of a democratic regime. The two other southern cone countries with bureaucratic-authoritarian regimes, Chile and Uruguay, are the two South American countries that did have the strongest democratic traditions. As of 1984, however, in neither country had authoritarian rule lost its legitimacy and effectiveness to the point where it could no longer be maintained and a replacement process could occur (as in Argentina). Nor had the leaders of either regime embarked on a meaningful tranformation process to democratize their system (as in Brazil). The Brazilian and Argentine changes, however, cannot fail to have impact on political development in the smaller countries.

The probability of movement in a democratic direction in the East Asian newly industrializing countries is considerably less than it is among the Latin American B-A states. The economic basis for democracy is clearly coming into existence, and if their economic development continues at anything like the rates it did in the 1960s and 1970s, these states will soon constitute an authoritarian anomaly among the wealthier countries of the world. The East Asian countries generally have also had and maintained a relatively equal distribution of income. In addition, the United States, Britain, and Japan are the principal external influences on these societies. All these factors favor democratic development. On the other side, cultural traditions, social structure, and a general weakness of democratic norms among key elites all impede movement in a democratic direction. In some measure, the East Asian states dramatically pose the issue of whether economics or culture has the greater influence on political development. One can also speculate on whether the spread of Christianity in Korea may create a cultural context more favorable to democracy.

Among other less economically developed East Asian societies, the prospects for democracy are undoubtedly highest but still not very high in the Philippines. The Marcos government is not likely to attempt to transform itself, and hence efforts to create a democratic system must await its demise. At that time, American influence, previous experience with democracy, social pluralism (including the influence of the Catholic Church), and the general agreement among opposition political leaders on the desirability of a return to democracy, should all provide support for movement in that direction. On the other hand, military leaders may not support democratic norms, and the existence of a radical insurgency committed to violence, plus a general proclivity to the use of violence in the society, might make such a transition difficult. Conceivably, Philippine development could follow the lines of the dialectical model referred to earlier, in which (as in Venezuela) an initial experience with democracy is broken by a personalistic authoritarian interlude that then collapses and a new, more stable democratic regime is brought into existence by agreement among political leaders. The Philippine Betancourt, however, may well have been gunned down at the Manila airport.

Among Islamic countries, particularly those in the Middle East, the prospects for democratic development seem low. The Islamic revival, and particularly the rise of Shi'ite fundamentalism, would seem to reduce even further the likelihood of democratic development, particularly since democracy is often identified with the very Western influences the revival strongly opposes. In addition, many of the Islamic states are very poor. Those that are rich, on the other hand, are so because of oil, which is controlled by the state and hence enhances the power of the state in general and of the bureaucracy in particular. Saudi Arabia and some of the smaller Arab oil-rich Gulf countries have from time to time made some modest gestures toward the introduction of democratic institutions, but these have not gone far and have often been reversed.

Most African countries are, by reason of their poverty or the violence of their politics, unlikely to move in a democratic direction. Those African and Latin American countries that have adhered to the cyclical pattern of alternating democratic and authoritarian systems in the past are not likely to change this basic pattern, as the example of Nigeria underlines, unless more fundamental changes occur in their economic and social infrastructure. In South Africa, on the other hand, the relatively high level of economic development by African standards, the intense contestation that occurs within the minority permitted to participate in politics, the modest expansion of that minority to include the Coloureds and Asians, and the influence of Western democratic norms, all provide a basis for moving in a more democratic direction. However, that basis is countered on the other side by the inequalities, fears, and hatreds that separate blacks and whites.

In some small countries, democratic institutions may emerge as a result of massive foreign effort. This did happen in the Dominican Republic; in 1984 it was, presumably, happening in Grenada; it could, conceivably, happen at extremely high cost in El Salvador.

The likelihood of democratic development in Eastern Europe is virtually nil. The Soviet presence is a decisive overriding obstacle, no matter how favorable other conditions may be in countries like Czechoslovakia, Hungary, and Poland. Democratization could occur in these societies only if either the Soviet Union were drastically weakened through war, domestic upheaval, or economic collapse (none of which seems likely), or if the Soviet Union came to view Eastern European democratization as not threatening to its interests (which seems equally unlikely).

The issue of Soviet intervention apart, a more general issue concerns the domestic pattern of evolution within Communist states. For almost four decades after World War II, no democratic country, with the dubious possible exception of Czechoslovakia in 1948, became Communist and no Communist country became democratic through internal causes. Authoritarian regimes, on the other hand, were frequently replaced by either democratic or Communist regimes, and democratic regimes were replaced by authoritarian ones. In their early phase, Communist states usually approximated the totalitarian model, with ideology and the party playing central roles and massive efforts being made to indoctrinate and mobilize the population and to extend party control throughout all institutions in the society. Over time, however, Communist regimes also tend to change and often to become less totalitarian and more authoritarian. The importance of ideology and mobilization declines, bureaucratic stagnation replaces ideological fervor, and the party becomes less a dedicated elite and more a mechanism for patronage. In some cases, military influence increases significantly. The question thus arises: Will Communist authoritarian regimes, absent Soviet control, be more susceptible to movement toward democracy than Communist totalitarian regimes?

The answer to that question may well depend on the extent to which Communist authoritarian regimes permit the development of a market-oriented economy. The basic thrust of communism suggests that such a development is unlikely. Communism is not, as Karl Marx argued, a product of capitalist democracy; nor is it simply a "disease of the transition" to capitalist democracy, to use Rostow's phrase.[41] It is instead an alternative to capitalist democracy and one whose guiding principle is the subjection of economic devolopment to political control. Even if it becomes more authoritarian and less totalitarian, the Communist political system is likely to ensure that economic development neither achieves a level nor assumes a form that will be conducive to democracy.

## The United States and Global Democracy

The ability of the United States to affect the development of democracy elsewhere is limited. There is little that the United States or any other foreign country can do to alter the basic cultural tradition and social structure of another society or to promote compromise among groups of that society that have been killing each other. Within the restricted limits of the possible, however, the United States could contribute to democratic development in other countries in four ways.

First, it can assist the economic development of poor countries and promote a more equitable distribution of income and wealth in those countries. Second, it can encourage developing countries to foster market economies and the development of vigorous bourgeois classes. Third, it can refurbish its own economic, military, and political power so as to be able to exercise greater influence than it has in world affairs. Finally, it can develop a concerted program designed to encourage and to help the elites of countries entering the "transition zone" to move their countries in a more democratic direction.

Efforts such as these could have a modest influence on the development of democracy in other countries. Overall, however, this survey of the preconditions for and processes of democratization leads to the conclusion that, with a few exceptions, the prospects for the extension of democracy to other societies are not great. These prospects would improve significantly only if there were major discontinuities in current trends—such as if, for instance, the economic development of the Third World were to proceed at a much faster rate and to have a far more positive impact on democratic development than it has had so far, or if the United States reestablished a hegemonic position in the world comparable to that which it had in the 1940s and 1950s. In the absence of developments such as these, a significant increase in the number of democratic regimes in the world is unlikely. The substantial power of anti-democratic governments (particularly the Soviet Union), the unreceptivity to democracy of several major cultural traditions, the difficulties of eliminating poverty in large parts of the world, and the prevalence of high levels of polarization and violence in many societies all suggest that, with a few exceptions, the limits of democratic development in the world may well have been reached.

## Notes

1. Michael W. Doyle, "Kant, Liberal Legacies, and Foreign Affairs, Part I," *Philosophy and Public Affairs* 12 (1983), pp. 213ff.

2. Peter Bachrach, *The Theory of Democratic Elitism: A Critique* (Washington, D.C.: University Press of America, 1980), pp. 24, 98ff.; Robert A. Dahl, *Polyarchy: Participation and Opposition* (New Haven: Yale University Press, 1971), p. 2. For a useful analysis of "rationalist" and "descriptive" concepts of democracy, see Jeane J. Kirkpatrick, "Democratic Elections, Democratic Government, and Democratic Theory," in *Democracy at the Polls*, ed. David Butler, Howard R. Penniman, and Austin Ranney (Washington, D.C.: American Enterprise Institute for Public Policy Research, 1981), pp. 325–348.

3. Dahl, *Polyarchy*, pp. 4–9. See also Joseph A. Schumpeter, *Capitalism, Socialism, and Democracy*, 2d ed. (New York: Harper & Row, 1947), p. 269: "The democratic method is that institutional arrangement for arriving at political decisions in which individuals acquire the power to decide by means of a competitive struggle for the people's vote."

4. James Bryce, *Modern Democracies*, 2 vols. (New York: Macmillan, 1921), vol. 1, p. 24.

5. The proportion of independent states that were democratic was roughly 19 percent in 1902, 34 percent in 1920, 32 percent in 1929–30, and 24 percent in 1960. See G. Bingham Powell, Jr., *Contemporary Democracies* (Cambridge, Mass.: Harvard University Press, 1982), p. 238.

6. See "The Comparative Survey of Freedom" compiled annually for Freedom House, [a private research organization in New York City], by Raymond D. Gastil, particularly *Freedom at Issue*, no. 17 (1973), pp. 2–3; no. 70 (1983), p. 4; no. 76 (1984), p. 5. Freedom House classifies a state as "free" if it rates in first or second place on a seven-place scale for both political rights and civil liberties. The countries so classified all have the minimum features of a democratic political system, at least at the time of classification. While recognizing the importance of institutionalization, the Freedom House survey does not attempt to measure the extent to which democracy has become institutionalized. Thus, its 1984 survey, published at the very beginning of 1984, rated both New Zealand and Nigeria as "free," although the latter had presumably left the category as a result of the coup on New Year's Day.

7. Dankwart A. Rustow, "Transitions to Democracy: Toward a Dynamic Model," *Comparative Politics* 2 (1970), p. 337ff.

8. Seymour Martin Lipset, "Some Social Requisites of Democracy: Economic Development and Political Legitimacy," *American Political Science Review* 53 (1959), p. 75.

9. James S. Coleman, "Conclusion," in *The Politics of the Developing Areas*, ed. Gabriel A. Almond and James S. Coleman (Princeton: Princeton University Press, 1960), p. 538.

10. World Bank, *World Development Report 1981* (New York: Oxford University Press, 1981), pp. 134–135; and *Freedom at Issue*, no. 64 (1982), pp. 8–9. See also Seymour Martin Lipset's update of his earlier analysis, *Political Man: The Social Bases of Politics*, 2d ed. (Baltimore: The Johns Hopkins University Press, 1981), pp. 469–476.

11. This is not to argue that authoritarian regimes necessarily have higher economic growth rates than democratic ones, although they may. See Robert M. Marsh, "Does Democracy Hinder Economic Development in the Latecomer Developing Nations," *Comparative Social Research* 2 (1979), pp. 215–248; G. William Dick, "Authoritarian Versus Nonauthoritarian Approaches to Economic Development," *Journal of Political Economy* 82 (1974), pp 817–827; and Erich Weede, "Political Democracy, State Strength and Economic Growth in LDCs: A Cross-National Analysis," (Paper presented at the Annual Meeting of the American Political Science Association, Chicago, Ill., September 1983).

12. Jonathan Sunshine, "Economic Causes and Consequences of Democracy: A Study in Historical Statistics" (Ph.D. diss., Columbia University, 1972), p. 115ff.

13. John F. Coverdale, *The Political Transformation of Spain after Franco* (New York: Praeger Publishers, 1979), p. 1.

14. Guillermo A. O'Donnell, *Modernization and Bureaucratic-Authoritarianism: Studies in Latin American Politics* (Berkeley: University of California, Institute for International Studies, 1973), pp. 3–15, 113–114. For analysis of this theory, see David Collier, ed., *The New Authoritarianism in Latin America* (Princeton: Princeton University Press, 1979).

15. World Bank, *Development Report 1981*, pp. 134–135, and *World Development Report 1983* (New York: Oxford University Press, 1983), pp. 148–149.

16. Those who hold a more Rousseauistic conception of democracy will, of course, tend to see intermediate groups as obstacles to the realization of true democracy. For a balanced analysis of these issues, see Robert A. Dahl, *Dilemmas of Pluralist Democracy: Autonomy vs. Control* (New Haven: Yale University Press, 1982). For a general argument for intermediate groups as a bulwark against totalitarianism, see William Kornhauser, *The Politics of Mass Society* (New York: Free Press, 1959).

17. See Lloyd I. and Susanne Hoeber Rudolph, *The Modernity of Tradition: Political Development in India* (Chicago: University of Chicago Press, 1967), passim.

18. For elaboration of these themes, see among others: Louis Hartz, *The Liberal Tradition in America* (New York: Harcourt Brace Jovanovich, 1955), and Louis Hartz, ed., *The Founding of New Societies* (New York: Harcourt Brace Jovanovich, 1964), especially chap. V, Richard M. Morse, "The Heritage of Latin America"; James M. Malloy, ed., *Authoritarianism and Corporatism in Latin America* (Pittsburgh: University of Pittsburgh Press, 1977); Howard J. Wiarda, "Toward a Framework for the Study of Political Change in the Iberio-Latin Tradition," *World Politics* 25 (1973), pp. 206–235; Claudio Veliz, *The Centralist Tradition of Latin America* (Princeton: Princeton University Press, 1979).

19. Barrington Moore, Jr., *Social Origins of Dictatorship and Democracy* (Boston: Beacon Press, 1966), p. 418.

20. Charles E. Lindblom, *Politics and Markets* (New York: Basic Books, 1977), pp. 161–169.

21. See primarily the works of Arend Lijphart, particularly *The Politics of Accommodation: Pluralism and Democracy in the Netherlands*, 2d ed. (Berkeley: University of California Press, 1975) and *Democracy in Plural Societies: A Comparative Evaluation* (New Haven: Yale University Press, 1977).

22. *Freedom at Issue*, no. 76 (1984), pp. 8–9.

23. Myron Weiner, "Empirical Democratic Theory," in *Comparative Elections in Developing Countries*, ed. Myron Weiner and Ergun Ozbudun (Washington, D.C.: American Enterprise Institute, manuscript, 26 [italics in original]).

24. Samuel P. Huntington, *American Politics: The Promise of Disharmony* (Cambridge, Mass.: Harvard University Press, 1981), pp. 246–259.

25. Sidney Verba, "Comparative Political Culture," in *Political Culture and Political Development*, ed. Lucian W. Pye and Sidney Verba (Princeton: Princeton University Press, 1965), p. 513.

26. For the statistical correlation between Protestantism and democracy, see Kenneth A. Bollen, "Political Democracy and the Timing of Development," *American Sociological Review* 44 (1979), pp. 572–587.

27. See Daniel Pipes, *In the Path of God: Islam and Political Power* (New York: Basic Books, 1983), pp. 48–69, 144–147.

28. David E. Apter, *The Politics of Modernization* (Chicago: University of Chicago Press, 1965), p. 85.

29. S. N. Eisenstadt, "Transformation of Social, Political and Cultural Orders in Modernization," *American Sociological Review* 30 (1965), p. 668. In contrast to the Hindu tradition, Eisenstadt writes, "the identity between political and religious communities represents a very important similarity between the Chinese and Islamic societies" (p. 663).

30. See Pye and Verba, *Political Culture*; Dahl, *Polyarchy*, pp. 124–187; Gabriel A. Almond and Sidney Verba, *The Civic Culture* (Princeton: Princeton University Press, 1963); David McClelland, *The Achieving Society* (New York: Van Nostrand Reinhold, 1961).

31. For arguments on the priority of democratic values, see the case Dahl makes on Argentina, *Polyarchy*, pp.132–140, and Jonathan Tumin's amendment of Barrington Moore in "The Theory of Democratic Development: A Critical Revision," *Theory and Society* 11 (1982), pp. 143–164.

32. Rustow, "Transitions to Democracy," p. 361.

33. Samuel P. Huntington, *Political Order in Changing Societies* (New Haven: Yale University Press, 1968), pp. 72–78.

34. Eric A. Nordlinger, "Political Development: Time Sequences and Rates of Change," *World Politics* 20 (1968), pp. 494–530; Dankwart A. Rustow, *A World of Nations* (Washington, D.C.: Brookings Institution, 1967), p. 126ff.; Leonard Binder et al., *Crises and Sequences in Political Development* (Princeton: Princeton University Press, 1971), pp. 310–313.

35. Dahl, *Polyarchy*, pp. 33–40; Huntington, *Political Order*, esp. pp. 32–59, 78–92. See also Richard A. Pride, *Origins of Democracy: A Cross-National Study of Mobilization, Party Systems, and Democratic Stability*, Comparative Politics Series, Vol. 1, (Newbury Park, Calif.: Sage Publications, 1970).

36. Rustow, "Transitions to Democracy," pp. 355–357

37. John H. Herz, "On Reestablishing Democracy after the Downfall of Authoritarian or Dictatorial Regimes," *Comparative Politics* 10 (1978), pp. 559–562.

38. Juan Linz, "Crisis, Breakdown, and Reequilibration," in *The Breakdown of Democratic Regimes*, ed. Juan Linz and Alfred Stepan, (Baltimore: The Johns Hopkins University Press, 1978), p. 35.

39. Moore, *Social Origins*, p. 508.

40. Dahl, *Polyarchy*, p. 45.

41. Walt, W. Rostow, *The Stages of Economic Growth* (Cambridge: Cambridge University Press, 1960), p. 162.

# 10

# Democracy in Africa

*Richard L. Sklar*

I am often asked to explain what possessed me, a white American political scientist, to undertake African studies. Usually, I reflect upon my state of mind in the mid-1950s and mention the allure of a new horizon for democracy, limned by the doctrine of self-determination for subject peoples. Even then, however, realists warned that democracy in Africa, as in Asia, would bleed and die on the altars of national consolidation and social reconstruction.[1] But democracy dies hard. Its vital force is the accountability of rulers to their subjects. Democracy stirs and wakens from the deepest slumber whenever the principle of accountability is asserted by members of a community or conceded by those who rule. Democracy cannot be destroyed by a coup d'etat; it will survive every legal assault upon political liberty. The true executioner of

SOURCE: Richard L. Sklar, "Democracy in Africa," Presidential address to the African Studies Association, 1982, *African Studies Review 26*, nos. 3/4 (September–December 1983), pp. 11–24. Reprinted by permission of the African Studies Association and the author. Notes and references abridged by the editors.

democracy has neither sword nor scepter, but a baneful idea. Ironically, the deadly agent is an idea about freedom.

In Africa today, freedom from want is a universal goal. Millions of lives are blighted by the effects of poverty, unemployment, malnutrition, untended illness, and inadequate education. In all countries, political leaders dedicate themselves to the cause of economic and social development. Most leaders also claim to respect the principle of accountability to the people. However, the imperatives of development are far more demanding than the claims of democracy. Appalled by the human condition and waste of resources in Africa and other nonindustrial regions, many intellectuals proclaim the validity of an antidemocratic idea, to which the term "developmental dictatorship" is aptly applied.

According to A. James Gregor the principles of developmental dictatorship were first formulated by Italian Marxists during the course of intense theoretical debates before the outbreak of World War One.[2] Eventually, they came to understand that orthodox Marxism was not relevant to the social realities of their underdeveloped country. Left to itself, they reasoned, the feeble Italian bourgeoisie, fettered by its dependence upon foreign capitalists, would not create an industrial society. Fatefully, they forsook the ideal of proletarian internationalism and embraced statist nationalism in order to mobilize all talents and resources for a program of forced and rapid industrialization. With heretical abandon, they entrusted responsibility for the direction of events to an "audacious minority" or "vanguard elite."[3] Faced with a similar predicament in the 1920s, the postcapitalist regime in Moscow adopted a similar nationalist and statist strategy. Ever since, national struggles to overcome economic backwardness in many parts of the world have been intensified if not actually led by proponents of developmental dictatorship.

The hardships of developmental dictatorship are well known: liberty is suppressed; labor is regimented and exploited; freedom of movement is curtailed; personal choice is severely restricted. From his pre-revolutionary vantage point, Karl Marx advised his readers to anticipate painful transitions or "birth pangs," during the creation of new social orders. "The country that is more developed industrially only shows, to the less developed, the image of its own future." [4] Must we, now, believe that Africa, rid of external rule but bowed-down in social and economic agony, with burgeoning populations and a dearth of jobs, should or will resort en masse and in extremis to developmental dictatorship? Shall we avert our eyes from an unforeseen alternative and disregard an abundance of evidence for the thesis that Africa today is a veritable workshop of democracy?

Democracy in Africa is as varied as the ever-changing forms of government in more than 50 sovereign states. Democracy in Africa is an experimental process in a new generation of countries. We should study this process not only to learn about Africa, but also to refresh our knowledge about the meaning of democracy itself. As the African philosopher, Edward Wilmot Blyden, might have said, in our time, these experiments in democracy constitute "Africa's service to the world." [5]

For this assessment of democracy in Africa, I have distinguished four existing types at the level of national government and one other which has been proposed. The first type is liberal democracy, wherein the powers of government are limited by law and citizens enjoy freedom of association to compete for office in free elections at regular intervals. Numerous liberal democracies were bequeathed to Africa by the former colonial rulers; all but a few of them, however, were rudely swept away by military coups, political usurpations, and constitutional changes shortly after (or within a decade of) independence. A few hardier breeds of liberal democracy have been planted and nurtured by African statesmen themselves.

At the present time, one person in five on the continent of Africa lives in a truly liberal democracy with genuine freedom of expression and freedom of political association. (Among black Africans the percentage is higher: one in four.) The citizens of liberal democracies include an estimated 100 million Nigerians plus the citizens of five other states, namely, Botswana, The Gambia, Mauritius, Senegal, and Zimbabwe. However, the serious qualifications to which this observation is liable underscore the experimental and highly contingent nature of liberal democracy in Africa.

During the past two years, ventures in liberal democracy have been aborted by paternalistic military guardians in Upper Volta, (arguably) the Central African Republic, and Ghana. At present, liberal democracy lingers in Zimbabwe, but the political leaders of that country have expressed their strong preference for a democracy without party competition. Until the electoral victory of Mauritian socialists in June 1982, no national government in an independent African state had ever been transferred to an opposition by electoral means. Confirming the historic importance of this event, the Mauritian socialists have pledged to strengthen a constitutional guarantee of free elections at regular intervals. In the Gambia, liberal democracy nearly succumbed to an insurrection in July 1981. It has since been fortified by the establishment of a confederation with a protective sister-republic, Senegal. Since the retirement of President Léopold Sédar Senghor in January 1981, Senegal has emerged as a full-fledged liberal democracy. President Abdou Diouf leads a moderate socialist party which enjoys a commanding majority in the national assembly. The party is also a haven for conservative and parasitical interest groups. To rejuvenate this party for the urgent tasks of economic reconstruction, and to defuse a potentially revolutionary opposition, President Diouf has opened the door of legality to all political parties. Inevitably, the opposition parties sparkle, like the fragments of a Roman candle, in splendid sectarian isolation. Diouf's open air treatment of illiberal dissent is a milestone for democratic socialists in Africa.

Given the large number of sovereign entities in today's Africa, and the preponderance of illiberal governments, the crucial accounting for

African liberal democracy must be rendered in populous Nigeria. Scholars have pondered and variously explained the remarkable resilience of constitutional liberty in Nigerian government. Without prejudice to the importance of other explanations, notably the influence of indigenous constitutional traditions, I am particularly impressed by the impact of federalism upon Nigerian political thought. While the number of states in Nigeria's federation has varied and remains contentious, federalism per se is an article of national faith, the virtually unquestioned premise of national unity. It is instructive to recall that federalism was a shared value for rival nationalists during the colonial era;[6] it was the indispensable basis for Nigerian unity under military rule, when the threat of national disintegration loomed large. At present, nineteen states accommodate a richly textured and wondrously complex tapestry of democratic political life.

Truly federal governments are necessarily liberal governments, predicated on the division and restraint of power. In Nigeria, the rights of citizens and constituent states alike are protected by a staunchly independent judiciary. In fact, Nigeria is an exceptionally legalistic society; many political issues of great moment are finally resolved in the courts, for example, the outcome of the 1979 presidential election. Nor did the courts lose their vitality under military rule. Shorn, temporarily, of their formal constitutional independence, the judges still retained their authority in the states, where, in the words of a legal scholar, they performed "prodigious feats of courage" defending the rights of citizens.[7] Should constitutional government in Nigeria be suppressed once again, the potential for its early revival would be preserved by federalism, the legal profession, and the determined practice of judicial independence.

Despite its apparent vigor, liberal democracy in Nigeria is debilitated by the effects of economic anarchy and social distemper. A small minority of the population is conspicuously wealthy and privileged while the vast majority seethes with discontent. Keepers of the national conscience frequently deplore the plunder and waste of Nigeria's wealth by corrupt officials in collusion with unscrupulous businessmen. Scholars discern the portents of revolutionary mass action, particularly in the northern states, where class conflict is pronounced.[8] Disillusioned intellectuals renounce democracy and urge the merits of developmental dictatorship in one form or another. Both the Leninist and the corporatist, or Brazilian, versions have their advocates. In Nigeria, as in Senegal, liberal democracy is democracy with tears and many reservations.

A second type of democracy in Africa accepts the principle that rulers should be accountable to their subjects but dispenses with the political method of multiparty electoral competition. I shall adopt the term guided democracy for this type of government by guardians of the public weal who insist upon political uniformity. Guided democracy is, to be sure, a form of developmental dictatorship; it is classified separately because the other forms of developmental dictatorship make little or no pretense of accountability to the people on the part of exalted persons or national saviors.

The late President Jomo Kenyatta of Kenya was one of a number of African presidents who have ruled beyond the reach of accountability. When he died, in 1978, the barons of Kenyan politics and society could not imagine, nor would they have tolerated, another episode of such highly personal rule. Kenya had become a de facto one-party state in 1969, when the sole opposition party was banned. Yet the one-party political process in that country has been highly competitive; the triumphal party itself has been described as a "confederation of arenas" where the bosses of rural factions "collide" and "collude" in their "perennial struggle" for power.[9] Survey research on the electoral process tells of a well informed electorate which imposes the norm of accountability upon its representatives; for example, in 1979, 45 percent of the incumbent members of Parliament were defeated at the polls.[10] When, in 1982, Kenya became a one-party state de jure, her commitment to guided rather than liberal democracy was decisively confirmed.

During the course of a purely formal parliamentary debate on the establishment of a one-party state, the Vice-President, Mr. Mwai Kibaki, explained that constitutional change was needed to preclude the election of persons who would favor experiments based upon Marxist theories. Such theories, he argued, have been disproved by the poor economic performances of communist systems.[11] This kind of reasoning, from a different ideological perspective, is used by the leaders of those authoritarian regimes which have socialist orientations to preclude the practical advocacy of capitalist ideas. In such cases, political monopolies are justified by persons who assert the moral necessity or scientific truth of an official doctrine, e.g., "Humanism" in Zambia, the "Third Universal Theory" in Libya, and Marxism-Leninism in several countries.

The touchstone of guided democracy is the existence and operation of a political mechanism which can be expected to ensure the accountability of rulers to the people. Various developmental dictatorships in Africa, both capitalist and socialist, do not pass muster as guided democracies because their leaders rule without regard to the principle of accountability. Those which do qualify as guided democracies include a variety of political forms and ideological orientations. Some, such as Guinea-Bissau, Tanzania, and (arguably) Zambia, have mass-mobilizing parties with open memberships. Others, including Congo People's Republic, Angola, and Mozambique, have created Leninist parties with doctrinal restrictions on membership and statutes on the required accountability of leaders. In these and other instances of one-party or, as in Libya, no-party rule, the degree of democracy varies with the intensity of passion for political accountability and its effective enforcement.

In socialist thought, the concept of democracy extends beyond the precept of accountability to the idea of social justice. From that perspective, democracy implies the effective pursuit of an egalitarian social order in addition to a government which is accountable to the people. For the principal instance of social democracy (my third type for this survey) in Africa I turn, necessarily, to Tanzania.

Ever since the famous Arusha Declaration of 1967, the Tanzanian Government has endeavored to minimize social inequality and to counteract various tendencies toward class division. In the commentaries of President Julius K. Nyerere, two aspects of the quest for social equality are strongly emphasized: first, the problem of privilege, or differentials in both personal consuming power and access to public services; second, the importance of popular participation in the decision-making processes of both political and economic organizations. On the first count, impressive achievements have been recorded in reducing income differentials and providing economic, educational, health, and other essential services to the public at large. Furthermore, the conversion of public trust into personal wealth has been checked by progressive taxation, lean salary scales for the administrators of public agencies, and the enforcement of a socialist code of conduct for leaders and officials.

On the second count, that of progress toward popular and democratic participation in governmental and economic decision-making, Tanzania's record is more difficult to assess. In 1967, the sole legal party accepted an historic challenge: to build socialism in an agrarian country without resorting to coercive methods of collectivization. At the same time, every effort would be made to raise the standard of living and enhance the quality of life in peasant and working class communities. However, the vast majority of rural dwellers did not respond favorably to the party's call for collectivization on a voluntary basis. Finally, at the end of its patience, the government used compulsion to move and resettle millions of peasants from their dispersed homes and farms into clustered villages between 1974 and 1976. That process, known as "villagization," has made it possible for the government to reach the entire rural population with basic services. However, the related aim of socialist farming—the collectivization of production—

was, at first, deemphasized and then virtually abandoned in the face of peasant resistance, a food crisis, and the critical views of potential donors, notably the World Bank, at a time of dire need for foreign aid.

Suddenly, the socialist venture in Tanzania was awash in a sea of academic and intellectual doubt. Could rural socialism be reconciled with an acceptable level of agricultural efficiency? Had the socialist venture been sabotaged by non- or pseudo-socialist officials and their class allies in concert with antisocialist foreign powers? Those who seek honest answers to these hard questions and still believe in the viability of socialist policies in Tanzania have set great store by the party's avowed commitment to popular and democratic participation in economic and political life. They also view with concern the lack of evidence to show that workers and peasants participate effectively in the formulation and adoption of public policies. At the center of power, the ruling party itself sets a decisive example for all other institutions. In his empathetic assessment of party life, Cranford Pratt finds an "oligarchic" and "profound bias against any opposition to the leadership." [12]

If, as Nyerere maintains, democratic participation is a cornerstone of social equality, sincere socialists cannnot disregard the inevitably repressive effects of legal barriers to freedom of association. Socialists of participative conviction cannot sidestep a pluralist question: Is democratic participation viable in a one-party state, where political competition is severely restricted by the virtual elimination of group rights to pursue self-determined political aims? This question, which reflects the liberal critique of guided democracy, has engaged the attention of intellectuals in several other African countries where the search for social democracy is less resolute than it has been in Tanzania. An illuminating example is the constitutional declaration of a "One-party Participatory Democracy" in Zambia. It signifies experimentation with a fourth, familiar but elusive, type of democracy, namely, participatory democracy.

The theory of participatory democracy is a product of the current era. It affirms the existence of a reciprocal relationship between democratic political institutions and participative social institutions, with particular emphasis upon the educative effects of democratic participation in the workplace.[13] In Zambia, the concept of participatory democracy was introduced as a national goal by President Kenneth D. Kaunda in 1968. Subsequently, Kaunda construed the concept to connote democratic participation in all spheres of life, so that "no single individual or group of individuals shall have a monopoly of political, economic, social or military power." To his mind, the public interest suffers when politicians monopolize political power, or soldiers monopolize military power, or intellectuals and technocrats monopolize knowledge, or publishers and writers monopolize the power of the pen, or workers monopolize power through strikes, or chiefs monopolize the power of tradition. In the near future, he forecast, participatory democracy would be practiced in all Zambian institutions, including the civil service and the army.

Objectively considered, however, the record of participatory democracy in Zambia has fallen far short of Kaunda's expectations. Careful studies attest to the very low levels of popular attachment to, or involvment in, participatory institutions in rural Zambia. The sole legal party has dwindled to fewer than 5 percent of the population despite its availability to Zambians without restriction. A "commandist" and "paternalistic" style of administration at the local level is magnified at the national level by a domineering office of the president. As William Tordoff observes, "Ironically, no one emphasizes the virtues of participatory democracy more than the President himself, yet his own style of increasingly personalized decision-making renders its realization difficult." [14] As in Tanzania, the party-state in Zambia abhors the very idea of political pluralism. Yet the Zambian government, unlike the Tanzanian, must contend with a formidable and resourceful labor movement; indeed, the Mineworkers Union of Zambia, 60,000 strong, has never accepted the hegemony of the party in the sphere of industrial relations.

Its long-term struggle for autonomy from an imperious government lies at the very heart of conflict in Zambian politics.

Truly democratic participation is self-motivated and self-determined; it is not coerced. In Africa, participatory democracy implies a commitment to the self-motivated assertion of peasant and working class interests in political affairs. But the Zambian leadership has tried to induce popular participation into channels which would be controlled by a monopolistic political party. From a democratic standpoint, however, induced participation comes close to being a contradiction in terms; indeed it is a form of coercion. And it has been rejected by the Zambian workers and peasants.

In 1981, following a spate of wildcat strikes, four leaders of the labor movement, including the chairman and secretary-general of the Zambia Congress of Trade Unions, and an eventually successful aspirant for the presidency of the Mineworkers' Union, were detained for nearly three months on charges of plotting against the government. Announcing this action, Kaunda accused the labor leadership of capitalist deviations. In 1982, Kaunda turned a corner in his personal ideology. Much to the amazement of Kaunda-watchers, most of whom were confident of his apparently unshakable commitment to nondoctrinaire "humanist" socialism, he decided that Zambia's official ideology should be Marxist (or "scientific") socialism. But this is not, after all, an arbitrary choice. Scientific socialism marks a strictly logical progression in ideology for a ruling group of socialist inclination which intends to control the working class. It also signifies the maturation of basic tendencies toward an undiluted developmental dictatorship in Zambia.

As a result of Kaunda's ideological demarche, the beleaguered labor movement has acquired a powerful ally in its bid for autonomy, namely the interdenominational Christian Council of Zambia. Following his release from detention, Frederick Chiluba, chairman of the Congress of Trade Unions, is reported to have "made a point of going to church almost every day." As in Poland, the struggle for participatory democracy in Zambia has forged an alliance between two social institutions which are second to none other in popularity, namely the labor movement and the churches. Like his Polish counterpart, Lech Walesa, Chiluba stands for participatory democracy from without, rather than from within, the party.

In Zambia, as in Tanzania, the acid test for participatory democracy is the attitude of the national leadership toward self-assertion by the working class and the peasantry. Neither regime has passed that test; each has chosen to promote induced, rather than spontaneous, participation. It may be instructive to contrast these instances with the noteworthy practice of worker self-management in Algeria, inaugurated spontaneously by urban and rural workers at the end of the war for independence. For 20 years, this genuine expression of working class democracy has survived the rigors of interaction with an authoritarian government. The vitality and lasting effect of this participatory institution in Algeria is attributable to its spontaneous, as opposed to induced, genesis. By contrast, a memorable episode of induced participatory democracy under revolutionary conditions in Guinea-Bissau, called by Amilcar Cabral "revolutionary democracy," appears to have faded in the post-revolutionary, one-party state.

A fifth type of democracy has no legal guardian in Africa, but its adoption is often contemplated. Its name is consociational democracy, so christened by a Dutch political scientist, Arend Lijphart, and widely celebrated by like-minded scholars. This type of democracy is prescribed by its advocates as a long- or short-term solution to the problem of cultural, i.e., ethnic, racial, or religious, group conflict in deeply divided societies. In fact, it is a version of liberal democracy with the addition of special arrangements to protect the vital interests of cultural groups. In culturally plural societies, such as Switzerland, federalism and cantonal autonomy are exemplary consociational devices; the principle of proportionality for both political representation and the distribution of benefits is also important. In Nigeria, the constitutional requirement that political parties must reflect the federal character of the country in order to qualify for registration is one of several consociational devices which have been designed to prevent sectional domination. Consociational mechanisms and techniques are routinely used by the governments of plural societies. According to Lijphart, however, the hallmark of specifically consociational democracy, as a distinct type, is effective and voluntary political cooperation among the elites and truly representative leaders of the main cultural groups.[15]

In South Africa, the banner of consociationalism has been unfurled by legal opponents of the ruling National Party, principally the white Progressive Federal Party and *Inkatha*, a Zulu-based mass organization, acting through a multiracial commission appointed by Gatsha Buthelezi, Chief Minister of Kwazulu, in 1980. Drawing upon the ideas of Professor Lijphart, who served as a member, the commission has proposed a consociational constitution for the Province of Natal as an example for the country as a whole. The key features of this proposal include universal adult suffrage, a legislative assembly elected by means of proportional representation in electoral districts, and an executive body chosen in accordance with consociational principles. These recommendations have been rejected by the government. Meanwhile proposals for consociational democracy in South Africa have also been criticized by rigorously democratic thinkers. Heribert Adam, for one, notes that group identities and ethnic labels in South Africa have been imposed upon subject groups by the dominant group. "For example," he observes, "there are no enthusiastic Coloureds in the self-perceptions of those classified as Coloureds."[16] Furthermore, a growing number of black liberation leaders are social revolutionaries with little or no interest in consociational compromising. Increasingly, the liberation struggle involves collective demands for "redistributive" or social and, in the workplace, participatory democracy.

In divided societies, like South Africa, where revolutionary action involves a large and increasing measure of class struggle, consociational democracy cannot fulfill its promise of stabilizing social satisfaction. Yet it would be mistaken to believe that the consociational idea of self-determination for self-regarding communities is counterrevolutionary per se. Insofar as subnational group rights command general respect, democratic movements which disregard consociational precepts do so at their peril. In Africa, the value of consociational democracy would be more clearly apparent in countries, such as the Democratic Republic of the Sudan, where the nature of cultural cleavage is less ambiguous than it is in the apartheid republic. This type of democracy should not be underappreciated because of its current association with moderate reform in South Africa.

Democracy in Africa is widely approved but everywhere in doubt. Democratic dreams are the incandescent particles of current history which gleam brightly in the sunlight of liberation only to fade beneath the lengthening shadow of grim economic realities. This survey of types may help to sort some of the problems of democracy in Africa. Liberal democracy founders in a rising tide of tears and social despair. Reflecting on two recent setbacks for liberal democracy in West Africa, an acute observer offered this judgement: "it was only the appalling economic situations in Ghana and Upper Volta, and the impotence of the respective governments faced with this situation that led to the collapse of their parliamentary systems."[17]

Social democracy introduces a standard for the just distribution of wealth and material benefits; but its success and survival cannot be ensured by redistributive policies alone. In an age of social optimism, people will not settle for the redistribution of misery and poverty. Everything depends upon the timely creation of national wealth and wealth-producing assets by means of public and collective, rather than private, enterprise. In many African countries, however, statist economic policies, espoused in the name of socialism, have discouraged or prevented the release of creative, wealth-generating energies. In Guinea, for example, the regime outlawed all private markets in 1975; private trading was made a criminal offense. State agencies were supposed to fill the void, but they were riddled with corruption and proved to be hopelessly inefficient. Economic collapse and starvation were avoided only because the law was erratically enforced and eventually allowed to lapse. In this and many other cases, statism has been mistaken for socialism.

For reasons that are, in the main, historical and contingent rather than theoretical or necessary, socialism has often been identified with statism by friends and foes alike. Increasingly that identification discredits socialism as a mode of development in the eyes of the world on the ground that statist strategies are plainly impractical and unrealistic apart from their troubling political aspects. In the past, a few countries, notably the Soviet Union and China, have constructed socialist economies with capital extracted from the countryside and appropriated by the state for purposes of investment and essential purchases abroad. That classic strategy is plainly unsuited to conditions in the agrarian countries of Africa for several reasons, among them rural resistance to collectivization, exponential population growth, the high cost of critical imports, and endemic problems of statist economic management. Furthermore, socialism is supposed to signify the democratization of economic life. Coercion is contrary to the spirit of socialism. Statism, the most general form of coercion, is the graveyard of socialism as well as democracy.

Participatory democracy is a logical response to the challenge of statism. Its appearance and reappearance in Africa should be a source of inspiration to democrats and, in particular, democratic socialists. However, the practice of participatory democracy cannot be regimented by the state without detriment to its integrity. Where participatory institutions have been created in factories and farms by self-motivated and self-directed workers, as in the case of Algeria, they countervail the power of the one-party state. By contrast, where participative

decision-making is narrowly restricted and subject to close supervision by a party-state, as in Tanzania and Zambia, participatory democracy succumbs to the assault of guided democracy and developmental dictatorship.

Shall we conclude, with Gregor, that developmental dictatorship is the wave of the future for Africa?[18] The empirical support for that viewpoint is weak. Its sole rationale—the presumed power to produce rapid economic development —is scarcely tenable. Democracy is a far more popular alternative, but democracy must take up the challenge of development where dictatorship has failed. Africa needs a developmental democracy, a democracy without tears. Developmental democracy could represent a synthesis of all that has been learned from the many experiments with simpler types. It would probably be liberal and social, participatory and consociational all at once. From guided democracy it could inherit an appreciation for the function of leadership. The core of guided democracy could even be refined and transformed into preceptoral democracy, or leadership without political power.[19] In a complex, developmental democracy, intellectual guidance would operate by means of persuasion alone; its efficacy in Africa would be ensured by that immense respect for learning and scholarship which is a characteristic quality of modern African societies.

Developmental democracy does not imply a specific formulation of democratic principles based upon distinctive core values, such as political liberty for liberal democracy, social equality for social democracy, popular participation for participatory democracy, or group rights for consociational democracy. The content of developmental democracy would vary with the views of democratic theorists. One such theorist, the Canadian, C.B. Macpherson, introduced the term to designate a stage in the evolution of liberal democracy, marked by the emergence, in theory and practice, of equal opportunity for "individual self-development."[20] This advance was promoted by the political doctrines of John Stuart Mill and his early 20th century successors. In our time, it is surely appropriate to broaden the meaning of developmental democracy so that it will accommodate the goals of social reconstruction in the nonindustrial countries. Developmental democracy today, should, I believe, be enlarged to encompass the core values of social, participatory, and consociational democracy as well as the specifically liberal elements of limited government and individual self-development.

Broadly conceived, developmental democracy would evoke fresh and original responses to the problems of economic underdevelopment, social stagnation, and political drift. Original thought is the heart of the matter. Gregor has shown, convincingly, that the essential ideas of developmental dictatorship were formulated during the first decade of this century by revolutionary syndicalists in Italy. By the ninth decade these ideas have surely run their course. There is no good economic reason for Africans today to propitiate the European gods of developmental dictatorship.

From the early stirrings of modern African nationalism to the onset and consolidation of political independence, Africa has resisted foreign intellectual domination. In all but a few countries, African governments conduct their foreign relations on the basis of a deep and abiding commitment to the principle of nonalignment in world politics. African statecraft reflects a determination to formulate the challenges of international relations from a self-defined standpoint. In the social thought of 20th century Africa, intellectual self-reliance is a paramount theme; it spans the ideological spectrum as indicated by its prominence in the francophonic philosophy of Negritude, the Africanist tradition of Anton Lembede and his followers in South Africa, the "African" and democratic socialism of Nyerere, and the revolutionary socialism of Amilcar Cabral. Students of social thought should recognize the quest for an intellectual synthesis and transcendence of capitalism and socialism in their classical and contemporary, or neoclassical, forms. In an essay entitled, "The Emancipation of Democracy," W.E.B. Du Bois assessed the contribution of black people in America to democracy thus:

It was the black man that raised a vision of democracy in America such as neither Americans nor Europeans conceived in the 18th century and such as they have not even accepted in the 20th century; and yet a conception which every clear sighted man knows is true and inevitable.[21]

Might this not be written of Africa's contribution to democracy in our time?

Where shall we look for the signs of intellectual and political synthesis which would signify the emergence of a new democracy? Where have the forms of developmental democracy begun to take shape? Every national workshop bears inspection, for each, in its own way, contributes to the aggregate of democratic knowledge and practice. Consider Zimbabwe, where revolutionary socialists in power prepare to terminate a transitional period of liberal government in favor of a more restrictive, one-party political formula. Their long-term objective has been described in an official document as "a truly socialist, egalitarian and democratic society." Zimbabwean leaders and theorists will be challenged by the fact that there are no models for that kind of social construction on the face of this earth.

In pacesetting Zambia, where wage labor constitutes a comparatively large component of the total work force (more than one third), the struggle for trade union autonomy is fundamental to the cause of developmental democracy. But for the democratic vitality of the labor movement, developmental dictatorship in the guise of "scientific socialism" could not be counteracted by other popular groups in Zambia. While clergymen, businessmen, intellectuals, and professional people are, in the main, opposed to the adoption of "scientific socialism" as an official doctrine, they could not resist it effectively without the firm support of democratic labor. In this matter of ideological choice, the principal restraining force on Zambia's political leadership is neither foreign capital nor the Zambian bourgeoisie; it is the Zambian labor movement.

In the Sahelian nation of Niger, a military government has proclaimed the institution of a new political order, known as "the development society." Founded upon the twin pillars of traditional youth organizations and village-based agricultural cooperatives, the new system of government functions through a series of elected councils, culminating in a National Development Council, which has been directed to frame an "original" and "authentically Nigerian" constitution. Here, too, the spirit of developmental democracy is abroad.

In neighboring Nigeria, the prospects for developmental democracy are enhanced by a federal system of government which provides a multiplicity of arenas for social and political experimentation. Federalism is also the essential foundation of Nigerian national unity. The relevance of that example to pan-African thought merits attention. Dictatorship may be the most formidable barrier to pan-African unity. Pan-African federalism would foster democracy at the expense of dictatorship in many countries. As a pan-African principle, federalism would also facilitate the exchange of democratic discoveries among African polities and thereby promote the growth of developmental democracy. Increasingly, African freedom would radiate African power.

Metaphorically speaking, most Africans today live under the dictatorship of material poverty. The poverty of dictatorship in Africa is equally apparent. It offends the renowned African tradition of community-wide participation in decision-making. By contrast with dictatorship, democracy is a developing idea and an increasingly sophisticated form of political organization. The development of democracy in Africa has become a major determinant of its progress in the world.

## Notes

1. See the sensitive assessment by Rupert Emerson, *From Empire to Nation* (Cambridge, Mass.: Harvard University Press, 1960), pp. 272–292.

2. A. James Gregor, *Italian Fascism and Developmental Dictatorship* (Princeton: Princeton University Press, 1979).

3. Ibid., p. 87.

4. Karl Marx, *Capital*, Vol. I (New York: International Publishers, 1967), pp. 8–10. Preface to the First German Edition, 1867.

5. The title of an address, delivered in 1880, in which Africa's contribution to world culture is judiciously assessed. See Edward Wilmot Blyden, *Christianity, Islam and the Negro Race*, 2d ed. (London: Whitingham, 1888).

6. Nnamdi Azikiwe, *Political Blueprint of Nigeria* (Lagos: African Book Company Limited, 1943); Obafemi Awolowo, *Path to Nigerian Freedom* (London: Faber, 1947); James S. Coleman, *Nigeria: Background to Nationalism* (Berkeley and Los Angeles: University of California Press, 1958), pp. 323–324.

7. Okay Achike, *Groundwork of Military Law and Military Rule in Nigeria* (Enugu: Fourth Dimension Press, 1978), p. 184.

8. Larry Diamond, "Cleavage, Conflict and Anxiety in the Second Nigerian Republic," *The Journal of Modern African Studies* 20:4 (1982), pp. 629–668.

9. Robert H. Jackson and Carl G. Rosberg, *Personal Rule in Black Africa* (Berkeley: University of California Press, 1982), p. 103.

10. Ibid., p. 111; Joel D. Barkan, "Legislators, Elections, and Political Linkage," in Joel D. Barkan with John D. Okumu, eds., *Politics and Public Policy in Kenya and Tanzania* (New York: Praeger Publishers, 1979), pp. 83–84.

11. *The Weekly Review* (Nairobi), June 11, 1982, p. 5.

12. Cranford Pratt, "Tanzania's Transition to Socialism: Reflections of a Democratic Socialist," in Bismarck U. Mwansasu and Cranford Pratt, eds., *Towards Socialism in Tanzania* (Toronto: University of Toronto Press, 1979), pp. 211, 219.

13. As Carole Pateman observes in her pathbreaking exposition of participatory democracy, "most individuals spend a great deal of their lifetime at work and the business of the workplace provides an education in the management of collective affairs that is difficult to parallel elsewhere." *Participation and Democratic Theory* (Cambridge, England: Cambridge University Press, 1970), p. 43.

14. William Tordoff, "Introduction," in William Tordoff, ed., *Administration in Zambia* (Manchester, England: Manchester University Press, 1980), p. 25; and Ian Scott, "Party and

Administration Under the One-Party State," ibid., p. 157.

15. Arend Lijphart, *Democracy in Plural Societies* (New Haven: Yale University Press, 1977). The theory of consociational democracy has a partly African pedigree, namely, the classic analysis of West African politics by the Jamaican Nobel Laureate, Sir W. Arthur Lewis, *Politics in West Africa* (London: Allen and Unwin, 1965). Lijphart, pp. 143–146, 177–181, 216–222.

16. Heribert Adam, "Political Alternatives," in Adam and Hermann Giliomee, eds., *Ethnic Power Mobilized: Can South Africa Change?* (New Haven: Yale University Press, 1979), p. 288.

17. *West Africa* No. 3377 (April 26, 1982), p. 1111.

18. A. James Gregor, *Italian Fascism and Developmental Dictatorship* (Princeton: Princeton University Press, 1979), pp. 327, 333.

19. This differs from Charles E. Lindblom's concept of a "preceptoral system," which denotes the fusion of intellectual leadership and political power by dictatorial means. *Politics and Markets* (New York: Basic Books, 1977), pp. 52–62.

20. C. B. Macpherson, *The Life and Times of Liberal Democracy* (Oxford, England: Oxford University Press, 1977), pp. 44–76.

21. W. E. Burghardt Du Bois, *The Gift of Black Folk* (New York: Washington Square Press, 1970), p. 65.

# 11

# The Asian Road to Democracy

*Nathan Keyfitz*

In daily reports on the Indonesian election campaign of last March the BBC, like the Voice of America and the American press, translated the several episodes into Western terms. The

SOURCE: Published by permission of Transaction Publishers, from *Society*, vol. 26, no. 1 (November/December 1988), pp. 71–76. © 1988 by Transaction Publishers. Article abridged by the editors.

translation made the present regime appear like a strongman dictatorship in Latin America, based on political manipulation backed by crude force. One commentator spoke of the "emasculated Parliament" and President Suharto as a "master political strategist," who had just retired General Moerdani, "the second most powerful man in Indonesia" against his will, and this to control "unease in the armed forces."

We should proceed differently. Before translating the events into Western terms, and then basing a judgment on how the translation sounds to English-speaking listeners, we ought to describe the phenomenon as it looks within the tradition that produced it, as far as possible without initially submitting it to alien judgment. To understand the phenomenon in its own terms is a necessary preliminary to judging it properly by more universal values.

We should think of the alternatives: if not Suharto, what political regime is viable? Bear in mind that parliamentary democracy was tried in the early 1950s, and there were seventeen governments in five years. The impotence of the system brought Sukarno's left-leaning "guided democracy." Aristotle tells us how anarchy leads to tyranny. Guided democracy was just as ineffective at home as its liberal predecessor, but it differed in expensively playing at war with Holland, then with Malaysia.

The country has now had more than twenty years of stable progress, nearly a record in the Third World, under auspices close to the Hindu-Javanese tradition. Income is rising, population growth is slowing. Liberalism could not provide that for Indonesia, or for most other Third World countries. The constitution of the Philippines provides for American-style politics more nearly than in any other part of Asia, and turmoil has been the outcome. Some of the countries that are the least liberal politically are making great progress: South Korea and Taiwan are conspicuous.

All this should make us want to know what the Indonesian arrangement looks like from the inside. By "inside" I mean the political theory implicit in Hindu-Javanese literature and thought. This thought exhibits many features that are broadly Asian, with heavy contributions from ancient India.

Unity, wholeness, was and is the supreme virtue in traditional Java. Anything that divides, whether "individual rights" or "division of powers" or "provincial autonomy," diminishes solidarity, weakens the community. Everyone will be looked after, not as a right held against the community, but insofar as one is a member of the community. One will be less secure, not more, if the community is opposed by people asserting rights against it. Equality and fairness are important and they will be attained not as individual entitlements, but rather through the community as long as the community is healthy and unified. Such is the ideal of social order not only of Java but also of ancient India and China.

We know that Asian history is replete with bloody insurrections; and every village has stories of cliques, personal enmities, family feuds, even killings. That by no means lessens the need for consensus. The hatred and chaos beneath the surface, in Asia just as elsewhere in the world, is exactly what prompts the desire for consensus, for the covering over of differences.

## MAGICAL ESSENCE

The all-essential order is only to be created by the concentration of power, as traditional Asia sees the matter. Power is no result of mere wealth; if there is any relation, it is the other way—wealth comes to the person of power. Nor is it the result of politics; it is in principle never attained by building coalitions or organizing a political party or attracting votes.

Power is a magical essence that comes down from above, rather than being yielded by those below. Just as his regime ends when the Chinese emperor loses the mandate of Heaven, so the Javanese sovereign's downfall is heralded by fighting in his court and in his dominions—fighting that he cannot control. The same principle holds all the way down; the village headman has a mandate not from heaven but from the patron above him, and his main task is to preserve harmony.

How do we know who has the mandate? By the behavior of the sovereign as much as by the state of his kingdom. The ideal ruler is *halus*, gentle, serene, slow-moving, quiet spoken. The divisive opponent is *kasar*, rough, uncouth, noisy, with jerky movements. The magical essence of power in the person is revealed by his undisturbed calm, his suppressed emotion. Its loss can show as dissolute behavior or as a defeat in battle. Loss of face, any assault on one's dignity, whether provoked by others or by oneself, becomes truly important when it is interpreted as a sign that one's position in society and in the universe is in jeopardy.

For the Javanese, power is not merely Weber's abstract probability that one will get one's way; it is a concrete entity existing independently of all use of it. In fact, according to Lucian W. Pye in *Asian Power and Politics*, "It is too precious to be contaminated by purposeful activities.... [Rather than] making power holders responsible for the causes they support, the Indonesian way of checking the evil effects of power has been to uphold the idea that power should not be used at all."

"Power is status; it is a matter of being above others and of being treated in a deferential manner." Yet it is by no means merely a matter of personal standing; it enmeshes the entire social order. The individual, the society, and the universe have to be in unison, and the stability of all of them is in danger when anyone behaves in a fashion that is not in accord with one's position.

The ruler must not appear to seek the concentration of power in himself. The mantle is thought more likely to fall on one who is indifferent to it and ascetic in behavior; the Indian view that prayer, fasting, and going without sleep in themselves give one power is by no means absent. It is from the ruler that all other power should devolve. Ideally no one is independent, in the sense of the independent professions among us. One gathers power in proportion as one is close to the ruler or is a client of someone who is close to the ruler.

The economy is embedded in the society, just as Karl Polanyi said. Devices are approved by which persons with prestige become rich; it is thought wrong for wealth in itself to lead to power. The incomes of those lower down in the hierarchy are not typically salaries or profits from trade, but benefices—the right to draw income from land pertaining to the office, for instance, or if not land then some other privilege. Land is never owned by the beneficiary, but enjoyed only while he holds office. To be given an income-providing benefice—perhaps an import permit—falls well within the tradition. Such favors for services go down the line. At each point the recipient is not supposed to use the benefice for personal luxury, but for the support of his own retainers and clients, to gather to oneself status and respect, through a tenure wholly dependent on the pleasure of the one above, and ultimately on the sovereign. At each level the relation is that of patron to clients, analogous to the relation of a father to his children. The most common address of respect today is *bapak,* 'father.'

Parallel to the tradition that power is a magical essence distributed unequally there is a high value placed on equality and fairness. Many of the problems of ancient times, and even more those of today, arise out of trying to reconcile the ideal of equality with that of the concentration of power.

For the Javanese tradition, power must be concentrated if things are to go well. When the empire starts to decay there will appear separate pools of power; perhaps distant provinces will refuse to deliver their surplus and instead put it to their own uses.

In modern terms any separation, any move toward autonomy, of an individual or a group is a similar dispersal of power, the creation of a separate pool. A division of constitutional responsibility between government, parliament, and the courts would be a dispersal of power, a sign that the community was breaking up. Individual rights against the sovereign are an even worse dispersal.

## PRESENT ARRANGEMENTS

This tradition is clearly exemplified by some of the features of the present government in Indonesia. As things now stand the 3,000,000 or so government employees must as the condition of their employment adhere to the Golongan Karya (Golkar), the official party. An opposition press is not permitted, and foreign papers that come into the country are examined by the censor, who occasionally blacks out an article or part of an article and sometimes suppresses a whole issue. Other political parties are permitted, but not outside a narrow ideological range.

An opposition newspaper with its readers would be a small pole of power. An opposition party could be a larger pole. A business concern that could do what it liked free of government regulation would be out of place; the current vogue of deregulation runs into enormous difficulties of implementation just because it is unacceptable that any individual or corporation, foreign or national, Indonesian or Chinese, should operate free of control by the collectivity. Efficiency has indeed become a value, but control by the community retains its importance. What the resting position will be is not clear, but one supposes that deregulation will be governed by some compromise between ancient norms of subordination and the modern need for efficiency. . . .

One wonders why all this gathering of power is necessary, given that the ruling party would win an open election conducted according to American rules. It would probably win with at least the 55:45 ratio that is familiar to us. But that would mean that 45 percent would be losers, only 55 percent winners; and that is not considered good enough. The ideal is not a fair contest like a football game with winners and losers, but a theatrical performance in which everyone plays a part. . . .

## FEAR OF CHAOS

Part of what sustains all this is a sense that the social order is fragile, and once it is weakened anything could happen. The opposite of the existing order is not some alternative order but chaos. Individuals could run amok; whole populations could take to senseless violence. History shows that the fear is not groundless.

We do not need to go back in history but just to look around the world today. Ceylon, now Sri Lanka, when I lived there thirty years ago was a model of democracy in the English style. If one sat in its Parliament and closed one's eyes one could imagine being in Westminister. The Ceylonese spoke of themselves as black Englishmen. Individuals had rights, political parties competed, there were fair elections, the economy was more or less competitive. It took less than two decades for Tamils and Singhalese to start shooting one another, and the outcome as of now includes an Indian occupying force that keeps the chaos going. This is exactly what Javanese political theory would have predicted: majority voting and the encouragement of self-interest led to division and to the final humiliation of a foreign army. It happened that the split was along the Singhalese/Tamil fault line, but it could have been between social classes or at some other point where solidarity cracked.

The attitudes and problems extend to economics, as we can see from the language itself. The everyday Indonesian word for competition is *persaingan*. Its root is *saing*, a fang or tusk; and the same root gives rise to a word for bite. Thus not only is competition compared to fighting, but to animal rather than human behavior. When the well-intentioned expatriate counsels an open system with free competition, the traditional hearer thinks of elephants fighting in the jungle, tearing one another apart with their tusks. That is hardly a model for civilized people, and the notion that good can come of it strains credulity. Other Asian languages have words for competition with similar derivations related to fighting.

The root of the English word *competition* is *petere*, seeking, so the concept is people peacefully seeking the same thing. French is *concurrence*, from *correre*, to run; the image is a race, and this is also the German and the Italian

etymology. The identical Latin root gives concourse. The absence of any implication of hostility in these words contrasts with the Indonesian etymology.

Consistent with all this the Asian model for the economy is not competition but cooperation, solidarity among producers. That applies on the village scale, where the ideal is producers working together to make their coconut oil or whatever, and then selling the product at a fair price. On the national scale the ideal is production according to a plan that will produce plenty and divide its benefits fairly among the people. It is all very well to point out that the cooperatives suffer from every kind of inefficiency, and that much of the advance that occurs is unplanned. Asians can see the difficulties of cooperation and planning just as well as we can, and we ought instead to be asking why despite inefficiencies cooperatives and planning remain their ideal.

The answer to this question seems to lie once again in the fear of chaos. In the Javanese view, self-seeking will assuredly bring chaos. That part of the social theory is well developed in the concept of *pamrih*.

## PERSONAL MOTIVES

*Pamrih*, concealed personal motives in Benedict R. Anderson's translation, means doing something to satisfy one's personal interests or desires. Again and again the sacred Hindu-Javanese books, and the *waying* plays based on them, allude to the importance of doing things because they have to be done, and not because of any expected gain. "To action alone hast thou a right and never at all to its fruits; let not the fruits of action be thy motive," says the Gita. Duty and loyalty are the virtues. When the Westerner talks about installing incentives to get people to do thus and so he is urging *pamrih*, reasons for action opposed to the knightly ideal, indeed to the ideal of all layers of the society.

Not only is there a loss of virtue in individual antisocial action, but even the immediate selfish end is not attainable by such means. Ultimately there is no gain to the person from responding to base motives. In fact, according to Anderson in Claire Holt's *Culture and Politics in Indonesia,* "the *pamrih* of the administrator or the military man is really a threat to his own ultimate interests, since the indulgence of personal, and therefore partial, passions or prejudices means interior imbalance and a diffusion of personal concentration and power."

The seeking for unanimity contrasts in many small ways with the Western preference for a contest. Expatriates forever complain that they cannot have a good discussion with their counterparts or other local people. They state a proposition, and there is a silence; no one talks back. How can they show how smart they are unless the local people will speak up so that they can down them in argument? There is indeed a tradition of arguing the sacred texts, but in most parts of Asia it is subordinate to an even stronger tradition of just repeating the texts. A high level of scholarly accomplishment is to recite the four books of the Bhagavad Gita; reciting them backwards is even better.

Above all, argument with a social superior is disapproved. To contradict a superior is to challenge his mandate, and through that to challenge the social order. There is no way of voicing such a challenge lightly or gracefully. In the presence of superiors who are speaking, whether to one person alone or to a larger audience, approving silence is the proper response, the approval occasionally voiced as a gentle murmur of assent, *inggih* in Javanese.

If the individuals present are of several levels, the sequence in which they speak is predetermined by their standing. The most senior, whether of rank or age, will speak first, and then the less senior on a descending scale; those at the bottom will only listen.

When the American goes to a meeting his object is to show how smart he is. When the Asian goes to a meeting,...his object is to achieve consensus. An American writing on this thirty years ago would have drawn the conclusion that the Asian will just have to change if he is to make headway in the modern world. Now Japan, Korea, Hong Kong, and other countries have made the rest of us less sure of this proposition.

## VOTING VERSUS PERSUASION

The fast way of coming to a decision in any deliberative body, whether a factory committee or the House of Representatives, is to call a vote. Once the issue has been debated sufficiently that most points have been heard there is no use going over the ground again. People's interests differ, and to talk a person into disregarding his own interests is brainwashing. The vote is a democratic decision, and the minority will just have to go along with the outcome. Those individuals who are voted down this time can take consolation, if they need it, in hoping to be on the winning side next time.

That way of cutting through to a decision does not seem right in traditional Asia, whether in Japan or in Indonesia. The outvoted ones lose face, solidarity is broken. The minority should rather be persuaded, not out-voted, and compromises should be sought. Time taken to do this is regarded as well spent if it achieves harmony and consensus.

This political philosophy, the preference for solidarity as against contest, reaches down to many of the smaller aspects of life. One that is conspicuous to an academic observer is the style of argument and presentation. In any debate Americans take for granted that not everyone is going to agree. Fudging the issues so that all will find the argument unexceptionable is for them no virtue. In fact, academics are expected to present issues in their starkest form, to show them as concretely and unambiguously as possible, to seek out disagreement; only when everyone does this will the truth emerge.

For traditional Asia that is the way to division and discord. It is better to be less incisive, to emphasize points of agreement. Some vagueness is preferable to aggressive concreteness. Explicitness is no virtue when it ends up with one group fighting another. It is better to write that memorandum so that the whole meeting can accept it, even at the expense of expression so broad or so indirect that it may not be understood; certainly there is no need for it to be understood by outsiders.

The difference of style between Indonesians and Westerners in discussion and in the criteria for decision making is so great that on serious matters expatriates and the local authorities cannot meet together. Expatriates will be heard, but at the point where a decision is to be taken they cannot be present. Once expatriates are excluded, the discussion resumes in Asian style. I can only imagine what that is, but I surmise that any sharp parts of the argument that are impossible to avoid are embedded in some wider give and take....

The Indonesian Parliament was in session from March 1 to March 9, and it tussled with six pieces of legislation, one of which was nothing less than the lines of state policy for the next five years. For a while disagreement was rampant, but some minor modifications were made and all ended well. A single expression of approval was provided for all six, with 795 voices in favor, none against.

Was the performance futile? By no means; it showed that the society was holding together; power was suitably concentrated when there was a danger that it might be dispersed; duty and loyalty triumphed over disruptive self-interest. There had indeed been a contest, but not the one between those for and those against the proposed lines of state policy that the Western observer thought was going on. Rather, it was a contest between the forces of concentration and of disruption, not alone in the Parliament but in the society. Like a *wayang* performance it reflected the perpetual struggle between unity and disorder in the cosmos as a whole.

## WHEN INTERESTS ARE OPPOSED

What happens in circumstances in which clearly opposed interests confront one another? Farmers A and B at the start of the rainy season both want water on their fields as soon as possible so they can start to plough, and there is only enough water for one. They stand around discussing the matter, with the *penjaga air*, the water guard, present more in the capacity of judge and arbitrator than as irrigation technician. One way to avoid a dispute would be open bidding, with the village collecting the fee offered by the higher bidder. That kind of quick resolution I have never seen applied.

What fits better is a discussion in which the criteria of relevance are loose; it is not irrelevant who had the water last year, even what my father did for your father many years ago, or that my brother married your sister. Efficiency may come into it—who can make better use of the water—but that alone will not decide the matter. Indirection is important in the securing of agreement—never go directly and brutally to the point, but always talk about those things, only more or less germane, on which an atmosphere of friendliness and agreement can be created. One can at the end glide into the decision; opposition is disarmed. As Lucian Pye says, "Although almost all Asian cultures, and especially those of Southeast Asia, praise the ideal of consensus, the Indonesians are the ones who carry it to an extreme at the village level."

Daniel Lev, in Claire Holt's book, describes what is likely to happen when a major conflict looms, over a property line, for instance, or an inheritance division. If the disputants cannot settle it themselves it may be referred to a close friend or a village elder or the village headman: "He will try to discover the facts at issue, while at the same time playing down the facts and playing up personal relationships.... The hope is that the disputants themselves will come up with a compromise, but if not, various possibilities will be proposed to them.... There is usually minimum reference to 'rights.' ... When the dust has finally settled, sometimes after weeks or months, no decision occurs, only a coming to terms in which both parties have presumably lost something." The public view is that both sides are wrong for having quarreled, but they have redeemed themselves by their concessions.

Anyone who says that all this is wrong, and what "should" be done is to install genuine parliamentary democracy, is well advised to study the history of the 1950s, when parliamentary democracy was given a thorough tryout and was a conspicuous failure. What happened could have been predicted by Javanese political theory. Before the war there was unity, but once the Dutch had gone, everyone sought his own interest; there was no center to take over the Dutch power. The multitude of parties, intermittent constitutional crises, rapid succession of governments—these were not themselves evil, but they were signs that the society was in trouble, the newly formed state was crumbling.

What must be kept in mind is that majority government requires assimilation of certain rules of the game—analogous to Durkheim's subcontractual conditions of contract in the economic sphere. The majority, for instance, has to learn to vote the interests of the community; if it votes its own interest alone the 51 percent will dispossess the 49 percent. That was Sukarno's contention (he often talked scornfully of 50 percent plus one), and if he were alive today he could point to Sri Lanka as an example. Until the necessary conditions have been thoroughly assimilated into the deepest layers of people's minds, pluralism will indeed lead to chaos. Far from being a protection against corruption, pluralism could increase the opportunities for it. The mental apparatus to cope with the divisiveness of a competitive polity and economy is not to be taken for granted.

From the depths of Javanese history and thought has come an alternative provisional solution to the problem of order and progress. It cannot expect the adherence of Westerners, but it is entitled to their respect. Without that inheritance, Indonesia would have no defense against disorder on the one side and naked force and manipulation on the other. Fundamentalist Islam would battle communism.

Underlying traditions so far in existence support persuasion where they do not support competition. The principle of persuasion and unanimity fits better, in Indonesia and apparently in some other countries as well, than

the principle of majority decision. Politics as theater in the present stage gives better results than would be given by politics as the contest that it is in the West.

## Suggested Readings

ANDERSON, BENEDICT R. "The Idea of Power in Javanese Culture." In Claire Holt, ed. *Culture and Politics in Indonesia*. Ithaca: Cornell University Press, 1972.

GEERTZ, CLIFFORD. *The Religion of Java*. New York: Free Press, 1964.

LEV, DANIEL S. "Judicial Institutions and Legal Culture in Indonesia." In Claire Holt, ed. *Culture and Politics in Indonesia*. Ithaca: Cornell University Press, 1972.

PYE, LUCIAN W. *Asian Power and Politics: The Cultural Dimensions of Authority*. Cambridge: Harvard University Press, 1985.

# 12

# The Quest for Economic Democracy

*M. Donald Hancock and John Logue*

Throughout much of the 20th century, reform-minded politicians and trade unionists in Western Europe and North America have sought to extend worker participation in both macro- and micro-economic decisions. They have done so, as Edward S. Greenberg has observed, for a variety of potentially inconsistent reasons: to integrate employees more fully into the productive process with a view to mitigating labor conflict, to humanize the workplace, and to democratize relations between labor and private capital.[1]

SOURCE: M. Donald Hancock and John Logue, "Sweden: The Quest for Economic Democracy," *Polity* 17, no. 2 (Winter 1984), pp. 248–269. By permission. Article and Notes abridged by the editors.

Modes of participation used to promote these objectives range from collective bargaining to worker representation in consultative bodies on the shop floor as well as at top levels of company management, various forms of profit-sharing, and worker ownership.

The forms and degree of worker participation in economic decisions vary considerably among the Western democracies. Workers' and union officials' access to managerial councils in Britain and the United States—"liberal" polities lacking highly centralized national trade union movements—is not securely institutionalized. But then there are corporatist systems such as Austria, West Germany, Denmark, Norway, and Sweden where strong national trade-union associations—in alliance with Social Democratic parties continuously garnering 30 percent or more of the popular vote—have achieved comprehensive and highly effective forms of worker participation. Numerous American and European scholars discern in these differences a principal explanation for contrasting patterns of policymaking and socioeconomic performance.[2]

Beyond efforts to explain the underlying causes of different policy outcomes in various nations or subsystems lies the necessity to assess the practical and theoretical implication of increased worker participation for ongoing processes of political change in the advanced democracies. Academic observers and policy actors alike concur that continuing efforts to extend employee influence in company and national economic decisions promise long-term systemic consequences—but they differ profoundly on what these will be. Most mainstream Social Democrats anticipate that increased worker participation will lead to a more equitable balance between capital and labor. This achievement would have the dual effect of lessening employee dissatisfaction and facilitating cooperation among labor, management, and government officials to sustain economic growth in the decades ahead. Radical left critics, in contrast, denounce Social Democratic "reformism," alleging that it merely co-opts workers into the established capitalist order and thereby helps ensure its survival. On

the right, many conservative politicians and spokesmen for employer interests fear just the reverse: economic democracy bringing about the eventual expropriation of private property and transforming capitalism into some as yet undefined form of "labor socialism."

Among the advanced industrial democracies, Sweden provides a crucial test of these alternative prospects. Since the late 1960s, leaders of the national Federation of Trade Unions (*Landsorganisation*, or LO) and the Social Democratic Party (SAP) have sponsored successive reform initiatives whose cumulative effect has been to extend substantially the individual and collective rights of workers. They have also proposed a system of compulsory wage-earner funds that will still further increase employee influence vis-à-vis private capital. The resulting public debate voicing intense non-socialist criticism of the proposal and revealing widespread ambivalence concerning its merits even within Social Democratic ranks underscores Sweden's distinctive status as a "threshold nation" confronting an historical choice between opposing strategies of system change.

We shall attempt here to clarify the substance and likely consequences of that choice. This will entail, first, an assessment of workplace reforms enacted during the 1970s—ranging from job redesign efforts to parliamentary legislation. We will then consider whether the implementation of a national system of wage-earner funds in fact promises a fundamental transformation of Sweden's existing economic system. We focus on Sweden not for its own sake but as an instance of distinctive policy and structural innovation in response to changing economic conditions that confront all industrial democracies. Accordingly, in our conclusion we will try to look at the Swedish experience in comparative perspective.

## DEMOCRATIZING WORK LIFE: "THE THIRD STAGE"

Aspirations to democratize work life in Sweden are a direct consequence of the electoral strength, ideological values, and long years of governance by the Social Democratic Party. Organized in 1889, in tandem with proliferating trade unions in the wake of rapid industrialization, the SAP soon became an important political force. In cooperation with the Liberals, Social Democratic leaders agitated successfully for suffrage reform and political democratization. The two parties formed Sweden's first democratic government in 1917 and, during three years of coalition rule, proceeded to institutionalize the present parliamentary system and introduce universal suffrage. After a desultory period of ministerial instability during the 1920s, when no party or coalition could command a stable parliamentary majority, the Social Democrats assumed long-term executive power in 1932 with the tacit backing of the Agrarian Party (now known as the Center). They governed either in coalition or alone for the next 44 years, during which time they initiated and expanded a whole array of social services, including universal retirement benefits, a national health system, and multiple financial benefits to lower-income workers and families.

Throughout their long tenure in power, the Social Democrats consistently polled nearly half of the national vote in successive national and local/regional elections—peaking at 53.8 percent in 1940 and 50.1 percent in 1968. One of their principal political assets is the LO, which represents some 90 percent of the industrial work force through its 25 member unions and contributes the bulk of the SAP's membership. In return, LO spokesmen have been allowed considerable influence in shaping party (and hence government) policy at key junctures in the nation's economic and social development. Leading examples include the formation and implementation of Sweden's highly effective active labor market policies in the early postwar period and the adoption of a controversial system of supplementary pension benefits during the late 1950s.

The Social Democrats claim historical credit for their leadership role in achieving political democracy and creating the welfare state in what they call the first two stages in Sweden's progressive democratization. Their goal for a third stage is to democratize work-place relations. Justifying it on the basis of "the traditions of the labour movement" and a "desire to humanize industrial society and make proper use of its enormous potentialities," the Social Democrats formally assert their intention

> to replace the present concentration of economic power in private hands by an order of things in which each individual is entitled as a *citizen, wage earner* and *consumer* to determine the direction and distribution of production, the shaping of the productive apparatus, and the conditions of working life. This will be done by engaging the *citizens* in the national planning of resource management in order to make the best use of the country's potentialities. It will be done by guaranteeing the *wage earners* influence on their work places and firms and by expanding their participation in the formation of capital and the administration of collective savings. It will be done by strengthening the position of *consumers* in relation to producers and by putting consumers themselves on a more equal footing where influence over production is concerned.

Placing the democratization of work life on par with political democracy or the welfare state may strike many outside observers as farfetched. Yet, in light of the actual developments in Sweden, the linkage is not inappropriate. After a decade of systematic reforms, even cursory visits to Swedish plants reveal that authority relations on the job are undergoing a transformation. This is not to say that Sweden has become a workers' paradise. Workers still work; managers still manage. But they do so in the context of new rules that reflect a basic shift in the balance of power at the work place.

Since the late 1960s a series of reforms has significantly strengthened the rights of individual workers and local unions vis-à-vis management. They include private and public measures to (1) redesign jobs to fit workers rather than vice versa; (2) guarantee individual rights at work; (3) increase employee influence on health and safety issues; (4) expand the scope of union-management bargaining to include the organization of production, investment policy, selection of managerial personnel, and other managerial prerogatives; and (5) institute employee representation on company boards. Together with the SAP-LO's efforts to establish a national system of wage-earner funds, these measures promise a democratization of authority on the job and in economic life as revolutionary as the centralization of power that resulted from the introduction of the factory system in the 19th century.

## ERODING TAYLORISM: MANAGEMENT ADAPTS TO THE WELFARE STATE

The industrial revolution introduced not only mechanical power to replace labor but also a new pattern of work organization. The transformation of skilled crafts into repetitive, unskilled jobs demanded the imposition in industry of almost military discipline and a clear hierarchy of command. The hermetic separation of supervision and planning responsibilities from manual work was as much a cornerstone of "Scientific Management" as was the subdivision of jobs into their smallest components. Indeed, Frederick Winslow Taylor, whose name has come to grace the theory invoked to justify the maximum division of labor, cautioned that "one type of man is needed to plan ahead and an entirely different type to execute the work." [3]

In retrospect it is clear that the emphasis Taylor and his successors placed on fragmenting and disciplining labor had to do with adapting complex production processes to an unskilled labor force. In Sweden the movement away from Taylorism's modern incarnations reflects the realization that highly regimented, monotonous work processes are badly matched with the expectations and abilities of a highly educated labor force. By the late 1960s the confluence of that realization with full employment, one of the world's highest per capita income levels, high marginal tax rates, and ample welfare provisions generated employee discontent that expressed itself in alarming rates of absenteeism and

turnover in routine, unpleasant production jobs. Costs soared while quality plummeted.

Management responded to these symptoms of worker malaise with a series of experiments in job redesign. Inspired by pathbreaking Norwegian precedents during the 1960s, Swedish managers proceeded to reverse the fragmentation of labor by expanding the work cycle of individual employees and organizing them into production teams which assumed many of the supervisory tasks, training functions, and quality control responsibilities previously exercised by foremen and white-collar personnel.

The most dramatic departure has been the introduction of semi-autonomous work groups in the auto industry—the very citadel of job fragmentation and industrial discipline. The best publicized example is the assembly plant that Volvo opened in 1974 in the Baltic coastal town of Kalmar. Designed from the outset for team assembly, rather than the traditional assembly line, all aspects of the physical plant—including the division of work areas and the placement of coffee rooms and even entrances—were intended to encourage group cohesion. The plant attracted immense domestic and international attention as soon as it opened, and continues to be viewed favorably by local management and labor. Volvo officials calculate that production costs in Kalmar—despite higher transportation expenses and a lower utilization of capacity—are competitive with Volvo's more traditional and far larger Torslanda plant in Gothenburg on the west coast. According to one semiscientific study conducted at the plant, workers approve of every aspect of the job innovations but one: the steady stream of visitors, experts, students, foreign scholars, and journalists who have descended on the new facility to see it in operation.[4]

\* \* \*

These examples from Volvo...are not unique; the movement away from Taylorism has been general throughout Swedish industry. That job redesign has been more common and more radical in Sweden than elsewhere reflects less the idealism of Swedish management than the fact that Sweden's comprehensive welfare services and full employment policies have provided workers the freedom (within limits) to pick and choose among jobs. Though job redesign does not quite recreate the kind of independence and skill that 19th-century craftsmen are supposed to have possessed, it has gone far toward restoring autonomy to production workers on the job.

## EXTENDING WORKER RIGHTS

Parallel with experiments in job redesign instigated by management during the 1970s, the governing Social Democrats, prodded by union leaders, legislated a spate of reforms that have significantly enhanced the individual and collective rights of employees. Some of the bills, such as the prohibition of sex discrimination in employment (1979), are the subject of legislation in the United States. Other measures cover benefits that are governed by contract in the United States, although their terms and scope are generally much more extensive than in the latter case. Examples include provisions for seven months of paid maternity/paternity leave (1975), five weeks of paid vacation (1977) plus paid holidays, and the right to paid leaves of absence for study purposes if the study assignment is related to union work (1975). A special legislative provision accords foreign workers—who make up 7 percent of Sweden's population and a quarter or more of the labor force in many plants—the right to 240 hours of Swedish language instruction on company time at full pay (1975).

One of the most ambitious reforms enacted during the 1970s was the Employment Security Act (1974) prohibiting the dismissal of individual workers without factual basis. Under this statute, employers may not fire an employee simply because of his or her reduced ability to work; instead, an employer is obligated to reassign the worker to lighter duties. Nor are

"incompatibility," "problems in cooperation," or other euphemisms for managerial caprice sufficient grounds to dismiss a worker. Where legitimate grounds for dismissal (such as the inability of a person to work at all, permanent cutbacks in production, or a plant closure) do exist, the act stipulates that individual workers receive prior notice ranging from one month for those under 25 to six months for those 45 and over. In addition, employers are required to pay full wages for layoffs exceeding two consecutive weeks or 30 days in a calendar year. The consequence of these provisions *is that the employer's interest in production stability matches that of the employee.* While the full effects of the Employment Security Act have yet to be measured, an immediate result has been to force large firms to improve their planning—at least as far as it affects unemployment levels.[5]

Alongside the extension of individual rights of workers, new legislation has accorded the unions themselves greater authority with regard to employers. Some statutory measures have simply extended contractual provisions previously restricted to local union bastions to the nation-at-large. For example, the right of shop stewards at some plants to perform union work on company time was made general by legislation in 1974. Under pressure of the threat of legislation, the LO and the SAF negotiated an agreement in 1975 that accorded local unions the right to hire outside consultants at company expense. In 1973 unions obtained the right, on a trial basis, to appoint two representatives to the boards of Sweden's larger industrial firms; the provision became permanent in 1976. While worker representation on company boards is largely symbolic in that the employee representatives are easily voted down by management, the practice does provide local unions an important source of information concerning company intentions.

Significantly broader channels of information were established with the passage of the Employee Participation Act (*Medbestämmandelagen,* or MBL) in 1976. Described by some observers as the most far-reaching piece of legislation concerning employee influence in the industrial West, the MBL inspired expectations of revolutionary change when it went into effect on January 1, 1977. The revolution did not in fact occur, but the key provisions of the law are worth noting:

1. The employers' traditional prerogative "to direct and allocate work," which had been enshrined in the statutes of the Swedish Federation of Employers (SAF) since 1906 and included in virtually every major labor contract negotiated thereafter, was struck down. The MBL eliminates the legal concept of managerial prerogatives common to other industrial democracies. Instead, all important managerial decisions —from hiring managerial personnel to investment—are subject to collective bargaining.

2. The employer is obligated to provide the union with continual information about production, personnel policy, and the economic status of the company. In addition, unions have the right to examine corporate accounts and other records relevant to their members' interests. As a result the union can have substantial insight into the real situation of the firm and management's intentions.

3. Management is required to negotiate with the unions all major changes prior to their implementation. If, or when, negotiations become deadlocked on the local level, and remain deadlocked after appeal to the national negotiating level, management can finally impose its decision. But it cannot do so without negotiation.

4. The union's interpretation of contractual provisions concerning codetermination and employee rights is binding until the national Labor Court rules to the contrary.

5. The union has veto rights over subcontracting under most circumstances.

* * *

Another far-reaching extension of collective influence involves health and safety. The Work Environment Act of 1974 (strengthened in 1978) brought a dramatic shift in the balance of power between employers and workers in the day-to-day operation of industrial firms. Key provisions of the law called for safety stewards on the shop floor empowered to enforce strict health and safety standards. They are accorded the same protection against dismissal as shop stewards, receive full pay from their company while in training and performing their duties, and possess the authority to shut down dangerous work processes at their own discretion. The latter provision constitutes a direct transfer of power from management to workers: the safety steward's judgment of health and safety requirements prevails over that of management until either changes are made or the steward is overruled by a government safety inspector.

The Draconian provisions of the Work Environment Act are rarely invoked. Interviews in four major plants in the metal trades in 1980, for example, revealed only one instance in which work had been shut down for safety reasons. But the threat implicit in the law has clearly induced management to improve the work environment. Most importantly, the law substantially redefines the traditional meaning of occupational health and safety. Going beyond the avoidance of industrial accidents and illness, it stresses the adaptation of work to human and social needs. Thus, it seeks to minimize monotony, stress, and isolation while according individual employees maximum influence over their work situation. Its objective, in short, is to make work congenial to those who perform it.

* * *

## THE WAGE-EARNER FUND CONTROVERSY

The wage-earner fund proposal, which was first advanced in 1975, points toward the possibility —though not yet the certainty—of an even more sweeping change in employer-worker relations than that achieved through the reforms of the 1970s. The proposal has, therefore, become the object of an extended ideological controversy between the LO and the Social Democrats, on the one hand, and leaders of the three non-socialist parties, the SAF, and spokesmen for individual firms, on the other. Even within Social Democratic ranks, opinions vary widely concerning the scope, timing, and even the desirability of such a system.

The controversy began—paradoxically, in light of Sweden's current economic doldrums—when the LO initiated steps to deal with the problem of "excess profits" in private industry. By the late 1960s, union spokesmen discovered that as an unintended consequence of the LO's postwar practice of "solidaristic wage policies" —defined as equal pay for equal work regardless of the profitability of particular firms—Sweden's more efficient companies had amassed considerable capital that might otherwise have been paid out in wages. Accordingly, the 1971 LO congress approved the formation of a study group to investigate the concentration of wealth and recommend steps to redistribute a portion of company profits to the advantage of employees. Rudolf Meidner, a senior LO economist, was appointed chairman of the study group. Together with two other union economists, Meidner proceeded to evaluate proposals which had been advanced earlier in Denmark and West Germany to establish branch or worker funds as a form of mandatory profit-sharing. The LO team published a Swedish blueprint for a similar venture in 1975, recommending the creation of a general and collective system of employee funds.[6] These would be generated through the transfer of a percentage of company profits in the form of shares and would be administered by union representatives. Dividend income from the shares could be used to acquire additional stock, thereby suggesting the prospect that employees could eventually acquire majority ownership of individual firms. The basic purpose of the wage-earner funds would be to enable wage-earners "to obtain not only greater influence over economic decisions but also greater power over their own work situation."[7]

The "Meidner plan," and its unanimous endorsement in a slightly modified version by the 1976 LO congress, sparked an extended public debate, both in Sweden and abroad. Rejecting the LO's concept of a compulsory system of funds based on collective ownership and control, a group of conservative economists, employed by the SAF and the Swedish Federation of Industry, proposed a voluntary program of individualized profit-sharing. In the political arena, leaders of the Center and the Moderate Unity (conservative) parties denounced the LO plan as posing a long-term threat to both the rights of private ownership and pluralist democracy. Discomforted by the fact that these attacks came on the eve of the September 1976 parliamentary election, Social Democratic chairman and Prime Minister Olof Palme sought to diffuse the controversy by referring the issue of wage-earner funds to a Royal Commission on Employees and Capital Growth which had been appointed the previous year to consider means of increasing employee influence through worker participation in capital formation. Palme's tactic failed to allay either nonsocialist criticism of the Meidner plan or widespread confusion among rank-and-file Social Democrats concerning its alleged merits. Because of public uncertainty about the fund proposal, a spirited attack by the Center Party on the Social Democrats' intention to expand Sweden's nuclear energy program, and the negative effects of various election-eve scandals, SAP strength fell to its lowest point in more than four decades (42.7 percent) in the September election. As a result, the Social Democrats had to relinquish the government to a coalition of the Center Party, the Liberals, and the Moderates.

During the subsequent six years of "bourgeois" rule, which saw considerable governmental instability, the Social Democrats and their nonsocialist opponents continued their verbal battle over the proposed wage-earner fund system. The SAP and the LO appointed a joint committee in 1977 to revise Meidner's original proposal in light of both nonsocialist and Social Democratic criticism. Responding to charges that the fund would concentrate economic power in the hands of union officials, the SAP-LO study group proposed in 1978 that the funds be established on a decentralized basis: a minimum of 24 funds, one apiece in each of Sweden's regional provinces. The committee also added an important new goal to the concept. Alongside the LO's original intention that the wage-earner funds should "complement the solidaristic wage policies," "mitigate the concentration of wealth," and "enhance worker influence in economic decisions," they were now envisaged as a means to "contribute to collective savings and capital formation for productive investments."

\* \* \*

Ideological differences concerning the fund issue intensified from the fall of 1981 onward. Both the Social Democrats and the LO formally endorsed a more detailed version of their earlier proposals at national congresses held in September/October. They proposed that 24 funds should be established, each with its own governing board. Initially, a majority of the members of the boards would be designated by the unions, while the remainder would be chosen by elected regional and local government bodies. In time, the boards could conceivably be elected directly. Each of the regional funds would be financed on a dual basis: (1) through a 1 percent increase in the amount that employers pay on behalf of each worker into the ATP system, and (2) through the annual transfer of one fifth of company profits above a certain percentage of its annual income. The wage-earner funds would be invested in Swedish industries through the purchase of company shares on the open stock market. Voting power conferred by share ownership would be divided between the governing boards of the various regional funds and the local unions. As initially proposed by the SAP and the LO in 1980, dividend income would be paid into the supplementary pension system.

\* \* \*

# CONCLUSION

None of the workplace reforms described above is in itself revolutionary or even dramatic. Other democratic nations have enacted more sweeping measures in particular areas of the industrial process. West Germany's system of codetermination (*Mitbestimmung*), for instance, offers workers and unions significantly more direct influence over company decisions than is the case in Sweden. Some of the American "humanization of work-life" projects are far more radical in terms of job redesign than the experiments at Volvo.[8] French and Italian judges have sentenced employers to jail for manslaughter when fatalities occurred in industrial accidents. That Sweden has become a recognized model for the democratization of work life is not due to the radicalism of any single reform; instead, it is a consequence of the scope and cumulative effect of the various measures taken together. The whole of Sweden's work-place reform, in short, is greater than the sum of its parts.

The LO has officially described this achievement as "reformism in the best sense of the word," aiming at a "fundamental transformation of society." In practice, it corresponds to Gunnar Adler-Karlsson's concept of "functional socialism": the socialization of some aspects of private ownership without touching the fact of ownership itself.[9] According to this definition, managerial privileges constitute a bundle of rights which, far from being indivisible, can be split in a variety of ways between management and labor. Among those affecting employees collectively, some—such as overseeing the day-to-day operations of the firm—remain the province of management. Other rights, such as those concerning health and safety, have become the prerogative of workers. Those affecting managerial personnel and employment have become the object of joint management-labor consultation and collective bargaining. The result is that many more functions of management have become "socialized" in Sweden than in other industrial democracies, despite the absence of a significant degree of public owner-ship comparable, for instance, to that in France and the United Kingdom.

In terms of the historical objectives of in-creased worker participation, Sweden has thus attained not only the "integration" of employees into the productive process but also far-reaching humanization and democratization of workplace relations. As such, Sweden has achieved—alongside West Germany—one of the world's most fully developed systems of industrial democracy. At the same time, it should be noted that job redesign and the reforms of the 1970s —however striking in international comparison—have not yet fundamentally altered existing property relations. Just as managers still manage and workers still work, private citizens and corporations still own nearly 90 percent of Swedish industry. Whether this will remain true in the decades ahead is another matter.

The pending test of the Social Democrats' ability to move beyond industrial democracy on the level of individual plants to a more com-prehensive system of economic democracy affecting the productive process of the nation as a whole is the wage-earner fund issue. Ideological conservatives speaking on behalf of individual firms, the SAF, and the nonsocialist parties who perceive wage-earner funds as a threat to private property have their ardent counterparts among those Social Democrats who support the proposal for precisely that reason. For "system-changers" within the LO and the SAP, the wage-earner funds promise the eventual transfer of ownership of Sweden's larger industrial firms from private to collective hands. Party and union moderates, on the other hand, have continually urged caution in for-mulating, and above all implementing, a fund system. Among them are Prime Minister Palme and other cabinet officials who have repeatedly emphasized the need for finding a compromise solution to the fund question. While the former SAF chairman, Curt Nicolin, categorically rejected the idea of an agreement with the Social Democrats in the aftermath of the 1982

election—saying, "We will not negotiate our own destruction," he subsequently relented some-what and said: "We have our own views on the fund question but we're good Swedes and will participate in the discussion."

Despite intense nonsocialist criticism and rank-and-file ambivalence, the Social Democrats have proceeded to implement the fund pro-posal. As one of its first acts upon resuming office, the Palme government introduced a 20 percent tax on dividends as an initial step toward creating a wage-earner fund system. Simultan-eously, the cabinet decreed that Swedish firms must deposit 20 percent of their pre-tax profits in noninterest bearing accounts with the national pension fund. (They may draw on their deposits for investment purposes but only after prior con-sultations with local union officials.) In April 1983, the Swedish parliament endorsed the new "profit tax" by a substantial margin (156–133).

During the summer of 1983, the Social Democrats formally proposed the creation of five regional wage-earner funds (rather than the 24 provincial funds, as envisioned in 1978). The funds are to be financed through a combination of a 20 percent tax on company profits and a marginal increase in the percentage of employer contributions to the ATP system. Moderate Social Democratic views prevailed with respect to the intermediate effects of the fund system: the government's bill restricted both the total capitalization of the regional funds to 17.5 billion Swedish crowns (the equivalent of approxi-mately $2.19 billion) and the percentage of company shares that each of the funds may purchase (namely, 8 percent per fund for a hypothetical total of 40 percent among the five regional funds together). The Swedish parlia-ment acted on the proposal in December 1983 along predictably partisan lines. The Social Democrats voted unanimously in favor, VPK delegates abstained, and nonsocialist deputies voted against. The plan went into effect in January 1984.

The next national election...will offer the Swedish electorate an opportunity to pass interim judgment on the prospective transformation of the nation's current economic system into a new mix of public and private ownership promised by the introduction of the wage-earner fund system. If the voters so endorse, the result will in fact be a threshold move toward an unprecedented version of economic democracy.

## Notes

1. Edward S. Greenberg, "Industrial Self-Management and Political Attitudes," *American Political Science Review* 75 (1981), pp. 29–42.

2. Among them are David R. Cameron, "The Expansion of the Public Economy: A Comparative Analysis," *American Political Science Review* 72 (December 1978), pp. 1243–1261; Cameron, "On the Limits of the Public Economy," *The Annals* 459 (1982), pp. 46–62; Francis B. Castles, *The Social Democratic Image of Society* (Boston: Routledge & Kegan Paul, 1978); Arnold J. Heidenheimer, Hugo Heclo, and Carolyn Teich Adams, *Comparative Public Policy: The Politics of Social Choice in Europe and America*, 2d ed. (New York: St. Martin's Press, 1983); Douglas A. Hibbs, Jr., "Political Parties and Macroeconomic Policy," *American Political Science Review* 71 (1977), pp. 1467–1487; Walter Korpi, *The Working Class in Welfare Capitalism: Work, Unions and Politics in Sweden* (Boston: Routledge & Kegan Paul, 1978); and Manfred G. Schmidt, "Does Corporatism Matter?" in *Patterns of Corporate Policy-Making*, ed. Gerhard Lehmbruch and Philippe C. Schmitter (Newbury Park, Calif: Sage Publications, 1982).

3. Frederick Winslow Taylor, *The Principles of Scientific Management* (New York: Harper & Row, 1916), p.38.

4. Stefan Aguren, Reine Hansson, and K. G. Karlsson, *The Volvo Kalmar Plant: The Impact of New Design on Work Organization* (Stockholm: Rationalization Council, 1976).

5. The act apparently also deters small firms from hiring new employees as quickly as they otherwise might.

6. Rudolf Meidner, in collaboration with Anna Hedborg and Gunnar Fond, *Löntagarfonder* (Stockholm: Tidens förlag, 1975).

7. Ibid., p. 20.

8. The General Foods Gravy Train plant in Topeka, Kansas, for example, encourages workers to learn *every* job in the plant, including those normally relegated to lab technicians and production engineers. Work teams handle hiring, what firing there is, and most of the direct management of the production process, even to the point of starting production during the graveyard shift in the absence of managers or team leaders. See Daniel Zwerdling, *Democracy at Work* (Washington, D.C.: Association for Self-Management, 1978), pp. 19–29.

9. Gunnar Adler-Karlsson, *Funktionssocialism*, 2d ed. (Stockholm: Prisma, 1970).

# CHAPTER FOUR

# Authoritarianism: Old, New, Transitional

## 13

## On Democracy and Tyranny

*Aristotle*

### PREREQUISITES OF DEMOCRACY

We proceed now to inquire what form of government and what manner of life is best for communities in general, not adapting it to that superior virtue which is above the reach of the vulgar, or that education which every advantage of nature and fortune only can furnish, nor to those imaginary plans which may be formed at pleasure; but to that mode of life which the greater part of mankind can attain to, and that government which most cities may establish: for as to those aristocracies which we have now mentioned, they are either too perfect for a state to support, or one so nearly alike to that state we are now going to inquire into, that we shall treat of them both as one.

The opinions which we form upon these subjects must depend upon one common principle: for if what I have said in my treatise on Morals is true, a happy life must arise from an uninterrupted course of virtue; and if virtue consists in a certain medium, the middle life must certainly be the happiest; which medium is attainable by every one. The boundaries of virtue

SOURCE: Aristotle, "On Democracy and Tyranny," in *A Treatise on Government*, trans. William Ellis (London: George Routledge and Sons, 1888). Abridged by the editors. Aristotle taught from 335 to 323 B.C. His writings are drawn from notes taken by his students.

and vice in the state must also necessarily be the same as in a private person; for the form of government is the life of the city. In every city the people are divided into three sorts; the very rich, the very poor, and those who are between them. If this is universally admitted, that the mean is best, it is evident that even in point of fortune mediocrity is to be preferred; . . .

It is also the genius of a city to be composed as much as possible of equals; which will be most so when the inhabitants are in the middle state: from whence it follows, that that city must be best framed which is composed of those whom we say are naturally its proper members. It is men of this station also who will be best assured of safety and protection; for they will neither covet what belongs to others, as the poor do; nor will others covet what is theirs, as the poor do what belongs to the rich; and thus, without plotting against any one, or having any one plot against them, they will live free from danger: for which reason Phocylides wisely wishes for the middle state, as being most productive of happiness. It is plain, then, that the most perfect political community must be amongst those who are in the middle rank, and those states are best instituted wherein these are a larger and more respectable part, if possible, than both the other; or, if that cannot be, at least than either of them separate; so that being thrown into the balance it may prevent either scale from preponderating.

. . .The middle state is therefore best, as being least liable to those seditions and insurrections which disturb the community; and for the same reason extensive governments are least liable to these inconveniences; for there those in a middle state are very numerous, whereas in small ones it is easy to pass to the two extremes, so as hardly to have any in a medium remaining, but the one half rich, the other poor: and from the same principle it is that democracies are more firmly established and of longer continuance than oligarchies; but even in those when there is a want of a proper number of men of middling fortune, the poor extend their power too far, abuses arise, and the government is soon at an end.

Other particulars we will consider separately; but it seems proper to prove, that the supreme power ought to be lodged with the many, rather than with those of the better sort, who are few; and also to explain what doubts (and probably just ones) may arise: now, though not one individual of the many may himself be fit for the supreme power, yet when these many are joined together, it does not follow but they may be better qualified for it than those; and this not separately, but as a collective body; as the public suppers exceed those which are given at one person's private expense: for, as they are many, each person brings in his share of virtue and wisdom; and thus, coming together, they are like one man made up of a multitude, with many feet, many hands, and many intelligences: thus is it with respect to the manners and understandings of the multitude taken together; for which reason the public are the best judges of music and poetry; for some understand one part, some another, and all collectively the whole....

...For the multitude when they are collected together have all of them sufficient understanding for these purposes, and, mixing among those of higher rank, are serviceable to the city, as some things, which alone are improper for food, when mixed with others make the whole more wholesome than a few of them would be.

* * *

Since in every art and science the end aimed at is always good, so particularly in this, which is the most excellent of all, the founding of civil society, the good wherein aimed at is justice; for it is this which is for the benefit of all. Now, it is the common opinion, that justice is a certain equality; and in this point all the philosophers are agreed when they treat of morals: for they say what is just, and to whom; and that equals ought to receive equal: but we should know how we are to determine what things are equal and what unequal; and in this there is some difficulty, which calls for the philosophy of the politician. Some persons will probably say, that the employments of the state ought to be given according to every particular excellence of each citizen, if there is no other difference between them and the rest of the community, but they are in every respect else alike: for justice attributes different things to persons differing from each other in their character, according to their respective merits....

Now the first thing which presents itself to our consideration is this, whether it is best to be governed by a good man, or by good laws? Those who prefer a kingly government think that laws can only speak a general language, but cannot adapt themselves to particular circumstances; for which reason it is absurd in any science to follow written rule; and even in Egypt the physician was allowed to alter the mode of cure which the law prescribed to him, after the fourth day; but if he did it sooner it was at his own peril: from whence it is evident, on the very same account, that a government of written laws is not the best; and yet general reasoning is necessary to all those who are to govern, and it will be much more perfect in those who are entirely free from passions than in those to whom they are natural. But now this is a quality which laws possess; while the other is natural to the human soul. But some one will say in answer to this, that man will be a better judge of particulars. It will be necessary, then, for a king to be a lawgiver, and that his laws should be published, but that those should have no authority which are absurd, as those which are not, should. But whether is it better for the community that those things which cannot possibly come under the cognizance of the law either at all or properly should be under the government of every worthy citizen, as the present method is, when the public community, in their general assemblies, act as judges and counsellors, where all their determinations are upon particular cases. For one individual, be he who he will, will be found, upon comparison, inferior to a whole people taken collectively: but this is what a city is, as a public entertainment is better than one man's portion: for this reason the multitude judge of many things better than any one single person. They are also less liable to corruption from their numbers, as water is from its quantity: besides, the judgment of an individual must necessarily be perverted if he is overcome by anger or any other passion; but it would be hard indeed if the whole community should be misled by anger. Moreover, let the people be free, and they will do nothing but in conformity to the law, except only in those cases which the law cannot speak to. But though what I am going to propose may not easily be met with, yet if the majority of the state should happen to be good men, should they prefer one uncorrupt governor or many equally good, is it not evident that they should choose the many? But there may be divisions among these which cannot happen when there is but one. In answer to this it may be replied that all their souls will be as much animated with virtue as this one man's.

. . . As for an absolute monarchy as it is called, that is to say, when the whole state is wholly subject to the will of one person, namely the king, it seems to many that it is unnatural that one man should have the entire rule over his fellow-citizens when the state consists of equals: for nature requires that the same right and the same rank should necessarily take place amongst all those who are equal by nature: for as it would be hurtful to the body for those who are of different constitutions to observe the same regimen, either of diet or clothing, so is it with respect to the honours of the state as hurtful, that those who are equal in merit should be unequal in rank; for which reason it is as much

a man's duty to submit to command as to assume it, and this also by rotation; for this is law, for order is law; and it is more proper that law should govern than any one of the citizens: upon the same principle, if it is advantageous to place the supreme power in some particular persons, they should be appointed to be only guardians, and the servants of the laws, for the supreme power must be placed somewhere; but they say, that it is unjust that where all are equal one person should continually enjoy it. But it seems unlikely that man should be able to adjust that which the law cannot determine; it may be replied, that the law having laid down the best rules possible, leaves the adjustment and application of particulars to the discretion of the magistrate; besides, it allows anything to be altered which experience proves may be better established. Moreover, he who would place the supreme power in mind, would place it in God and the laws; but he who entrusts man with it, gives it to a wild beast, for such his appetites sometimes make him; for passion influences those who are in power, even the very best of men: for which reason law is reason without desire.

## TYRANNY

It now remains to treat of a tyranny. . . In the beginning of this work we inquired into the nature of kingly government, and entered into a particular examination of what was most properly called so, and whether it was advantageous to a state or not, and what it should be, and how established; and we divided a tyranny into two pieces when we were upon this subject, because there is something analogous between this and a kingly government, for they are both of them established by law; for among some of the barbarians they elect a monarch with absolute power, and formerly among the Greeks there were some such, whom they called aesumnetes. Now these differ from each other; for some possess only kingly power regulated by law, and rule those who voluntarily submit to their government; others rule despotically according to their own will. There is a third species of tyranny, most properly so called, which is the very opposite to kingly power; for this is the government of one who rules over his equals and superiors without being accountable for his conduct, and whose object is his own advantage, and not the advantage of those he governs; for which reason he rules by compulsion, for no freemen will ever willingly submit to such a government. These are the different species of tyrannies, their principles, and their causes.

...Tyrannies are preserved two ways most opposite to each other, one of which is when the power is delegated from one to the other, and in this manner many tyrants govern in their states. Report says that Periander founded many of these. There are also many of them to be met with amongst the Persians. What has been already mentioned is as conducive as anything can be to preserve a tyranny; namely, to keep down those who are of an aspiring disposition, to take off those who will not submit, to allow no public meals, no clubs, no education, nothing at all, but to guard against everything that gives rise to high spirits or mutual confidence; nor to suffer the learned meetings of those who are at leisure to hold conversation with each other; and to endeavour by every means possible to keep all the people strangers to each other; for knowledge increases mutual confidence; and to oblige all strangers to appear in public, and to live near the city-gate, that all their actions may be sufficiently seen; for those who are kept like slaves seldom entertain any noble thoughts: in short, to imitate everything which the Persians and barbarians do, for they all contribute to support slavery; and to endeavour to know what every one who is under their power does and says; and for this purpose to employ spies....

...A tyrant also should endeavour to engage his subjects in a war, that they may have employment and continually depend upon their general. A king is preserved by his friends, but a tyrant is of all persons the man who can place no confidence in friends, as every one

has it in his desire and these chiefly in their power to destroy him....

These and such-like are the supports of a tyranny, for it comprehends whatsoever is wicked. But all these things may be comprehended in three divisions, for there are three objects which a tyranny has in view; one of which is, that the citizens should be of poor abject dispositions; for such men never propose to conspire against any one. The second is, that they should have no confidence in each other; for while they have not this, the tyrant is safe enough from destruction. For which reason they are always at enmity with those of merit, as hurtful to their government; not only as they scorn to be governed despotically, but also because they can rely upon each other's fidelity, and others can rely upon theirs, and because they will not inform against their associates, nor any one else. The third is, that they shall be totally without the means of doing anything; for no one undertakes what is impossible for him to perform: so that without power a tyranny can never be destroyed.

# 14
# Notes on the Theory of Dictatorship
*Franz L. Neumann*

## DEFINITION OF DICTATORSHIP

Strange though it may seem, we do not possess any systematic study of dictatorship. The historical information is abundant, and there are many analyses of individual dictators in various countries. But there is no analysis that seeks to

SOURCE: Reprinted with permission of The Free Press, a division of Macmillan, Inc. from *The Democratic and Authoritarian State* by Franz L. Neumann. Copyright © 1957 by The Free Press; copyright renewed 1985.

generalize not only from the political experience of the 20th century, but from the political systems of the more distant past. The present paper attempts to outline the theoretical problems encountered in the analysis of dictatorship and to indicate whatever answers now can be supplied.

By dictatorship we understand the rule of a person or a group of persons who arrogate to themselves and monopolize power in the state, exercising it without restraint.

The first question raised by this definition is whether the Roman dictatorship and the absolute monarchy should be included in its scope.

It seems more appropriate to classify the Roman dictatorship (prior to Sulla) not as a dictatorship properly speaking, but as a form of Crisis Government. This may seem arbitrary, for the very word "dictator" derives from Roman constitutional law. Nevertheless, the Roman dictatorship was a magistracy, clearly defined in authorization, scope, and duration, and it ought not to be confused with a political system in which power is arrogated by an individual or a group, and which does not circumscribe either the scope or the duration of dictatorial power. The Roman dictator was appointed by one of the consuls for a period not to exceed six months, to defend the country against an external enemy or to cope with internal dissension. He was duty-bound to appoint at once a Master of the Horse for the command of the cavalry; he had no authority to change the constitution, to declare war, to intervene in civil law suits, or to impose new fiscal obligations upon Roman citizens. Within these limits, the sovereign power of the Roman people was concentrated in his hands. The consuls became his subordinates; the tribunician power of intercession did not apply against his acts; nor could a citizen condemned in a criminal trial invoke the normal right of appeal (*provocatio*) against him.

The Romans resorted to dictatorship because the collegiate nature of the magistracy, including the consulate, and the one-year restriction on its term, made the conduct of war extremely difficult. But the dictatorship itself was to prove unsuitable for wars of long duration. By the end of the fourth century it was already in decline, reappearing in irregular forms during the Punic Wars and disappearing at the end of the Second Punic War (201 B.C.). From then on, the Roman dictatorship (e.g., Sulla's and Caesar's) changes its character radically.

The second problem that our definition raises is the relation between monarchy and dictatorship. The title of the absolute ruler— whether he is designated King, Emperor, Leader, or Duce—is not decisive here. This was already recognized by Aristotle, who held the rule of kings among non-civilized (non-Hellenic) peoples to be "similar to that of tyranny" and who defined his fifth type of kingship, the case "where a single power is sovereign on every issue, with the same sort of power that a tribe or a polis exercises over its public concerns," as a *Pambasileia*, an all-kingship or super-kingship.

Actually, from the standpoint of the exercise of power the absolute monarch is a dictator, but from the standpoint of the legitimacy of power, he is not. We may speak of legitimate monarchical rule whenever accession to power is constitutionally regulated by heredity or by election and monarchical rule is generally accepted as the normal form of government. These criteria are rather vague—but so is the actual situation. In the history of political and constitutional thought, the ruler who comes to power through a *coup d'état* (*absque titulo*) is held to be an usurping tyrant, but he may rid himself of this stigma if he succeeds in formally establishing his rule and that of his line, which then becomes "legitimate." On the other hand it was also generally held that a monarch who acceded to the throne legitimately could degenerate into a tyrant through his acts (*quoad exercitio*). Thus, while one may distinguish in principle between monarchy and dictatorship, one must realize that the principle suffers many exceptions and that, consequently, certain forms of the absolute monarchy must also be treated as forms of dictatorship.

Our definition, furthermore, envisages dictatorship only in the state, and in no other social organization. There may be situations in which absolute power of a party boss or of the *pater familias* may help us understand the mechanisms leading to a dictatorship or serving to maintain its power. But there is as yet no convincing evidence that the dictatorial structure of social organizations necessarily leads to or facilitates political dictatorship. An example is the ambiguity of the social and psychological role of the so-called "authoritarian family."[1] The authoritarian (quasi-dictatorial) family may lead, as some maintain, to a more ready acceptance of political dictatorship,[2] but dictatorship may also be promoted (and more frequently, perhaps) by the decay of traditional authority, by the very undermining of the authority of the father. The relation between political and social forms of authoritarianism must, therefore, be taken as a special problem, and not as an automatic correlation.

Moreover, we deliberately do not distinguish among a dictator, a tyrant, and a despot. Tyranny and despotism have no precise meaning. One usually associates despotism with oriental dictatorships, whereas tyranny is often used to designate any system of government that either in its origin or in its practice is tainted by unconstitutional practices or characterized by lack of restraints. Both words are emotionally charged and exhibit in varying degrees rejection and resentment of these systems of government.

Rejection of the terms *tyranny* and *despotism* does not mean, however, that within the general definition of dictatorship there are no subtypes. A number of distinctions are significant.

The first pertains to the scope of the political power monopolized by the dictator. The dictator may exercise his power through absolute control of the traditional means of coercion only, i.e., the army, police, bureaucracy, and judiciary. We may call this type a *simple dictatorship*.

In some situations, the dictator may feel compelled to build up popular support, to secure a mass base, either for his rise to power or for the exercise of it, or for both. We may call this type a *caesaristic dictatorship*, which, as the name indicates, is always personal in form.

Even this combination of monopolized coercion and popular backing may be insufficient as a guarantee of power. It may be necessary to control education, the means of communication and economic institutions and thus to gear the whole of society and the private life of the citizen to the system of political domination. The term for this type is *totalitarian dictatorship*. It may be either collective or personal, that is, it may or may not have a caesaristic element.

It need hardly be mentioned that these classifications are ideal types which will only approximate historical realities. They will help us, however, to understand the structure of the various cases of dictatorship.

## CAESARISTIC DICTATORSHIP

The simple dictatorship—whether it be military or bureaucratic, the rule of a junta, a caudillo, or even an absolute monarch—is exercised primarily through the control of what one may call the classical instruments of rule: army, police, bureaucracy, judiciary. This limitation is due less to self-imposed restraints than to the absence of any need for more extensive controls. Simple dictatorship usually occurs in countries where the masses of the people lack political awareness, where politics is the affair of small cliques who compete for favors and hope to gain prestige and wealth by association with the dictator. The mass of the people pay taxes and may have to serve in the army, but otherwise have little to do with political life. The only social controls which may be needed are bribery and corruption of a few influential individuals in order to tie them closely to the system.

In the *caesaristic dictatorship* a new element enters: the need for popular support. The term *caesarism* was apparently coined by Romieu in his little book *L'Ere des Cesars* (1950) and its climate most adequately described by Guizot, Louis Philippe's Prime Minister after the revolution of 1830.

"Chaos," says Guizot, "is now hiding under one word—democracy. This is now the ultimate and universal word all seek to appropriate as a talisman. The Monarchists say: Our Monarchy is a Democratic Monarchy; it differs essentially from the ancient monarchy and is adapted to modern conditions of society. The Republicans say: The Republic is Democracy governing itself. This is the only form of government in harmony with democratic society, its principles, its sentiments, and its interests.

"Socialists, Communists, Montagnards wish that the Republic should be pure and absolute democracy. This is for them the condition of its legitimacy.

"Such is the power of the word democracy that no government or party dares to exist or believes it can exist without inscribing that word upon its banner."[3]

Caesarism becomes a necessity when the masses tend to become politically articulate.

\* \* \*

## TOTALITARIAN DICTATORSHIP

Totalitarian dictatorship, to which our attention now will be directed, ought not to be confused with caesarism. Up to the 19th century at least, caesaristic dictatorship does not necessarily lead to a totalitarian system, nor is the totalitarian state necessarily the result of a genuine caesaristic movement. Totalitarianism is thus a separate problem. For the purpose of a brief discussion the modern totalitarian dictatorship may be reduced to five essential factors.

The first of these is the transition from a state based upon the rule of law (the German *Rechtsstaat*) to a police state. The rule of law is a presumption in favor of the right of the citizen and against the coercive power of the state. In the totalitarian state this presumption is reversed. Details need not concern us here, since the power of executive agencies in totalitarian states to interfere at discretion with life, liberty and property may be taken as the best-known feature of this kind of dictatorship.

The second factor is the transition from the diffusion of power in liberal states to the concentration of power in the totalitarian regime. This concentration may vary in degree as well as form. But there is no role in any totalitarian state for the various liberal devices of diffusing power, such as separation of powers, federalism, a functioning multiparty system, bicameralism, etc.

These first two elements, however, are to be found in the absolute monarchy as well as in the totalitarian dictatorship. What distinguishes totalitarianism politically is the third element, namely, the existence of a monopolistic state party. Such a party is required because the traditional instruments of coercion do not suffice to control an industrial society, and all the less so since bureaucracies and armies may not always be reliable. The monopolistic party is a flexible instrument which provides the force to control the state machine and society and to perform the gigantic task of cementing the authoritarian elements within society together.

Moreover, the monopolistic party involves a socio-psychological aspect pertaining to what is commonly called a "mass" society. Since modern totalitarian dictatorships arise, almost without exception, within and against democracies (weak though the democratic structures may have been), the totalitarian clique has to assume the shape of a democratic movement and to retain this façade even after it has come to power. In other words, it is forced to practice the ritual of democracy even though the substance is totally denied.

The role of the monopolistic party involves the fourth element of the totalitarian dictatorship: the transition from pluralist to totalitarian social controls. Society ceases to be distinguished from the state; it is totally permeated by political power. The control of society, now as important as the control of the state, is achieved by the following techniques:

1. The leadership principle—to enforce guidance from the top and responsibility to the top.

2. The "synchronization" of all social organizations—not only to control them, but to make them serviceable to the state.

3. The creation of graded elites—so as to enable the rulers to control the masses from within and to disguise manipulation from without, i.e., to supplement bureaucracies in the narrow meaning of the term with private leadership groups within the various strata of the population.

4. The atomization and isolation of the individual, which involves negatively the destruction or at least weakening of social units based on biology (family), tradition, religion, or cooperation in work or leisure; and positively the imposition of huge and undifferentiated mass organizations which leave the individual isolated and more easily manipulable.

5. The transformation of culture into propaganda—of cultural values into saleable commodities.

The final factor in totalitarianism is the reliance upon terror, i.e., the use of noncalculable violence as a permanent threat against the individual. Care must be taken, however, not to define a totalitarian dictatorship simply as rule of violence. Without it, it is true, such regimes could not survive. But they could not endure for any length of time without considerable identification by the oppressed people with its rulers.

These, in brief outline, are the features of the most repressive of political systems. What distinguishes it from absolutism is not primarily the caesaristic element, for this was also characteristic of the absolute monarchy in certain periods of its history, but rather the destruction of the line between state and society and the total politicization of society by the device of the monopolistic party. This is not merely a question of more or less political power. The difference is one of quality, not quantity. Where, as in the absolute monarchy, power is primarily exercised through the traditional bureaucratic instruments of coercion, its operation is governed by abstract, calculable rules, although their execution often may be arbitrary.

Absolutism, therefore, already contains the major institutional principles of modern liberalism. Totalitarian dictatorship, on the other hand, is the absolute negation of these principles because the main repressive agencies are not courts and administrative bodies, but the secret police and the party.

A fully developed totalitarian dictatorship is the form an industrial society may adopt if it should become necessary to maximize its repressive elements and eliminate its liberal ones. But totalitarian dictatorship is not the child of modern industrialism alone. Sparta...may be...an illuminating earlier experiment.

\* \* \*

## DEMOCRACY AND DICTATORSHIP

If we review the various types of dictatorships outlined above, we are forced to conclude that the usual confrontation of liberal democracy vs. dictatorship as an antithesis of good and evil, cannot be maintained from a historical point of view. Moralizing about political systems makes it difficult to understand their functions. The relationship between democracy and dictatorship is not as simple as is sometimes stated.

1. Dictatorships may be an implementation of democracy. But this refers to emergency dictatorships with functions similar to the classical Roman type, which we prefer to classify as a kind of magistracy.
2. Dictatorships may be the preparation for democracy. We may then speak of an educational dictatorship.
3. Dictatorships may be the very negation of democracy and thus be a totally regressive system.

Pisistratus' rule is probably a classical example of an educational dictatorship. As Werner Jaeger puts it: "The masses were still politically inexperienced, so that democracy was far away: it could not come until the aristocracy had been brought low by the Pisistratic tyrants." We may add that the great function of the Pisistratidae was the creation of an Athenian national (or collective) spirit. This was done by facilitating the emergence of a "middle class," which Aristotle believed to be the social prerequisite of democracy. Hence, without the work of Pisistratus the regimes of Cleisthenes and Pericles would hardly be conceivable.

It is well to remember that the Marxist-Leninist conception of a dictatorship of the proletariat was democratic precisely in this sense of a preparatory dictatorship. The concentration of power in the hands of the proletariat was to be used to abolish class rule altogether and to herald a new epoch of freedom in a classless society. That it was not this expectation but the very opposite which materialized cannot be discussed in detail here. However, we may cite the basic reasons why, under modern conditions, every dictatorship tends to be a totalitarian dictatorship and to involve the negation of democracy.

The democratic ideology has become so universal that Guizot's statement seems even truer today than it did in 1848. All modern dictatorships arose from democratic conditions. This is true of Italy, Germany, Spain, Argentina, and perhaps even of the USSR, although to a lesser degree.

The dictator is therefore compelled to seek mass support and, having obtained it, to practice the ritual of democracy even if its substance is withheld. As Engels already saw, a *coup d'état* seems hopeless against a modern army; the dictator can come to power only with the help or toleration of the army, but to sustain his power, he depends on a mass base.

There is, however, an important distinction between the Fascist-Nazi type and the Bolshevik. In the former, the dictator could rely upon substantial sectors of the traditional ruling groups (industry, finance, agrarians, army, bureaucracy, judiciary) which were committed to a minimum of formal legality since overt rebellion would have jeopardized their own status and security. Consequently, the dictatorship in its rise to power had to play the democratic game (compare Hitler's strategy before his Beer Hall Putsch of 1923 and afterwards). And once it had attained this goal, the requirements of competition with the outside world and the need to secure the active or passive co-operation of industrial labor, led the Nazi-Fascist type of dictatorship to present itself as a higher and nobler form of democracy.

For the Bolsheviks the need for mass support is of a different nature. The original theory of the dictatorship of the proletariat as the dictatorship of the majority over a minority was compatible at least with one version of democracy. But the Russian proletariat was a small minority in 1917, and with the Bolshevik rejection of Trotsky's theory of a permanent revolution, the democratic mass base had to be secured from among the peasants. When this was not voluntarily forthcoming the Bolshevik regime evolved into a full-blown totalitarian dictatorship.

But even in agrarian, colonial, and semi-colonial countries, where democracy did not exist or was inadequately practiced, modern dictatorship tends to become totalitarian. Today every nation experiences democracy vicariously. Due to the world-wide scope of communications, even the most backward peoples have become aware of democracy and want it, awakening mass consciousness usually taking the form of a demand for national emancipation. Consequently, here too a dictator must attempt to be a Caesar by acting out the democratic ritual even if he is compelled to go on towards a totalitarian regime.

## THE SOCIAL FUNCTION OF DICTATORSHIP

Neither the attraction of a democratic ideology nor the scope of the dictatorship can fully explain the phenomena of caesarism and totalitarianism. An understanding of the social function of dictatorship would require a comprehensive analysis based upon the following elements:

1. The economic system.
2. The class relationship.
3. The personality structure.

In each historical situation these factors—economic, social, and psychological—must be treated as a unity, not as isolated, independent causes. An index of changes in these elements will frequently—I would even say invariably—be found in the intellectual and artistic trends of a given period, i.e., in philosophy, literature, and the arts. I should like to indicate certain principles that may help in the search for the causes and functions of the various types of dictatorships.

In terms of *class relationships*, the function of dictatorship may be related to three basic and recurring situations:

1. Disenfranchised and insurgent social classes demand recognition of their interests which the political power-holders refuse to grant. There are two alternatives, depending upon the political maturity of the ascending classes:

If they are politically mature—as the bourgeoisie in England in the 17th or in France in the 18th century—caesarism will be merely a transitory phenomenon (Cromwell and Robespierre). The new classes, in power and commanding a majority, will for various reasons demand a liberal political system.

But if they are not mature, or too weak, the caesaristic movement will become a dictatorship as in the case of Pisistratus, Cola di Rienzo, or Lenin.

2. The second case is the attempt of a social class threatened with decline and striving to preserve its status and power. Dictatorship may then arise as an attempt to preserve the status quo. The most striking examples are Sparta, to a lesser extent the half-hearted efforts of Napoleon I, and probably the regimes of Franco and Perón.

3. The third possibility is the attempt of what one might call doomed classes to change radically the socioeconomic situation, to reverse it, and to install a political system that would restore them to their old preeminence. This is the kernel of the German and Italian Fascist movements.

These class relationships must be studied in the light of changing economic systems. Totalitarianism, although not a new phenomenon, is determined in its modern form by the features of an industrial society. Modern industrialism is politically ambivalent because it contains and intensifies two diametrically opposed trends in modern society: the trend toward freedom and the trend toward repression. Sociologists usually define this as the problem of "moral lag," holding that the growing potentialities of modern technology outstrip the progress of "morality." This may or may not be true, but it is not, in my opinion, the decisive factor.

It is easy to say that technology is neutral politically and socially, so that any desired result can be attained depending upon the persons who use it and upon their aims. Technological optimists (like Georges Sorel and Thorstein Veblen) hold that only the full development of technological resources and their efficient utilization (e.g., exclusion of "conspicuous consumption"), can bring mankind to its highest perfection. We do not challenge this statement, but should like to explore some of its implications.

Large-scale technology on the one hand may imply the total dependence of the industrial population upon a complex, integrated mechanism, which can be operated only in a highly organized, stratified, and hierarchic system. This system must instill the virtues of discipline, obedience and subordination—no matter who owns the means of production. Thus, modern industrialism preaches the very virtues which every authoritarian political system seeks to cultivate. These virtues are repressive because they are opposed to man's self-determination.

On the other hand, the very opposite virtues may also be strengthened by technology: self-reliance, awareness of one's power and, most particularly, the feeling of solidarity—

that is, a spirit of cooperation as opposed to authoritarianism.

## THE PSYCHOLOGICAL PROCESSES OF DICTATORSHIP

These two antagonistic trends of industrialism are, in my opinion, essential for the understanding of modern dictatorship. The authoritarian element facilitates the rise of a dictatorship. But the cooperative aspect forces the dictatorship to find some way of replacing solidarity based on a rational interest (such as class interest) with some other identification that does not undermine but rather strengthens the dictatorship. Mussolini tried corporatism; Hitler, the doctrine of folk-community; Stalin, that of the classless socialist state. But in varying degrees all these identifications were a fake. That they nonetheless "succeeded" leads us to our final problem: the psychological processes connected with dictatorship. The basic problem is anxiety and fear and their function in political life.

Freud has defined anxiety as an "increase in tensions arising from nongratification of [the individual's] need."[4] Anxiety is thus always present—at least potentially—as a situation or a state of indefiniteness. Fear, in turn, is the recognition of a specific danger.

Therefore, external dangers, arising in specific situations and from specific objects, are experienced in the light of internal anxiety, which then becomes externalized and activated.

But this externalization of anxiety through fear is by no means always dangerous to the personality. One may distinguish three functions of fear:

1. Fear as a warning.
2. Fear as protection.
3. Fear as destruction.

Thus, an external danger may well have a kind of monitoring function: it may warn the individual that something terrible may happen to him. And the reaction to the threat may then perform a protective or even cathartic function. It may not only remove the concrete danger, but allay the anxiety as well and thus make the individual more free. On the other hand, fear may activate anxiety (particularly neurotic anxiety) to the point of making it destructive. (Indeed there are psychoanalysts who derive anxiety from destructive impulses.) Hence, in some individuals, fear becoming operative or latent anxiety may either paralyze the personality and make it incapable of defense (depressive anxiety) or heighten its aggressive instincts (persecutory anxiety).

This bare (and rather thin) analysis of certain terms of individual psychology may now be put to use in understanding the rise of totalitarian movements and the operation of the totalitarian state.

As an illustration let me again take the Spartan state. Plutarch says, " . . . [T]he Spartans dealt with them [the Helots] very hardly: for it was a common thing to force them to drink to excess, and to lead them in that condition into their public halls, that the children might see what a sight a drunken man is; they made them to dance low dances, and sing ridiculous songs. . . ." Then they assassinated them. There is little difference between the Spartan aristocracy's behavior toward the Helots and the Nazis' treatment of the Jews. The ancients were well aware of the fact that the passive element in the Spartan character was fear, that this fear was systematically cultivated and that the Spartans' famous courage in battle was nothing but fear of being stigmatized if they failed in their military duty. The actual or feigned fear of the Helots is the integrating principle of the Spartan ruling class, their anxieties being activated into aggressiveness and destruction. The totally repressive character of Sparta (as compared to Athens) rests precisely in this fact.

In totalitarian movements (as contrasted with totalitarian states), there appears a similar element. A distinction should be made between the Nazi-Fascist movement and Lenin's party prior to 1917. The Bolshevik party at that time was not a totalitarian movement, nor may Lenin (in contrast to post-1928 Stalin) be considered a totalitarian leader. The Bolshevik party then did not manipulate fear; this is a later development which began with the defeat of the revolutionary movements in Western Europe.

In contrast, the Nazi-Fascist movement activated the anxieties of the middle classes and turned them into channels of destruction which were made legitimate by means of the masses' identification with a leader, the hero. The nature of such identification has already been discussed by Freud.[5] This phenomenon appears in all caesaristic and totalitarian movements, in various degrees, of course, and with varying historical functions.

## Notes

1. Which, however, need not necessarily be a dictatorial family, because the power of the *pater familias* may well be founded in reason: "rational authority."

2. T. W. Adorno et al., *The Authoritarian Personality* (New York: W. W. Norton, 1950).

3. Guizot, *La Démocratie en France* (Leipzig, 1849), p. 2.

4. Sigmund Freud, *The Problem of Anxiety,* trans. H. A. Bunker (New York: W. W. Norton, 1936), p. 76.

5. Sigmund Freud, *Group Psychology and the Analysis of the Ego,* trans. S. J. Strachey (New York: W. W. Norton, 1949).

# 15

# From Authoritarianism to Democracy

*Myron Weiner*

Few issues are more likely to seize world attention for the remainder of this century than the

SOURCE: Myron Weiner, "Empirical Democratic Theory and the Transition from Authoritarianism to Democracy," *PS,* vol. XX, no. 4 (Fall 1987), pp. 861–866. Reprinted by permission of the American Political Science Association and the author.

question of whether authoritarian countries in the third world will make a transition to democratic civilian rule. The Philippine experience and the promising developments in South Korea have heartened democrats in Bangladesh, Indonesia, Pakistan, and Taiwan. In each of these countries democrats are pondering over what is the appropriate strategy for pressing authoritarian rulers and their military supporters to open up the political system to competitive politics. What coalitions against authoritarian rulers are most likely to succeed? Is a centrist or leftist stance likely to win maximum popular support? Is popular support sufficient or is it also necessary to win over sections of the military and if so, how is that to be done? Is external support helpful or harmful? Is a popular, mass, non-violent movement sufficient or are there circumstances when an armed struggle is necessary to force an authoritarian ruler to step down?

Alas, empirical democratic theory offers little of use to those who seek answers to these questions. The many attempts to formulate a theory on the prerequisites or conditions for the creation and persistence of democratic regimes have not stood well the test of time. The various theories are by now familiar to political scientists: the efforts by Seymour Martin Lipset, Phillips Cutright, Daniel Lerner, Deane Neubauer, and Leon Hurwitz to correlate modernization, economic growth and the development of democracy; the related work by Philip Coulter testing the hypothesis that social mobilization produces liberal democracy; neo-Marxist theories focusing on the nature of dependent development in the context of world capitalism to explain why democratic regimes have been replaced by bureaucratic authoritarian states; and Barrington Moore's efforts to identify the class configurations that emerge during the process of development, refining Aristotle's thesis that a strong urban middle class is indispensable in the growth of parliamentary democracy.

The relationship between rates of growth (or rates of social mobilization), class structure, and the development and persistence of democratic institutions in low-income countries has had several variant contradictory hypotheses. One is that a high rate of economic development is a precondition for democratic development, and hence that a *low* rate is destabilizing. A variant hypothesis (indeed, its antithesis!) is that a *high* rate of development can be destabilizing, especially when rapid social mobilization occurs without a commensurate increase in institution building and power sharing. Still another variant is the famous "J curve" hypothesis which asserts that stagnation or low growth following a period of high growth is destabilizing. For each of these hypotheses one can find examples, suggesting that they have little explanatory power.

Other theories have focused on the kinds of values essential for the maintenance of a democratic system, then looked at the value patterns of particular societies to see how good is the fit. Among the more sophisticated and influential of these theories was the work of Harry Eckstein on the congruence (or lack of it) between the authority patterns of democratic regimes and the social norms of intermediate institutions such as the family, the school and voluntary organizations. Gabriel Almond, Sidney Verba, and Robert Dahl, among others, have argued that attitudes and beliefs are ultimately decisive in whether democratic institutions can be made to work. There is, of course, some circularity in these arguments as John Stuart Mill suggested: the character of a people may shape political institutions, but it is also the case that democratic institutions shape attitudes toward political participation and can create a spirit of public-mindedness, tolerance for opposing viewpoints and interests, and increasing competence among citizens.

A list of countries in the contemporary third world that have sustained democratic institutions suggests how difficult it is to find an explanation that fits all the cases. They include India, Sri Lanka (its current ethnic turmoil notwithstanding), Costa Rica, Venezuela, Colombia, Malaysia, Jamaica, Trinidad and Tobago, Papua New Guinea, and the small states of the Bahama Islands, Barbados, Botswana, Nauru, Gambia, Mauritius and, until recently, Fiji. They include several countries that have slipped back

and forth between military and civilian democratic rule: Nigeria, Turkey, and, in Europe, Greece. The list has grown in recent years to include the Philippines, Argentina, Brazil, and several other Latin American countries. Paradoxically, many of these cases are often cited by democratic theorists as exceptions to their propositions, but for those of us trying to understand the conditions and prospects for democracy in the third world these are the very cases which theories need to explain!

One of the few generalizations that appears possible from this diverse list is that the British colonial model of tutelary democracy has been more successful than other colonial models in creating democratic institutions and processes in newly independent countries. Almost every country that has emerged from colonial rule since the second World War with a continuous democratic experience is a former British colony. Not a single newly independent country that lived under French, Dutch, American or Portuguese rule has continually remained democratic. This finding undermines the assumption that political institutions and procedures cannot be transplanted from one society to another, that such transplants would be rejected as alien to the body. But the success of the British model, limited as it is since not all former British colonies have remained democratic, suggests that we need to reexamine our assumptions. Robert Dahl, in his wonderful book, *Polyarchy, Participation and Opposition*, pointed out that foreign rule does not necessarily impede the emergence of a democratic system and may even make it possible. He noted that of the twenty-nine countries with polyarchical regimes in 1970, seventeen were inaugurated during a period of foreign domination, including Austria, West Germany, Italy, Japan, Australia and Canada, as well as some of the developing countries!

It ill serves the cause of democracy in the third world for countries to be told that their growth rates are too low, their middle class not large enough, their political culture inappropriate for democracy to thrive, or that an independent judiciary, a free press, and political pluralism are alien to their political tradition, Imagine if Lenin and Mao, after reading Marx, had concluded that communism was not possible in their countries because the proletariat was too small, capitalism had not yet reached an advanced enough stage for a revolution, and that one could not leap from "feudalism" and "semi-feudalism" to socialism. Marxist theory proved to be useless for predicting the rise of Marxist-Leninist regimes among low-income countries. Perhaps it is time to recognize that democratic theory, with its list of conditions and prerequisites, is a poor guide to action as well.

The characteristics of societies that have become democratic are sufficiently diverse to suggest that less attention should be paid to conditions and prerequisites, more to the strategies available to those who seek a democratic revolution. A review of the experiences of countries that have made successful transitions may point to workable strategies. There are, of course, unique features to every case and one must know the concrete circumstances before one can devise an appropriate strategy. But enough countries have made the transition from authoritarian regimes to democracy to suggest some of the major features of a strategy. I shall focus exclusively on transitions involving military and military-supported regimes since we do not as yet have any cases of transitions to democratic rule of authoritarian countries run by Marxist-Leninist parties. Efforts to end the domination of the communist parties in Poland, Czechoslovakia, Hungary, Afghanistan, Cuba, Nicaragua, Angola and Mozambique (not all, of course, in a democratic direction) have not thus far been successful.

While the successful historical struggles for democracy were largely against absolute monarchies, in the twentieth century they have primarily been against military regimes or military-backed regimes. Overthrowing the military is quite different from overthrowing a monarchy. A monarchy that is overthrown can be removed from the scene, but the military remains even after its political domination has ended. For this reason popular mobilization against a military regime is not sufficient.

Sections of the military must be won over, and for democracy to be sustained military acquiescence to democratic civilian rule must continue. While power almost never reverts back to a monarchy after it has been deposed there are numerous instances of alternations in power between the military and civilians. Greece, for example, has had a relatively long history of democratic politics in modern times, beginning in the middle of the nineteenth century, with frequent interventions by the military. The military coup of 1967 and the reversion to democratic government in 1974 is the most recent example of this pattern of alternation.

Turkey inaugurated its democratic process with its first competitive elections in 1946, but there was a brief military takeover in 1960 for a year, another military takeover in 1971, a period of civilian rule, and still another coup in 1980. A new constitution was installed by the military regime in 1982 and civilian government was once again established with democratic elections in 1983.

The Nigerian experience is instructive as a post-colonial example of a regime shifting back and forth from civilian to military rule. Nigeria was one of a handful of African countries to sustain competitive parties and elections after independence, but democratic politics came to an end with a military coup in 1966. In 1979 civilian party rule was reestablished with competitive elections. Elections were held again in 1983 but an elected government was subsequently overthrown by the military a few months later.

There are other examples where a return to civilian rule proved to be brief: one need only recall the military overthrow of the elected government of Bhutto in Pakistan and the overthrow of an elected president of Bangladesh, two instances in which civilian government had been preceded by military rule. Latin America is, of course, full of such examples of alternations in power between civilian forces (not always democratic) and the military.

Two developments increase the likelihood that the military will no longer acquiesce to civilian rule. One is a renewal of societal violence and the failure of a civilian government to keep adversarial politics within an orderly framework. A second is an effort by the government to sharply restrict the military, by cutting its budget, giving it too subordinate a position within the state bureaucracy or humiliating its senior leaders.

Popular support for democratic government has rarely been sufficient for ending military rule or for keeping the military in the barracks. Successful transitions have taken place when popular support for democratic rule has been combined with a willingness of the military to relinquish power. For the military to step down it is necessary that the military be assured that the conditions of disintegration that precipitated the decision to take power not be reestablished. Sometimes the military rewrites the rules of government in such a way as to enable it to accept the restoration of civilian democratic rule. The Nigerian military, for example, eager to prevent the recurrence of ethnic conflicts that might lead to renewed civil war, reconstructed the constitutional framework to discourage the formation of tribal parties. They set new ground rules under which political parties could run, including how many votes each had to obtain from the several regions of the country to be declared a political party. It was the failure of the elected government of President Shagari to play by the democratic rules—the elections of 1983 were badly marred by violence and charges of rigging, and corruption was widespread—that made the return to military rule popular.

Other military regimes feared the return of radical parties. Outlawing the Communists and other radical groups has enabled the military to set constraints on who could participate in the political arena. In Greece, Turkey and Spain the Communist parties were declared illegal. Such a ban need not persist, of course. In Spain the centrist government of Suarez ended the ban on the Communists imposed earlier by the military and thereby deprived the left of the political advantages of martyrdom. Similarly, in Greece the Papandreou government restored civil rights to the parties of the left.

In Latin America the pressure of the center and of right-wing parties to redemocratize politics has generally proven to be a more potent force than pressure from left-wing parties, which often only brought on increased repression. Pressure for political participation by the center and the right tends to reassure a military that has justified its domination as a means of preventing the rise to power of radical forces. In Greece, Turkey, Colombia, Argentina, Portugal, Spain and the Philippines the transition to democratic rule was made possible by the presence of a centrist or conservative party to which power could be transferred. In Greece, for example, the miltary transferred power to Constantine Karamanlis, a right-wing politician who assured the military of many of its perquisites. The conservatives may, of course, prove to be a transition to a more left-of-center government, as in Greece. Moreover, elections permitted by the military may not result in the election of the military's choice, as was demonstrated in Turkey in 1983 when the Motherland party, led by Turgut Ozal, won over the objections of President (and General) Kenan Evren. Still, Ozal was acceptable to the military, for the Motherland party was committed to a liberal economic policy and took no positions threatening to military interests.

Another consideration is whether the military is assured that if civilian rule is restored the military will not be prosecuted for crimes it committed when in power. The Nigerian military, for example, wanted assurances from the political elites before it turned over power to them in 1980. A similar concern shaped the attitude of the Argentinian military toward the question of whether to democratize politics, particularly in the light of the military record of forcing the "disappearance" of many of its opponents. Again, it should be noted that these assurances may be modified by a post-military civilian regime. In Greece, for example, Karamanlis placed some key military figures under arrest. And in Argentina President Raul Alfonsin's government prosecuted military officers for killings committed when they were in power, though the government subsequently suspended further arrests rather than risk military intervention.

The military also wants to be assured that its budget will not be decimated by a civilian regime and that the military continues to have a decisive voice in determining the magnitude of military expenditures, the disposition of forces, control over internal promotions, the kind of military technology to be acquired, and from what countries equipment should be purchased. Mujib Rahman's open denunciation of the military on virtually all of these matters after his election victory in early 1971 united the Pakistan military against him. The attitude of the opposition toward American military assistance or American bases is often a touchstone for the military, an indication of whether a post-military regime will undermine its access to financial resources and to military hardware. Corazon Aquino's conservative stance on this matter was an important element in disarming opposition from within the military; Benazir Bhutto's caution on this issue similarly reflects her desire to win over sections of the military and to place the United States in a position to signal the military that it does not regard democratization as a threat to a continued military relationship. American support for democratization in Brazil, Argentina, the Philippines and now South Korea, though not often welcomed by opposition groups embittered at earlier U.S. support for the regimes, has been important in politically disarming the military. Again, it should be noted that assurances made during the transitional phase do not necessarily constrain a post-authoritarian democratic regime. The Papandreou government, for example, has been asserting a hard line on the issue of U.S. military bases in Greece and on Greece's continued membership in NATO.

If a substantial section of the military is allied with forces pressing for a return to civilian rule, the military rulers or the authoritarian leaders whom they back must choose between internecine warfare within the military or a transfer of power. In the Philippines military leaders supporting President Marcos were reluctant to turn their guns against a faction of the military supporting Corazon Aquino with the result that

President Marcos went into exile and a popular government was able to take power ultimately under the protection of the military itself.

Finally, in any consideration of the strategies which facilitate a transition to democracy it is necessary to distinguish between military regimes that regard themselves as temporary guardians of authority, running the state only until conditions are ripe for a transfer of power to forces within the society, and military regimes that see themselves as legitimately, hence permanently, in power. The military governments of Turkey, Greece, Pakistan and Bangladesh regularly promised a return to elections, but not so the military-dominated or military-dependent governments of Syria, Iraq, and Libya. It is easy to be cynical when a military ruler promises, as President Zia of Pakistan and President Ershad of Bangladesh regularly did, that elections would be held in a matter of months, but such promises are a restatement by a regime that it does not consider its authority legitimate and that it defines its political task as one of creating conditions within society that would permit the formation of a legitimately elected government. Indeed, after much delay, national parliamentary elections were held in Pakistan in 1985 and in Bangladesh in 1986 and while neither has satisfied the democratic opposition, in both countries there has been a resumption of party politics even as the military rulers continue to retain power. When the military calls elections in an effort to legitimize its authority, that is a good sign for democrats, for it suggests that the military regards itself in competition with democratic forces for mass support. An election window opened by the military, even under the constraints usually imposed by a martial law regime, provides democratic forces with an opportunity to mobilize their supporters, to erode the claims of the military that civilian politicians are too divided to govern, and to seek international oversight of elections through the presence of foreign journalists.

The challenge for democrats living in a military-dominated regime is to find a strategy that will mobilize popular support against military domination that simultaneously will lead a significant section of the military to acquiesce to democratic rule. A popular movement under leftist control, sharply antagonistic to the military, and committed to punishing officers for their misdeeds, is less likely to succeed than a popular centrist movement willing to accommodate itself to some of the corporate interests of the military. A democratic movement must persuade sections of the military that democratic government is less a risk than are the dangers of a massive clash between the citizenry and the regime or armed conflict within the military itself. For those who seek democratization the lessons are these: mobilize large-scale non-violent opposition to the regime, seek support from the center and, if necessary, from the conservative right, restrain the left and keep them from dominating the agenda of the movement, woo sections of the military, seek sympathetic coverage from the western media, and press the United States for support. So far, this has proven to be the most successful winning strategy.

# 16

# Paths Toward Redemocratization

*Alfred Stepan*

The tasks of this [essay] are conceptual and historical. The goal is to explore the following questions concerning authoritarianism and redemocratization. How should we conceptualize the types of paths by which redemocratization can occur? What are the particular strengths and weaknesses of each path for the institutionalization of political democracy? What theoretically predictable implications does each

SOURCE: Alfred Stepan, "Paths Toward Redemocratization: Theoretical and Comparative Considerations," in Guillermo O'Donnell, Philippe Schmitter, and Laurence Whitehead, eds., *Transitions From Authoritarian Rule: Comparative Perspectives* (Baltimore: The Johns Hopkins University Press, 1986), pp. 64–84. Reprinted by permission of The Johns Hopkins University Press. Article and Notes abridged by the editors.

path have for reactionary, status quo, progressive, or revolutionary policies? What can we learn from the history of the most important cases of redemocratization since World War II? And finally, what insights can we derive from our abstract and historical analysis that will illuminate instances of authoritarianism and redemocratization before us now?. . .

On abstract and historical grounds, we can propose eight particularly plausible and distinctive paths leading to the termination of authoritarian regimes and the process of redemocratization. Obviously. . .a complex variety of causes—economic, historical, political, and international—are involved in the outcome of the redemocratization process. Yet it is my contention that the actual route taken toward that redemocratization has an independent weight: serious comparative analysis must attempt the difficult task of isolating and assessing this distinctive contribution.

The first three paths are ones in which warfare and conquest play an integral part in the redemocratization process. The great majority of historical examples of successful redemocratization, most of them European, in fact fall into these first three categories. The balance between prior democratic strength, the political unity and disunity of the conquered country, and the role of external powers in the redemocratization process can be sufficiently different to warrant the identification of three distinct categories: (1) internal restoration after external reconquest; (2) internal reformulation; and (3) externally monitored installation.

For the last three decades, and for the conceivable future, the overwhelming majority of cases of redemocratization have been and will be ones in which sociopolitical forces rather than external military forces play the key role, though international and economic forces, as well as political blocs, play an important role. We can divide these paths toward redemocratization into two general categories. In the first category, the termination of authoritarian regimes and the move toward redemocratization could be initiated by the wielders of authoritarian power themselves. Authoritarian power-holders may attempt to relieve pressure on themselves while at the same time preserving as many of their interests as possible by: (4) redemocratization initiated from within authoritarian regimes. (This important path has three subtypes. Each subtype is differentiated by the distinctive institutional base of the power group within the authoritarian regime that initiates the redemocratization attempt. The initiating group can be drawn from the civilianized political leadership [4a], the military-as-government [4b], or the military-as-institution which acts against either the military as government or the civilianized political leadership [4c].)

In the final category, oppositional forces play the major role in terminating the authoritarian regime and in setting or not setting the framework for redemocratization. The following oppositional routes would seem the most important: (5) society-led regime termination; (6) party pact (with or without consociational elements); 7) organized violent revolt coordinated by democratic reformist parties; and (8) Marxist-led revolutionary war.

## INTERNAL RESTORATION AFTER EXTERNAL RECONQUEST (1)

Internal restoration after external reconquest means that redemocratization takes place when a functioning democracy that has been conquered in war restores democracy after the conqueror is defeated by external force. Here the key questions seem to be whether the leaders of the original regime are deemed culpable for the conquest, whether there is an issue of collaboration by the democratic leadership, whether a resistance movement unconnected or antagonistic to the defeated democratic leadership becomes a competing center of national identification and authority, and whether, during the occupation, enduring changes occur in the social, economic, and political structures of the country. The more the answer is in the negative for all questions, the more likely it is that the outcome after reconquest will be the restoration of the previous democratic system, with full legal continuities between the old and new democratic regimes. Such restoration would entail few pressures or incentives for major socioeconomic change. The more the answer is positive for these four questions, the less likely it will be that restoration (Path 1) is possible and the more likely that internal reformulation (Path 2) or even externally monitored installation (Path 3) will be the outcome.

The obvious cases that fit Path 1 are the Netherlands, Belgium, Norway, and Denmark....

## INTERNAL REFORMULATION (2)

In this category redemocratization takes place after a conqueror has been defeated largely because of external force. However, the more internal circumstances cause the previous democratic regime to collapse, or the previous regime is deemed culpable for the conquest, or there is a perception of collaboration, or a powerful resistance movement unconnected or antagonistic to the previous democratic leadership emerges, or profound changes occur during the occupation, then: the more impossible simple restoration of the previous democratic system becomes, and the more likely that redemocratization will entail deep, constitutional reformulation. Further, the more the above factors (collaboration, autonomous resistance, etc.) are positive, the more likely the outcome will be civil war among the competing groups. This path toward redemocratization obviously has much greater potential for political instability than Path 1. It also has much greater potential for rightist reaction or leftist structural change than Path 1. Depending on the outcome of the struggle among the competing groups and classes, there is greater potential for popular forces to gain important changes such as nationalizations, legalization of popular control of unions, or the right to full participation in elections. On the other hand, there is also a greater likelihood that the outcome of the struggle could be repression, the exclusion of groups from the political system, and the denial of their rights to organize; that is, that there will be only partial redemocratization.

The two cases closest to Path 2 are post-liberation France and Greece. Italy combines Path 2 and Path 3. . . .

## EXTERNALLY MONITORED INSTALLATION (3)

This category includes cases in which democratic powers defeat an authoritarian regime and play a major role in the formulation and installation of a democratic regime.

The major political weakness of this path toward redemocratization would seem to be its foreign imposition. It would appear to have a problem of legitimacy not found in the first path. However, it does share with the Marxist revolutionary path, described later, the power to dismantle the military and political institutions and other features of the authoritarian state apparatus. Such dismantling removes an important obstacle to redemocratization, an obstacle that looms large in many of the other paths analyzed in this chapter. If the authoritarian regime has been severely discredited, nationalistic reaction against foreign imposition might be dampened. However, if imposition occurs by capitalist powers, the range of socioeconomic and political changes supported by the monitoring powers will fall within broadly predictable limits.

The purest case of this category is West Germany, followed by Japan. Austria and Italy fall partially into this category, but Austria has elements of the consociational path described later, and Italy, as we have shown, had strong elements of the internal reformulation of Path 2. Rather surprisingly, especially in view of the element of foreign imposition, all four countries that redemocratized by this route have had an unbroken history of democratic rule since World War II. What explains this historical

outcome, and why should we be extremely skeptical about the ease with which it could be reproduced?

The historically specific fact of worldwide repugnance against Fascism meant that the defeated regimes had almost no overt domestic political defenders. Also, because all four countries were part of the core of the world capitalist system, even though they had been defeated in the war, the successor democratic systems were the beneficiaries of unprecedented financial support from the United States. The United States emerged from the war as the unchallenged economic, political, and military leader of the world and used these powers—especially after the cold war began in 1947—to create economic and ideological allies against Communism.

The democratic imposition by the United States and other Western powers also helps to account for the consistency of the fundamental outlines of the supported model with the social and economic patterns of the conquering powers, though there were significant social changes and economic reforms during the reconstruction (especially the agrarian reform in Japan).

Despite the concrete outcome in all four of the existing cases, it is virtually impossible—even with the advent of a war—for these conditions to reappear. Given the political and economic evolution of the world system, no single capitalist country today or plausible group of core capitalist countries is ever again likely to have the hegemonic power the United States had in the period immediately after the war. For countries outside the core of capitalism, instead of Marshall Plan integration, there is likely to be a much more complex set of factors, involving nationalism, dependency, North-South and East-West conflicts.

The first three categories are ones in which warfare and conquest played integral parts in redemocratization. The majority of historical examples of successful redemocratization (most of them European) fall into these three categories. The connection between successful redemocratization, World War II, and the legacy of democracy and capitalism is apparent.

Equally apparent is that redemocratization today and in the future will almost always occur via very different paths.

## REDEMOCRATIZATION INITIATED FROM WITHIN THE AUTHORITARIAN REGIME (4)

By this category I do not mean a once-and-for-all decision to devolve power. Such a decision seldom happens. What often does happen, however, is that some major institutional power-holders within the ruling authoritarian coalition perceive that because of changing conditions their long-term interests are best pursued in a context in which authoritarian institutions give way to democratic institutions.

On the surface, it would appear that this path has at least three characteristic constraints and predictable problems that should be given special attention. First, the power-holders can attempt to reverse their initial liberalizing decision if—in Dahlian terms—the opening of the political system contributes to situations in which the costs of toleration are much greater than the costs of repression.[1] Second, the power-holders can attempt to construct formal and informal rules of the game that guarantee their core interests even in the context of the successor democratic regime, and thus yield only a limited democracy. Third, more than in any other path, the security apparatus from the authoritarian regime can attempt to preserve its prerogatives intact.

The path of redemocratization initiated from within the authoritarian regime, however, is quite broad and for analytic and historic purposes it is useful to identify three subtypes, each of which has a somewhat different institutional base.

In any authoritarian regime, the security apparatus and specifically the military play a major role. However, there can be an authoritarian regime in which the political component (civilian or civilianized-military) is dominant over the military-as-institution.[2] In such a case it is possible to have a redemocratization subtype we could call "redemocratization initiated by the civilian or civilianized political leadership." The institutional base of such a redemocratization effort is thus the political leadership of the authoritarian regime.

Another kind of authoritarian regime is one in which a clear military government is the central base of power. If the attempt to redemocratize originates from within such an institutional base, we would call the subtype "redemocratization instituted by the 'military-as-government.'"

Finally there is a case in which the military-as-institution, though at one time a component part of the authoritarian regime, seeks to overthrow either the civilian political leadership or the military-as-government because it comes to believe that the continuation of the authoritarian regime is detrimental to its long-term core institutional interests. I call this subtype "redemocratization led by the 'military-as-institution.'"

In concrete empirical cases these three subtypes may be difficult to disentangle, but there are analytic gains for attempting to distinguish them. For example, in cases in which the institutional base of the redemocratization effort is the civilianized political leadership, there will tend to be a preoccupation on the part of the political leadership with potential vetoes from the military-as-institution and a corresponding preoccupation with obtaining nonmaximalist behavior from the democratic opposition. Likewise, if the institutional base of redemocratization is the military-as-government, the military-as-institution can play an important veto role which predictably can impede, slow, or severely constrain redemocratization. However, if the institutional base of the redemocratization effort is a highly threatened military-as-institution, which for its own preservation thinks it must terminate the authoritarian regime rapidly, there is a potential for a speedier process of redemocratization and greater purges against the authoritarian government than in either of the other two subtypes. Let us therefore examine each of the three major subtypes of redemocratization initiated from within an authoritarian regime.

# REDEMOCRATIZATION INITIATED BY THE CIVILIAN OR CIVILIANIZED POLITICAL LEADERSHIP (4a)

If one accepts as axiomatic that power-holders will retain power unless forced by circumstances to alter the power-sharing formula, then one would predict that (1) the more there are new socioeconomic and political demands from below or from former active supporters, (2) the more there is doubt or conflict about regime legitimacy rules (especially among those who have to enforce obedience), and (3) the more there is the chance that the power-holders will retain and ratify much of their power via competitive elections (or at a minimum be able to remain active in political life), the greater the chance that this path will be initiated and will arrive at redemocratization.[3]

What are the implications of this path for policy and democratic stability? The first point to consider is that even when civilians or civilianized leaders are in control of the state apparatus the military-as-institution is still a factor of significant power. Thus the civilian leadership is most likely to persist in its democratizing initiative (and not to encounter a military reaction) if the democratic opposition tacitly collaborates with the government in creating a peaceful framework for the transition. However, even if the initial transition is successful, much of the coercive apparatus of the authoritarian state will remain intact after the election. There is therefore strong potential for severe constraints against policies that might introduce greater control over the state apparatus via democratic procedures. The stability of the newly democratized regime is particularly vulnerable to an internal coup by the bureaucratic apparatus of the previous authoritarian regime, or an actual coup

by the security forces, should members of the coercive apparatus come to believe that democratic procedures are creating security risks.

The clearest case of this path is Spain. A major factor in facilitating the internal transformation of the authoritarian regime was the death in November 1975 of the only chief executive the regime had ever known, General Franco, and before that the December 1973 death of the only potential heir apparent. Franco's death inevitably raised fundamental questions about the regime's legitimacy rules even for many of those charged with enforcing obedience. Very important, the pressures of demands from below kept the process of internal transformation of the authoritarian regime going forward.... The Spanish opposition at strategic moments shrewdly alternated between pushing and compromising, and the democratizing process went from the initial modest "reform" (*reforma*), initiated by the government, to a reform worked out with the democratic opposition (*reforma-pactada*), to a rupture with the past negotiated with the opposition (*ruptura-pactada*).

This cooperation between the government and the opposition in the transition decreased the chances of a military reaction. Also the agreement of the opposition to the system of electoral laws meant that leaders of the authoritarian regime like Suarez, whose careers had been made almost entirely within the regime's political organization, believed they had at least some chance of winning the first election; or, even if they lost, that they would have a chance to continue in political life. Despite these many favorable factors, however, Spanish democracy is fragile, and its fragility is in part a consequence of the path taken to redemocratization. The most sensitive issue is the Basque one. The consolidation of Spanish redemocratization has been greatly complicated because it has involved not only a change to democracy but also a change in the regional nature of the state. The security apparatus was left virtually intact by the transition, and views the Basque conflict as a major threat to order and a threat exacerbated by the style and context of democratic legal and electoral procedures. . . .

## REDEMOCRATIZATION INITIATED BY "MILITARY-AS-GOVERNMENT" (4b)

In this subpath, the primary drive for regime termination would come from the individual leaders of the military government. Since most modern authoritarian regimes are military regimes, this would seem to be a relatively secure and numerically predominant path. However, the important point to stress here is that if it is not perceived to be in the interests of the military-as-corporate-institution to extricate itself from power, and if there is not a strong societal demand for the termination of the authoritarian regime, this is an extremely precarious path. The redemocratization effort may falter because of military institutional resistance, and no actual transfer of power may occur.

Possibly because of these problems, I know of no pure empirical case in which redemocratization has been achieved by this path alone. Indeed, on theoretical grounds, we can say that, though the leaders of a military government may voluntaristically begin a process of liberalization, the process cannot cross the threshold of redemocratization without the additional support of societal push or corporate pull. Let us explore the complexities of this assertion by assessing liberalization and democratization in Brazil.

The Brazilian opening began in conditions of voluntaristic fragility. In the months before they assumed office in March 1974, President Ernesto Geisel and his chief ally, General Golbery, the head of the Civil Household, virtually by themselves initiated a controlled series of liberalizing steps which by late 1974 were increasingly turned into liberalizing policies, including a less constricted right to contest elections, less censorship, and fewer arbitrary arrests and tortures. In terms of our eight paths, Brazil is a clear case of liberalization commencing under the aegis of the military-as-government.

However, liberalization was sustained and broadened by a complex process involving governmental concessions and societal conquest. Despite the unquestioned growth of the power of civil society, the military-as-institution (particularly the security forces who are now an integral part of the institution) does not yet believe that devolution of power is necessary for the preservation of its institutional interests. Given this perspective, when the security apparatus concluded in November 1981 that the elections scheduled for November 1982 raised the possibility of crossing the threshold from liberalization to redemocratization, the military altered the rules of the political game to complicate this prospect greatly. Because opposition parties had only weak organic connections to the forces of civil society—the lawyers, the base communities, the church, entrepreneurs, and even the new unions—and because the November package did not threaten the fundamental achievements of liberalization (no one was tortured, no censorship was imposed), the parties were unable to rally sufficient support against the new barriers to redemocratization. In the first five days after the passage of the new regulations there was not a single political demonstration against them.

Brazil is a clear example in which lack of support is not a sufficient case for the military-as-institution to yield power. The task of the democratic opposition would seem to be to forge more organic links between the new organizations in civil society and the political parties so that demands for redemocratization become a combined social and political force which raises the cost of rule for the military-as-institution and which presents at the same time a clear governing alternative. Should the strategy lead to success, redemocratization (notwithstanding the origins of liberalization in the military-as-government's policies) would have actually been achieved, not by Path 4b, but by a complex series of forces emanating from Paths 4c, 5, and 6, involving the calculation of the military-as-institution, the diffuse demands of civil society, and the more politically channeled pressures of the opposition parties.

## REDEMOCRATIZATION LED BY "MILITARY-AS-INSTITUTION" (4c)

In this category, the primary motivation for the termination of the authoritarian regime derives from corporate factors of the military-as-institution.

It is a peculiar category. If the military-as-institution wants to return to democracy in order to protect its fundamental corporate interests, this is an extremely powerful force for the termination of authoritarian rule. In cases in which the military-as-institution sees the leaders of the authoritarian government (be they civilian or military leaders) as carrying out policies that create a crisis for the military-as-institution, it may be willing to sacrifice many of its own fellow officers—especially the leaders of the military-as-government—in order to transcend the crisis and reequilibrate the situation. However, there are also special risks attached to this form of extrication. Unless this path is augmented by other factors such as societal pressure, the military may retain a number of emergency powers. Also, once the crisis is past, there may not be major obstacles to reentry. The institutional factor is so powerful that we should be aware that in cases in which there is military rule, if there is no reason why the military-as-institution feels it is in its interest to relinquish power, redemocratization, short of foreign imposition (Path 3) or opposition-led armed violence (Paths 7 and 8) will almost certainly not occur. I mean to stress that loss of civilian support alone is not enough for the government to fall. Authoritarian regimes, unlike monist regimes, do not have high active support requirements. Apathy and acquiescence will suffice. Loss of civilian support must somehow be transformed into a tangible cost or a direct threat to the military-as-institution.

The two sharpest examples in which perception of intense threat to the military-as-institution played a fundamental role in the termination of authoritarian regimes were Greece in 1973 and Portugal in 1974. The Greek military government was born in 1967 as a colonels'—as opposed to a generals'—coup. But since the generals were never purged, the military government began with a relatively poor base in the military-as-institution. By 1973, the leader of the military government was politically isolated, possibly for this reason, and he became engaged in an extremely risky intervention in Cyprus. This intervention immediately put the military institution under the grave security threat of a war with Turkey, for which it was completely unprepared. Under these circumstances, with an acceptable civilian conservative alternative in former Prime Minister Constantine Karamanlis, the military institution negotiated an extremely rapid extrication. For those officers associated with the military-as-government, the military-as-institution accepted harsh terms. Over one hundred high-ranking military officers from the military government were still in jail eight years later. The combination of speed and purges would seem to be virtually impossible to achieve in either Paths 4a or 4b.

However, notwithstanding the unpopularity of the government and the university uprising in 1973, there was not much pressure from society for the military to withdraw from government. Under these conditions, the military-as-institution insisted that the military-as-government withdraw from political power, but retained substantial institutional prerogatives that only began to be challenged by the Socialist coalition elected in 1981. However, the Greek case is important because it illustrates that the rules of the game for extrication can be renegotiated if democracy endures and if a new political force mobilizes new sources of power in the electoral arena.

The other case is Portugal. As a number of authors have documented, the colonial wars in Africa generated a series of what were perceived by Portuguese career officers as increasingly severe problems for their military-as-institution. The length of the war generated manpower shortages at the officer corps level. Conscripted university graduates and sergeants were more frequently made officers, and this practice was resented by the permanent corps of officers. The army, which was closest to the war, also saw the war in the long run as fundamentally unwinnable. The termination of the African colonial war, and of the Portuguese authoritarian government that persisted in waging the war, became a central goal of the Portuguese military institution. The Portuguese case is unusual in two respects. The colonial war radicalized a section of the army, and the Armed Forces Movement played an important role in the initial structure of the state after the overthrow of the authoritarian regime. Even after democratic elections in 1975, 1976, and 1980, the military retained sufficient power to warrant labeling Portugal a "dyarchial" system of government. The Constitution of 1976 gave the military's "Council of the Revolution" de jure veto power over the National Assembly in that its members had the power to judge the constitutionality of acts of that elected chamber. In conditions of conflict between the president and the prime minister, latent dual power conflicts in the 1976–82 period could have precipitated a constitutional crisis for Portuguese democracy. The dyarchy ended only in 1982.

The Peruvian case is another example in which corporate, institutional factors in the military played an important role in redemocratization in 1980. As I have argued elsewhere, by 1977 the military-as-institution felt it faced external security problems on all its borders with Chile, with Ecuador, and with Bolivia (a Bolivia possibly backed by Brazil). It also felt that it had achieved much of its initial program (settlement of the IPC [International Petroleum Corporation] conflict, some agrarian reform, strengthening of state structures) and that the continuation of the military government created internal conflicts that further aggravated its external security position. More than in Greece or Portugal, societal threats were present in Peru in the form of general strikes and growing pressures from diverse groups and classes for the military to withdraw. In these circumstances, when the Peruvian military withdrew, it retained fewer prerogatives than its Greek or Portuguese counterparts.

In all three cases, external threats played a central role in extrications led by the military-as-institution. Of course, a variety of internal pressures could become contributing factors in

a decision by the military-as-institution to relinquish power. The most common of these are policy pressures and divisions that shake the internal unity of the military so that extrication is the safest path to internal cohesion. Sudden internal upheavals often initiate a "return to barracks" movement within the military. Also major reputational or budgetary costs borne by the military-as-institution can erode its support for the military-as-government. In most of these instances of internal pressures, society-initiated demands characteristic of Path 5 are vital.

## SOCIETY-LED REGIME TERMINATION (5)

The key phrase here is "society-led" as opposed to party-, pact-, or revolutionary-induced transformation of an authoritarian regime. In theory, such a transformation could be brought about by diffuse protests by grass roots organizations, massive but uncoordinated general strikes, and by general withdrawal of support for the government. However, upon closer analysis this is a path toward government change rather than a path toward full redemocratization. The most likely outcome of sharp crises of authoritarian regimes stemming from diffuse pressures and forces in society is either a newly constituted successor authoritarian government, or a caretaker military junta promising elections in the future.[4] In the latter case, the actual transition involves the extrication by the military-as-institution, and many of the elements of Path 4 obtain. The key factor is that despite societal resistance to authoritarianism, many of the rules of transition are set by the caretaker junta.

On theoretical grounds, therefore, one is tempted to argue that society-led upheavals *by themselves* are virtually incapable of leading to redemocratization but are, nevertheless, often a crucial, or in some cases an indispensable, component to the redemocratization.

Greece in 1973 had elements of this path, led by the student uprising, but the need of the military-as-institution rapidly to alleviate the security crisis with Turkey was the major reason for the rapid redemocratization. Argentina after the massive but uncoordinated revolt in Córdoba in 1969, a revolt that spread quickly to other parts of the country, and Peru after the general strike of 17 July 1977 also fall into this category in some important ways.

The power of civil society to create and channel social pressures is extremely important in successful redemocratization, particularly for all three subtypes of Path 4. Without demands from civil society, in Path 4a (redemocratization initiated by civilian or civilianized political leadership) and in Path 4b (redemocratization initiated by "military-as-government"), the soft-liners within the authoritarian regime will almost certainly not be able to convince the hard-liners that extrication or redemocratization is an institutional necessity: the best the soft-liners can achieve is liberalization. For Path 4c (redemocratization led by "military-as-institution"), the smaller the social pressures, the greater the prerogatives the military can demand in the postextrication period. Finally, for most paths, the politically organized strengths and weaknesses of civil society determine to a large extent the barriers to military reentry in the post-redemocratization period.

# PARTY PACT (WITH OR WITHOUT CONSOCIATIONAL ELEMENTS) (6)

By this category is meant the internal construction of a grand oppositional pact, possibly with some consociational features. The pact members unite to defeat the authoritarian regime and lay the foundation for a successor democratic regime in which power is open to most opposition forces.

In theory, this path, especially in its full-blown consociational form, would appear to be one of great interest for strategies of redemocratization, because it simultaneously addresses two critical issues. First, the construction of such a pact helps erode the bases of the authoritarian regime, especially if the rationale for the authoritarian regime is that a bloody conflict would ensue in the absence of authoritarianism. Second, it helps lay the foundation for the successor democratic regime with elaborate formulas for power-sharing, mutual vetoes, and grand coalitions.

Despite its apparent attractiveness, a strict consociational path presents several problems of a political nature. Pact *creation* does not necessarily imply pact *maintenance*—pacts can fall apart. Also, even when the pact is maintained, social change may occur and important new groups that were not a part of the original pact will be excluded. This possibility would represent not a case of consociational redemocratization but an example of exclusionary consociational authoritarianism.

When we explore the predictable policy consequences of a strict consociational path toward redemocratization, it should be clear that the "mutual vetoes" and the "purposeful depoliticization" of some major substantive issue areas, which are a part of Arend Lijphart's classic definition of consociationalism, would appear to build in systemic constraints to rapid socio-economic change. The recognition of such constraints may in turn explain why, if the fundamental conflict in society relates to socioeconomic issues, as opposed to religious, ethnic, or linguistic disputes, it will be difficult for warring classes to walk the consociational path together.

If we start our empirical examination with a reading of Arend Lijphart's *Democracy in Plural Societies: A Comparative Perspective,* we note the rather surprising fact that of the consociational or semiconsociational cases he fully discusses (the Netherlands, Belgium, Austria, Nigeria, Cyprus, Malaysia, and Lebanon), only Austria is a case of redemocratization of an authoritarian regime.[5] All other cases are of consociationalism first emerging as a conflict regulation device to avoid democratic breakdown or of consociationalism in the process of the decolonization of new states. In the only case of consociationalism emerging for redemocratization, Austria, the defeat of the authoritarian regime is accomplished by foreign powers; this external factor played a role, along with consociationalism, in the creation of democratic institutions. Lijphart mentions Colombia twice in passing, but does not examine it in detail because he claims it is not a plural society. For our purposes, however, both Colombia (1958) and Venezuela (1958) were cases of redemocratization in which party pacts and even some consociational practices—mutual guarantees, vetoes, and purposeful depoliticization—were crucial. Both Venezuela and Colombia are cases that conform to our theoretical expectation, in that, though pacts for a long time contributed to the stability of political democracy, these same pacts kept socioeconomic change within a narrow range. In Spain, the negotiated agreements on economic policy contained in the Moncloa Pact of 1977 and the consensual working out of the constitution are evidence of the role of party pacts and some consociational practices in the redemocratization process.

Pacts—with or without consociational elements—cannot be created in all political systems. Party pacts by their very nature have two indispensable requirements: first, leaders with the organizational and ideological capacity to negotiate a grand coalition among themselves; second, the allegiance of their political followers to the terms of the pact.

## ORGANIZED VIOLENT REVOLT COORDINATED BY DEMOCRATIC REFORMIST PARTIES (7)

On theoretical grounds this path appears to have a number of advantages for the process of redemocratization. Because the revolt against authoritarianism has a party base, the parties can provide a continuous political direction unavailable to the diffuse society-led path. The political core is also one that is committed to democracy and whose most probable internal political allies will be drawn from democratic forces. If we ask how far this path can go in terms of socioeconomic change, it clearly has

greater potential than a party pact with consociational elements because it does not have the mutual vetoes, depoliticization of key issues, and institutionalized power-sharing that are part of the consociational formula. Likewise, the fact that the authoritarian regime has been defeated in a political-military struggle gives some scope to the parties to restructure the state apparatus.

This path has predictable constraints, however. The most likely type of reformist parties, in Europe and Latin America at least, are Social Democratic or Christian Democratic parties. The range of international political and economic allies and role models of either type of party keeps socioeconomic change within the boundaries of the international capitalist system. Because Social Democrats, and especially Christian Democrats, do not have a strong tradition of clandestine, violent party activity, the most likely paramilitary formula appears to be one that coopts a wing of the military to its cause of overthrowing the authoritarian government. Even though the military is a junior partner, it still sets limits to the degree to which the military and security apparatus can be dismantled.

Historically, there are no successful examples of this path leading to redemocratization in Europe, Africa, the Middle East, or Asia. In Latin America, the closest case is the 1948 revolt in Costa Rica. . . .

## MARXIST-LED REVOLUTIONARY WAR (8)

This path has the greatest theoretically predictable potential for fundamental socioeconomic change because the revolutionary forces come to power only after defeating the state apparatus and a sector of the social order is displaced without waiting for the results of elections. In theory, the revolutionary forces also have an ideology and a social base supportive of fundamental change.

Theoretically, there can be a space for democratic revolutionary Marxist reconstruction. However, the doctrinal and organizational tradition of revolutionary Leninism, which has been the most effective and prestigious modern revolutionary model, rejects two of the requirements of a minimalist definition of political democracy—the relatively unrestricted right to organize and the relatively unrestricted right to open contestation. The Leninist party model in power therefore virtually precludes the existence of other parties advocating alternative conceptions of society and having a legitimate chance to gain power through electoral means.

Historically, there are many cases—such as China, Yugoslavia, the Soviet Union, Vietnam, and Cuba—in which revolutionary Marxism has overthrown authoritarian regimes and introduced fundamental change. However, to date there has not yet been even one election with full rights of organization and contestation (and with the right to make the government accountable to the electorate) after a revolutionary Marxist triumph.

Nonetheless, since the 1970s there seems to be greater doctrinal and geopolitical space for this option to be realized than before. There has been greater doctrinal space because the Leninism that dominated revolutionary Marxism from 1917 until the early 1970s began to have serious Marxist critics who drew on Italian Eurocommunism and the antivanguardist critique of democratic centralism, for example, Rosa Luxemburg's and Leon Trotsky's writing against *What Is to Be Done?*, and on some of the participatory themes emerging in Marxism.

There has been greater geopolitical space in the world for democratic revolutionary socialism because neither the functional equivalents of the capitalist encirclement that threatened the Soviet Union after World War I nor the Stalinist encirclement of Eastern Europe after 1945 seemed likely to be repeated. In the multipolar, post-OPEC world since the 1970s, new revolutionary regimes had greater opportunities than before for piecing together aid, trade, and security relationships with a variety of countries.

The country in the world with the greatest opportunity to arrive at revolutionary democratic Marxism was Nicaragua. Given its initial international support from the then financially strong oil powers as politically diverse as Mexico, Libya, and Venezuela, from the ruling Social Democratic party in Germany, good relations with the strong Socialist parties in France and Spain, as well as support from Leninist party systems such as Cuba and the Soviet Union, Nicaragua had the potential to maintain degrees of independence which would have allowed it to construct its own path to democracy within the revolution. International capitalist bankers accepted the new power relations in the region; and, under the aegis of Mexico, and with the initial tolerance of the Carter government, they entered into an unprecedented and creative debt-rescheduling process for the revolutionary government. Domestically, in Nicaragua the participation of the post-Vatican II Catholic church and an important wing of the national bourgeoisie in making the revolution seemed to give the Sandinista regime the possibility of at least a loyal opposition to the construction of democratic revolutionary Marxism.[6] However, the triumph of President Reagan in the United States elections of 1980, the incorporation of El Salvador into the East-West struggle, economic difficulties, and the emergence (in a country without a rich tradition of Marxist debate) of classical Leninism as an important component of the core model of the Sandinista rule of organization have made revolutionary Marxist democracy problematic.

Regardless of the outcome in Nicaragua, some democratic currents within Marxism and new geopolitical realities have created somewhat greater theoretical space for a democratic, revolutionary Marxist alternative. The unfortunate way in which Nicaragua was caught in the East-West conflict reconfirmed capitalist hard-liners and Leninist hard-liners alike in their skepticism about the possibility of democratic revolutionary Marxism.[7]

## Notes

1. Robert A. Dahl, *Polyarchy: Participation and Opposition* (New Haven: Yale University Press, 1971), p. 15.

2. Some examples of authoritarian regimes in which the civilian or civilianized military is dominant over the military-as-institution are Spain after the death of Franco, the first Vargas regime in Brazil (1930–45), the Mexican government since the late 1930s, and Turkey in the 1940s.

3. For example, in terms of these three factors, the conditions in Egypt and Cuba after Nasser and Castro came to power were such that factor 3 was supportive of a choice for democratization (both Nasser and Castro would have won), but factor 2 pressure was absent in both countries, and in neither country was there significant pressure for democratization from below (factor 1).

4. Two cases of society-led regime transition were Iran during the movement against the shah and the French Revolution before Napoleon. Korea during the revolt against General Park was an attempted case but it reverted to a military regime.

5. Arend Lijphart, *Democracy in Plural Societies: A Comparative Perspective* (New Haven: Yale University Press, 1977).

6. For the important role of the domestic bourgeoisie in the struggle against Somoza see Harold Jung, "Behind the Nicaraguan Revolution," *New Left Review* 117 (September–October 1979), pp. 69–90. All the Nicaraguan bishops signed the important statement in support of the then still unresolved revolutionary struggle. See Conferencia Episcopal de Nicaragua, *Mensaje al Pueblo Nicaragüense: Momento Insurreccional, 2 de Junio 1979*. Even more significant was a pastoral letter, again signed by every Nicaraguan bishop, almost four months after the revolution was successful, explicitly acknowledging, if a few key safeguards were maintained, a role for the Sandinistas in carrying out the postrevolutionary government. See Carta Pastoral del Episcopado Nicaragüense, *Compromiso Cristiano para Una Nicaragua Nueva* (Managua, 17 November 1979).

7. For a thoughtful discussion of the dilemmas of the Nicaraguan Revolution by an important thinker and participant see Xabier Gorostiaga, "Dilemmas of the Nicaraguan Revolution," in *The Future of Central America: Policy Choices for the U.S. and Mexico*, ed. Richard R. Fagen and Olga Pellicer (Stanford: Stanford University Press, 1983), pp. 47–66. See also Richard R. Fagen, "The Nicaraguan Revolution," Working Paper no. 78, Wilson Center, Latin American Program, (Washington, D.C., October 1980).

# CHAPTER FIVE

# Communist Regimes

## 17

## The Post-Revolutionary Phase in China and Russia

*Richard Lowenthal*

The death of Mao Zedong in 1976 was, as everybody felt at once, the end of an epoch in the evolution of Communist China—and that in more senses than one. It was the death of the leader of the long drawn-out revolutionary struggle that had established communist rule in China, and of the man who, by breaking up the alliance with the Soviet Union he had signed from a less than equal position, had destroyed the last of the unequal treaties in China's modern history. It also marked the end of the same man's failed attempt, in the last decade of his life, to establish despotic personal rule over the party's institutions, and potentially opened the way to restoration of institutional party rule. But it could not be foreseen with certainty at once that this restoration of party institutions would also coincide with the end of the effort to continue the "institutionalized revolution" of which Mao had been the unbending exponent.

It is the thesis of this paper that both the tendency to institutionalize revolution as a recurrent phenomenon due to the utopian impulses of communist ideology, and the necessity for the

SOURCE: Richard Lowenthal, "The Post-Revolutionary Phase in China and Russia," *Studies in Comparative Communism* 16, no. 3 (Autumn 1983), pp. 191–201. By permission. Notes abridged by the editors.

revolutionary process finally to exhaust itself due to the requirements of economic modernization, are inherent in communist party regimes—at least if they are created by the victory of a revolutionary mass movement and not imposed by a great power from outside. The tendency for a personal despotism to paralyze or replace institutional party control in the course of this long-drawn out revolutionary process, but for "normal" party control eventually to be restored after the death of the despot or would–be despot, is not equally general for communist regimes, but is typical enough to have manifested itself in the two leading communist powers—Russia and China. It is my intention to discuss the general phenomenon of the exhaustion of the revolutionary process from the angle of its interaction with the post-despotic normalization in Russia and China.

## INSTITUTIONALIZED REVOLUTION

Permit me first to explain briefly what I mean by the process of institutionalized revolution and by the need for its eventual exhaustion.... Communist revolutionary movements are motivated by visions of a society of perfect equality excluding all social conflict, which are utopian in the strict sense of being impossible to achieve among human beings. In the real world, all their power cannot prevent that every step forward in the planned revolutionary destruction of formerly or potentially "ruling classes" is followed by unplanned, spontaneous processes of new social differentiation—as in the rise of a class of prosperous peasants after the expropriation of the landowners in Russia, or in the rise of a new privileged bureaucracy in Soviet industry with its growth under Stalin's five-year plans. Hence new "revolutions from above" were undertaken first against the "kulaks" in the form of Stalin's forced collectivization, and later against important parts of the bureaucratic, industrial and military elites in the form of his notorious blood purge, and were projected by him still in the final year of his life in the form of replacing the right of the collective farms to sell their produce to the state by some kind of centrally controlled barter. You can easily draw the parallel first to Chinese agricultural collectivization, then to the tightening of party control over the industrial managers in the course of the "Great Leap Forward" and to the creation of the "People's Communes" by Mao, finally to his desperate struggle against differentiated material incentives as a form of "Capitalism" and his attempt to uproot, by the "Cultural Revolution," the underlying mentality in the masses and the inclination of the party and state bureaucracy to make concessions to it.

Yet communist revolutions have only taken place in underdeveloped countries under the pressure of their economic problems: hence all communist regimes have faced the need to combine the struggle for equality with the struggle for economic modernization, which necessarily requires social differentiation and material incentives—thus striving to reconcile the irreconcilable. Accordingly, a tendency to restrict, stop or finally reverse the extreme egalitarian measures has arisen both from the more productive part of the working classes and from the administrative elites responsible for economic success, and has found at different times and in different places more or less of a hearing among the leadership. Stalin, for instance, while destroying the more prosperous peasants by his mass deportation of "kulaks" with disastrous economic consequences and severely holding down the general wage level under his first five-year-plan, took a stand early in favor of differentiated incentive wages, and in his great purge

favored the well-trained industrial managers and technicians without a revolutionary past over the "Red Directors" with a party tradition but poor technical knowledge—and after the purge of the "Reds" opened the party ranks wide to the "experts." Mao Zedong, on the other hand, the more he freed himself from the Soviet model after Khrushchev's de-Stalinization, became more and more critical of differentiated material incentives as spoiling the people's chances of developing a true socialist consciousness, and while originally coining the slogan that managers and technicians should be both "red and expert," in practice became increasingly determined to favor non-expert reds over not-so-red experts: this was true during the Great Leap, and central to the Cultural Revolution.

However, the more a country has already begun to overcome primitive economic conditions, to develop industrial technology and train technicians, the higher becomes the cost of insisting, in the name of the ideological imperative of egalitarianism, on continuing the institutionalized revolution at the expense of the economic imperative of modernization. Over time, then, the tendency is bound to grow for the dynamics of the revolutionary process to run down and the dynamics of the pressure for modernization to gather momentum. We have long known that it is impossible to invent a *perpetuum mobile* in the physical world; the communists, first in Russia and later in China, have had to learn that no *perpetuum mobile* exists in the world of political revolution either.

## THE RUNNING DOWN OF INSTITUTIONALIZED REVOLUTION IN RUSSIA AND CHINA

Let me now try to recall in somewhat more detail how the running down of the institutionalized revolution occurred first in Russia and then in China. It has often been said that Stalin turned essentially conservative in the course of World War II, if he had not already in his Great Purge; above all, those people who are convinced that a revolution must be something humane and beautiful, naturally consider the Great Purge a counter-revolution rather than a revolution. But the Great Purge was no attempt to restore a previous state of affairs: apart from inaugurating Stalin's personal despotism above the party institutions, it largely destroyed the traditional revolutionary elite, but replaced it by a new one by no means averse to further revolutionary upheavals. The bureaucrats, technicians and army officers trained since the end of the civil war eagerly entered the gates of the party now widely opened for them by Stalin; and the party, though now subject to the despot's every whim, had not abandoned its program of social transformation: there had been no "Thermidor," as Trotsky believed.

It is true that during the war, Stalin made important concessions both to the material demands of the peasants and to the ideological traditions of Great Russian nationalism and orthodoxy—but from necessity, not from conviction. The concessions to the peasants and to non-communist ideologies and literature were revoked as soon as the war was over. By 1950, planned social transformation restarted with the merging of the collective farms to greater units: this reduced their number to little more than one-third within two years, thus making sure at last that there should be a party unit in most collective farms. A year later, Nikita Khrushchev, then responsible for agriculture in Stalin's Politburo, suggested the next step: the peasants should be uprooted from their villages and rehoused in one central "agrotown" for each of the new merged farms, losing access to their former private plots and getting much smaller gardens in the process. But this met opposition within the leadership, both because of the risk of a disincentive effect on the peasant's work and of the lack of the needed masses of building materials. Stalin did not back Khrushchev, and the project was cancelled.

Yet in 1952, Stalin himself came forward with a far more revolutionary project. In a series of essays published as a pamphlet on the eve of the 19th Party Congress—the first since the war and the last in his lifetime—he proposed a plan for replacing all trade between the cities and the countryside by centrally organized barter! The idea was that as long as the peasants owned their produce, even collectively, there was a danger of a return to capitalism. The new plan was aimed to cut out market and money altogether from the relations between town and country—and Stalin's final essay on the subject urged that first steps toward this gigantic revolutionary change should be taken at once. But strangely, the plan was not discussed, let alone approved at the party congress: for the first time in years, there seems to have been resistance in the Politburo against the despot's idea, which would have made any comparison of the collective farms' income and expenditure, difficult as it was anyhow, completely impossible. At any rate, at the end of the Congress Stalin replaced the Politburo by a much larger Presidium, and Khrushchev later told us that Stalin planned a purge of some of its members and that the "doctor's plot" affair, announced in January 1953 but planned at the time of the congress, was his preparation for that. But by 5 March 1953, the despot was dead.

Clearly, while institutionalized revolution had not been abandoned by Stalin, its continuation had become increasingly difficult in his later years. During the struggle for his succession, which ended with the restoration of party primacy under Khrushchev, the rival leaders were indeed more interested in initiating popular reforms than unpopular revolutionary upheavals. But by 1959, the victorious Khrushchev unveiled at the 21st Party Congress his plan for another turn of the revolutionary screw, though this time a nonviolent one: he resumed his campaign for the resettlement of the peasants in "agrotowns," now combined with a drive for the "voluntary" sale of the peasants' private cattle to the collective farms. Yet early successes of the campaign announced in the press soon turned out either to have been faked by the local officials or to have been achieved with so much pressure that the peasants slaughtered most of their cattle rather than sell them—and within less than two years the campaign was abandoned. It was the Soviet communist party's last attempt to continue the institutionalized revolution: the new party program presented by Khrushchev to the 22d Party Congress in October 1961 treated further changes in the direction of "the higher stage of communism" no longer as a task for the revolutionary transformation of the social structure, but as an expected by-product of the party's concentration on the increase in productivity and the improvement of the general standard of living. Modernization had finally won over utopianism, and the post-revolutionary period had definitely begun in Russia.

However, it turned out that Khrushchev, with his dynamic urge for innovating changes, was not the right kind of leader for a post-revolutionary communist party regime. The party's bureaucratic oligarchy, consolidated in their physical security by Khrushchev's denunciation of Stalin's purges, now wanted the security of regular procedures of decision within their circle, without a dynamic leader inclined to appeal over their heads to "public opinion." It was their discontent with Khrushchev's uncontrollable improvizations that finally led to his overthrow by a central committee formed under his primacy and led by men of his choice— drawing the final conclusion of his transition to the post-revolutionary phase which he had failed to draw himself. As the 18 years of the Brezhnev era have shown, that conclusion was oligarchic rule bringing to the Soviet Union stable procedures of decision for the first time in its history— with the advantages of unprecedented stability, and the setbacks of unprecedented stagnation.

In China, the struggle for or against continuing the institutionalized revolution started at the time of the Great Leap Forward and the inauguration of the People's Communes: it formed the core of what Mao Zedong and his followers came to call "the struggle between two lines." Its beginning coincided with the beginning of Mao's political estrangement from post-Stalin Russia, which sharpened as the Chinese leader came to attribute the—in his view—

insufficiently militant character of Soviet foreign policy to an abandonment of revolutionary principles inside the Soviet Union itself; he saw this symbolized by the statement in the Soviet party program of 1961 that, owing to the disappearance of hostile classes in the Soviet Union, it could no longer be described as a "dictatorship of the proletariat." Mao correctly perceived that this formula was an expression of Russia's entrance into a post-revolutionary period.

You will recall that the policies of the Great Leap and the People's Communes were explicitly justified by the doctrine of "uninterrupted revolution," and that this doctrine was not abandoned by Mao when the early illusions that the Communes would make possible a quick transition to communism faded by the end of 1958, and when a number of adjustments to harsh economic realities had to be made in the policies based on the doctrine, particularly between 1960 and 1962. In 1964, parallel to his twin campaigns for "socialist education" and for "learning from the army," Mao further developed the doctrine in his famous reply to "Khrushchev's Phoney Communism," laying down that the danger of a capitalist restoration, such as had allegedly taken place in Russia, would persist in China throughout the period preceding the achievement of full communism, which he now expected to last for "5 to 10 generations or one or several centuries," and to require new revolutionary struggles throughout this period. It was in the context of this vision that he came to prepare the "Cultural Revolution" as a struggle not only against non-revolutionary thought, but against "people in authority walking the capitalist road"—in other words, against all members of the party leadership who opposed his priority for institutionalized revolution in the name of a priority for economic modernization—and that he launched it, probably without the support of a majority of the Central Committee, in 1966.

I do not have to retell here the phases of the Cultural Revolution, nor the lasting damage it did both to the party regime and to the Chinese economy. What matters in our context is that even after Mao decided in 1968 to end the chaos caused by the Red Guards and restore the paralyzed party with the help of the same armed forces on which he had previously relied to back the Red Guards against the institutions of party rule, he still expected the army under the leadership of Lin Biao (from 1969 his deputy and designated successor) to pursue a course of continuing revolution if by different means. After Lin Biao's death following an alleged plot, the "struggle between the two lines" continued in a divided leadership, with Mao's authority visibly fading and Zhou Enlai, who had in the past both supported Mao against his opponents and tried to moderate his policies, now assuming the leadership in the struggle for a turn towards modernization (and rehabilitation of surviving victims of the Cultural Revolution), but being attacked by the Maoist diehards in an abstruse campaign allegedly directed "against Lin Biao and Confucius." As Zhou succumbed to an illness a few months before the death of Mao, those diehards got a final opportunity to resume their struggle for uninterrupted revolution.

The death of Mao in September 1976 was thus the precondition for China's entry into a post-revolutionary period, but that entry did not take place immediately. While Hua Guo-feng, who now assumed power, was able to arrest Mao's widow and his most extremist followers, and was unwilling to continue "revolutionary" measures, he was equally unwilling to break openly with the late-Maoist doctrine and continued to mouth the formulas of continuing revolution and class struggle used by the "infallible" leader. It took two years until a decision of the Central Committee in late 1978 actually opened the post-revolutionary period by disavowing those formulas as absurd in the absence of hostile classes and giving priority to a policy of modernization, and another two years and a half until another Central Committee meeting in mid-1981 demonstrated the finality of the turn by passing a resolution on the history of Communist China which recognized the lasting merits of the early Mao on the road to communist power and in the building of the new

society, but clearly condemned the doctrinal and political errors of the late Mao and admitted the damage they had done both to the nation and to its communist regime. The same meeting also replaced Hua Guo-feng as leader of the party. The new leader, not in title but in fact, had been already for some time Deng Xiaoping, once ousted as general secretary of the party and banished during the Cultural Revolution, then rehabilitated by Zhou Enlai but banished once more by the Maoist extremists after Zhou's death, and finally rehabilitated a second time as the party moved towards a post-revolutionary priority for modernization.

## DESPOTISM IN RUSSIA AND CHINA

So far, this rapid survey has shown that both in Russian and in Chinese communism, the conflict between the tendency to institutionalized, recurrent revolution and the tendency to give priority to modernization has in some way been intertwined with another drama—the rise of a despotic or would-be despotic leader paralyzing or even temporarily destroying the institutions of party rule for a period, and the restoration of the normal functioning of party institutions after the death of the despot or would-be despot. I shall now attempt to suggest some reasons for the appearance of this type of drama in some major communist party regimes, and to ask just how it has affected the struggle between revolutionary and post-revolutionary forces which is my main theme.

I should like to start from a difference between communist party regimes and fascist regimes, with which the rules of Stalin and of Mao have been frequently compared.[1] The fascist regimes of Mussolini and Hitler were based from the start on the *Führerprinzip*, the principle of one-man leadership. Legitimacy in those regimes was attached primarily to the person of the leader rather than to the institution of the party. Hence a conflict of authority in those regimes could only arise in case of a crisis of succession—and neither regime lasted long enough for this to happen.

Communist regimes, being run by highly centralized parties organized from the top downward, also depend for their functioning on a single leader; but their ideology does not proclaim that. Legitimacy is not primarily attached to the person of the leader but to the institution of the party, which is supposed to be governed by a principle called "democratic centralism." Under this principle, the leadership is elected by a party congress, but the leadership also "proposes" the candidates for leading the party's regional and local units who, in turn, "propose" delegates to the party congress; hence a united leadership can always be sure both to perpetuate itself with minor changes and to get its policies approved "democratically." The system works as smoothly as the fascist one—on condition of unity in the leadership. But this unity can only be assured, amidst the crucial policy issues that have to be decided in the course of a revolutionary process, if there happens to be a leader who enjoys virtually uncontested authority. That was the case with Lenin, who had led the Bolsheviks to power; and it also applied to Mao, who had led the Chinese communists to victory, for many years. But it was not the case with any of the candidates for Lenin's succession, and it no longer applied to the aging Mao from 1958 onwards.

Yet if the leadership of a ruling communist party is not united, it turns out that there is also no generally accepted procedure for decision making. There is, originally, no duty for a communist that he must follow the leader, as there is for a fascist. But neither is there a clear duty that he must follow the majority in all conditions. For Lenin, in building his party and leading it to power, taught that the majority can err, and that the true revolutionary must not submit to an erring majority, but rather split or refound the party, as he did repeatedly himself before he was in power. But the same Lenin, when later leading a party that ruled a dictatorial state and that therefore could not tolerate a split, taught that "factional" opposition to decisions once passed by the highest party organs was a danger to the party's monopolistic rule—hence

potentially counter-revolutionary. Thus well-trained communists grow up with two contradictory lessons going back to Lenin—that it is better to fight an erring majority than to submit to it, and that it is better to submit to the ruling majority than to endanger the unity of a ruling party.

As I said before, those problems do not become acute while the party leadership is united behind a generally respected leader. But if there is no longer such a leader, and if policy disputes arise about the "correct" solution, on which the fate of the revolution may depend, minorities may feel authorized by the "early" Lenin to oppose majority decisions on vital issues and found factions, and majorities will feel authorized by the "later" Lenin to suppress them. It is from such factional struggles on vital issues of the revolutionary road to take, that an internal power struggle in the ruling party may arise—and may end in personal despotism.

The rise of personal despotism, or of attempts at personal despotism, is thus an inherent *possibility*, though not, as far as we can observe, an inherent *necessity* in communist regimes. An all-powerful leader is not demanded by their ideology. But the fact that ideology neither forces all communists to submit to the leader whatever he does, nor forces them to submit to a majority whatever it decides, means that communist ideology offers no clear system of rules for the procedures of decision within the party; and this lack of procedural clarity may lead to inner-party conflicts sharpening to a point where a despot seeks to achieve general submission no longer based on ideologically motivated discipline, but on force. Clearly, such conflicts are most likely to arise on the need for another phase of the institutionalized revolution.

Lenin had been unable to designate a successor enjoying his unique authority, and none was available at his death. In the factional quarrels now arising within the "collective leadership," Stalin enjoyed the double advantage that as general secretary he had the decisive influence on appointments, and that he saw more clearly than his rivals that as the share of members who had joined the party after the seizure of power increased with the lapse of time, the late-Leninist stress on the need for party unity was bound to seem more convincing to the rank and file than the early-Leninist argument for the right to defy an erring majority. Accordingly, he used in each conflict the tactics of presenting his policies from the start as those of "the party," and his critics as a "factional" opposition. It worked successively first against Trotsky, then against the "left opposition" of Zinoviev and Kamenev, and finally, after some initial difficulty, also against Bukharin and his supporters once Stalin had maneuvered them into the role of a "right opposition."

By 1929, when Stalin had defeated all inner-party opposition and initiated a new "revolution from above" by the "dekulakization" and forced collectivization of Soviet agriculture and the first five-year plan for forced industrialization, he had become the effective single leader of the party, but still by the use and abuse of his statutory powers—not yet by the use of despotic force inside the party. The massive use of force against the peasants and the resulting widespread misery and discontent, by seeming to endanger the survival of the regime, even increased the feeling in the party that Stalin's strong arm was indispensable for saving it. Yet as late as 1932 the Politburo, by rejecting Stalin's demand that a communist who had secretly circulated a pamphlet calling for Stalin's replacement by the party, should be tried and executed for allegedly calling for his assassination, showed that Stalin was not yet a despot above the party institutions; and when the crisis was over, the Seventeenth Party Congress of 1934, as part of an effort to restore a more normal atmosphere, apparently made an attempt to reduce his powers: it renamed him "First Secretary" instead of "General Secretary," sought to strengthen the collective character of the party secretariat by electing the popular Leningrad secretary Kirov to become his colleague, and in a secret ballot is said to have given Stalin the lowest vote of all Central Committee members.

It was this apparent threat to Stalin's institutional power that evidently decided him to move towards establishing despotic power above the party institutions. He put men beholden to him into key positions in the secret police, the prosecutor's office and the judiciary; he at the very least did nothing to make the secret police prevent a second and successful attempt on Kirov's life in December 1935 after a first attempt by the same man had failed; and he used Kirov's assassination to start the Great Purge, which began with measures against former oppositionists, culminating in the notorious show trials, and extended quickly to his own former supporters who had shown doubts about his new methods: the victims finally included the majority of members both of the 1934 Party Congress and of the Central Committee elected there, as well as the most outstanding army leaders and a large part of the industrial leadership. With that purge, Stalin had assumed the full powers of a despot; the party remained the bearer of legitimacy in name, but henceforth was no more than one of the instruments of the *Vozhd*—less important than the secret police, and no more important than the government bureaucracy and the army during the war.

From the 18th Party Congress in March 1939 which announced the end of the mass purge to the 19th Party Congress in the fall of 1952, the Central Committee met only rarely and the Politburo mostly in *ad hoc* groups selected by Stalin's whim; during the war, the highest collective organ under Stalin, who had become head of government as well, was not a party organ at all, but the "State Defense Committee." Smaller purges in the post-war period affected particularly the party organizations of Leningrad and the Caucasus as well as prominent Jewish communists. But the party was never dissolved, and after Stalin's death in 1953, Khrushchev's struggle for the succession was at the same time a struggle for the restoration of the primacy of the party over the other machines of power, of which the overthrow of Beria and the subordination of the secret police, the replacement of Malenkov as head of the government, the "de-Stalinization" started by the disclosure of Stalin's crimes at the 20th Party Congress, the partial decentralization of the economic bureaucracy and the defeat of the "anti-party group," i.e., the Politburo majority which tried to oppose it, and finally the demotion of Marshal Zhukov for excessive independence as head of the Soviet armed forces were the principal stages. By late 1957, Khrushchev in his capacity as first secretary of the party was the unmistakable political leader of the Soviet Union—without attempting or indeed needing to become a despot; and as we have seen, it was under him that the decision to end the process of institutionalized revolution was taken in 1960–61.

When Khrushchev's method of leadership, while far from despotic, proved too irregular and incalculable for a post-revolutionary period, he was overthrown in 1964—without serious resistance, and without another succession crisis. In the post-revolutionary phase, disagreements within the leadership, while no more absent than in Western governments, were now fought without the revolutionary fervor that could have justified a refusal to submit to the majority, in a new type of communist "cabinet discipline"—and the post-revolutionary phase in Russia, as I said before, became a period of generally accepted, clear procedures of decision making and of oligarchic normality and stability.

China, as you know, went through the early stages of institutionalized revolution without major leadership conflicts, thanks largely to the unique authority of Mao Zedong as the leader of the original struggle for power. But that authority, somewhat diminished by the failed experiment of the "Hundred Flowers" campaign in 1957, was seriously shaken by the results of the "Great Leap Forward" in 1958 and after. Despite Mao's willingness to retire from day-to-day decisions to the "second line," his stubbornness in defending and extending the principle of the "uninterrupted revolution" led to a sharpening "struggle between two lines." It was the increasing difficulties Mao encountered in trying to win this struggle by normal inner-party

methods which caused him to launch the Cultural Revolution by seeking once more to make inner-party power grow out of the barrel of the gun—as he had done in Tsunyi in 1935. The Cultural Revolution, carried out by mobilizing the Red Guards of university and high school students with the help of the army and intimidating and paralyzing the regular party organs with their help, was Mao's attempt to establish a form of personal despotism.

This attempt differed from Stalin's in its aims, its means and the degree of its success. It was motivated by a determination to continue the institutionalized revolution regardless of the damage this might do to economic modernization, while Stalin had long tried to combine new revolutionary transformations in particular fields with such concessions to economic needs as differentiated material incentives and authority for technical and managerial experts. It was based on temporarily mobilizing not the secret police, but the armed forces and an ideologically inspired youth movement against the party bureaucracy. And while succeeding temporarily in breaking the party's resistance and dissolving the communist youth organization as well as the trade unions, it failed to create a *stable* despotism. Stalin, while for a time primarily relying on the secret police, had been able repeatedly to depose and execute their heads. Mao became dependent on the army for taming the anarchic youth movement he had mobilized with its help, and reorganizing the near-dissolved party with the cooperation of a mixture of old cadres and young rebels selected as supposedly reliable. Even after the fall of Lin Biao, Mao remained to his death dependent on an uneasy and unstable balance of military leaders, surviving party "moderates" around Zhou and Deng and unrepentant revolutionary ultras around his wife—not only not a despot, but not even any longer an effective leader with a clear line of policy.

The death of Mao was followed with remarkable speed by the restoration of the primacy of the weakened party—mainly from lack of serious rivals, as the army little had proud memories of its intervention in the domestic power struggle. But within the party, the struggle for or against continuing the institutionalized revolution went on for at least two more years, and only its end with a clear victory of the modernizers around Deng created the conditions for the kind of oligarchic stability with regular procedures of decision making suitable to a post-revolutionary phase.

## CONCLUSION

It is time to attempt to draw some conclusions from the facts of the conflict, inherent in communist systems, between the needs of institutionalized revolution and the requirements of modernization, and of the less inherent, but not atypical conflict between a tendency to establish a personal despotism above the party institutions and the counter-tendency to restore the primacy of those institutions after the death of the despot. Can we say anything general about the causal connection or interaction of the two processes? I think we can.

First of all, it seems clear that the major obstacle to disciplined acceptance of majority decisions in communist political systems is the ideological passion connected with the struggle for new stages of the institutionalized revolution. It follows that despotism, or an attempt at despotism, is likely to arise in communist systems only as long as the belief in an institutionalized revolution has not been finally abandoned. To put it more bluntly, the turn to despotism remains likely only while utopianism is still alive.

Second, and to some extent conversely, the abandonment of the institutionalized revolution has occurred both in Russia and China only after the death of the despot or would-be despot. In both cases, the liberation from his terror has made it easier for the desire for a more normal life to come to the surface, particularly among the party oligarchy; and the security of an oligarchy is best assured by the renunciation of further revolutionary change.

Third, and turning now to the present and future consequences, we are now dealing in the Soviet Union and the Chinese People's Republic with two communist party regimes that are both in their post-revolutionary and post-despotic phase. That means that both are governed by bureaucratic oligarchies with more or less generally accepted procedural rules of decision making, whose domestic policies are no longer marked by ideological conflicts, but by the conflict between the goal of economic modernization and the tendency towards bureaucratic stagnation. Both oligarchies stick to their party monopoly, and both are firmly opposed to political liberalization; but neither tends to return to the experiments in mass annihilation of the revolutionary period.

Fourth, a vital *difference* between the two countries concerns the stage of development at which the revolutionary process was stopped. When Khrushchev announced his 1961 program, the Soviet Union, for all its structural weaknesses, had become one of the major industrial countries of the world. China at the present time is still far from that stage, and her difficulties in reaching it are still tremendous—for reasons of lack of capital compared to the pressure of the population, of lack of scientific and technical cadres proportionate to the size of the problems, and perhaps also of the repercussions of the absurdities of the period of the Cultural Revolution on working morale and general confidence. But this last must be a tentative judgment.

Finally, the fact that China, almost two decades after Russia, has entered her post-revolutionary phase, has one major international consequence: the power conflict between those two neighbors has lost its ideological component. The Chinese communists can no longer accuse the Russians of having abandoned their revolutionary principles, and the Russians can no longer blame the Chinese for utopianism and adventurism in domestic affairs. The fact that both sides are aware of that post-revolutionary change has made it easier for them to discuss a possible normalization of their relations. But that does not and cannot mean that those relations will, at some future date, be characterized by an apparent ideological community, as they were a long time ago, instead of by ideological conflict. They will be determined, like other relations between great powers, by their interests—and that means important conflicting interests, but potentially some common interests as well.

## Notes

1. Cf. above all the description of Stalin's and Mao's rule as a system of "Führerism" essentially similar to that of Hitler and Mussolini and sharply distinct from the "Bolshevism" of Lenin in Leonard Schapiro and John Wilson Lewis, "The Role of the Monolithic Party Under the Totalitarian Leader," in *Party Leadership and Revolutionary Power in China,* ed. John Wilson Lewis (London: Cambridge University Press, 1970). The same argument is also used for a *definition* of totalitarianism by this type of leader in Leonard Schapiro, *Totalitarianism* (New York: Macmillan, 1972).

# 18
# China's Political Evolution
*Michel Oksenberg and Richard Bush*

In the past decade, but especially since Mao Zedong's death in 1976, the Chinese political system has experienced a spectacular sequence of events: the arrest of Mao's wife Jiang Qing and her associates in the "gang of four," one month after his death; the return to political power of Deng Xiaoping in mid-1977, a reversal of fate after his removal but 15 months earlier; the

SOURCE: Michel Oksenberg and Richard Bush, "China's Political Evolution: 1972–82," *Problems of Communism* (September–October 1982), pp. 1–19. Reprinted by permission. Article and Notes abridged by the editors.

proclamation by Premier and party Chairman Hua Guofeng in early 1978 of the ambitious goal of transforming China into a modern state by the year 2000; the quiet abandonment of these unrealistic targets 10 months later, although the leaders still remained committed to rapid economic growth and openness to the outside world; the normalization of relations with the United States in late 1978; the incursion into Vietnam in late February 1979; the political experimentation epitomized by the "democracy wall" movement in the spring of 1979; the sharpening tension between Hua Guofeng and Deng Xiaoping; the erosion of Hua's position as well as the purge of Politburo members who had advanced during the Cultural Revolution; the proclamation of sharp economic retrenchment and the postponement of several multimillion-dollar import purchases in December 1980; the major reassessment of Mao Zedong in June 1981, which enumerated his many policy errors while reaffirming the essential wisdom of his beliefs; the replacement of Hua as party chairman by Hu Yaobang and as premier by Zhao Ziyang in 1980–81, thereby marking Hu and Zhao as Deng's chosen successors; a major shake-up of personnel in the party and state structure in early 1982; and finally, the 12th Congress of the Chinese Communist Party, in September 1982, which consolidated the gains of the previous three years in establishing a more durable political order.

Quieter developments have also occurred. Seven deserve to be specially emphasized:

• The strategy of economic development was changed. The leaders have cut the rate of capital accumulation sharply and allowed the nation's wage bill to increase. Furthermore, they have sought to alter the balance among heavy industry, light industry, and agriculture, moving away from the Stalinist emphasis upon heavy industry toward light industry. Within agriculture, cropping patterns have been changed to boost production of crops used in light industry.

• The methods of organizing agricultural production have undergone sweeping change.

The incomes of peasant households in many regions are now based on the crops raised on specific plots of land assigned to the households. The institutions which directed peasant activity (commune, production brigade, and production team) have had their powers significantly curtailed. Changes of equal magnitude are being attempted in industrial management, although the obstacles in this area may be greater.

• The country has been opened to foreign commerce and foreign influence. Special economic zones now exist as a means of encouraging investment in China, and foreign firms enjoy special privileges. Foreign books in translation, classical and popular music, films, and clothing styles—all controlled and in limited scope, to be sure—are now available.

• Class labels and other terms of opprobrium (e.g., "landlord," "reactionary," "rightist") are being removed from several million Chinese. The government has promised to restore these people to their previous positions and, in some cases, has offered restitution for the damages they suffered.

• A major corpus of laws and regulations has been enacted which offers some promise of making life for Chinese more just and predictable. This includes criminal, civil, marriage, and tax laws.

• The government has vigorously encouraged family planning. Major programs have been enacted to achieve the goal of the one-child family.

• A growing energy problem has arisen due to a levelling-off in coal and petroleum production. Energy shortages now constitute a major brake on rapid industrial expansion.

Without denigrating the importance of these developments, this essay eschews a focus on either the factional power struggles or the specific economic and legal reforms. Instead, we wish to step back and to ask questions about the decade 1972–82, from the eve of Mao's decline to the arrangement of an initial succession after Deng. How does the Chinese political system today differ from that of a decade ago? What remains the same? More important, why the

changes? Has the system reached an equilibrium point? Are aspects of the Maoist system that have been abandoned likely to be restored? Is the political evolution of the past 10 years likely to continue?

Our core argument can be summarized succinctly. During the decade under scrutiny, China passed a watershed. In 1972, totalitarian revolutionaries ruled the nation; by 1982, China's rulers had become authoritarian reformers. The totalitarian revolutionaries had acted upon their belief that rapid, violent, and comprehensive transformation of elites and institutions was the most effective mode of change. The leaders had unleashed upon society and themselves a reign of terror. They had constructed a totalitarian regime which sought to deny privacy or cultivation of individuality in society. They expected all citizens, especially those in urban areas, to express their belief in the integrating ideology of the regime, to participate in political life, and to surrender their individuality to a collective identity.

By contrast, in 1982, the top Chinese leadership appears to be committed to gradual and peaceful change within a framework of continuity of elites and institutions. The leaders have shifted their emphasis in implementing policy from mobilization of the populace to action through the bureaucracy. They have also sought to end the terror. While seeking orthodoxy to which all intellectuals and creative artists are expected to adhere, the authoritarians do permit individual silence and a limited withdrawal or distancing from politics. Also, orthodoxy is less well defined and broader in scope.

Being authoritarian, to be sure, China's leaders today maintain extensive surveillance over the population and tolerate no organized opposition or challenges to their rule. They value hierarchy and discipline and are not hesitant to employ force in ordering their realm. Yet, individuals may cultivate personal pursuits and are encouraged to plan their careers. The current leaders no longer measure their own performance by their progress in nurturing a new "socialist man" or in creating a classless society. Instead, they wish their performance to be judged by their ability to improve the material well-being of the populace.

This evolution can be attributed to several interrelated factors. The passing of Mao and the advent of a leadership group who had suffered during the Cultural Revolution is a key factor. More than personnel changes at the top are involved, however. The developments in China bear a great resemblance to trends in other societies after sustained periods of terror and politically induced social change. The case of the post-Stalin Soviet Union and the Khrushchev era comes immediately to mind. Yet, societies can manifest different types of Thermidor, and China's post-Mao moderation reveals the reassertion of certain deeply rooted traditions which the Maoist system had challenged. China's evolution since Mao's death represents the continued adaptation of Communist revolution to the Chinese cultural context.

We note that the process of domesticization has not yet ended. In some respects, the present reforms are not fully congruent with some aspects of the cultural heritage. Furthermore, certain bureaucracies of the Maoist era remain strong and resistant to change, while power is still vested as much in people as in institutions. Finally, China is undergoing massive economic changes, and the exposure to the outside world will also have its impact. For all these reasons, we conclude that the Chinese political system has yet to reach an equilibrium, and further evolution can be anticipated.

## THE MAOIST SYSTEM BEFORE ITS DECAY

. . . As its principal architect, Mao had designed a system that supported not only his power needs but also his larger goals for China in the late 1960s, and his strategy for attaining those goals. Put in its best light, the policy process which Mao shaped through 1972, when for the last time it escaped his control, had this rationale.[1] It was meant to downplay economic interdependence among regions, the national use of material rewards, and the regular, formal promotion system as the best means of preserving China's unity. Instead, Mao relied on coercion and the propagation of a single ideology as his principal instruments for integrating his heterogeneous nation. To be sure, the central economic agencies retained a role in redistributing resources from the more developed to the less developed regions of the country, a process which may have reduced interprovince tensions and promoted unity. Nonetheless, in terms of allocating power among the organizational hierarchies in China, Mao assigned primacy in integrating the society to the propaganda apparatus, the public security forces, and the military. With Mao's proxy, those who presided over these hierarchies wielded great power.

The emphasis on the inculcation of values was related to the diagnosis of the major impediments to China's modernization made by Mao in his later years. Mao always had been sensitive to certain deeply ingrained cultural attributes which seemed to him inimical to China's modernization. These were fatalism, passivity, familialism, a preference for harmony and the avoidance of conflict, and a disdain for physical labor. But after achieving power in 1949, Mao chose to give more emphasis to the establishment of an economic infrastructure as the prerequisite for China's growth. Hence, he embraced the Stalinist development model, with its emphasis on steel, machine-building industries, and energy production. Then, in the late 1950s and early 1960s, Mao increasingly concentrated on institutional issues: the role of the party, the creation of rural communes, and the refinement of campaigns as a technique for implementation of policy. But from the early 1960s until the end of his life, Mao considered the attitudes of Chinese bureaucrats and the populace generally to be the major impediment to China's modernization. Hence he launched a cultural revolution. Mao had concluded that a new culture would emerge only through the deliberate fostering of class struggle, pitting portions of the populace against his own bureaucracy. By the mid-1960s, Mao had also decided that many of his associates and their subordinates were beyond salvation and were unworthy of succeeding him. Not only a cultural revolution but a massive purge of the unredeemable was necessary in his view to keep China on his path to modernity.

Similarly, Mao came to view the organizational web of party, government, and armed forces as an inherently conservative repository of the values he was seeking to eradicate. Distrustful of bureaucracy, he sought ways of administration which minimized its role. Hence, his attraction to campaigns (*yun-dong*) as an alternative mechanism of policy implementation. With the encouragement of his more radical supporters, especially Zhang Chunqiao, Mao deliberately promoted a primitive economy. His demand for maximum local self-sufficiency, the restrictions on the number of commodities that could be traded on the regulated free market, and his simultaneous curtailment of the capacity of planning agencies to allocate goods according to plan—all sought to minimize commerce and the division of labor in society. To bring about such an unstratified social and economic structure, Mao realized, would require enormous change. Thus, instead of the incremental, inherently cautious, fragmented decision making which a bureaucratic policy process tends to yield, Mao sought sweeping, bold, utopian policies that a mobilization system is more likely to engender.

Mao sought a system in perpetual change. According to his dialectic and idealist vision of history, thesis could be turned into antithesis, which in turn would become synthesis. What appeared irreconcilable today could be reconciled tomorrow. To name Mao's three favorite polarities—discipline and freedom, centralism and democracy, a general will and the individual spirit—they were viewed by him as equally desirable but contradictory qualities at this stage in history. However, Mao thought that wise leaders could drive their society forward, raising the material standard of living and altering the consciousness of the populace. Ultimately, the

polarities could be reconciled in a classless, abundant society, provided that the greatest threat to the attainment of this vision—the calcification of the social structure—was overcome.

This brings us to the core of Mao and the policy process he structured. As noted earlier, he was to the end of his life a revolutionary and a totalitarian ruler. He believed that the only way to transform China was rapidly, violently, comprehensively; its elites and institutions would have to be subjected to continual change. China's problems were so vast that efforts to attain peaceful, gradual change could not be sustained and would eventually be lost in the morass of bureaucracy. In his view, to transform China required vision and extraordinary confidence that a politically involved Chinese populace—given no respite to cultivate individual pursuits—could overcome its plight of poverty and weakness. To unleash portions of the populace in all their fury required leaders capable of interacting directly with the forces in society without mediation by intervening bureaucracies. Mao saw little intrinsic value in institutions like the party, government, or army. They were to serve as instruments whose credibility and authority could be expended in his larger effort to transform China into a strong, prosperous, socialist nation.

## EVOLUTION OF THE SYSTEM, 1972–82

Since early 1972, the Chinese system has evolved through several stages: (1) a concerted effort to restore order and to rebuild institutions based on an amalgam of pre-1966 and Cultural Revolution values, a period lasting until late 1973; (2) an unbridled struggle for political survival and succession to Mao, from late 1973 to October 1976, when the "gang of four" were arrested; (3) a period of uncertainty lasting until mid-1978, with some of the leaders seeking to establish a neo-Maoist system; (4) introduction of broad institutional reforms and a moderation and rationalization of economic goals, a stage that began with the emergence of Deng Xiaoping as the dominant political leader in mid-1978; (5) from late 1980 to mid-1982, the appearance of resistance to reforms and the resultant efforts by Deng and his associates to weaken and remove the points of resistance.

## September 1971–August 1973.

Mao sought to preserve his rule and surmount the Lin Biao affair by incorporating the two principal factional groupings—led by Zhou Enlai and Jiang Qing respectively—that had supported him in the attack on Lin. Mao turned to Zhou to create order out of the economic chaos, but he gave preeminence to the "radicals" in the cultural domain to preserve his ideological gains of the previous five years. As the military's role in civilian institutions declined, the rebuilding of the state and party apparatuses began, and a number of supposedly chastened "capitalist roaders" returned to help staff them (the most prominent returnee was Deng Xiaoping, who first reappeared in public in April 1973). They began to work with officials who had come to the fore during the Cultural Revolution.

This modus vivendi in personnel was accompanied by an attempt in a range of policy areas to introduce more pragmatic methods while retaining Cultural Revolution values. In industry, for example, limited material incentives were introduced, although mobilization continued to be used to stimulate output. In the educational sphere, examinations were reintroduced to judge the academic competence of students, even though ideological considerations remained important in the admissions process. In design, the policy process remained Mao-centered; in fact, the physically declining Chairman was unable to achieve the coherence he sought or to control the conflict he had built into the system.

## September 1973–October 1976.

In the wake of the Tenth CCP Congress in August 1973, struggle between the Zhou-Deng and Jiang factions intensified, each side trying to secure advantage for the day that Mao died. (The military and public security factions maneuvered on the sidelines.) Each faction offered competing programs for China's development. Each tried to put through its policy in various sectors. And each seemed to enjoy moments of political ascendancy: the Jiang forces during the first half of 1974 (the "Criticize Confucius–Criticize Lin Biao" campaign); the Deng forces from late 1974 to late 1975 (under the slogan of the "four modernizations"); and the radicals again from late 1975 until Mao's death in September 1976 (a period in which the more pragmatic policies were again set aside). The three years of unabated conflict left behind a weak and largely ineffective political system that had come to rely very heavily on coercion.

## October 1976–October 1978.

After the euphoria that ensued from the arrest of "the gang of four" had somewhat abated, a long list of neglected economic problems came to attention. It became clear that, without major changes in the policy process, the nation would meet with disaster. The disparate groups that had combined to oust the radicals attempted to work together (as had been the case after the Lin Biao affair). Neo-Maoists, led by Hua Guofeng, and the pragmatists who supported the newly rehabilitated Deng Xiaoping could agree on the priority of economic growth and the need for some ideological liberalization in the fields of science, education, and culture. Material incentives and the purchase of foreign technology were again deemed acceptable. A mere 18 months after Mao's death, this leadership presented an ambitious program in pursuit of the "four modernizations" (in agriculture, industry, national defense, and science and technology).

However, the coalition was inherently unstable. The neo-Maoists were willing to accept modernization, especially when described as "a new leap forward." But they were less prepared to accept dilution of Maoist values or methods of rule. With Hua Guofeng as their principal spokesman, the neo-Maoists essentially advocated continuing the mobilization process, sustaining class struggle, propagating Mao's ideology, and implementing policy through campaigns. The pragmatist camp believed that Maoist values and Mao's style of rule were at the root of China's problems. They also judged that nothing less than an open attack on Mao was necessary to regain popular support. Also, some of Deng's followers came to question whether the leadership had the resources, institutional capacity, and popular support to pursue a policy of forced-draft industrialization. After some fencing over these issues during the spring and summer of 1978, the leadership dispute came to a head in December at the Third Plenum of the CCP Central Committee. In the streets of Beijing, an increasingly bold public began writing posters which attacked the Cultural Revolution and Mao.

## November 1978–November 1980.

Both in China and abroad, the Third Plenum is now regarded as the crucial watershed of the post-Mao era. It was at that session (and the central work conference preceding it) that Deng Xiaoping unquestionably gained the upper hand in China's leadership. His colleagues living (Chen Yun and Peng Zhen, for example) and dead (Peng Dehuai, Tao Zhu) were rehabilitated. The case of Liu Shaoqi was reopened, and he was rehabilitated in February 1980. The neo-Maoists came under attack, historical verdicts on such issues as the Tiananmen Incident were reversed, and an evaluation of Mao was promised.

Equally important were the new directions charted for the country's institutional life. In law, politics, and economics, liberalization would, it was predicted, have a positive, energizing effect and engender popular support for the regime. In this spirit, the Third Plenum promised that "socialist modernization" was China's long-term priority, and that mass political campaigns and all that came with them were no longer appropriate. In

order to promote "socialist legality" and limit police abuses, the criminal justice system was reformed, and economic laws were drafted. To promote "socialist democracy," direct popular vote was mandated for the election of delegates to county-level people's congresses, and plans to end the rubber-stamp nature of the National People's Congress were circulated. Life tenure in office, perceived to be the root of many of the problems of the late-Mao era, came under attack. Even the closing of Democracy Wall and the later ban on wall posters constrained but did not reverse this democratizing trend.

In addition, a major shift in economic policy became apparent especially after Chen Yun, an economic specialist and a top party official in the 1940s, joined the Politburo Standing Committee in December 1978. This "readjustment" entailed the abandonment of the investment policy stressing high rates of accumulation and development of heavy industry. It also entailed a "restructuring" in the Soviet-style system of central control, in the direction of allowing greater play of market mechanisms.

## December 1980–Spring 1982.

By late 1982, the institutional reforms and related policies had achieved success in some areas (for example, boosting agricultural production and peasant income), but fostered difficulties on other fronts (for example, generating inflation and a large government deficit). These economic difficulties prompted the declaration of a policy of economic retrenchment in 1980. Perhaps equally unsettling for the leadership, however, were the political and ideological repercussions of reforms. In 1979, elements of the public began to question the necessity for one-party rule and the socialist system itself, while in 1980, the leadership began to perceive a disruptive Western impact upon Chinese thought and behavior.

Indeed, Deng Xiaoping and Chen Yun themselves concluded that reform of institutions without a workable national consensus on ideology would not succeed. The issue was widely discussed during 1981, in the context of an evaluation of the filmscript "Unrequited Love," written by Bai Hua, who worked in the military's large cultural establishment. The film's sympathetic portrayal of a Chinese intellectual victimized during the Maoist era epitomized for the more orthodox party officials the damaging effects of cultural freedom. The leadership tried to disarm the critics with a rebuke of Bai Hua and a general attack on "bourgeois liberalism." In this context, the official verdict on Mao, adopted at the Sixth Plenum in June 1981, was less condemnatory than it might otherwise have been. In the absence of a clearcut ideological alternative to Mao's thought, the Deng regime had to soft-pedal its criticism of Mao the man in order to be able to espouse elements of his thought.

Writers and artists were not the only group affected by the new stress on values and ideology. Focusing on poor preparation of the party cadres, Chen Yun termed the problem of party work-style a "life-and-death matter," and a drive against economic crimes by officials began in early 1982. Young people were told more and more frequently that a "spiritual civilization" must accompany material progress. Fearing "the corrosive influence of capitalist ideas," the regime tightened restrictions on contacts between Chinese and foreigners.

In short, the parameters of institutional reform were more clearly etched. The Chinese system would remain highly centralized and authoritarian. The Communist party would retain its monopoly of power and be revitalized in order to perform well its distinctive role. The instruments of totalitarian rule—the public security forces and the propaganda apparatus—would be curbed but not dismantled. The economy would remain largely under state plan; the role of the market would be secondary. Within these constraints, the Maoist system would be significantly altered.

## THE SYSTEM IN 1982

The tortuous path of development from 1972 to 1982 reveals that no single vision of rule—and

certainly not Mao's—guided China during the entire decade. Differences existed among the leaders on many issues. Moreover, the twists and turns in policy suggest that the same leaders, even Deng Xiaoping, changed policy positions as they confronted new problems, learned new lessons, and faced shifting constellations of opponents. . . . In spite of all this, one can say that since 1978 an effective consensus has existed among the top leaders concerning broad political and economic objectives and the major methods to achieve them.

The dedication of the leadership to the attainment of a strong and prosperous China is as firm as that of Mao. However, their appraisal of the disastrous consequences of the Great Leap Forward and the Cultural Revolution, as well as their sensitivity to the excesses of the anti-rightist and rectification campaigns of 1957—which Deng himself had helped direct—caused them to depart sharply from Mao's view of the way to achieve the goal.

Instead of seeking to unite China primarily through coercion and propaganda, they encouraged unity through increased economic interdependence among regions, through reliance on effective, planned allocation of material goods and capital, and through a regularized promotion and personnel management system. The immediate bureaucratic beneficiaries of this emphasis were the leading economic agencies—the State Planning Commission, the Ministry of Finance, the People's Bank of China—and the central agency responsible for managing a regular personnel system, the Organization Department of the Chinese Communist Party (CCP). The losers were the Propaganda Department of the CCP, the Ministry of Public Security, and the military. Billboards that once displayed Mao's sayings now advertise various merchandise. Tens of thousands were released from the labor camps of the public security apparatus, while millions more lost their "labels" and ceased being under continual supervision by the public security forces. The military lost many of its privileges and suffered a reduced budget. Abandoning Mao's totalitarian demand for the positive involvement of everyone in politics,

Deng has been willing to permit individuals to withdraw from politics and to pursue their private interests, be it careers or avocations, and to create works of art, provided these do not exhibit opposition to the rule of the party.

Deng and Chen saw the need for regularity and predictability. Their pledge has been: no more campaigns, no more Maoist dialectical swings between periods of mobilization and stability. The goal has been steady rule through a professional bureaucracy, untainted by corruption and personal ties. The object has been to eliminate the immobilism, the factionalism, and the reliance on personal ties (*guan-xi*) in the bureaucracy which had thrived during the Cultural Revolution. The establishment of the Academy of Social Sciences and the reestablishment of professional associations are intended to generate a more empirical policy process and to encourage greater communication among professionals working in different units or systems (*xi-tong*).

To guard against bureaucratism in the pejorative sense, the leaders have reestablished the disciplinary control commissions within the party that existed in the 1950s and again during the post-Great Leap Forward recovery. They have sought more vigorous monitoring of the bureaucracy through elected congresses. For a brief span in 1978-79, they encouraged open petitioning over accumulated grievances, in mid-1979 permitting petitioners to assemble at the entrance to Zhongnanhai (the state and party headquarters) and in late 1978 and the spring of 1979 sponsoring the Democracy Wall. They assigned close aides to high positions on newspapers and gave them a mandate to undertake investigative journalism. They saw expansion of the marketplace as a further check on bureaucratic slothfulness. There was even discussion in those heady days of 1979 about establishing a bicameral legislative system, with invigorated minor democratic parties playing a serious political role in the revitalized Chinese People's Political Consultative Conference. They have given considerable publicity to many cases of corruption and abuse of power and have punished the offending bureaucrats.

The major immediate objective domestically has been to improve the standard of living of the populace. Deng, Chen, and their associates clearly felt that the justification of party dictatorship and socialist rule in China rested on the party's ability to improve the welfare of the people. In this regard, performance in the past has been lackluster: the average income, diet, or availability of material goods in 1977 were hardly better than in 1957. Without improvement in the quality of life, the leaders believe, the Chinese people would not embrace more advanced socialist or collectivist forms of social organization. Deng and his associates also have envisioned a more lively, diversified cultural life than the narrow range of theater, literature, and movies offered in Mao's last years. In short, the reformers have staked their popular standing on improving the material and cultural quality of life in China now and have promised a more abundant tomorrow. Mao had avoided basing his legitimacy on such tangible promises and, except in 1955 and 1958, tried not to arouse expectations about a more abundant life in the near future. Deng and his associates have felt it necessary to do so in order to restore morale in the country and reestablish the confidence of the populace in the efficacy of their government. Only in this way, they believe, can China's major problems of productivity and modernization be solved.

When one looks at the program of reform espoused by the present leadership and at their strategy for implementing it, one has to conclude that the leadership has already succeeded in changing the system significantly from what it had been in 1972. First, China has begun to recover from the trauma of the Cultural Revolution and its aftermath. Though this is very difficult to judge, it does seem that the totally benumbed quality of much of the populace has begun to disappear. To be sure, cynicism and apathy are widespread, especially in urban areas. Some of the enthusiasm and optimism for the "four modernizations" generated among the urban intellectuals in 1978-79 appear to have dissipated. Nonetheless, the current leaders seem to have inspired some popular confidence in their capacity to steer a steadier course toward gradual economic growth. The fears of a return to the excesses of the Cultural Revolution so prevalent in 1976–78 appear to be subsiding. The leaders probably have done much to restore their ability to rule effectively, though they have yet to regain the power and authority which the system enjoyed in the 1950s.

China today has collective rule, in contrast to Mao's one-man rule. To be sure, Deng has enjoyed periods where the initiative was almost totally his; nonetheless, no one ruler can bend the entire system to his will, as Mao was able to do on many occasions. One cannot envision Deng, Chen, or any ruler at this stage being able to launch a Great Leap Forward or a Cultural Revolution as Mao did. The legitimacy of the regime is not rooted in the thought and writings of a single leader, as in the Maoist era. Most major decisions in China today appear to be based on the building of a consensus within the Politburo and Secretariat, and—in a formal sense—even minor decisions frequently require the approval of several members of the State Council's Standing Committee.

Power still appears rooted more in people than in institutions, and indications remain of factional alignments at the top. Nonetheless, factional strife has been dampened; it is no longer a Hobbesian struggle for survival. Progress has been made in rebuilding institutions. The streamlining of the State Council in early 1982, the drafting of the 1982 state constitution, and the restructuring of the apex of the party apparatus at the 12th CCP Congress represent major steps in this process. Appointment of Zhao Ziyang as premier and Hu Yaobang as party general secretary, as well as the anticipated naming of a head of state—i.e., a chairman of the People's Republic—will also contribute to the institutional revival. A smoother succession can now be anticipated following the deaths of Deng and Chen than occurred in 1976 when Zhou and Mao died. The leaders have begun to reveal how their policy process actually works—how documents are drafted and issued, how leaders live and work, how meetings are convened. Furthermore, they have begun to obey the rules governing the stages through which discussion of policy ought to proceed before a policy is formally promulgated.

Yet, certain aspects of the system remain the same. Different factional groupings on the Politburo and Secretariat still have their distinctive sources of power in the capital, based in different organizational hierarchies. *Guan-xi* networks of people still link leaders in Beijing to provinces, counties, and primary units. The power of middle-level bureaucrats remains intertwined with the waxing or waning influence of their bosses and protectors. Many bureaucrats continue to believe that the single most important factor determining their fate is the political strength and interest of the State Council Standing Committee member responsible for their agency.

Yet, in terms of the principal mechanisms for integrating the country, major changes have occurred since 1972. In Mao's last years, China's essential unity, severely tested to be sure, was retained primarily through coercion, the propagation of ideology, and the personal ties linking individual leaders in Beijing to leaders in different parts of the country. By 1982, the economic planning apparatus had been substantially reestablished, fiscal and monetary controls had been revitalized, and a national personnel management system, with promotions and dismissals based on merit, had begun to be restored. Meanwhile, the range of responsibilities of both the military and the public security forces has contracted. In particular, the public security forces have lost their direct control over millions of people previously in labor camps or under surveillance because they were charged with being one of the "five black elements." The establishment of a judicial system and procuracy and the proclamation of legal codes offer hope that some checks would eventually exist on the powers of the police. With the acknowledgment that Mao's body of writings was germane to his time, had to be reinterpreted to suit new conditions, and contained flaws in any case, no identifiable, authoritative, current doctrine prevails on which behavior has to be firmly based. . . .

Three additional developments have accompanied and undergirded the reemergence of the economic bureaucracies. First, campaigns as an alternative mode of policy implementation have been essentially abandoned. Since the death of Mao, the Chinese have not been subjected to one hallmark of the Chairman's rule: the designating of a particular task or set of tasks as central; the organization of ad hoc committees to direct the campaign, staffed by bureaucrats seconded to the committee; the supply of study documents to enlighten the populace about the campaign's objectives; and the struggle against people whom the ad hoc committees identified as obstacles to the campaign—all done in an atmosphere of frenzy. The campaigns totally disrupted bureaucratic routine, as budgets and personnel were altered. Perhaps no other development so clearly accounts for the reassertion of bureaucratic rule as does the abandonment of campaigns.

A second development has been some progress in rebuilding the state statistical network. . . .

The third development was the amelioration of tensions within the bureaucracies. From 1972 to 1976, the "cultural revolutionaries" and the rehabilitated "capitalist roaders"—the tormenters

and the tormented—worked side by side in the various agencies. Since 1978, those officials who had risen during the Cultural Revolution have been gradually weeded out, while more of the officials who had been purged have returned to office. Of course, a renewal of fragmentation among the top leaders could revive intra-agency strife around Cultural Revolution cleavages. However, personnel changes, new issues, and somewhat dimmed memories, as well as greater leadership cohesion at higher levels seem to have dampened animosities within agencies. This generalization does not apply to all agencies. Bureaucracies which were at the vortex of the Cultural Revolution—for example, the ministries of Culture and Education—manifested more evident scars than those which were either totally destroyed and had to be rebuilt (e.g., the Statistical Bureau), or which had been somewhat isolated from the turmoil (e.g., some of the machine-building ministries).

The developments from 1972 to 1982 we have sketched can be summarized in tabular form (see table 1). Though the table is oversimplified, it vividly underscores the considerable change over the decade. The extent of the changes immediately raises two questions: Why did the changes occur? Will they endure?

**TABLE 1**  Evolution of the Chinese political system, 1972–82

| Attribute of the system | In 1972 | In 1982 |
|---|---|---|
| Method of change preferred by leader(s) | Revolution | Reform |
| How leader(s) view process of change | Dialectical | Linear |
| Preferred method of policy implementation | Mobilization of populace; class struggle | Rule by bureaucracy; regularity |
| Intrusiveness of state | Total | Pursuit of some private interests and withdrawal tolerated |
| Main tasks of governance | Restoration of order; attitudinal change; elimination of lingering bourgeois influences | Raising economic production and living standards |
| Mechanisms for integrating the policy | Networks of personal relations; coercion; ideology | Networks of personal relations; regularized personnel system; planned allocation of material goods and capital; coercion |

**TABLE 1 (Continued)**  Evolution of the Chinese political system, 1972–82

| Attribute of the system | In 1972 | In 1982 |
|---|---|---|
| Techniques for controlling "bureaucratism" | Campaigns | Experimentation with numerous techniques, none successful |
| Extent of "institutionalization" | Low; rule of men rather than institutions | Low; major efforts under way to rebuild institutions |
| Nature of politics at top level | Unbridled factionalism below top leader | Struggle among factions and opinion groups governed by unwritten rules |
| Rule at top | One-man rule | Collective leadership |
| Empirical bases of decisions | Prior preferences demonstrated in model units | Investigation; statistical compilation; model units |
| Popular confidence in political system | Low | Somewhat improved |
| Dominant organizational hierarchies | People's Liberation Army, public security forces; party Propaganda Department | Party committee chain of command; party Organization Department; State Planning Commission; Ministry of Finance; army; public security forces |

## CAUSES OF CHANGE AND ITS DURABILITY

Three interrelated factors help to explain the evolution of the system: the change in the top leaders, the course of revolution, and China's specific development problems. The human factor is the passing of Mao and the rise of Deng and Chen. Many of the changes only took place after Mao's death, the arrest of his principal allies in revolution, and the subsequent eclipse of his lingering beneficiaries (e.g., Hua Guofeng). The Chinese system remains one which reflects the aspirations and techniques of rule of the top officials. To that extent, the system will continue to evolve and take on the coloration of Deng's and Chen's successors.

A second, more systemic factor is also at work, namely, the course of any totalitarian revolution.[2] The reform-oriented, institutionalized polity which had begun to emerge by 1982 bears a great resemblance to the Chinese system which was making its appearance in the mid-1950s and then again in the early 1960s, after the

Great Leap Forward campaign (1958–60). By launching the Cultural Revolution in 1966, Mao sought to postpone in China the inevitable aftermath of revolutions—be they in France, Russia, Germany, Cuba, or Vietnam—that is to say, the strengthened grip of bureaucracy over society. Mao deliberately sought mechanisms to keep society in constant turmoil so as to prevent a bureaucratic domination in China.

Nevertheless, it appears as though societies reach a limit beyond which they do not welcome turmoil and become exhausted by it. Problems of legitimacy and compliance come to the fore as the leaders must grapple with a cynical, disenchanted population which has been coerced for too long. Yet, upon closer examination, no revolutionary or totalitarian regime has followed exactly the same path. What is common among totalitarian regimes, as Richard Lowenthal has noted, is their

> call for mobilization to be directed toward development of one sector [of the nation], while totalitarian instruments of control and repression are used to demobilize the other sectors....

Herein lies the dilemma of the totalitarian regime that has successfully mobilized its system's assets to attain a single developmental objective. . . . Its very success has led to mounting pressures to bring the system into balance, to allow development in the hitherto unauthorized areas; yet, if it does so, it will be sanctioning the end of the revolution from above, the end of the movement toward the goal culture.[3]

Lowenthal's insight implies that the post-totalitarian phase in each case will be a specific reaction to the particular emphases of the mobilization effort. In sum, since each revolutionary effort to transform a society has its own emphasis, it will leave its own particular legacy. For this reason, while focusing on the post-Mao era, this essay laid initial stress on Mao's goals and techniques of rule. To an extraordinary extent, the pressing problems now, even six years after Mao's death, are precisely the ones Mao neglected as he directed the nation's energies elsewhere. The contours of the 1982 political system are, to a considerable degree, a reaction to the Maoist system. The political institutions and process Deng and his associates have called into being have been designed to cope with the particular set of problems Mao had neglected and thus bequeathed to his successors:

- Lagging agricultural production.
- An inefficient industrial system.
- High unemployment among youth.
- A low standard of living.
- Widespread apathy and cynicism.
- An inadequate scientific and technological manpower base.
- Specific bottlenecks in transportation, communications, and energy.
- An unacceptably high rate of population increase.

So pressing are these problems and so seemingly supportive to their solution is the political system Deng, Chen, and their associates have designed, that the observer might be tempted to assume that rationality has prevailed and an equilibrium may have been reached. Such a conclusion is unwarranted on several grounds.

To begin with, the major instruments of totalitarian rule have been weakened but not eliminated. The military, the public security forces, and the propaganda apparatus have yet to acquire roles in domestic affairs commensurate with the objective resources under their command. They are potentially destabilizing institutions and focal points of resistance to the system which Deng and Chen have forged.

In addition, the current system and set of policies generate their own, new set of problems, and it is not yet clear that the Deng–Chen system is capable of handling these problems. . . .

Another potential source of instability stems from the promise the leadership has made to raise the standard of living of the populace. From 1978 to 1982, real income has gone up dramatically for many, particularly in the countryside, and moderately for others, especially in the cities. Not only have wages gone up, but construction of housing has increased significantly, as has the production of many consumer durables (watches, bicycles, portable radios, television sets, etc.). The slightly more affluent urban Chinese populace is beginning to press upon scarce leisure-time facilities, such as theaters, parks and sports grounds. Therefore, questions remain. Are expectations rising more rapidly than the expansion of consumer goods industries? Is it in fact wise to stimulate support for the regime through such a heavy reliance on material incentives? What might happen if the economic strategy does not succeed, the growth rate falters, and standards of living stagnate? In that case, the fundamental stability of the Chinese regime would not necessarily be at stake, but many of the changes made since 1972 would be threatened, particularly in the relative importance of various bureaucracies and the mechanisms for integrating the society.

In addition to the leadership, the natural course of totalitarian revolutions, and the concrete problems facing the Chinese leaders, another consideration bears mention in explaining the change from 1972 to 1982 and in assessing the future: Chinese cultural traditions. One way of looking at the last years of Mao and the post-Mao era is in the light of China's cultural heritage. In many respects, what has transpired is a reassertion of certain dominant strands in the Chinese tradition. In particular, as W. Theodore deBary has argued, the two dominant models of rule in China have been harsh dictatorship or benevolent but still authoritarian bureaucracy, with the latter being more common through the centuries.[4] Ironically, the Cultural Revolution helped revive the traditional culture it had been intended to destroy. The harsh dictatorship under Mao strengthened people's desire to confide in those whom they trusted, i.e., those with whom they shared ties. Thus, the immediate family in many ways became more important; school, native place, or early career connections became tickets to survival. The disillusionment with the formal Maoist ideology led to increased interest in traditional religion, especially Buddhism and Taoism. Thus, what makes current China at least superficially resemble the imperial system is the twin reassertion of formal bureaucracy and the informal means (especially use of *guan-xi* and the prevalence of factions) for coping with the state.

The present leadership swiftly jettisoned those aspects of the Maoist system which ran especially counter to the dominant strands in the Chinese tradition. These were its denial of the cultivation of individual pursuits, its emphasis on class struggle, and its extreme denigration of bureaucracy and hierarchy. To be sure, such concepts as "privacy" and "individualism," so central to Western political thought, were not well developed in the Chinese tradition; on the other hand, notions of "withdrawal," "quietude," and particularly, "self-cultivation" were quite well developed. Not privacy but scholarship, meditation, and detachment were esteemed values, and rule which prevented cultivation of talent—poetry, painting, carving of seals—was threatening to culture and the attainment of virtue. Mao's fostering of struggle also ran counter to a deeply ingrained preference for harmony. Campaigns and the brawling that accompanied them brought disorder instead of the preferred regularity and order.[5]

To the extent that the Deng-Chen system represents a reassertion of "Chineseness," several exceptions must also be noted: collective leadership, the idea of linear progress, the downplaying of ideology, and the empirical basis of policy choice. Let us briefly identify each of these very complicated matters. When unified, China always has had a single, discernible ruler. It remains to be seen if a system of shared power will work. The traditional Chinese view of history being cyclical has more in common with Mao's dialectic conceptions than with the current leadership's notions that progress can be gradual and evolutionary. As to ideology, in the absence of extensive, formal religion, the state always played a major role in the inculcation of morality; this had a major role in helping unify the country. The current system would seem to leave a vacuum in the propagation of a unifying, coherent set of beliefs.

Turning to epistemological matters, the current leaders are trying to build methods of research and analysis derived from Western social sciences into the empirical procedures of the bureaucracy. Many students of China would argue that these methods are antithetical to dominant Confucian precepts: the view that most facts are infused with values and hence that truly "neutral" social and policy sciences cannot be developed; the preference to learn through the emulation of models rather than through the understanding of scientific principles. It remains open to question, therefore, whether the current effort to develop an empirically based policy process will really succeed.

Deng and his associates seem to have rekindled the century-old debate over how best to root the quest for modernity in the nation's intellectual heritage. In fact, as Benjamin Schwartz has stressed, it is incorrect to speak of a single or even dominant Chinese intellectual tradition.[6] Rather, aspects of Confucianism, legalism, Buddhism, and various popular religions offered China's rulers a diversity of traditions upon which to draw. The real question was which of these diverse strands should be combined with which Western ideas to create an ideological amalgam suited to Chinese needs. China's rulers and their thinkers were confronted by a series of dualities each of which was sustained by an eclectic mixture of Chinese and Western thought. Among these polarities spurring debate were:

• The notion that societies can be egalitarian versus the notion of a hierarchical natural order.

• The notion that hierarchy is inevitably oppressive versus the idea that hierarchy is essential for order and the attainment of morality.

• The view that only external controls can order a society versus the idea that fostering of virtue in each person is the requisite for order.

• The notion that China can attain modernity through self-reliance and exclusion of the outside world versus the belief that the West and Japan have much to offer.

• The belief that mankind can swiftly create a utopian community if properly motivated versus the view that economic conditions basically shape the social structure and that economic conditions can be changed only gradually.

• The belief that theory—abstract knowledge—is acquired in practice versus the notion that theory can arise from reflection.

The distinctive and complex response to each of these polarities which was provided by Mao became the official ideology of the nation.

The reassertion of "Chineseness" in post-1976 China has meant a partial return to examining these polarities in ways which had absorbed Chinese intellectuals before 1949. To be sure, the precise terminology and the centers of gravity have changed in the intervening years, thus revealing the impact of Marxism-Leninism and Maoism. But the polarities that are being explored and the syntheses that are being sought echo the debates of an earlier period.

As we have already noted, Deng and his associates have exhibited an ambivalent attitude toward renewed intellectual ferment. On the one hand, they acknowledge its necessity since Mao's prescriptions seem inadequate for dealing with China's current problems. On the other hand, they fear that the ferment will escape their control—with unpredictable consequences. No matter what the ideological proclivities of the leaders, they are unlikely to be able to provide

the same continuity and coherence in ideology that Mao had achieved. Until a consensus on ideology exists, it is improbable that China's political system will be fully stable.

## Notes

1. See Stuart Schram, "Introduction: The Cultural Revolution in Historical Perspective," in *Authority, Participation and Cultural Change in China*, ed. Schram (Cambridge: Cambridge University Press, 1973), pp. 1–108; and John Bryan Starr, *Continuing the Revolution: The Political Thought of Mao* (Princeton: Princeton University Press, 1979).

2. On this topic, see Crane Brinton, *The Anatomy of Revolution* (Englewood Cliffs, N.J.: Prentice-Hall, 1965). See also Robert Tucker, *Marxian Revolutionary Idea* (Princeton: Princeton University Press, 1969), pp. 172–214.

3. Richard Lowenthal, "Development vs. Utopia in Communist Policy," in *Change in Communist Systems*, ed. Chalmers Johnson. (Stanford: Stanford University Press, 1970), p. 14. See also David E. Apter, *The Politics of Modernization* (Chicago: University of Chicago Press, 1965), esp. chap. 10, and Seweryn Bialer, *Stalin's Successors* (New York: Cambridge University Press, 1980), especially pp. 5–62.

4. See DeBary's contribution to *China's Future and Its Implications for U.S.–China Relations*, Occasional Paper No. 2, Washington, D.C. East Asian Program, The Wilson Center, August 1980, pp. 1–11.

5. On these points see Donald J. Munro, *The Concept of Man in Contemporary China* (Ann Arbor: University of Michigan Press, 1977); and Richard H. Solomon, *Mao's Revolution and the Chinese Political Culture* (Los Angeles: University of California Press, 1971).

6. Benjamin Schwartz, *In Search of Wealth and Power: Yen Fu and the West* (Cambridge, Mass.: Harvard University Press, 1964), and his "Some Polarities in Confucian Thought," in *Confucianism in Action*, ed., David Nivison and Arthur Wright (Stanford: Stanford University Press, 1959), pp. 50–62.

# 19

# Achieving Qualitative Change in Soviet Society

*Aleksandr N. Yakovlev*

In the spring of 1985, the USSR embarked upon an undertaking unprecedented in its novelty, complexity and scale, and in the responsibility it entails. The in-depth process of *perestroika*—restructuring—is moving ahead, but its progress is fraught with contradictions and difficulty. One among many factors slowing it down is the lack of a sufficient theoretical basis for the reforms already begun and for those that lie ahead.

The period since April 1985 has been marked by energetic efforts in the field of theory; a set of ideas concerning social development has been formulated. The efforts are resulting in the emergence of a new way of envisaging the socialist future and a general comprehension of the aims and character of the revolutionary changes involved. . . .

The period of restructuring is one of fundamental change and a continuation, in changed historical circumstances, of the work of the October Revolution. Restructuring, a moment of revolutionary truth following upon a certain stagnation in social processes, has necessitated an objective examination of the state of Soviet society and of world development, taking in all the basic problems of the life of man and of mankind. . . .

A concept of new political thinking has been put forward, based on an analysis of the dialectical relationship between class factors and factors common to humanity as a whole in present-day circumstances, and on the premise that socialism, in alliance with all revolutionary, progressive and democratic forces, is capable of preserving and enhancing the humanist values of civilization and of taking historic initiatives in the main

SOURCE: Aleksandr N. Yakovlev, "Achieving Qualitative Change in Soviet Society: The Role of the Social Sciences," *International Social Science Journal* (February 1988), pp. 149–162. © Unesco 1988. Reproduced by permission of Unesco.

avenues of social progress. Questions have been raised regarding the complex dialectical relationship between the internal progress of socialism and world development as a whole.

In its basic essentials, an ideological and theoretical platform has been established for accelerating the socioeconomic development of the country and thereby bringing about a qualitative change in society.

The concept of acceleration is not only an answer to the question of how to increase the rate of economic growth: it is an attempt to find effective ways and means of giving a fitting response to the challenge of the times, in order that our society may truly become the embodiment of all that is forward-looking and humane in world progress, and a model of social efficiency. This concept is a theoretical and practical expression of the objective requirements of the development of society at its present stage, directed towards a renewal of socialism that produces results at all levels—the basis and the superstructure, the social sphere and culture, and the life of society as a whole. This is what is meant by qualitative change. . . .

## AN ASSESSMENT OF THE RESPONSIBILITY OF THE SOCIAL SCIENCES

The present political and moral climate makes it possible to examine dispassionately and honestly how far and how deep the awareness of the role and responsibility of the social sciences in the new circumstances goes. We must speak about everything openly and conduct affairs with the utmost sincerity. . . .

It is very important that our social scientists carry out a critical examination of the mistakes of the past. To put it mildly, our philosophers, political economists, historians and literary critics have seldom played the part of pioneers and champions of what is new and progressive. They have in the past had a hand in the discrediting of cybernetics and genetics, and later in declaring the use of mathematical modelling methods in economics to be almost anti-scientific, and in deriding the idea of forecasting. It is clear in retrospect that too much effort was wasted on what in fact turned out to be a theoretical justification for complacency, for an outward show of well-being and thereby also for stagnation in the country's socioeconomic and political development. This is a 'legacy' that needs to be resolutely renounced; this must be done thoroughly so that lessons can be drawn for the future, both in terms of outlook and in moral terms.

But it is also true that, along with the processes that have now been condemned by society, other, opposite processes were developing. A civic conscience, without which today's political and moral shake-up would have been unthinkable, was hard at work. A search for ideas on a wide range of issues concerning the economy, management, the life of society and socialist legality was being conducted. The ideological and moral potential for future fundamental changes was breaking through and gradually growing. A demand developed in society and in the scientific community for an end to inertia and indifference, to political irresponsibility and mindless drifting with the current, to dogmatism and scholastic theorizing....

## THE ABSENCE OF CREATIVE SOCIAL SCIENCES

The criticism that has recently grown up of social science as being remote and cut off from social practice, criticism levelled at its style and working methods and at the moral and psychological climate of scientific activity, is legitimate. Social science has not simply reflected the condition of society but has also taken an active part in its formation. The ideology of stagnation and its camouflaging had no need of an exact knowledge of life. Anything that did not fit into the Procrustean bed of dogmatic thinking or did not fit in with the practice of 'universal admiration' was accounted—openly or tacitly—dubious and suspect.

The concept of developed socialism was subjected to an expedient interpretation leading in the direction of leisurely, timid and inconsistent piecemeal improvement, thus sanctioning complacency and blunting awareness of the urgent need for cardinal changes.

Disregard for the socialist principles of co-operation and the attitude of treating individual holdings and individual enterprise as something alien deprived society of significant potential resources.

The glorification of one single component part of the principle of democratic centralism—albeit a necessary and most important part, to wit centralized forms of management—shackled initiative, independence and socialist entrepreneurial spirit, producing a narrow departmentalism and bureaucracy that became the main control levers of the economic machine.

The ideas of the 'anti-commodity' theorists, which were more like political accusations, turned out to be an impediment to economic development. It was thought that these were merely academic disputes, but in fact disregard for the law of value prevailed both in theory and in practice. Disregard for the principles of cost-benefit accounting, together with the use of subsidy-based methods in a number of economic sectors, did a disservice to the economy that had all sorts of consequences.

Harm has been done by the disparagement of socialist self-management and by systematic scare-mongering about the 'unpredictable' consequences of wider democracy.

The absence of a wide degree of *glasnost*—openness—and genuine control from below, the fall in the level of criticism and self-criticism and the inconsistency between word and deed have fostered the growth of undesirable phenomena in society: social passivity and corruption, irresponsibility and moral depravity, careerism and consumerism.

There can be no successful progress along the path of restructuring without an elucidation of the reasons why such phenomena became possible. Those reasons are to be found both in the realm of practice and in that of consciousness.

The country set out on the road of socialist construction and the conditions it encountered along the way were extremely complicated. As it progressed it had to make theoretical sense of the problems and contradictions of the new path-breaking society and to elaborate concepts for the future. There were no ready-made blueprints for socialism, nor indeed could there have been any.

At a certain point, however, preference began to be given not to the creative development of theory but to scholasticism and the dogmatic interpretation of some of the tenets of Marxism–Leninism. Some of the Leninist propositions on socialism were interpreted simplistically and their theoretical depth and significance were emasculated. For instance, the idea that with the advance towards communism there would be increasing uniformity, that diversity would disappear or wither away, imposed itself: in the economic field, there was to be only state ownership and a single pattern of economic management; in the social sphere, all differences whatsoever were to be effaced; in politics, the structures were to be immutable, and so on and so forth. The proponents of this approach saw progress as the increasing simplification and straightening-out of everything under the sun.

What most distinguishes the works of Marx, Engels and Lenin is a vision of the real dialectical relationships of life and of the complexity and diversity of historical development. The whole of experience testifies that in no instance has history ever advanced by way of simplification. On the contrary, each successive structure and socioeconomic or political system has turned out to be internally more complex than the previous one, and there are no grounds for supposing that socialism and communism constitute an exception to this rule. The concept of uniformity nevertheless took hold with persistence both in practice and in theoretical constructs. Its influence is still to be seen today in approaches to a number of economic, social and cultural issues.

Looking at capitalism, one can see the complex, fluctuating nature of its internal processes and mechanisms; but as soon as we start to talk about socialism, it seems that things run almost entirely automatically, independent of man: production relations fall by themselves into line with the development of productive forces; the planned, balanced development of the economy and the resolving of social problems are self-regulating processes; and the mechanisms of development of social consciousness, social justice, relations between nationalities and much else besides operate automatically.

These and other notions were combined with processes in social life tending to erect existing theoretical formulae into absolutes, to identify transient features of a given phase in history with the substantive characteristics of socialism as a system, and to elevate a number of propositions and concepts to canonical status. The outcome was a persistent tendency to minimize the role of social science in the process of socialist construction.

The capacity for critical self-analysis was gradually being eroded. Instead of the study of real, living socialism, preference was given to constructing speculative models. Theory became ever more tautologous. The demands made upon social science became demands of pure expediency so that it too was losing its real function.

These trends became particularly noticeable in the 1970s, when the study of living, developing socialism began to be ever more openly replaced by far-fetched formulae and schemes. Furthermore, as a result of a non-critical attitude to stagnation, many influences distorting the course of theoretical thinking developed and became ossified.

We thus entered the 1980s not only with serious practical omissions and miscalculations, but also with a theoretical consciousness which was in many respects still at the level of the 1930s, when our society was at a relatively early stage of its formation. Such a situation was objectively conducive to dogmatic, scholastic and doctrinaire attitudes and, on the other hand, it made a creative approach to the issues of present-day socialism more difficult. In the same way that enclaves closed to criticism were formed, there was also an increase in the number of areas closed to scientific research. The idea predominated that only partial, evolutionary modifications could be made, and then in practice rather than in theory, whereas it should be clear to every Marxist that any weakening of revolutionary theory, with the enormous intellectual capital it represents for mankind, has dire consequences and leads to stagnation not only in the theory but also in the practice of the building of a new society.

What is required of social science today is to take an unbiased attitude, to be self-critical, to acknowledge honestly and openly the past consequences of the opportunistic interpretation of a number of the propositions of revolutionary theory which contradicted its essentials, and to mobilize the scientific research towards looking for answers to the questions that life raises. . . .

## ISSUES IN THE DEVELOPMENT OF THE SOCIALIST SOCIETY

Restructuring inevitably spills over into the area of basic questions regarding the political economy of socialism, and requires that they be examined as they relate to conditions at the present stage of development of social production.

In any structure known to us and at every stage in past history, the contradiction between productive forces and their social form, i.e., production relations, generates revolutions and accelerates progress; but instead of subjecting that contradiction in socialist society to thorough investigation, there were those who dogmatically asserted that under socialism the basic contradiction was between the 'visible shoots of communism' and the 'survivals of capitalism'. Into the category of 'survivals' went everything that got in the way of administrative-bureaucratic methods of management: collective farm and co-operative property; individual plots and personal subsidiary holdings; individual enterprise; commodity production and commodity-money relations; the market; profit and cost–benefit accounting.

Lenin used to draw a distinction between formal and real achievements in the development of socialist society. Let us remember that he emphasized the fundamental difference between formal, legal, socialist socialization and the real thing. Continuing this Leninist tradition, we have to strive for real conformity to plan in the development of production, real centralism and real democracy in economic management.

The real degree of conformity to plan is gauged by the extent to which we succeed in maintaining and regulating the proportions between different parts. Real centralism is gauged by the extent to which economic processes are subordinated to the economic centre. Real democracy in management is measured not simply by the granting of rights to a given body of workers but by the creation of the necessary socioeconomic and political conditions for the effective exercise of such rights.

It seems that the creation of an inhibitory mechanism is to be traced back to those causes that led gradually, from the 1930s onwards, to a certain shift in the balance between objective conditions and practical actions, a shift in favour of the latter. The path of extensive economic development was at the time an objective requirement, it corresponded to the tasks that had then to be accomplished, and it produced considerable results, but that same path and the methods of management, planning, distribution and so on connected with it came in effect to represent a brake on development at its subsequent, higher stage, when quality factors came to the fore and when the need to go over to intensive forms of economic management arose. Inertia in thinking and practice proved too obdurate, however, and the efforts made to overcome it were patently inadequate. As a result, in recent decades a system has in effect been established that undermines the material bases of socialism: economic *zatratnost*.*

---

* Translator's note: a neologism applied to a high-expenditure approach, disregarding cost-effectiveness, dealing with problems by 'throwing money at them'.

One reason was that state ownership was made an absolute and equated with the supreme form of ownership, that of the whole people. In practice this resulted in primacy being given to administration by injunction, and it left the field even wider open for bureaucracy.

Bureaucracy needs dogmatism, and vice versa. Like bureaucrats, dogmatists can exist only by infringing on the interests of society; if the state apparatus lays claim to a sort of omnipotence, they use their membership of the apparatus for that purpose, whence the endeavour to 'statize' everything in sight and to attribute any successes and achievements to administrative methods of management.

Dogmatism, committing an act of violence on life, dragged the co-operative system into the state by the ears. A stereotyped attitude to state property gradually developed: 'ours is not mine, it is nobody's.' This caused trouble, indifference and mismanagement, though it was certainly not the only cause. In our opinion, however, it is precisely the co-operative system which can take over functions that the state is not obliged to fulfil, thereby contributing to the normalization and effective functioning of the socialist market and, in conjunction with the state, strengthening the rouble.

No social form disappears until its potential has been exhausted. If the family contract system results in a two-fold or three-fold increase in productivity over other forms of labour organization, how can it be regarded as a historically obsolete form with no place in the structure of socialist production? If individual enterprise can produce results, why should ideological and practical obstacles be put in the way of its development? Only one restriction needs to be strictly maintained: not to allow exploitation. In practical terms, the strengthening of socialism must be regarded as the principal task, to which every effort and all forms of the organization of labour and social life should be subordinated.

One of the most acute contradictions at the present stage of the restructuring process is the contradiction between the quantity and the quality of labour. In economic practice, priority continues to be given to quantity, whereas the demand today is for an optimum combination of quantitative and qualitative growth indicators. The essence of the 'strategy of quantity' is high-expenditure, deficit-inflationary production. The scrapping of the high-expenditure mechanism and its replacement by a fundamentally new cost-benefit mechanism, suited to the nature of developing socialism, is a top priority in restructuring.

In philosophical terms, *zatratnost* is a subjective factor slowing down the objective transition from quantity to quality, and represents the priority of the former over the latter. In economic terms, *zatratnost* means a minimum end result with maximum intermediate expenditure and increasingly acute contradictions between productive forces and production relations, with anarchy reigning in the former and bureaucracy taking over the latter, the perpetuation of scientific and technological backwardness and, at the end of the road, stagnation. When the producer's word is law, *zatratnost* is constantly generated, cost-benefit accounting is rejected and the consumer comes to be looked upon not as an interested partner but as a troublesome companion.

Let us take another group of deep-rooted contradictions, contradictions in labour itself. As Marx put it, 'society will never be able to reach a balance until it begins to rotate around the sun of labour.' Under developing socialism, the division of labour into abstract and concrete is not eliminated; but the postulate that the absence of private property and even the mere existence of a state plan ensure in advance that any work, be it useful or harmful, is *ipso facto* social, necessary work, has become ingrained in the social consciousness and in practice.

This dogma is, objectively, one of the catalytic factors of *zatratnost*. All kinds of work are remunerated on wage-levelling principles, and the results are cooking of books, report-padding and other deceitful practices; the national income is haphazardly and fraudulently redistributed; the morality and ethics of labour are deformed and its standard declines. The remuneration of labour is distorted, and this undermines workers' motivation and social motivation.

At the same time, a division has been established between productive work (in the material sphere) and non-productive work (in other spheres). This has resulted in application of the 'residual' principle to investments in the social infrastructure, in technocracy and in undervaluation of the human factor; it has resulted also in a decline, in material and moral terms, in the status of the highly qualified doctors, teachers, engineers and scientists whose services the scientific and technological revolution requires, and in a lowering of the social prestige accorded to knowledge and genuine professionalism.

The high-expenditure mode of economic management, generating as it does irresponsibility, also weakens the moral content of work, which is bound to affect attitudes to it on the part of some of the urban and rural workers, members of the intelligentsia and, in particular, young people. The problem of the standard of work and workers' motivation is acquiring a new significance since the criteria of labour relations are inevitably being transformed in the context of self-financing and self-management.

## DEMOCRATIZATION

Democracy is the most important and indeed the only possible means of achieving socialism as a social organism. Marxism by no means reduces the socioeconomic essence of socialism to social ownership of the means of production. Socialized production is genuinely socialist when the decisive role in managing production and other public affairs actually belongs to the working people and when the workers' collectives themselves resolve vital economic and social development issues.

In the Leninist political vocabulary, 'democracy,' 'self-management' and the 'lively initiative of the masses' are key concepts, particularly for discussing socialism. Convincingly, and in

detail, Lenin substantiated the meaning of democracy, revealed its essential nature and defined its content: the participation of working people in discussing the state's legislation and planning; the nomination and election of their representatives for membership of bodies exercising full authority, and control from below of their activity; openness, criticism and self-criticism as methods of political guidance; responsibility and conscious discipline and the equality of all citizens before the law.

The restructuring process has also raised questions of socialist democracy in connection with the demand for new approaches to the problem of management. Suitable forms and incentives for real participation by people in working out both basic and day-to-day decisions at the level of the country as a whole, of the community and of the collective, need to be found, and the mechanism whereby democracy operates as a means of resolving emergent contradictions at all levels and of all kinds needs to be identified as precisely as possible. There is a crying need for theoretical studies of the whole range of questions of democratic development and its effects on other areas of life, on man, on the formation of political awareness in society and on managerial and administrative organizations.

Special attention needs to be given to improving the quality of the legal sciences. This covers a huge range of problems, from laying the juridical basis for economic reform to introducing the cardinal changes needed in those sectors of jurisprudence that underpin the economic, political and social rights and freedoms of Soviet citizens. In other words, theorists must come up with dialectically developed organizational, juridical and political methods, suited to present requirements, for ensuring ever full democracy.

There remains the extremely complex relationship between legal science and current political and economic practice. The attempts of certain leaders to avoid dealing with pressing problems, coupled with half-hearted departmentalism and parochialism, did nothing to promote interest in a serious scientific treatment of the issue. Of the recommendations made by scientists, only those which could confer a quasi-scientific respectability on the decisions taken—even wrong ones—and justify them on legal grounds were taken into account.

The situation can and must now change. The time has come for an understanding of the real value of giving juridical form to social relations and for the all-round development and effective utilization of the humanist and moral potential of socialist law. Without law, legality and justice, social progress cannot be achieved, the normal functioning of material production and of the institutions of political democracy cannot be ensured, effective management cannot be instituted and incentives for the development of the individual cannot be provided.

The legal status and the rights and freedoms of citizens are rooted in the totality of social relations, while the law sets down and safeguards what has been formed in real life. A conception of the rights of citizens as a bonus granted from above still persists, however, reflecting a failure to grasp the real link that exists in our country between the individual, society, law and the state.

To steer the law in the direction of common sense, turning respect for human dignity into an unconditional priority, constitutes today a most serious task for legal science and practice. An equally significant task for the future is to work out the forms of organization needed by society for its activity, drawing up blueprints for society, as it were.

## TAKING INTO ACCOUNT THE GLOBAL INTERDEPENDENCE

...Until recently, the concept of mankind as a worldwide historical and generic entity was still regarded in many philosophical and economic studies as being some kind of lofty abstraction, with no practical application in our socially divided world. But in the new circumstances, whilst emphasizing the basic class differences and the historic confrontation of the two socio-economic systems, we should also take account of the exceedingly complex dialectics of their interaction. A dialectical materialist way of looking at the present can neither deny the profound opposition of the two existing systems and modes of production nor disregard the essential oneness of contemporary mankind, with its common interests and values.

The concept of one interdependent world is also closely linked to the ecological problem. We have not yet fully realized, I think, that to continue with the present approaches to the utilization of natural resources is to run the risk of catastrophic global consequences. The development of a technological civilization on the basis of the reckless subjugation of nature has considerably impaired the capacity of natural systems for self-regeneration. We must devise a comprehensive scientific strategy for saving mankind from the ecological disaster which, unless enormous efforts are made by the whole international community, may, according to some forecasts, be upon us in literally a few decades.

The problem is not just a matter of increased expenditure on environmental protection: a new level of political and ecological standards needs to be reached. From the political point of view, this means peace and co-operation between states on a reliable basis of international law. From the economic point of view it means switching the world economy over to non-polluting technologies and the preservation and enhancement of the environment. From the social point of view, it means stepping up the fight against those age-old scourges of mankind: hunger, disease, poverty and illiteracy. From the philosophical point of view, it means harmony in man's relationship with nature, the cleansing of hearts and minds of all forms of social evil, the protection and development of the genuine achievements of culture and the prevention of its degradation.

A fresh development in the theory of international relations is the formulation of the question of the creation of a system of security to be based on values common to the whole of mankind and on large-scale initiatives to usher in a nuclear-free world. A comprehensive system of views needs to be elaborated, a political philosophy that would prompt states to transcend existing contradictions where the survival of mankind is at stake.

The creation of a demilitarized, nuclear-free world requires elimination of the deep-seated causes and sources of mistrust, tension and enmity in the modern world. Specialists in international affairs are faced with the question of how to transcend traditional confrontational approaches in international relations. It is important to find, for the development of such relations, common reference points that correspond to the interests of all the states making up the international community. International economic security should also provide a sound basis for a world free from violence.

New approaches are also needed to the problem of co-operation in the humanitarian field. The spirit of restructuring and democratization that is moving in our socialist homeland must also be fully felt outside it. This gives Soviet specialists in international affairs new opportunities for theoretical elaboration of the question of the moral and spiritual factors involved in a comprehensive system of international security.

The concept of the sufficiency of military capacities, *inter alia* in a situation of total elimination of nuclear weapons, needs to be clarified, and its factual content amplified. No less important is the task of analysing, jointly with military experts, our military doctrine based in its strategic essence on a policy of prevention of nuclear war.

## CHALLENGES FOR PHILOSOPHY, SOCIOLOGY, AND HISTORY

Restructuring presents major problems for philosophy. Philosophy gave the divorce from reality a specific 'theoretical substantiation.' A similar trend has been clearly apparent in the distorted interpretation and application of Lenin's epistemological principle of proceeding 'from living perception to abstract thought, and from this to practice,' a principle which in practice had excised from it that part which pointed

to the need, in the course of theoretical inquiry, for constantly addressing the real subject of study. Another noticeable tendency occurring at the same time has been a slide into empiricism and descriptivism. Many published works by philosophers and other social scientists report observed facts and particular events without attempting to make theoretical sense of them.

I believe that we should be seriously worried by the backwardness of social science regards the integral study of the problems of man and ways of activating the human factor. Problems connected with man's inner life are becoming of great importance, and it is precisely over such matters that the ideological battle is most intense. Unfortunately, the whole area of moral and philosophical issues remains virgin territory.

Instead of investigating the real structure of society, the dynamics of social and class changes, changes within classes, and the complex and contradictory process whereby social homogeneity is created in Soviet society, works on scientific communism, philosophy and sociology merely intone the thesis concerning that homogeneity. Instead of studying the highly complex process of forming and educating the socialist individual, they give only scholastic disquisitions on an almost ideal Soviet man, leaving one to wonder where, in that case, the phenomena of stagnation, the unworthy people, the degenerates infected with consumerism and acquisitiveness, the spiritually empty, careerism, bureaucracy and indifference all come from.

The situation in sociology is equally complex. The professional standard of many sociological studies is still low, while descriptivism and the simplistic treatment of questions of social development and public opinion are widespread. Uncertainty persists as to the place of sociology in the social sciences.

The study of relations between the nationalities is also divorced from reality. In this area, more perhaps than in any other, many outdated and dogmatic assessments with little bearing on actual practice have accumulated.

Basically, sociologists have failed to investigate the real contradiction inherent in the fact that, as class differences wither away and the people's way of life and spiritual make-up continue to develop common features, differences of a non-class character, whether based on occupation, culture and custom, age, nationality or language, become more apparent. Serious work needs to be done to conceptualize this process and forecast developments, and adjustments need to be made in advance to political activity, social development plans and educational measures.

In history, a sizeable proportion of scholars specialize largely in exposing the pseudo-scientific conceptions of bourgeois authors without undertaking an independent study of sources, without developing scientific ideas and without critically rethinking outdated notions. Vulgar sociologizing has re-emerged on a new basis. On the pretence of eradicating triviality, some historians in fact merely undertake to fill out sociological schemata with 'historically' arranged factual illustrations.

Party history is facing serious problems. Despite the large number of specialists in the history of the Soviet Communist Party and of Soviet society, many crucial issues of primary importance remain unexplored. There has recently been growing criticism of party historians for sinning against the truth. Violation of the principle of historicity, depersonalization of the historical process, 'blanks' in the history of entire periods, sketchy and lacklustre writing—these are but a few of the justified reproaches expressed.

What is needed is a fresh approach to the elucidation of many important and complex periods in the party's history, drawing the necessary lessons from each, and adhering strictly to the principles of historicity and truth. In the specific context of the restructuring process, a thorough knowledge of the past is an invaluable help for the present and the future.

Many and vast are the tasks ahead. But how far can a thorough restructuring of social science in the spirit of the times be carried out with the sort of organization and set-up of research work and the sort of moral atmosphere that exists in our research institutions? This today is one of the most crucial questions.

The main concern is with the development of democracy in science and with scientific ethics. Democracy in science is a salutary form of civilized, instead of coercive, resolving of contradictions. Tolerance and respect for the other person's point of view are by no means tantamount to abandoning one's own position. They are based on a sense of one's own dignity, respect for this feeling in others, and an ability to understand problems and people, which is to say that they are based on a genuine adherence to principles that is inseparable from an elevated moral sense.

*Glasnost*—transparence or openness—is the instrument whereby society controls the situation in all areas of life, including science. Unless changes are made here, there will be no fundamental, substantive improvements in the work of research institutions. Too many things that give cause for concern have accumulated. The situation where officialdom holds a monopoly of the truth, where not truth but deference to authority has the last word, in theoretical work, cannot be tolerated. Many abuses of authority take place, such as the practice of unjustifiably forcing ghost-writing work on subordinates, encouraging scientific subservience among them, covering-up for one another, a lenient and undemanding attitude towards one's 'cronies' and ostracism of those who are not compliant.

The forms of organization of science must themselves be democratized, the role of academic councils and scientific conferences and discussions increased, scientific criticism given a new lease of life, and the authority of office subordinated to the authority of thought.

Scientific ethics and rules of conduct are matters of particular importance. Our social scientists fall, as it were, into two groups: while one group works and formulates problems, those in the other group watch attentively and wait for the first group to make a mistake or suffer a setback; then, having bided their time, they try to make out that they knew the truth all along.

Science can develop only through the cut and thrust of constructive debate. If scientific discussions are to become an active ingredient of acceleration, it has to be realized that neither in formulating nor in answering new questions does anyone hold a monopoly of the truth.

Perhaps the most acute problem in the development of the social sciences is their connection with life. As Lenin put it, 'the historical moment has arrived when theory is being transformed into practice, vitalized by practice, corrected by practice, tested by practice' (*Collected Works*, Vol. 26, p. 413). Active work and real efficiency are at one and the same time the result and one of the most important safeguards of democracy, openness and a healthy atmosphere in social science itself.

It is time social science was included as a permanent component in the system of nationwide work. The practice of expert scientific assessments of technical, economic and social projects should be widely introduced and the consultancy role of research establishments should be stepped up. The time has also come to give serious consideration to the setting up of financially autonomous consultancies dealing with management, social planning, sociological analysis, ecology and the like. This area of the scientific potential of higher education should be broadened as well.

The system of scientific research planning requires basic restructuring. Such plans at present consist of little more than the preparation of collective monographs, many of which are not the result of research and contain no new information, no new syntheses, no new conclusions or forecasts. Much of the research undertaken is unconnected with social requirements. The present planning and reporting system in social science amounts to piling publication upon publication, thus absorbing huge creative and material resources.

Publishing requires radical democratization. The need for a rebirth of scientific ethics and for outspokenness and openness in science is extremely acute, especially as regards scientific journals. Particular dangers here are such phenomena as clannishness and the weakening role and importance of editorial boards and councils. Most scientific journals restate things that are

generally known, are reluctant to call on new authors, and continue to be nervous about publishing controversial material raising new issues. Journals are still crammed with complimentary reviews written in a bland and even eulogistic tone.

On all fronts, Soviet society is on the move. A start has been made. There can be no turning back. We can and must break through into the unknown and provide a response to the complex questions of the day and of socialist development. There is no other way.

*(Translated from Russian)*

# 20
# Reforms and Civil Society in the USSR

*James P. Scanlan*

Among the more dramatic signs of *perestroyka* or restructuring in the Soviet Union today are the liberalizations in thought and expression that fall under the heading of *glasnost'* or openness. Without question, *glasnost'* has brought some striking changes to the Soviet cultural scene. Soviet commentators speak of an intellectual atmosphere very different from that which prevailed only a few years ago. . . .

In his book *Perestroika*, General Secretary Mikhail Gorbachev stresses the functions of *glasnost'* in promoting two prime requisites of democratic government—an open quest for truth and the answerability of government to the people. In tones reminiscent of the English champion of liberty John Stuart Mill—whose writings, however, are still unpublished in the USSR—Gorbachev insists that no one can claim a monopoly on truth and that dissenting opinions must be heard out: "Even the most extreme

SOURCE: *Problems of Communism*, vol. 37 (March–April 1988), pp. 41–46. By permission of *Problems of Communism*. Article and Notes abridged by the editors.

viewpoint," he writes, "contains something valuable and rational." Similarly, publicity concerning policies and the airing of public criticisms of policies are said to be necessary as a form of popular control over the activities of government: "We won't be able to advance if we don't check how our policy responds to criticism, especially criticism from below, if we don't fight negative developments, don't prevent them and don't react to information from below." In brief, Gorbachev advocates a measure of free expression as an essential condition of democratic government: "There is no democracy, nor can there be, without *glasnost'*."[1]

In this connection, *glasnost'* must be seen as a part of a broader concern in the Soviet reform movement with a range of individual rights and freedoms. Although liberalizations relating to freedom of information and expression have received the most attention outside the Soviet Union, other developments of equal potential significance for the expansion of civil rights either appear to be under way or are being discussed—in particular, measures to strengthen legal safeguards of rights and freedoms. . . .

One of the most original and penetrating analyses in the Soviet literature of both the origin of ultra-collectivism in the USSR and the means of overcoming it is contained in a discussion of the idea of "civil society" published in the journal *Voprosy Filosofii* by the historian Andranik Migranian. If the socialist revolution were to take place in a fully developed capitalist society (as Marx envisaged), Migranian argues, the socialist system would be supported by a developed "civil society"—that is, by a broad network of non-political relations among individuals and groups who spontaneously and independently carry out a great many economic and social functions. But if, he states in an obvious reference to the 1917 situation in Russia, it takes place in a country where "not all the possibilities inherent in the old system have been fully developed," the result is quite different. The country's economic and cultural backwardness make it difficult for civil society to develop, and so the state steps in: "The state takes on not only its own functions

but those of society. The state in effect 'swallows up' both society and the individual, in the sincere belief that the essentially bureaucratic solutions it has adopted are the most adequate to reflect the interests of individuals and of society." Although a start was made on a civil society in the Soviet Union during the New Economic Policy (NEP) period in the early 1920's, Migranian contends that the way in which the subsequent policies of industrialization and collectivization were carried out led to virtually total regulation of social activity, reducing "almost to zero" the opportunities for spontaneous, non-sanctioned activity. Politically, the result was the loss of democracy: the state controls society rather than being controlled by it.[2]

In such a situation, Migranian continues, the only solution is for civil society to be strengthened and its possibilities for action institutionalized, so that it comes to have a real opportunity to act effectively on the organs of state power. In effect, the state itself must create "a new civil society" by progressively reducing government interference in economic and social life and giving individuals and groups the legal means to act independently of the state. In this light Migranian welcomes the various pieces of economic and social reform legislation already introduced or proposed by the Gorbachev administration. It is through such measures, he believes, that civil society will be activated and democracy established: "The principal task of revolutionary restructuring in the political sphere," he writes, "is the attainment of full control over the state by civil society, with the help of all the means now at its disposal and the means which it acquires as it is progressively strengthened and institutionalized."

The protection of individual rights and liberties is fundamental to this process, Migranian insists. In a remarkable concession to "bourgeois" doctrine, he affirms that "in the West, society's control over the state is largely conditioned by the fact that a civil society consisting of diverse social institutions is under the active control of individuals." Hence, he regrets that in the heat of the Marxist struggle against bourgeois individualism, "we have thrown out the baby with the bath water"; individualism has its positive side, which is as beneficial to democratic socialism as it is to capitalism. Democracy, socialist or otherwise, requires a strong and institutionalized civil society, and the latter cannot be achieved without "radical extension of the autonomous sphere of the personal freedoms of the individual."[3]

This is the vision of a new open society in the USSR, of a state held in check by vigorous social forces, as sketched by some exponents of the "new thinking." To what extent is this concern for individuality and for the establishment of a firmly protected sphere of rights and liberties shared by Soviet policy makers? Can we say that it reflects anything resembling a serious ideological commitment on the part of the Communist party leadership?

Certainly, Gorbachev has spoken favorably not only of *glasnost'* but of individual diversity, of the need to respect individual interests, and of the independent activity of social organizations. One of his favorite themes when addressing citizens' groups is to urge them to become more socially active: "No one will do it for you," he tells them. Moreover, some of the reform measures already introduced do move in the direction of easing restrictions on individual and group activity and expanding the nongovernmental sphere, as Migranian notes.

On the other hand, neither Gorbachev nor his close political associates have waxed lyrical on the subject of "civil society" or elaborated what could be called an ideology of individual rights. Speaking in his book *Perestroika* of "grass-roots activities," Gorbachev says weakly that the democratic process does not rule them out. Though he speaks a great deal about interests, he rarely mentions rights (except in the context of the economic reforms—"the rights of enterprises," etc.) and he hardly ever speaks of liberty or freedom (one word—*svoboda*—serves in Russian for both English words). Thus it is difficult to say how genuine is the commitment of those in power to the assurance of a sphere of "independent activity" on the part of individuals and groups.

Perhaps a more manageable question is this: how genuine could a commitment to individual rights and liberties be given the political circumstances as well as the constraints of other Soviet attitudes and views? How far can one realistically expect *perestroyka* to go toward creating a society in which individual rights and freedoms are held inviolate and powerful social organizations restrain the actions of government? Three considerations in particular suggest that expectations cannot be high.

The most obvious problem is the paradox of expecting the state to create civil society—that is, expecting the power that is said to need control to yield its power so that such control can be established. On Migranian's own analysis, it is capitalism that historically has created civil society, in the absence of which the socialist state "swallows up" society and the individual. Without capitalism or a comparable nonpolitical force, how can that omnivorous state be expected to shed its natural inclinations, including its "sincere belief" that it is pursuing the interests of society and its members? Is not *perestroyka* itself—state conceived and state executed—simply one more example of that belief and that dominance? Migranian apparently sees no absurdity in saying in the same breath that society must tear itself from the grip on the state and that "the CPSU as the true leader of the working class and the Soviet people has become the initiator and director of this revolutionary *perestroyka*." His defense, of course, might be that in the USSR there is simply no other way to proceed—given the realities of the political situation, the state is the only power available to do the job. But that regrettable fact does not make the prospects of success any brighter.

A second, more complex problem concerns the meaning that "civil society" can have within a Soviet Marxist theoretical framework. Gorbachev, like other Soviet leaders after Stalin, denies the existence of "antagonistic" interests in socialist society, and the "new thinking" follows this lead in retaining the assumption of a fundamental harmony of interests among all groups and individuals in the Soviet Union. Migranian, for example, contrasts the political theory of Marxism, which he characterizes as aiming at the attainment of consensus on the basis of overriding common interests, with the Western political process, which he describes as being based on "the legitimized conflict of interests" in which one set of special interests either triumphs over others or effects a "temporary compromise" with them.

Migranian admits that in the Marxist model, too, consensus is reached through "conflict," and in the statements of other Soviet theorists as well there are sometimes suggestions of a Western, pluralist model of political life. Gorbachev himself, though rejecting "antagonisms," speaks of diverse and even "contradictory" interests as being unavoidable in socialist society, and he has exhibited such inclinations toward pluralism as scolding trade unions for not defending the interests of workers.

On the other hand, it is said that only "legitimate" interests need defending; and in the new thinking as well as the old, "special" interests are never legitimate. For example, the real, long-term interests of the workers—interests that should be defended—are equated with the interests of society as a whole, and are opposed to "the immediate, narrow, even egoistic interests of separate individuals and groups"; selfish interests and actions must be "resolutely combated," Gorbachev insists. Characteristic of this view is the context of Gorbachev's statement about the worth of even the "extreme viewpoint" quoted earlier: the value of the extreme opinion, Gorbachev goes on to say, is that "the person who upholds it honestly and who cares for the common cause in his own way reflects some real aspects of life." Without a concern for the common cause, the opinion would apparently be "selfish" and valueless. With regard, specifically, to the debate over *perestroyka*, Gorbachev writes that "for us this is not an antagonistic class struggle; it is a quest, a debate on how we can really get going with the restructuring effort." And for Migranian, too, the "conflict" through which Marxist consensus is reached is not really a conflict of interests but "the collision of various

approaches to the resolution of problems." Thus, in the new Soviet thinking the political process consists in the expression, on the part of different individuals and groups, not so much of their own interests as of their different ideas as to what is in the general interest—a trace, incidentally, of the philosophical legacy of Jean-Jacques Rousseau as transmitted by Karl Marx.

How does this approach affect the notion of civil society and the likelihood of genuine social control over the state? Chiefly through the fact that in Soviet ideology—new thinking and old—the assumption of a fundamental harmony of interests in society is linked with the case for a one-party political system. As Migranian presents the link, the attainment of socialist consensus through "conflict" is made possible by the absence not only of antagonistic interests but of competing political parties. Competing parties, presumably, can exist and function only by representing divisive "special" interests. A single party, on the other hand, joins all "legitimate" interests into a harmonious whole from which selfishness is eliminated, just as the multinational Soviet Union is said to unite all nationalities and liberate them from their exclusiveness. Since the true interests of society are basically harmonious, they are adequately and properly represented by a single political leadership. Thus a one-party system, far from being incompatible with popular government, is the only way of guaranteeing the dominance of the general interest.

The unanswered question, of course, is whether an active civil society can flourish where a one-party system is enforced. If individuals and groups lack the right to seek alternative political representation of their interests—or even express their ideas as to how best to achieve the general interest—it is uncertain how "institutionalized" their powers can be, or will remain even if once established. It is not clear that civil society can operate effectively on the organs of the state if it cannot threaten to withdraw its political support from the group administering those organs. Thus a conception of civil society that limits society and its components to a single channel of political expression offers little promise of producing effective social control over the state.

A third, related obstacle to the establishment of a viable "civil society" with protected individual rights in the USSR is the Marxist-Leninist view of the nature of rights—a view the "new thinking" gives no indication of abandoning. This view, in deliberate opposition to the "bourgeois" conception dominant in capitalist societies, rejects any notion that individual rights have an extra-social basis; that is, it denies that rights are "absolute," "God-given," "natural," or in any other way independent of society with respect to their origin, scope, or sanction. Rather, rights are held to exist only in society and to change as society changes; they grow out of concrete social relationships and are defined in terms of those relationships. Consequently, their content changes with social development. Furthermore, just as people have no rights independently of social conditions, they have no rights without corresponding social duties and obligations. A distinguishing feature of the socialist conception of the rights of man, according to the Soviet jurist Ye. A. Lukasheva, is "the indissoluble union of rights and duties"—a feature also emphasized in the Soviet Constitution.[4]

A question that naturally arises in connection with the Marxist-Leninist view of rights is this: at a given point in the life of a society, how is it to be determined just what the content of a given right is and what duties go along with it? Soviet jurists insist that this is not an arbitrary or subjective matter but is dictated by impersonal circumstances. Rights are not "a gift of the state," according to Lukasheva: "their scope and content is objectively determined by the economic and social-class conditions of society, by the state of democracy and legality." Thus, as Soviet society advances, the extent of citizens' rights grows: "Each new stage in the development of the Soviet state, the strengthening of its economic basis, the extension of democracy, and the growth of culture create the objective preconditions for enriching the content of the rights and liberties of the individual, for strengthening their guarantees." At the same time, Lukasheva cannot deny that these "objective circumstances" must be identified and assessed by someone—that decisions must be made by flesh-and-blood human beings as to what rights are now appropriate for the citizens of a socialist society. This task she assigns to "the legislator" and she acknowledges that the extent of rights granted not only is but must be confined by his decisions. The legislator, she writes, "may proclaim only those rights for which the real economic, political, and sociocultural preconditions have matured. At this point, of course, it becomes hard to see the distinction between a "gift of the state" and the "objective dictates of circumstances."

Perhaps the most important implication of this view of rights, however, is that the legislator must seek to adjust rights to the state of society, rather than adjust society to the demands of rights. The inevitable result of an approach of this sort is that the rights and duties "proclaimed" by the legislator will be those considered by state authorities to be consonant with the needs of society at a given stage of its development—the needs of its present condition and of its future advance. Rights and freedoms, in other words, are conceived not as independent values that it is the purpose of social and political organizations to serve, but, quite the contrary, as instrumental to society and its progressive advance toward some future condition. Despite the occasional use by Soviet writers now of such expressions as "inalienable rights" and "basic freedoms," the instrumental conception of rights prevails in the theoretical presentations and policy proposals concerning the individual sphere of activity that are advanced as part of the "new thinking."

This instrumental approach to *glasnost'* and the whole range of individual rights is indicated from the very outset in the notion that the social and political reforms are "guarantees" of economic *perestroyka*—that is, that they are conceived as strengthening and assuring the success of the transformations in the economic sphere. Like the reforms in economics, they are directed above all to motivational concerns, to acting on the interests of individuals in such a way as to enlist those interests in the creation of a dynamic, more productive economy. Speaking of the need to take personal interests into account in re-energizing the Soviet economy, Gorbachev clearly ties political *perestroyka* to economic *perestroyka* in these words: "It is imperative to strike a balance of interests, and we are doing so through the new economic mechanism, through greater democracy, through the atmosphere of openness, and through public involvement in all aspects of restructuring."

In part this attention to individual interests through democratization is counted on simply to energize socioeconomic activity by giving people stronger motives for engaging in it. But it is no less an instrument of social control, a way of motivating not only managers, directors, and officials, but workers themselves to work more effectively and responsibly. Thus, Gorbachev calls *glasnost'*, for example, "an effective form of public control over the activities of all government bodies without exception, and a powerful lever in correcting shortcomings."[5]

From this perspective, rights and freedoms are not ends in themselves but instruments to be utilized for a social purpose, and consequently they are constrained by that purpose and its accompanying obligations. No one has stated these constraints more forcefully than Gorbachev himself when he discussed *glasnost'* in the media during a meeting of the Central Committee in June 1987: "There is a political line, there are principles, there are demands, there are criteria—for socialism, for restructuring in the interests of the people, and not against socialism, not against the people. This is what must guide us in debates and in the magazines' work." The continued stress that criticism must be "constructive" and show "party spirit" reflects the instrumentalist approach: what is "constructive" is directed toward the proper end as defined by the party. As the Uzbek Republic prosecutor put it in *Pravda Vostoka*, giving people the opportunity to express their opinions "makes it all the more important to distinguish the voicing of constructive ideas aimed at the improvement

of our life from malevolence and all kinds of inflammatory fuss. It should be the job of the press, Gorbachev has written, to "unite and mobilize people," not divide them.

Indeed the instrumentalist conception of rights and freedoms perpetuates the mentality of devotion to the cause that has consistently characterized Soviet Communist party programs since the Bolshevik revolution. It imparts to *glasnost'* and *perestroyka* themselves the style of a military campaign, complete with inspirational exhortations, the servile repetition by lieutenants (even as they extol the virtues of independent thinking) of a stock of catch phrases—"the braking mechanism," "the period of stagnation" "the democratization of all social life," and so on—as well as the repeated assurances from the leadership that "there is simply no alternative, comrades" and "there is no turning back."

All these features of the *perestroyka* atmosphere, plus Gorbachev's insistence that Soviet pluralism must be socialist pluralism, suggest rights and liberties constrained, rather than enriched, by socialism, and suggest that the slogan "more socialism, more democracy" masks a hidden conflict, since in order to have more "socialism" it may be necessary to have more discipline and hence less democracy. For the three reasons cited above, it seems unlikely that *glasnost'* and other expansions of individual and group rights and liberties in the USSR, however dramatically they now affect the climate of Soviet intellectual life, will in themselves proceed far enough to alter fundamentally the existing relationship between society and the state in the Soviet Union.

## Notes

1. Mikhail Gorbachev, *Perestroika: New Thinking for Our Country and the World*, (New York: Harper and Row, 1987), pp. 78–79, 82.

2. A. M. Migranian, "The Relations Among the Individual, Society, and the State in the Political Theory of Marxism and the Problems of the Democratization of Socialist Society," *Voprosy Filosofii* (Moscow), No. 8, 1987, pp. 78–80.

3. Ibid., pp. 79, 87–91.

4. Human Rights: Two Views, Two Approaches," *Kommunist* (Moscow), no. 13, 1987, p. 111.

5. Gorbachev, op. cit., pp. 75–76, 97.

# 21

# Soviet Union: A Civil Society

*S. Frederick Starr*

What better way is there to initiate a program of reforms than to persuade the public that life stagnated under a predecessor's policies? There is no better evidence of Soviet leader Mikhail Gorbachev's political prowess than the thoroughness with which he has accomplished this discrediting. In his view, the vitality of the post-Stalin thaw gave way to a period of turgid bureaucratism during which not only the Soviet government and economy but also the society at large succumbed to a profound malaise.

Successful political slogans must contain at least a grain of truth, and the notion of general stagnation under the late Soviet leader Leonid Brezhnev meets this test. Long before the economy went flat about 1978, the regime had become petrified and oligarchic, thereby repressing the very forces that might have stimulated economic renewal. Where Gorbachev is seriously wrong—and where many Americans err in accepting his view—is in his claim that the manifest stagnation in the Communist party and bureaucracy pervaded Soviet society as well.

Much of what happened in Soviet society under Brezhnev was bound to strike a provincial bureaucrat like the young Gorbachev as decadent, but this says as much about the mentality of officialdom as about the social dynamic itself. For

SOURCE: Reprinted with permission from *Foreign Policy*, no. 70 (Spring 1988), pp. 26–41. © 1988 by the Carnegie Endowment for International Peace. Article and Notes abridged by the editors.

while the official economy lagged, an entrepreneurial "second economy" burgeoned. In unprecedented numbers young Soviets became contributing participants in the global youth culture, forcing the government to accept what it could not alter. Individual citizens in countless fields plunged into innovative work, blithely ignoring official taboos and following wherever their interests led them. Torpor may have reigned in the official world, but Soviet society in Brezhnev's time experienced great ferment. To be sure, corruption abounded. But the rise of corruption must be laid directly to the regime's failure to open legitimate channels for the new energies rather than to some cancerous venality that had entered the body politic. Indeed, the social energies that were marginalized or suppressed under Brezhnev provide much of the impetus to today's economic and political reforms.

Gorbachev may be excused for playing down the dynamic element in Soviet society. To accept it he would be acknowledging that much of the initiative for change has shifted from the Communist party to society. Gorbachev then would appear not as the revolutionary leader calling a somnolent nation to action but as a conservative reformer trying to save a system facing pressures beyond his control.

Western analysts cannot so easily be excused for their narrow concern with Kremlin politics to the neglect of the social realities underlying them. To their credit, American researchers first identified the impact of alcoholism on the life expectancy of Russian men, as well as the demographic trends creating a labor shortage in European Russia and a baby boom in Soviet central Asia. But most have dismissed the broader changes occurring in Soviet society as not germane to explaining Moscow's actions to U.S. television viewers and members of Congress.

Gorbachev's June 1986 statement to Moscow writers that "Soviet society is ripe for change" exemplifies his sleight of hand and reveals the source of westerners' analytic errors. For Soviet society was already in the process of change; what is "ripe for change," but until recently unaffected by it, is the governmental apparatus. Economic stagnation, like its kin, corruption, occurred because the system failed to adjust to the emerging values of the populace, especially its best educated and technically most competent elements. Today Gorbachev is not creating change so much as uncorking it. The measure of his reform program is whether it adapts the party and government to the dynamic elements in Soviet society.

Fundamental shifts in Soviet society are going forward, and these increasingly define the national agenda. Since most recent analyses minimize this factor, a fuller review of the causes and character of the social transformations is in order.

Among the causes, none is more fundamental than the rapid urbanization of the past 30 years. A rural society at Joseph Stalin's death in 1953, the Soviet Union today is only about 10 per cent less urban than the United States and about as urban as Italy. This change occurred in spite of official policy rather than because of it. Boldly defying severe residency laws and internal passport controls, peasants flooded into the cities.

This great migration marked the waning of peasant Russia and the passing of a controversial national archetype. Long-suffering Russian peasants are a fixture of both Russian and Western writing. For centuries they seemed to epitomize all that made their country different and distinctive—they bowed to authority, engaged in elemental and anarchistic rebellion, were natural communists in their village communes, and strove desperately to escape the extended family's despotic might. In the eyes of Slavophiles they were noble savages, and to westerners, a barrier to Russia's integration into the community of modern countries. Today, fewer than one in four Soviets is a peasant, and the number continues to plummet.

City air may not have made all rural migrants free, but it has emancipated their offspring. Sons and daughters of Russia's collectivized peasantry have plunged into urban life with a vengeance, pulling strings to get their children into the right schools, hustling for better apartments, and cutting deals for everything from seaside vacations to birth-control pills. In the process, the new urbanites have grown more independent than their forebears. Those who have gained access to the best goods and services can give credit as much to their own initiative as to the largess of the system. As their expectations rose they grew more critical. Dissatisfaction is more common in the city than in the poorer countryside and is greater in large and more affluent metropolises than in smaller centers, where the peasant mentality still holds sway. Responding to their new environment, Soviet urbanites assert their individual rights in the face of what officialdom sees as their collective duties. As this happens they cross, albeit unconsciously, the ideological fault line running in Western political theory between the writings of Thomas Hobbes, who stressed the individual's need for security, and those of John Locke, who stressed the right to liberty.

Rapid economic development spurred this shift in outlook. Notwithstanding its recent stagnation, the Soviet economy remains the world's second largest and has grown faster than the U.S. economy through the postwar years. Millions of new jobs have been created, many requiring great expertise and sophistication. Important responsibilities have been entrusted to tens of thousands of people far outside the narrow circles of party, bureaucracy, and military that controlled national life in the Stalin era. No longer does the Communist party enjoy the relative monopoly on skills it had when the economy was smaller and simpler. Today's professional elite is for the most part staunchly loyal but far less beholden to the party and state bureaucracy than was its Stalinist predecessor. Brezhnev, by withholding from technocrats and intellectuals the rewards he extended to labor, hastened the growing autonomy of these elements.

The Soviet Union still lags behind the United States on many key educational indicators, but progress in this area, too, has been significant. Advances in education have fostered the individuation and sense of autonomy unleashed by urbanization and economic growth. In 1987, 245 million people, or 89 per cent of the Soviet population, had at least a

10th-grade education. The comparable figure in 1939 was 10 per cent; in 1959 it was 32 per cent. As the number of those able to read has expanded, so has the number of those capable of reading between the lines. Millions are now acquiring and assessing critically information that their grandparents would have found utterly inaccessible, the object of fear or awe. Not surprisingly, the rising levels of education have been accompanied by a proportionate erosion of faith in the state's ability to organize and micromanage such diverse functions as medicine, specialized manufacturing, and the provision of services.

Paradoxically, the recent economic slump has fostered the sense of individual autonomy that prosperity generated. As the sociologist Vladimir Shlapentokh showed in a 1986 study, applicants to Soviet universities now have less than one-half as good a chance of gaining admission as they did 20 years ago, and graduates have access to fewer positions in the ranks of bosses and managers. As the escalator of social mobility has slowed, especially at the upper floors, the young, educated, and ambitious increasingly have been thrown on their own resources.

The exercise of personal choice was once a privilege offered by urban life. Today it is a necessity. The State Planning Agency (Gosplan) may still bear formal responsibility for formulating comprehensive plans embracing all of the country's material and human resources, but in today's organizationally more complex environment it has lost the ability to carry out this task effectively. As a result, life decisions formerly made by the state—such as the selection of a career, employer, and place of residence—are either subject to personal influence or left fully to individual choice. The Soviet system of planning remains distinguished for its coerciveness and paternalism when compared with even the most socialized advanced industrial countries elsewhere. Compared with its own past, however, the Soviet system today devolves far more decisions to individual initiative.

All inhabitants of the peasant village knew where their neighbors were and what they were doing. But in the modern metropolis millions of urbanites rush about like unplottable electrons in an atom. Such circumstances have lowered the level of regimentation and surveillance the regime can expect to maintain. True, the Soviet Union remains a police state. Most of the laws and institutions created under Stalin are still in place. Now, however, the KGB has no choice but to focus its surveillance on a few individuals and groups. Many recent articles on criminality prove that police tactics often fail. That draft dodging could reach unprecedented proportions during the war in Afghanistan attests to the difficulty of operating a police state when the inhabitants are determined and resourceful in pursuing their own interests. The decline of fear as an instrument of control is both a cause and an effect of this situation.

Some future revisionist historian will remind the world how much Brezhnev and former Prime Minister Aleksei Kosygin did to reward the laboring men and women of the USSR. Whether from a sense of social justice or from concern that Soviet workers might follow the example of their Polish counterparts, they increased salaries steadily throughout their term in office. However, they failed to bring about commensurate growth in the supply of consumer goods, with the result that individual Soviet citizens had no choice but to salt away billions in savings accounts. Although total savings in 1960 equaled only 50 rubles for each Soviet citizen, by the 1980s this figure had risen to more than 600 rubles, equal to nearly three-fourths of the country's entire annual outlay for salaries.

This development, too, has advanced the process of individuation. For half a century Soviet workers were encouraged to identify with the progress of a command economy in which the state was the sole producer. Now workers with bank accounts of unspendable rubles have a personal stake in prodding the economy toward responding to their own demands as consumers. Of course, the government would be foolish to alienate the owners of so significant a source of investment capital.

When the regime has failed to produce desired goods and services, citizens have not hesitated to create them. Thus enters the twilight second economy, which is estimated to account for one-seventh of the USSR's nonagricultural output. Whether semilegal or fully underground, this privatized economy has come of age. Pioneered by young people 30 years ago, it now touches every segment of the population. Hence when Gorbachev talks of expanding the small private sector he really means extending legal legitimacy—and taxability—to areas of the gray or black markets. After all, as a former general administrator, he scarcely can be ignorant of the fact that industrial firms and communes throughout the Soviet provinces rely on the services of semilegal *sabashniki*, free-lance teams of builders and laborers who outperform their official counterparts in spite of bureaucratic harassment.

During the Brezhnev regime Soviet society moved steadily in the direction of individuation, decentralization of initiative, and privatization. A virtual revolution in personal communications in that supposedly stagnant era dramatically strengthened these processes of change. V.I. Lenin and Stalin both labored to establish "top-down" vertical systems of communication. They nationalized and imposed strict political controls over such technologies as radio, film, sound recording, and modern postal services. More important, they limited or suppressed such horizontal technologies as the private telephone and the intercity telegraph. Their successors did the same with xerographic machines and desktop computers. In the 1970s the USSR was the only country moving toward advanced industrialization that successfully braked the spread of private automobiles. All forms of international communication—radio, travel, mail, and telephone—were restricted or muzzled. As a result, society was left unable to communicate with itself. It was atomized and, in theory at least, rendered passive.

Extensive controls on the dissemination of information remain in effect today, yet millions of Soviet citizens routinely evade them. Over many years they have been astonishingly resourceful in their efforts to gain access to whatever information they desire. In the process

they have taken advantage of such officially sanctioned major technologies as intercity telephones, whose number has increased rapidly but which are still in short supply. Equally important, they have skillfully exploited such seemingly innocuous "small technologies" as the cassette-tape recorder, the personal camera, the videocassette recorder (VCR), and the ham radio. In each case the state tried to suppress or strictly curb access to the new information technology. Outwitted by the public, it then sought a face-saving avenue of retreat. In the 1960s it had to reckon with a wave of illegally imported cassette-tape recorders that transformed their owners into publishers. The state then fell back on producing and selling its own. In the 1980s the process was repeated with imported VCRs. Eventually the Soviet government began producing its own VCRs in the hope that it at least could influence the use of a technology it no longer could prohibit.

By such steps the Soviet state lost its monopoly on information. A privatized system embracing large segments of the population now exists alongside the controlled official system of communications. What one Soviet writer, Vladimir Simonov, called "technotronic *glasnost*" was a fact long before Gorbachev took up the latter word for his own purposes. Thanks to this *glasnost*, or "openness," instituted by the public itself, members of Soviet society have gained the ability to communicate with one another and, increasingly, with the outside world. With or without official *glasnost*, few events in the USSR or abroad long escape notice. Even the darkest corners of Soviet history eventually will be illuminated by the more resourceful members of society, whatever the party and state may desire.

Improved communications have made possible a degree of "networking" among Soviet citizens that would have been inconceivable a generation ago. Controls over the freedom of assembly are still in place and enforced sometimes with extreme severity. Yet persons with common interests throughout the Soviet Union can readily locate one another and enter into communication by means of the legal and semilegal technologies available to them.

Whether model-airplane enthusiasts, rock music fans, Hare Krishnas, Afghanistan war veterans, or ecologists, interest groups of like-minded people form with relative ease and establish regular channels of communication among their devotees.

What began in the 1950s with networks of underground jazz fans spread in the 1970s to the sphere of public affairs. The Communist party newspaper *Pravda* acknowledges the existence of more than 30,000 *neformaly,* grass roots voluntary associations dedicated to various types of civic improvement. What Western political scientists call "interest group articulation" reached a record high in August 1987, when a conference of some 600 politically oriented clubs and associations—in this case, all nominally socialist in their program—convened in Moscow under the aegis of the city's party boss at the time, Boris Yeltsin.

The existence of such entities testifies to the ability of the Soviet people to generate ideas independently on virtually any topic and to air them broadly. It also confirms that the state's powers to form and inculcate social values from above are strictly limited. This sea change took place in the arts more than a generation ago and in recent years has occurred in many other areas of endeavor. Although manifestations of official ideology remain ubiquitous, by the early 1980s the initiative for ideas had shifted from state to society in a process of de facto democratization. In the sphere of ideology, this democratization has been accompanied by a de facto secularization, in which revolutionary myths retain their status and even some of their evocative power but have yielded much of their day-to-day relevance to that yeasty body of ideas being generated by, and circulated among, the public at large.

The void left by a waning ideology is filled by an ever more assertive and potent public opinion. The growing importance of public opinion can be gauged by the progress of efforts to measure it. Tentative contact with American public-opinion research firms was made as early as the 1960s. The legitimation of sociology as a field of research was achieved in the 1970s, by which time Soviet newspapers and official organs had begun analyzing public opinion to seek feedback.

The ability of Soviet public opinion to influence decision making is exemplified in the field of ecology. The conquest of nature has been a sacred ideal of Russian communism since before the revolution. Yet when government agencies proposed over the past decade to divert water from Siberian rivers to water the arid steppes of central Asia, educated public opinion succeeded in killing the project. In 1987 a water-control scheme for the Kamchatka Peninsula was thwarted in the planning stage by local activists, many of them blue-collar workers.

As public opinion gained in strength it grew in diversity. The public's increased facility at networking has brought to the fore a bewildering range of views on virtually every issue of the day. That some virulent forms of Russian nationalism, extreme by any standard, are among them is not surprising, since the USSR lacks the regularized public forums at which advocates of maximalist positions might moderate them through interchange with people representing other views. But even the most extreme manifestations of public opinion are important because they attest to the living diversity and pluralism beneath the surface of the "unbreakable unity of Party and people" today in the USSR.

## BECOMING A "CIVIL SOCIETY"

These, then, are some of the fundamental changes that took place during the otherwise stagnant Brezhnev era. Together they constitute part of the social reality that the Gorbachev administration will ignore only at its peril.

Clearly the new tendencies in Soviet life will soften many features of the social system forged by Lenin and Stalin. The old society's tendency was for everything outside the party and state apparatus to be turned into an amorphous mass, the whole country becoming "as if déclassé," in the words of the historian Moshe Lewin.[1] The emerging society, by contrast, includes large numbers of autonomous and assertive personalities among both the rulers and the ruled. The sense of duty that the late anthropologist Margaret Mead found so characteristic of the

Soviet public under Stalin is being balanced by millions of individuals actively trying to affirm their rights under law. People who formerly viewed themselves as subjects are taking on the mentality of citizens.

Gorbachev has declared his goal to be the democratization of society. But Soviet society already has moved far in this direction thanks to developments fostered or tolerated by his predecessors. The key question is whether the party and state will follow suit. To the extent they do, the Soviet Union will move toward becoming a radically different type of society than it has been for 70 years—namely a "civil society."

This concept has a rich history in Western political thought, most notably in the writings of Locke, Alexis de Tocqueville, and John Stuart Mill. It is grounded in ideals of citizenship under law; in freedom of speech, of the press, of assembly, and of worship; and in the protection of minority rights under majority rule. Above all, it holds that society is distinct from government and that government is but one of several institutions coexisting in a pluralistic social fabric.

So greatly do these ideals differ from the current situation in the Soviet Union that it might be tempting to dismiss as utopian all talk of civil society there. The Communist party still exercises a degree of control over the citizenry that is antithetical to notions of civil society. Whatever amelioration has taken place in recent years has occurred de facto and not de jure.

It might also be objected that the very idea of civil society is too narrowly Western in origin to be applied appropriately beyond Western Europe and North America. Clearly civil society in the Soviet Union will be shaped by Russian traditions, just as those in Great Britain and France bear the very different mark of their national heritages. Starkly different structures, however, can fulfill similar functions. To acknowledge the differentness of Russia's political heritage does not disqualify it from experiencing evolutionary change. For someone in 16th-century England, 18th-century France, or 19th-century Japan to have claimed that those countries would someday become civil societies would have seemed no less

outrageous than for someone to make a similar claim today for the USSR. . . .

Arguably the most astonishing utterance from any member of Gorbachev's inner circle was Aleksandr Yakovlev's declaration last year, that the Soviet Union "should operate more by the common law principle that everything not explicitly forbidden by law is permitted." As if acting on the general secretary's advice, Soviet courts in the first half of 1987 sent back more cases for further investigation, handed down more acquittals, and threw out more suits than in any previous 6-month period in Soviet history. Such words and deeds would seem to reflect an understanding of civil society at the highest levels in the Kremlin.

Yet the suspicion remains that Gorbachev's démarche toward the new social realities is merely a tactic. What will happen when *glasnost* is directed not against the Brezhnev legacy but against Gorbachev's own record? How quickly will his administration pull back when the extension of openness to non-Russian peoples in the Soviet Union unleashes centrifugal forces incompatible with Great Russian pretensions? And how sharply will Gorbachev shift directions when the cycle of reform is played out, as must inevitably happen?

Such questions are intriguing but premature. Most of the announced reforms, particularly in the crucial area of law, are still being prepared. Until the first drafts emerge it will be impossible to determine how much substantive wheat is mixed with the rhetorical chaff. But there are serious grounds for doubting that legislation embodying principles of a civil society will get very far. First, Gorbachev has declared his commitment to maintaining all the inherited prerogatives of the Communist party. Second, he fully shares the traditional Marxist opposition to private property. Indeed, his limited acceptance of a private sector seems designed more to co-opt the unruly second economy than to affirm the right to property that Locke posited as the basis of citizenship in a civil society.

Third, and most important, Gorbachev's highest priority is not to introduce liberal reforms but to revive the bedraggled Soviet economy. That administrative decentralization and sharp staff cutbacks in planning organs spell disaster for thousands of bureaucrats is well known. Less often noted is the way the economic reforms might hurt the interests of labor. To put it bluntly, Gorbachev's economic program contains many facets that, if crudely imposed on the Soviet public, would sour the atmosphere for reform in other areas. How, after all, is a Soviet worker to view proposals calling for deregulation, the suspension of wage and price controls, the expansion of the powers of local managers, compulsory job reassignments for millions of blue-collar laborers, and the stretching out of salary scales for the purpose of rewarding diligence and punishing sloth? The economy may desperately need such measures, but to the Soviet worker they can only appear as a speedup.

Any other reforms put forward when such controversial measures are being implemented will be tarred with an antilabor brush. If the economy fails to respond to Gorbachev's stimuli—and 1987's results give little reason for optimism—then many common Russians will pine for the good old days when labor was not punished for the country's economic malaise. That serious problems with poverty and unemployment in the USSR are only waiting to be discovered by the public simply adds to the risks. It will be all too easy to draw the conclusion that the inevitable price of political freedom and civil rights is an unacceptable level of economic inequality. If embittered bureaucrats forge ties with alienated labor, the reform program will face formidable opposition that will test Gorbachev's powers as a political broker.

Reviewing such arguments, some Western observers have begun penning Gorbachev's political obituary and have written off the prospects for basic change in the civic sphere. In rushing to the latter conclusion, if not the former as well, they reveal the analytic bias discussed earlier. Such factors as the erosion of planning, the progress of decentralization, the spread of privatization in the service sector, the information revolution leading to openness, and the overall individuation of society—what Gorbachev calls the "human factor"—all call for a different perspective, one emphasizing change from below rather than from above. At issue is not whether such fundamental developments will be erased or thwarted, but when, to what degree, and by what political processes the ruling party and government will make their peace with them.

It might be argued that it is not too late for these changes to be reversed and for the political superstructure thereby to escape their effects. This scenario is possible, but its cost rises daily. Citizens in a civil society are less malleable and less subject to manipulation by the state than subjects under an authoritarian regime. And as society becomes less malleable, society and the state grow more interdependent, each gaining the power to limit and influence the other. Since the state has long wielded broad power over Soviet society, the focus of change today is for society to gain reciprocal powers over the Soviet state—that is, to reach a condition in which "every branch of [the] civil policy supports and is supported, regulates and is regulated, by the rest," as the 18th century English jurist Sir William Blackstone wrote in his *Commentaries.* In July 1986 Gorbachev himself decried those "who try to put the Party and society at loggerheads." If he is to avoid this, Gorbachev must take steps to accommodate the system to the new social reality.

The thesis presented here holds that profound changes have taken place in Soviet society and that these changes eventually will exert an influence upon both the traditional institutions of government and what George Kennan, in his "Mr. X" article in *Foreign Affairs* in July 1947, called "the mental world of the Soviet leaders." Only time will tell how deeply these new conditions will alter the political superstructure....

## Notes

1. Moshe Lewin, *The Making of the Soviet System* (New York: Pantheon, 1985), p. 265.

# PART THREE

# Political Dynamics and Processes

In every political system, we have noted, individuals and groups seek to influence the state and thereby translate their interests into authoritative political decisions. An indispensable condition for the efficient functioning of political systems is widespread acceptance of the decision-making process—which we shall call "consensus." Wherever this kind of consensus exists, the state itself becomes legitimized. Legitimacy and consensus are key indicators of the effectiveness and performance of the system and conversely of the existence of basic instabilities that may undermine it. Ultimately, the phenomenon of government—what Mosca calls "the political fact"—is a matter of will as well as force; that is, political relations are willed relations.

## POLITICAL AUTHORITY

One aspect of legitimacy is the use of the power of the state by officials in accordance with prearranged and agreed upon rules. A legitimate act is also legal, but a lawful command is not always legitimate. For example, the commands issued by the Nazi government in Germany were legal, and presumably subordinate officials down to the private soldier or individual citizen had to obey them. But at the same time, these orders violated a code of civilized behavior and morality that brought into question their legitimacy. Legality refers to the letter of the law as decreed by a state organ, whereas legitimacy involves the very character of the state and the substance and purpose of a legal enactment. But who will decide when there is a difference between legality and legitimacy? No clear answer

can be given. On the one hand, the state always claims legitimacy for its legal commands: "What is pleasing to the prince has the force of law," according to an old axiom of the Romans. On the other hand, many individuals see a higher law beyond the formal law of the state. Ultimately, they obey their own conscience and consider some acts of the state to be illegitimate; this is the justification of civil disobedience as advocated by Thoreau, Tolstoy, and Gandhi.

But these extreme formulations are hypothetical. In actual political life, legality, legitimacy, and consent *tend* to converge. Consensus is more than agreement; it denotes acceptance of a given political system. Acceptance may be due to individual consent stemming from recognition of the beneficent purposes of the state; acceptance is also the product of tradition and habit. Consensus is generally addressed to the basic rules that establish, define, limit, and channel political power—that is, to the constitution. It is not limited to specific laws or specific acts of the government, or even to governmental forms. Consensus transforms power into authority, and the legal enactments emanating from the government into legitimate orders.

Democratic theory postulates canons of legitimacy that clarify the distinctions we are trying to make. Force can be used only in accordance with certain previously agreed upon procedures. There is an elaborate setting of limitations upon the exercise of power, which can be used only by persons elevated to office through elections. Individuals agree to the basic rules so long as they are not violated. The government derives its authority from these basic rules; whenever disagreements about the government and its policies erupt, they are resolved through popular choice. The substance of political life, therefore, is the consensus—or "agreement on fundamentals"—that binds the citizens into an organized common political life.

The contract theory as developed by John Locke is a classic formulation of this consensual model. According to it, the formation of a political community is an act of will embodying the cardinal rule that the majority of the people, acting through their legislature, govern. However, property rights and individual freedoms may not be infringed upon by the majority, and there must be periodic free elections of the legislative body. In such a political community, a minority can be coerced only in order to implement the basic agreement entered into by the whole community. But such coercion cannot be used to destroy or silence the minority. The consensus on a free and open society gives the majority the right to act while allowing the minority the right to protest peacefully and ultimately to appeal to the community at large in favor of its positions—in other words, the right to become the majority. This model, then, incorporates the obligation to obey and the right to protest, criticize, and oppose. It allows the force of the state to be transformed into authority, deriving its legitimacy from the basic agreement. Individual dissent is expressed not in disobedience, but through organized opposition seeking to present alternative policies. Thus, opposition in the democratic scheme is harnessed to the total political system, which is strengthened, not weakened, by dissent.

The model helps us to see clearly the distinctions between force and authority, consensus and legitimacy. It also has analytic value in calling our attention to the conditions under which consensus is likely to emerge or be disrupted. But most political systems at present are not based on the Lockean model. Force rather than authority is frequently the rule, and this is an indication of a lack of consensus binding the citizens together. More important, values other than free elections, including national or ethnic identity, may serve to legitimize the state.

Political decisions may be accepted by a population for a variety of reasons. Freely given consent is only one basis of legitimacy, and in the modern world it remains precarious.

## Consensus Building

The contract theory that Locke used to illustrate the formation of a political community—all citizens agree to form it through a solemn compact—is at best a fiction or simply an illustration with no historical foundation. It holds that, under certain conditions, a state of mind develops among a given people to establish a set of fundamental rules about the manner in which they would cooperate and live peacefully together. But what accounts for such a state of mind? And why was it reached in some societies and not in others? When and under what conditions does a community become a political one accepting a common agreement?

There are no simple answers to these questions, but some general indications may be given. First, there must be a fairly extensive acceptance of common norms of social conduct. Customs must begin to develop—even become everyday habits—before we can begin to talk of a community. Second, social behavior must be predictable, at least to the extent that makes human intercourse possible. If all parishioners spied upon one another while celebrating mass, for fear that each might carry a gun, a functioning community would hardly be likely. Third, a political community requires common expectations of material benefits for all members. The utilitarian argument was put forward by Thomas Hobbes and, later, more persuasively by James Mill and John Stuart Mill. Put simply, this means that the chances for achieving consensus are greater in political communities that enjoy economic prosperity.

Finally, the role of the elite is crucial in the formation of consensus. It is axiomatic that leadership is always lodged in the hands of a few. In all countries that have experienced the

Industrial Revolution, rule by a relatively small traditional elite was challenged by new groups, in particular the bourgeoisie and the working class. This was a momentous period in the evolution of political systems, because claims to political leadership had to be subordinated to the requirements of popular participation and support. Two developments can be discerned. In some cases, the ruling groups became restrictive and negative, attempting to thwart participation and to maintain themselves in a position of control and leadership through the use of repressive measures. In other cases they became permissive and supportive, allowing their claims to leadership to be qualified and indeed ultimately subverted by new symbols, forms, and practices deriving from popular participation. The greater the degree of permissiveness on the part of the traditional elite, the smoother was the transition to a consensual and participant society; the greater their tendency to reject newcomers, the more difficult and the less likely was the emergence of consensus.

In Britain, for example, ever increasing participation and influence was offered to the citizenry at large throughout the nineteenth century. But in Russia, despite some half-hearted reforms, autocratic rule was maintained. The result was that in Britain the people began to value and accept their system as an instrument for the satisfaction of their wants, whereas the rising groups in Russia either rejected their government or remained apathetic to it. In the one case, consensus was built; in the other, its very preconditions were denied. Thus, we may postulate that the congruence between mass demands for participation and influence and a positive elite response to these demands is a fundamental condition for the development of consensus.

This hypothesis is equally relevant for developing societies today. Throughout Asia, Latin America, and Africa, many of the preconditions of consensus—the sense of national identity, compatibility of values, and predictability of behavior—are lacking. In all these societies demands for material progress have been stimulated through exposure to more advanced societies. The role of the elite then becomes critical for the development of political consensus. Rejection of new groups may lead to sharp conflict between the few and the many, and to a state of virtual civil war. Complete permissiveness, on the other hand, may thrust unprepared and unqualified groups into power prematurely. Inability to advance industrialization produces popular disenchantment and apathy.

In the last analysis, it is the interplay among a great number of factors that accounts for the development of a consensual society or for the failure of consensus to emerge. We have emphasized the relationship between mass and elite under conditions of economic modernization in order to illustrate the complexity of the phenomenon rather than to identify it as a single causal factor. For the very attitude of the elite—whether it is permissive and open or restrictive and negative—in turn depends upon many other historical and social factors. Common linguistic or religious bonds, prolonged community life behind natural barriers that deter attack or invasion, feelings of ethnic or racial identity, continuing economic progress, and the impact of technology and science upon the society are all factors that we subsumed earlier under the general terms of common values, predictability of behavior, and perception of common material benefits. It is only when these factors materialize at the proper time that the conditions for consensus also emerge and that the Lockean model is relevant.

Consensus is always under stress, even in systems with a long tradition of legitimacy. Efforts to create an independent Quebec, the conflict between the Flemish and Walloons in Belgium, the appearance of a black power movement in the United States, and Scottish nationalism in the United Kingdom are all threats to the basic consensus in previously stable systems. In these cases, dissidence stems from the conditions we have discussed—repressive or rejective measures by the elite and a relative inability to fulfill the demands for economic well-being aroused by the elite themselves and the ideology prevalent in the whole system. A theory of consensus therefore can be used to assess and to measure degrees of alienation, including the emergence of revolutionary situations.

The processes of socialization and politicization—whereby individuals are conditioned to accept their society and government—are of special importance in consensus building. No society can exist for long unless its norms are transmitted to the young. In early childhood the pattern of transmission is sheer habit. The young simply accept the behavior of their parents, on pain of discipline, and identify with their symbols and values. There can be no rational inquiry into the fundamental rules of the system. Within the entire educational establishment an overt effort is made to inculcate favorable attitudes toward the state. Through ceremony, ritual, and outright indoctrination, the young learn to cherish their national community and their political system. The manner in which national history is taught and the emphasis upon the unique and superior traits of the national culture are calculated to create an emotional acceptance of the political system.

Generally, the young begin to assume a critical attitude toward authority in secondary schools and universities. In many societies there is a tradition of unrest and political alienation among university students, though radical students of middle-class backgrounds frequently tend to be absorbed readily into the system once they complete their studies and enter the job market. But revolutions can rarely, if ever, be traced to intergenerational strife. They stem rather from discontinuities in historical development and basic divisions within the society that split the generations internally. In revolutionary situations consensus is already undermined. Disagreement about norms and symbols of authority is sharp, and the young are inducted into a system that is embroiled in conflict. The agencies of socialization, including the family, school, and church, speak with different tongues and cultivate contradictory ideas involving the very nature and character of the system itself.

## Effectiveness and Performance

All social groups have goals or purposes in terms of which their discipline is justified. The effectiveness of the organization—be it church, trade union, corporation, or state—must be appraised in relation to its success in achieving stated goals. An army, for example, has well-defined goals: the application of superior firepower at a given point or, more broadly, defense of the country. An army is disciplined—command and obedience relations are established in unequivocal fashion, and criticism of its code is severely limited. It is an organization geared to performance, so that an order by a single chief moves masses of men and equipment. The efficiency of the "army model" accounts for widespread admiration of autocratic and authoritarian political systems and constantly feeds the antidemocratic schools of thought. Lenin fashioned his theory of the Communist party after the army model, calling for rigorous discipline and total commitment of its members. Many of the symbols of fascist and other authoritarian parties are borrowed from the military. Order, discipline, and unquestioning obedience are equated with performance and effectiveness.

The army is a single or limited-purpose organization. Politics, on the other hand, entails regulation and control of a society that contains many organizations, each striving to attain unique and frequently divergent goals. The family, school, church, corporation, and university are concerned with such distinctly different activities as reproduction of the species, rearing of the young, education, religion, industrial production, and the acquisition of scientific knowledge. The state is not only a relationship of command and obedience; it also involves conciliation and supports. For example, throughout Europe in the nineteenth century new groups were created in the course of industrialization and sought entry into the political system. Complex societies are participant societies. The "army model" is relevant only to the coercive aspect of a political system.

As Karl Deutsch suggests in his *Nerves of Government*,[1] a political system may be viewed as complex sets of messages with a communication system that has been learned and internalized by all members of the society. A structured and learned communication system makes the government a sensitive instrument for the satisfaction of demands and interests of the citizens, and it also makes the citizens receptive to the needs and directives of the government. The government and citizens are mutually supportive.

The "communications model" is useful in analyzing performance. It points to the following: that obedience to commands is learned and willed; that the government is constantly listening to the messages that come from all social groups and individuals; that so long as official directives are generally consonant with demands and expectations they are likely to be obeyed—indeed, obedience is taken for granted; and that if such a pattern of relations is established over a period of time the relationship between government and citizens will become intimate and positive, characterized by marked interdependence and mutual trust. The capabilities of the government to act are immense because it can count on popular support. It can mobilize the citizenry for common purposes.

But what are these common purposes? In terms of what criteria is the effectiveness of a political system to be appraised? Every political society sets for itself varying goals, both specific (such as the creation of the infrastructure of a modern economy) and broad (the realization of values like equality or freedom). Comparison of political systems in terms of performance is difficult: What is considered success in one society may be failure in another, for their goals or values may be entirely different. There are, however, some generally accepted ends to which all political systems are committed—the survival

of their societies in a hostile world; the maintenance of order; and the resolution of conflicting demands and the allocation of goods in a manner that provides maximum satisfaction for all. The system must be able to maintain itself as it adjusts to constantly changing environmental factors. It must resolve problems as they arise and provide mechanisms for settling them.

A consensual democratic system derives its strength from the open communication between state and society. It contains a responsive mechanism that permits the articulation of interests and demands on the part of the governed, gears its decisions to those demands, and, by so doing, elicits supports that can again be converted into a resource for the achievement of common ends. Emerging conflicts engage the attention of government and citizens so that the way is paved for their resolution. Broad participation in the system and the open nature of communications guarantee acceptance of policy and help legitimize the state. A consensual system does not hesitate to arm the citizens, to draft them into the army, and to decree stringent measures calling for individual restraints in order to safeguard collective ends.

But, as we noted earlier, consensus is never universal in complex societies. The very openness of communications in democratic regimes permits dissident elements ample opportunity to clash with each other and with the government. Indeed, dissidence may be so widespread that no majority can form, and the ability of the political system to formulate public policy is reduced. Nonconsensual democracies tend to be ineffective in achieving socially accepted goals or may even collapse altogether—as in Russia in October 1917, Italy in 1922, and Germany in 1933.

Authoritarian regimes do not enjoy the advantages of an open communication system between leaders and the people. Because the citizens do not have the right to express their criticism, it is difficult for those in power to understand the nature of popular expectations and to assess the effectiveness of policy. There is always a danger of solving political problems by violence, which includes popular uprisings as well as repression by the state. But some dictatorships have demonstrated a remarkable ability to mobilize popular energies and resources and to promulgate effective policy. This requires exceptional dynamism and perspicacity on the part of the leaders, who in effect give the people what they want without going through the bother of inquiring beforehand or afterward. The citizens may be reasonably content, even if they have no opportunity to criticize, under conditions of full employment and material progress, and especially if the regime succeeds in embodying nationalistic sentiment. Military victory is also a good way of arousing popular enthusiasm for any regime, democratic or authoritarian. Popular support for authoritarian regimes is most likely in countries that have been governed previously by ineffective parliamentary democracies. It is noteworthy that the most important dictatorships in modern Europe—bolshevism in Russia, fascism in Italy, and nazism in Germany—all replaced nonconsensual and ineffective democracies.

The student will find that analysis of any aspect of a given political system—such as the interest groups, parties, political institutions, administration, and ideologies—always leads back to the critical question of consensus.

## POLITICAL DYNAMICS

The pursuit of power—the capacity to command the actions of others—by individuals and groups is a universal phenomenon. Individuals and groups are organized through specialized associations representing their interests; they also promulgate or associate themselves with ideological orientations. By *political dynamics* we mean the interplay of social groups, organized interests, and ideologies that generally takes place through political parties and institutions in order to shape public policy.

The process whereby groups compete for positions and advantage takes place in all political systems, and hence it can be studied functionally and comparatively. In some political systems, groups press their demands and claims mainly through "interest" or "pressure" groups; others use the parties or administration. Comparative analysis can be conducted by studying the diverse patterns of interest articulation. Interest groups can be considered in terms of their size, membership, leadership, organization, relations with political parties, and means used to mobilize public opinion, gain access to the state, and influence decisions. Group analysis has the merit of bringing the student directly into the heart of the political process— social conflict and its resolution. By studying the "interest group universe" in a given political system, we gain a good insight into the distribution of power in that society and the manner in which interests are organized and expressed.

One of the striking features of industrialized societies is the development and proliferation of specialized groups. In a modern society they represent every conceivable social, economic, religious, and professional interest. The largest and most powerful groups speaking on behalf of the major social classes are the business, labor, and agricultural organizations. Every modern political system must provide these associations or interest groups with the opportunity to gain access to the policy makers and make known their proposals or demands.

Reconciliation of the demands of interest groups and, broadly speaking, of social forces, is perhaps the most serious single challenge confronting any political system. We are not referring here to the demands, say, of trade unions and management for a minimum wage fixed at a particular level, though this kind of conflict is quite intense. We refer rather to the attitude of social groups toward the political process itself, the acceptance of the "rules of the game" by all the players. For example, there is a complex network of specialized associations in both Great Britain and France. In both countries we find powerful trade unions, business groups, churches, and associations of farmers, veterans, teachers, and so on. Some French groups are more powerful than their opposite numbers in Britain (for example, farmers, small merchants, lay Catholics) and vice versa (British trade unions and business groups are more highly organized than their counterparts in France). Yet the basic attitudes of the groups are significantly different. In spite of their political rivalry, expressed through support of the Labor and Conservative parties, the trade unions and management groups in Great Britain accept a commitment to parliamentary institutions. With a few exceptions (such as the Irish nationalists), they are willing to work within the existing system in order to realize their goals and do not turn against it when they lose. The habits of compromise are solidly established in British society; the actors abide by fundamental rules that are embodied in the constitutional system.

In France, however, the same economic or social interests are *not* in agreement on the values of the state or on political procedures to be used in the resolution of group conflicts. The labor and business groups are fundamentally hostile to each other and constantly strive to change the rules of the game or the system itself so as to secure a more advantageous position. The most powerful trade union in France, the General Confederation of Labor, is Communist-controlled and Communist-oriented; that is, the industrial proletariat in France expressed its demands until recently, through a party that rejected the system. Important elements of the business community, on the other hand, not only distrust the workers, but wish to introduce a "strong" state to deal with them. The parliamentary system is held in low repute by other important interests as well. Political debates and meetings are marked by verbal and physical violence. In practice the disaffected groups are generally unable to overthrow the system and accept it provisionally. Compromise is difficult to achieve and breaks down altogether during political crises. There is a distinct tendency to change the rules of the game (usually by promulgating a new constitution) whenever the balance shifts and one constellation of groups or forces gains the upper hand. Thus, one of the most important questions to pose about a political system is the attitude of the principal organized groups toward each other and toward the system itself.

## Political Parties

Max Weber's definition of party is useful for placing the subject in broad social and historical perspective. The term political party, he suggested,

> will be employed to designate an associative type of social relationship, membership in which rests on formally free recruitment. The end to which its activity is devoted is to secure power within a corporate group for its leaders in order to attain ideal or material advantages for its active members. These advantages may consist in the realization of certain objective policies or the attainment of personal advantages or both.[2]

As Weber uses the term, a "party" can exist in any corporate group—unions, fraternal orders, churches, university faculties, and corporations. It can be oriented toward personal interest or toward broad policy. When the rules of the corporate group provide for campaigns and elections, the parties coalesce around interests. Political victory in party terms means that its adherents, in assuming direction of the state, can realize party proposals. Political parties thus tend to be complex social institutions holding together those who have a common program and those who strive for power and personal advantage. In a sense they are specialized associations *within* specialized associations and become more complex, organized, and bureaucratic as a society approaches the "modern" type.

It is therefore understandable that political parties were not studied systematically until the modern period, when they were fully developed. John Stuart Mill's treatise *On Representative Government*, written in 1861, contained an extensive plea for proportional representation but no analysis of parties. Insofar as parties were brought under scrutiny, they were generally denounced as expressions of factionalism. In a classic criticism of political parties, James Bryce expressed his fear that insofar as parties are permitted to run the government a community falls below the level of ideal democracy:

> In the ideal democracy every citizen is intelligent, patriotic, disinterested. His sole wish is to discover the right side in each contested issue, and to fix upon the best man among competing candidates. His common sense, aided by a knowledge of the constitution of his country, enables him to judge easily between the arguments submitted to him while his own zeal is sufficient to carry him to the polling booth.

But, Bryce continues, the electorate is *not* informed or interested. Hence, politicians discover the advantages of organization. "Organization and discipline mean the command of the leaders, the subordination and obedience of the rank and file; and they mean also the growth of a party spirit which is in itself irrational, impelling men to vote from considerations which have little to do with a love of truth or a sense of justice."[3]

Most students of political parties at the turn of the century, like Bryce, were concerned with the shortcomings and deficiencies of the political parties: with bossism, corruption, and the inability of the parties to put forward coherent programs and implement them once in power. M. I. Ostrogorski's classic treatise on *Democracy and the Organization of Political Parties* emphasized especially the sordid side of politics—above all, the politicians' craving for spoils. The thesis argued by Bryce and Ostrogorski concerning American parties was strengthened by Robert Michels's study of the German Social Democratic party, *Political Parties*. From the viewpoint of comparative analysis Michels's work marked an advance, for his "iron law of oligarchy" could be construed as a general theory in the light of which all political parties may be examined. Bryce, Ostrogorski, and Michels, taken together, offered a full-fledged theory of parties and their role in democracies. They fully documented the growth of mass political parties with complex structures in the United States, Britain,

and Germany. They assumed that democracy somehow involves meaningful participation by the masses in the making of important decisions. They agreed that parties were controlled by a handful of politicians and leaders. Democracy therefore becomes less and less feasible as parties become more and more complex.

Theory regarding the role of parties in a democracy has undergone sweeping change since then. The widespread view of parties as destructive of democracy has given way to an almost equally widespread view that parties are indispensable to the operation of democratic institutions. American political scientists were especially affected by the New Deal, which seemed to demonstrate the potential utility of political parties in mobilizing public support for a program of social reform. Also, the hostile reaction to the Nazi regime included searching appraisal of the one-party system. In defense of Western democracy against the challenge of fascism and communism, it was discerned that democracy was bound up somehow with the existence of at least two parties. The previously despised parties were elevated to positions of great prestige by political philosophers and researchers.

The role of parties in the democratic process was emphasized by such writers as A. D. Lindsay, R. M. MacIver, C. J. Friedrich, Joseph Schumpeter, and Walter Lippmann, to name but a few.[4] They argued that a distinct element of democracy, as contrasted with fascism and communism, was the existence of an opposition. But it is not sufficient to grant an abstract right of opposition to individuals. To be effective, opposition must be enabled to organize—that is, to form a party. In the absence of parties, there would be no check upon the egoistic impulses of the rulers. Also, the masses can participate effectively in government only through the agency of parties. Thus, parties organize the "chaotic public will," educate the private citizens to public responsibility, connect government with public opinion, and select the political leadership. In answer to Michels's criticism of oligarchy, it has been argued that even oligarchical parties may serve democratic purposes

—provided that there is free competition among the parties.[5] Thus, Gwendolyn Carter concludes her survey of parties in the Commonwealth: "Political parties...are not only an aid to democracy but an essential element in making it possible." Similarly, E. E. Schattschneider on the American parties: "The major parties have become the crucial and competing channels of policy formulation in our national democracy." And Maurice Duverger contends that in all advanced societies, "liberty and the party system coincide."[6] The contrast with Bryce, Ostrogorski, and Michels is complete!

However, the pervasive crisis of parliamentary democracy since World War II has been reflected in a revival of criticism of political parties. This is especially the case in countries where large social groups have not been fully integrated into the political system, as evidenced by massive support for antiparliamentary parties. In France, for example, there is an extensive literature critical of the role played by parties in the democratic process.

In developing nations, competitive political parties generally have fallen into disrepute. In many countries, as in Burma, Turkey, South Korea, Pakistan, Egypt, Ghana, and Nigeria, the army seized power professedly in order to defend the national interest against the corrupt parties. In India, disciples of Mahatma Gandhi urge the conversion of Congress into a national movement and the creation of a "party-less democracy." Ben Bella declared after coming to power that the "Front" ruling Algeria should never degenerate into a mere party. But it would be misleading to consider all criticism of parties as manifestations of a dictatorial impulse. Most students of developing nations recognize that in fact there are genuine difficulties in transferring democratic institutions from Europe and North America to the rest of the world. Democracy does not appear appropriate in societies in which the overwhelming majority of the people is illiterate and therefore not in a position to judge intelligently among candidates and programs. Different kinds of questions about both parties and democracy are raised: how the elite

is recruited, what role is played by the party in mobilizing the masses and breaking up the traditional society, what kind of values are held by the educated elite, and so on. The trend in interpreting the democratic nature of parties in developing nations is to assess their role in the transition from traditional to more modern forms of social organization. Mass participation in politics is one of the social conditions of democratic government. In some cases the party asserts a monopoly of power in order to create a modern society with the support, even if without the understanding, of the peasantry. In other cases, the party seeks to preserve the power of a traditional group. Dominant parties may seek to crush opposition or may tolerate criticism and respect an independent judiciary. Theory concerning the role of parties in a democracy is thus being modified in the light of the experience of the developing nations.

The political party is the most important single link between groups, the people, and the government in a democracy. Through the party, leadership is able to reach out into the masses for support and new sources of strength, while the masses in turn are able to focus criticism and make demands upon it. The party, if backed by a majority of the electorate, coordinates the multifarious functions of the government in order to achieve coherently stated aims. A minority party gives like-minded individuals and groups an opportunity to rally their forces, develop a program, and prepare for the day when power might be wielded or at least shared.

But the mass party also characterizes modern dictatorships. In the Soviet Union the Communist Party attempts to coordinate the activities of all major interests in the nation, whereas in Great Britain the majority party recognizes the right of other parties to seek the support of the electorate. Yet in both countries the party remains the most important instrument used by social groups in their quest for power. In a dictatorship the overriding task of the party is to mobilize the masses. This is the dominant trend also in developing nations, where a small, educated elite is determined to bring about modernization. Even in parliamentary democracies parties must be able to generate widespread popular support for the policies of the executive, or else the regime is in serious trouble. Totalitarian parties in particular secure the adherence of masses of people by offering them an opportunity to gratify social impulses, but democratic parties likewise engage in some of the same activities. Most studies of totalitarian parties have emphasized the role of the party as an instrument of the leadership, whereas most studies of democratic parties stress the role of the party in limiting leadership and permitting popular participation in the decision-making process. Yet, all parties may be viewed and compared in both ways.

Thus, groups organize, present their claims to the parties, and are in turn courted by party leaders. Decision makers are themselves members of parties and are dependent upon the support of groups for maintenance in office. The delicate process involving compromising pressures must take place somewhere within the political system: Is it within the single party, or the major party of a two-party system, or a parliamentary assembly? Does the nature of the relationship between leaders and followers in British, American, French, and Russian parties reveal differences or similarities? If we compare parties as regards function, we may discover that social conflict is expressed and resolved in different ways in these countries. Comparative study of party structure may reveal the existence of common organizational trends in all party systems.

## Classification of Party Systems

Classification is a first step in comparison of party systems because it enables the observer to select for analysis the like elements of various political systems. One such classification is based on the means employed in appealing to the electorate and organizing opinion. Some commentators distinguish between parties of interest and parties of principle, or parties of

personalities and parties of program, "broker" parties and "missionary" parties. American parties would thus be considered examples of interest appeal and personalities, whereas British and continental parties would be programmatic. Yet this classification does not fully explain modern trends. American parties reflect ideological orientations, and continental parties represent interests and may be led by forceful personalities. As Sigmund Neumann has persuasively argued:

> The reality of modern politics represents a much more complex picture than is suggested by the simple array of insiders and outsiders, of parties of patronage and parties of principles, of expediency, interests and Weltanschauung, of personages and programs. Such precise but utterly imaginary partitions fail to reveal the inner dynamics and tensions of a functioning democracy. In fact, it is the inexhaustible mixture of all these elements that comprises the life of modern political parties—and perhaps escapes any rigid classification.[7]

A more useful scheme of classification is in terms of degree of centralization and discipline. Robert Michels, in his classic study of *Political Parties*, argued that the dominance of the leadership characterizes *all* mass parties, including those whose ideology is militantly democratic. Michels raised a significant problem of democratic theory. Democracy obviously involves some kind of control over the rulers by the people. Every democracy is run by political parties. But who runs the parties? To what extent can the leaders be controlled by those who hold subordinate positions in the organization?

Democratic parties vary greatly as regards the relative power of local units, members, national agencies, and leaders. American parties, for instance, are federations of state political organizations. There is no formal chain of command. National leadership results from coalitions among local party leaders, not from the directives of a powerful center. British parties, on the other hand, are national organizations with local branches. In both the Conservative and Labor parties decision making is vested in the leaders. Parties in parliamentary democracies run the gamut from the British model to the American. The two large parties of the Federal Republic of Germany are structurally similar to the British parties. Leadership in both the Social Democratic party and the Christian Democratic Union is concentrated at the national level and personalized. On the other hand, conservative and moderate parties in multiparty systems have relatively few active members and are run almost exclusively by parliamentarians.

In authoritarian systems the parties are always highly centralized and serve as admirable instruments of coordination and control. In all communist parties relations between local units and national bodies are proclaimed to be "democratic"—that is, each local unit elects delegates to the next highest organization, and all delegates are urged to "discuss" party policy. The impression is carefully cultivated that "democratic centralism" enables the party to act as a unit on the basis of widespread debate within the party ranks. In practice, however, "democratic centralism" vests plenary control of the party in the leadership and confines the role of militants to the execution of policy.

The degree of centralization and discipline within parties largely determines the "style" of the political process—that is, the level of the political system at which compromises are made, the degree of cohesion of parliamentary groups, and the nature of electoral appeals. Yet in all parties there is a sharp distinction between the leadership and the followers, and the latter are rarely in a position to shape or control policy.

Perhaps the most popular classification of party systems is in terms of the number of parties in the field. In his influential book, *Political Parties*, Maurice Duverger points out that the one-party, two-party, and multiparty systems tend to correspond to the major types of contemporary regimes. Thus, dictatorships are characterized by the single party, and democracies by either a two- or multiparty system. The two-party system is frequently held up as a model form, permitting the majority to govern and the minority to criticize. Multiparty systems

are usually considered less stable but offer the voter a greater choice of alternatives. However, this classification has come under attack. Some observers have suggested that one-party systems may serve as transitional forms, making possible the creation of a more democratic regime at a later time. Mexico is frequently cited as an instance in which one-party rule is compatible with democracy because debate can take place within the dominant party.

The customary distinction between two- and multiparty systems has also been questioned, particularly with regard to France and Scandinavia. French political scientists have called attention to the agreements (electoral alliances and cabinet coalitions) between parties of the same political family, which provide a measure of coherence. Thus, Francois Goguel speaks of the "party of order" and the "party of movement" in interpreting the conflict among the various parties of the Third Republic, in his *La Politique des partis sous la IIIᵉ République* (1946). In run-off elections under the Third and Fifth Republics the French voter has virtually been presented with a choice between only two (rarely three) serious candidates. Similarly, students of Scandinavia have pointed out that these multiparty systems are capable of sustaining dynamic and stable governments. The parties form coalitions in the same way that wings of a major party in Britain or the United States come to agreement on a common policy or leader. It may be more fruitful to view party systems in terms of the nature of the national consensus—that is, whether or not the major parties (within either a two- or multiparty system) and in turn the major social groups on which they are based share the same attitudes toward basic values and goals and the means by which they are to be attained.

In recent years party systems have been reappraised in the context of the general process of modernization. As a traditional society breaks up and takes on the characteristics of "modernity," it goes through a series political crises. The first is a crisis of *legitimacy*. Values sanctioning rule by a traditional monarchy or aristocracy are called into question and are eventually replaced by values such as parliamentary democracy or nationalism that are more consonant with mass participation in the political system. This goes hand-in-hand with a crisis of *participation*. New social groups, in particular an industrial middle class and a working class, make their appearance and demand entry into the political system. In mature industrial societies there is a continuing crisis of *conflict management*. The political system is confronted by the need to facilitate economic growth, reconcile the claims of powerful social groups for a greater share of wealth and power, and ensure the continued adherence of these groups to the system itself.

Political parties, it may be argued, have gone through stages of development that correspond to the successive crises of legitimacy, participation, and conflict management. Parties throughout Europe in the early part of the nineteenth century were primarily concerned with new principles of legitimacy and the representation of fairly narrow interests. With the extension of suffrage in the course of the nineteenth century the parties created mass organizations outside of parliament. Mass parties, like the German Social Democrat, British Liberal, and, later, Labor parties, sought to defend the interests of the new middle and working classes and to mobilize popular support for their policies. At this stage the parties tended to reflect sharp ideological orientations. The "parties of participation" had to make adjustments in order to cope with the demands of late industrialization, when problems became more complex and less susceptible to ideological solutions. They became more concerned with the management of conflict and tensions when in power, and more pragmatic in their appeals to the electorate.

One of the most noticeable trends affecting parties at present is the development of plebiscitary government. Its main trait is the bypassing or the diminution of the powers of all representative bodies in favor of personalized leadership stemming from direct popular support in periodic elections. In France under the Gaullist constitution, the President, as the political leader and head of the executive, now derives his powers from direct election. This is also the case for the American president and the British cabinet under the leadership of the prime minister, who is head of the majority party. The political parties select and nominate a leader who then appeals directly to the public. Although the parties may set broad policy guidelines, the personal appeal of the leader and his ability to secure widespread support may, in the last analysis, be the decisive factor for victory or defeat at the polls.

In France, plebiscitary government has an old and venerable lineage that goes back to Bonapartism. In all countries it is a reflection of profound social changes that have led to an increasingly homogeneous body politic. Under these altered circumstances the parties can no longer sell their ideological or policy programs. Large national formations vie for support on the basis of broadly similar appeals to consumer interests. As a result, identification with the party becomes weaker, or, to put it another way, the personality of a leader becomes more important. Correspondingly, the ratio of party members to voters, for the whole community and for each party, goes down, while there are growing numbers of independents or "floaters."

In totalitarian systems the ruling party excludes competition and uses the election as a well-controlled plebiscitary instrument. The leader in a communist system is likely to emerge only after he has proven himself within the party, which remains a powerful recruitment and screening agency. In presidential democracies nonparty people may, without any prior screening or testing, avail themselves of the plebiscitary character of the election. Even in Britain and other parliamentary democracies the struggle for leadership of the party, and certainly the general election itself, is greatly influenced by the personal qualities of the contending leaders. The logic of plebiscitary government applies to both Western democracies and totalitarian systems. The intermediary organs—including the parties and representative assemblies—

are weakened, and power is concentrated in the political executive. A continuing problem in all modern political systems is to create institutions that might counterbalance the tremendous political and decision-making powers of plebiscitary leaders.

## Interests

There are three basic models in terms of which the relationship between the state and interests can be viewed: pluralist, corporatist, and totalitarian. Each model, in turn, has versions reflecting the unique traditions and circumstances of individual nations.

In the pluralist (or democratic) model, interests (whether trade unions, business groups, professional associations, or churches) are autonomous and free to act. They make demands through publicity, electoral pressure, and direct or indirect action on the state. Their aim is to maximize their own interests at the expense of others, but in most cases there is accommodation and compromise. According to this model the state and its agencies respond to the constant demands of interest groups, and the public good is the sum total of particular interests. Under certain conditions pluralism may lead to stalemate—when competing interests are evenly matched. Some observers attribute recent indications of crisis in democracies to the inability of political institutions, including parties, to create a synthesis among competing and conflicting interests. The state becomes a captive of an interest universe that it cannot transcend.

In the corporatist authoritarian model it is assumed that clashes among interests are prejudicial to the public good. It is therefore necessary to secure cooperation among interests (and classes) under the overall direction and often control of the state. Some specific powers are delegated to interests—for example, to fix prices and wages, organize production in various sectors of the economy, and assume responsibility for social and welfare services—but all interests and associations operate under state control. Interest groups do not enjoy autonomy; their relations with other groups are structured and supervised by public agencies. They are not free to pressure the state, nor to communicate among themselves in order to make compromises or strike bargains. They function as part of the state structure, not as free agents acting upon the state.

In the totalitarian model interests and professional associations are taken over physically or are absorbed by the state. This is notably the case in communist systems in which the means of production and virtually all economic and entrepreneurial activities are run by the state and its agencies. The interest groups have no independent resources, no freedom to take their case to the public, and no autonomy. The political elite dominates the interest universe and infuses it with its own purpose and imperatives; how effectively depends on a number of factors: the strength of the single political party, the appeal of the official ideology, the tenacity of past political culture, and the level and degree of economic modernization. The Soviet Union, Rumania, China, and Vietnam differ markedly, though they all propose the same subordination of interests to an official ideology and party.

These models rarely exist in a "pure" or ideal form. In most democracies the pluralist model has been qualified by corporatist practices whereby interest groups and professional associations work closely with state agencies in the making and carrying out of public policy. We speak of corporate pluralism in evidence in Scandinavia. In communist systems interest groups have been able to interact with the party and state agencies, and in some cases have acquired a modicum of autonomy. Corporatist practices have become current everywhere as groups assert their identity.

## POLITICAL INSTITUTIONS

Interests and interest groups are the raw material of politics. Through the political parties, or through other larger groupings, they press their claims upon the governmental structures and the decision-making organs of the political system. Policy is often the result of such claims. The farmers wish protection, the workers ask for wage increases, the military for special appropriations, the church for subsidies, and the business community for lower taxes. To the uninitiated the striving for satisfaction by various interest groups, the multiplicity and the intensity of conflicts, and the incompatibility of the interests involved often make a political community seem something like a jungle in which the survival of the fittest or the strongest appears to be the only rule.

Yet over and above interest and interest conflict there is a basic consensus on the fundamental rules of the game—that is, the acceptance of certain rules according to which conflict will be waged, interests articulated, and conflict resolved. All political systems are characterized by the existence of these rules—what A. D. Lindsay in his book *The Modern Democratic State* calls "operative ideals." That is, in every political society there is an organ that makes decisions according to certain procedures, and these decisions are accepted and obeyed. The state has authority and prestige, not only force.

## Constitutions

The general organization and structure of authority is in essence a "constitution." Whether written or unwritten a constitution expresses the "fundamental agreement" of the political society on how it will be governed. It usually defines the scope of governmental authority, the way in which decisions are made, and the manner in which decision makers are selected and held accountable. It both creates and limits power. The legacy of the Middle Ages was to define what today we call rights that limit arbitrary power and narrow the scope of the state's authority. With the beginning of the nineteenth century most political systems began to establish responsibility of the governors to the governed

through representative assemblies and periodic elections.

A system in which a constitution is widely accepted may be referred to as *consensual*; that is, the people in it agree on how they will resolve their differences. They do not "bicker about fundamentals." Political systems may well be classified, therefore, in terms of this criterion. In some systems the agreement on fundamentals is not widely shared or intensely felt—they have a *low degree of consensus or legitimacy*. In others, there is no such agreement—they are *highly divided or transitional systems*. In still others, the agreement is overtly manufactured through the control of the media of communication by a small group of political leaders—this is the case in authoritarian systems. But authoritarianism is not in itself evidence of low consensus, for in some cases leadership may bring about a high degree of unity and perhaps popular support.

The distinction between consensual and highly divided systems may be illustrated by the cases of Great Britain and France. In both countries the feudal scheme was disrupted, the traditional monarchy was severely restricted or overthrown, and parliamentary democracy was introduced. The British monarchy during the seventeeth century proved to be less adaptable than the French. The loss of its prerogatives was registered in the Declaration and Bill of Rights of 1689. That is, by the end of the seventeenth century parliamentary sovereignty was enunciated as the basic principle of the British constitution. Political conflict did not disappear, and the monarch continued to exert great influence upon his ministers and the Parliament. With the extension of suffrage in the nineteenth century, the political base of the House of Commons was transformed. Its legitimacy now derived from the people, whose will was expressed and shaped by mass political parties. These new forces accepted the venerable principle of parliamentary sovereignty and the practice of parliamentary government.

The new interests and classes created by the Industrial Revolution thus found a ready-made instrument for the resolution of their conflicts.

Slowly the system absorbed, or rather integrated, the new groups, notably the industrial middle class and the workers. But in so doing the political institutions were themselves greatly modified. The country was governed not by an independent and narrowly based House of Commons, but rather by disciplined parties, the cabinet, and the civil service. The need for strong leadership and the increasing importance of the personality of the leader strengthened the position of the prime minister; on the other hand, the growing complexity of administration made it difficult for the cabinet to function as a collective agency. The trend in the modern era has been toward the concentration of power in the prime minister, who dominates the cabinet much as the cabinet previously dominated Parliament.

In France and other countries of the continent, a radically different situation prevailed. Parliaments in these countries knew an uneasy and eventful life, becoming the source of unresolved opposition to the powers of the king or the nobility. The French representative assemblies were not allowed to meet for over a century and a half. When finally they met in 1789, they set aside the powers of the king and ushered in a period of turmoil. A democratic constitution was accepted only by a part of the population. The nineteenth century was a period of conflict and struggle in which sometimes democracy and sometimes monarchy or personal government (Bonapartism) triumphed. The working classes found it impossible to accommodate themselves to one or the other form and developed a utopian or revolutionary outlook. Thus by the end of the nineteenth century there was no widespread agreement in France about any constitution; sizable fractions of the population had not been integrated into the system; and people remained divided not only about interests and aspirations but also on how they should resolve their conflicts. The French found it difficult to "agree on how they were to disagree."

Throughout the nineteenth and twentieth centuries, constitutional instability was also the rule in most other European countries where sharp incompatibilities and ideological divisions were very much in evidence. The threat of revolutionary uprising by the underprivileged groups that had never been fully integrated into the system was ever present. The Bolshevik Revolution of 1917 gave sharpness and meaning to their demands. The Nazi system in Germany and, to a lesser degree, the Fascist system in Italy, gave hope to the wealthier groups, to the military, to some of the conservative elements of the Church, and to the many lower-middle-class groups that a "strong" government based on one-party rule could provide stability and unity. Both the Bolshevik and Fascist movements imperiled democratic constitutionalism and provided their followers with an armed vision that undermined the tolerance and agreement on which democracy rests.

## Governmental Institutions

The decision-making functions of all political societies have been divided traditionally into three separate types: the executive, the legislative, and the judicial. However, this threefold division is not a realistic guide to the exercise of political power. In some systems the legislature assumed the totality of decision-making power, with the executive simply executing the will of the lawmakers and the judiciary applying and interpreting the law in case of litigation. In other instances, a precarious balance between the executive and the legislature was established, with the executive slowly assuming increased powers and independence of action. In other systems—notably those with a federal organization of power—the judiciary emerged as a genuinely independent organ with wide latitude to interpret the constitution and in so doing to limit the powers of the legislature and the executive.

The nineteenth century was the period of legislative supremacy in most of the Western constitutional democracies. Walter Bagehot, writing in the latter part of the century, pointed out that the Parliament nominated the members of the executive, passed laws, prepared and voted the budget, supervised the cabinet, and finally aired grievances and ventilated issues, thus helping to mold and shape public opinion. It was primarily a body of people who represented the upper and middle classes of the community, who fundamentally agreed about the policies to be pursued unharried, and who embodied the complacency and stability of the Victorian period. They usually debated broad political problems—educational reform, extension of the franchise, the rights of associations and individuals, and international treaties. Controversy was resolved in compromise that could be spelled out in general parliamentary enactments. This was also the case in some other systems in which parliamentary democracy developed—Sweden, Holland, Norway, and Denmark. In the United States the pendulum swung between "presidential" government, especially in times of crisis, and "congressional" government.

On the continent representative assemblies were often regarded as the instruments of popular rule against the privileged groups. They claimed on behalf of the people the totality of political power, and they relegated the executive to the role of an agent. This was notably the case of France, where the legislative assemblies reduced the cabinet to a subservient role.

Outside of Western Europe, North America, and the British Dominions, representative government in the nineteenth century was virtually unknown. In the Balkans and Latin America, constitutions and parliamentary institutions were provided on paper, but the practice belied the constitutional forms. Most of these systems were oligarchies in which political power, irrespective of the forms, was in the hands of the landowners, the military, or the church. Others were traditional societies, in which political rule was hereditary. They had not experienced the conflicts and modernization, associated with the French Revolution and industrialization, that led to progressive political emancipation of the masses in Europe. Their political systems were encrusted in tradition and immemorial custom.

With the beginning of the twentieth century, an important change in the organization and functioning of democratic institutions can be discerned. The internal balance of power between the three organs—executive, legislative, and judicial—began to shift in favor of the executive. This trend reflects profound modifications in the social and political structures of modern societies.

Representative institutions operated well when the pressure upon them to make decisions was light. The free-market system provided an automatic mechanism of decision making. Matters of wages, hours of work, employment, social security, education, technological improvement, investment, and economic development were to remain outside of the province of the state. The increasing complexity of the industrial society called, however, for regulation of economic activity. The need for state intervention grew and demanded special knowledge and skill. The legislature proved singularly unfit to perform these tasks. The legislature was cumbersome; its members had neither technical knowledge, nor expertise, nor time. Slowly the burden of decision making shifted to the political executive and the civil service.

Political reasons also accounted for this shift. Most significant were the extension of suffrage and the growth of large national parties. The two phenomena are historically associated. Elections increasingly became confrontations between two or more parties appealing to a mass electorate on specific issues or on a general program for action. Thus the legislature was bypassed, for victory at the polls meant that the leadership of the majority party would form a government to carry out its pledges. Whenever party discipline was strong, therefore, popular elections were equivalent to the selection of the "government," i.e., the executive.

Political and technical trends reinforced each other, and during the interwar years the executive assumed more and more powers. Representative assemblies have lost virtually all of the functions attributed to them by Walter Bagehot in the nineteenth century. The vast majority of legislative projects emanate from the executive; the preparation of the budget has become an executive function in which the cabinet, in association with the top civil service or independent executive bodies, drafts the specifications involving public expenditures and revenue. Parliament has even virtually lost the power to nominate the cabinet. Finally, the very scope of lawmaking has changed. Special laws or regulations are needed that can best be made by those in touch with the problems of developed industrial societies—that is to say, by the executive departments and the civil service. Thus the legislature has fallen into the habit of drafting general laws in which regulatory powers are generously delegated to the executive. For all practical purposes such delegation is so broad as to invest the executive and civil service with virtual lawmaking powers.

In modern political systems, then, leadership has shifted to the executive, with the legislature acting mainly as a forum for the airing of grievances. The executive has taken the initiative as regards general lawmaking, foreign and defense policy, and direction of the economy. Assumption of these responsibilities and the concentration of these functions in the executive branch have led to a proliferation of new agencies and bureaus. The political executive has become "bureaucratized." It initiates policy, coordinates policy decisions, and is responsible for their implementation and execution. Institutions corresponding to these three phases of the policy-making process have developed within the executive.

In both presidential and parliamentary systems, a small group of political leaders is in charge of overall policy initiation and formulation. They are the president (or the prime minister) and his or her immediate advisers. To assist the top leaders in the formulation of policy there are a number of "adjunct" administrative staff organizations. They draft policy papers on economic planning, foreign policy, defense, and the budget. In the United States, the Office of Management and the Budget, the National

Security Council, and the Council of Economic Advisers perform important deliberative and policy-initiation functions. In Britain and France, presidential and cabinet committees are responsible for similar activities. Thus deliberation is institutionalized at the executive level.

Policy proposals put forward by various executive agencies must then be coordinated. Suggestions and countersuggestions are thrashed out in the cabinet, or in small ministerial committees made up of top civil servants, the chiefs of staff, and the personal advisers to the president or prime minister. Reconciliation of conflicting proposals may require the ultimate personal intervention of the president or prime minister. The interdependence of military, economic, and foreign policy has called increasingly for such interdepartmental coordination.

Finally, it is necessary to implement decisions. This is the task of the vast majority of civil servants—to inspect, repair, perform, and check. They do what the employees of any large corporation do—they perform on the basis of orders and regulations decided by their superiors.

## THE BUREAUCRACY

It is one of the characteristics of industrial societies, irrespective of their form of government, to develop a civil service recruited on the basis of specific technical requirements. "Bureaucratic administration means fundamentally the exercise of control on the basis of knowledge," observed Max Weber. It is above all a rational organization characterized by: (1) a clearly defined sphere of competence subject to impersonal rules; (2) a hierarchy that determines in an orderly fashion relations of superiors and subordinates; (3) a regular system of appointments and promotions based on free contract; (4) recruitment on the basis of skills, knowledge, or technical training; and (5) fixed salaries.

The Prussian civil service was an early example of a professional service with clear-cut demarcation of spheres of competence, rigid rules of recruitment, and allocation of posts on the basis of skills. It reflected the high degree of military organization and centralization of that country. After the unification of Germany the same standards were made applicable to the whole German bureaucracy.

In Great Britain professionalization was introduced officially in 1853 by the Northcote-Trevelyan Report on the "Organization of the Permanent Civil Service," which opened the civil service to talent through competitive examinations. Until then civil service appointments were made on political considerations and were, by and large, restricted to the nobility. The civil service was divided into three "classes," each corresponding to a distinct function: (1) the administrative class, which is the highest policy-making group within the departments; (2) the executive class, whose main task is the execution of policies; and (3) the clerical or manipulative class, whose work is primarily clerical and manual.

In France it was only after the Liberation in 1944 that drastic reforms—inspired in large measure by the organization of the civil service in Britain—were made. First, a general entrance examination has been established for all candidates: previously, each department did its own recruiting. The examination stresses law, political science, economics, and social sciences in general. Second, the civil service was broadly divided into two classes: (1) civil administrators (approximating the British administrative class) and (2) "secretaries of administration" (corresponding to the executive class). Third, the *Ecole Nationale d'Administration* has been founded to serve as the training school for all prospective civil administrators. Students are considered public officials from the moment they enter, they receive a stipend, and after successful completion of their studies and the passing of the final examinations they are assigned to an executive department. Throughout their training, which is jointly offered by civil servants and academicians, an effort is made to depart from the formalistic and legalistic approach so typical of the past and to create a self-reliant and imaginative civil servant.

The American civil service has also been "professionalized," beginning with the Pendleton Act of 1883. Recruitment is by competitive examinations, but the emphasis tends to be on specialized knowledge rather than a broad, liberal education. There is no clear-cut division between an administrative and an executive class in terms of rigidly separate educational requirements and examinations, though of course those who occupy the highest "general classes" within the hierarchy in effect perform the policy-making function. The American civil service thus is not as homogeneous as its European counterparts. American top-level administrators are graduates of universities all over the nation and are drawn from a wider range of social classes. There is also considerable movement of individuals between the civil service and private life (business, universities, and law practice, for example), not common in Europe. The undoubted advantage of the European system is the creation of a corps of administrators who have demonstrated brilliance in academic studies during their youth and who have shared common experiences; the result is a remarkable *esprit de corps*. In the United States, on the other hand, it is easier to invigorate the administrative establishment by providing new recruits from private life, and also to make use of talented individuals who may not have distinguished themselves in universities.

Traditionally "bureaucracy" has been viewed as an instrument of enforcement and execution of the law. Impartial and neutral—at least in theory—it was also remote, incarnating the authority and majesty of the state. It emphasized legality rather than equity, application of rules rather than innovation, continuity rather than change. The civil servant (or "mandarin," as called by the French) remained aloof from everyday affairs, saw more files than citizens, and made decisions of a quasi-judicial character.

But in some respects modern bureaucracy has departed from the Weberian model of a legal–rational organization. The increase in sheer numbers and the expansion of functions produced profound changes. The civil servant became ubiquitous and, as a result, less aloof and remote from the society that was governed. By taking on new responsibilities, bureaucrats were transformed from guardians of the law into quasi legislators. Their powers became increasingly political and had immediate consequences for those affected by their decisions and for the whole society. The bureaucrats' world was expanded, and they began to view their constituency not as a host of individual plaintiffs who sought redress in accordance with the law, but as groups and interests pressing for decisions affecting the very nature of social relations. They found themselves confronted with conflicts among interests that called for political analysis and choice among alternatives. While still clinging to the tradition of statism and neutrality, the bureaucrat and the bureaucracy as a whole became integral parts of the policy-making process.

The civil servants' mentality inevitably changed when they entered the realm of direct action in the world of commerce and industry. The skills required to set regulations for, let us say, credit, are different from those needed to apply laws in individual cases. The people responsible for the use of atomic energy to produce electricity, for construction of new cities, for settlement of labor disputes, or for maintenance of full employment no longer resemble their nineteenth-century counterparts. The requisites of bureaucratic decision making are knowledge, expertise, originality, inventiveness, and an ability to gain cooperation and support from the interests involved. Civil servants who participate in the drafting of an economic plan must not only know their own jobs, but must be in touch with the interest groups that are affected by the plan.

Consultation with the organized interests and mutual interpenetration of interests and the civil service has become general. The old bureaucracy based on "imperative coordination" has become a "consultative" bureaucracy making decisions that affect the whole society, thoroughly permeated by the interests it serves. Although links have always existed between organized interests and bureaucracy, the open consultative process is a central feature of modern political systems. Interest groups in the past have attempted to colonize, influence, or neutralize the bureaucracy, and they usually tried to maintain anonymity while doing so. Now the dialogue is open, the anonymity has been shed, and decisions engage the responsibility of the civil servants who make them. The bureaucracy thus takes on some of the characteristics of political parties in seeking close ties with specific interests (like business or labor) and broad popular support from all consumers and citizens. The "mandarin" has become a manager and a politician, whereas the spokepersons of interest groups and executives of private corporations are directly involved in the decision-making process. A "new corporatism" seems to be emerging in all modern political systems.

The executive has thus become in all contemporary industrialized societies a huge bureaucracy in which millions of people work and perform thousands of interrelated tasks. A small group of people are ultimately responsible for the policies made and the manner in which they are implemented. They alone have to confront the public in periodic elections and give an account of their activities. They have to answer questions raised in the representative assemblies and reply to criticism. They have the burden of political responsibility—and this applies to authoritarian and democratic systems alike, though the forms of enforcement may differ.

But political responsibility, even when enforced through periodic elections and accountability to legislative assemblies, is not enough. The magnitude and the complexity of modern government are so great that no legislature (not even through its committees) can take full cognizance of them. Legislative control has often proven inadequate for effective supervision of the operations of nationalized industries, the performance of regulatory agencies, and many other technical decisions.

The crucial problem facing all democratic systems today is to devise other forms and techniques of executive accountability. One possibility is the development of a sense of "internal responsibility" within the civil service itself. This can be inculcated by education and the development of strict rules of performance and rules of accountability of subordinate to superior. Another technique often suggested is the creation of specialized legislative committees to deal with specific areas of executive activity— nationalized industries, delegated legislation, defense, and the budget. A third one is the establishment of advisory bodies in which the major interests affected by policy decisions may participate. Recently there has been considerable discussion concerning the parliamentary Ombudsman (or Grievance Person) in Scandinavia and the possibility of transplanting this office in other parts of the world. None of these techniques, however, appear to be fully successful, and the truth of the matter is that they cannot be. The notion of "political responsibility" appears to be increasingly anachronistic in an era of massive technological development. The leaders of any modern society—democratic or authoritarian—confront the challenge of implementing common aspirations. Success or failure depends mainly upon the technical competence and skill of the political leadership.

The growth of the executive and its assumption of policy-making functions, the tremendous expansion of public services coupled with the ineffectiveness of political controls over the bureaucracy, pose serious threats to individual freedom. A highly complex bureaucratized apparatus geared to performance is potentially an ever-present danger to the individual, even when it claims to serve his or her interests. To the old "reason of state" may be added a new, perhaps even more dangerous "reason of service." Managerialism or *technocratie*, as the French call it, may finish by exalting efficiency, skill, and organization over criticism, freedom, and individualism. It may encourage conformity rather than eccentricity, unity rather than pluralism, action rather than thought, and discipline rather than freedom. An astute author writing some forty years ago predicted that managerialism would be the political form of the future in all contemporary industrialized societies—democratic or not.[8]

The rise of the large bureaucratized state as well as the example of totalitarianism have aroused widespread concern for the protection of individual rights and freedoms. In some post-Second World War constitutions, higher courts were given power to scrutinize legislative acts and see to it that the legislative and executive branches remained strictly within the confines of the constitution. In West Germany, Italy, Austria, and recently in France, constitutional courts were established for this purpose. In both Britain and the United States administrative courts have been created to try cases involving litigation between the state and individuals. "Administrative law," long misunderstood by American and British observers of the French scene, has developed slowly as a guarantee of the rights of individuals in their dealings with the administrative and regulatory agencies of the state.

Other safeguards have also been sought. Federalism, for instance, has as a major purpose internal limitation upon the omnicompetence of the state. Even in unitary states like Britain and France, efforts have been made to revitalize local governments in order to stimulate experimentation and avert uniformity and rigidity of centralized control.

However, the technique of judicial review and the effects of administrative courts and federalism have not proved capable of bringing central bureaucracies under effective political or legal control. The problems of modern society are so complex and far-ranging that protecting the governed by enforcing responsibility of the governors remains a central political problem.

## Notes

1. Karl Deutsch, *Nerves of Government*, rev. ed., (New York: Free Press, 1966).

2. See Max Weber, *The Theory of Social and Economic Organization* (London: Oxford University Press, 1947), pp. 407–412.

3. From James Bryce's preface to M. Ostrogorski, *Democracy and the Organization of Political Parties* (New York: Macmillan, 1902).

4. See A. D. Lindsay, *The Modern Democratic State* (New York, 1947); R. M. MacIver, *The Web of Government* (New York, 1947); Carl J. Friedrich, *Constitutional Government and Democracy* (Boston, 1946); Joseph Schumpeter, *Capitalism, Socialism and Democracy* (New York, 1947); and Walter Lippmann, *Public Opinion* (New York, 1945).

5. See the argument in R. T. McKenzie, *British Political Parties* (London, 1955).

6. See contribution by Gwendolyn Carter and E. E. Schattschneider in Sigmund Neumann, ed., *Modern Political Parties* (Chicago: University of Chicago Press, 1956), pp. 103 and 215; and M. Duverger, *Les partis politiques* (Paris: Armand Colin, 1954), p. 465.

7. Sigmund Neumann, ed., *Modern Political Parties* (Chicago: University of Chicago Press, 1956), p. 401.

8. J. Burnham, *The Managerial Revolution* (New York: John Day, 1941).

# CHAPTER SIX

# Groups, Parties, and Elections

## 22

## Groups and Group Theory

*Roy C. Macridis*

Without attempting to enter into a detailed discussion it would seem to me that group analysis is (epistemological labels may be used without implying any guilt by association) a crude form of determinism. Interest is the primary propelling force and every action is based upon sharing of interest. Power configuration is basically the configuration of competing and struggling interests organized into groups. Ideology, values, the state, the formal organization of political decision making, and the content of decisions are determined by the parallelogram of group forces. Perhaps this may be an oversimplification, but I do not think that it does violence to the scheme of group analysis. It is interesting, for instance, that not only concern with the state recedes into the background in the writings of all proponents of the group theory, but also the role of ideology, of extra-economic and non-rational motivational patterns, and of the political system as an independent factor influencing group behavior.

But while Marx with his class theory and its deterministic underpinnings provided a broad theory of history and development through which man would ultimately be able to shed

SOURCE: Roy C. Macridis, "Interest Groups in Comparative Analysis," *The Journal of Politics*, vol. 23, no. 1 (February 1961). By permission.

interest in order to attain freedom—that is, while Marxist determinism led progressively to higher stages of consciousness and perception of the environment, group theorists anchor man's life into the perennial group conflict which by their very nature groups can never transcend. Not only our lives remain intolerably and unredeemably "nasty and brutish," but our theoretical universe in terms of which we can explain behavior becomes unduly restricted. Interest is the propelling force and man is forever destined to live in an environment that mirrors interest. It may be argued that group theory is "realistic" and, furthermore, that the "group" is a far more useful concept analytically than "class." I doubt it very much—first, because group analysis as I have noted has normative implications and second and more important, because the concepts of "interest" and "group" are fuzzy analytically, perhaps just as much as that of the "class."

But the above criticisms involve philosophic questions that are highly controversial. What is more important for our discussion is that group theory puts exaggerated demands upon empirical research and data collection. If an understanding of a political system at a given moment depends upon the study of the total configuration of interests the task of the political scientist becomes stupendous. We have to study every and all interest groups, index them and measure carefully and constantly the increments of power and influence they generate before we can make any statements about the most meaningful aspects of politics—the resolution of conflict and policy making, including foreign policy. We would have to elaborate precise units of power in order to assess and reassess continuously group power. But such a measurement would involve so many variables that meaningful measurement and quantification would become hopeless.... Where then do we start and even more important where do we stop indexing and measuring group power and interaction: business interests, economic interests, labor interests, religious interests, local interests, bureaucratic interests, organized interests, to say nothing of potential groups that hide in their bosom potential interests that are ready to blossom forth? How many of them do we study and exactly for what purpose? The index of power at any given moment would be inaccurate unless we measure the potential counter-power that can be generated by the potential groups. How can we tell exactly under what conditions groups will compromise? What can we learn about the perception that groups have of other groups or the total group configuration? How can we measure the adherence of groups to the "rules of the game" that in all political systems curb, limit, and often shape group action? What I am saying, of course, is that group analysis may prove to be both self-defeating and misleading. We cannot know the power configuration in a society unless we have studied all groups as they interact, and when we do so we still do not know why groups interact in one manner rather than another.

Finally, group analysis seems to beg rather than answer the very question it purports to ask—to give us an explanatory frame of reference in terms of which we can account for differences and uniformities in political behavior and action. This is the central problem of comparative analysis. Group theory assumes the existence of organized groups or interests that can be defined in objective terms; labor, business, and agriculture are some of the more obvious and frequently studied ones. It is further assumed that their members have a common perception of the interest involved which accounts for the very formation of the group and its organization and articulation. So far so good. Descriptive and comparative study immediately presents us with extreme variations in the organization, cohesiveness, membership strength, forms of action, and patterns of interaction among these groups. It reveals some striking differences in the manner in which interest groups in various political systems relate to the political parties and the political processes.

To attempt to explain such differences in terms of a group theory is impossible. Why are, for instance, agricultural groups so well organized under the National Farmers Union in England, to which more than 90 percent of the farmers belong, but dispersed and relatively unorganized in the United States and France? Why are more than 85 percent of all manufacturing concerns in England represented in their national association while not more than 6 percent are so represented in the United States? Why do more than 50 percent of the British workers belong to trade unions which are almost all represented in their peak organization, the TUC, while in France membership remains low and articulation of labor interest dispersed in at least four trade union organizations? Why is it that in England interest groups avoid large publicity campaigns and center their attention on the party and the cabinet, while in the United States interest groups perform important publicity and propaganda functions through the media of communications and center their efforts on the electorate and the legislature, primarily, while French interest groups shy publicity and center their activities upon the legislature and the administration?

A number of answers can be given to these questions in the form of propositions to be carefully investigated, but I submit none of them are researchable in terms of group analysis. The answers are often given (without adequate evidence, to be sure) in terms of other categories: the American political system *with multiple foci* of decision making, for instance, makes the legislature and more particularly individual legislators more susceptible to pressure either directly or indirectly; *the diffusion of power* in the political party in the United States makes any effort to control or influence the party unrewarding for pressure groups; the same applies for France, where it is often pointed out that "interest" and "interest groups" are divided and sub-divided and lose their "objective" or "real" interest *because of political reasons*. The workers, the farmers, the teachers have no spokesmen and no cohesive and disciplined interest articulation because they are divided into a number of "political" or "ideological" families. As for group interaction, again the differences are striking: in some cases, groups interact within a given political party and compromise their differences; in other cases, compromise is made outside of the political parties, or is not made at all, leading to immobility; elsewhere compromise is made impossible by virtue of the fact that interests are "colonized" by ideological parties so that interest groups mirror the ideological divisions of the society instead of causing them.

*In all cases the reasons advanced for a given pattern of group organization, action and interaction derive from categories other than group analysis would suggest:* the formal organization of power; the cohesiveness or dispersal of political power; the two-party or multiparty configuration; the "climate of public opinion"; the intensity of consensus or lack of same in given political systems. . . .

Let me further illustrate the shortcomings of group analysis as an explanatory theory by borrowing from the conclusions of authors interested in comparative study or who did field work in foreign political systems. Professor Ehrmann writes in his introduction to *Interest Groups on Four Continents*: "The political system, as well as the social structure, will often decide whether claims raised in the name of special interests will be successful or not; it may determine the "style" used by pressure groups when raising their demands."[1] Professor Lavau, after indicating in detail the fragmentation of many French interests because of ideological reasons, points out that "this hostile ideological and moral climate surrounding pressure groups in France reacts in turn upon their behavior." He

indicates that some pressure groups if *not politicized* play an aggregative and integrative role that the French political parties do not play. This is, for instance, the case with some peak organizations that include a variety of professional groups. "Since it is [their] function to arbitrate or mediate possible conflicts between different member organizations, this role confers upon [them], in the eyes of the administration and the politicians, a considerable dignity."[2] In fact one of the most pervasive efforts of the French interest groups is to liberate themselves from a divided political culture and be able to organize their membership on the basis of interest alone. That they fail more often than they succeed is an indication of the importance, and what is more, the independence, of political and ideological factors. Professor Sam Finer accepts Beer's emphasis upon the British "consensus" and the general agreement of the British leadership on a number of policy issues as a factor that shapes and structures group action. He adds that such beliefs are brought together in English political life by the myth of "public interest" which provides a yardstick in terms of which interest claims are judged. The image of the national interest acts as a cohesive force. Professor Beer in an excellent analysis points to the parallel development in Great Britain of well organized and integrated political parties with well organized national interest groups.[3] For the purpose of our discussion this parallelism between interest organization and party organization is striking and one cannot avoid the impression that British interests gradually evolved a pattern of organization and cohesiveness *that corresponds* to and *parallels* the highly centralized and cohesive political system; that perhaps their "style" of action was conditioned by the cohesiveness of the political culture and the organization of political parties very much as the dispersion of the French interest groups may well have been shaped by the diversity of the French political culture and multipartism. Joseph LaPalombara[4] points out bluntly that many interest groups in Italy (and the same applies to France) operate within the political sub-cultures of the system (communist, catholic, socialist, etc.) resulting in an enormous proliferation (and the same applies to France) of pressure groups. Writing for the Swedish pressure groups Gunnar Heckscher points out that "there is hardly any point at which this term (politics of compromise) seems more definitely warranted than with regard to interest organizations: an equilibrium is maintained chiefly through the willingness of each of them to make concessions in order to achieve important results." But why? Because "the pluralistic character of the Swedish society is openly accepted on all sides." [5] Back we come to the general values of the community in terms of which the role of pressure groups and pressure group action and interaction can be explained. Jean Meynaud, in his comprehensive study of French pressure groups in France comes very close to a very important theoretical insight, when he points out that the fragmentation of parties like the fragmentation of the groups has its origin in the divisions in the public mind. [6] Political ideologies and religious considerations destroy the unity that would result from objective professional and interest considerations. A number of organizations mushroom *within the same* professional sector because of ideological reasons. One might hypothesize indeed that this parallelism between the political system and the interest configuration is true everywhere. *Whenever the political governmental organization is cohesive and power is concentrated in certain well-established centers the pressure groups become well organized with a similar concentration of power and vice versa.*

Despite the reputed advantage of concreteness, groups appear to be as elusive as some of the much criticized terms used in the past—such as the state, consensus, social structure, national character, or class; implicitly accepting the power theory, group analysts tend to embrace a theory of group determinism in which interest groups appear to be the most significant actors within a system with the individual, on the one hand, and the state on the other, receding in the background; from the standpoint of research in a political system group analysis compels the student, if he is to gain a solid view of a system, to study all groups and all patterns of group interaction—no clear-cut discrimination of what is relevant and what is not being offered. Indeed, when David Truman brings the potential groups into the picture any discriminating feature that group analysis might offer goes to the winds; finally, and what is very revealing, researchers who start with a group orientation finish by admitting the inadequacy of their approach—they tell us that in order to understand how groups behave and how they interact, we must study the political system, the overall behavior patterns, the values and beliefs held by the actors, the formal organization of authority, the degree of legitimacy, etc., etc. Without realizing it, they reverse their theoretical position. They start with the groups only to admit the primacy of the political phenomenon and suggest that in order to explain group behavior we must start with what group behavior purported to explain—the political system!

\* \* \*

The road to theory in comparative politics is a long one. Group theory claims that it is more "comprehensive" and "operational" in that it directs the student to the study of concrete and observable entities—the groups—and leads him immediately to the promised heaven of data-accumulation and explanation. When the real test of the utility of the theory comes, however—field work—groups prove to be just as stubborn in yielding their secrets as other structures and units of a system. Their pulsating reality often proves to be nothing but a ghost that haunts the field worker from one interest group office and organization to another, from one interest group publication to another. In some cases, especially in the underdeveloped systems where interest articulation is weak, the office may be vacant. Even where interest articulation and interest groups pulsate with life and vigor the student soon discovers that the "interest universe" overlaps with the political universe; that it is indeed enmeshed with the political universe in which tradition, values, habits, styles, and patterns of leadership and the governmental organization must be carefully studied before we begin to understand the system as a whole. The dichotomy between "interest" and "government" appears increasingly tenuous and the student has often to study the latter in order to understand better not only the manifestations and actions but also the motivation and organization of the former. He is soon forced to the conclusion that "interest" like any other activity in a system is conditioned by secular forces that have shaped the political culture of the community and that the best way to a theory of comparative politics is at this stage a comprehensive comparative look at the main features of a political system—political culture, social configuration, leadership, and governmental institutions. It is only such an approach, which requires a good understanding of the historical dimension of any and all political systems, that may help us differentiate between political systems and isolate those factors that may account for the diversities and similarities we observe.

## Notes

1. Henry Ehrmann, ed. *Interest Groups on Four Continents* (Pittsburgh: University of Pittsburgh Press, 1959), p. 1.

2. Ibid., pp. 61 and 78.

3. Samuel Beer, "Group Representation in Britain and the United States," *The Annals*, September 1958.

4. "The Utility and Limitations of Interest Group Theory in Non-American Field Situations," *Journal of Politics*, February 1960.

5. Gunnar Heckscher, "Interest Groups in Sweden," in Ehrmann, *Interest Groups on Four Continents*, p. 170.

6. Jean Meynaud, *Les Groupes de Pression en France* (Paris: Armand Colin, 1959), particularly chaps. 1 and 5.

# 23
# The Formation of Political Preferences
*Aaron Wildavsky*

The formation of political preferences ought to be one of the major subjects of political science. Although it is eminently reasonable to study—as most of us, including myself, have throughout our professional lifetimes—how people try to get what they want through political activity, it is also *unreasonable* to neglect the study of why people want what they want. To omit or slight the most important reason all of us have for studying politics, namely, educating our preferences, is a particularly unfortunate lapse for scholars.

I am making a double argument: first, on behalf of the usefulness of a cultural approach in general (rooting explanation in social life) and, second, on behalf of a particular cultural theory (cultures characterized by boundedness and prescription). Readers might find the first more persuasive than the second. There may be better formulations. My brief for the cultural theory that follows is based upon the usual criteria of parsimony and power, that is, getting the most explanatory and predictive capacity from the fewest variables. Challenges and improvements are welcome....

## PREFERENCES ARE ENDOGENOUS, NOT EXOGENOUS

...Cultural theory...is based on the premise that preferences are endogenous—internal to

SOURCE: Aaron Wildavsky, "Choosing Preferences by Constructing Institutions: A Cultural Theory of Preference Formation," *American Political Science Review*, vol. 81, no. 1 (March 1987), pp. 3–21. This essay is the presidential address presented in 1986 at the 82nd annual meeting of the American Political Science Association. Reprinted by permission of the American Political Science Association and the author. Essay, notes, and references abridged by the editors.

organizations—so that they emerge from social interaction in defending or opposing different ways of life. When individuals make important decisions, these choices are simultaneously choices of culture—shared values legitimating different patterns of social practices. Always, in cultural theory, shared values and social relations go together: there are no disembodied values apart from the social relations they rationalize, and there are no social relations in which people do not give reasons for or otherwise attempt to justify their behavior. When choices are not completely controlled by conditions (cultural theory holds), people discover their preferences by evaluating how their past choices have strengthened or weakened (and their future choices might strengthen or weaken) their way of life. Put plainly, people decide for or against existing authority. They construct their culture in the process of decision making. Their continuing reinforcement, modification, and rejection of existing power relationships teaches them what to prefer.

"If political preferences are molded through political experiences, or by political institutions," James March and Johan Olsen (1984) state, "it is awkward to have a theory that presumes preferences are exogenous to the political process" (p. 739). Cultural theory, by contrast, gives preferences an endogenous political explanation: preferences are formed through opposing and supporting institutions.

Rejecting a social science that begins at the end by assuming interests, I wish to make *what people want*—their desires, preferences, values, ideals—into the central subject of our inquiry. By classifying people, their strategies, and their social contexts into the cultural biases that form their preferences, cultural theory attempts to explain and predict recurrent regularities and transitions in their behavior. Preferences in regard to political objects are not external to political life; on the contrary, they constitute the very internal essence, the quintessence of politics: the construction and reconstruction of our lives together.

## DERIVING PREFERENCES FROM CULTURES: FOUR WAYS OF LIFE

Culture theory is based on the axiom that what matters most to people is their relationships with other people and other people's relationships with them. It follows that the major choice made by people (or, if they are subject to coercion, made for them) is the form of culture—shared values legitimating social practices—they adopt. An act is culturally rational, therefore, if it supports one's way of life.

A basic proposition of this cultural theory (which cannot be demonstrated here) is an impossibility theorem: there are only a limited number of cultures that between them categorize most human relations. Though we can imagine an infinite number of potential cultures, only a relatively small number (here I shall work with four) are filled with human activity; the rest are deserted. What makes order possible is that only a few conjunctions of shared values and their corresponding social relations are viable in that they are socially livable.

The dimensions of cultural theory are based on answers to two questions: Who am I? and What shall I do? The question of identity may be answered by saying that individuals belong to a strong group, a collective, that makes decisions binding on all members or that their ties to others are weak in that their choices bind only themselves. The question of action is answered by responding that the individual is subject to many or few prescriptions, a free spirit or a spirit tightly constrained. The strength or weakness of group boundaries and the numerous or few, varied or similar, prescriptions binding or freeing individuals are the components of their culture.

Strong groups with numerous prescriptions that vary with social roles combine to form hierarchical collectivism. Strong groups whose members follow few prescriptions form an egalitarian culture, a shared life of voluntary consent without coercion or inequality. Competitive individualism joins few prescriptions with weak group boundaries, thereby encouraging ever new combinations. When groups are weak and prescriptions strong—so that decisions are made for them by people on the outside—the controlled culture is fatalistic (see figure 1).

The social ideal of individualistic cultures is self-regulation. They favor bidding and bargaining in order to reduce the need for authority. They support equal opportunity to compete in order to facilitate arrangements between consenting adults with a minimum of external interference. They seek opportunity to be different, not the chance to be the same, for diminishing social differences would require a central, redistributive authority.

Hierarchy is institutionalized authority. It justifies inequality on grounds that specialization and division of labor enable people to live together with greater harmony and effectiveness than do alternative arrangements. Hence, hierarchies are rationalized by a sacrificial ethic: the parts are supposed to sacrifice for the whole.

Committed to a life of purely voluntary association, those from egalitarian cultures reject authority. They can live a life without coercion or authority only by greater equality of condition. Thus egalitarians may be expected to prefer reduction of differences—between races, or income levels, or men and women, parents and children, teachers and students, authorities and citizens.

An apathetic culture arises when people cannot control what happens to them. Because their boundaries are porous but the prescriptions imposed on them are severe, they develop fatalistic feelings: what will be, will be. There is no point in their having preferences on public policy because what they prefer would not, in any event, matter.

But none of these modes of organizing social life is viable on its own. A competitive culture needs something—the laws of contract—to be above negotiating; hierarchies need something—anarchic individualists, authority-less egalitarians, apathetic fatalists—to sit on top of; egalitarians need something—unfair competition, inequitable hierarchy, nonparticipant fatalists—to criticize; fatalists require an external source of control to tell them what to do. "What a wonderful place the world would be," say the adherents of each culture, "if only everyone were like us," conveniently ignoring that it is only the presence in the world of people who are not like them that enables them to be the way they are. Hence, cultural theory may be distinguished by a necessity theorem: conflict among cultures is a precondition of cultural identity. It is the differences and distances from others that define one's own cultural identity.

Alone, no one has power over anyone. Power is a social phenomenon; power, therefore, is constituted by culture. But the form and extent of manipulation vary. Apathetic cultures are manipulated; fatalists live by rules others make and impose upon them. Manipulation is built into hierarchies; orders come down and obedience presumably flows up. The evocative language of New Guinea anthropology (the "big men" versus the "rubbish men") expresses the growth of manipulation in market cultures as some people cease to possess the resources

| Number and Variety of Prescriptions | Strength of Group Boundaries | |
| --- | --- | --- |
| | Weak | Strong |
| Numerous and varied | Apathy (Fatalism) | Hierarchy (Collectivism) |
| Few and similar | Competition (Individualism) | Equality (Egalitarianism) |

**FIGURE 1**  Models of four cultures
SOURCE: Adapted from Douglas 1970; 1982.

to regulate their own lives. Egalitarians try to manipulate the other cultures by incessant criticism; they coerce one another by attributing inequalities to corruption and duplicity.[1]

To identify with, to become part of a culture, signifies exactly that: the unviable void of formlessness—where everything and therefore nothing is possible—is replaced by social constraint. Even so, individuals keep testing the constraints, reinforcing them if they prove satisfactory in practice, modifying or rejecting them, when possible, if unsatisfactory. It is individuals as social creatures, not only being molded by but actively molding their social context—shaping the maze as well as running it—that are the focus of cultural theory.

Suppose a new development occurs. Without knowing much about it, those who identify with each particular way of life can guess whether its effect is to increase or decrease social distinctions, impose, avoid, or reject authority—guesses made more definitive by observing what like-minded individuals do. Of course, people may be, and often are, mistaken. To seek is not necessarily to find a culturally rational course of action. Gramsci's would-be capitalists may try to establish hegemony over others, but they are often mistaken about which ideas and actions will in fact support their way of life. They may, for instance, use governmental regulation to institute a pattern of cumulative inequalities that convert market arrangements into state capitalism, leading to their ultimate subordination. To be culturally rational by bolstering one's way of life is the intention, not necessarily the accomplishment.

If social life is the midwife of political preferences, how do people get from culture to preferences? Perhaps politics is too complicated to allow many people to figure out what they prefer.

## "PREFERENCES NEED NO INFERENCES"

...How does the social filter enable people who possess only inches of facts to generate miles of preferences? What is it about cultures that makes them the kind of theories that ordinary folk can

use to figure out their preferences? The ability of people to know what they prefer without knowing much else lies at the crux of understanding preference formation. Culture codes can be unlocked, I maintain, because its keys are social. By figuring out their master preferences, as it were—who they are and are not, to what groups they do and do not belong—they can readily figure out the rest. A basic reason people are able to develop so many preferences is that they actually do not have to work all that hard. A few positive and negative associations go a long way.

It is no more necessary for a person to verbalize about culture than it is necessary to know the rules of grammar in order to speak. The stock phrases "one of us" versus "one of them" goes a long way. Preferences might come from insight into general principles, but, because meanings have to be shared, ideologues and theorists often discover that their views are rejected or modified by others. Preferences can and do come sideways, from identifications, experiences, and conversations. What matters is not how preferences are first proposed (many are called but few are chosen) but how they are ultimately disposed through the presence or absence of social validation. It is not the lone individual, after all, who creates what is called *ideological constraint* ("one thing entailing another") among preferences but social interaction among adherents of a particular culture in contrast to other cultures whose identifiers have different preferences....

## TWO TESTS OF CULTURAL THEORY: IDEOLOGY AND RISK

...One test of cultural theory is conceptual-historical; I contend that the cultural categories described here fit far better in accounting for political preferences than the usual left-right, liberal-conservative dimensions. A second test is both contemporary and future-oriented; I claim that perception of danger and disposition toward risk—from technology and from acquired immune deficiency syndrome—are better explained and predicted by cultural theory than by competing theories.

## A CONFUSION OF CULTURES: COMPETITIVE INDIVIDUALISM VERSUS EGALITARIAN COLLECTIVISM

The single worst misunderstanding about U.S. politics, in my opinion, is the joining together as a single entity, called "individualism," two separate and distinct political cultures with opposing preferences for policies and institutions—competitive individualism and egalitarian collectivism. Between equality of opportunity (enabling individuals to accentuate their differences) and equality of results (enabling them to diminish their differences), there is a vast gulf. To say that equal opportunity is empty without more equal results is to say that the latter is more important than the former.

Individualistic cultures prefer minimum authority, just enough to maintain rules for transactions, but they do not reject all authority; if it leaves them alone, they will leave it alone. While egalitarians also like to live a life of minimal prescription, they are part and parcel of collectives in which, so long as they remain members, individuals are bound by group decisions. This critical distinction in group-boundedness, the freedom to transact for yourself with any consenting adult vis-à-vis the requirement of agreement with group decisions, makes for a radical difference in the formation of political preferences.

The confusion to which I am objecting manifests itself more generally in the use of dichotomous instead of triangular designations of political cultures. The most infamous of these is left versus right. Left, or liberal, presumably designates a tendency toward greater use of central government for policy purposes, including an inclination to welfare state measures designed to be at least somewhat redistributive. Presumably, right, or conservative, signifies a

disposition against central governmental intervention in the economy but of greater respect for collective authority. As political shorthand, these terms have their uses. But for purposes of political analysis, they obfuscate more than they clarify. The preference for greater use of government may stem from a hierarchical culture in which the individual is subordinated to the group. Yet the very same preference for central governmental action may be rooted in a desire to reduce all social distinction, including those on which hierarchies are based. Hierarchies and egalitarian collectives may, in certain historical contexts, ally themselves in favor of redistributive measures, yet they may also, at the same time, be bitter opponents in regard to respect for authority. For equalization of statuses would destroy hierarchy. It is not easy, as the Catholic Church is learning, to say that all forms of inequality are bad but that popes and bishops are good. . . .

The left-right distinction is beset with contradictions. Hierarchical cultures favor social conservatism, giving government the right to intervene in matters of personal morality. Thus egalitarians may support intervention in the economy to reduce economic differences but not intervention in social life to maintain inequality. Libertarians, who are competitive individualists, oppose both social and economic intervention.

A division of the world into left and right that is equally inapplicable to the past and to the present deserves to be discarded. Efforts to read back the left-right distinction into U.S. history, for instance, succeed only in making a hash of it. In the early days of the republic, egalitarians pursued their objectives through severe restrictions on central government because they then regarded the center as monarchical, that is, hierarchical. Nowadays, after decades of dispute and struggle, they regard the federal government as a potential source for increasing equality. Their egalitarian objectives remain constant, but their beliefs about what will be efficacious instruments of policy vary according to the conditions of the times.

Without knowledge of the historical context, and therefore, without being privy to the internal discussions through which shared meanings are worked out, it is impossible to explain why a given culture prefers certain institutional arrangements and instruments of policy at one time and different ones on other occasions. How, nowadays, make sense of the Republican alliance of economic free markets and social conservatism or the Democratic combination of statism with distrust of authority? Is it the "left" that supports the authority of central government and the "right" that opposes it, or is it the "right" that respects authority and the "left" that denigrates it?

The division of the political universe into liberals and conservatives, when based on innate tendencies toward change, is bound to be misleading because historical context alters whatever the various political cultures wish to preserve. Given the current extent to which most proposals for government action involve redistribution of income or regulation of business, it is not surprising that people who are opposed to these policies have learned to dislike change. So, when asked, they reply that most change is for the worse. People who prefer these programs respond that they like change. Were the tables turned, so that most legislation was in favor of maintaining social and economic differences, say anti-abortion and anti-inheritance taxes, contemporary liberals would learn that most change is bad and their conservative opponents that change is by and large good.

In a rich analysis of differences and similarities among left- and right-wing activists, McClosky and Chong (1985) conclude that "thus, paradoxically, despite its patriotic fervour, spokesmen of the radical right are profoundly antagonistic to the status quo" (pp. 346–47). It is paradoxical if conservatism is identified with resistance to change but not if desire for change depends on perceived distance from desired behavior. Those who look at life from the conservative perspective "continually lash out against what they consider to be the government's conciliatory stance towards Communism,

its support for welfare programmes, (which, in their view, rewards laziness and lack of initiative), its encouragement of moral depravity (sexual license, tolerance of abortion, homosexuality, etc.), and its lenient treatment of criminals" (pp. 346–47). If readers believed that, they might also want big changes. What kind of changes we want depends not nearly so much on our predispositions toward change per se, as if the destination did not matter, but on the gap between desired and actual power relationships.[2]

The further the distance between the real and the ideal, the greater the desire for rapid and radical change. If this proposition is correct, it should follow that "left" or "progressive" forces, when they consider existing power relationships more desirable than proposals for change, should cling to the status quo with as much passion as any reactionary who prefers the last century to the present. Wandering in the void between the Articles of Confederation (interpreted as minimal central authority) and the Constitutional Convention (which, by comparison, elevated central power), the antifederalists preferred the past to the future. Worrying about the return of monarchy or, just as bad, monarchical principles, the individualist Jacksonians (who believed that equality of opportunity, rigorously enforced, would lead to relative equality of condition), fought a rearguard action against commercial capitalism.[3] Similarly, the Federalist party (a hierarchy coalescing with market forces to form an establishment) fought to achieve and maintain the relative centralization of the Constitution—a radical change from the immediate past.

An advantage of cultural theory is that it handles both economic and social issues without strain. Conover and Feldman (1981) wrote that

> traditionally, it was assumed that the meaning of ideological labels and self-identifications could be easily summarized in terms of a single dimension: the liberal/conservative continuum. In recent years, however, this viewpoint has undergone some modification. The decade of the 1970s ushered in a variety of "social" issues—abortion,

marijuana use, the Equal Rights Amendment—which did not fit easily into the traditional liberal/conservative spectrum. Because of this, many researchers now posit that the meaning of ideological labels and self-identification must be interpreted within the context of two liberal/conservative dimensions: one economic and one social. (p. 168)

Using cultural concepts, however, makes such ad hoc category massage unnecessary. Individualists, being nonprescriptive and anticollectivist, prefer minimal economic and social regulation. Egalitarians, combining nonprescription with collective decision, prefer strong economic but weak social regulation. And adherents of hierarchy, joining hard group boundaries to heavy prescription, desire strong social and economic regulation. Presumably, students of cultural theory would not be surprised at a U.S. president who (combining market individualism with social hierarchy, like his party) urges compulsory urine tests to detect drug users.

## CULTURE AND RISK

Comparing perceptions of danger is especially useful as a test of cultural theory. The subject abounds with anomalies; it is fiercely contested; rival theories are already in place; and, best of all, readers can check out the performance of cultural theory vis-à-vis its competitors by reading their daily newspapers. . . .

In discussions of technological danger, one theory is that people are reacting to the actual dangers; they are risk-averse because the risks are rising. Another theory is psychological; there are risk-taking and risk-averse personalities. Still another theory concerns an intuitive sense of justice: people are willing to accept dangers that are voluntarily undertaken, but they reject risks that are imposed on them. In *Risk and Culture* (1982), Mary Douglas and I argue that perception of danger is a function of political culture, risk acceptance going along with approval of individualistic and hierarchical cultures and

risk aversion with egalitarian opposition to these other cultures on the grounds they are coercive and domineering. Put briefly, we contend that the debate over risk stemming from technology is a referendum on the acceptability of U.S. institutions. The more trust in them, the more risk acceptance; the less trust, the more risk rejection.

Consider, in this context of competing explanations, a variety of survey findings. The first, a survey of the feelings of a variety of elites about the safety of nuclear power plants shows, among other things, an immense gap (far greater than survey research usually produces) between nuclear energy experts (98.7%) and the military (86.0%) saying "safe" compared to relatively tiny proportions of leaders of public interest groups (6.4%), movie producers and directors (14.3%) and elite journalists (29.4%). The difference between people expected to support and to oppose authority is very great.

A second poll compares the general public to executives of small and large corporations and environmentalists on a variety of preferences related to politics and public policy. Whereas around two-thirds of the general public and executives favor a strong defense, only a quarter of environmentalists give it a high priority. Maintaining order in the nation gets around 80% or more from everyone else but just 47% from environmentalists. On an egalitarian issue, such as having more say at work, the situation is reversed. Two-thirds of environmentalists and the general public give it a high priority but only a quarter of executives in large companies and two-fifths in small ones do the same (Bloomgarden, 1983). Polarization of elites is evident.

A third study surveys business and ecology activists vis-à-vis the general public in West Germany in regard to their political positions on a left-right basis. It is obvious that ecologists and business elites are divided (twice as sharply as the general public) on ideological grounds. . . .

Nuclear war may well be the greatest contemporary risk of all. Glenn Sussman (1986) has conducted a survey of U.S. and British anti-nuclear weapons activists in which he asked them to rate four goals: fighting rising prices, giving the people more say in important governmental decisions, maintaining order in the nation and protecting freedom of speech. A priori there is no reason to believe that these activists have anything else on their minds except opposition to nuclear war. Yet approximately two-thirds valued more say in government as their first priority while maintaining order got less than 5%.[4] If one posits a cultural connection between this "anti" activism and opposition to existing authority as inegalitarian, the low ranking of "order" makes more sense. Viewing environmentalists as protestors against inegalitarian institutions (recall their concern about "endangered species" and corporations that cause cancer) helps us understand their political alliances. Because Berkeley [California] constitutes a kind of political-medical museum for this purpose, we can observe a member of the city council, accused of spending too much time on foreign affairs instead of local concerns, respond, "You can't explain one without the other. If the money was not going to Central America, we would have the money to fix the sewers."

Why, if we are dealing with a reasonable adaptation to emerging knowledge, do attitudes to political authority distinguish so well positions on nuclear power? Why, if there are major personality differences, do ecologists and environmentalists and businessmen divide so neatly on general ideological grounds? Why, if it is the voluntary/involuntary distinction that matters, are there such strong and similar differences on public order and defense? Rooting explanation

in adherence to several different ways of life rather than the usual left-right dichotomy, I think, makes more sense out of the data.

A striking contemporary example connecting culture and risk comes from perceptions of acquired immune deficiency syndrome. The more hierarchical the group, I hypothesize, following cultural theory, the more it minimizes technological danger as the price of progress while maximizing fear of casual contact with people who have AIDS. For, in its view, when people violate divine commandments, the Lord brings plague. Conversely, egalitarians tend to grossly overestimate the dangers from technology (on grounds that the social and economic relationships they dislike are bad for your health) while minimizing the dangers from casual contact with carriers of AIDS. Gays are good in the egalitarian view because they are antiestablishment and because they reduce differences among people. Only cultural theory explains why, when we know a group's general ideology, we can tell how much danger they will impute to technology versus AIDS.

Now this conclusion, which is sure to be contested, depends on a substantial scholarly apparatus. How can laymen, that is, most of us most of the time, figure out what our preferences ought to be?

## THE CALCULATION OF PREFERENCES

How do people make so much, derive so many preferences, from so few clues? We know that

**TABLE 1** The double polarization in West Germany, 1980: Left versus right

| Respondents | (n) | "How would you describe your political attitude?" | | | | | |
|---|---|---|---|---|---|---|---|
| | | Strong left | Middle left | Center | Middle right | Strong right | No position |
| **Ecology activists** | (98) | 9% | 27% | 29% | 15% | 3% | 14% |
| **General public** | (1,088) | 3 | 16 | 39 | 23 | 6 | 12 |
| **Business leaders** | (130) | 1 | 8 | 30 | 49 | 8 | 3 |

SOURCE: Milbrath 1981a, 1981b; Lauber 1983.

most people are not interested in or knowledgeable about most issues most of the time. Consequently, the clues must be exceedingly simple. Even the highly educated and interested cannot know much about most matters of politics and policy, yet they are able to generate and express preferences when necessary. Indeed, the educated may well be getting more than their due from social scientists. Though they do know more about a few major issues than the less educated, people with high levels of formal education have many more preferences than they can know much, if anything, about. It is likely, therefore, that the highly educated have many more unfounded preferences than do those who have far fewer preferences about subject matter of which they know little.

Rational people, I have argued, support their way of life. By answering two questions, they are able to discover their cultural identity: Who am I? (free to negotiate or bound by a group?) and What should I do? (follow detailed prescriptions that vary with role or decide for myself?). Knowing who they are and are not—the cultures to which they do and do not belong—helps them to begin sorting their preferences. Cultural identity enables individuals to answer for themselves the crucial quantitative and qualitative questions about preferences: How many are they expected to have? What kind should these be? Fatalists know that they do not need to know anything (it won't matter) except what others tell them to do. They are prescribed to, not prescribing. Members of hierarchies can rule in whatever goes with their station and rule out whatever does not. By relying on others whose duty it is to take care of whatever they neglect and by positive reinforcement of this nonparticipation—it is normative not to act above (or, for that matter, below) your station—both groups come to learn how much of what kind of preferences they are expected to have and how much they can leave to the authorities. Individualists are expected to figure out for themselves whether and to what extent participation is worthwhile. There is no onus on nonparticipation.

Overall, it cannot be too difficult to arrive at preferences on most matters, because everyone does it. Just as we consider our connections with those who advocate petitions as a quick way of determining whether we would feel comfortable in signing, so do people in general learn how to know what they ought to prefer without knowing much about it. People who do not pay much attention to politics or public policy can nevertheless develop preferences by getting them from Berelson, Lazarsfeld, and McPhee's (1954) well-known ("But," as James Stimson [1986] reminds us, "we keep forgetting it") two-step flow of communication from activists to less attentive citizens. Stimson (1986) shows that "mass perceptions track activist positions." His thesis is that this social connection "accounts for the riddle of inattentive electorates who seem to know much of what they need to know to make policy informed choices." Wholly in the spirit of cultural analysis, Stimson concludes "that many of the things that matter in political life...have very little to do with individual psychological processes. They are macro behaviors, such as mediated cognitions, that require for understanding a focus on 'between' rather than 'within' individual effects" (pp. 4, 19, 20). All I would add is that "between...individual effects" *become* "within individual effects."

"System" or "person" blame are dead giveaways. The slightest clue as to whether the authorities and the institutions vis-à-vis individuals are at fault helps people know whether they want to go along with egalitarian or hierarchical or market policies. Anyone who thinks that attribution of blame to "the system" or to individuals is not diagnostic should consult table 2 from Verba and Orren, in which they address that very question to a variety of elites. The differences could hardly be greater.

If it were necessary to go back to the cultural source each time a new preference is involved, building back up to the actual preference through some sort of chain of inference, many people could not manage the complexity; hence there would be far fewer preferences.

**TABLE 2**  Poverty in the United States

| Group | Fault of poor | Fault of system |
|---|---|---|
| **Business** | 57% | 9% |
| **Labor** | 15 | 56 |
| **Farm** | 52 | 19 |
| **Intellectuals** | 23 | 44 |
| **Media** | 21 | 50 |
| **Republicans** | 55 | 13 |
| **Democrats** | 5 | 68 |
| **Blacks** | 5 | 86 |
| **Feminists** | 9 | 76 |
| **Youth** | 16 | 61 |

SOURCE: Verba and Orren 1985, p. 74.

Consequently, concerted political action would be a rarity. Near universal preference formation requires that preferences be inferred from all possible directions. Culture is the India rubber man of politics, for it permits preferences to be formed from the slimmest clue. By knowing who or what is involved, the arena or institution of involvement, the subject or object of involvement, people know whether they are supposed to have preferences and what these preferences ought to be.

What is it that enables everyone to come up with reliable solutions to the problem of preference formation whenever, it arises? The one source all human beings know something about is their social relations.

## CULTURES CONSTITUTE OUR POLITICAL SELVES

> Even when I carry out *scientific* work—an activity which I seldom conduct in association with other men—I perform a *social*, because *human* act. It is not only the material of my activity—like language itself which the thinker uses—which is given to me as a social product. *My own existence is a social activity.*
>
> —Karl Marx

The view of human life as suffused in social relations makes the study of institutions central to political science. To use Elkin's apt expression,

"Values are thus 'in' politics, not above or outside it. Michael Oakeshott's (1962) insistence on good form and better manners, his "idioms of conduct," is based on the understanding that the purposes institutions create are expressed in their practices (Elkin 1985, 17–18). Elkin goes on to say that "the institutions are a way in which citizens experience each other and for different institutions the form of experience is different. . . . Political institutions constitute the citizenry in the sense of. . .giving it an organized existence" (pp. 16–17). Wolin (1986) defines democracy as I would a political culture: "Democracy involves more than participation in a political process. It is a way of constituting power" (p. 2). Similarly, Connell and Goot explain that "politics must be invoked not merely as the outcome of political socialization but a cause thereof as well" (Cook 1985).

On the level of ideas, a research program on political culture would seek to increase our understanding of how opposed visions of the good life are selected, sustained, altered, and rejected. As social scientists following Robert Merton and knowing, therefore, that unanticipated consequences are a staple of social life, we want to understand what else we choose when we choose our political cultures. The Great Depression was a market phenomenon. The great holocaust was perpetrated by a hierarchy (the Nazi party) that tolerated no rivals. The second greatest holocaust was perpetrated by egalitarians (the Cambodian Khmer Rouge). . . . Deadly visions as well as virtues are also rooted in our public lives. Appraising the consequences of living lives of hierarchical subordination or of the purely voluntary association of egalitarian liberation or of the self-regulation of individualistic cultures, at different times, on different continents, with different technologies, languages, and customs would be a remarkably productive research program. So would comparing cultures rather than countries or, put precisely, comparing countries by contrasting their combinations of cultures. Such a research program would enable us to test the general hypothesis that how people organize their institutions has a more powerful effect on their preferences than any rival explanation—wealth, technology, class, self-interest, tradition, you name it. The field of preference formation is open to all comers.

## Notes

1. Michael Thompson argues in favor of the viability of his hermit category, a market-like people who, however, seek subsistence rather than domination, to escape (a) from manipulating others and (b) from being manipulated themselves. I wish them luck (see Thompson, 1982).

2. For the reasons given, I disagree with the view that liberals are pro- and conservatives anti-change (see McCloskey and Chong, 1985; and Robinson and Holm, 1980).

3. The widespread belief among those who theorized about Jacksonian democracy in this time, a belief apparently shared by their supporters in the citizenry as well, was that equality of opportunity, meticulously followed would lead to an approximation of equality of result. The operation of economic markets, unimpeded by the federal government, would eventually approximate real equality of condition as closely as innate differences in human ability permitted. At the very least, central government would not add artificial to natural inequality, thereby preserving representative government. Individuals would be allowed, indeed encouraged, to keep all gain that resulted from the unfettered use of their own talents. But everything artificial and unnatural, everything government imposed on man in his free state, such as charters, franchises, banks, and other monopolies, became anathema. It is this belief—not in equality undefined nor in just one kind of equality but in the *mutual reinforcement of opportunity and result*—that I think made the United States truly exceptional. Another way to describe U.S. exceptionalism is to say that liberty (i.e., individualism) is held to be compatible with equality (egalitarianism). Just as supporters of hierarchy understand that their organizations are likely to

be rigid and egalitarians recognize that perfect equality is unattainable, so adherents of U.S. individualism understand that liberty can conflict with equality and vice versa. What they deny is that this conflict is immutable, and what they affirm is that their two cherished passions, liberty and equality, can reinforce one another (see Wildavsky 1986).

4. The actual figures are 1) more say: U.S. citizens 64.5%, British 68.6%; 2) order: U.S. citizens 4.3%, British 2.1%; 3) freedom of speech scored a little over 25%; 4) rising prices were 4% or below.

## Author's References

BERELSON, BERNARD R., PAUL R. LAZARSFELD, and WILLIAM N. McPHEE. 1954. *Voting: A Study of Opinion Formation in a Presidential Campaign.* Chicago: University of Chicago Press.

BLOOMGARDEN, KATHY. 1983. Managing the Environment: The Public's View. *Public Opinion* 6: 47–51.

CONOVER, PAMELA JOHNSON, and STANLEY FELDMAN. 1981. The Origins and Meaning of Liberal/Conservative Self-Identifications. *American Journal of Political Science* 25:617–645.

CONOVER, PAMELA JOHNSON, and STANLEY FELDMAN. 1984. How People Organize the Political World. *American Journal of Political Science* 28:93–126.

COOK, TIMOTHY E. 1985. The Bear Market in Political Socialization and the Costs of Misunderstood Psychological Theories. *American Political Science Review* 79:1079–1093

DOUGLAS, MARY. 1970. *Natural Symbols.* Harmondsworth: Penguin.

DOUGLAS, MARY. 1982. *In the Active Voice.* London: Routledge & Kegan Paul.

DOUGLAS, MARY. 1983. *Identity: Personal and Socio-Cultural*, Uppsala Studies in Cultural Anthropology, vol. 5, ed. Anita Jacobson-Widding, 35–46.

DOUGLAS, MARY, and AARON WILDAVSKY. 1982. *Risk and Culture.* Berkeley: University of California Press.

ELKIN, STEPHEN. 1985. Economic and Political Rationality. University of Maryland, College Park. Typescript.

ELKIN, DAVID J., and RICHARD E. B. SIMEON. 1979. A Cause in Search of Its Effect; or, What Does Political Culture Explain? *Comparative Politics* 11:127–145.

LAUBER, VOLKMAR. 1983. From Growth Consensus to Fragmentation in Western Europe: Political Polarization over Redistribution and Ecology. *Comparative Politics* 15:329–350.

MARCH, JAMES G., and JOHAN P. OLSEN. 1984. The New Institutionalism: Organizational Factors in Political Life. *American Political Science Review* 78:734–749.

McCLOSKY, HERBERT, and DENNIS CHONG. 1985. Similarities and Differences between Left-Wing and Right-Wing Radicals. *British Journal of Political Science* 15:329–363.

MILBRATH, LESTER W. 1981a. Beliefs about Our Social Paradigm: Are We Moving to a New Paradigm? Paper presented at the twenty-second annual conference of the International Studies Association, Philadelphia.

MILBRATH, LESTER W. 1981b. The Relationship of Environmental Beliefs and Values to Politics and Government. Paper presented at the fourth annual conference of the International Society for Political Psychology, Mannheim, Germany.

ROBINSON, JOHN, and JOHN HOLM. 1980. Ideological Voting Is Alive and Well. *Public Opinion* 3: 52–58.

ROTHMAN, STANLEY, and S. ROBERT LICHTER. 1985. Elites in Conflict: Nuclear Energy, Ideology, and the Perception of Risk. *Journal of Contemporary Studies* 8:23–44.

STIMSON, JAMES A. 1986. The Process of Perception of Party Issue Position: A Longitudinal and Regional Perspective. Paper presented at the annual meeting of the Midwest Political Science Association, Chicago.

SUSSMAN, GLENN. 1986. Postindustrialism and Antinuclear Weapons Activism. Paper presented at meetings of the Western Political Science Association, Eugene, Oregon.

THOMPSON, MICHAEL. 1982. The Role of the Centre. In *Essays in the Sociology of Perception*, ed. Mary Douglas. London: Routledge and Kegan Paul.

VERBA, SIDNEY, and GARY R. ORREN. 1985. *Equality in America: The View From the Top.* Cambridge, MA: Harvard University Press.

WILDAVSKY, AARON. 1985a. Idolatry and "The Poor." *Catholicism in Crisis* 3:42–44.

WILDAVSKY, AARON. 1985b. A World of Difference: The Public Philosophies and Political Behaviors of Rival American Cultures. University of California, Berkeley. Typescript.

WILDAVSKY, AARON. 1986. Industrial Politics in American Political Cultures. In *The Politics of Industrial Policy*, ed. Claude E. Barfield and William A. Schambra, 15–32. Washington, DC: American Enterprise Institute.

WOLIN, SHELDON S. 1986. Democracy and the Welfare State: Staatsrason and Wohlfahrtsstaatsrason. University of Wisconsin, Madison. Typescript.

# 24

# The Transformation of the Western European Party Systems

*Otto Kirchheimer*

[Editors' Note. *Mention is made in this excerpt of parties of "individual representation" and "mass integration." Professor Kirchheimer explains earlier that parties of individual representation, such as the bourgeois parties of the Third French Republic, are based on "the local parish pump and the operation of the parliamentary factions." These parties are unable to function as transmission belts between the population and the government. By political integration he means "the capacity of a political system to make groups and their members previously outside the official fold full-fledged participants in the political process." A mass integration party is one that helps perform this function.*]

SOURCE: Otto Kirchheimer, "The Transformation of the Western European Party Systems," in Joseph LaPalombara and Myron Weiner, eds., *Political Parties and Political Development* (Princeton University Press, 1966). © 1966 by Princeton University Press. Excerpt, pp. 184–200, reprinted with permission of Princeton University Press.

# THE POSTWAR CATCH-ALL PARTY

Following the Second World War, the old-style bourgeois party of individual representation became the exception. While some of the species continue to survive, they do not determine the nature of the party system any longer. By the same token, the mass integration party, product of an age with harder class lines and more sharply protruding denominational structures, is transforming itself into a catch-all "people's" party. Abandoning attempts at the intellectual and moral *encadrement* of the masses, it is turning more fully to the electoral scene, trying to exchange effectiveness in depth for a wider audience and more immediate electoral success. The narrowed political task and the immediate electoral goal differ sharply from the former all-embracing concerns; today the latter are seen as counter-productive since they deter segments of a potential nationwide clientele.

For the class-mass parties we may roughly distinguish three stages in this process of transformation. There is first the period of gathering strength lasting to the beginning of the First World War; then comes their first governmental experience in the 1920s and 1930s (MacDonald, Weimar Republic, *Front Populaire*), unsatisfactory if measured both against the expectations of the class-mass party followers or leaders and suggesting the need for a broader basis of consensus in the political system. This period is followed by the present more or less advanced stages in the catch-all grouping, with some of the parties still trying to hold their special working class clientele and at the same time embracing a variety of other clienteles.

Can we find some rules according to which this transformation is taking place, singling out factors which advance or delay or arrest it? We might think of the current rate of economic development as the most important determinant; but if it were so important, France would certainly be ahead of Great Britain and, for that matter, also of the United States, still the classical example of an all-pervasive catch-all party system. What about the impact of the continuity or discontinuity of the political system? If this were so important, Germany and Great Britain would appear at opposite ends of the spectrum rather than showing a similar speed of transformation. We must then be satisfied to make some comments on the general trend and to note special limiting factors.

In some instances the catch-all performance meets definite limits in the traditional framework of society. The all-pervasive denominational background of the Italian *Democrazia Cristiana* means from the outset that the party cannot successfully appeal to the anticlerical elements of the population. Otherwise nothing prevents the party from phrasing its appeals so as to maximize its chances of catching more of those numerous elements which are not disturbed by the party's clerical ties. The solidarity element of its doctrinal core has long been successfully employed to attract a socially diversified clientele.

Or take the case of two other major European parties, the German SPD (Social Democratic Party) and the British Labour party. It is unlikely that either of them is able to make any concession to the specific desires of real estate interests or independent operators of agricultural properties while at the same time maintaining credibility with the masses of the urban population. Fortunately, however, there is enough community of interest between wage-and-salary earning urban or suburban white- and blue-collar workers and civil servants to designate them all as strategic objects of simultaneous appeals. Thus tradition and the pattern of social and professional stratification may set limits and offer potential audiences to the party's appeal.

If the party cannot hope to catch all categories of voters, it may have a reasonable expectation of catching more voters in all those categories whose interests do not adamantly conflict. Minor differences between group claims, such as between white-collar and manual labor groups, might be smoothed over by vigorous emphasis on programs which benefit both sections alike, for example, some cushioning against the shocks of automation.

Even more important is the heavy concentration on issues which are scarcely liable to meet resistance in the community. National societal goals transcending group interests offer the best sales prospect for a party intent on establishing or enlarging an appeal previously limited to specific sections of the population. The party which propagates most aggressively, for example, enlarged educational facilities may hear faint rumblings over the excessive cost or the danger to the quality of education from elites previously enjoying educational privileges. Yet the party's stock with any other family may be influenced only by how much more quickly and aggressively it took up the new national priority than its major competitor and how well its propaganda linked the individual family's future with the enlarged educational structures. To that extent its potential clientele is almost limitless. The catch-all of a given category performance turns virtually into an unlimited catch-all performance.

The last remark already transcends the group-interest confines. On the one hand, in such developed societies as I am dealing with, thanks to general levels of economic well-being and security and to existing welfare schemes universalized by the state or enshrined in collective bargaining, many individuals no longer need such protection as they once sought from the state. On the other hand, many have become aware of the number and complexity of the general factors on which their future well-being depends. This change of priorities and preoccupation may lead them to examine political offerings less under the aspect of their own particular claims than under that of the political leader's ability to meet general future contingencies. Among the major present-day parties, it is the French UNR...[Union for the New Republic] a late-comer, that speculates most clearly on the possibility of its channeling such less specialized needs to which its patron saint

De Gaulle constantly appeals into its own version of the catch-all party. Its assumed asset would rest in a doctrine of national purpose and unity vague and flexible enough to allow the most variegated interpretation and yet—at least as long as the General continues to function—attractive enough to serve as a convenient rallying point for many groups and isolated individuals.

While the UNR thus manipulates ideology for maximum general appeal, we have noted that ideology in the case of the *Democrazia Cristiana* is a slightly limiting factor. The UNR ideology in principle excludes no one. The Christian Democratic ideology by definition excludes the nonbeliever, or at least the seriously nonbelieving voter. It pays for the ties of religious solidarity and the advantages of supporting organizations by repelling some millions of voters. The catch-all parties in Europe appear at a time of de-ideologization which has substantially contributed to their rise and spread. De-ideologization in the political field involves the transfer of ideology from partnership in a clearly visible political goal structure into one of many sufficient but by no means necessary motivational forces operative in the voters' choice. The German and Austrian Social Democratic parties in the last two decades most clearly exhibit the politics of de-ideologization. The example of the German Christian Democratic Union (CDU) is less clear only because there was less to deideologize. In the CDU, ideology was from the outset only a general background atmosphere, both all-embracing and conveniently vague enough to allow recruiting among Catholic and Protestant denominations.

As a rule, only major parties can become successful catch-all parties. Neither a small, strictly regional party such as the South Tyrolian Peoples' party nor a party built around the espousal of harsh and limited ideological claims, like the Dutch Calvinists; or transitory group claims, such as the German Refugees; or a specific professional category's claims, such as the Swedish Agrarians; or a limited-action program, such as the Danish single-tax Justice party can aspire to a catch-all performance. Its raison d'être is the defense of a specific clientele or the lobbying for a limited reform clearly delineated to allow for a restricted appeal, perhaps intense, but excluding a wider impact or—once the original job is terminated—excluding a life-saving transformation.

Nor is the catch-all performance in vogue or even sought among the majority of the larger parties in small democracies. Securely entrenched, often enjoying majority status for decades—as the Norwegian and Swedish Social Democratic parties—and accustomed to a large amount of interparty cooperation,[1] such parties have no incentive to change their form of recruitment or their appeal to well-defined social groups. With fewer factors intervening and therefore more clearly foreseeable results of political actions and decisions, it seems easier to stabilize political relations on the basis of strictly circumscribed competition (Switzerland, for instance) than to change over to the more aleatory form of catch-all competition.

Conversion to catch-all parties constitutes a competitive phenomenon. A party is apt to accommodate to its competitor's successful style because of hope of benefits or fear of losses on election day. Conversely, the more a party convinces itself that a competitor's favorable results were due only to some nonrepetitive circumstances, and that the competitor's capacity of overcoming internal dissension is a temporary phenomenon, the smaller the overall conversion chance and the greater the inclination to hold fast to a loyal—though limited—clientele.

To evaluate the impact of these changes I have found it useful to list the functions which European parties exercised during earlier decades (late in the 19th and early in the 20th centuries) and to compare them with the present situation. Parties have functioned as channels for integrating individuals and groups into the existing political order, or as instruments for modifying or altogether replacing that order

(integration-disintegration). Parties have attempted to determine political-action preferences and influence other participants in the political process into accepting them. Parties have nominated public officeholders and presented them to the public at large for confirmation.

The so-called expressive function of the party, if not belonging to a category by itself, nevertheless warrants a special word. Its high tide belongs to the era of the 19th century constitutionalism when a more clear-cut separation existed between opinion formation-and-expression and the business of government. At that time the internally created parliamentary parties expressed opinions and criticism widely shared among the educated minority of the population. They pressed these opinions on their governments. But as the governments largely rested on an independent social and constitutional basis, they could if necessary hold out against the promptings of parliamentary factions and clubs. Full democratization merged the opinion-expressing and the governmental business in the same political parties and put them in the seat either of government or an alternative government. But it has left the expressive function of the party in a more ambiguous state. For electoral reasons, the democratic catch-all party, intent on spreading as wide as possible a net over a potential clientele, must continue to express widely felt popular concerns. Yet, bent on continuing in power or moving into governmental power, it performs this expressive function subject to manifold restrictions and changing tactical considerations. The party would atrophy if it were no longer able to function as a relay between the population and governmental structure, taking up grievances, ideas, and problems developed in a more searching and systematic fashion elsewhere in the body politic. Yet the caution it must give its present or prospective governmental role requires modulation and restraint. The very nature of today's catch-all party forbids an option between these two performances. It requires a constant shift between the party's critical role and its role as establishment support, a shift hard to perform but still harder to avoid.

In order to leave a maximum imprint on the polity a party has to exercise all of the first three functions. Without the ability to integrate people into the community the party could not compel other powerholders to listen to its clarions. The party influences other power centers to the extent that people are willing to follow its leadership. Conversely, people are willing to listen to the party because the party is the carrier of messages—here called action preferences—that are at least partially in accord with the images, desires, hopes, and fears of the electorate. Nominations for public office serve to tie together all these purposes; they may further the realization of action preferences if they elicit positive response from voters or from other powerholders. The nominations concretize the party's image with the public at large, on whose confidence the party's effective functioning depends.

Now we can discuss the presence or absence of these three functions in Western society today. Under present conditions of spreading secular and mass consumer-goods orientation, with shifting and less obtrusive class lines, the former class-mass parties and denominational mass parties are both under pressure to become catch-all peoples' parties. The same applies to those few remnants of former bourgeois parties of individual representation which aspire to a secure future as political organizations independent of the vagaries of electoral laws and the tactical moves of their mass-party competitors.[2] This change involves: *(a)* Drastic reduction of the party's ideological baggage. In France's SFIO, for example, ideological remnants serve at best as scant cover for what has become known as "*Molletisme*," the absolute reign of short-term tactical considerations. *(b)* Further strengthening of top leadership groups, whose actions and omissions are now judged from the viewpoint of their contribution to the efficiency of the entire social system rather than identification with the goals of their particular organization.

*(c)* Downgrading of the role of the individual party member, a role considered a historical relic which may obscure the newly built-up catch-all party image. *(d)* Deemphasis of the *classe gardée,* specific social-class or denominational clientele, in favor of recruiting voters among the population at large. *(e)* Securing access to a variety of interest groups. The financial reasons are obvious, but they are not the most important where official financing is available, as in Germany, or where access to the most important media of communication is fairly open, as in England and Germany. The chief reason is to secure electoral support via interest-group intercession.

From this fairly universal development the sometimes considerable remnants of two old class-mass parties, the French and the Italian Communist parties, are excluding themselves. These parties are in part ossified, in part solidified by a combination of official rejection and legitimate sectional grievances. In this situation the ceremonial invocation of the rapidly fading background of a remote and inapplicable revolutionary experience has not yet been completely abandoned as a part of political strategy. What is the position of such opposition parties of the older class-mass type, which still jealously try to hold an exclusive loyalty of their members, while not admitted nor fully ready to share in the hostile state power? Such parties face the same difficulties in recruiting and holding intensity of membership interest as other political organizations. Yet, in contrast to their competitors working within the confines of the existing political order, they cannot make a virtue out of necessity and adapt themselves fully to the new style of catch-all peoples' party.[3] This conservatism does not cost them the confidence of their regular corps of voters. On the other hand, the continued renewal of confidence on election day does not involve an intimate enough bond to utilize as a basis for major political operations.

The attitudes of regular voters—in contrast to those of members and activists—attest to the extent of incongruency between full-fledged participation in the social processes of a consumer-goods oriented society and the old political style which rested on the primordial need for sweeping political change. The latter option has gone out of fashion in Western countries and has been carefully eliminated from the expectations, calculations, and symbols of the catch-all mass party. The incongruency may rest on the total absence of any connection between general social-cultural behavior and political style. In this sense electoral choice may rest on family tradition or empathy with the political underdog without thereby becoming part of a coherent personality structure. Or the choice may be made in the expectation that it will have no influence on the course of political development; it is then an act of either adjusting to or, as the case may be, signing out of the existing political system rather than a manifestation of signing up somewhere else.

## THE CATCH-ALL PARTY, THE INTEREST GROUP, AND THE VOTER: LIMITED INTEGRATION

The integration potential of the catch-all mass party rests on a combination of factors whose visible end result is attraction of the maximum number of voters on election day. For that result the catch-all party must have entered into millions of minds as a familiar object fulfilling in politics a role analogous to that of a major brand in the marketing of a universally needed and highly standardized article of mass consumption. Whatever the particularities of the line to which a party leader owes his intraparty success, he must, once he is selected for leadership, rapidly suit his behavior to standard requirements. There is need for enough brand differentiation to make the article plainly recognizable, but the degree of differentiation must never be so great as to make the potential customer fear he will be out on a limb.

Like the brand whose name has become a household word, the catch-all mass party that has presided over the fortunes of a country for some time, and whose leaders the voter has therefore come to know on his television set and in his newspaper columns, enjoys a great advantage. But only up to a certain point. Through circumstances possibly outside the control of the party or even of the opposition—a scandal in the ranks of government, an economic slump—office-holding may suddenly turn into a negative symbol encouraging the voter to switch to another party as a consumer switches to a competitive brand.

The rules deciding the outcome of catch-all mass party competition are extremely aleatory. When a party has or seeks an almost nationwide potential constituency, its majority composed of individuals whose relation to politics is both tangential and discontinuous, the factors which may decide the eventual electoral outcome are almost infinite in number and often quite unrelated to the party's performance. The style and looks of the leader, the impact of a recent event entirely dictated from without, vacation schedules, the weather as it affects crops—factors such as these all enter into the results.

The very catch-all character of the party makes membership loyalty far more difficult to expect and at best never sufficient to swing results. The outcome of a television contest is dubious, or the contest itself may constitute too fleeting an exposure to make an impression that will last into the election. Thus the catch-all mass party too is driven back to look out for a more permanent clientele. Only the interest group, whether ideological or economic in nature or a combination of the two, can provide mass reservoirs of readily accessible voters. It has a more constant line of communication and higher acceptance for its messages than the catch-all party, which is removed from direct contact with the public except for the comparatively small number intensively concerned about the brand of politics a party has to offer these days—or about their own careers in or through the party.

All the same, the climate of relations between catch-all party and interest groups has definitely changed since the heyday of the class-mass or denominational integration party. Both party and interest group have gained a greater independence from each other. Whether they are still joined in the same organization (like British Labour and the TUC [Trades Union Congress]) or formally enjoy complete independence from each other (like the German SPD and the DGB [Workers' Federation]), what matters most is the change of roles.[4] Instead of a joint strategy toward a common goal there appears an appreciation of limited if still mutually helpful services to be rendered.

The party bent on attracting a maximum of voters must modulate its interest-group relations in such a way so as not to discourage potential voters who identify themselves with other interests. The interest group, in its turn, must never put all its eggs in one basket. That might offend the sensibilities of some members with different political connections. More important, the interest group would not want to stifle feelings of hope in another catch-all party that some moves in its direction might bring electoral rewards. Both party and interest group modulate their behavior, acting as if the possible contingency has already arrived, namely that the party has captured the government—or an important share in it—and has moved from the position of friend or counsellor to that of umpire or arbitrator. Suddenly entrusted with the confidence of the community as a whole, the government–party arbitrator does best when able to redefine the whole problem and discover solutions which would work, at least in the long run, in the favor of all interest claimants concerned.

Here there emerges a crucial question: What then is the proper role of the catch-all party in the arbitration of interest conflicts? Does not every government try to achieve the best tactical position for exercising an effective arbitration between contending group claims? Is the catch-all party even needed in this connection? Or —from the interest viewpoint—can a society dispense with parties' services, as France now does?

A party is more than a collector of interest-group claims. It functions at the same time as advocate, protector, or at least as addressee of the demands of all those who are not able to make their voices felt as effectively as those represented by well organized interest groups: those who do not yet have positions in the process of production or those who no longer hold such positions, the too young and the too old, and those whose family status aligns them with consumer rather than producer interests.

Can we explain this phenomenon simply as another facet of the party's aggregative function? But functionalist phraseology restates rather than explains. The unorganized and often unorganizable make their appearance only on election day or in suddenly sprouting pre-election committees and party activities arranged for their benefit. Will the party be able and willing to take their interests into its own hands? Will it be able, playing on their availability in electoral terms, not only to check the more extreme demands of organized groups but also to transcend the present level of intergroup relations and by political reforms redefining the whole political situation? No easy formula will tell us what leader's skill, what amount of pressure from objective situations has to intervene to produce such a change in the political configuration.

In this job of transcending group interests and creating general confidence the catch-all party enjoys advantages, but by the same token it suffers from an infirmity. Steering clear of sectarianism enhances its recruiting chances in electoral terms but inevitably limits the intensity of commitment it may expect. The party's transformation from an organization combining the defense of social position, the quality of spiritual shelter, and the vision of things to come into that of a vehicle for shortrange and interstitial political choice exposes the party to the hazards of all purveyors of nondurable consumer goods: competition with a more attractively packaged brand of a nearly identical merchandise.

## LIMITED PARTICIPATION IN ACTION PREFERENCE

This brings us to the determination of action preferences and their chances of realization. In Anthony Downs's well-known model, action preference simply results from the party's interest in the proximate goal, the winning of the next election. In consequence the party will arrange its policies in such a way that the benefits accruing to the individual members of the community are greater than the losses resulting from its policy.[5] Downs's illustrations are frequently, though not exclusively, taken from fields such as taxation where the cash equation of political action is feasible. Yet Downs himself has occasionally noted that psychological satisfactions or dissatisfactions, fears or hopes, are elements in voters' decisions as frequently as calculations of immediate short-term benefits or deprivations. Were it different, the long-lasting loyalty of huge blocks of voters to class-mass integration parties in the absence of any immediate benefits from such affiliation could scarcely be explained. But can it be said that such short-term calculations correspond much more closely to the attitudes connected with the present-day catch-all mass party with its widely ranging clientele? Can the short-term benefit approach, for example, be utilized in military or foreign-policy issues?

In some countries in the last decade it has become the rule for catch-all parties out of office simply to lay the most recent shortcomings or apparent deterioration of the country's military or international position at the doorstep of the incumbent government, especially during election campaigns; thus in the United States the Republican party in 1952 with regard to the long-lasting indecisive Korean War, or in Germany more recently the Social Democrats with regard to Adenauer's apparent passivity in the face of the Berlin Wall. In other instances, however, the opposition plays down foreign or military issues or treats them in generalities vague enough to evoke the image of itself as a competitor who will be able to handle them as well as the incumbent government.

To the extent that the party system still includes "unreformed" or—as in the case of the Italian Socialist party—only "half-reformed" class-mass integration parties, foreign or military issues enter election campaigns as policy differences. Yet even here the major interest has shifted away from areas where the electorate could exercise only an illusory choice. The electorate senses that in the concrete situation, based in considerable part on geography and history, the international bloc affiliation of the country rather than any policy preference will form the basis of decision. It senses too that such decisions rest only partially, or at times nominally, with the political leadership. Even if the impact of the political leader on the decision may have been decisive, more often than not election time-tables in democracies are such that the decision, once carried out, is no longer contested or even relevant to voter choices. As likely as not, new events crowd it out of the focus of voters' attention. Few voters still thought of Mendès-France's 1954 "abandonment" of Indo-China when Edgar Faure suddenly dissolved the Assembly in December 1955. While a party may benefit from its adversary's unpopular decisions, such benefits are more often an accidental by-product than the outcome of a government-opposition duel with clearly distributed roles and decisions.

A party may put up reasonably coherent, even if vague, foreign or military policies for election purposes. It may criticize the inept handling of such problems by the government of the day, and more and more intensively as it gets closer to election day. But in neither case is there a guarantee of the party's ability to act as a coherent body in parliament when specific action preferences are to be determined. Illustrative of this dilemma are the history of EDC in the French Parliament and the more recent battles within the British parties in regard to entrance into the Common Market (although the latter case remains inconclusive because of De Gaulle's settling the issue in his own way, for the time being). Fortuitous election timetables and the hopes, fears, and expectations of the public do not intermesh sufficiently with the parliamentary representatives' disjointed action on concrete issues before them to add up to the elaboration of clear-cut party action preference.

The catch-all party contributes general programs in the elaboration of domestic action preferences. These programs may be of a prognostic variety, informing the public about likely specific developments and general trends. Yet prognostics and desirability blur into each other in this type of futurology, in which rosy glasses offer previews of happy days for all and sundry among the party's prospective customers. These programs may lead to or be joined with action proposals in various stages of concretization. Concrete proposals, however, always risk implying promises which may be too specific. Concretizations must remain general enough so that they cannot be turned from electoral weapons to engines of assault against the party which first mounted them.

This indeterminacy allows the catch-all party to function as a meeting ground for the elaboration of concrete action for a multiplicity of interest groups. All the party may require from those who obtain its services is that they make a maximal attempt to arrive at compromises within the framework of the party and that they avoid coalescing with forces hostile to the party. The compromises thus elaborated must be acceptable to major interest groups even if these groups, for historical or traditional reasons, happen not to be represented in the governing party. Marginal differences may be submitted to the voter at elections or, as older class-mass parties do on occasion, via referenda (Switzerland and Sweden). But expected policy mutations are in the nature of increments rather than major changes in intergroup relations.

It is here that the difference between the catch-all and the older form of integration party becomes most clearly visible. The catch-all party will do its utmost to establish consensus to avoid party realignment. The integration party may count on majority political mechanisms to implement its programs only to find that hostile interests frustrate the majority decision by the economic and social mechanisms at their disposal. They may call strikes (by labor or farmers or storekeepers or investors), they may withdraw capital to safe haven outside the country, they may undermine that often hypocritically invoked but real factor known as the "confidence of the business community."

## INTEGRATION THROUGH PARTICIPATION IN LEADERSHIP SELECTION—THE FUTURE OF THE POLITICAL PARTY

What then remains the real share of the catch-all party in the elaboration of action preferences? Its foremost contribution lies in the mobilization of the voters for whatever concrete action preferences leaders are able to establish rather than a priori selections of their own. It is for this reason that the catch-all party prefers to visualize action in the light of the contingencies, threats, and promises of concrete historical situations rather than of general social goals. It is the hoped-for or already established role in the dynamics of action, in which the voters' vicarious participation is invited, that is most in evidence. Therefore the attention of both party and public at large focuses most clearly on problems of leadership selection.

Nomination means the prospect of political office. Political office involves a chance to make an impact via official action. The competition between those striving to influence official action puts into evidence the political advantage of those in a position to act before their political adversaries can do so. The privilege of first action is all the more precious in a new and nonrepetitive situation where the political actor can avoid getting enmeshed in directives deriving from party action preferences. Much as the actor welcomes party support on the basis of revered (but elastic) principles, he shuns specific direction and supervision. In this respect the catch-all party furnishes an ideal background for political action. Where obtaining office becomes an almost exclusive preoccupation of a party, issues of personnel are reduced to search for the simplest effective means to put up winning combinations. The search is especially effective wherever the party becomes a channel by which representatives of hitherto excluded or neglected minorities may join in the existing political elite.

The nomination of candidates for popular legitimation as office-holders thus emerges as the most important function of the present-day catch-all party. Concentration on the selection of candidates for office is in line with an increasing role differentiation in industrial society. Once certain levels of education and material welfare are reached, both intellectual and material needs are taken care of by specialized purveyors of communications and economic products. Likewise the party, which in less advanced societies or in those intent on rapid change directly interferes with the performance of societal jobs, remains in Western industrial society twice removed—through government and bureaucracy —from the field of direct action. To this state of affairs correspond now prevailing popular images and expectations in regard to the reduced role of the party. Expectations previously set on the performance of a political organization are now flowing into different channels.

At the same time, the role of the political party as a factor in the continued integration of the individual into the national life now has to be visualized in a different light. Compared to his connection with interest organizations and voluntary associations of a non-political nature and to his frequent encounters with the state bureaucracy, the citizen's relations with the political party are becoming more intermittent and of more limited scope.

To the older party of integration the citizen, if he so desired, could be closer. Then it was a less differentiated organization, part channel of protest, part source of protection, part purveyor of visions of the future. Now, in its linear descendant in a transfigured world, the catch-all party, the citizen finds a relatively remote, at times quasi-official and alien structure. Democratic society assumes that the citizen is finally an integral and conscious participant in the affairs of both the polity and the economy; it further assumes that as such he will work through the party as one of the many inter-related structures by which he achieves a rational participation in his surrounding world.

Should he ever live up to these assumptions, the individual and society may indeed find the catch-all party—non-utopian, non-oppressive, and ever so flexible—an ingenious and useful political instrument.

What about the attitude toward the modern catch-all party of functional powerholders in army, bureaucracy, industry, and labor? Released from their previous unnecessary fears as to the ideological propensities and future intentions of the class-mass party, functional powerholders have come to recognize the catch-all party's role as consensus purveyor. In exchange for its ability to provide a clear-cut basis of legitimacy, functional powerholders are, up to a point, willing to recognize the political leadership claims of the party. They expect it to exercise certain arbitration functions in intergroup relations and to initiate limited political innovations. The less clear-cut electoral basis of the party's leadership claim and the closer the next election date, the smaller the credit which functional powerholders will extend to unsolicited and non-routine activities of the political powerholders impinging on their own positions. This lack of credit then sets the stage for conflicts between functional and political leadership groups. How does the catch-all party in governmental positions treat such conflicts? Will it be satisfied to exercise pressure via the mass media, or will it try to recreate a militant mass basis beyond the evanescent electoral and publicity levels? But the very structure of the catch-all party, the looseness of its clientele, may from the outset exclude such more far-reaching action. To that extent the political party's role in Western industrial society today is more limited than would appear from its position of formal pre-eminence. Via its governmental role it functions as coordinator of and arbitrator between functional power groups. Via its electoral role it produces that limited amount of popular participation and integration required from the popular masses for the functioning of official political institutions.

Will this limited participation which the catch-all party offers the population at large, this call to rational and dispassionate participation in the political process via officially sanctioned channels, work?

The instrument, the catch-all party, cannot be much more rational than its nominal master, the individual voter. No longer subject to the discipline of the party of integration—or, as in the United States, never subject to this discipline—the voters may, by their shifting moods and their apathy, transform the sensitive instrument of the catch-all party into something too blunt to serve as a link with the functional powerholders of society. Then we may yet come to regret the passing—even if it was inevitable—of the class-mass party and the denominational party, as we already regret the passing of other features in yesterday's stage of Western civilization.

## Notes

1. . . . For both weighty historical and contemporary reasons the Austrian Social-Democratic party forms a partial exception to the rule of less clear-cut transformation tendencies among major class-mass parties in smaller countries. It is becoming an eager and rather successful member of the catch-all club. For the most adequate treatment see K. L. Shell, *The Transformation of Austrian Socialism* (Albany, N.Y.: State University of New York, 1962).

2. Liberal parties without sharply profiled program or clientele may, however, make such conversion attempts. Val Lorwin draws my attention to the excellent example of a former bourgeois party, the Belgian Liberal party, which became in 1961 the "Party of Liberty and Progress," deemphasizing anticlericalism and appealing to the right wing of the Social Christian party, worried about this party's governmental alliance with the Socialists.

3. However, even in France—not to speak of Italy—communist policies are under pressure to accommodate to the new style. For a concrete recent example see W. G. Andrews, "Evreux 1962: Referendum and Elections in a Norman Constituency," in *Political Studies* 11 (October 1963), pp. 308–326. Most recently, Maurice Duverger, "L'Eternel Marais, Essai sur le Centrisme Francais," in *Revue Francaise de Science Politique* 14 (February 1964), pp. 33 and 49.

4. See the conclusions of Martin Harrison, *Trade Unions and the Labour Party Since 1945* (London: Allen and Unwin, 1960).

5. "It always organizes its action so as to focus on a single quantity: its vote margin over the opposition is the test at the end of the current election period." In A. Downs, *An Economic Theory of Democracy* (New York: Harper & Row, 1957), p. 174.

## 25

# From Consensus to Dissensus: Britain and Japan

*Brent Steel and Taketsuga Tsurutani*

Much of the postwar period in advanced industrial democracies was characterized by a consistent decline of ideological asperity and substantive policy conflict between major parties of the right and of the left. The decline was so palpable in the eyes of some analysts that they once confidently spoke of "the end of ideology." Politics in these democracies lost the traditional "hot" political climate of combat and struggle and instead became, in the words of one European journalist, "boring."[1] Thus arrived an era of political consensus—convergence of the right

SOURCE: Brent Steel and Taketsuga Tsurutani, "From Consensus to Dissensus: A Note on Postindustrial Parties," *Comparative Politics*, vol. 18 (January 1986), pp. 235–248, © The City University of New York. Reprinted by permission. Article and notes abridged by the editors.

and the left—and an age of "depoliticization."[2] Indeed, during the postwar period through the 1950s, and 1960s, and perhaps into the first years of the 1970s, it did not seem to matter much in these nations whether government was in the hands of the party of the right or that of the left. Whatever differences remained between them were tactical—questions of "how" and "how much"—and not substantive, that is, not of objectives. Khrushchev's caustic observation about party competition in the United States, that it did not make any difference which horse won because both were from the same stable, was basically accurate and applied to most of the western democracies. Major parties, of the right as well as of the left, had ceased to be the agents of differing visions of societal destiny and had instead become instruments of intermediation and consensus-building, and they appeared to be quite successful.

That age of policy consensus seems to have deteriorated, however. In its place, there have emerged in some democracies trends toward repoliticization and dissensus. Ideological contentiousness is on the rise again. Resurgence of policy differences between some parties of the right and those of the left, as a consequence, is becoming noticeable. And which party is in power seems again to make differences in policy outcome. These trends are, of course, not uniform among advanced industrial democracies. In some, such as Britain, they are quite pronounced; in others, for example West Germany, they may be considered incipient; in still others, they are not ascertainable at all. Why in some but not in others? This essay attempts first to summarize briefly the causes of consensus that obtained during much of the postwar period (and still obtains in a number of these democracies) and then to examine those of new dissensus and repoliticization where this new trend seems more noticeable. . . .

. . .What has become noticeable since the latter part of the 1970s in some western democracies is a trend away from consensus and convergence between the parties of the right and the left. It is particularly noticeable in Britain,

the nation where that historical convergence and consensus were achieved first among major western democracies in the postwar period and where the two major parties during much of this period were the paradigmatic examples of consensus, intermediation, and instrumentalism. In this paper, we will use the case of the two major British parties as examples in our attempt to explicate what we think is the most direct and immediate cause of redivergence and reradicalization.

. . .convergence and consensus between the major parties of the right and the left in the past were variously promoted by certain intraparty and external socioeconomic developments. The intraparty development here had to do with the evolution in the character and objective of leadership, while the socioeconomic change related to the evolution of modern industrialism. It is tempting to think that there is some necessary causal relationship between the two. A relationship there obviously is, but whether or not it is necessary or inevitable is a bit problematic. There is no doubt that the evolution in the character and objective of party leadership was abetted and reinforced by the socioeconomic development as described above. This in itself, however, does not lead us to the conclusion that party leadership necessarily synchronizes its evolution with that of its socioeconomic environment. Coincidence of the two developments is far from universal. British Labour perhaps exemplified such coincidence; so, it may be argued, did the Tories. Scandinavian socialist parties may also be said to have approximated such coincidence. The West German SPD, on the other hand, was, at least, much slower, and its leadership remained quite ideological and doctrinaire until 1959. And the Italian Socialist Party (under Nenni and his successors) did not follow the pattern until much later. The point we are trying to make here is that there is nothing deterministic about either deradicalization or reradicalization of parties. There are only chance, contingency, and accident, and a party's political fortune is the function of interaction between it or its leadership on the one hand and its internal and external environment on the other. This, we hope, will become clear in the remainder of the present paper, which focuses on the cause and process of redivergence and reradicalization.

It is quite true that the external environment for the major parties of the right and of the left has become considerably less hospitable to the politics of consensus and intermediation. Since the first Arab oil shock of 1973, the performance of western economies has shown a decline and stagnation. Economic growth, employment, and the consumer price index, to take but a few major statistical measures of economic health, have all taken a negative turn from the days of stable consensus and the continuing expansion of the consumption-oriented economy. Persistent stagflation and recurring recession have changed the popular perception of the advanced industrial economy as well as the ability of the political system to meet the popular redistributive demands that have continued to expand in the face of the adverse economic circumstances. That equilibrium between the rate of economic growth and the rise in popular expectations that underlay and, in an important sense, sustained the stable consensus came to be eroded. The growing disequilibrium has led to what some analysts worry about as "overload"[3] which translates itself, for example, into massive and chronic deficit spending. What is feared as declining fiscal integrity and worsening economic health has in the meantime revived the old conflict between the secure, the contented, and the well-to-do, on the one hand, and the insecure, the poor, the marginal, and the impatient, on the other. Some economic analyses even suggest a shrinking in the size of the "middle class." One may well be tempted to conclude that the central precondition for the politics of consensus and compromise is declining. Under the circumstances, it is perhaps only natural that the erstwhile or latent radical elements in the party of the left as well as that of the right should feel reinvigorated. And, to the extent that environmental inclemency encourages ideological asperity and particularistic

stridency, consensus-building and intermediation become more difficult.

While this general environmental change has occurred in all advanced industrial democracies, albeit with differential impact, redivergence and reradicalization have not. In short, where such redivergence and reradicalization have become noticeable, we should seek their more immediate and crucial cause in phenomena other than the socioeconomic environmental change. This is not to discount the abetting or reinforcing effect of that environmental change on redivergence and reradicalization. But the immediate and crucial cause we think we find in the relationship among various levels of party organization or personnel, especially in party leadership selection.

Where one stands, as noted by Graham Allison and others, depends on where one sits, and this dictum applies to those different levels of the party. It can be postulated, for example, that the more practical experience one has had in the arena of electoral politics and that of policy negotiation, bargaining, and compromise, the more pragmatic and instrumental one becomes. This would seem particularly to be the case with successful politicians whose ambitions for power are abetted by their successes. Given this consideration, it is not unreasonable to argue that there is a positive general correlation between the combination of experience and success on the one hand and pragmatism, moderation, and instrumentalism on the other. If this is true, then we can posit the following: members of the parliamentary party (of the right or of the left) are less radical (conservative or leftist) and more consensus-oriented, more instrumentalist, and thus more moderate than members of the constituency party, and more noticeably so than activists within the constituency party of extra-parliamentary organizations. Now, the distinction in this regard between the parliamentary party and the extraparliamentary organization (or constituency party) is not difficult to see. The former consists of individuals—politicians—who were baptized in pratical electoral competition and tempered by pragmatic tasks of negotiation, bargaining, and compromise in policymaking with relevant groups in society and government. In this process, they have learned, through existential osmosis as well as conscious observation, strategies, tactics and vocabulary required for maximizing the prospects of achieving their individual as well as collective ambitions and the imperative of intermediation and consensus-building among these groups for the making of workable policies and programs. They are thus predisposed, as many analysts note, to sacrifice ideological fidelity for power[4] In short, they know and adhere to the need for more instrumental programs and less ideological or sectoral posture in order to produce favorable electoral and policy payoffs for themselves and for their party. It is only natural, then, that they should be committed to a political perspective and policy orientation that are compatible with the modal values, preferences, and aspirations of the citizenry at large, even though they might continue to employ, albeit with declining authenticity, their traditional class or ideological rhetoric on occasion.

Members of the party's extraparliamentary organizations, however, suffer no such constraints for moderation and instrumentalism because they do not sit in the arena where practical electoral considerations, wider perspectives, and pragmatic cross-sectoral intermediation and consensus-building are imperative. They can, in short, afford to remain ideologically pure. This is particularly the case with more partisan and ideological activists among them, and they differ, as noted by many observers, significantly from most party voters in this regard. Hence their description as militants. One prominent student of western political parties observed:

> The voluntary and amateur nature of these associations ensures that they attract zealots in the party cause, and particularly so at the local leadership level, where there are many routine political chores which only the devoted are likely to perform. Principles, not professional careers, are what matter here[5]

Where these activists stand, there is no compelling pressure to be flexible and pragmatic, to adapt to larger realities. The modal pattern of popular expectations and preferences is one of these realities, and it differs from the narrow particularistic reality of those partisan and ideological activists.

Within the parliamentary party, too, there is an important difference in attitude and orientation between its senior stratum (front bench in parliamentary argot) and its rank-and-file membership (back bench), essentially because of the diversity between the two in experience, responsibility, and constituency pressure. Junior parliamentarians do not engage in direct negotiations, intermediation, and consensus-building as their seniors do; they do not have the responsibility for success or failure of policies as their leaders do; and they are more amenable to pressures and wishes of local party activists who have selected them as candidates while their seniors are more secure in this regard by virtue of their prestige, influence, and stature. That there is some considerable difference in attitude and orientation between the front bench and the back bench of the party, for example, in Britain, can be seen in the fact of frequent backbench dissent from its leadership.

Differences among these various levels of the party and between them and the general electorate may be summarized in the following illustration of a radical-moderate (or ideological-instrumental) spectrum. Now, these differences among various levels of the party are extremely relevant to the issue of leadership selection. To the extent that the party is deradicalized, consensus-building, and centrist, its intermediative and instrumental capability can be retained if it maintains leadership independence from its backbenchers. And even more important, it must retain its independence from the constituency activists. This is imperative because "the logic of electoral competition will force each party to allow its 'centrist' wing to shape policies, as a necessary condition of winning a parliamentary majority."[6] But this imperative can be met only so long as the frontbenchers or senior leaders of the party retain effective control of party leadership selection. In an important

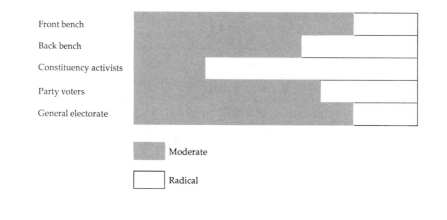

FIGURE 1

---

sense, the Labour and the Conservative parties of Britain may be viewed as paradigmatic examples of "reradicalization," one caused by the shift of leadership selection power to constituency activists, and the other caused by the same to backbenchers.

Traditionally, there was, in the case of Britain as in other democratic nations, some superficial difference between the Conservatives and Labour. Inasmuch as Labour was presumably rooted in commitment to egalitarian democracy, its formal internal operation was more open than that of the Conservatives. Its rank-and-file members were theoretically sovereign, and the party leadership was accountable to them. Rules were made on the basis of constituency party membership consultation and vote; party officials were elected by the constituency party membership; and party proceedings were noisily democratic and at times unwieldily participatory. Internal operations of the Tories, in contrast, were more often than not characterized by procedural secrecy, leadership elitism, and membership deference. During the period of mutual convergence on the center of the political spectrum, however, the parties actually shared one critical internal feature in common, and that was relative independence of party leadership from more partisan and ideological activist strata of their respective constituencies. The core party leadership at the apex was insulated and therefore

relatively free to conduct itself in the arena of interparty competition for electoral support and policymaking more or less as it saw fit. This independence of party leadership was insured so long as the manner in which the party leadership was effectively selected was compatible with such independence. Indeed, in neither the Conservative nor the Labour party were constituency activists permitted to participate, let alone play a crucial role, in such leadership selection. Hence the insulation of the party leadership from the influence and potential power of the constituency party and, more specifically, from its more narrowly partisan strata was insured. It was indeed this leadership insulation and independence that in turn insured the leadership stability, policy continuity, and instrumental pragmatism of the party.

This equation concerning convergent, moderate, and instrumental intermediative policy unravels when the locus of power for party leadership selection shifts downward—from senior leaders to backbenchers in the case of the Tories after 1965, and from the parliamentary Labour Party (PLP) to the National Conference in the case of Labour after 1980. Prior to its 1965 procedural change concerning party leadership selection, the Conservative leader was selected by a consensus among senior Tory leaders, including some members of the House of Lords, after informal and secretive consultation with backbenchers and extraparliamentary groups. In this process of leadership selection, the views and preferences of those senior leaders were decisive. By the same token, the process had in the meantime come to be viewed with increasing unhappiness by the more conservative backbenchers who more directly reflected "grass roots discontent" of constituency-association activists. The normative basis for the demand for rule change in party leadership selection, of course, was different and was justified in the name of democratic principles. Hence the 1965 change, which subjected leadership selection to votes by all the Conservative MPs. Tory backbenchers as an aggregate were understandably more radical (conservative) than frontbenchers. For reasons we have already alluded to, backbenchers were more amenable to pressures and preferences of local constituency activists who had selected them as candidates, and, as one observer noted, "it [was] MPs of 'moderate' opinions in both the main parties who seem[ed] most likely to antagonize their local party... because the local party activists m[ight] tend to be more extreme in their views than their MPs, or...because moderate opinions held by an MP [could] be taken as indicating sympathy with the opposing party."[7] Reflecting this phenomenon, there were numerous instances of Tory backbench revolts in the 1960s and the 1970s, with as many as two-thirds of the backbenchers voting against their government. It was to these backbenchers that the effective power of leadership selection gravitated ultimately as the result of the 1965 reform. The first party leadership election under the new rule took place in 1965, and, promptly, Enoch Powell, an arch-conservative, ran against the more centrist Edward Heath and Reginald Maudling. Heath was finally elected with a small majority of votes and continued in the post until 1975 (when the rule was amended to subject the leader to annual reelection) when he was successfully challenged by Margaret Thatcher, who was supported by a majority of backbenchers. As one observer noted, she could not have become party leader had it not been for the change in leadership selection

rules.[8] Today, the Conservative Party (or its leadership) seems to be anything but consensualist or centrist; instead its posture and rhetoric have become radical and confrontational as well as ideologically strident. And the party has embarked on a program of reversing the postwar welfare state and of reprivatizing some of the large, publicly owned industries. The former party of the right seems to be gravitating toward its old self.

If the Tories constitute an example of reradicalization as a result of the shift in effective power of leadership selection from the front bench to the back bench within the parliamentary party, then Labour may be viewed as an archtypal instance of reradicalization as a result of a power shift from the parliamentary party to constituency activists. With the January 1981 change in party rules in the name of greater democracy and public accountability,[9] the selection of Labour leadership, which had traditionally been made by the PLP, was effectively transferred to the Labour Conference where the PLP now holds only 30 percent of the votes. The remaining 70 percent are cast by extraparliamentary groups—40 percent by trade unions and 30 percent by the constituency party. Those union and constituency party activists who participate in the Labour Conference are typically more ideological, particularistic, and militant than the rank-and-file Labour voters and, of course, PLP members. Their radicalism or militancy was palpable long before the reform. In the 1960s and the 1970s, even when Labour was in power, these extraparliamentary activists demonstrated their ideological and political disaffection with the party leadership by choosing "left-wing candidates to replace outgoing Labour MPs,"[10] for they controlled, as they continue to do, the party's local "management committee" which in effect selects each candidate. And that, of course, increased the number of more "radical" backbenchers within the PLP. Backbench dissent within the PLP was thus no less frequent than within the Conservative Party. Thus, by 1976, Michael Foot was capable of mounting a serious challenge to the moderate party leadership by garnering 43 percent of votes by Labour MPs in the second ballot for party leader. In any event, the 1981 rule change transformed the intra-PLP competition between a moderate majority and a radical minority into essentially a constituency activist stratum struggle between a vast radical majority and a declining moderate minority. The result seems obvious. Michael Foot and Neil Kinnock have not much in common with James Callaghan, Harold Wilson, Hugh Gaitskell, and Clement Attlee. According to one recent analysis by an authoritative source, Labour today is more than ten times as radical as the West German SPD.[11] It is this development that led to the exodus of centrist Labourites from the party to form the Social Democratic Party in late 1981.

Decline of centrist policy orientation and intermediative capability through "democratization" of party leadership selection is not entirely novel as a political phenomenon. Demands for intraparty democracy are irresistible because democracy is the twentieth-century doctrine of legitimacy. Duverger observed that "parties must in consequence take the greatest care to provide themselves with leadership which is democratic in appearance. . . . Democratic principles demand that leadership at all levels be elective, that it be frequently renewed, collective in character, weak in authority." [12] But this imposition of intraparty democracy can have dramatic results upon party policy and electoral fortune. There is at least one major example emanating from an industrial and democratic society that had preceded, and hence should have warned, the British Labour Party of 1981—the case of the Japan Socialist Party (JSP).

The Japan Socialist Party—a party of the left consisting largely of amateurs in electoral competition and policymaking at the time—had its first taste of power (and the burden of policymaking responsibility) as the fortuitous senior partner of a coalition government in 1947–48. Much to the chagrin of its more pragmatic leaders, the party was quite unprepared for the task. (One of its most powerful leaders, upon being informed that the party had won a

plurality of votes in the 1947 general election and that it could finally form a government, was said to have involuntarily reacted by uttering a mournful "Oh, no!") It managed to cling to power for less than one year because of its inexperience as a ruling party and its understandable incompetence compounded by the horrendous difficulties the war-devastated nation faced. This experience as a short-lived ruling party was quite sobering to many of its members, and it precipitated serious debates within the party on its doctrines and policy direction. For a while it split into two parties of left socialists and right socialists. But the desire for power, once tasted, was irresistible ("leadership ambition"), and in 1955 the Socialists reunited into a single party (which in turn compelled the two warring conservative parties to merge as the current Liberal Democratic Party a few months later) and promptly garnered 35 percent of the electoral vote in the general election held later that same year (as opposed to less than 24 percent in the immediately preceding election). The reunited JSP raised a widespread popular expectation (and fear among conservatives) that it would soon grow into a genuinely viable alternative governing party, an expectation entirely justified by the experience of some European socialist parties, for example British Labour. Industrialization and urbanization were presumed to result in a rising popular support for "progressive" or "socialist" parties when those parties of the left "deradicalized" themselves. And, indeed, by the latter half of the 1950s, the Japanese Socialists had had a decade of experience in practical electoral competition and pragmatic parliamentary tasks. In the 1958 general election, they increased their electoral support to 36 percent, thus further reinforcing the popular expectation for the growth of the JSP as an alternative governing party. There was talk among politicians, analysts, and citizens alike of a "British-style two-party system" emerging in the country. Such a system never materialized because of the JSP's unintended reradicalization and the subsequent decline of electoral support for the party.

The principal cause of the JSP's reradicalization was the shift of power of leadership selection from the parliamentary JSP to its extraparliamentary organizations, that is, the constituency JSP. The constituency JSP consisted, as it still does, of some 50,000 members (a miniscule fraction of the total popular JSP voters), most of whom were members of the militantly Marxist public-sector labor federation called the General Council of Trade Unions (*Sohyo* in Japanese abbreviation) and of the doctrinaire revolutionary ideological "study group" called "Socialism Association."[13] As we indicated in the illustration earlier, there was a sharp divergence in attitude and orientation between the parliamentary JSP (or its majority) and its constituency party activists. In 1959, in the name of greater democracy and participatory egalitarianism in party affairs, party convention rules were changed. Until then, the JSP MPs, by virtue of their parliamentary status, were automatically voting delegates to the party convention which chose the party leadership (party chairman, secretary-general, central executive committee members), and their preferences prevailed as to candidates for these leadership posts. The party leadership, therefore, consisted largely of moderate MPs intent on enhancing the party's electoral fortune. The 1959 rule change deprived the MPs of their power to select their leadership by requiring that all convention delegates (one for every one hundred constituency party members) be elected by their respective local party organizations. These local organizations were naturally controlled by partisan and ideological *Sohyo* and Socialism Association radicals, and moderate MPs had little chance of being elected by them as convention delegates. Most JSP MPs were thus reduced to being hapless bystanders at the most important party gathering. The result of this rule change was the immediate transformation of the JSP leadership, and hence the JSP policy and public posture as well, from the moderate, increasingly

intermediative, and pragmatic to the incorrigibly doctrinaire and trenchantly ideological, for the leftist minority within the parliamentary JSP came to be heavily favored by the radical majority of the constituency JSP activists now dominant in the party convention. The electoral impact of this reradicalization of the JSP was a quick and steady decline in the party's share of popular votes in subsequent elections (to 27 percent in 1960 and 21 percent in 1969), and the party has since stagnated with tepid support of under or barely above 20 percent of voters. The reradicalization of the JSP has thus insured permanent dominance of the LDP in Japanese politics.

It does appear that in advanced industrial democracies today the socioeconomic environment has to varying degrees become less hospitable to the pattern of consensualist and centrist political competition that characterized their politics throughout much of the postwar period. While popular expectations for greater material equity and improvement remain high, resources required to meet them are more limited than before. Relations between government and governed are inevitably strained, as evinced in the decline of popular confidence in government, the erosion of regime legitimacy, and, in some cases, the rise of extremist forces on the right and/or the left. Party competition cannot help being affected by these developments, for they have the effect of strengthening certain elements in the party of the right and that of the left and making certain others vulnerable. Thus, environmental inclemency may be said to have an inherently abetting impact on party reradicalization. Insofar as we can ascertain, however, it has such an impact only when reradicalization is under way, precipitated by intraparty change in itself quite unrelated to any environmental change. The seed of reradicalization of the British Tories was the 1965 rule change initiated at the time of perhaps the best socioeconomic circumstances in postwar British history. And the single ascertainable cause of quick reradicalization of the Japan Socialist Party was that drastic convention rule change of 1959, at the very time when the nation had achieved such astonishing recovery from the devastation of war and was about to enter a period of even more astonishing growth toward international economic superstardom. Reradicalization of British Labour formally coincided with the still continuing period of economic downturn, but it was a matter of internal changes within the party which its activist strata had wanted all along. And the same condition of downward socioeconomic change elsewhere in the advanced industrial world has not created a similar phenomenon of party reradicalization. From these experiences, therefore, it does seem that the most crucial and immediate cause of reradicalization is internal to the party concerned. When that cause materializes, then the declining socioeconomic environment most likely will abet and reinforce it.

To the extent that we are worried about the actual trend (for example in the examples we examined) as well as incipient or potential trend (for example in the West German SPD)[14] toward reradicalization and repolarization, we cannot but concern ourselves with the crucial role the major political parties play in these democracies in preventing instability from arising in the arena of negotiation, intermediation, and policymaking. Reradicalization would seem to deprive the party, in power or out, of its critical ability to perform this role. These parties, during much of the postwar era, played a valuable role in promoting stability by reducing the area in which strident ideological combat and rigid sectoral struggle would be the norm of political competition. And the key to this role was the convergence and consensus between their leadership strata. And such convergence and consensus were the function of party leadership insulation or autonomy from the pressures and preferences of constituency parties and particularly their more ideological and partisan activists.

## Notes

1. Quoted in Seymour Martin Lipset, *Political Man: The Social Basis of Politics* (Garden City: Doubleday, 1963), p. 422.

2. Ulf Torgersen, "The Trend toward Political Consensus," in Erik Allardt and Stein Rokkan, eds., *Mass Politics: Studies in Political Sociology* (New York: Free Press, 1970), pp. 93–94.

3. Samuel Beer, "Political Overload and Federalism," *Polity,* 10 (Fall 1977); Anthony King, "Overload: Problems of Governing in the 1970s," *Political Studies,* 23 (June–September 1975); and Samuel Brittan, "The Economic Contradictions of Democracy," *British Journal of Political Science,* 5 (1975).

4. Dinis G. Sullivan, Jeffrey L. Pressman, Benjamin I. Page, and John J. Lyons, *The Politics of Representation: The Democratic Convention 1972* (New York: St. Martin's, 1974), pp. 2–3.

5. Leon D. Epstein, "British MPs and Their Local Parties," *American Political Science Review,* 54 (1960), p. 385.

6. Richard Rose, *Do Parties Make a Difference?* (Chatham: Chatham House, 1980), p. 24.

7. R. M. Punnett, *British Government and Politics* (London: Heinemann, 1980), pp. 266–267.

8. Robert Behrens, *The Conservative Party from Heath to Thatcher: Policies and Politics 1974–79* (London: Saxon House, 1980), pp. 30–31.

9. Robert McKenzie, "Power in the Labour Party: The Issue of 'Intra-Party Democracy,' " in Dennis Kavanagh, ed., *The Politics of the Labour Party* (London: Allen & Unwin, 1982), p. 191, and Dennis Kavanagh, "Representation in the Labour Party," in ibid., pp. 202–222.

10. Hugh Berrington, "The Labour Left in Parliament: Maintenance, Erosion and Renewal" in Kavanagh, ed., p. 91.

11. *The Economist* (London), June 11, 1983, p. 71.

12. Maurice Duverger, *Political Parties* (New York: Wiley, 1963), p. 134.

13. Taketsuga Tsurutani, *Political Change in Japan: Response to Postindustrial Challenge* (New York: McKay, 1977), pp. 118–134.

14. Gerard Braunthal, *The West German Social Democrats 1969–1982* (Boulder: Westview Press, 1983).

# 26
# Postmaterialist Politics

*Ronald Inglehart*

It is time to redress the balance in social analysis. Since the late 1960s, rational choice models based on economic variables have become the dominant mode of analysis; while cultural factors have been deemphasized to an unrealistic degree. This approach has made major contributions to our understanding of how politics works; nevertheless, it underestimates the significance of cultural factors, if only because while economic indicators are readily available for these models, cultural data generally are not.

The incompleteness of models that ignore cultural factors is becoming increasingly evident. In Catholic societies from Latin America to Poland, the church plays a major role despite the demise often predicted by economic determinists. In the Islamic world, Muslim fundamentalism has become a political factor that neither East nor West can ignore. The Confucian-influenced zone of East Asia manifests an economic dynamism that outstrips any other region of the world. By economic criteria one of the *least*-favored regions on earth, it is virtually impossible to explain its performance without reference to cultural factors. Even in advanced industrial societies religion not only outweighs social class as an influence on electoral behavior (Lijphart 1979) but actually seems to be widening its lead: while social class voting has declined markedly in recent decades, religious cleavages remain astonishingly durable.

There is no question that economic factors are politically important, but they are only part

SOURCE: Ronald Inglehart, "The Renaissance of Political Culture," *American Political Science Review*, vol. 82, no. 4 (December 1988), pp. 1120–1130. Reprinted by permission of the American Political Science Association and the author. Article abridged by the editors. Professor Inglehart's reviews of the literature on political culture and of cross-national surveys on life and political satisfaction have been omitted by the editors.

of the story. I argue that different societies are characterized to very different degrees by a specific syndrome of political cultural attitudes; that these cultural differences are relatively enduring, but not immutable; and that they have major political consequences, being closely linked to the viability of democratic institutions....

## CULTURAL CHANGE AND ECONOMIC DEVELOPMENT

...Max Weber (1958) argued at the turn of the century that the rise of capitalism and the subsequent rapid economic development of the West were made possible by a set of cultural changes related to the emergence of Calvinist Protestantism. His Protestant ethic thesis gave rise to a controversy that endured for decades. Some of the criticisms seem well founded; and the thesis that economic achievement was linked with Protestantism may seem unconvincing today, when predominantly Catholic countries have higher economic growth rates than Protestant ones. Nevertheless, though I would not defend Weber's thesis in its entirety, I believe that important aspects of it were correct, provided his work is viewed as an analysis of a specific historical phenomenon (as was clearly Weber's intention) and not as asserting an immutable relationship between economic achievement and Protestantism. Particularly crucial is Weber's insight that culture is not simply an epiphenomenon determined by economics but an autonomous set of factors that sometimes shape economic events as well as being shaped by them.

I utilize the dominant religious tradition of a given society as an indicator of its preindustrial cultural heritage. This is, of course, an oversimplified indicator though not as oversimplified as it may seem from today's perspective. Contemporary social scientists tend to underestimate the historical importance of religion, both because they are social scientists, habituated to viewing the world from a secular and scientific viewpoint, and because they are contemporary and live in societies in which the functions of religion have diminished drastically. In most agrarian societies, religion is an overwhelmingly important force, filling the functions that educational and scientific institutions, the mass media, art museums, and philanthropic foundations, as well as religious institutions, now fill in advanced industrial societies. In modern societies, religion is a far less adequate indicator

of the culture as a whole, which becomes more differentiated and subject to more rapid change. But my interest here is on the impact of the *preindustrial* cultural heritage of given societies. Though religion is only a rough indicator of this heritage, I use it for want of more refined measures of the value systems prevailing at given times and places in the past.

Figure 1 diagrams a long-term process of economic and cultural change that led to the

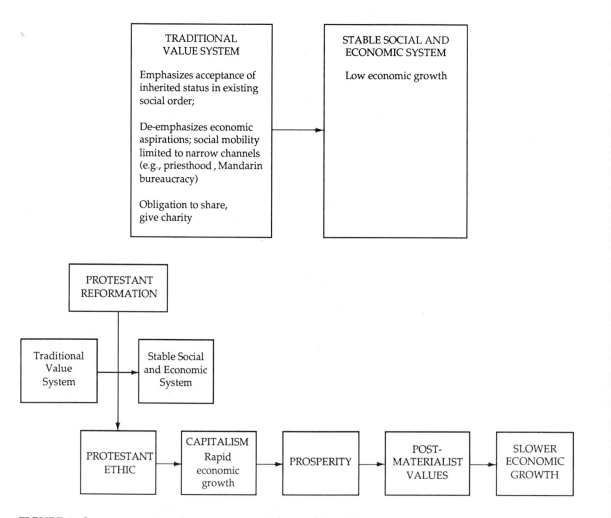

**FIGURE 1**  Long-term economic consequences of rise of Protestant ethic

NOTE: With varying time lags, the impact of the industrialized nations serves as a functional equivalent to the Protestant Reformation for the rest of the world, though the value system that emerges is shaped by the traditional value system that precedes it.

emergence of democracy in the West as one consequence. As this figure suggests, the relationship between economic and cultural change is one of complex reciprocal causality, with cultural factors not only being influenced by economic change, but also influencing it. Weber argues that Calvinist Protestantism gradually evolved into a value system that viewed the accumulation of wealth for its own sake (and not as a means to survive or acquire luxuries) as a sign of divine grace and encouraged an ascetic self-control conducive to the accumulation of wealth. This led to an entrepreneurial spirit and an accumulation of capital that facilitated the Industrial Revolution in the eighteenth and nineteenth centuries, which in turn had immense consequences for global economic development in the twentieth century.

I suggest that the Protestant Reformation was only one case of a more general phenomenon: the breakdown of traditional cultural barriers to economic modernization. For as the top half of Figure 1 suggests, one feature common to traditional value systems is that they emerge in, and are adapted to, economies characterized by very little technological change and economic growth. In this situation, social mobility is a zero-sum game, heavily laden with conflict and threatening to the social system. In a society undergoing rapid industrialization and expansion, by contrast, social mobility may be widespread. But in traditional agrarian societies, social status is hereditary, except when an individual or group forcibly seizes the lands and social status of another. To preserve social peace, virtually all traditional cultures discourage upward social mobility and the accumulation of wealth. These cultures perform an integrating function by providing a rationale that legitimates the established social order and inculcating norms of sharing, charity, and other obligations that help to mitigate the harshness of a subsistence economy.

By their very nature the traditional value systems of agrarian society are adapted to maintaining a stable balance in unchanging societies. Accordingly, they tend to discourage social

change in general and the accumulative entrepreneurial spirit in particular. One of the important functions of the Protestant Reformation was to break the grip of the medieval Christian world view on a significant portion of Europe. It did not accomplish this alone. The emergence of scientific inquiry had already begun to undermine the anthropocentric cosmos of the medieval Christian tradition. But it is difficult to avoid the conclusion that Weber's emphasis on the role of Protestantism captures an important part of reality. For prior to the Protestant Reformation, southern Europe was economically more advanced than northern Europe. During the three centuries after the Reformation, capitalism emerged, mainly among the Protestant regions of Europe and among the Protestant minorities of Catholic countries. Protestant Europe manifested a subsequent economic dynamism that was extraordinary, moving it far ahead of Catholic Europe. Shifting trade patterns, declining food production in southern Europe, and other variables played a role in this shift, but the evidence suggests that cultural factors were also important.

As capitalism led to industrialization and eventually to historically unprecedented levels of prosperity, emulation became more and more attractive, and increasing amounts of cross-cultural diffusion took place. But to a truly remarkable degree, throughout the early stages the Protestant cultural zone was markedly more receptive to industrialization and economic development than any other part of the world. The Industrial Revolution began in England, spreading rapidly to predominantly Protestant Scotland and Wales but leaving Catholic Ireland largely untouched except for the Protestant region around Belfast. Industrialization spread from England to nearby France but lagged there in comparison with its rapid implantation in more distant but more receptive areas such as the United States and Germany, both of which soon became far more industrialized than France. At the start of the twentieth century, the correlation between Protestantism and economic development was still remarkably strong. In

Europe, the economically most dynamic nations were Great Britain, Germany, Sweden, Denmark, Norway, The Netherlands, and Switzerland, all of which were predominantly Protestant at that time. The only non-Protestant countries that had attained even roughly comparable levels of economic development were Belgium and France, both of which were geographically near the original core area from which the Industrial Revolution spread and in both of which Protestant minorities played a disproportionately important role in the process of economic development. In the New World, the United States and Canada had also emerged as developed industrial societies, while virtually all of Latin America remained almost totally unaffected by the Industrial Revolution. Even within Canada, the predominantly Catholic region developed much less rapidly than the rest of the country. Economic development seemed wedded to Protestantism.

But culture is not a constant. It is a system through which a society adapts to its environment. Given a changing environment, in the long run culture is likely to change. One major change that took place was the secularization of Catholic (and other non-Protestant) cultures. In much of the world, the role of the merchant and the profit-making entrepreneur became less stigmatized. In some settings the entrepreneur even became the cultural hero, as the captain of industry had been in the United States of the late nineteenth century.

A contrasting process of cultural change began to take place in the more advanced industrial societies during the second half of the twentieth century. The lower half of figure 1 diagrams this process. Precisely in those regions that had earlier been most strongly influenced by the Protestant ethic, the long-term consequences of economic development began to be felt, as generations emerged that had been raised in unprecedented prosperity and economic security and were characterized, increasingly, by the presence of postmaterialist values. . . .

This thesis implies that as a result of the historically unprecedented prosperity and the absence of war that has prevailed in Western countries since 1945, younger birth cohorts place less emphasis on economic and physical security than do older groups, who have experienced a much greater degree of economic insecurity. Conversely, the younger birth cohorts tend to give a higher priority to nonmaterial needs, such as a sense of community and the quality of life. Cohort analysis carried out from 1970 through 1987 in six Western countries confirms the presence of substantial differences in the basic societal priorities of younger and older generations. Moreover, it demonstrates that as intergenerational population replacement has occurred, there has been a gradual but pervasive shift in the values of these publics from predominantly materialist priorities toward postmaterialist goals. One consequence of this shift has been a diminishing emphasis on economic growth in these societies together with increasing emphasis on environmental protection and preserving the quality of life—if necessary, even at the expense of economic growth. Postmaterialists place markedly less emphasis on economic growth than do those with materialist or mixed values. And they emphasize a high salary and job security less than working with people they like or doing interesting work. Conversely, postmaterialists place more emphasis on protecting the environment and are far more likely to be active members of environmental organizations than are materialists. Finally, postmaterialists are economic underachievers; that is, *controlling* for the fact that they come from more prosperous families and receive better education, postmaterialists earn significantly lower incomes than those with materialist values. All this suggests that as societies become increasingly influenced by the growing postmaterialist minority, they will tend to give economic growth a lower priority. Figures 2 and 3 test this prediction at the societal level.

Evidence from a cross-national perspective converges with evidence from the individual level, pointing to a long-term cultural process of negative feedback linked with economic growth. On one hand, as figure 2 demonstrates, the

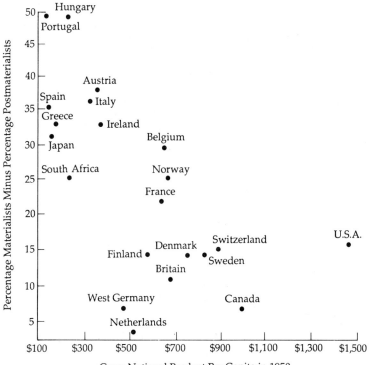

**FIGURE 2** Economic development and the decline of materialist values
SOURCE: Value priorities data from World Values survey, 1981; Euro-Barometer surveys 19–25 (1982–1986); and Political Action study, 1974. Gross national product per capita calculated from *UN Statistical Yearbook, 1958* (New York: UN, 1959).
NOTE: $r = -.63$.

publics of relatively rich societies are least likely to emphasize materialist values and most likely to emphasize postmaterialist ones. Since one's values tend to reflect the conditions prevailing during one's preadult years, I allow a lag of about 30 years between the independent variable (level of development in 1950) and the dependent variable (mass value priorities in 1981–86). Since the median age in my adult sample is about 45, my economic indicator taps conditions when the median individual was about 15 years of age, I find a correlation of $-.63$ between a society's per capita GNP in 1950 and the proportion of materialists among that society's public in the 1980s. Not only does this result have the predicted polarity and significant strength, but it is stronger than the correlation

obtained when I use GNP per capita in 1980 as the independent variable. The time lag assumed to exist between economic cause and cultural effect seems to reflect reality.

Figure 3 is a mirror image of figure 2. The wealthier societies are least likely to produce materialist publics, but materialist publics seem to produce high economic growth rates. Or, to reverse labels, though wealthier societies are most likely to produce postmaterialists, after an appropriate time lag the more postmaterialist societies have the lowest growth rates. The long-term result is that high growth rates eventually lead to lower growth rates. Prosperity engenders a cultural shift toward postmaterialist values, which eventually leads to a less intense emphasis on economic growth.

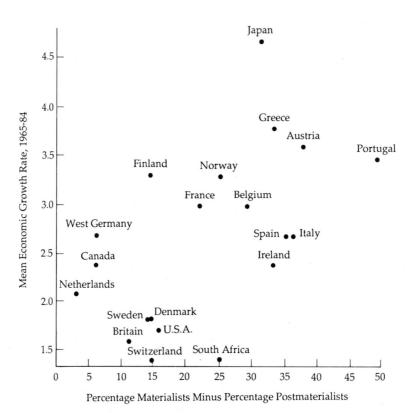

**FIGURE 3**   Materialist values and economic growth, 1965–84

SOURCES: Growth rates 1965–1984 from *World Development Report, 1986* (Washington: World Bank, 1986). Growth rates 1870–1913 from Angus Maddison, *Economic Growth in Japan and the USSR* (London: Allen & Unwin, 1969).

NOTE: $r = .51$ (correlation between 1870–1913 growth rates and 1981–1986 values = $-.38$, i.e., the countries that are most postmaterialist today had relatively high growth rates in 1870–1913).

---

Data from 21 societies reveal a consistent cultural-economic syndrome that was originally linked with the Protestant ethic: the wealthier nations and those with highly developed tertiary sectors are most likely to be long-established democracies, *and* the publics of these societies tend to show a "civic" political culture, have less materialist value priorities, and tend to be Protestant in religion (cf. Huntington 1984). But the Protestant ethic seems to be unraveling: for the linkage between Protestantism and economic achievement is a thing of the past. While the Protestant ethic syndrome was strongly correlated with high levels of economic growth in 1870–1913 (the earliest period for which we have

data), this correlation weakens and then becomes strongly negative as we move into historically more recent periods.

Among those countries for which we have long-term historical data, those that had relatively high growth rates a century ago tend to have relatively low growth rates today. Table 1 illustrates this phenomenon. In 1870–1913, nearly all Protestant countries had growth rates that were higher than those of almost all Catholic countries. My table actually understates the extent to which this was true, because the few Catholic countries from which we have historical data are precisely the ones that were *most* developed in the nineteenth century.

**TABLE 1**  Economic growth rates in Protestant versus Catholic countries and Japan, 1870–1984

| Rank | 1870–1913 | 1913–1938 | 1949–1965 | 1965–1984 |
|---|---|---|---|---|
| 1 | U.S.A. (P) | Japan (B) | Japan (B) | Japan (B) |
| 2 | Canada (P) | Norway (P) | W. Germany (P) | Norway (P) |
| 3 | Denmark (P) | Netherlands (P) | Italy (C) | France (C) |
| 4 | Sweden (P) | U.S.A. (P) | France (C) | Belgium (C) |
| 5 | Germany (P) | Switzerland (P) | Switzerland (P) | Italy (C) |
| 6 | Belgium (C) | Denmark (P) | Netherlands (P) | W. Germany (P) |
| 7 | Switzerland (P) | Sweden (P) | Canada (P) | Canada (P) |
| 8 | Japan (B) | Italy (C) | Denmark (P) | Netherlands (P) |
| 9 | Norway (P) | Canada (P) | Norway (P) | Denmark (P) |
| 10 | Gt. Britain (P) | Germany (P) | Sweden (P) | Sweden (P) |
| 11 | Netherlands (P) | Gt. Britain (P) | U.S.A. (P) | U.S.A. (P) |
| 12 | France (C) | France (C) | Belgium (C) | Gt. Britain (P) |
| 13 | Italy (C) | Belgium (C) | Gt. Britain (P) | Switzerland (P) |
| **Mean economic growth rate in Protestant countries*** | 152 | 120 | 98 | 72 |

SOURCES: 1870–1965 standings calculated from data in Angus Maddison, *Economic Growth in Japan and the U.S.S.R.* (London: Allen & Unwin, 1969), pp. 148–149; 1965–1984 standings from data in *World Development Report, 1986* (Washington: World Bank, 1986).
NOTE: (P) = countries in which a majority of the population was Protestant in 1900; (C) = countries having a Roman Catholic majority in 1900; (B) = Buddhist majority in 1900.
*Percentage of rates in Catholic countries.

Protestant countries still had more dynamic economies in the interwar years. But in the past few decades, this situation has reversed itself; during 1965–84, the Catholic countries in our sample had *higher* growth rates than most of the Protestant ones. Within the United States, as recently as 1958, Catholics and Protestants manifested different values concerning various aspects of economic and family life (Lenski 1963). But these differences have been dwindling (Alwin 1986).

In part, this reflects the fact that it is easier for a poor country to attain a high growth rate than for a rich one. By importing technology that has already been proven in more developed countries, one can catch up rapidly. But in global perspectives it is clear that this is only part of the story. For plenty of poor societies are *not* showing rapid economic growth, while others (like those of East Asia) have been growing at an extraordinary pace. Clearly, some societies

are more receptive to economic development than others. Conversely, some rich nations (like Japan) continue to develop relatively rapidly—even when they can no longer rely on imported technology but are increasingly developing their own —while others have become relatively stagnant.

High economic growth was once an almost uniquely Protestant phenomenon; today it has become global in scope and is *less* likely to be found in the Protestant societies than elsewhere. This does not mean that the civic culture that emerged in these societies will disappear. On the contrary, these countries are still becoming richer and on the whole, life satisfaction, political satisfaction, and trust have been gradually rising in recent years. The syndrome that linked Protestantism with wealth and democracy has become less distinctively Protestant because it is permeating other regions of the world.

It is doing so unevenly, however, with its spread being shaped by the cultural traditions of given societies. The Confucian system was virtually unique among traditional cultures in that it institutionalized a socially accepted and even honored channel for upward social mobility, based on nonviolent individual achievement rather than ascription. By passing a series of difficult academic examinations that were open to any promising young male, one could attain power, status, and wealth as a government official. Consequently, in the sixteenth century a social scientist from Mars might have ranked East Asia, with its Confucian tradition, as the region of the world that was culturally most conducive to economic development. Though narrowly circumscribed, social mobility through individual achievement was accepted to a degree virtually unknown elsewhere. Education, rather than armed force, was the principal means to rise in society. And a secular orientation was relatively conducive to technology and worldly achievement.

I suspect that the Confucian cultural tradition, its traditional rigidity having been shattered by the impact of the West, is an important element underlying the current economic dynamism of certain portions of Asia. During the period from 1965 to 1984, 5 of the 10 fastest-growing nations in the world were countries shaped by the Confucian and Buddhist traditions: Singapore, South Korea, Hong Kong, Taiwan, and Japan. China ranked thirteenth. Moreover, three more of the top 20 countries had significant Chinese minorities that in each case played disproportionately important economic roles: Malaysia, Thailand, and Indonesia. Finally, immigrants of East Asian origin have shown disproportionately high rates of economic achievement throughout Southeast Asia and in the United States, Canada, and Western Europe. It is difficult to avoid the conclusion that the Confucian cultural tradition is conducive to economic achievement today. It would be unrealistic to view these traits as indelible, however. My broader thesis suggests that the intense emphasis on economic achievement now found among peoples shaped by the Confucian

tradition could emerge only when the static orientation of traditional society was broken and is likely to gradually erode when future generations have been raised in high levels of economic security. For the present, however, it may be a key factor in the world economy.

## CONCLUSION

Both social analysis and social policy would be much simpler if people from different societies were interchangeable robots. But a large body of evidence indicates that they are not. The peoples of given societies tend to be characterized by reasonably durable cultural attributes that sometimes have major political and economic consequences. If this is true, then effective social policy will be better served by learning about these differences and about how they vary cross-culturally and over time than by pretending that they don't exist.

Rational choice models constitute one of the most promising tools now available for political analysis. As currently applied, they are effective in analyzing short-term fluctuations within a given system, taking cultural and institutional factors as constant. But these factors are not constant, either cross-nationally or over time. And current models cannot deal with long-term changes in the basic goals and nature of a system. One of the central debates in the field of political economy seems to reflect this fact. When it was found that political support responded to fluctuations in the economy, it was taken for granted that this reflected the workings of economic self-interest among the electorate. Subsequent research has made this interpretation increasingly doubtful. The linkage between economics and politics seems largely shaped by sociotropic concerns. The classic model of economically determined behavior has a strong grip on the minds of social analysts, probably because, throughout most of the history of industrial society, it provided a fairly accurate description of human behavior. In recent decades, the rising role of postmaterialist concerns may have helped make sociotropic concerns increasingly important, particularly among the politically more aware segments of the electorate.

Political economy research has demonstrated convincingly that short-term economic changes have significant political consequences. But the long-term consequences of economic change have barely begun to be analyzed in comparable fashion, though they may be at least equally significant. Evidence presented here indicates that the emergence and viability of mass-based democracy is closely related to economic development *and* that the outcome is contingent on specific cultural changes. Though mass democracy is almost impossible without a certain amount of economic development, economic development by itself does not produce democracy. Unless specific changes occur in culture and social structure, the result may not be democracy but a variety of alternatives ranging from the Libyan to the Soviet. A large body of cross-national survey evidence indicates that enduring cultural differences exist. Though these differences may be related to the economic level of a given nation, they are relatively independent of short-term economic changes. These cultural factors have an important bearing on the durability of democracy, which seems to result from a complex interplay of economic, cultural, and institutional factors. To neglect any of these components may compromise its survival.

Finally, it appears that economic development itself is influenced by cultural variables. In my brief analysis of this, I have utilized one indicator of materialist and postmaterialist values that is available from only the past two decades and another indicator—the dominant religious or philosophic tradition of a given society—that is a greatly oversimplified indicator of prevailing worldviews at a given time and place but goes back over centuries. Clearly, this analysis cannot be regarded as conclusive. But the available evidence tends to confirm Weber's insight that culture is not just a consequence of economics but can shape the basic nature of economic and political life.

## Author's References

ALMOND, GABRIEL, and SIDNEY VERBA. 1963. *The Civic Culture.* Princeton: Princeton University Press.

ALWIN, DUANE F. 1986. "Religion and Parental Childrearing Orientations: Evidence of a Catholic-Protestant Convergence." *American Journal of Sociology* 92:412–440.

ANDREWS, FRANK, and STEPHEN WITHEY. 1976. *Social Indicators of Well-Being in America.* New York: Plenum.

BANFIELD, EDWARD. 1958. *The Moral Basis of a Backward Society.* Chicago: Free Press.

CANTRIL, HADLEY. 1965. *The Pattern of Human Concerns.* New Brunswick: Rutgers University Press.

DALTON, RUSSELL J. 1977. "Was There a Revolution? A Note in Generational versus Life-Cycle Explanations of Value Differences." *Comparative Political Studies* 9:459–475.

DALTON, RUSSELL J., SCOTT FLANAGAN, and PAUL ALLEN BECK, eds. 1984. *Electoral Change in Advanced Industrial Democracies.* Princeton: Princeton University Press.

DETH, JAN W. van. 1984. *Politieke Waarden: Een Onderzoek naar politieke waardeorientaties in Nederland in de periode 1970 tot 1982.* Amsterdam: CT Press.

EASTERLIN, RICHARD A. 1974. "Does Economic Growth Improve the Human Lot? Some Empirical Evidence." In *Nations and Households in Economic Growth,* ed. Paul A. David and Melvin W. Reder. New York: Academic.

FLANAGAN, SCOTT C. 1982. "Changing Values in Advanced Industrial Society." *Comparative Political Studies* 14:403–444.

GALLUP, GEORGE H. 1976. "Human Needs and Satisfaction: A Global Survery." *Public Opinion Quarterly* 41:459–467.

HUNTINGTON, SAMUEL P. 1984. "Will More Countries Become Democratic?" *Political Science Quarterly* 99:193–218.

IKE, NOBUTAKA. 1973. "Economic Growth and Intergenerational Change in Japan." *American Political Science Review* 67:1194–1203.

INGLEHART, RONALD. 1971. "The Silent Revolution in Europe: Intergenerational Change in

Postindustrial Societies." *American Political Science Review* 65:991–1017.

INGLEHART, RONALD. 1977. *The Silent Revolution: Changing Values and Political Styles among Western Publics.* Princeton: Princeton University Press.

INGLEHART, RONALD. 1981. "Post-Materialism in an Environment of Insecurity." *American Political Science Review* 75:880–900.

INGLEHART, RONALD. 1985. "Aggregate Stability and Individual-Level Change in Mass Belief Systems: The Level of Analysis Paradox." *American Political Science Review* 79:97–117.

INGLEHART, RONALD. N.d. *Culture Change in Advanced Industrial Society.* Princeton: Princeton University Press. Forthcoming.

KAASE, MAX, and HANS-DIETER KLINGEMANN. 1979. "Sozialstruktur, Wertorientierung, und Parteiensysteme." In *Sozialer Wandel in West Europa,* ed. Joachim Mattes. Frankfurt: Campus Verlag.

LAFFERTY, WILLIAM M., and ODDBJORN KNUTSEN. 1985. "Postmaterialism in a Social Democratic State: An Analysis of the Distinctness and Congruity of the Inglehart Value Syndrome in Norway." *Comparative Political Studies* 17:411–431.

LENSKI, GERHARD. 1963. *The Religious Factor.* New York: Anchor-Doubleday.

LIJPHART, AREND. 1979. "Religious vs. Linguistic vs. Class Voting: The Crucial Experiment of Comparing Belgium, Canada, South Africa, and Switzerland." *American Political Science Review* 73:442–461.

MARSH, ALAN. 1975. "The Silent Revolution, Value Priorities, and the Quality of Life in Britain." *American Political Science Review* 69:1–30.

MOORE, BARRINGTON. 1966. *Social Origins of Dictatorship and Democracy.* Boston: Beacon.

PUTNAM, ROBERT D., ROBERT LEONARDI, RAFFAELLA Y. NANETTI, and FRANCO PAVONCELLO. 1983. "Explaining Institutional Success: The Case of Italian Regional Government." *American Political Science Review* 77:55–74.

THOMASSEN, JACQUES et al. 1983. *De Verstomde Revolutie.* Alphen aan den Rijn: Samsom Uitgeverij.

WEBER, MAX. 1958. *The Protestant Ethic and the Spirit of Capitalism.* New York: Scribners.

# 27

# Democratic Theory and Neocorporatist Practice

*Philippe C. Schmitter*

## NEOCORPORATISM

The concept of corporatism, usually accompanied by some prefix such as "societal-," "liberal-," "bargained-," or, more recently, "neo-," burst upon the social-science scene in 1974[1] and has since grown in prominence to the point that it has been described by one author as "a growth industry."[2] Confused in political discourse with fascism and authoritarian rule—not to mention with the French-Italian polemic usage which identifies it with the pursuit of narrow and immediate sectoral interests—and confounded in academic discussion by competing definitions and theoretical approaches, it has become a controversial subject, an "essentially contested" concept. Neocorporatism (the *neo* is intended both to separate it from its historical predecessors—whether medieval or interwar—and to indicate its relative novelty) has been found everywhere—and nowhere. It has been credited with producing all sorts of goods—and charged with promoting all manner of evils. It has been described as an inexorable political trend—and called a passing academic fancy. Most of all, it has been difficult to define neocorporatism clearly and consensually. One of its strengths has been its ability to speak to the concerns of scholars from different disciplines and orientations—each of whom, however, has tended to give his or her own twist to the concept. It has become virtually impossible to tell whether all of the contributors to this growth industry are

SOURCE: Philippe C. Schmitter, "Democratic Theory and Neocorporatist Practice," *Social Research* 50, no. 4 (Winter 1983), pp. 885–928. By permission. Article and notes abridged by the editors.

talking about related, much less identical, phenomena.

For purposes of this essay, neocorporatism refers to a recently emergent *political* arrangement—not to a new way of running the economy or ordering the entire society. It is concerned primarily with the activities of permanently organized and specialized *associations*—not units of production (firms, enterprises, corporations, etc.), not units of consumption (individuals, families, cooperatives, etc.), not units of status or affect (corps, colleagues, cliques, etc.), and not units of public authority (state agencies, ministries, parliaments, local governments, etc.). These associations seek to advance or defend interests by influencing and contesting collective choices. And they do this by intermediating between members and various interlocutors (mostly the State) without presenting candidates for electoral approval or accepting direct responsibility for the formation of governments (i.e., they are not parties, caucuses, coalitions, etc.). Any or all of the other above-mentioned units of political action may have a significant effect on the emergence or viability of neocorporatism by supporting, opposing, or circumventing it, but they are not an integral part of its defining properties. Indeed, it is arguable that neocorporatist practices have proven compatible with a rather wide range of surrounding units.

However, neocorporatist arrangements are not the only way in which intermediation between interest associations and authoritative interlocutors can be institutionalized. Indeed, if one leaves aside medieval precedents and the short period of state-enforced corporatization under interwar dictatorships, they are relatively recent and rare. For a considerable period, the predominant way of conceptualizing interest intermediation was "pluralism," and a very substantial and impressive literature on that topic was devoted to demonstrating that its arrangements were not just compatible with but actively promotive of democracy. Much of the "cloud of suspicion" which hangs over neocorporatism is due, not just to the objections of

those "utopians" who reject organized intermediation and incorporation of partial interests into policymaking on the grounds that it is destructive of the direct citizen role in public affairs and of government by popular assembly, but to the suspicions of "realists" that these new arrangements represent a serious distortion and perversion of "proven" pluralist processes. . . .

## NEOCORPORATIST PRACTICES AND THE CITIZENSHIP PRINCIPLE

In our effort to develop normative standards for evaluating its performance, we defined modern, representative democracy as a general principle in search of a certain qualitative relationship between rulers and ruled. Connecting the two are decision rules, procedural norms, and political institutions which have varied considerably over time—no matter how established and definitive they may appear at a given moment. Except in instances of dramatic refounding after the collapse of an authoritarian regime or in periods of deliberate reform in the face of manifest crisis, these specific rules, procedures, and institutions tend to change slowly, often imperceptibly, and usually by consensus under the pressure of opportunistic situations, internal diffusion, or evolutionary trends.

Neocorporatism is a good example of such a transformation within democratic polities in which the "procedural minimum" has been respected but substantial changes in such things as majority rule, parliamentary sovereignty, public deliberation, etc. have occurred. Perhaps precisely because these contemporary trends in the organizational structure of interests and in their relation to policymaking have not been backed by an explicit ideology—again in contrast to interwar state or authoritarian corporatism—and because they evolved in such a piecemeal, uneven, and almost surreptitious manner within distinct policy arenas, they have largely escaped evaluative scrutiny. Only once they have accumulated over time, so to speak, and are manifestly affecting a wide range of producer and consumer—as well as citizen—behaviors is the question of their compatibility with democracy likely to arise and to attract the attention of scholars as well as activists.

Our first and most diffuse evaluative standard is whether these arrangements violate the principle of citizenship. Do they diminish the extent to which individuals have equal opportunities to act as citizens and to be treated as equals by their fellow citizens? Do they reduce the extent to which citizens feel obligated to respect choices made by collective deliberation among equals (or their representatives)?

If one equates the opportunity to act as citizen only with voting and the obligation to conform only to laws which have been certified by a sovereign legislature, then neocorporatism is manifestly contrary to the citizenship principle. It introduces elements of "weighted" calculation and consensual bargaining with privileged minorities which clearly violate the sacred norms of "one man, one vote" and "the most votes win." It generates binding commitments which either are never subject to parliamentary approval or involve a mere officializing of package deals hammered out elsewhere. However, if one broadens the notion of equal political opportunity and treatment to include intraelectoral periods and extraelectoral processes, then neocorporatism can be interpreted as extending the citizenship principle.

Basically, what it does is to resolve "the paradox of liberal associability," the fact that where the freedom to associate is equally accorded but the capacity to exercise this freedom is unequally distributed, those that most need to act collectively in defense of their interests are the least likely to be able to do so. Small, compact, and privileged groups who are already better able to advance their interests through existing economic and social exchanges than larger, more dispersed, and equally endowed ones, will find it easier to recruit members and extract contributions for a further defense of their interests in the political realm—if and when such a response is required. Hence comes the

theme of the "institutionalization of bias" in pressure politics which has been decried by so many critics of pluralism.[3] What neocorporatism does is shift the basis of associability from a predominantly voluntaristic and individualistic calculus to one where contributions become more generally binding on all members of a relevant category (or more difficult to avoid), and mutual recognition and official certification protect the role of specific collectivities at the expense of competing fragments or individual actors. In short, as "free riding" and "freebooting" became increasingly difficult under such arrangements, virtually everyone can be made to contribute and conform to associative action. This can have the effect of evening out considerably the organizational capacity of competing groups, particularly capital and labor. In addition, most neocorporatist forums are based on highly formalized systems of parity in representation and, not infrequently, produce policies which make the participating "social partners" co-responsible for their implementation. Under such conditions, organized socioeconomic interests may never be equally counted, but they are likely to be more equally weighed than they would be if citizens invested voluntarily and individually their own disparate resources and personal intensities in the liberal "art of association."

The normative problem with applying this "science of organization" to interest intermediation is that it may make more equal the capacities for exerting influence of incorporated collectivities at the same time that it purposively excludes others which may be affected by their deliberations. So far, neocorporatism has privileged interests organized along functional lines of production within a capitalist economy—classes, sectors, and professions. Its relative success has depended on restricting the number and identity of participants and passing on the costs to those not directly represented in its deliberations: consumers, taxpayers, youths, feminists, irregular workers, foreigners, cultural minorities, nature lovers, pedestrians, prohibitionists, etc. Granted that the more comprehensive scope of the associations engaged in neocorporatist bargaining may encourage them to take into account some of these "marginal" interests—for example, when a comprehensive trade union calculates the effect of its demands on its member interests as consumers or when a national business association agrees to moderate its position in deference to the need for environmental protection[4]—but this is a tenuous and contingent relationship, hardly reliable enough in the long run to lead to an effective equalization of influence for such categories of citizens. Existing corporatist associations which defer too much to such interests risk a paralysis of their own internal decision structures and/or a defection of their own core supporters.

One "democratic" answer would be to extend the process of corporatization to cover interests structured along distributional lines or causes generated by cultural and ideological diversity, but that hardly seems feasible. Establishing monopolistic, hierarchically coordinated, and topically differentiated national associations for, say, consumers, taxpayers, youths, environmentalists, and foreign residents would likely involve such extensive state intervention and subsidization that it would be difficult to avoid the appearance, not to mention the reality, of manipulation and cooptation from above. The officially recognized associations would be simply disavowed by their nominal members and lose all credibility for contracting in their names. In addition to which, many of these groups define their very existence in ways that defy professionalized representation and bureaucratic *encadrement*. To be organized corporatistically would destroy the very basis of their collective identity. Finally, even if the organizational problem could be solved, bringing such a quantity and variety of recognized interlocutors into the policy-making process on a coequal basis would destroy the properties of small-group interaction, specialized competence, reciprocal trust, and propensity for compromise which have contributed so much to the viability of existing neocorporatist arrangements.

In summary, a pattern of more equalized and formally structured exchange among associations has emerged in some democratic countries—a sort of corporatism for the functionally privileged—which could be defended as a direct extension of the citizenship principle outside the electoral-parliamentary arena in ways that go beyond the formalistic opportunities afforded by pluralist associability. Moreover, its operation has undoubtedly had the indirect effect of promoting policies which have extended citizen rights to protection against unemployment, to more extensive welfare services, and to representation within institutions previously governed by other authority principles, especially business firms and state agencies. Citizens of pluralistically structured polities have suffered significantly greater inequalities in all these domains. Its unintended consequence, however, has been to consolidate a disparity between these more equally *competent* and privileged class, sectoral, and professional interests and less equally *competent* and organized ones—leaving a sort of residual pluralism for the distributionally disadvantaged and the culturally underprivileged. Since there appear to be serious impediments to extending neocorporatist practices to these latter interest domains and since at least some of these appear to be of genuine concern to the citizenry of contemporary democracies, neocorporatism is neither fully compatible with the citizenship principle nor are decisions made under its auspices likely to go unchallenged by those who are expected to obey them. However, like so many of its forerunners in the history of democratic development, its norms and institutions may long be tolerated as a second-best compromise: "a better system than those that preceded it and those that have hitherto followed it."[5]

## A SHIFT IN THE QUALITY OF DEMOCRACY?

...Neocorporatist arrangements shift performance away from a concern with *participation* and *accessibility* toward a greater emphasis on *accountability* and *responsiveness*. Individual citizens become less intensely and directly involved in political life; at the same time, organizations active in their interests became increasingly integral components of the policy process. The number and type of interlocutors with equivalent and effective access to authorities decrease considerably due to the recognition of monopolies, the creation of associational hierarchies, and the formalization of functional systems of representation; at the same time those that are able to obtain such privileged status acquire more resources and become more indispensable to the management of public affairs so that arbitrary (and often self-serving) actions by state officials become less likely. Subjects of collective choice which were highly politicized—that is, subject to intense citizen concern, public debate, group mobilization, and extensive pressure—become less so, at the same time as institutions of administrative and market allocation which were previously defined as outside the realm of democratic polities become subject to greater scrutiny by political associations.

In the midst of this shift from participation/accessibility to accountability/responsiveness lies a phenomenon which modern democratic theory has been ill prepared to analyze or even to recognize, namely, the development of "private" or "class governance." Perhaps one major reason for this stems from its historical roots in liberalism. Democratic theory was originally closely identified with the liberal struggle against the constraints that obligatory associability had placed on the economic and social behavior of individuals: guild restrictions, state-chartered monopolies, licensing provisions, etc. It continued to regard all associations which subsequently grew up under its tolerance and encouragement as purely voluntary and autonomous, an embodiment of that original resistance to regimentation and loss of individual freedom.

Neocorporatism changes not merely the resources of associations and the nature of policymaking. It can also radically alter the relationship between interest groups and their members. Instead of merely aggregating independently formed preferences and articulating them before authorities, its associations acquire an enhanced capacity for defining the interests of members and controlling their behavior. In the pluralist idiom, *information* is the key resource involved in interest exchange; in the corporatist mode, it becomes *compliance*. Associations do not just inform policymakers about the intensities of preference and likely reactions of their members, expecting officials to react accordingly; they also agree—for a price—to deliver member compliance to contracts negotiated with the approval of public authorities. All this presumes, of course, that it will be to the long-term benefit of members to be forced to cooperate irrespective of their individualistic, short-term preferences. Occasionally and always reluctantly, neocorporatist organizations may even have to wield directly the coercive powers necessary to keep dissident members (and even nonmembers where contracts are extended to cover a whole category) in line: fines, expulsions, refusal to provide services, loss of license, etc. Whether this authority is generated consensually from within or devolved legally upon it from without, the net result is the same. The society acquires a set of parallel institutions of semiprivate and semipublic governance capable of coordinating the behavior of some large social aggregates—classes, sectors, professions—without directly burdening or involving state authorities. This may provide one element for explaining why the more neocorporatist polities have proven demonstrably more "governable" in recent decades than pluralist ones at a similar level of capitalist development and organizational complexity.

This leaves us with competitiveness, the quality of democracy which putatively ties all the others together. What happens to it under the auspices of neocorporatism? Obviously, some forms are eliminated altogether or reduced to insignificance. Groups with overlapping domains no longer compete for members or for access to public authorities on the same issues.

Factions within associations are less likely to risk investing their resources in founding alternative organizations, if only because other public and private interlocutors will persist in recognizing only the officially monopolistic one. Under a general process of incorporation, highly specialized or very particularistic "maverick groups" will find it increasingly prudent to merge with larger and more established units or to accept coordination from overarching "peak associations" if they do not wish to suffer a progressive margination from the policy process.

It is not clear whether the politics *within* neocorporatist organizations is likely to become more competitive as that between them diminishes. Certainly the rewards for winning office become more substantial with the increase in associational resources and semi-public functions, but that may only encourage entrenched oligarchies to defend their positions more assiduously and tempt state and party officials to intervene in order to ensure that interest interlocutors will continue to play the responsible and respectful role assigned to them. At the level of national peak associations, executive leaders become highly visible and influential figures who can count on help from "outsiders" provided they agree to stay within the rules of the corporatist game.

But this does not mean that competitiveness disappears altogether under such arrangements. Rather its effect tends to become more implicit than explicit, more potential than observable. One must never forget that neocorporatism is a chosen, not an imposed, strategy for the promotion and defense of interests and that it is not the only mode of intermediation between citizens and authorities. Associations can withdraw from negotiations patterned this way—and they can survive, even prosper, by engaging in classic pressure politics. Specific issues can be taken to other arenas—and they can be articulated through single-issue movements or spontaneous protest actions. Association members are also voting citizens—and they can express their dissatisfaction by switching allegiance among existing parties or by supporting new

ones. Parties which have promoted corporatist arrangements can lose elections—and their successors in government may choose to dismantle or ignore those arrangements. Parliaments can assert their legal sovereignty—and they can refuse to ratify the social contracts which are put before them. Members can refuse to obey the directives of their associations—and the sanctions available may be so weak or difficult to wield that they can get away with such defections. The fact that such occurrences have been relatively rare in neocorporatist polities does not alter the latent role that competitiveness continues to play in setting boundaries upon such arrangements. Participants in them are forced to anticipate that such reactions could occur and to adjust their bargaining behavior accordingly. They cannot act as if neocorporatism were the only game in town. Observers, however, who predicted its imminent demise after each wildcat strike or electoral failure of Social Democracy have been generally disappointed. It even appears to be surviving under the conditions of increased national and international competitiveness induced by protracted recession and consequent failure to meet such performance goals as full employment and economic growth. Nevertheless, the politics of these countries has not settled into some "postproblematic" consensus. Controversial items still manage to get on their agenda for collective deliberation; citizens continue to be offered real choices; associational leaders know they must be accountable to member preferences—just as they know they must be responsive to system imperatives.

Moreover, one cannot ignore the fact that many of the polities where neocorporatist practices have become most firmly entrenched have either inherited (e.g., Switzerland) or experimented with (e.g., Sweden, Norway, Denmark, Austria, West Germany) a wide range of institutional innovations which have extended the equal rights of individual citizens in their direct interaction with public officials and partisan representatives: referenda, proportional representation, ombudsman systems, subsidies for political parties and citizen groups, elections to works councils, public-disclosure laws, decentralized administration, protection of personal data, profit-sharing arrangements, and so forth. One can argue that not all of these have had that much of an impact (and some have been very selectively implemented), but one can hardly fault these systems for not trying. It is at least plausible that discussion of them and their eventual presence in political life has effectively compensated for some of the more insidious and less positive effects that creeping neocorporatism has had upon the other democratic qualities of participation, accessibility, and competitiveness.

Finally, one must acknowledge the almost complete absence of popular resistance to neocorporatist trends in those countries. This is all the more remarkable since they have rarely been defended explicitly and globally. Ordinarily they have been sanctioned only pragmatically on a case-by-case basis. No one confesses to being a "corporatist," or even to some euphemism thereof. There exists no explicit justification of its practice in terms of its conformity to democratic principles or procedures. And yet citizens have by and large accepted it upon reflection. They might recognize that its emergence has altered their rights and obligations, and they might occasionally grumble to survey researchers that "organized business," "organized labor," or "organized professions" seem to have too much influence, but few if any seem to feel that they have lost more than they have gained by entrusting the management of their interest politics to such intermediaries. Ironically, it is in those countries whose interest associations have been least corporatized that one hears the epithet "corporatist" thrown most often at opponents and that intellectuals denounce all signs of its prospective emergence as a threat to traditional freedoms and democratic institutions.

## THE SPECTER OF VICARIOUS DEMOCRACY?

So does this mean that the more neocorporatist polities are already headed toward some new form of postindividualistic, vicarious democracy, with other advanced industrial/capitalist societies soon to follow? That the famous myth of the rational, well informed, and active citizen has finally been put to rest and been replaced by the specter of the reasonable, well staffed, and recognized association as the basic unit of democracy? That the notion of a civil society composed of natural groups voluntarily entering into exchanges in the pursuit of their own autonomously defined preferences and capable of reproducing itself without the constant intromission of the state has given way to a vision of a semipublic society composed of artifactual organizations compulsorily negotiating compromises in the pursuit of their members' imputed interests and capable of sustaining itself only by symbiotic interdependence with public authorities?

Let us leave aside the probability that neocorporatism and vicarious democracy may well be a solution to the problem of modern interest conflict confined to particular countries and national circumstances. Small size, high international vulnerability, well-established state legitimacy, centralized administrative structures, clear preponderence of class cleavage over other bases of social and cultural conflict, ideological hegemony of social democratic over bourgeois values are all factors which seem to have contributed to the emergence of such a pattern, although they may not all necessarily be prerequisites for such an outcome in the future.

I suspect that the answer to the "paradox of corporatist associability"—to its ambiguous impact on the *practice* of democracy—eventually lies in the truth of what is one of the most central tenets of the *theory* of democracy, namely, that for a polity to be really responsive to the needs and concerns of its citizens, these citizens must *participate* actively and freely in the definition of those needs and the expression of those concerns. They must not only have the "enlightened understanding" of their interests which Robert Dahl so rightly stressed, but they must also have the resources *and* the desire to engage in the political struggle necessary to make sure their preferences are taken into consideration by those who govern or by seeking themselves to govern. Specialized experts, organic intellectuals, designated spokespersons, professional intermediaries, benevolent rulers, etc. may, in some contexts and for some period of time, be better informed and more capable of interpreting the interests of social groups, but unless they are kept accountable by an active citizenry, their theories and suppositions about what is good for their members, clients, followers, etc. are likely to prove erroneous in the long run. What is more, the organizational and political "rents" which these intermediaries extract for the service they perform will systematically distort the very content of demands made upon the polity.

The progressive assertion of interest politics, its conversion from an "art of association" into a "science of organization," may have greatly changed the identity of relevant actors. It may have expanded the resources and extended the range of such intermediaries. The emergence of a neocorporatist mode may have increased the immediate governability, improved the aggregate economic performance, and equalized access to policymaking in advanced capitalist societies, but the "vicarious democracy" which has accompanied these transformations may not prove so satisfying and in the long run so governable. Rulers may become more accountable under such arrangements, but to the wrong collectivities—not necessarily to the units with which persons voluntarily identify and from which they naturally derive a sense of shared existence, but to those which struggle, convenience, connivance, and luck have allowed to become formally organized, often at levels of aggregation far above that which would have been spontaneously forthcoming. *Governments may also be more responsive, but to the wrong needs*—not necessarily to those which individuals would themselves feel and become concerned about, but to those which professional intermediaries have defined and promoted as the "real" interests of their respective memberships or clienteles—often while including substantial

side payments for themselves and the organizations which they control.

Whatever impact the organization of interest politics has had upon political performance, whatever has been the relationship between neocorporatism and governability, whatever both have done to growth, equality, and democracy, it is difficult to imagine that these changes have completely voided the old liberal adage that "each individual person is the best judge of his or her own interests." Ultimately, if not immediately, the polity will be judged by its ability to satisfy *these* interests—not just *those* which have been identified, given generic labels, and packaged collectively by intermediaries and to which authorities have presumably been dutifully accountable and responsive. Moreover, if among these "really felt" interests of individual citizens are distinctively political needs for active participation and close access to rulers, then one would have even more grounds for suspecting that the sort of "vicarious democracy" promoted by neocorporatism will prove to be but a passing phase—hopefully, an appropriate and proportionate (if temporary) adjustment in the "art of association" that Tocqueville thought was so necessary to keeping our collective existence "civilized" while our individual conditions were becoming "equalized."

# Notes

1. Gerhard Lehmbruch, "Consociational Democracy, Class Conflict and the New Corporatism," in *Trends Toward Corporatist Intermediation*, ed. Schmitter and Lehmbruch (Newbury Park, Calif.: Sage, 1979), pp. 53–62; Philippe C. Schmitter, "Still the Century of Corporatism?" *Review of Politics* 36 (January 1974), pp. 85–131; R. E, Pahl and J. T. Winkler, "The Coming Corporatism," *New Society* 10 (October 1974).

2. Leo Panitch, "Recent Theorizations of Corporatism: Reflections on a Growth Industry," *British Journal of Sociology* 31 (June 1980), pp. 159–187.

3. Peter Bachrach and Morton S. Baratz, *Power and Poverty: Theory and Practice* (New York: Oxford University Press, 1970), esp. pp. 3–66.

4. Mancur Olson, *The Rise and Decline of Nations: Economic Growth, Stagflation and Social Rigidities* (New Haven: Yale University Press, 1982), attempts to elevate this contingent point into a major explanatory factor.

5. Norberto Bobbio, "Are There Alternatives to Representative Democracy?" *Telos*, no. 35 (Spring 1978), p. 29.

# CHAPTER SEVEN

# Political Institutions

## 28

## Legitimation Crisis

*Jürgen Habermas*

### THREE DEVELOPING CRISES

The rapid growth processes of late-capitalist societies have confronted the system of world society with new problems. These problems cannot be regarded as crisis phenomena specific to the system, even though the possibilities of coping with the crises *are* specific to the system and therefore limited. I am thinking of the disturbance of the ecological balance, the violation of the personality system (alienation), and the explosive strain on international relations.

### The Ecological Balance

If physically economic growth can be traced back to the technologically sophisticated use of more energy to increase the productivity of human labor, then the societal formation of capitalism is remarkable for impressively solving the problem of economic growth. To be sure, capital accumulation originally pushes economic growth ahead, so there is no option for the conscious steering of this process. The growth imperatives originally followed by capitalism have meanwhile

SOURCE: Jürgen Habermas, "What Does a Crisis Mean Today? Legitimation Problems in Late Capitalism," *Social Research* 40, no. 4 (Winter 1973), pp. 643–667. By permission. Article abridged by the editors.

achieved a global validity by way of system competition and worldwide diffusion (despite the stagnation or even retrogressive trends in some Third World countries).

The mechanisms of growth are forcing an increase of both population and production on a worldwide scale. The economic needs of a growing population and the productive exploitation of nature are faced with material restrictions: on the one hand, finite resources (cultivable and inhabitable land, fresh water, metals, minerals, etc.); on the other hand, irreplaceable ecological systems that absorb pollutants such as fallout, carbon dioxide, and waste heat. Forrester and others have estimated the limits of the exponential growth of population, industrial production, exploitation of natural resources, and environmental pollution. To be sure, their estimates have rather weak empirical foundations. The mechanisms of population growth are as little known as the maximum limits of the earth's potential for absorbing even the major pollutants. Moreover, we cannot forecast technological development accurately enough to know which raw materials will be replaced or renovated by future technology.

However, despite any optimistic assurances, we are able to indicate (if not precisely determine) *one* absolute limitation on growth: the thermal strain on the environment due to consumption of energy. If economic growth is necessarily coupled with increasing consumption of energy, and if all natural energy that is transformed into economically useful energy is ultimately released as heat, it will eventually raise the temperature of the atmosphere. Again, determining the deadline is not easy. Nevertheless, these reflections show that an exponential growth of population and production—i.e., an expanded control over external nature—will some day run up against the limits of the biological capacity of the environment.

This is not limited to complex societal systems. Specific to these systems are the possibilities of warding off dangers to the ecology. Late-capitalist societies would have a very hard time limiting growth without abandoning their principle of organization, because an overall shift from spontaneous capitalist growth to qualitative growth would require production planning in terms of use-values.

## The Anthropological Balance

While the disturbance of the ecological balance points out the negative aspect of the exploitation of natural resources, there are no sure signals for the capacity limits of personality systems. I doubt whether it is possible to identify such things as psychological constants of human nature that inwardly limit the socialization process. I do, however, see a limitation in the kind of socializing that societal systems have been using to create motives for action. Our behavior is oriented by norms requiring justification and by interpretative systems guaranteeing identity. Such a communicative organization of behavior can become an obstacle in complex societies for a simple reason. The adaptive capacity in organizations increases proportionately as the administrative authorities become independent of the particular motivations of the members. The choice and achievement of organization goals in systems of high intrinsic complexity have to be independent of the influx of narrowly delimited motives. This requires a generalized willingness to comply (in political systems, such willingness has the form of legitimation). As long as socialization brings inner nature into a communicative behavioral organization, no legitimation for norms of action could conceivably secure an unmotivated acceptance of decisions. In regard to decisions whose contents are still undetermined, people will comply if convinced that those decisions are based on a legitimate norm of action. If the motives for acting were no longer to pass through norms requiring justification, and if the personality structures no longer had to find their unity under interpretative systems guaranteeing identity, then (and only then) the unmotivated acceptance of decisions would become an irreproachable routine, and the readiness to comply could thus be produced to any desirable degree.

## The International Balance

The dangers of destroying the world system with thermonuclear weapons are on a different level. The accumulated potential for annihilation is a result of the advanced stage of productive forces. Its basis is technologically neutral, and so the productive forces can also take the form of destructive forces (which has happened because international communication is still undeveloped). Today, mortal damage to the natural substratum of global society is quite possible. International communication is therefore governed by a historically new imperative of self-limitation. Once again, this is not limited to all highly militarized societal systems, but the possibilities of tackling this problem have limits specific to the systems. An actual disarmament may be unlikely because of the forces behind capitalist and postcapitalist class societies. Yet regulating the arms race is not basically incompatible with the structure of late-capitalist societies if it is possible to increase technologically the use-value of capital to the degree that the capacity effect of the government's demand for unproductive consumer goods can be balanced....

## DISTURBANCES SPECIFIC TO THE SYSTEM

...In my opinion, the late-capitalist state can be properly understood neither as the unconscious executive organ of economic laws nor as a systematic agent of the united monopoly capitalists. Instead, I would join Claus Offe in advocating the theory that late-capitalist societies are faced with two difficulties caused by the state's having to intervene in the growing functional gaps of the market. We can regard the state as a system that uses legitimate power. Its output consists in sovereignly executing administrative decisions. To this end, it needs an input of mass loyalty that is as unspecific as possible. Both directions can lead to crisis-like disturbances. Output crises have the form of the efficiency crisis. The administrative system fails to fulfill the steering imperative that it has taken over from the economic system. This results in the disorganization of different areas of life. Input crises have the form of the legitimation crisis. The legitimation system fails to maintain the necessary level of mass loyalty. We can clarify this with the example of the acute difficulties in public finances, with which all late-capitalist societies are now struggling.

The government budget, as I have said, is burdened with the public expenses of an increasingly socialized production. It bears the costs of international competition and of the demand for unproductive consumer goods (armament and space travel). It bears the costs for the intrastructural output (transportation and communication, scientific and technological progress, vocational training). It bears the costs of the social consumption indirectly concerned with production (housing, transportation, health, leisure, general education, social security). It bears the costs of providing for the unemployed. And finally, it bears the externalized costs of environmental damage caused by private production. Ultimately, these expenses have to be met by taxes. The state apparatus thus has two simultaneous tasks. It has to levy the necessary taxes from profits and income and employ them so efficiently as to prevent any crises from disturbing growth. In addition the selective raising of taxes, the recognizable priority model of their utilization, and the administrative performance have to function in such a way as to satisfy the resulting need for legitimation. If the state fails

in the former task, the result is a deficit in administrative efficiency. If it fails in the latter task, the result is a deficit in legitimation.

## THEOREMS OF THE LEGITIMATION CRISIS

I would like to restrict myself to the legitimation problem. There is nothing mysterious about its genesis. Legitimate power has to be available for administrative planning. The functions accruing to the state apparatus in late capitalism and the expansion of social areas treated by administration increase the need for legitimation. Liberal capitalism constituted itself in the forms of bourgeois democracy, which is easy to explain in terms of the bourgeois revolution. As a result, the growing need for legitimation now has to work with the means of political democracy (on the basis of universal suffrage). The formal democratic means, however, are expensive. After all, the state apparatus does not just see itself in the role of the supreme capitalist facing the conflicting interests of the various capital factions. It also has to consider the generalizable interests of the population as far as necessary to retain mass loyalty and prevent a conflict-ridden withdrawal of legitimation. The state has to gauge these three interest areas (individual capitalism, state capitalism, and generalizable interests), in order to find a compromise for competing demands. A theorem of crisis has to explain not only why the state apparatus encounters difficulties but also why certain problems remain unsolved in the long run.

First, an obvious objection. The state can avoid legitimation problems to the extent that it can manage to make the administrative system independent of the formation of legitimating will. To that end, it can, say, separate expressive symbols (which create a universal willingness to follow) from the instrumental functions of administration. Well known strategies of this sort are: the personalizing of objective issues, the symbolic use of inquiries, expert opinions, legal incantations, etc. Advertising techniques, borrowed from oligopolistic competition, both confirm and exploit current structures of prejudice. By resorting to emotional appeals, they arouse unconscious motives, occupy certain contents positively, and devalue others. The public, which is engineered for purposes of legitimation, primarily has the function of structuring attention by means of areas of themes and thereby of pushing uncomfortable themes, problems, and arguments below the threshold of attention. As Niklas Luhmann put it: The political system takes over tasks of *ideology planning*.

The scope for manipulation, however, is narrowly delimited, for the cultural system remains peculiarly resistant to administrative control. There is no administrative creation of meaning; there is at best an ideological erosion of cultural values. The acquisition of legitimation is self-destructive as soon as the mode of acquisition is exposed. Thus, there is a systematic limit for attempts at making up for legitimation deficits by means of well aimed manipulation. This limit is the structural dissimilarity between areas of administrative action and cultural tradition.

A crisis argument, to be sure, can be constructed out of these considerations only with the viewpoint that the expansion of state activity has the side effect of disproportionately increasing the need for legitimation. I regard such an overproportionate increase as likely because things that are taken for granted culturally, and have so far been external conditions of the political systems, are now being drawn into the planning area of administration. This process thematizes traditions which previously were not part of public programming, much less of practical discourse. An example of such direct administrative processing of cultural tradition is educational planning, especially the planning of the curriculum. Hitherto, the school administration merely had to codify a given naturally evolved canon. But now the planning of the curriculum is based on the premise that the tradition models can also be different. Administrative planning creates a universal

compulsion for justification toward a sphere that was actually distinguished by the power of self-legitimation.

In regard to the direct disturbance of things that were culturally taken for granted, there are further examples in regional and urban planning (private ownership of land), health planning ("classless hospital"), and family planning and marriage-law planning (which are shaking sexual taboos and facilitating emancipation).

An awareness of contingency is created not just for contents of tradition but also for the techniques of tradition—i.e., socialization. Among preschool children, formal schooling is already competing with family upbringing. The new problems afflicting the educational routine, and the widespread awareness of these problems, are reflected by, among other indications, a new type of pedagogical and psychological writing addressed to the general public.

On all these levels, administrative planning has unintentional effects of disquieting and publicizing. These effects weaken the justification potential of traditions that have been forced out of their natural condition. Once they are no longer indisputable, their demands for validity can be stabilized only by way of discourse. Thus, the forcible shift of things that have been culturally taken for granted further politicizes areas of life that previously could be assigned to the private domain. However, this spells danger for bourgeois privatism, which is informally assured by the structures of the public. I see signs of this danger in strivings for participation and in models for alternatives, such as have developed particularly in secondary and primary schools, in the press, the church, theaters, publishing, etc.

These arguments support the contention that late-capitalist societies are afflicted with serious problems of legitimation. But do these arguments suffice to explain why these problems cannot be solved? Do they explain the prediction of a crisis in legitimation? Let us assume the state apparatus could succeed in making labor more productive and in distributing the gains in productivity in such a way as to assure an economic growth free of crises (if not disturbances). Such growth would nevertheless proceed in terms of priorities independent of the generalizable interests of the population. The priority models that Galbraith has analyzed from the viewpoint of "private wealth vs. public poverty" result from a class structure which, as always, is still being kept latent. This structure is ultimately the cause of the legitimation deficit.

We have seen that the state cannot simply take over the cultural system and that, in fact, the expansion of areas for state planning creates problems for things that are culturally taken for granted. "Meaning" is an increasingly scarce resource. Which is why those expectations that are governed by concrete and identifiable needs —i.e., that can be checked by their success— keep mounting in the civil population. The rising level of aspirations is proportionate to the growing need for legitimation. The resource of "value," siphoned off by the tax office, has to make up for the scanty resource of "meaning." Missing legitimations have to be replaced by social rewards such as money, time, and security. A crisis of legitimation arises as soon as the demands for these rewards mount more rapidly than the available mass of values, or if expectations come about that are different and cannot be satisfied by those categories of rewards conforming with the present system.

Why, then, should not the level of demands keep within operable limits? As long as the welfare state's programming in connection with a widespread technocratic consciousness (which makes uninfluenceable system-restraints responsible for bottlenecks) maintains a sufficient amount of civil privatism, then the legitimation emergencies do not have to turn into crises. To be sure, the democratic form of legitimation could cause expenses that cannot be covered if that form drives the competing parties to outdo one another in their platforms and thereby raise the expectations of the population higher and higher. Granted, this argument could be amply demonstrated empirically. But we would still have to explain why late capitalist societies

even bother to retain formal democracy. Merely in terms of the administrative system, formal democracy could just as easily be replaced by a variant—a conservative, authoritarian welfare state that reduces the political participation of the citizens to a harmless level; or a Fascist authoritarian state that keeps the population toeing the mark on a relatively high level of permanent mobilization. Evidently, both variants are in the long run less compatible with developed capitalism than a party state based on mass democracy. The sociocultural system creates demands that cannot be satisfied in authoritarian systems.

This reflection leads me to the following thesis: Only a rigid sociocultural system, incapable of being randomly functionalized for the needs of the administrative system, could explain how legitimation difficulties result in a legitimation crisis. This development must therefore be based on a *motivation crisis*—i.e., a discrepancy between the need for motives that the state and the occupational system announce and the supply of motivation offered by the sociocultural system.

## THEOREMS OF THE MOTIVATION CRISIS

The most important motivation contributed by the sociocultural system in late-capitalist societies consists in syndromes of civil and family/vocational privatism. Civil privatism means strong interests in the administrative system's output and minor participation in the process of will-formation (high-output orientation vs. low-input orientation). Civil privatism thus corresponds to the structures of a depoliticized public. Family and vocational privatism complements civil privatism. It consists of a family orientation with consumer and leisure interests, and of a career orientation consistent with status competition. This privatism thus corresponds to the structures of educational and occupational systems regulated by competitive performance.

The motivational syndromes mentioned are vital to the political and economic system. However, bourgeois ideologies have components directly relevant to privatistic orientations, and social changes deprive those components of their basis. A brief outline may clarify this.

## Performance Ideology

According to bourgeois notions which have remained constant from the beginnings of modern natural law to contemporary election speeches, social rewards should be distributed on the basis of individual achievement. The distribution of gratifications should correlate to every individual's performance. A basic condition is equal opportunity to participate in a competition which is regulated in such a way that external influences can be neutralized. One such allocation mechanism was the market. But ever since the general public realized that social violence is practiced in the forms of exchange, the market has been losing its credibility as a mechanism for distributing rewards based on performance. Thus, in the more recent versions of performance ideology, market success is being replaced by the professional success mediated by formal schooling. However, *this* version can claim credibility only when the following conditions have been fulfilled:

- Equal opportunity of access to higher schools.
- Nondiscriminatory evaluation standards for school performance.
- Synchronic developments of the educational and occupational systems.
- Work processes whose objective structure permits evaluation according to performances that can be ascribed to individuals.

"School justice" in terms of opportunity of access and standards of evaluation has increased in all advanced capitalist societies at least to some degree. But a counter trend can be observed in the two other dimensions. The expansion of the educational system is becoming more and more independent of changes in the occupational system, so that ultimately the connection between formal schooling and professional success will most likely loosen. At the same time, there are more and more areas in which production structures and work dynamics make it increasingly difficult to evaluate individual performance. Instead, the extrafunctional elements of occupational roles are becoming more and more important for conferring occupational status.

Moreover, fragmented and monotonous work processes are increasingly entering sectors in which previously a personal identity could be developed through the vocational role. An intrinsic motivation for performance is getting less and less support from the structure of the work process in market-dependent work areas. An instrumentalist attitude toward work is spreading even in the traditionally bourgeois professions (white-collar workers, professionals). A performance motivation coming from outside can, however, be sufficiently stimulated by wage income only:

- If the reserve army on the labor market exercises an effective competitive pressure.
- If a sufficient income differential exists between the lower wage groups and the inactive work population.

Both conditions are not necessarily met today. Even in capitalist countries with chronic unemployment (such as the United States), the division of the labor market (into organized and competitive sectors) interferes with the natural mechanism of competition. With a mounting poverty line (recognized by the welfare state), the living standards of the lower income groups and the groups temporarily released from the labor process are mutually assimilating on the other side in the subproletarian strata.

## Possessive Individualism

Bourgeois society sees itself as an instrumental group that accumulates social wealth only by way of private wealth—i.e., guarantees economic growth and general welfare through competition between strategically acting private persons. Collective goals, under such circumstances, can be achieved only by way of individual utility orientations. This preference system, of course, presupposes:

- That the private economic subjects can with subjective unambiguity recognize and calculate needs that remain constant over given time periods.
- That this need can be satisfied by individually demandable goods (normally, by way of monetary decisions that conform to the system).

Both presuppositions are no longer fulfilled as a matter of course in the developed capitalist societies. These societies have reached a level of societal wealth far beyond warding off a few fundamental hazards to life and the satisfying of basic needs. This is why the individualistic system of preference is becoming vague. The steady interpreting and reinterpreting of needs is becoming a matter of the collective formation of the will, a fact which opens the alternatives of either free and quasi-political communication among consumers as citizens or massive manipulation—i.e., strong indirect steering. The greater the degree of freedom for the preference system of the demanders, the more urgent the problem of sales policies for the suppliers—at least if they are to maintain the illusion that the consumers can make private and autonomous decisions. Opportunistic adjustment of the consumers to market strategies is the ironical form of every consumer autonomy, which is to be maintained as the facade of possessive individualism. In addition, with increasing socialization of production, the quota of collective commodities among the consumer goods keeps growing. The urban living conditions in complex societies are more and more dependent on an infrastructure (transportation, leisure, health, education, etc.) that is withdrawing further and further from the forms of differential demand and private appropriation.

## Exchange-Value Orientation

Here I have to mention the tendencies that weaken the socialization effects of the market, especially the increase of those parts of the population that do not reproduce their lives through income from work (students, welfare recipients, social-security recipients, invalids, criminals, soldiers, etc.) as well as the expansion of areas of activity in which, as in civil service or in teaching, abstract work is replaced by concrete work. In addition, the relevance that leisure acquires with fewer working hours (and higher real income), compared with the relevance of issues within the occupational sphere of life, does not in the long run privilege those needs that can be satisfied monetarily.

The erosion of bourgeois tradition brings out normative structures that are no longer appropriate to reproducing civil and family and professional privatism. The now dominant components of cultural heritage crystalize around a faith in science, a "postauratic" art, and universalistic values. Irreversible developments have occurred in each of these areas. As a result, functional inequalities of the economic and the political systems are blocked by cultural barriers, and they can be broken down only at the psychological cost of regressions—i.e., with extraordinary motivational damage. German Fascism was an example of the wasteful attempt at a collectively organized regression of consciousness below the thresholds of fundamental scientistic convictions, modern art, and universalistic law and morals.

## Scientism

The political consequences of the authority enjoyed by the scientific system in developed societies are ambivalent. The rise of modern science established a demand for discursive justification, and traditionalistic attitudes cannot hold out against that demand. On the other hand, short-lived popular syntheses of scientific data (which have replaced global interpretations) guarantee the authority of science *in the abstract*.

The authority known as "science" can thus cover both things: the broadly effective criticism of any prejudice, as well as the new esoterics of specialized knowledge and expertise. A self-affirmation of the sciences can further a positivistic common sense on the part of the depoliticized public. Yet scientism establishes standards by which it can also be criticized itself and found guilty of residual dogmatism. Theories of technocracy and of democratic elitism, asserting the necessity of an institutionalized civic privatism, come forth with the presumption of theories. But this does not make them immune to criticism.

## Postauratic Art

The consequences of modern art are somewhat less ambivalent. The modern age has radicalized the autonomy of bourgeois art in regard to the external purposes for which art could be used. For the first time, bourgeois society itself produced a counterculture against the bourgeois life style of possessive individualism, performance, and practicality. The *Bohème*, first established in Paris, the capital of the 19th century, embodies a critical demand that had arisen, unpolemically still, in the aura of the bourgeois artwork. The alter ego of the businessman, the "human being," whom the bourgeois used to encounter in the lonesome contemplation of the artwork, soon split away from him. In the shape of the artistic avant-garde, it confronted him as a hostile, at best seductive force. In artistic beauty, the bourgeoisie had been able to experience its own ideals and the (as always) fictitious redemption of the promise of happiness which was merely suspended in everyday life. In radicalized art, however, the bourgeois soon had to recognize the negation of social practice as its complement.

Modern art is the outer covering in which the transformation of bourgeois art into a counterculture was prepared. Surrealism marks the historical moment when modern art programmatically destroyed the outer covering of no-longer-beautiful illusion in order to enter life desublimated. The leveling of the different reality degrees of art and life was accelerated (although not, as Walter Benjamin assumed, introduced) by the new techniques of mass reproduction and mass reception. Modern art had already sloughed off the aura of classical bourgeois art in that the art work made the production process visible and presented itself as a made product. But art enters the ensemble of utility values only when abandoning its autonomous status. The process is certainly ambivalent. It can signify the degeneration of art into a propagandistic mass art or commercialized mass culture, or else its transformation into a subversive counterculture.

## Universalist Morality

The blockage which bourgeois ideologies, stripped of their functional components, create for developing the political and economic system, is even clearer in the moral system than in the authority of science and the self-disintegration of modern art. The moment traditional societies enter a process of modernization, the growing complexity results in steering problems that necessitate an accelerated change of social norms. The tempo inherent in natural cultural tradition has to be heightened. This leads to bourgeois formal law which permits releasing the norm contents from the dogmatic structure of mere tradition and defining them in terms of intention. The legal norms are uncoupled from the corps of privatized moral norms. In addition, they need to be created (and justified) according to principles. Abstract law counts only for that area pacified by state power. But the morality of bourgeois private persons, a morality likewise raised to the level of universal principles, encounters no barrier in the continuing natural condition between the states. Since principled morality is sanctioned only by the purely inward authority of the conscience, its claim to universality conflicts with public morality, which is still bound to a concrete state-subject. This is the conflict between the cosmopolitanism of the human being and the loyalties of the citizen.

If we follow the developmental logic of overall societal systems of norms (leaving the area of historical examples), we can settle that conflict. But its resolution is conceivable only under certain conditions. The dichotomy between inner and outer morality has to disappear. The contrast between morally and legally regulated areas has to be relativized. And the validity of *all* norms has to be tied to the discursive formation of the will of the people potentially affected.

Competitive capitalism for the first time gave a binding force to strictly universalistic value systems. This occurred because the system of exchange had to be regulated universalistically and because the exchange of equivalents offered a basic ideology effective in the bourgeois class. In organized capitalism, the bottom drops out of this legitimation model. At the same time, new and increased demands for legitimation arise. However, the system of science cannot intentionally fall behind an attained stage of cumulative knowledge. Similarly, the moral system, once practical discourse has been admitted, cannot simply make us forget a collectively attained stage of moral consciousness.

I would like to conclude with a final reflection.

If no sufficient concordance exists between the normative structures that still have some power today and the politicoeconomic system, then we can still avoid motivation crises by uncoupling the cultural system. Culture would then become a nonobligatory leisure occupation or the object of professional knowledge. This solution would be blocked if the basic convictions of a communicative ethics and the experience complexes of countercultures (in which postauratic art is embodied) acquired a motive-forming power determining typical socialization processes. Such a conjecture is supported by several behavior syndromes spreading more and more among young people—either retreat as a reaction to an exorbitant claim on the personality-resources; or protest as a result of an autonomous ego organization that cannot be stabilized without conflicts under given conditions. On the activist side we find: the student movement, revolts by high-school students and apprentices, pacifists, women's lib. The retreatist side is represented by hippies, Jesus people, the drug subculture, phenomena of undermotivation in schools, etc. These are the primary areas for checking our hypothesis that late-capitalist societies are endangered by a collapse of legitimation.

# 29

# On the Governability of Democracies

*Ralf Dahrendorf*

These are times when we are forcefully reminded of the basic functions of government—law and order, and external defence. These are by the same token bad times for liberty. Liberty flourishes when reforms of the criminal justice system and reductions in defence expenditure are possible without any threat to people's safety at home and security abroad. Safety and security are never a sufficient condition of liberty; but they are a necessary condition. And today there is a smell of war in the air.

Chancellor Schmidt of West Germany tells us that 1980 is one long July 1914. We remember: when Archduke Ferdinand was assassinated at Sarajevo on June 28, 1914, everyone commiserated with the Austrian Emperor (never mind the unpopularity of the Archduke), and most gave the Austrian Government to understand that they would tolerate certain reprisals against Serbia. A month, endless diplomatic contacts, and quiet military preparations later, the world had changed out of recognition. One word, above all, was heard in the capitals of Europe, the word "inevitability": war, it was said, was

SOURCE: Ralf Dahrendorf, "Effectiveness and Legitimacy: On the 'Governability' of Democracies," *The Political Quarterly*, October–December 1980, pp. 393–410. By permission.

now "inevitable"; and so it began. In his recent article in *Foreign Affairs*, Professor Miles Kahler has taken the analogy further.[1] He sees Russia today in the position of Germany 1914, the United States in the position of Britain, the Middle East as the Balkans of 1980, and above all once again the unwilling slide into inevitability everywhere.

There is, however, at least one major difference. It may be that once again there are those who believe that war can be "localised." One might even argue that John Hackett in his book on the *Third World War* has done us a disservice by suggesting that once Birmingham and Minsk have been wiped out by nuclear devices, all will be over, so that those of us who are lucky enough not to live in these doomed cities will be all right (provided, of course, we let NATO arm to the hilt).[2] In fact, the doctrine of limited war in the nuclear age is infinitely more dangerous than the equally mistaken doctrine of localised war was in 1914. The fact is that today mankind can destroy itself, or rather, can be destroyed by the decisions of a small number of governments. Never has there been as dramatic a mismatch between the potential of destruction and the frailty of men, including those who command the potential. Neither red telephones nor double-check command systems nor the fantasy of a monastic order of moral physicists who guard the dangerous material can bridge the mismatch. The fact is—to quote one of those responsible for these dangers, though one who has since given much thought to coping with them, the physicist-philosopher Carl Friedrich von Weizsäcker—that "the Third World War is probable," because nothing has changed in the hegemonial contest which leads to war; indeed "the Third World War will take place once it can be won."[3]

This is a gloomy beginning. It might even be called somewhat melodramatic, were it not for the fact that either the hegemonial contest, or the proliferation of nuclear weapons to nations threatened for survival, or a mere accident might well lead to widespread destruction. And if it is true that it is unlikely that there is any government which can be counted on to control the ultimate threat, then this presents clearly also the ultimate problem of governability: it appears that we have created technical possibilities of destruction which no conceivable human government can contain. We have reached limits of governability. I shall return to this point at the end of my lecture. For the moment, let me take refuge in a statement by the philosopher of desperate optimism, Karl Jaspers, in his book on *The Atom Bomb and the Future of Man*: "Reason tells us: it shows little courage to make statements on the end and the inevitable downfall. It shows courage to do what is possible, given our knowledge and our ignorance, and not to abandon hope as long as one lives."[4] Let us leave the dark cloud of war in the distant, or even not-so-distant sky then and turn to areas of life which are more obviously within the orbit of government action, or would seem to be so. Inflation is a topical and important example. One of the many things which seem to have gone wrong with the economies of OECD countries in the 1970s, is the apparent inability to contain inflation. Several recipes have been tried. First, there was the stimulation of growth, in order to catch up with inflation, as it were; but for a variety of reasons, growth itself has become more difficult and never did catch up, quite apart from the fact that it is doubtful whether it contains or generates inflation. Then, there were tricks designed to cushion the effects of inflation, and perhaps to expose its absurdity, such as indexation; but examples like Israel show that while this may expose the absurdity it does not remove it. Then, there was the "social contract," an agreement to hold down expectations on the wages front, and sometimes on that of prices as well; but whether "contract," "policy" or even "law," it does not seem to work for any length of time. Finally, there is the control of the money supply (whatever that is), by high interest rates, cuts in public expenditure, growing unemployment, and the like; but the more technical the policy is, the less does it come to grips with the real problem of people's expectations. Those who have tried a mix of the various policies have been most successful; though even their success is limited, and may have been achieved for different reasons, a strong industrial base, favourable terms of trade, and other comparative advantages. Thus, inflation, one of the banes of the OECD world, seems to have escaped the ability of governments to cope. It is clearly a test of governability.

## THE SCHIZOPHRENIA BETWEEN PERSONAL AND POLITICAL WELL-BEING

James Alt has recently looked at what might be called the subjective side of the story, people's perceptions (in Britain since 1964), in his book, *The Politics of Economic Decline*.[5] His findings are a goldmine for analysis. For instance, he can show that people's inflationary expectations exaggerate existing trends considerably, thus making the monetarist remedy even less effective.[6] He also shows that wage controls are the most popular remedy,[7] though he does not tell us whether people want to see the wages of others controlled, or their own. But in our context, another of his findings is the most important. For a long time, Alt tells us (in line with Butler and Stokes, and others),[8] people have distinguished quite clearly between their personal well-being and that of their country. And with a curious schizophrenia, they did not associate their personal well-being with politics, but took it for granted that by and large they have never had it so good. On the well-being of the country, on the other hand, views varied, and changed, and these changes and variations determined the electoral success of the parties. Then comes inflation; and suddenly personal and national well-being merge. Not only the country, but people themselves are doing badly if inflation rates run into two figures. So naturally, people expect government to do something about it. However, governments, successive governments of different parties, fail. "In 1970," James Alt reports, "nearly 60 percent felt that 'a government can do a lot to check rising prices.' In early 1974, only a quarter of the electorate felt that way."[9]

Alt's conclusions may be far reaching, but they are not implausible: people have ceased to expect government to deliver the goods:

> In large measure, then, the story of the mid 1970s is the story of a politics of declining expectations. People attached a great deal of importance to economic problems, people saw clearly the developments that were taking place, and people expected developments in advance and thus were able to discount the impact of the worst of them. However, in unprecedented numbers, people also ceased to expect the election of their party to make them better off, largely because they also ceased to expect it to be able to do very much about what they identified as the principal economic problems of the time. The result of this. . .was not a politics of protest, but a politics of quiet disillusion, a politics in which lack of involvement or indifference to organised party politics was the most important feature.[10]

If there is a problem of governability—and the examples given leave little doubt that there is—most of its elements are probably assembled in this illustration. However, before examples are taken further, there is a case for making sure that it is clear what we are talking about. Our concern is with governments, and essentially with national governments, or perhaps I should say with central governments of the units which we have come to recognise as countries, or states. For them to work—or so I shall argue without any claim to originality—two things have to be present: effectiveness and legitimacy. Effectiveness is a technical concept. It simply means that governments have to be able to do things which they claim they can do, as well as those which they are expected to do; they have to work. Legitimacy, on the other hand, is a moral concept. It means that what governments do has to be right. This takes us straight into the confusions of moral philosophy, of course.

Suffice it to say here that what is "right" in the sense of giving legitimacy to governments has at least two aspects. One is that of absolute moral imperatives, or, slightly less ambitiously put, that of values which may be assumed to apply to all human societies. What we call human rights, even, in the most general sense, the rule of law, belongs in this category. Then there are values which, while still of long-term validity, are culturally determined; they vary, and they change. We have to assume that democracy belongs in this category, that is the institutions which, by enabling all citizens to express their views, make change possible without revolution. The category also includes Max Weber's patterns of legitimation, at any rate those of "traditional" and of "legal" or "rational authority." A government is legitimate if what it does is right both in the sense of complying with certain fundamental principles, and in that of being in line with prevailing cultural values. Written constitutions, where they exist, usually begin by spelling out the values which make the actions of the state legitimate, and then proceed to describe the institutions which are intended to guarantee effectiveness. A Bill of Rights has to do with legitimacy, electoral reform has to do with effectiveness in this sense.

How do we measure effectiveness, and legitimacy? The temptation has always been great to be too idealistic in this respect. Political education has tended to emphasise general consent and participation as a condition of effectiveness; in fact, it would seem that the absence of effective protest is good enough. People are not political beings except as political "fleets in being"; in the normal course of events, participation is nice, but not indispensable. What is important, is the possibility of participation in order to veto developments, to express dissent. (Admittedly, to mention this practical point in passing, it is difficult to assess how much of James Alt's "lack of involvement or indifference" is normal disinterest, and how much is dissent or opposition by abstention.) Legitimacy, similarly, should be measured not in terms of the active will of all, or even some fictitious general will, but in terms of doubt, of a perceived dissociation of government action and basic as well as cultural values. Again, the distinction is important. When governments violate values which apply to all societies, they may not meet

with doubts by the majority. This is where minorities have a crucial function: dissidents, human rights groups, underground publications, "flying" universities. By contrast any dissociation of government action and prevailing cultural values, be it due to the imposition of an alien government, the alienation of an indigenous government or changes in cultural values, is bound to find expression in widespread doubts of one kind or another. In our context, the important question is whether changes in prevailing values are taking place which, while barely perceptible as yet, may well in due course expose the alienation of traditional democratic governments. I do not want to take the conceptual discussion too far, but one further point is indispensable for the following argument. I said that a Bill of Rights has to do with legitimacy, and electoral reform with effectiveness. Could it not be the other way round? Is not electoral reform intended to re-establish belief in the fundamental fairness of the political system, whereas a Bill of Rights merely regulates effective relations between politics and the judiciary? Conceptual sophistry apart, it is clear that effectiveness and legitimacy are related. The relationship is asymmetrical. Unfortunately, governments can be effective without being legitimate. Totalitarian rule offers the main example. Hitler's rule was certainly effective, but it was not legitimate in that it violated the rule of law deliberately and systematically. It is more difficult to imagine governments which are legitimate without being effective. One is tempted to think of Weimar Germany which has so often been described as the purest democracy of them all; though "pure democracy," like "inner freedom," has a suspicious ring of deception. Over time, ineffectiveness will probably erode legitimacy. A government which cannot do its job, and seems systematically unable to do so, will not only be shown up by protest and dissent, but in the end also by spreading doubt in the name of underlying values, whether they be universal like the rule of law, or culturally specific like the rational or traditional exercise of power.

# WHAT IS UNGOVERNABILITY?

The notion of governability has to do with the effectiveness of government. In the first instance, it tells us whether governments can cope with what they have on their plate. There is a useful definition of the concept by the historian, Theodor Schieder, who says that "ungovernability" is given if:

1. there is a weakness or complete absence of the expression of a uniform political will because political consensus is lacking,
2. the process of political decision making is thereby seriously endangered or made impossible,
3. existing institutions based on written or traditional constitutional law and functioning accordingly prove insufficient or completely unsuitable, and
4. thus the function of self-preservation of a political unit—internal and external security, satisfaction of needs in the context of the prevailing, at present steadily growing level of expectations, adaptability to historical change in its different forms as social change, change of values—is put in jeopardy.[11]

This is a tall order. According to Schieder the statement that a society is ungovernable means that it can no longer preserve itself as a polity because it is unable to protect its integrity, to satisfy the needs and expectations of its citizens, and to accommodate change. This in turn reflects on the usefulness of institutions.

Schieder's definition appears in a German collection of essays on our subject, entitled *Regierbarkeit* (governability). Its publisher, eager to raise the appeal of the book, printed a laconic statement on the title page: "*The problem:* A horrifying slogan has for some time come to articulate the growing political defeatism of the West: ungovernability of democracies. *The solution:* we must counter technocratic megalomania and the political pusillanimity of the slogan 'ungovernability' by enlightenment about the conditions of reasonable government and the

limits of what politics can do."[12] A splendid project—or is it perhaps "reasonable government" itself which has brought about the ineffectiveness of government in the democracies of the OECD countries? And is it "enlightenment" that we need, or are there requirements for tangible institutional reform? Leaving the "horrifying slogan" on one side for the moment, it appears from the (vast) literature as well as from immediate observation that there are three main processes which begin to impair the effectiveness of democratic governments.

The first of these is what has come to be called "overloading." This is, of course, Michael Crozier's great preoccupation; but in his or in other words it has been observed by many.[13] It has been argued that this is not so much an overloading with new objectives of the state (*Staatsziele*) that is at issue as one with new tasks within traditional objectives (*Staatsaufgaben*).[14] Either way, there are few today who would doubt that modern governments have taken on more than they can cope with, and in doing so have partly responded to, and partly generated expectations which were bound to be disappointed. Such disappointments need not be as extreme as those of the gambler who, as he was losing all his savings in a casino, told himself that surely the State, which had given the casino its licence, would not wish him to be impoverished to the point of destitution. He actually wrote a book about his experience which contains the ringing—and telling—accusation: "What kind of State is it that does not prevent people who have been caught by the gambling passion from falling into the certain abyss and which then leaves them miserably alone?"[15] What kind of State indeed? One begins to understand why Milton Friedman not only opposes the licensing of casinos, but even the banning of marijuana, indeed of heroin, so that the state is not involved at all in people's misery.

More seriously (though the example is not to be dismissed lightly), there are two areas in particular in which the State has taken on responsibilities, and has come to be expected to deliver, in which it is now apparent that its limits are closer than many expected: economic policy, and social policy. In the field of economic policy, governments appear to have come up against human values, and the difficulties of manipulating them. There is no simple answer to the problem of inflation; and Alt may well be right that it is bound to lead to further estrangement from the political system. But this much is clear that there is no endemic inflation as long as people's expectations of their standard of living, and their ability to produce coincide. The ability to produce—productivity—can, of course, be raised. But if it is not raised enough, expectations will have to come down to cope with the problem. Yet there is relatively little that government can do to dampen expectations. In the field of social policy, at least two restrictions of the effectiveness of government are apparent today. One is financial. The systems of social policy built into most welfare states involve an automaticity almost like the Common Agricultural Policy of the European Community. This means that they reach ceilings of taxability, especially if demographic changes take place which tilt the balance further towards recipients of help and against contributors.

## THE PRICE OF BUREAUCRATISATION

The other limit of social policy has to do with the clumsiness of planning, and the price of bureaucratisation. It is probably an impermissible extrapolation to predict that by the year 2000 there will be, in the National Health Service, one administrator for every patient; but there is a trend not only towards larger but towards less effective organization.

The first problem of governability, then, is that of "overloading." The second process which has begun to impair the effectiveness of modern government has to do with the space in which it operates. Few institutions seem more jealous of their position than the nation state. Government and Parliament make a great song and dance about "sovereignty" whenever the question

of a redistribution of powers arises. But of course they cannot prevent it. Issues are stronger than institutions; and the "productive forces" of the time tend away from national governments to two opposing directions. One is, decentralisation. Most European societies have been through a paradoxical period of institutional change. On the one hand, people were promised more rights of participation at all levels, and were encouraged to become active citizens. On the other hand, "rationalization" was the order of the day; in the name of this suspicious slogan, local government was all but destroyed in many places. Whether it can be re-established is uncertain. But it is certain that today the pendulum is swinging towards participation rather than rationalization. It may be that "small is beautiful"; certainly it is more effective in many respects. We have somehow gone over the top of all economies of scale, in human terms, but also in technical terms. Thus, government, industry and organisations alike are rediscovering the smaller dimension; and I have little doubt that in democratic countries the battle for devolving authority will in the end be won.

But, of course, not everything can be devolved. Scotland alone cannot guarantee an international monetary system. Small firms need access to wider markets. In an age of Super Powers, even Middle Powers are too weak to defend themselves. No one country can hope to win the fight against poverty in the world. Monetary stability, trade rules, defence organisations, and development are but four examples of subjects which have irreversibly emigrated from the political units to which we have grown accustomed. There is a case for European co-operation, even if the European Communities sadly fail to live up to its requirements. There is a case for a Western alliance. There is a case for joint action on the part of the rich to make sure that at the very least people's basic needs are met everywhere. There is a case for world-wide rules of monetary stability, free trade and a number of other fields. Whoever resists such needs will find himself poorer, weaker, less responsible and, before long, less secure.

But governments resist both the forces for devolution and those for international co-operation. We have noted already that such resistance does not quench the forces themselves; or put differently, governments are not all-important. There is in fact a revival of local politics. Many groupings have emerged in recent years around specific concerns at the local level. The "black economy" at least provides many an example of the success of small businesses. If this is not too far-fetched a comment: people want to belong, which they do neither as cogs in the wheel of a big organisation nor as men and women in the street nor as inhabitants of a high-rise monster. Thus they build their own ligatures where they live and work and play. At the other end, the forces of change have pushed their way through a less popular though equally effective fashion. In the absence of flexible governmental arrangements transcending nations and continents, private organizations have stepped into the breach. Whatever issues the accountability of transnational companies, or its absence, may raise, there can be no doubt that they have discovered and exploited the potential of wider spaces for action. They demonstrate beyond doubt that ineffective government and effective private action can exist side by side. Suspicions of transnational companies may be well-founded in some respects. It is irresponsible to make fortunes out of the production and sale of cheap tobacco in developing countries. Windfall profits as well as currency manipulations and the sudden closure of factories for reasons of corporate convenience raise many a question. But when all is said and done, there is a case for acknowledging that transnationals have been more effective in recognising the need for wider spaces of action than our rigid and tired governments.

Is there a lesson here? Is it possible that ungovernability, at least with respect to overloading and the stubborn defence of a useless political space, will be overcome by autonomous development? Is there a case for assuming that the hidden hand of new social forces will in the end correct the arrogance of traditional structures of power? The point is worth bearing in mind, though before we pursue it we have to consider the third and most serious process contributing to the declining effectiveness of government.

## THE BRITISH EXAMPLE

If one wants to give it a name, one could call it the arteriosclerosis of government, though there are more familiar descriptions, such as corporatism, group politics, even collectivism. Britain has provided the preferred subject of the study of this phenomenon which has to do with Schieder's fourth point, the ability of political communities to absorb new forces and change. The first stage of the process was the gradual dissipation of the Westminster Model which John Mackintosh has described so vividly in his *Government and Politics of Britain*.[16] He shows, above all, "how the executive gained control over parliament," and how government thus became identified with the executive. But the executive did not remain suspended in mid-air. It was soon surrounded by a number of groups, of which political parties are only one, with which arrangements had to be made. At least some of these groups, such as the TUC and the CBI, gradually became "governing institutions." This is Keith Middlemas's term who uses it to describe the development of a "corporate bias" in Britain in the 1920s and 1930s.[17] By the 1950s, a system had come to full bloom which engaged in a veritable "cult of the equilibrium." Decisions were taken, not by adversary politics growing out of the class struggle, but by an organised consensus between government and governing institutions. More extreme analysts of this development have argued that there is a sense in which the end government came to be but one group among others, indeed several groups if one considers the bargains between government departments.[18] These analysts may be right in the world of effectiveness, as it were: this is how things happen. But they are wrong in the world of legitimacy: without government, decisions lack two crucial ingredients, authority and money. Nevertheless, there remains the central point that the Westminster Model has been turned into a bargain process between government and important organisations the result of which is a more-or-less harmony in place of strife.

This is the British example. Others, who have never followed the Westminster Model, have reached the same destination by different routes. In the United States, quite contrary to its constitutional assumptions, there is no simple notion of "the executive"; parts of congress are involved in the great consensus. In continental countries, the state itself has been regarded as an instrument of consensus, if not as the "reality of the moral ideal," and non-adversary consensus is backed up by legal systems of the Roman Law tradition. Everywhere, however, the terms in which Keith Middlemas, in his *Politics in Industrial Society*, describes the way in which the great consensus has gone sour, are applicable. From the "high aspirations" which accompanied the consensus when it was built, it has now sunk to being "the lowest common denominator of policies designed to avoid trouble." [19] And this does not work for very long. The "stagnant mediocrity" of an inflexible system of consensus has revived, or generated for the first time, doubts and conflicts with which the system itself cannot cope. The consensus was meant to bring about massive social changes, the new deal of a just society; but in the end it became a thoughtless administration of the past. In the 1970s, the rigidity of the system became fully exposed, "Like an overloaded electrical circuit, the system began to blow more fuses than electricians could cope with in that dismal decade." [20]

There is a danger in metaphorical language. It evokes images, and plays on preconceptions without proving anything. However, there are quite fundamental issues which support the point that the "corporate bias" creates new problems without necessarily solving old ones. Such a bias was an appropriate response to a condition in which overriding class interests had dissolved into multiple interests of a more specific character. It could be assumed that there would be, for each of the major concerns of people, an organised group which had access to, or formed itself, "governing institutions." All seemed well, because the bargaining system reflected, or was capable of reflecting, the relative weight of different interests at different times. New concerns could always be absorbed into the system. But then, a new kind of interest emerged. It is the desire of individuals to check the power of large organizations, and to be free of their domination. The concern is paradoxical; the same people feel represented by, say, trade unions and resent their bigness and power. Thus the question is not how to weaken the unions, but how to have them strong and yet safeguard individual liberty. However, the corporate bias cannot make any provisions for this. There cannot be an anti-group group which becomes one of the "governing institutions." Even political parties fail to play this role. As a result, an important concern remains unexpressed in official politics, and that means, it is expressed in unofficial and unpredictable ways, by massive abstention, by votes for parties and candidates outside the consensus, by situational protest, ecological, fiscal or otherwise. This is where the corporate system blows its fuses.

## WHY IS ECONOMIC GROWTH DIFFICULT?

The example provides a partial answer to the question of whether the processes which have impaired effective government are important. They are. Their symptoms are everywhere, and there is little reason to believe that they will go away. This becomes even more clearly evident if we ask ourselves why it is that we have reached this position.

There are at least two answers to this question, one conjectural and one structural. Samuel Huntington was the first to argue that the "crisis of democracy" is a reflection of changing economic circumstances.[21] Democracy worked as long as the contest for higher expectations built into its structures promised some success. As long as a governing party could deliver at least some of the goods, all was well. But once economic growth—the necessary condition of the ability of governments to respond to expectations the increase of which they themselves had to stimulate—became more difficult, democratic governments were in trouble. If there is, say, the beginning of a Kondratieff cycle which means a quarter-century of low growth or even decline, democratic politics has no way of coping. It is only—thus Huntington's conclusion—by introducing elements of authoritarianism that we can survive the long slump. Leaving this conclusion on one side, there is much that seems persuasive in the argument. Yet in a crucial sense it begs the question: why is it that economic growth has become more difficult?

The point can be made in a different way. Britain has a great deal of experience with the politics of economic decline. Yet a century of low, at times "negative" growth has in fact not led to the decadence of political democracy. On the contrary, Britain is one of a mere handful of countries in the world in which democracy has survived the ups and downs of this century. Economic growth is in fact no more than one symptom of a much deeper process. Growth, too, has become difficult for reasons which have to do with its own assumptions; unmanageable size and the accompanying cost of research, development and investment, provide but one significant example; changes in values (from a "protestant" to a hedonist ethic) and satiation if not of markets then of human capacity to absorb innovation are others. The same principle applies to the processes of government as well: the very assumptions on which modern, "reasonable" government is based have created the problems to which we have spoken.

John Mackintosh has seen this clearly: "Thus while the Westminster Model was never reconstructed or revised, the continuation of trends such as the extension of the right to vote, the consequent growth of parties, the new demands of the electorate and the complex

administration required to fulfil these demands all affected it, introducing new elements and finally altering the balance between institutions."[22] By developing its own assumptions, parliamentary democracy turned into corporate democracy. The machine of corporate democracy in turn has run hot and is about to crank to a halt. Similarly, the assumptions of a community of citizens whose rights extended from the legal to the political and the social sphere led of necessity to an increase in government activity, to big government, until in the end its very bigness prevents government from moving ahead. And the vested interests, that go with big government and the "governing institutions" which surround it, are such that a change in relevant spaces of action goes unnoticed, or rather is resisted in the hope that no one will notice. In the end, as we have seen, government itself wears the Emperor's new clothes. The declining effectiveness of democratic government is, in other words, endemic, or structural. It is a result of its own assumptions; it is one of the contradictions of modernity. The central point is not that too many fuses have been blown for electricians to cope; the point is that we need a different system of fuses and retrained electricians to cope.

It has become fashionable to make proposals for change. Not only is the boundary between description and prescription, analytical and normative statements no longer respected, there is in fact an expectation that the academic lecturer will come up with remedies, the more radical, even outrageous, the better. I shall disappoint those who expect such a conclusion. There are, to be sure, important proposals to discuss. In passing at least, I have mentioned some of them: a Bill of Rights, electoral reform, the devolution of powers, a new internationalism. But in a sense, programmes are easy to come by, whereas analysis is not. At the risk of appearing unduly gloomy, I propose to take my argument a last step further without pretending to have answers.

There are today serious limitations of the effectiveness of democratic government. They concern (to return to Theodor Schieder's definition yet again) both the ability of governments to satisfy rising expectations and their ability to absorb changes in values and social structure. Such limitations are serious. They mean that governments are weak at a time at which it could be argued that we can ill afford such weakness. They also mean that reforms are necessary without it being evident where the ideas of the future should come from. For the moment, not only political parties, but intellectuals, too, seem to have run out of ideas. Keith Middlemas involuntarily sums up the problem when at the end of a critical tirade about the ills of democracy, he admits that while change is necessary "the form it will take cannot be seen."[23] We need thought and discussion, publications and even policy research institutes, but they are merely the shell of thought and designs of the future.

Yet there is no reason to think that the dearth of ideas about the future and the resistance of institutions to necessary change must be fatal. In the end, as transnationals, or the "black economy" show, the imagination of reality is greater than that of professors or ministers. For this seems beyond doubt: Neither the "unloading" of functions nor recognition of appropriate spaces nor the acknowledgment of individual rights in a group society are in principle outside the orbit of democratic governments. Changes are likely to be painful, but they are not impossible. Robert Heilbroner has made this point with respect to inflation. Inflation is, in his analysis, the latest malady of capitalism. But capitalism has coped before: with poverty, with trusts and cartels, with depressions. In every case, coping was costly. Again with inflation, major cataclysmic events are likely before the obvious solution is implemented: "permanent wage and price controls" and "a sufficiently heavy and well-directed structure of taxation [to] prevent a buildup of purchasing power."[24] But, Heilbroner adds: "in the end, I believe that capitalism will again evidence its extraordinary institutional and ideological flexibility and will accept the necessary text 'socialistic' steps as the only means by which it can extend its nervous, expansionary life." It

is not just capitalism which has this ability to adjust, but even more so the open society and its political institutions which are, after all, designed to accommodate change without revolution.

Yet, when this is said, and even done, one wonders: is this all? What about the famous "crisis of legitimacy" of modern, late capitalist, democratic corporatist societies? Are we not faced with a deeper malady? Are there not endemic threats greater than the challenges of reform of which we have spoken? Has the declining effectiveness of government not begun to affect its legitimacy in the democratic countries of the world?

There is evidently a great temptation to deduce the answer from one's political preconceptions. Habermas, for example—and Middlemas tends to follow him—would like to think that we are faced, if not with a proletarian revolution, then with some other great historical earthquake; and as a result he tends to introduce the notion of a "crisis of legitimacy" first and then seek material to support it.[25] Heilbroner, on the other hand, allows his social democratic pragmatism to reject the notion of a crisis of legitimacy out of hand; he assumes that somehow or other problems will be worked out, or will work themselves out. If one is neither a critical theorist nor a dogmatic pragmatist, the answer is less easy. It is really that we do not know for sure, but that there are signs which point to more serious cataclysms than a mere crisis of effectiveness would suggest. There are in particular threats to liberty which arise from the unpredictability— dare one say, the predictable unpredictability?—of governments which are alienated from people's values, worried about self-preservation, and faced with the ultimate threats to governability and to survival.

I have hinted once or twice at a condition which I have described as the alienation of government. What this means is quite simple. On the one hand, a certain system and practice of government produces problems, endemic problems like, say, the inability to satisfy expectations which the process of government has raised or implied. On the other hand, people's expectations turn away from government. While government desperately, and vainly, attempts to live up to its self-imposed aims, people have long decided to look for other ways to safeguard their life chances. It is as if the carpet is pulled away from underneath government. But government tries to resist: a situation in which it is not surprising that Samuel Huntington and others demand a return to authority, if not authoritarianism.

This is most dramatically evident if we consider the basic functions of government. It seems that today the conflict between the prevailing social democratic consensus which informs the ineffectual actions of government, and the values which haltingly and tentatively, but no less clearly inform people's actions, has reached the social contract itself (Thomas Hobbes's social contract, not Jack Jones's, to be sure). Government is still very largely, and understandably, about increasing people's options, about what has come to be called, somewhat misleadingly, "liberalisation." People, on the other hand, begin to wonder what these options are for. They find that options make little sense if one is not anchored in a framework of social ties, ligatures. So they look for ligatures, often desperately, as in Jonestown, or perversely, as in drug abuse, or in criminal gangs. There is, in other words, a real problem of holding society together, of social control, and it could be argued that few things are clearer indices of declining legitimacy than problems of the fundamental social contract. The return of a war of all against all documents doubt in the ability of governments to do what they were initially set up to do. Governments are not unaware of this dilemma. So they translate the social contract into "law and order," and this in turn into the "short, sharp treatment" of offenders, only to find that it makes matters worse. Once again, there is a great danger that the response to a crisis of legitimacy will be authoritarianism and illiberty.

This, then, takes us back to the frightening question with which I began this lecture. Who will save us from disaster? Karl Jaspers's recommendation, not to lose hope, is fine but hardly enough. Raymond Aron—not, to be sure, a Hegelian, despite his somewhat abstract terminology—gave what is the only possible answer: "In the nuclear age, the only chance that mankind will be saved from itself is that the intelligence of the personified state will bring armaments under control."[26] The "intelligence of the personified state," that is the capacity of governments to comprehend and to do the right thing. But does it exist? The potential of destruction, so we said, takes us to the limits of governability; it is too great for the moral and intellectual weaknesses of man. These weaknesses need, of course, not be tempted. The intelligence of the personified state can be such at least that the ultimate threat remains remote and unlikely. This is where the effectiveness, and above all, the legitimacy of governments comes in. Illegitimate governments are worried governments. The new authoritarianism documents their worries with respect to security within societies. Outside, with respect to external security, worried governments are liable to make every mistake in the book. This is why the danger is so great that widespread doubts in the effectiveness of governments turn into doubts in their legitimacy. A free society does not need a strong government.

It may indeed fare better if government is fairly inactive and quiet. But a free society needs an unworried government, and that means one which is effective where necessary and legitimate throughout.

## Notes

1. Miles Kahler, "Rumours of War: the 1914 Analogy," *Foreign Affairs*, New York, Winter 1979–80, pp. 374–396.

2. Sir John Hackett, *Third World War* (London: Sidgwick & Jackson, 1978).

3. Carl Friedrich von Weizsäcker, *Wege in der Gefahr* (Munich: DTV, 1979), pp. 110, 118.

4. Karl Jaspers, *Die Atombombe und die Zukunft des Menschen* (Munich, 1968).

5. James E. Alt, *The Politics of Economic Decline* (Cambridge: Cambridge University Press, 1979).

6. Ibid., chap. 7.

7. Ibid., p. 206.

8. *Cf.* D. Butler and D. Stokes, *Political Change in Britain* (New York: Macmillan, 1975).

9. Alt, *The Politics of Economic Decline*, p. 157.

10. Ibid., p. 270.

11. Theodor Schieder, "Einmaligkeit oder Wiederkehr," in *Regierbarkeit. Studien zu ihrer Problematisierung,* ed. Wilhelm Hennis, Peter Graf Kielmannsegg, and Ulrich Matz (Stuttgart: Klett-Cotta, 1977), p. 31.

12. Hennis, *Regierbarkeit.*

13. *Cf.* M. Crozier's contribution to *The Crisis of Democracy* by Michael J. Crozier, Samuel P. Huntington, Joji Watanuki (New York: New York University Press, 1975).

14. Thus by Ulrich Matz, "Der überforderte Staat," in Hennis, *Regierbarkeit.*

15. Frank Hordan, *Die Banken des Satans* (Tirschenreuth: Hordan-Verlag, 1980).

16. John Mackintosh, *The Government and Politics of Britain* (London: Hutchinson, 1977).

17. Keith Middlemas, *Politics in Industrial Society* (London: Andre Deutsch,1979).

18. *Cf.* J. J. Richardson and A. G. Jordan, *Governing Under Pressure* (Oxford: Martin Robertson, 1979).

19. Middlemas, *Politics in Industrial Society,* p. 429.

20. Ibid., p. 459.

21. *Cf.* Samuel Huntington's contribution to Michel Crozier et al., *The Crisis of Democracy.*

22. Mackintosh, *The Government and Politics of Britain*, p. 28.

23. Middlemas, *Politics in Industrial Society,* p. 463.

24. Robert Heilbroner, "Inflationary Capitalism," *The New Yorker,* October 8, 1979, pp. 121–141.

25. *Cf.* Jürgen Habermas, *Legitimationsprobleme im Spätkapitalismus* (Frankfurt: Suhrkamp, 1979). See also Middlemas, *Politics in Industrial Society,* chap. 15.

26. Raymond Aron, *Penser la Guerre, Clausewitz* (Paris: Gallimard, 1978), vol. 2.

# 30

# Presidents and Prime Ministers

*Richard Rose*

The need to give direction to government is universal and persisting. Every country, from Egypt of the pharoahs to contemporary democracies, must maintain political institutions that enable a small group of politicians to make authoritative decisions that are binding on the whole of society. Within every system, one office is of first importance, whether it is called president, prime minister, führer, or dux.

There are diverse ways of organizing the direction of government, not only between democracies and authoritarian regimes, but also among democracies. Switzerland stands at one extreme, with collective direction provided by a federal council whose president rotates from year to year. At the other extreme are countries that claim to centralize authority, under a British-style parliamentary system or in an American or French presidential system, in which one person is directly elected to the supreme office of state.

To what extent are the differences in the formal attributes of office a reflection of substantive differences in how authority is exercised? To what extent do the imperatives of office—the need for electoral support, dependence upon civil servants for advice, and vulnerability to events—impose common responses in practice? Comparing the different methods of giving direction to government in the United States (presidential), Great Britain (prime ministerial and Cabinet), and France (presidential and prime ministerial) can help us understand whether other countries do it—that is, choose a national leader—in a way that is better.

To make comparisons requires concepts that can identify the common elements in different offices. Three concepts organize the comparisons

SOURCE: Published by permission of Transaction Publishers, from *Society,* vol. 25, no. 3 (March–April 1988), pp. 61–67. © 1988 by Transaction Publishers.

I make: the career that leads to the top; the institutions and powers of government; and the scope for variation within a country, whether arising from events or personalities.

## CAREER LEADING TO THE TOP

By definition, a president or prime minister is unrepresentative by being the occupant of a unique office. The diversity of outlooks and skills that can be attributed to white, university-educated males is inadequate to predict how people with the same social characteristics—a Carter or an Eisenhower; a Wilson or a Heath—will perform in office. Nor is it helpful to consider the recruitment of national leaders deductively, as a management consultant or personnel officer would, first identifying the skills required for the job and then evaluating candidates on the basis of a priori requirements. National leaders are not recruited by examination; they are self-selected, individuals whose driving ambitions, personal attributes, and, not least, good fortune, combine to win the highest public office.

To understand what leaders can do in office we need to compare the skills acquired in getting to the top with the skills required once there. The tasks that a president or prime minister must undertake are few but central: sustaining popular support through responsiveness to the electorate, and being effective in government. Success in office encourages electoral popularity, and electoral popularity is an asset in wielding influence within government.

The previous careers of presidents and prime ministers are significant, insofar as experience affects what they do in office—and what they do well. A politician who had spent many years concentrating upon campaigning to win popularity may continue to cultivate popularity in office. By contrast, a politician experienced in dealing with the problems of government from within may be better at dealing effectively with international and domestic problems.

Two relevant criteria for comparing the careers of national leaders are: previous experience of government, and previous experience of party and mass electoral politics. American presidents are outstanding in their experience of campaigning for mass support, whereas French presidents are outstanding for their prior knowledge of government from the inside. British prime ministers usually combine experience in both fields.

Thirteen of the fourteen Americans who have been nominated for president of the United States by the Democratic or Republican parties since 1945 had prior experience in running for major office, whether at the congressional, gubernatorial or presidential level. Campaigning for office makes a politician conscious of his or her need for popular approval. It also cultivates skill in dealing with the mass media. No American will be elected president who has not learned how to campaign across the continent, effectively and incessantly. Since selection as a presidential candidate is dependent upon winning primaries, a president must run twice: first to win the party nomination and then to win the White House. The effort required is shown by the fact that in 1985, three years before the presidential election, one Republican hopeful campaigned in twenty-four states, and a Democratic hopeful in thirty. Immediately after the 1986 congressional elections ended, the media started featuring stories about the 1988 campaign.

Campaigning is different from governing. Forcing ambitious politicians to concentrate upon crossing and recrossing America reduces the time available for learning about problems in Washington and the rest of the world. The typical postwar president has had no experience working within the executive branch. The way in which the federal government deals with foreign policy, or with problems of the economy is known, if at all, from the vantage point of a spectator. A president is likely to have had relatively brief experience in Congress. As John F. Kennedy's career illustrates, Congress is not treated as a means of preparing to govern; it is a launching pad for a presidential campaign. The last three presidential elections have been won by individuals who could boast of having no experience in Washington. Jimmy Carter and

Ronald Reagan were state governors, experienced at a job that gives no experience in foreign affairs or economic management.

A president who is experienced in campaigning can be expected to continue cultivating the media and seeking a high standing in the opinion polls. Ronald Reagan illustrated this approach. A president may even use campaigning as a substitute for coming to grips with government; Jimmy Carter abandoned Washington for the campaign trail when confronted with midterm difficulties in 1978. But public relations expertise is only half the job; looking presidential is not the same as acting like a president.

A British prime minister, by contrast, enters office after decades in the House of Commons and years as a Cabinet minister. The average postwar prime minister had spent thirty-two years in Parliament before entering 10 Downing Street. Of that period, thirteen years had been spent as a Cabinet minister. Moreover, the prime minister has normally held the important policy posts of foreign secretary, chancellor of the exchequer or both. The average prime minister has spent eight years in ministerial office, learning to handle foreign and/or economic problems. By contrast with the United States, no prime minister has had postwar experience in state or local government, and by contrast with France, none has been a civil servant since World War II.

The campaign experience of a British prime minister is very much affected by the centrality that politicians give Parliament. A politician seeks to make a mark in debate there. Even in an era of mass media, the elitist doctrine holds that success in the House of Commons produces positive evaluation by journalists and invitations to appear on television, where a politician can establish an image with the national electorate. Whereas an American presidential hopeful has a bottom-up strategy, concentrating upon winning votes in early primaries in Iowa and New Hampshire as a means of securing media attention, a British politician has a top-down approach, starting to campaign in Parliament.

Party is the surrogate for public opinion among British politicians, and with good reason.

Success in the Commons is evaluated by a politician's party colleagues. Election to the party leadership is also determined by party colleagues. To become prime minister a politician does not need to win an election; he or she only needs to be elected party leader when the party has a parliamentary majority. Jim Callaghan and Sir Alec Douglas-Home each entered Downing Street this way and lost office in the first general election fought as prime minister.

The lesser importance of the mass electorate to British party leaders is illustrated by the fact that the average popularity rating of a prime minister is usually less than that of an American president. The monthly Gallup poll rating often shows the prime minister approved by less than half the electorate and trailing behind one or more leaders of the opposition.

In the Fifth French Republic, presidents and prime ministers have differed from American presidents, being very experienced in government, and relatively inexperienced in campaigning with the mass electorate. Only one president, Francois Mitterrand, has followed the British practice of making a political career based on Parliament. Since he was on the opposition side for the first two decades of the Fifth Republic, his experience of the problems of office was like that of a British opposition member of Parliament, and different from that of a minister. Giscard d'Estaing began as a high-flying civil servant and Charles de Gaulle, like Dwight Eisenhower, was schooled in bureaucratic infighting as a career soldier.

When nine different French prime ministers are examined, the significance of a civil service background becomes clear. Every prime minister except for Pierre Mauroy has been a civil servant first. It has been exceptional for a French prime minister to spend decades in Parliament before attaining that office. An Englishman would be surprised that a Raymond Barre or a Couve de Murville had not sat there before becoming prime minister. An American would be even more surprised by the experience that French leaders have had in the ministries as high civil servants, and particularly in dealing with foreign and economic affairs.

The traditional style of French campaigning is plebiscitary. One feature of this is that campaigning need not be incessant, Louis Napoleon is said to have compared elections with baptism: something it is necessary to do—but to do only once. The seven-year fixed term of the French president, about double the statutory life of many national leaders, is in the tradition of infrequent consultation with the electorate.

The French tradition of leadership is also ambivalent; a plebiscite is, after all, a mass mobilization. The weakness of parties, most notably on the Right, which has provided three of the four presidents of the Fifth Republic, encourages a personalistic style of campaigning. The use of the two-ballot method for the popular election of a president further encourages candidates to compete against each other as individuals, just as candidates for the presidential nomination compete against fellow-partisans in a primary. The persistence of divisions between Left and Right ensures any candidate successful in entering the second ballot a substantial bloc of votes, with or without a party endorsement.

On the two central criteria of political leadership, the relationship with the mass electorate, and knowledge of government, there are cross-national contrasts in the typical career. A British or French leader is likely to know far more about government than an American president, but an American politician is likely to be far more experienced in campaigning to win popular approval and elections.

## LESS FOR THE PRESIDENT TO GOVERN

Journalistic and historical accounts of government often focus on the person and office of the national leader. The American president is deemed to be very powerful because of the immense military force that he can command by comparison to a national leader in Great Britain or France. The power to drop a hydrogen bomb is frequently cited as a measure of the awesome power of an American president; but it is misleading, for no president has ever dropped a hydrogen bomb, and no president has used atomic weapons in more than forty years. Therefore, we must ask: What does an American president (and his European counterparts) do when not dropping a hydrogen bomb?

In an era of big government, a national leader is more a chief than an executive, for no individual can superintend, let alone carry out, the manifold tasks of government. A national leader does not need to make major choices about what government ought to do; he inherits a set of institutions that are committed—by law, by organization, by the professionalism of public employees, and by the expectations of voters—to appropriate a large amount of the country's resources in order to produce the program outputs of big government.

Whereas political leadership is readily personalized, government is intrinsically impersonal. It consists of collective actions by organizations that operate according to impersonal laws. Even when providing benefits to individuals, such as education, health care, or pensions, the scale of a ministry or a large regional or local government is such as to make the institution appear impersonal.

Contemporary Western political systems are first of all governed by the rule of law rather than personal will. When government did few things and actions could be derived from prerogative powers, such as a declaration of war, there was more scope for the initiative of leaders. Today, the characteristic activities of government, accounting for most public expenditure and personnel, are statutory entitlements to benefits of the welfare state. They cannot be overturned by wish or will, as their tacit acceptance by such "antigovernment" politicians as Margaret Thatcher and Ronald Reagan demonstrates. Instead of the leader dominating government, government determines much that is done in the leader's name.

In a very real sense, the so-called power of a national leader depends upon actions that his government takes, whether or not this is desired by the leader. Instead of comparing the constitutional powers of leaders, we should compare the resources that are mobilized by the government for which a national leader is nominally responsible. The conventional measure of the size of government is public expenditure as a proportion of the gross national product. By this criterion, French or British government is more powerful than American government. Organization for Economic Cooperation and Development (OECD) statistics show that in 1984 French public expenditure accounted for 49 percent of the national product, British for 45 percent, and American for 37 percent. When attention is directed at central government, as distinct from all levels of government, the contrast is further emphasized. British and French central government collect almost two-fifths of the national product in tax revenue, whereas the American federal government collects only one-fifth.

When a national leader leads, others are meant to follow. The legitimacy of authority means that public employees should do what elected officials direct. In an era of big government, there are far more public employees at hand than in an era when the glory of the state was symbolized by a small number of people clustering around a royal court. Statistics of public employment again show British and French government as much more powerful than American government. Public employment in France accounts for 33 percent of all persons who work, more than Britain, with 31 percent. In the United States, public employment is much less, 18 percent.

The capacity of a national leader to direct public employees is much affected by whether or not such officials are actually employed by central government. France is most centralized, having three times as many public employees working in ministries as in regional or local government. If public enterprises are also reckoned as part of central government, France is even more centralized. In the United States and Great Britain, by contrast, the actual delivery of public services such as education and health is usually shipped out to lower tiers of a federal government, or to a complex of local and functional authorities. Delivering the everyday services of government is deemed beneath the dignity of national leaders in Great Britain. In the United States, central government is deemed too remote to be trusted with such programs as education or police powers.

When size of government is the measure, an American president appears weaker than a French or British leader. By international standards, the United States has a not so big government, for its claim on the national product and the national labor force is below the OECD average. Ronald Reagan is an extreme example of a president who is "antigovernment," but he is not the only example. In the past two decades, the United States has not lagged behind Europe in developing and expanding welfare state institutions that make government big. It has chosen to follow a different route, diverging from the European model of a mixed economy welfare state. Today, the president has very few large-scale program responsibilities, albeit they remain significant: defense and diplomacy, social security, and funding the federal deficit.

By contrast, even an "antigovernment" prime minister such as Margaret Thatcher finds herself presiding over a government that claims more than two-fifths of the national product in public expenditure. Ministers must answer, collectively and individually in the House of Commons, for all that is done under the authority of an Act of Parliament. In France, the division between president and prime minister makes it easier for the president of the republic to avoid direct entanglement in low status issues of service delivery, but the centralization of government necessarily involves the prime minister and his colleagues.

When attention is turned to the politics of government as distinct from public policies, all leaders have one thing in common, they are engaged in political management, balancing the interplay of forces within government, major economic interests, and public opinion generally. It is no derogation of a national leader's position to say that it has an important symbolic dimension, imposing a unifying and persuasive theme upon what government does. The theme may be relatively clear-cut, as in much of

Margaret Thatcher's rhetoric. Or it may be vague and symbolic, as in much of the rhetoric of Charles de Gaulle. The comparative success of Ronald Reagan, an expert in manipulating vague symbols, as against Jimmy Carter, whose technocratic biases were far stronger than his presentational skills, is a reminder of the importance of a national political leader being able to communicate successfully to the nation.

In the United States and France, the president is both head of government and head of state. The latter role makes him president of all the people, just as the former role limits his representative character to governing in the name of a majority (but normally, less than 60 percent) of the voters. A British prime minister does not have the symbolic obligation to represent the country as a whole; the queen does that.

The institutions of government affect how political management is undertaken. The separate election of the president and the legislature in the United States and France create a situation of nominal independence, and bargaining from separate electoral bases. By contrast, the British prime minister is chosen by virtue of being leader of the largest party in the House of Commons. Management of Parliament is thus made much easier by the fact that the British prime minister can normally be assured of a majority of votes there.

An American president has a far more difficult task in managing government than do British and French counterparts. Congress really does determine whether bills become laws, by contrast to the executive domination of law and decree-making in Europe. Congressional powers of appropriation provide a basis for a roving scrutiny of what the executive branch does. There is hardly any bureau that is free from congressional scrutiny, and in many congressional influence may be as strong as presidential influence. By contrast, a French president has significant decree powers and most of the budget can be promulgated. A British prime minister can also invoke the Official Secrets Act and the doctrine of collective responsibility to insulate the

effective (that is, executive) side of government from the representative (that is, Parliament).

Party politics and electoral outcomes, which cannot be prescribed in a democratic constitution, affect the extent to which political management must be invested in persuasion. If management is defined as making an organization serve one's purpose, then Harry Truman gave the classic definition of management as persuasion: "I sit here all day trying to persuade people to do the things they ought to have sense enough to do without my persuading them. That's all the powers of the President amount to." Because both Democratic and Republican parties are loose coalitions, any president will have to invest much effort in persuading fellow partisans, rather than whipping them into line. Given different electoral bases, congressmen may vote their district, rather than their party label. When president and Congress are of opposite parties, then strong party ties weaken the president.

In Great Britain, party competition and election outcomes are expected to produce an absolute majority in the House of Commons for a single party. Given that the prime minister, as party leader, stands and falls with members of Parliament in votes in Parliament and at a general election, a high degree of party discipline is attainable. Given that the Conservative and Labor parties are themselves coalitions of differing factions and tendencies, party management is no easy task. But it is far easier than interparty management, a necessary condition of coalition government, including Continental European governments.

The Fifth Republic demonstrates that important constitutional features are contingent upon election outcomes. Inherent in the constitution of the Fifth Republic is a certain ambiguity about the relationship between president and prime minister. Each president has desired to make his office preeminent. The first three presidents had no difficulty in doing that, for they could rely upon the support of a majority of members of the National Assembly. Cooperation could not be coerced, but it could be relied upon to keep the prime minister subordinate.

Since the election of François Mitterrand in 1981, party has become an independent variable. Because the president's election in 1981 was paralleled by the election of a Left majority in the assembly, Mitterrand could adopt what J.E.S. Hayward describes in *Governing France* as a "Gaullist conception of his office." But after the victory of the Right in the 1986 Assembly election resulted in a non-Socialist being imposed as premier, Jacques Chirac, the president has had to accept a change of position, symbolized by the ambivalent term *cohabitation.*

Whether the criterion is government's size or the authority of the national leader vis-à-vis other politicians, the conclusion is the same: the political leaders of Great Britain and France can exercise more power than the president of the United States. The American presidency is a relatively weak office. America's population, economy, and military are not good measures of the power of the White House. Imagine what one would say if American institutions were transplanted, more or less wholesale, to some small European democracy. We would not think that such a country had a strong leader.

While differing notably in the separate election of a French president as against a parliamentary election of a British prime minister, both offices centralize authority within a state that is itself a major institution of society. As long as a French president has a majority in the National Assembly, then this office can have most influence within government, for ministers are unambiguously subordinate to the president. The linkage of a British prime minister's position with a parliamentary majority means that as long as a single party has a majority, a British politician is protected against the risks of cohabitation à la française or à l'américaine.

## VARIATIONS WITHIN NATIONS

An office sets parameters within which politicians can act, but the more or less formal stipulation of the rules and resources of an office cannot determine exactly what is done. Within these limits, the individual performance of a president or prime minister can be important. Events too are significant; everyday crises tend to frustrate any attempt to plan ahead, and major crises—a war or domestic disaster—can shift the parameters, reducing a politician's scope for action (for example, Watergate) or expanding it (for example, the mass mobilization that Churchill could lead after Dunkirk).

In the abstract language of social science, we can say that the actions of a national leader reflect the interaction of the powers of office, of events, and of personality. But in concrete situations, there is always an inclination to emphasize one or another of these terms. For purposes of exposition, I treat the significance of events and personality separately: each is but one variable in a multivariate outcome.

Social scientists and constitutional lawyers are inherently generalizers, whereas critical events are unique. For example, a study of the British prime ministership that ignored what could be done in wartime would omit an example of powers temporarily stretched to new limits. Similarly, a study of Winston Churchill's capacities must recognize that his personality prevented him from achieving the nation's highest office—until the debacle of 1940 thrust office upon him.

In the postwar era, the American presidency has been especially prone to shock events. Unpredictable and nonrecurring events of importance include the outbreak of the Korean War in 1950, the assassination of President Kennedy in 1963, American involvement in the Vietnam War in the late 1960s, and the Watergate scandal, which led to President Nixon's resignation in 1974. One of the reasons for the positive popularity of Ronald Reagan has been that no disastrous event occurred in his presidency—at least until Irangate broke in November 1986.

The creation of the Fifth French Republic followed after events in Vietnam and in Algeria that undermined the authority and legitimacy of the government of the Fourth Republic. The events of May 1968 had a far greater impact in Paris than in any other European country.

Whereas in 1958 events helped to create a republic with a president given substantial powers, in 1968 events were intended to reduce the authority of the state.

Great Britain has had relatively uneventful postwar government. Many causes of momentary excitement, such as the 1963 Profumo scandal that embarrassed Harold Macmillan, were trivial. The 1956 Suez war, which forced the resignation of Anthony Eden, did not lead to subsequent changes in the practice of the prime ministership, even though it was arguably a gross abuse of power vis-à-vis Cabinet colleagues and Parliament. The 1982 Falklands war called forth a mood of self-congratulation rather than a cry for institutional reform. The electoral boost it gave the prime minister was significant, but not eventful for the office.

The miner's strike, leading to a national three-day working week in the last days of the administration of Edward Heath in 1974, was perceived as a challenge to the authority of government. The prime minister called a general election seeking a popular mandate for his conduct of industrial relations. The mandate was withheld; so too was an endorsement of strikers. Characteristically, the events produced a reaction in favor of conciliation, for which Harold Wilson was particularly well suited at that stage of his career. Since 1979 the Thatcher administration has demonstrated that trade unions are not invincible. Hence, the 1974 crisis now appears as an aberration, rather than a critical conjuncture.

While personal factors are often extraneous to government, each individual incumbent has some scope for choice. Within a set of constraints imposed by office and events, a politician can choose what kind of a leader he or she would like to be. Such choices have political consequences. "Do what you can" is a prudential rule that is often overlooked in discussing what a president or prime minister does. The winnowing process by which one individual reaches the highest political office not only allows for variety, but sometimes invites it, for a challenger for office may win votes by being different from an incumbent.

A president has a multiplicity of roles and a multiplicity of obligations. Many—as commander in chief of the armed forces, delivering a State of the Union message to Congress, and presenting a budget—are requirements of the office; but the capacity to do well in particular roles varies with the individual. For example, Lyndon Johnson was a superb manager of congressional relations, but had little or no feel for foreign affairs. By contrast, John F. Kennedy was interested in foreign affairs and defense and initially had little interest in domestic problems. Ronald Reagan is good at talking to people, whereas Jimmy Carter and Richard Nixon preferred to deal with problems on paper. Dwight D. Eisenhower brought to the office a national reputation as a hero that he protected by making unclear public statements. By contrast, Gerald Ford's public relations skills, while acceptable in a congressman, were inadequate to the demands of the contemporary presidency.

In Great Britain, Margaret Thatcher is atypical in her desire to govern, as well as preside over government. She applies her energy and intelligence to problems of government—and to telling her colleagues what to do about them. The fact that she wants to be *the* decision-maker for British government excites resentment among civil servants and Cabinet colleagues. This is not only a reaction to her forceful personality, but also an expression of surprise: other prime ministers did not want to be the chief decision-maker in government. In the case of an aging Winston Churchill from 1951–55, this could be explained on grounds of ill health. In the case of Anthony Eden, it could be explained by an ignorance of domestic politics.

The interesting prime ministers are those who chose not to be interventionists across a range of government activities. Both Harold Macmillan and Clement Attlee brought to Downing Street great experience of British government. But Attlee was ready to be simply a chairman of a Cabinet in which other ministers were capable and decisive. Macmillan chose to intervene very selectively on issues that he thought important and to leave others to get on with most matters. Labor leader Neil Kinnock, if he became prime minister, would adopt a non-interventionist role. This would be welcomed in reaction to Thatcher's dominating approach. It would be necessary because Kinnock knows very little about the problems and practice of British government. Unique among party leaders of the past half-century, he has never held office in government.

In France, the role of a president varies with personality. De Gaulle approached the presidency with a distinctive concept of the state as well as of politics. By contrast, Mitterrand draws upon his experience of many decades of being a parliamentarian and a republican. Pompidou was distinctive in playing two roles, first prime minister under de Gaulle, and subsequently president.

Differences between French prime ministers may in part reflect contrasting relationships with a president. As a member of a party different from the president, Chirac has partisan and personal incentives to be more assertive than does a prime minister of the same party. Premiers who enter office via the Assembly or local politics, like Chaban-Delmas and Mauroy, are likely to have different priorities than a premier who was first a technocrat, such as Raymond Barre.

## FLUCTUATIONS IN LEADERS

The fluctuating effect upon leaders of multiple influences is shown by the monthly ratings of the popularity of presidents and prime ministers. If formal powers of office were all, then the popularity rating of each incumbent should be much the same. This is not the case. If the personal characteristics of a politician were all-important, then differences would occur between leaders, but each leader would receive a consistent rating during his or her term of office. In fact, the popularity of a national leader tends to go up and down during a term of office. Since personality is held constant, these fluctuations cannot be explained as a function of personal qualities. Since there is no consistent decline in popularity, the movement cannot be explained as a consequence of impossible expectations causing the public to turn against whoever initially wins its votes.

The most reasonable explanation of these fluctuations in popularity is that they are caused by events. They may be shock events, such as the threat of military action, or scandal in the leader's office. Alternatively, changes may reflect the accumulation of seemingly small events, most notably those that are reflected in the state of the economy, such as growth, unemployment, and inflation rates. A politician may not be responsible for such trends, but he or she expects to lose popularity when things appear to be going badly and to regain popularity when things are going well.

Through the decades, cyclical fluctuations can reflect an underlying long-term secular trend. In Europe a major secular trend is the declining national importance of international affairs. In the United States events in Iran or Central America remain of as much (or more) significance than events within the United States. In a multipolar world a president is involved in and more vulnerable to events in many places. By contrast, leaders of France and Great Britain have an influence limited to a continental scale, in a world in which international relations has become intercontinental. This shift is not necessarily a loss for heads of government in the European Community. In a world summit meeting, only one nation, the United States, has been first. Japan may seek to exercise political influence matching its growing economic power. The smaller scale of the European Community nations with narrower economic interests create conditions for frequent contact and useful meetings in the European arena which may bring them marginal advantages in world summit meetings too.

If the power of a national leader is measured, as Robert A. Dahl suggests in *Who Governs?*, by the capacity that such an individual has to influence events in the desired direction, then all national leaders are subject to seeing their power eroded as each nation becomes more dependent upon the joint product of the open international economy. This is as true of debtor nations such as the United States has become, as of nations with a positive trade balance. It is true of economies with a record of persisting growth, such as Germany, and of slow growth economies such as Great Britain.

A powerful national leader is very desirable only if one believes that the *Führerprinzip* is the most important principle in politics. The constitutions and politics of Western industrial nations reject this assumption. Each political system is full of constraints upon arbitrary rule, and sometimes of checks and balances that are obstacles to prompt, clear-cut decisions.

The balance between effective leadership and responsiveness varies among the United States, Great Britain, and France. A portion of that variation is organic, being prescribed in a national constitution. This is most evident in a comparison of the United States and Great Britain, but constitutions are variables, as the history of postwar France demonstrates. Many of the most important determinants of what a national leader does are a reflection of changing political circumstances, of trends and shock events, and of the aspirations and shortcomings of the individual in office.

# 31

# The New Institutionalism

*James C. March and Johan P. Olsen*

In most contemporary theories of politics, traditional political institutions, such as the

SOURCE: James C. March and Johan P. Olsen, "The New Institutionalism: Organizational Factors in Political Life," *American Political Science Review*, vol. 78, no. 3 (September 1984), pp. 734–749. Reprinted by permission of the American Political Science Association and the authors. Article and references abridged by the editors. The authors' extensive discussion of theoretical styles in contemporary political science has been omitted.

legislature, the legal system, and the state, as well as traditional economic institutions, such as the firm, have receded in importance from the position they held in the earlier theories of political scientists such as J. W. Burgess or W. W. Willoughby, economists such as Thorstein Veblen or John R. Commons, and sociologists such as Max Weber. From a behavioral point of view, formally organized social institutions have come to be portrayed simply as arenas within which political behavior, driven by more fundamental factors, occurs. From a normative point of view, ideas that embedded morality in institutions, such as law or bureaucracy, and that emphasized citizenship as a foundation for personal identity, have given way to ideas of moral individualism and an emphasis on conflicting interests.

In recent years, however, a new institutionalism has appeared in political science. It is far from coherent or consistent; it is not completely legitimate; but neither can it be entirely ignored. This resurgence of concern with institutions is a cumulative consequence of the modern transformation of social institutions and persistent commentary from observers of them. Social, political, and economic institutions have become larger, considerably more complex and resourceful, and *prima facie* more important to collective life. Most of the major actors in modern economic and political systems are formal organizations, and the institutions of law and bureaucracy occupy a dominant role in contemporary life....

## THEORETICAL RESEARCH AND POLITICAL INSTITUTIONS

Human actions, social contexts, and institutions work upon each other in complicated ways, and these complex, interactive processes of action and the formation of meaning are important to political life. Institutions seem to be neither neutral reflections of exogenous environmental forces nor neutral arenas for the performances of individuals driven by exogenous preferences and expectations. As a result, contemporary political theory is probably overly sanguine about the possibilities for a theory of politics that ignores political institutions.

For the most part, however, the relevant theoretical work remains to be done. It is interesting to suggest that political institutions and the society are interdependent, but that statement needs to find a richer theoretical expression. It is appropriate to observe that political institutions can be treated as actors in much the same way we treat individuals as actors, but we need more detailed demonstrations of the usefulness of doing so. There is good sense in noting that history is not necessarily efficient, but it would be of greater help if we were able to show the specific ways by which specific history-dependent processes lead to outcomes that are either non-unique or long delayed under some conditions. It is plausible to argue that politics is filled with behavior that is difficult to fit into a utilitarian model, but the plausibility would be augmented if we could describe an alternative model. And it is provocative to note the importance of symbols, ritual, ceremony, and myth in political life, but we cannot sustain the provocation without a clearer specification of how theories of politics are affected by such a vision.

Moving from the subtle judgments of empirical knowledge to an appropriate theoretical formulation is no easier in the analysis of politics than it is elsewhere. It requires not only further empirical studies but also theoretical research. By theoretical research we mean primarily the development of ideas, concepts, and models based on empirical observations and relevant to a behavioral understanding and prescriptive ordering of political life. The objective is not impossible. Thirty years ago, empirical students of organizations made two major criticisms of the existing theory of organizational decision making. The first criticism was that the theory made extraordinary time and information demands on organizations (March & Simon, 1958; Simon, 1957a, b). Information and time were treated as freely available resources. To ask that all consequences of all alternatives be known precisely seemed unreasonable in the face of empirical evidence that organizations considered only a small number of alternatives, examined only a small number of consequences related to only a subset of organizational goals, and made relatively imprecise estimates.

The second criticism was that the theory assumed that all participants in an organization shared the same goals, or if they did not, that conflict among them could be readily managed through the terms of some prior agreement (Cyert & March, 1963; March, 1962). In the case of a political organization, the agreement was a coalition contract, or constitution, by which all members of a coalition or polity agreed to be bound to the policies specified through bargaining or legislation. Thus, the familiar distinction between "politics" and "administration." In the case of an economic organization, the agreement was an employment contract by which employees, in return for the payment of wages, agreed to act as though they had the same goals as the owner or other legitimate policy maker. Empirical studies seemed to indicate that conflict was endemic in organizations and that it tended to be interminable rather than settled by prior agreements.

These criticisms began to have serious impact on formal theories of organized action when they were translated into useful theoretical statements through the development of information economics and theories of agency. Such theories consider information as a scarce resource subject to strategic action in a world populated by self-interested rational actors. Ideas drawn from organizational studies of bounded rationality and internal conflict permeate modern economic theory in the form of discussions of moral hazard, asymmetric information, agency, signalling, and optimal information strategies (Hirshleifer & Riley, 1979). Most students of organizations would argue that these theories are also incomplete, but it is clear that the earlier empirical criticisms have reformed theoretical thinking.

The new institutionalism would benefit from similar theoretical development if it could be accomplished. Like the early observations about bounded rationality and internal conflict, observations about the importance of institutions have generally taken the form of criticism of existing theoretical ideas rather than the delineation of an alternative set of precise theoretical concepts. Developing a comprehensive theoretical structure for institutional thinking is, of course, a prodigious and pretentious task, not one that will be undertaken here. We can, however, identify a few ideas associated with the new institutionalism that might warrant theoretical attention.

## INSTITUTIONAL CONCEPTIONS OF ORDER

Institutional thinking emphasizes the part played by institutional structures in imposing elements of order on a potentially inchoate world. Traditional political theory involved considerable attention to the order produced by political contracts and reflected in constitutions, laws, and other stable rules, or by a community of moral obligation, often inspired and buttressed by religious dogma (Berki, 1979; Waterstone, 1966). For the most part, modern political theory eschews such concerns and focuses on aggregation and historical efficiency superimposed on two other kinds of order: the order imposed by reason and the order imposed by competition and coercion. Reason is recognized in ideas of rationality and intentional action; it finds institutional expression in the hierarchical organization of means and ends (and thus in formally planned institutions). Competition and coercion are recognized in ideas of conflict of interest, power, bargaining, survival, and war; they find institutional expression in elections and policymaking. Theoretical research relevant to the new institutionalism would involve elaborating additional notions of political order. We believe it is possible to identify at least six such conceptions on which a modest amount of theoretical work might yield rewards.

## Historical Order

The concept of historical order implicit in contemporary theory emphasizes the efficiency of historical processes, the ways in which history moves quickly and inexorably to a unique outcome, normally in some sense an optimum. An institutional theory would specify how historical processes are affected by specific characteristics of political institutions, and it would provide greater theoretical understanding of the inefficiencies of history, i.e., historical processes that do not have equilibria, take extended periods of time, lead to non-unique but suboptimal outcomes. Theoretical attention to the inefficiencies of history involves a greater concern for the ways in which institutions learn from their experience (Etheredge, 1976) and the possibilities that learning will produce adjustments that are slower or faster than are appropriate or are misguided. It involves trying to specify the conditions under which they diverge. It involves characterizing the role of standard operating procedures, professions, and expertise in storing and recalling history.

## Temporal Order

In most theories of action, we assume things are ordered by their consequential connections. Means are linked to appropriate ends; causes are linked to effects they produce; consequences are linked to actions that lead to them and to preferences they affect; solutions are linked to problems they solve. Such concepts of order underlie theories of choice. Deviations from consequential order are viewed as interesting aberrations, disturbances, of a system otherwise held together by the way wanting something leads to doing something connected to the want, and doing something leads to consequences related to the intention. Temporal order provides an alternative in which linkages are less consequential than temporal. Things are connected by virtue of their simultaneous presence or arrival. In a culture with a strong sense of monthly or yearly cycles or of birth cohorts, we should not be overly surprised by temporal order. In many human situations the most easily identified property of objects or events is the time subscripts associated with them. Thus, students of time allocation in organizations have observed the ways in which attention to problems seems to be determined as much by the time of their arrival as by assessments of their importance. A classic form of temporal order is found in queuing theory, although most discussions of queuing are embedded in a consequential structure in which queues are either indistinguishable or distinguishable only by their processing times.

## Endogenous Order

Much of contemporary theory emphasizes the way order is imposed on political institutions by an external environment. From this perspective, for example, power within a political system is determined by possession of resources in the environment, interests are determined by position in the external world, and coherence within an institution is assured by the exigencies of existence. Thus, order is effectively exogenous to the institution and does not depend on properties of the institution or processes within it. Students of institutions have suggested a number of ways in which internal institutional processes affect things like the power distribution, the distribution of preferences, or the management of control. As a result, they invite theoretical development of models appropriate for understanding the ways in which interests and preferences develop within the context of institutional action, the ways reputations for power evolve as a result of the outcomes of politics, the ways in which the process of controlling purposive organizations produces unanticipated consequences, and the ways in which the course of decision making within political systems systematically, and endogenously, results in illusions of success and failure.

## Normative Order

It is a commonplace observation in empirical social science that behavior is constrained and dictated by cultural dicta and social norms. Although self-interest undoubtedly permeates politics, action is often based more on discovering the normatively appropriate behavior than on calculating the return expected from alternative choices. As a result, political behavior, like other behavior, can be described in terms of duties, obligations, roles, and rules. Such a description has not, however, been translated into any very compelling theoretical form. Some efforts have been made to rationalize normative rules, such as altruism (Kurz, 1978) and reciprocity (Axelrod, 1980), or to specify the conditions for their evolution (Axelrod & Hamilton, 1981; Trivers, 1971). From an institutionalist perspective, such efforts are exemplary, but they tend to limit attention to the comparative statics of individual norms. A broader theoretical examination of normative order would consider the relations among norms, the significance of ambiguity and inconsistency in norms, and the time path of the transformation of normative structures. A theoretical understanding of such conventional norms as those surrounding trust and legitimacy seems likely to be particularly germane to political analysis.

## Demographic Order

It is tempting for students of politics, as for students of other human endeavor, to find order defined in terms of the logic of their particular domain of interest. Thus, students of legislatures imagine that a legislature is best understood in terms of lawmaking, and students of courts imagine that a court is best understood in terms of adjudicating. Alternatively, a human institution can be studied and interpreted as the cross-section of the lives of the people involved. The idea that collective behavior can be understood as a mosaic of private lives links contemporary theoretical thought to similar ideas among qualitative students of human behavior and novelists (Krieger, 1983). A focus on institutional demography combines such a vision of organized life with attention to a property of individual lives that is itself a product of the institutional structure—the individual career (March & March, 1978; Pfeffer, 1981b). The theoretical requirements include useful concepts of the ways in which organizations adapt through turnover, institutions are driven by their cohort structures, and the pursuit of careers and professional standards dictates the flow of events.

## Symbolic Order

Students of formal organizations have called attention to the ordering force of symbols, rituals, ceremonies, stories, and drama in political life (March, 1981; March & Olsen, 1976, 1983; Meyer & Rowan, 1977; Pfeffer, 1981a; Pondy, 1978). Symbols permeate politics in a subtle and diffuse way, providing interpretive coherence to political life. Many of the activities and experiences of politics are defined by their relation to myths and symbols that antedate them and that are widely shared. At the same time, symbolic behavior is also a strategic element in political competition. Individuals and groups are frequently hypocritical, reciting sacred myths without believing them and while violating their implications. The traditional problem with such observations is not doubt about their veracity but about our ability to translate them into useful theoretical statements without excessive damage to their meaning. Theoretical development reflective of an institutional perspective would include an examination of the ways in which the tendencies toward consistency and inconsistency in beliefs affect the organization of political meaning, the ways in which "exemplary centers" (Geertz, 1980) create social order through ceremony, and the ways in which symbolic behavior transforms more instrumental behavior and is transformed by it. In particular, a serious theoretical understanding of myths, symbols, and rituals must include some attention to the dynamics of symbols, to the processes by which symbols shape the behavior not only of the innocent but of the society as a whole.

## EXAMPLES OF POSSIBLE THEORETICAL RESEARCH

Within these six conceptions of order, there are possibilities for theoretical research attentive to the insights of students of institutions. Such research is institutional in two respects: First, it is oriented to one or more of the institutionalist conceptions of order; second, it tries to illuminate how institutional and organizational factors affect political events. As examples, consider the following:

## Example 1: Policy Martingales

Many models of history recognize that specific historical events involve elements of chance. The unique historical happening may be a draw from some probability distribution of possible events. Even in cases where chance, strictly considered, is not viewed as vital, any specific event is seen as the consequence of a complicated interweaving of factors impossible to predict with precision in a single case. In the independent trial version of such models, any specific historical event is subject to various kinds of random fluctuations but, in the long run, unlikely events at a particular time are balanced by different unlikely events at a subsequent time. The specific realizations of the historical process that comprise the events of today are independent of the specific realizations that comprise the events of yesterday. Each specific event of an unfolding history is relatively difficult to predict, but prediction is not improved by knowledge of the history of past realizations of that process.

It is possible to see political policymaking as an independent trial process. Suppose we think of policy as the result of bargaining among political actors with prior preferences and resources, but subject to trial-by-trial variation attributable to specific, unpredictable and uncontrollable factors. Then understanding the short-run outcomes of a policy process would depend on considerable detail of the specific situation. A student of institutions might well observe that the details of the way attention is organized, how alternatives are presented, what information is available, which participants are free from other demands, how institutional memory is consulted, and a host of other factors would affect the specific political policy adopted at a specific time. At the same time, however, such factors are irrelevant (or redundant) to understanding the long-term mix of policies. Such an understanding is possible simply from a knowledge of the underlying political process and any systematic institutional biases.

Not all policymaking processes are independent trial processes. Many of them seem to be more in the nature of martingales (Feller, 1950). Like an independent trial process, a martingale process is subject to chance variation, but the variations accumulate. What distinguishes a martingale is the property that the *expected value* of the process at one time is equal to the *realization* of the process at the preceding time. This property makes the specific path of history important to understanding current historical events. In effect, the chance fluctuations of history change the baselines of the next step of the historical process. Common descriptions of incremental policy processes make them appear to be in the nature of martingales. The distribution of possible outcomes from a policy process is pictured as resulting from competition and bargaining over incremental adjustments in the current policy; the policy actually adopted is a draw from that distribution. This martingale property of policymaking is not independent of institutional factors. Indeed, it seems a prototypic institutional characteristic. Policies, once adopted, are embedded into institutions. They are associated with rules, expectations, and commitments. By affecting attention and aspirations, they affect the future search behavior of political participants.

Martingales diverge more rapidly than do independent trial processes; that is, for a given amount of chance variation in each time period, the variance across possible outcomes after some number of periods will be substantially greater in a martingale. As a result, the precision with which specific realizations of the process can be anticipated is considerably less. Thus, policy martingales are related to, but not identical to, various less precise ideas of forks in history, of critical events that made a difference. There is a sense in which the first step is more important than any subsequent one, but it is a limited sense. In a martingale process all events are forks; the policy paths of two political systems with identical underlying political conditions will be radically different simply because of the way in which (possibly small) perturbations shift the focus of political pressure.

## Example 2: Experiential Learning

It is a frequent observation of institutionalism that institutions accumulate historical experience through learning. The results and inferences of past experience are stored in standard operating procedures, professional rules, and the elementary rules of thumb of a practical person. These elements of historical knowledge have been portrayed both as forms of irrational retrogression and as carriers of wisdom, and it is not hard to specify environmental situations in which either characterization would be appropriate. What is less clear is whether we can model the processes of institutional learning. Although there have been some loose arguments that experiential learning will, in the long run, lead to the discovery and adoption of optimal strategies, little theoretical effort has been devoted to specifying precisely the conditions under which learning from experience leads to optimal behavior, or to relating those conditions to features of institutional structure or life.

Consider the following simple model of learning (Levinthal & March, 1982). A decision-making institution simultaneously learns along three dimensions. First it modifies its strategy; that is, it changes the likelihood of making one choice rather than another among the alternative activities available to it. Subjective success leads to increasing the chance of repeating a choice; subjective failure leads to decreasing the chance of repeating a choice (March & Olsen, 1976). Second, an institution modifies its competences; that is, it changes the skill it has at the various activities in which it might engage. Competence at an activity increases with experience at it; it decreases with time (Preston & Keachie, 1964). Third, an institution modifies its aspirations; that is, it changes its definition of subjective success. Aspirations move in the direction of past performance (Cyert & March, 1963). It is clear that institutional factors affect several of the key features of such learning. The learning rates associated with the three kinds of learning are partly a function of features of the institution. The degree of loose coupling in an organization affects the precision with which choices are made, outcomes observed, aspirations expressed, and competences realized. Thus, it can be expressed as various forms of noise in the process. Organizational slack affects the degree of centralization in the organization, and thus the linkage among subunits.

The three dimensions of learning obviously interact. For example, learning of aspirations affects the definition of subjective success, and thereby affects the learning of strategies. Learning of competences affects performance outcomes, and thereby affects the learning of both strategies and aspirations. Learning of strategies affects choices, and thereby affects the learning of competences. The model can be explored to discover the circumstances under which it reaches an equilibrium, and, among those the circumstances, those under which it reaches an optimum. It can also be combined into more complicated structures of learning where the choices of one institution affect the outcomes of another (e.g., competition and cooperation),

and where the learning institution is itself composed of learning subunits.

## Example 3: Garbage Cans

Garbage-can models of organizational choice have been suggested as a representation of a particular temporal order. In the form most commonly discussed in the literature, the garbage-can model assumes that problems, solutions, decision makers, and choice opportunities are independent, exogenous streams flowing through a system (Cohen, March, & Olsen, 1972). They come together in a manner determined by their arrival time. Thus, solutions are linked to problems primarily by their simultaneity, relatively few problems are solved, and choices are made for the most part either before any problems are connected to them (oversight), or after the problems have abandoned one choice to associate themselves with another (flight). This situation of extreme loose coupling, called an open structure in the original discussions of the garbage can, has attracted most of the attention in the literature, and empirical studies have revealed decision processes that appear to approximate such an open structure (March & Olsen, 1976).

Not all decision situations are quite so unstructured, however. We can characterize a choice situation in terms of two structures. The first is the access structure, a relation between problems (or solutions) and choice opportunities. The access structure may require, allow, or not allow a particular problem, if activated, to be attached to a particular choice. The second structure is the decision structure, a relation between decision makers and choice opportunities. This structure may require, allow, or not allow that a particular decision maker participate in the making of a particular choice. Access and decision structures can be imagined in any kind of arbitrary configuration, but two special forms have been considered formally. A specialized structure is one that is decomposed into substructures that are open. Thus, a specialized decision structure is one in which it is possible to divide choice opportunities and decision makers into subgroups and match the two sets of subgroups so that every decision maker in a particular subgroup of decision makers has access to every choice opportunity in the matched set of choice opportunities, but to no other. A hierarchical structure is one that expands access rights as a function of hierarchical rank. For example, in a hierarchical access structure, problems and choices are ordered, and each problem has access to choices of the same or lower rank. The differences made by these structures have been noted both formally (Cohen, March, & Olsen, 1972) and empirically (Egeberg, 1981; Olsen, 1983), but the empirical and theoretical examination of garbage-can processes within access and decision structures that are not completely open is barely begun.

## SUBTLE PHENOMENA AND SIMPLE THEORIES

These examples hardly exhaust the list. Empirical observations of reputations for power in politics suggest that such reputations depend heavily on the place of an individual in a political structure and on inferences about the relation between preferences and outcomes. Some simple models of the dynamic relations among reputations for power, institutional position, preferences, and social outcomes would provide a richer understanding of the ways in which power reputations affect politics. Empirical observations of post-decision surprises (i.e., deviations of realized outcomes from expected outcomes) suggest that there are systematic differences between the ways in which individuals experience the consequences of their actions and the ways in which institutions do. Some simple models of institutional expectations, choices, and post-decision assessments would clarify the occasions for expecting positive or negative surprises from deliberate action.

What characterizes all of the examples, as well as the others that might be added, is a relatively simple approach to institutional phenomena. The new institutionalism is often couched in terms of a contrast between the complexity of reality and the simplifications provided by existing theories, but theoretical research from an institutional perspective cannot involve the pursuit of enormous contextual detail. It is constrained by the capacity of human (and artificial) intelligence to cope with complexity, and although that capacity seems to expand with time, the rate of expansion continues to be modest relative to the demands of a fully contextual and institutional theory. From the point of view of theoretical research, consequently, the new institutionalism is probably better viewed as a search for alternative ideas that simplify the subtleties of empirical wisdom in a theoretically useful way.

## CONCLUSION

The institutionalism we have considered is neither a theory nor a coherent critique of one. It is simply an argument that the organization of political life makes a difference. Some of the things we have noted are fragments of ideas; others are somewhat more systematic in developing a theme or reporting a series of observations. They are held together by an awareness of a set of phenomena that are more easily observed than explicated. Insofar as the ideas are consistent, the consistency is sustained partly by ambiguity. Many of the core ideas seem plausible and have been durable, but plausible durability (as numerous students of the history of knowledge have observed) is neither necessary nor sufficient for good sense.

The new institutionalism is an empirically based prejudice, an assertion that what we observe in the world is inconsistent with the ways in which contemporary theories ask us to talk. Like other prejudices in knowledge, it may be wrong-headed or muddle-headed, but it may also be a useful continuation of that gentle confrontation between the wise and the smart that describes much of intellectual history. On the chance that it is the latter, which of course does not exclude the possibility that it is also the former, we have tried to draw some possible implications for theoretical research in political science. They are, at best, theoretical directions suggested by a sympathetic appreciation of a tradition of institutionalist thought. Such an effort is a little like trying to write a useful commentary on Heidegger in the form of a Shakespearean sonnet. If it has virtue, it is in attempting to encourage talking about a subtle body of thought in a way sufficiently naive to entice the technically proficient.

## Author's References

AXELROD, R. More effective choice in prisoners' dilemma. *Journal of Conflict Resolution*, 1980, *24*, 379–403.

AXELROD, R., & HAMILTON, W. D. The evolution of cooperation. *Science*, 1981, *211*, 1390–1396.

BERKI, R. N. State and society: an antithesis of modern political thought. In J. E. S. Hayward & R. N. Berki (Eds.), *State and society in contemporary Europe*. Oxford: Martin Robertson, 1979.

COHEN, M. D., MARCH, J. G., & OLSEN, J. P. A garbage can model of organizational choice. *Administrative Science Quarterly*, 1972, *17*, 1–25.

CYERT, R. M., & MARCH, J. G. *A behavioral theory of the firm*. Englewood Cliffs, N.J.: Prentice-Hall, Inc., 1963.

EGEBERG, M. *Stat og organisasjoner*. Bergen: Universitetsforlaget, 1981.

ETHEREDGE, L. S. *The case of the unreturned cafeteria trays*. Washington, D.C.: American Political Science Association, 1976.

FELLER, W. *An introduction to probability theory and its applications*, Vol. I. New York: Wiley, 1950.

GEERTZ, C. *Negara: the theater state in nineteenth-century Bali*. Princeton, N.J.: Princeton University Press, 1980.

HIRSCHLEIFER, J., & RILEY, J. G. The analytics of uncertainty and information—an expository survey. *Journal of Economic Literature*, 1979, *17*, 1375–1421.

KRIEGER, S. *Mirror dance*. Philadelphia: Temple University Press, 1983.

KURZ, M. Altruism as an outcome of social interaction. *American Economic Review*, 1978, *68*, 216–222.

LEVINTHAL, D., & MARCH, J. G. A model of adaptive organizational search. *Journal of Economic Behavior and Organization*, 1982, *2*, 307–333.

MARCH, J. C., & MARCH, J. G. Performance sampling in social matches. *Administrative Science Quarterly*, 1978, *23*, 434–453.

MARCH, J. G. The business firm as a political coalition. *Journal of Politics*, 1962, *24*, 662–678.

MARCH, J. G. Decisions in organizations and theories of choice. In A. H. van de Ven & W. F. Joyce (Eds.), *Perspectives on organizational design and behavior*. New York: Wiley, 1981.

MARCH, J. G., & OLSEN, J. P. *Ambiguity and choice in organizations*. Bergen: Universitetsforlaget, 1976.

MARCH, J. G., & OLSEN, J. P. Organizing political life: What administrative reorganization tells us about government. *American Political Science Review*, 1983, *77*, 281–296.

MARCH, J. G., & SIMON, H. A. *Organizations*. New York: Wiley, 1958.

MEYER, J. W., & ROWAN, B. Institutionalized organizations: formal structure as myth and ceremony. *American Journal of Sociology*, 1977, *83*, 340–363.

OLSEN, J. P. *Organized democracy*. Bergen: Universitetsforlaget, 1983.

PFEFFER, J. Management as symbolic action: The Creation and maintenance of organizational paradigms. In L. Cummings & B. M. Staw (Eds.), *Research in organizational behavior*. Vol. 3. Greenwich, Conn.: JAI Press, 1981(a).

PFEFFER, J. Some consequences of organizational demography: Potential impacts of an aging work force on formal organizations. In S. B. Kiesler, J. N. Morgan, & V. K. Oppenheimer (Eds.), *Aging: social change*. New York: Academic Press, 1981(b).

PONDY, L. R. Leadership as a language game. In M. W. McCall, Jr. & M. M. Lombardo (Eds.), *Leadership*. Durham, N.C.: Duke University Press, 1978.

PRESTON, L. D., & KEACHIE, E. C. Cost functions and progress functions: an integration. *American Economic Review*, 1964, *54*, 100–108.

SIMON, H. A. *Administrative behavior*. (2nd ed.) New York: Macmillan, 1957a.

SIMON, H. A. *Models of man*. New York: Wiley, 1957b.

TRIVERS, R. The evolution of reciprocal altruism. *Quarterly Review of Biology*, 1971, *46*, 35–57.

WATERSTONE, G. C. *Order and counterorder. Dualism in western culture*. New York: Philosophical Library, 1966.

# CHAPTER EIGHT

# Political Performance

## 32

## The Crisis of Embedded Liberalism

*Robert O. Keohane*

### INTRODUCTION

The political economies of modern Western European states do not exist in isolation, but within a context established by the international system. In pursuing policies designed to facilitate economic growth and social cohesion, governments react not just to the interests and power of domestic groups, but to constraints and incentives provided by the world political economy.

These international conditions affect each country differently: each economy occupies a particular location in the international division of labour, and changes in the environment (for example, increasing competitiveness of exports in a particular sector from newly industrializing countries) will affect each one in a distinctive way. This is most obvious with respect to oil: Britain and Norway, alone among Western European countries, are net exporters. In other sectors there are also differences in the sensitivity of different countries to external events:

SOURCE: Robert O. Keohane, "The World Political Economy and the Crisis of Embedded Liberalism, in *Order and Conflict in Contemporary Capitalism* John H. Goldthorpe, ed., (Oxford: Clarendon Press, 1984). © The Social Science Research Council (USA), 1984. Reprinted by permission of Oxford University Press. References abridged by the editors.

for instance, the effects of cheap Third World textile and clothing exports on a given European country will depend not only on the size of its textile and clothing industry, but also on whether it competes directly with such products or, as in the case of Switzerland, uses them as inputs in the production of high-quality final products.

Much of this volume seeks to explain the substantial differences among European countries in economic policy and performance during the 1970s. For this purpose it is important to understand their somewhat different locations in the world economy. This chapter, however, seeks to identify the international forces impinging on Western Europe as a whole, to establish a context for the comparison and evaluation of national policies. My argument is that these common forces are significant enough that they must be taken into account in any analysis of the European political economies, and the evolution of the welfare state, during the 1970s and 1980s.

Without an analysis of common patterns, comparative political-economic studies can be quite misleading. Analysts focusing on the domestic politics and economics of one or a few countries may ascribe patterns of behaviour and outcomes to distinctively national causes, without recognizing the degree to which common forces affecting a range of countries operate powerfully in each. Consider the example of inflation. One could have investigated inflation in the 1970s by considering it as a separate phenomenon in Britain, France, Germany, Holland, and Sweden, and by searching for its causes within each country. In each case, domestic forces could have been located that contributed to rapid increases in prices. But this would have missed a key point: that inflation was a worldwide phenomenon, which no country could singlehandedly resist. After understanding this, the analyst of domestic German policy would not seek to explain high rates of inflation simply on the basis of those policies, but would rather seek to solve the puzzle of why German inflation was so *low*, relative to the inflation rates of most other industrial countries.

An international-level analysis such as the one offered in this paper is therefore neither an alternative to studying domestic politics, nor a mere supplement to it—an afterthought in which "the international dimension" is introduced. On the contrary, it is a *precondition* for effective comparative analysis. Without a conception of the common external problems, pressures, and challenges facing European political economies in the 1970s and 1980s, we lack an analytical basis for identifying the role played by domestic interests and pressures in the various countries. Understanding the constraints imposed by the world political economy allows us to distinguish effects of common international forces from those of distinctive national ones.

My purpose in this paper is to locate the European economies in a changing world political economy, by analysing how changes in the world political economy during the last two decades have affected European societies and conditioned their policy reactions. I will emphasize constraints that the international political economy of modern capitalism places on domestic policy choices, and how these constraints may be changing.

My principal theme has to do with liberalism, or what I call, following John Ruggie, "embedded liberalism." I inquire about the preconditions for its emergence after the Second World War; the political biases that it may embody; and the sources of reactions against it that became apparent during the 1970s. My working assumption is that liberalism was acceptable in Europe for such an unprecedentedly long time largely because of the extended period of prosperity, associated with liberal policies, that lasted until the early 1970s. Conversely, in the absence of a strong ideological commitment to liberalism, economic adversity can be expected to lead to increased protectionism, as it did after the crises of 1873 and 1931. Thus my examination of the preconditions for, and reactions to, liberalism rests in part on an analysis of the international sources of economic growth. This involves a comparison between conditions in the 1950s and 1960s, which facilitated both liberalism and extensive systems of social welfare; and those of the 1970s, which sharpened conflicts between the maintenance of liberalism and the continued expansion of the welfare state.

I begin by indicating how conditions in the world political economy and American policy during the 1950s and early 1960s facilitated European economic growth and reduced the severity of dilemmas facing European governments seeking to combine capitalism, increased openness with respect to the world economy, and social welfare. Ironically, it was American hegemony that provided the basis for the development and expansion of the European welfare state.

The second section of the paper then considers the argument made by both Marxists and conservatives that international liberalism is biased in favour of conservative governments favouring capital, and against socialist or social-democratic regimes supported by labour. This claim has considerable force, although it suffers from failing to take into account different strategies that can be followed by social-democratic regimes, and different sets of institutions and policy networks that affect the feasibility of one strategy or another. Some of these strategies. . .have been much more effective than others. Thus the "bias against social democracy," allegedly inherent in international capitalism, can be reinterpreted as a bias against those forms of social democracy that do not sufficiently take account of the constraints of the market.

The third section of this paper directs our attention to some international forces that have helped to undermine liberalism (either through worsening the economic situation of Western Europe or otherwise) during the 1970s and early 1980s. I distinguish three sets of changes. First, features of the world economy that had been transmitting prosperity from one country to another began to transmit inflation and recession. The forces generating prosperity, inflation or recession can be regarded as in the first instance internal, endogenous to one society or another (although such developments in each country are surely influenced by observations of events elsewhere). Yet in an open world political economy their effects spread out beyond borders. Even if the international "transmission belts" did not change greatly, their impact was altered as they began to carry the virus of economic failure rather than the vaccine of success from one economy to another. The costs of interdependence became increasingly severe. A second change had more direct negative effects on the real incomes of Europeans: the terms of trade deteriorated after 1973, largely as a result of huge increases in oil prices. This negative shift in the terms of trade, compounded by indirect effects on aggregate demand, seems to have made liberalism more difficult to maintain, since it worsened the European economic situation. Finally, Europe was affected by the expansion of capitalism to the periphery, especially East Asia and Latin America, as reflected in the increases in exports of manufactured goods by less developed countries, especially the newly industrializing countries, to Europe over the last two decades. Although the direct economic effects of these exports may have been positive for Europe (as neo-classical economists claim), they seem to have provided a catalyst for intensified protectionism.

In the conclusion, I ask about the stability of a liberal world order. Liberalism can be regarded as a self-reinforcing system, in which declines in trade barriers both foster prosperity and weaken the inefficient sectors pressing for protection, thus creating political conditions for further liberalization. According to this perspective, disturbances and setbacks should be considered unpredictable "shocks," as the McCracken Report (OECD, 1977) suggested.[1] But liberalism can also be viewed as beset by contradictions, containing the seeds of its own destruction so that its very success undermines it. In so far as the latter is the case, the current problems of liberalism have their sources in the inherent dynamics of an open capitalist world political economy.

## EMBEDDED LIBERALISM AND AMERICAN HEGEMONY

Goldthorpe has suggested that an analysis of contemporary economic failure and social conflict in the advanced industrialized countries should begin with an understanding of the political bargains that provided a basis for the successful growth of their economies, and the expansion of their welfare states, during the 1950s and 1960s. Thus he writes (Memorandum to the Study Group):

> If the current problems of western capitalist economies are to be seen as grounded in institutional and other social changes [as opposed to the McCracken Report view emphasizing exogenous shocks], then it would appear only logical to see the success of these economies in the post-war years as being likewise grounded in some form of social order or "settlement": that is, one which could provide for conditions favourable to a higher level of economic performance than now prevails. Thus, the need is indicated to understand the nature of this post-war order, as it applied both internationally and—in differing versions—within western industrial societies, as a precondition for understanding the nature of its subsequent breakdown and, in turn, the possibilities for further collapse or for reconstruction or transcendence.[2]

In my view, this settlement is well characterized by Ruggie's felicitous phrase, "embedded liberalism."[3] To understand what this concept means, it is useful to think of the political-economic choices faced by governments as falling along two dimensions:

1. *The extensiveness of the welfare state:* that is, the extent to which the state reallocates resources to individuals, firms, and groups, as compared to the allocations that would be made by markets;
2. *The degree of liberalism or protectionism* in foreign trade and international monetary policy.

These two dimensions can provide the basis for a simple illustration, as shown in Table 1. In the top left of the diagram is found the classic *laissez-faire* state, characterized by market allocations and liberal foreign economic policies. This state neither reallocates income internally nor stands as a shield between world markets and the domestic economy. On the opposite end of the main diagonal is the ideal type of socialism, or closed welfare-state national capitalism, in which the state is both intimately involved in the domestic economy, and social welfare arrangements, and interposes itself between that economy and world markets.

The lower-left hand box of the diagram represents the location of a state pursuing *laissez-faire* policies at home but mercantilist ones abroad. I label this the "self-help" state. The most important example of this pattern is probably provided by the United States in the period between the Civil War and the Great Depression, culminating in the high Smoot-Hawley Tariff of 1930, enacted by a Congress and acquiesced in by an administration hostile to the development of an extensive welfare state at home. One still observes nostalgic tendencies in this direction on the part of some Americans, but the United States has not really fitted this category since the New Deal.

In combining liberalism in foreign economic relations and activist, welfare-oriented policies at home, European societies after the Second World War pursued policies that were diametrically opposed to the self-help model. These constitute what has previously been described as "embedded liberalism." Liberalism was "embedded" in the acceptance of an extensive role for the state, both in the steering of the

**TABLE 1** The two dimensions of embedded liberalism

| Policies Toward World Economy | Role of the State | |
|---|---|---|
| | Laissez-Faire | Interventionist |
| **Liberal** | classic liberalism | embedded liberalism |
| **Protectionist/ Mercantilist** | self-help | socialism or closed national capitalism |

economy and in assuring a decent life to citizens. Internationally, the form of liberalism agreed to after World War II had to be consistent with the welfare state rather than in conflict with it. Thus the constraints imposed on national economic policies by the classical gold standard were relaxed, and the pursuit of "free trade" replaced by the goal of non-discrimination. Furthermore, the goal of price stability was sacrificed, when this seemed necessary to maintain an open international economy.

Embedded liberalism did not develop automatically after World War II. And it certainly was not the product of purely domestic political bargains or settlements. On the contrary, the United States devoted a great deal of thought, and huge resources, to ensuring this outcome.

Part of the American effort was ideological. The United States propagated the view that the maintenance of capitalism and the welfare state could be rendered compatible by what Maier has called the "politics of productivity."[4] Cooperation among classes would ensure rising real wages and increasing opportunities, as well as extensive social welfare benefits, to the mass of the population. Liberalism, policies of macroeconomic management, and a limited form of welfare state would reinforce one another rather than be in conflict. Liberal trade would bring economic benefits through the international division of labour.

Yet the ideological appeal of the "politics of productivity" was not sufficient to persuade Europeans to support an open capitalist system based on non-discriminatory trade. Liberalism was not deeply rooted in continental Europe, and even Britain had turned in the 1930s to protectionism, in the form of the Ottawa System of Imperial Preference. The United States self-consciously set out to create a liberal system in Germany, and sought to promote the victory of pro-capitalist coalitions in Italy and France. Furthermore, it provided both positive and negative incentives for European countries to adopt liberal external policies and to renounce what Block has called "national capitalism."[5]

The groundwork for this American policy was laid during and after World War II, in successful U.S. attempts to gain political control over the two most crucial areas of the world economy: finance and energy. Before the Bretton Woods conference of 1944, the United States apparently sought to "fine-tune" British power, keeping Britain strong enough to be able to adopt liberal trade and payments policies after the war, but too weak to be in a position to renounce American credits and follow an independent economic strategy. At the conference itself, and later in negotiations on a loan to Britain, the United States pursued its interests as the only large creditor country in the world economy, and the chief international banking centre. At the same time, the United States sought to establish its control over Middle Eastern oil, whether through an agreement with Britain, which proved abortive or, successfully, through the rupture of the Red Line Agreement and the reinforcement of exclusive control over Saudi oil by American companies.

Finding its initial attempts quickly to construct a liberal world capitalist economy thwarted by the difficulties of reconstruction and the political influence of labour and the Left in Europe, the United States shifted its policies in 1947 without abandoning its basic objective: it provided massive financing through the Marshall Plan, and accepted trade and payments liberalization by stages rather than all at once. As Hirsch and Doyle comment, "such a policy was then possible because of the fundamental characteristic of the international political economy of the time: United States leadership on the basis of only qualified hegemony."[6] The United States was not strong enough to achieve its objectives exactly as it preferred; but it was sufficiently powerful to be able to find routes to achieve its goals, even if these were neither entirely direct, nor those originally preferred by the policy-makers themselves.

During the 1950s and 1960s the United States continued to pursue policies that reinforced embedded liberalism in Europe. It supported an international monetary regime of pegged exchange rates, in which it acted as the Nth country, keeping its currency tied to gold at a fixed price and allowing others to maintain exchange rates that enabled their exports to be competitive on world markets. In conjunction with the now-liberal European governments, the United States pressed for trade liberalization in a series of negotiations, culminating in the successful conclusion of the Kennedy Round, at least in so far as trade in manufactured goods was concerned, in 1967. American policy also sought, in the face of greater European reluctance, to secure most-favoured-nation treatment for Japan: between 1951 and the mid-1960s the United States pressed European governments first to admit Japan to the GATT, then to end discrimination against Japanese exports, which many of them had continued to maintain even after Japan became a Contracting Party of GATT in 1955. Yet even as it pressed for trade liberalization, the United States accepted the barriers erected by the Common Market, and its initial protests against the highly protective Common Agricultural Policy of the European Community—which itself had a major welfare component—were muted. American policy accepted the "embeddedness" of European liberalism in the welfare state.

By the mid-1960s it appeared that the prophets of productivity had been correct in their praise of liberalism. The development of a common market within Europe and the reduction, on the whole, of trade barriers between Europe and other industrialized areas of the world (particularly North America) had led to efficiencies resulting from economies of scale. Liberalization also increased competition within European economies, presumably resulting in positive dynamic effects. The combination of selective state interventionism and international openness seemed to have assured steady capitalist economic growth. Different countries could achieve this benign result by different combinations of demand management and export-led growth.

Europe also benefited from a peculiar sort of "invisible hand," in the form of improving terms of trade for Europe with other countries, particularly the raw materials-producing areas of the Third World. This was the counterpart to the worsening terms of trade faced by the Third World producers themselves. Such a trend was most striking in the case of oil. Prices of oil, which were around $3.00 a barrel shortly after the war, fell to $1.80 during the 1950s and remained quite stable in nominal terms until 1971. Since manufactured exports from the advanced indus-trialized countries were subject to inflation (albeit moderate compared to the 1970s) during this time, the real cost of oil fell between 1950 and 1971. Even after the rise in posted oil prices in 1971 from $1.80 to $3.00 per barrel, world prices of oil between 1963 and 1972 only rose at the same rate as for manufactures during that same period. The favorable trends in terms of trade that characterized the period between 1950 and 1971 provided resources that could be used by Western European governments both to enhance the benefits provided by the welfare state and to increase investment and growth. In effect, transfer payments from the primary-producing countries to the industrialized ones made it easier for the latter to satisfy the demands arising from groups within their societies.

Thus European economies in the 1950s and 1960s benefited both from liberalization of the world economy and from improving terms of trade, particularly with respect to oil. The pros-perity to which these trends contributed financed the expanding European welfare states that emerged during this period and that continued to grow during the 1970s. Yet neither liberalization on a world scale (as opposed to within the six-nation European Community) nor the improving terms of trade were principally the result of

European actions. On the contrary, both were highly dependent on the hegemonic leadership of the United States. American policy fostered liberal trade among the advanced industrialized countries: one could even say that the policies of the Truman administration were designed to "force Europe to be free." U.S. domination of the Middle East, and the willingness of the United States to use American oil reserves, in a crisis, to support Europe (as in 1956–57), kept oil prices low. The European welfare state was built on foundations provided by American hegemony.

## THE POLITICAL BIAS OF LIBERALISM

Both Marxist and neo-classical writers have recently contended that liberal capitalism exerts pressure against social-democratic solutions to economic problems in advanced industrialized countries. For the purposes of evaluating this argument, liberal capitalism can be defined as a world system embodying arrangements for the production and exchange of goods in which three conditions are met: (1) property rights to productive resources are vested principally in private individuals and corporations; (2) produc-tion for profit takes place predominantly with wage labour, to be sold on a market; and (3) pri-vately controlled capital and goods are able to move relatively freely across national boundaries. The hypothesis to be explored in this section is that liberal capitalism, thus defined, generates a systematic bias against social-democratic solu-tions to economic problems in advanced industrial countries. In so far as this hypothesis is correct, liberalism in Europe both constrained the Left from going as far as it would have liked to ensure welfare through public policy, and gave the Left (or at least its more radical elements) incentives to break out of the strait-jacket of liberalism, particularly when general economic conditions worsened.

The contention that international liberalism contains a bias against labour, and thus against social democracy and the extensive welfare state, has been employed by prominent Marxist writers. For instance, Hymer argued that openness in the world political economy favours capitalists *vis-à-vis* labour, since it leads capital to coalesce, but fragments labour.[7] Capitalists benefit politically from openness because capital is more mobile than labour and because they have superior access to information. In an open system, new investment can move abroad, and even established firms can relocate. Goods produced abroad can be exported back to home markets. Block, who also stresses the role of capital exports, argues that "the openness of an economy provides a means to combat the demands of the working class for higher wages and for economic and social reforms."[8]

Conservatives make a remarkably similar argument, albeit with different language and opposite normative implications. Thus the McCracken Report contends that the scope for social-democratic economic policies is limited by economic interdependence:

> Some governments may have underrated the consequence[s] of international interdependence and overrated their scope for independent action. With the improvement in international communications there are increasing signs of an international "demonstration effect" which, coupled with the greater mobility of skilled labour, may lead to a capital flight and a brain drain from countries pursuing equality strenuously with an inadequate growth rate, while in others failure to do enough about inequality creates political unrest.[9]

This argument develops, in different phrases, the essential Marxian claim that liberal capitalism benefits capital over labour and constrains governments from pursuing social-democratic policies much beyond the modal world level. In the first place, as explained further below, the transnationalization of financial flows, as capital movements become ever easier and cheaper, is likely to make it difficult for any country long to maintain a rate of profit significantly below the norm for the advanced countries, without suffering capital flight and loss of private investment. A sort of Gresham's Law may operate in

which policies that reinforce the position of capital drive out policies that reduce its dominance and distribute wealth more equally. Secondly, as capital becomes more mobile, labour in the industrialized countries comes more directly into competition with labour in the less developed countries, particularly the "newly industrializing countries." Immobile labour employed in manufacturing industry becomes particularly vulnerable to competition from much cheaper labour in places such as South Korea, Mexico, or Taiwan. Thus measures that increase the real wage of labour in the advanced industrialized countries, either through pay increases or increases in welfare payments borne in whole or part by employers, will increase the incentives for firms to relocate production abroad. In a liberal world economy, the price, in terms of employment, paid by labour in return for increasing its real wage, will tend to rise, as the mobility of capital, technology, and managerial expertise increases. This development corresponds, at the international level, to the development of economic dualism, in which migrant labour plays an important role, at the level of European (or American) society.

The conservative economists draw the conclusion from these international constraints not that international interdependence is harmful (which might imply that protectionist policies would be in order), but that national social welfare objectives should be trimmed. Acceptance of international liberalism reinforces the need for what I have elsewhere called the neo-orthodox conception of a "disciplinary state."[10]

Both Marxist and neo-classical political economists argue, implicitly or explicitly, that international openness improves the bargaining position of investors *vis-à-vis* governments and other groups in society. In a closed economy, governments interested in promoting private investment need only ensure that expected rates of profits from productive investment, discounted for risk, are higher than those to be gained from holding financial instruments or engaging in speculation, and higher than the rewards anticipated from consumption. For an open economy with capital mobility, however, investment at home must also bring profits higher than those anticipated from investment abroad. If the prospective marginal rate of profit at home falls below expected returns abroad, one can expect an investment outflow and a slowing down of economic activity at home, relative to activity abroad. As a result, the minimum ordinary rate of profit that the government must allow to be generated at home in order to avoid capital outflow and a lack of investment, will be determined not simply by convention, domestic interest rates, and the willingness of investors to defer consumption, but by the marginal world rate of profit. Thus the internationalization of capital flows—the ease with which financial capital can be transferred across national boundaries—makes it more difficult for any country to institute measures that change the distribution of income against capital and in favour of labour, if this implies a marginal rate of profit significantly below that for the world as a whole. Unless the government has the ability to withstand the short-term costs (as well as potential long-term efficiency costs) of closing off its economy from the world economy, it must keep profit rates from falling too far below the world standard. At the same time, the "exit" possibilities that capitalists have available are likely to increase the efficacy of their attempts at "voice"—their ability to influence policy through the political process at home.[11]

Once an open capitalist world system has been established, it may create a bias in favour of pro-capitalist, and against socialist-leaning, governments. When Thatcher or Reagan induces a recession through tight monetary policies, as part of a strategy to control inflation through reducing the rate of wage increases, the pound or dollar appreciates and funds flow into the country. This may be inconvenient for a country seeking to control its money supply or expand exports; but it does not lead to a loss of confidence in the government, and expands rather than contracts the resources at its disposal. No help needs to be sought from other governments as a result. When Mitterrand tries to stimulate demand and to nationalize selected industries,

by contrast, the franc declines, France's foreign reserves are jeopardized, and assistance may be needed from the IMF or selected governments of wealthy countries. Socialist and social-democratic governments are thus induced to maintain openness. The experience of Britain's Labour party during the 1960s and 1970s illustrates the dilemma. In the face of international economic problems, reflected in payments deficits, Labour sought to resolve the contradictions it faced by abandoning socialism, and even some elements of its plans for social democracy, in the interests of maintaining business confidence. This process culminated in the decision of James Callaghan's Labour Government, in 1976, to sign a Letter of Intent to secure an IMF loan.

This argument implies that an open capitalist world financial system tends to reinforce itself. When pro-capitalist governments are in power, they have strong incentives to promote openness, not only for the sake of efficiency and gains from trade, but to reinforce the power of capital *vis-à-vis* labour. They also find that reinforcing economic openness helps their own political fortunes, since the web of interdependence thus created makes it more difficult for subsequent left-wing governments to achieve their purposes. When socialist and social-democratic governments come into power, they soon find that to avoid runs on their currencies, and financial crises, they need to gain the confidence of the business "community," and that this may require that they abandon some of their more socialist objectives.

This argument is oversimplified and potentially misleading because it ignores variations in strategies followed by social-democratic governments, and in the policy institutions and networks that those governments can use. Indeed, the contrast between the substantial success of social democracy in both Scandinavia and Austria, on the one hand, and the difficulties encountered by attempts to move to the Left in Britain and France, on the other, suggests that variations in national strategies are important determinants of success or failure. From the standpoint of the Marxist/neo-classical argument about the bias of liberal capitalism, these variations are puzzling.

The answer to this conundrum may lie in the institutions of trans-sectoral concertation involving both labour and business, that some European countries have developed: that is, in "corporatism."[12] Indeed, it may be helpful to think of the problem in terms of two ideal-typical forms of social democracy. Type A is typical of large countries such as Britain and France. It is characterized by only sporadic control of government by socialist parties; by policies of socialist governments that seek rapidly to shift the distribution of rewards from private capital to labour; and by a lack of domestic corporatist institutions permitting trans-sectoral concertation. Type B, by contrast, which is most closely exemplified by Austria and Sweden, is typical of small, open economies that need to export to survive: it is characterized by continuous left-wing rule over a long period of time, on the basis of strong union movements; by policies designed to maintain employment and improve equity in ways consistent with market incentives; and by corporatist institutions linking the state with leaders of both business and labour.

This distinction could help us to reformulate the Marxist/neo-classical argument. International capitalism does seem to exert a bias against Type A social democracy. Capital flight, or the threat thereof typically leads to pressures on social-democratic governments in these countries to move toward the Right. That is, international capitalism *reinforces* the pressures exerted by the market against anti-capitalist policies in open, non-corporatist economies. Yet no such bias seems to exist against Type B social democracy. Capital flight does not seem to have been a serious problem for these countries during the 1970s; Sweden, for example, has maintained capital controls. Indeed, international capital markets *financed* Austrian and Swedish balance of payments deficits, permitting either an investment-led boom, as in Austria, or extensive job-training programmes, as in Sweden.

The McCracken Report suggested the existence of a "narrow path to growth" for the advanced industrialized countries after the first oil shock. This analysis by contrast, indicates that there may be a "narrow path to social democracy." Strategies for social democracy that exploit the market are more effective than those based on the assumption that market pressures can be ignored or over-ridden by the exercise of state power.

It is not clear whether small countries have an inherent advantage in designing appropriate strategies that reconcile social democracy with world capitalism. The Marxist/neo-classical argument seems to imply that small states should have more difficulty in coping with the pressures of world capitalism than large ones, because they are more open and because they have less power over the "rules of the game"— the international arrangements, such as those agreed to at Bretton Woods, that define the terms under which a given country can link itself to the world political economy. Furthermore, in bilateral relationships where both sides are involved with equal intensity, small states might be expected to be more constrained by the policies of larger ones than vice versa. Yet Cameron has shown that it is precisely the small European countries that have the largest state budgets, in proportion to their size: far from simply succumbing to the pressures of the world political economy, they seem to try, actively, to provide a buffer between the world political economy and their citizens.[13] Perhaps this is a result of the fact that as citizens of small countries their social democrats were acutely aware of the need to make social democracy consistent with export competitiveness. They therefore were willing to design domestic institutions and policy networks that facilitated mutual adjustment between labour and management.

In so far as a bias exists against Type A social democracy, socialist movements in such countries will have incentives to consider radical moves toward state intervention to sever key links with the world economy. Cutting oneself off from world capitalism may seem to be the only effective way of regaining autonomy, even if the economic costs are recognized as being enormous. As the international conditions fostering prosperity were undermined during the 1970s, such arguments regained some of their appeal. It is not surprising that the sympathy for measures such as these was greater on the British and French Left—especially in certain elements of the British Labour party and the French Socialists—than on the Right, or in countries which had developed effective strategies of social-democratic corporatism.

# INTERNATIONAL FORCES UNDERMINING EMBEDDED LIBERALISM

Embedded liberalism is now under pressure in Europe. Protectionism and state interventionism in the economy have increased in the last decade, and tendencies toward socialism, or national capitalism, are more evident than they have been since the 1940s. The question is not whether there is a "new protectionism," but what it represents, and why the previous trend toward increasing liberalism has been reversed. From the neo-classical liberal standpoint protectionism is an atavistic reaction by groups that refuse to adjust to the efficiency-creating pressures of competition. For instance, Olson regards protectionism as the result of the political influence of narrowly-based, self-serving "distributional coalitions," and Baldwin, and in more extreme form Brock and Magee, following the same long line of analysis, see it as an economically perverse outcome of the competition of groups in the political market-place. Conversely, from the standpoint of Polanyi and his followers, protectionism could be regarded as an effort at self-defence by "society," against the rampages of the market-place.[14]

Polanyi's notion of action by "society" is vague and could be regarded as a mystification of more concrete political processes. The neo-classical analysis of the political economy of protectionism, on the other hand, naively incorporates the political theory of pluralism: policy outcomes are simply the result of group and sectoral pressures; the state is a virtual cipher without a political stance or ideology of its own. As a basis for description and partial explanation, pluralism is a useful notion, but it begs issues of the role and structure of the state, the sources of group interests, and the role of ideology. In this section of the present paper, I will not consider the potential sources of protectionism within European societies but rather focus on features of the *international* political economy that seem to have had negative effects on the ability of these societies to attain economic growth and to manage social conflicts. These characteristics of the world system may have intensified pressures throughout Europe for protectionism. As indicated in the introduction, I will consider three forces: (1) the transmission of prosperity, inflation and recession; (2) the deterioration of the terms of trade; and (3) the expansion of capitalism to the periphery.

## From Transmission of Prosperity to Transmission of Stagflation

The construction of an increasingly open world economy in the 1950s and 1960s meant that economic growth in one country contributed to growth elsewhere. Demand for imports in prosperous economies created demand for exports in others, increasing incomes and the demand for imports in the latter. Until the late 1960s, this beneficent pattern of exchange took place in a world economy with pegged exchange rates and great confidence in the dollar as the key currency, yet with persistent United States payments deficits that helped to maintain world liquidity. America was the chief supporter of an international financial regime that facilitated non-inflationary economic growth.

In the 1970s, international transmission mechanisms had less benign effects. From 1966 onward the United States pursued an inflationary fiscal policy associated with the war in Vietnam, and in 1971 the United States ceased to support pegged exchange rates and formally cut the linkage between the dollar and gold. The international monetary system, which continued to be highly integrated despite the changes it went through during the next few years, then carried inflation from country to country. This occurred, although by different means and perhaps to a lesser extent, under flexible as well as fixed exchange rates. Particularly during the period of greatest uncertainty about the exchange rate regime, between August 1971 and March 1973, national monetary policies in the major OECD countries were highly inflationary, perhaps partly as a result of the absence of incentives from the international regime to follow more stringent policies.

In the 1970s the rules governing both exchange rates and oil prices were much less clear, and less constraining of national policy, than they had been during the Bretton Woods era. The changes in oil prices reflected a decline in American and European control over the terms of exchange; in money, they reflected an attempt by the United States to free itself from the burdens of the Bretton Woods regime. In both cases, the result was that the structure of authority became more decentralized. Neither a well-defined set of rules, nor a hegemonic power (in conjunction with its large corporations and its allies) determined outcomes.

From this decentralized authority structure emerged a pattern of relations that is similar to what Hirschman has described in another context as a "political tug-of-war."[15] In such a situation, organizations or groups can determine the prices for their own products (that is, they have market power), but there is no central authority capable of establishing a consistent set of non-inflationary prices for all goods. Each group would prefer stable prices if it could also be assured of its desired share of the social product; but since it cannot accomplish this on its own, it demands more, in nominal terms, in the hope of gaining, or at least not losing, in real terms. In this model, inflation is explained "in terms of social conflict between groups each aspiring to a greater share of the social product," and by the absence of an effective government that can authoritatively allocate shares of that social product.

Such an inflationary tug-of-war seems to have taken place between the major oil-importing countries and OPEC in the years immediately

following the major price increases of 1973–74. The *nominal* price of oil had an effective floor under it, since OPEC feared the consequences of initiating a downward spiral. But the *real* price of oil could be reduced either by increases in the prices of goods sold to OPEC countries, or by declines in the value of the dollar, either of which could be facilitated by inflation in the United States. This does not mean that the United States deliberately fostered inflation to reduce the real price of oil, but it does suggest that concern about oil prices and terms of trade reduced the incentives to deal decisively with inflation. To some extent, inflation was a face-saving device by which the demands of producers for high prices could be reconciled with the desire of consumers for lower prices.

Inflationary American macroeconomic policies in 1977–78 meant that European countries paid lower prices for imported oil, since the price of oil was denominated in depreciating dollars. Yet American policy also transmitted less welcome effects to Europe. Having been unsuccessful at persuading Germany and Japan to reflate more rapidly in early 1977, the United States sought to put pressure on them by letting the dollar depreciate, therefore making German and Japanese exports less competitive against those of the United States. This led eventually to an agreement at the Bonn summit, in July 1978, by which Germany and Japan were to stimulate their economies in return for phased decontrol of U.S. oil prices and a tightening of American monetary policy. Unfortunately for these governments, the Bonn summit did not lead to a resumption of the virtuous circle of non-inflationary growth: in the fall of 1978, the dollar came under severe pressure, requiring extensive exchange market intervention, and in early 1979 the effects of the Iranian Revolution began to lead to a new escalation of oil prices.

Since the tightening of American monetary policy that took place in the fall of 1979, and particularly since the Reagan administration took office, another vicious circle of international transmission has contributed to the difficulties faced by European governments. High American interest rates have led European governments and central banks to increase their interest rates, for fear of foreign exchange crises resulting from capital flight. The consequence, of course, is that American monetarism has been imitated even by governments that do not sympathize either with its economic logic or its political biases. This is not to say, of course, that these governments had no choices: they could have sought to reflate their economies regardless of American policy. But then they would have encountered difficulties similar to those experienced by the socialist government in France since 1981: foreign exchange crises and losses of reserves, as capital fled the country for areas where real rates of return (nominal interest rates adjusted for inflation and expectations of exchange rate movements) were higher. Faced with such dilemmas, governments that are unable to sustain strategies to counteract, or even take advantage of, international constraints are under severe pressure to return to orthodoxy.

Viewed politically, the point is that the pressures transmitted by the international monetary system are not merely the results of impersonal market forces but reflect the policies of political coalitions in major countries, particularly the United States. When these policies shift, the effects are transmitted quickly throughout the system.

Thus international transmission of economic forces has had a different impact since 1971 from that of the two previous decades. Often the shift to flexible exchange rates is cited as a major source of these changes, although flexible rates are really more symptoms of disorder than cause. If national fiscal and monetary policies diverge sharply in a highly interdependent world economy but politically fragmented world system, fixed exchange rates will be impossible to sustain for long. In some respects, flexible rates may enable governments to control the effects of international disturbances more effectively—for instance, a low-inflation country can counteract the effects of inflation emanating from other countries by letting its own currency appreciate. Nevertheless, even if flexible rates are unavoidable, and have certain advantages, they

do complicate the task of economic management by introducing another unpredictable variable into the managers' calculations.

The key issue, in my view, is not so much how economic effects are transmitted internationally, but what is being transmitted. Is it helpful or harmful to the recipient? The 1950s and early 1960s seem to have been characterized largely by "virtuous circles," in which non-inflationary growth in one area reinforced non-inflationary growth in another. In the last decade and a half, transmission has been characterized by "vicious circles," in which inflation and recession, perhaps generated originally within one society as a result of a combination of economic and political forces partly endogenous to it, are carried to others. International interdependence remains, but its consequences for social conflict and economic management are different.

## The Deterioration of the Terms of Trade

All significant changes in the world economy have uneven effects on various countries, groups, or sectors. Furthermore, those countries, groups and sectors adversely affected by changes have differential abilities to force the costs of adjustment to change on to others. Power is, by one measure, the ability not to have to adjust to change.

Governments, of course, have to allocate the costs of adjustment among their citizens, and in particular, between capital and labour. If they are powerful in the world system, this internal adjustment may be facilitated by their ability to force foreigners to bear some of those costs. Conversely, if they are weak (or become weaker from a formerly strong situation), their internal adjustments may be rendered more difficult by adverse shifts imposed on them by others.

During the 1950s, the industrialized countries, including Europe, benefitted substantially from improving terms of trade between manufactured goods, which they exported, and primary products, of which they were net importers: these terms of trade improved by about 25 percent (from the standpoint of exporters of manufactured goods) between 1950 and 1963.[16] During the next decade (1963-72), these terms of trade were essentially stable, continuing to improve slightly in favour of manufactures: the industrialized countries' terms of trade improved by about 3 percent. Between 1973 and 1982, however, the terms of trade for these countries worsened by about 20 percent. This dramatic shift, caused largely by the huge oil price increases of that period, reflected the inability of the industrialized countries to force the costs of adjustment to higher oil prices entirely on to others: indeed, during that decade, taken as a whole, the terms of trade of the non-oil developing countries were almost stable, deteriorating only after 1977, while the terms of trade of the oil producers improved sharply.[17]

Since the deterioration in the terms of trade was essentially a result of the huge oil price rises in 1973-74 and 1979-80, we need to look somewhat more closely at the effects of those price increases on the economies of the industrialized countries. The first set of price rises led to an increased import bill for the OECD countries of $65 billion, equivalent to about 1.5 percent of their collective GNP. The second price spiral led to increased import costs of about $150 billion, equivalent to about 2 percent of OECD GNP. In addition to these terms of trade effects, the oil shocks reduced aggregate demand. In 1980 the OECD countries lost about 3 percent of GNP as a result of the oil price increases of the previous year; in 1981 the loss was about 4 percent.[18]

Oil price increases therefore both made the industrialized countries poorer and directly reduced their levels of economic activity. But the price rises also, of course, had an inflationary effect in the short run. In an effort to counter inflation, governments contracted their monetary and fiscal policies. This led to a further reduction in real income in these societies, which was particularly pronounced after the second oil shock. The consequent reduction in GNP was about one-fourth of 1 percent in 1980 and almost 2 percent in 1981. Thus the combined loss of output from the second oil shock amounted to about 5 percent of Gross Domestic Product

(GDP) in 1980 and nearly 8 percent in 1981 for a two-year total of over $1 trillion.[19]

The immediate effects on worker-consumers in the OECD countries were cushioned by the fact that the distribution of income in 1974-75 shifted quite sharply from capital to labour, and from investment to consumption, throughout the area. Labour's share of total domestic factor income rose between 1970-73 and 1974-77 from about 69 percent to about 72 percent in Germany, from 64 to almost 70 percent in France, and from 76 to 80 percent in the United Kingdom. This had temporarily positive effects on consumption but very negative effects on private investment, with serious consequences for subsequent unemployment. After the second oil shock, in contrast, changes in labour's share of income, and in the balance between consumption and investment, were much less marked.[20] Although European societies responded to the first oil shock by trying to cushion their citizens against it, they were not able to repeat this performance. The reaction to the second oil shock, especially in Britain and the United States (in the latter, even before Reagan took office), was to follow tight monetary policies in an attempt to force the costs of adjustment on to the present population, rather than to impose it, through inflation and low investment, on the future. As we have seen, this policy was transmitted, through international markets, to other countries, even where their governments had different preferences or different theories about how the world looked.

The crucial point about this is a familiar one. Governments have to allocate costs among their people, between classes and sectors. Much of political analysis is about how this is done: "who gets what, when, how?" in Lasswell's phrase. But domestic allocations depend on the allocations resulting from political struggle at the international level. Weak countries have to bear the burdens of adjustment to change: they cannot impose them on others. Unless they are being subsidized by rich allies or politically naïve bankers, their governments must allocate costly adjustments among their people—inevitably leading to discontent—or else let them be inflicted through the market (for instance, in the form of inflation). Between the 1960s and the 1980s the willingness of the United States to maintain a stable international monetary system declined. Furthermore, its ability, in conjunction with selected European governments and major oil firms, to control petroleum prices virtually disappeared. As a result, the dependence of European governments on other countries increased. The higher petroleum prices that accompanied this loss of control reduced the ability of Europeans as well as people in other oil-importing areas to purchase manufactured goods: real incomes had to fall. The corollary of this process, thrusting adjustment costs on to Europe, was that domestic allocational dilemmas were sharpened, and the task of social conflict management made more difficult.

## The Rise of Exports from Less Developed Countries

During the last two decades, less developed countries (LDCs), and in particular the eight principal newly industrializing countries (NICs) of Asia and Latin America (Hong Kong, Singapore, South Korea, and Taiwan—the "gang of four"— in East Asia, India in South Asia, Argentina, Brazil, and Mexico in Latin America) have experienced rates of economic growth much above those in Europe and North America. This growth has been led by exports. Manufactured exports from LDCs rose annually by 16.2 percent between 1960 and 1976, a rate higher than the rate of export growth for industrialized countries (14.1 percent) or for all trade commodities (13.7 percent). The pace of LDC expansion was, at least at first, not seriously retarded by the oil crisis: largely as a result of the rapid growth of NIC exports, imports to both the EEC and the United States from non-OPEC developing countries increased threefold between 1973 and 1978. Although LDC exports accounted for less than 10 percent of the world market for manufactured goods in 1976, in sectors such as clothing and footwear they had increased by that time to over 30 percent of the market; and in the more technologically advanced sector of electrical machinery they increased from less than 1 percent in 1963 to 12 percent in 1977. This relative growth continued even in the recession: in 1981–82, the volume of industrial country exports remained roughly constant, but the exports of non-oil LDCs rose by about 7 percent; and preliminary figures for 1983 indicated that LDC exports continued to do relatively better than those of the industrial countries.[21]

Questions about the implications of this export growth for employment in the advanced industrialized countries have been raised with increasing urgency in recent years. Hager, for instance, has claimed that "the supply of industrial labour of the Third World will approach, for practical purposes, the infinite," and that "there is no natural equilibrium solution possible even in theory."[22] Yet OECD economists and others point out that exports from the advanced industrialized countries to the non-oil developing countries have increased almost as fast as imports in percentage terms; since exports to the LDCs of manufactured goods exceeded imports by almost a three to one ratio in 1973, the result was that the positive trade balance of the advanced countries with the LDCs, in manufactured goods, increased from $25 billion in 1973 to almost $70 billion in 1979.

These changes suggest that rapid adjustment to change has been taking place in the world trade system since 1973. Branson has documented this for the United States; whether similar patterns characterize Western European adaptation is not yet clear. Between 1973 and 1978 the United States trade surpluses in capital goods, chemicals, and agricultural products almost doubled, to approximately $26 billion, $7 billion, and $13 billion, respectively. During the same period of time, its trade deficits in consumer goods and automotive products also doubled, to about $18 billion in the former category and $10 billion in the latter. Branson infers that this reflects clear patterns of comparative advantage.[23]

The dominant view among economists is that this pattern of adjustment is good for the advanced industrialized countries as well as for the newly industrializing countries: both parties benefit, in Ricardian fashion, from trade and the associated investment. The conclusion of one analyst reflects the dominant neo-classical wisdom: "there seems little doubt that it is to the advantage of developed countries to absorb more LDC exports and to adjust their economies accordingly."[24] Thus the increasing economic interdependence between advanced countries and the newly industrializing countries is seen as a triumph of liberalism, only somewhat tarnished by economically irrational, politically inspired protectionism.

Yet if adjustment is a reality, so is protectionism. This has been evident both in the United States and Western Europe, but Europe has shown stronger tendencies to act in a protectionist manner, and considerably greater willingness to deviate from the rhetoric of liberal trade. In textiles, the EEC has taken the lead in tightening up the provisions of the Multi-Fiber Agreement, and in steel and shipbuilding it has also intervened to protect old industries. Individual European countries have gone further, particularly in areas such as automobiles and consumer electronics. The major target of European ire was Japan, but as Turner points out, "some of the NICs began to be sucked into such trade disputes."[25]

European resistance to Japanese and LDC imports is taking place at levels of import penetration below those already attained by these exporters in the U.S. market. Less than 16 percent of EEC imports (excluding intra-EEC trade) were accounted for in 1978 by the LDCs, while the corresponding figure for the United States was almost 22 percent. Even as a percentage of GDP, American imports from the LDCs were almost a third higher than Europe's. Perhaps partly as a consequence, the rate of growth of LDC imports into the EEC between 1973 and 1978 was lower than into the U.S. market.

It is not surprising that resistance to imports should increase during times of economic stress.

Workers facing unemployment are strongly motivated to use political action to preserve their jobs. If firms "satisfice," seeking to maintain customary levels of profits, many of them will redouble their lobbying efforts in a downturn as actual profits and earnings fall below these thresholds. Even if firms and workers act as maximizers, they may intensify their efforts to secure protection during depressions. In such a period, their gains are less likely to be competed away by new entrants, since rates of return even after protection may still be too low to justify new investment within the area enclosed by the trade barriers.

Imports into advanced countries from less industrialized ones can also be expected to stir up more opposition than imports from other advanced economies. Both tentative theoretical models and experience suggest that liberalization of trade is most likely where neither country has a strong comparative advantage in the industry and the products of different firms within the industry are highly differentiated, since under these conditions firms in *both* countries can benefit from liberalization. Where advantages are all on one side, however, one finds what Bhagwati calls the "growing dominance of external products" scenario, leading to protectionist demands both from entrepreneurs (especially if cheap migrant labour is not available) and from labour.[26] In so far as protectionism results from political pressures by affected groups, therefore, one can expect it to be particularly intense against imports from LDCs, especially the well-organized NICs, with their tendency to focus suddenly on one sector or another for massive import penetration.

The findings of the literature on the political economy of protectionism are ironic, if not paradoxical. Since Europe and the United States benefit economically from LDC exports, one might expect the changing international division of labour to reinforce embedded liberalism. However, the conjunction of surplus capacity and unemployment (the results overwhelmingly of other factors) with rapid increases in NIC exports makes the NICs obvious scapegoats for advocates of protection. Wages in the NICs are low, and many of these countries have highly repressive governments; so the charge of "unfairness" is easier to make than it is with respect to the Japanese.

Thus the significance of the newly industrializing countries for European liberalism may be more indirect than direct. The NICs serve as catalysts for action to scuttle non-discriminatory patterns of trade. Mercantilists can play down the importance of exports by the advanced countries to the NICs, arguing that these will only temporarily increase in response to gains by the less developed, lower-cost trading partners. Hager, for instance, characterizes Europe as "a high cost area with decentralized real-capital formation, and hence intrinsically on the defensive. Under free trade conditions, any of the low-cost producers can decide to produce anything for the European market, constrained only by other outside competitors."[27] He thus conjures up the extraordinary spectacle of the NICs having comparative advantages over Europe in *everything.*

From the protectionist standpoint, the existence of the welfare state makes international liberalism even more intolerable. Hager comments as follows:

> With unemployment approaching 10 percent, the full-employment-of-factors assumption of free trade welfare economics looks threadbare. The welfare state adds a twist to the classical story by insisting that the idled factor labour be paid nearly in full, as if it were still producing. The cheap shirt is thus paid for several times: once at the counter, then again in unemployment benefits for the idled workers. Secondary losses involve input industries (although in the short term their exports rise): machinery, fibres, chemicals for dyeing and finishing products.[28]

Western Europe seems more likely than the United States to follow protectionist policies during this decade. Ideological beliefs in liberalism are weaker in Europe than across the Atlantic, European industry is less dynamic technologically, and governments have more instruments available for intervention in the economy. "Industrial policy" is therefore more attractive to many European governments, especially that of France, than it is to the United States. As Woolcock notes "there are no specific trade-related adjustment policies in Western Europe. With extensive structural-policy instruments of both a selective and a non-selective nature, there is little need to introduce new policy instruments."[29]

Protectionism coupled with industrial policy is not inevitable. European protectionism would conflict with the fact that the huge debts of many less developed countries can only be serviced if those countries can continue to increase their exports. For this reason, as well as its own political-security concerns with countries such as Mexico, South Korea, and Taiwan, the United States is likely to resist pressures for extensive protection. Since not all European governments are as enthusiastic about industrial policy as the French, pressures against protectionism are likely to be strong.

Neo-classical economists have long held that a well-functioning liberal world economy provides opportunities for the poor and weak. Despite the denial of this argument by dependency theorists, the developments of the last decade in the world political economy strongly support it. The rise of the NICs was itself a consequence of liberalism. Yet the result is not the further increase in economic openness envisioned by liberals: on the contrary, the suddenness of the process, characteristic of capitalist uneven development, forces adjustment costs on to groups that are weak economically but relatively strong politically. Polanyi's metaphor captures the effects, if not the nature of the process: "society protects itself" against the ravages of the market. Or, to use the phrases of the literature on the political economy of protectionism, groups threatened by change lobby for protection in order to create rents for themselves. The policy connotations are different but the results are the same: unless its effects are cushioned by deliberate policy, the success of liberalism, even embedded liberalism, tends to destroy the conditions for its existence.

Even within the parameters of liberal assumptions about the best long-run path of the political economy, therefore, proponents of adjustment assistance, subsidies, and other forms of support for threatened industries and workers can make a strong case. Their argument is strengthened if these measures appear, in the medium to long run, to facilitate adjustment and maintain the conditions for liberalism. From this perspective, a reduction in the rate of increase in economic interdependence could be seen as a precondition for avoiding the demise of embedded liberalism in Western Europe.

## CONCLUSIONS

Behind the variety of international forces impinging on Europe from the world political economy, two closely related patterns of change seem to be crucial: the rise and erosion of American hegemony and the expansion of capitalism on a world scale. As we have seen, American dominance, and the willingness of the United States to use its resources to build a liberal international political economy, were crucial elements in the post-war triumph of embedded liberalism in Europe. Conversely, the adverse shifts in terms of trade and the transmission of economic distress that characterized the 1970s were aggravated, if not caused, by a decline in the ability and willingness of the United States to manage the world economy for its own benefit and that of its allies. Even when it would have been possible for the United States to continue managing the world political economy, to do so in a way that benefited Europe would have required more costly adjustments by the United States than it cared to make.

As American authority over the world capitalist system was eroding in the 1970s, the system itself continued to expand. The earlier expansion of the 1940s and 1950s, incorporating Europe into the Americano-centric world political economy, contributed to European economic growth and to the gradual expansion of the welfare state, even if it contained a bias

against rapid increases that went beyond the modal pattern of the time. The incorporation of Japan into the system as an advanced country during the 1960s and 1970s was received with less enthusiasm in Europe, since it imposed adjustment costs on their economic and political institutions and threatened the European position at or near the top of the international division of labour. Yet throughout this period, the political bias of liberalism benefited interests, groups, and political élites that were favourable to maintaining internationally oriented capitalism.

In conjunction with the economic crises of the 1970s (which had a variety of sources), the later rise of exports of manufactured goods from the newly industrializing countries, coupled with an increasing Japanese challenge, began to generate a powerful counter-reaction. Increasing state interventionism, designed at first to cushion societies from some of the adverse effects of interdependence, threatened to overwhelm liberalism itself. The problem was not the failure of capitalism but, in Schumpeterian fashion, its success. Uneven development again took place in the 1970s, as in the 1950s—but this time the most rapid rates of growth were in East Asia rather than Europe. Not surprisingly, the reactions of Europeans to this turn of events were quite different from their response to the Marshall Plan.

Against this background it is hard to regard the problems of the world political economy in the 1970s as exogenous, unpredictable shocks, as argued in the McCracken Report. Admittedly, not all of these events seem inevitable, and misguided American policies on both oil and monetary relations had a great deal to do with the subsequent crises. Nevertheless, there is an inherent logic to the decline of hegemonic powers in a capitalist system, since their technological and organizational advantages are inherently subject to diffusion to the periphery, driven by the incentives of profit and power.[30] Equally fundamental to the hegemon's position is the relationship between power and adjustment. As we have seen, power is in part the ability not to have to adjust to change. Adjustment is a "political bad": people do not like to have to change their habits, especially if the results are psychologically and financially distressing. Voters tend to punish politicians who seek to force adjustments on to them. Yet adjustment is an "economic good": neo-classical economists never tire of singing its praises as the principal engine of growth. The economy that does not adjust does not grow.

Hegemonic powers can avoid adjustment longer than others, precisely because they are powerful. Yet this ability to evade the necessity to make unpleasant changes can itself contribute to long-term decay. If weaker states adjust more readily than strong ones (not necessarily because they are more farsighted but because they have less choice), their economies will become more efficient, and they will become stronger. Japan's rapid adjustment to the 1973–74 oil shock, compared to that of the United States, is a case in point. No law prescribes that hegemonic powers will necessarily decline at any given time, but they are subject to the temptation to take the easy path. Their power gives them enough rope with which to hang themselves.

Even more than the decline of hegemony, the expansion of capitalism is the result of endogenous factors: unconstrained by state power, capitalism continuously reaches out not only for new markets and sources of raw materials, as in the past, but for new areas in which production for export can profitably take place. As new manufacturing centres enter the world system, the international division of labour becomes more extensive and interdependence grows rapidly. Yet the *political* economy of capitalism follows a more contorted path. Political reactions arise against what may seem, on efficiency grounds, to be a beneficial process. Europe, and to some extent the United States, are now going through such a reaction.

At the heart of this problem is a fundamental tension, or contradiction, in the international political economy of modern capitalism. International capitalism keeps expanding to the periphery, but depends on interventionist,

self-interested states in the centre for its maintenance and support.[31] Embedded liberalism is endangered because its peculiar combination of state interventionism and international openness rested on conditions—American political dominance and the pre-eminent position of Europe in the international division of labour—that can no longer be maintained, and that indeed were undermined by the success of liberalism itself. Major adjustments must now take place: to a new form of embedded liberalism that accepts the expansion of capitalism away from Europe, uncontrolled by the United States; or toward greater self-reliance and protectionism for Western Europe, perhaps in conjunction with selected areas of the Third World. Domestic political pressures point toward protectionism, yet its economic costs, and the threat it poses to transatlantic political relations, are well appreciated in Europe as well as in the United States. One plausible compromise would incorporate elements of both cooperation and protection. "Cooperative protectionism" could limit political friction through the use of multilateral agreements, while cushioning the costs of rapid economic change. Such a strategy could easily degenerate to a discordant and stringent protectionism if too many concessions were made to obsolescent industries and interest groups seeking to prevent, rather than merely to delay, painful adjustments to change. Yet it offers the promise of reconciling the realities of international political and economic interdependence with demands for protection at home. Europe may have to choose, not between liberalism and protectionism in stark forms, but between defensive and discordant, or adjustment-oriented and cooperative, variants of protectionism. Its future will be affected—one is tempted to say, determined—by its reaction to this fateful choice.

## Notes

1. *Towards Full Employment and Price Stability* (Paris: Organization for Economic Cooperation and Development, 1977). [Note by the editors:

The above-cited McCracken Report was produced by a group of distinguished economists from OECD countries and sought to defend the view that the economic problems that had emerged in these countries could be "largely...understood in terms of conventional economic analysis" and that what was needed to overcome them was "better use of existing instruments of economic policy and better functioning and management of existing market mechanisms."]

2. John Goldthorpe, "Introduction", in Goldthorpe, ed., *Order and Conflict in Contemporary Capitalism* (Oxford: Clarendon Press, 1984).

3. John Gerard Ruggie, "International Regimes, Transactions and Change: Embedded Liberalism in the Postwar Economic Order," *International Organization* 36 (1982).

4. Charles S. Maier, "The Politics of Productivity: Foundations of American Economic Policy after World War II," in Peter J. Katzenstein, ed., *Between Power and Plenty: Foreign Economic Policies of Advanced Industrial States* (Madison: University of Wisconsin Press, 1978).

5. Fred Block, *The Origins of International Economic Disorder* (Berkeley: University of California Press, 1977).

6. Fred Hirsch and Michael Doyle, "Politicization in the World Economy: Necessary Conditions for an International Economic Order" in Hirsch, Doyle and Edward L. Morse, eds., *Alternatives to Monetary Disorder* (New York: McGraw-Hill, 1977).

7. Stephen Hymer, "The Internationalization of Capital," *Journal of Economic Issues*, 6 (1972).

8. Fred Block, *The Origins of International Economic Disorder*, p. 3.

9. *Towards Full Employment and Price Stability*, pp. 136–137.

10. Robert O. Keohane, "Economics, Inflation and the Role of the State: Political Implications of the McCracken Report," *World Politics*, 31 (1978).

11. Albert O. Hirschman, *Exit, Voice and Loyalty: Responses to Decline in Firms, Organizations and States* (Cambridge, Mass.: Harvard University Press, 1970).

12. Gerhard Lehmbruch, "Concertation and the Structure of Corporatist Networks," in John Goldthorpe, ed. *Order and Conflict in Contemporary Capitalism*, pp. 60–80.

13. David Cameron, "The Expansion of the Public Economy: A Comparative Analysis," *American Political Science Review*, 72 (1978).

14. Mancur Olson, *The Rise and Decline of Nations* (New Haven: Yale University Press, 1982); Robert E. Baldwin, "The Political Economy of Protectionism," in Jagdish Bhagwati, ed., *Import Competition and Response* (Chicago: University of Chicago Press, 1982); W. A. Brock and S. P. Magee, "The Economics of Special Interest Politics: The Case of the Tariff," *American Economic Review, Papers and Proceedings* 68 (1978); and Karl Polanyi, *The Great Transformation* (Boston: Beacon Press, 1944).

15. Albert O. Hirschman, "The Social and Political Matrix of Inflation: Elaborations on the Latin American Experience," in *Essays in Trespassing: Economics to Politics and Beyond* (Cambridge: Cambridge University Press, 1981).

16. *Towards Full Employment and Price Stability*, Chart 9, p. 61.

17. *World Economic Outlook* (Washington, D.C.: International Monetary Fund, 1982), Table 9, p. 150.

18. *Annual Report* (Basle: Bank for International Settlements, 1981), p. 40; Sylvia Ostry, John Llewellyn, and Lee Samuelson, "The Cost of OPEC II," *OECD Observer*, 115 (1982), pp. 37, 38.

19. *Towards Full Employment and Price Stability*, p. 70; Sylvia Ostry et al., "The Cost of OPEC II," p. 38; *World Energy Outlook* (Paris: OECD, 1982), pp. 63–64.

20. *Annual Report*, pp. 41, 42, 44; ibid. (1982), p. 30.

21. *World Economic Outlook* (Washington, D.C.: International Monetary Fund, 1982), Appendix B, Tables 1 and 2, pp. 143–44; ibid. (1983), pp. 179, 185; Colin I. Bradford, Jr., "The NICs and World Economic Adjustment," in Louis Turner and Neil McMullen, eds., *The Newly Industrializing Countries* (London: Allen and Unwin, 1982), pp. 175–76; Leslie Stein, "The Growth and Implications of LDC Manufactured Exports to Advanced Countries," *Kyklos*, 34 (1981); *The Impact of the Newly Industrializing*

Countries on Production and Trade in Manufacturing (Paris: OECD, 1979), Table 5, p. 24.

22. Wolfgang Hager, "Protectionism and Autonomy: How to Preserve Free Trade in Europe," *International Affairs*, (Summer 1982), pp. 421, 420.

23. William H. Branson, "Trends in United States International Trade and Investment Since World War II," in Martin Feldstein, ed., *The American Economy in Transition* (Chicago: University of Chicago Press, 1980), Table 3.19, p. 220.

24. Leslie Stein, "The Growth and Implications of LDC Manufactured Exports to Advanced Countries," *Kyklos* 34 (1981), p. 57.

25. Louis Turner and Neil McMullen, eds., *The Newly Industrializing Countries*, p. 138.

26. Jagdish Bhagwati, "Shifting Comparative Advantage, Protectionist Demands and Policy Response," in Bhagwati, ed., *Import Competition and Response*, pp. 177–179.

27. Wolfgang Hager, "Protectionism and Autonomy," p. 423.

28. Ibid., p. 424.

29. Stephen Woolcock, "Adjustment in Western Europe," in Turner and McMullen, eds., *The Newly Industrializing Countries*, p. 236.

30. Robert Gilpin, *War and Change in World Politics* (Cambridge: Cambridge University Press, 1981).

31. Robert Gilpin, *U.S. Power and the Multinational Corporation: The Political Economy of Direct Foreign Investment* (New York: Basic Books, 1975).

# 33
# West Germany Compared

*Peter J. Katzenstein*

Forty years after the founding of the Federal Republic it is time to consider the pattern of

SOURCE: Peter J. Katzenstein, "The Third West German Republic: Continuity in Change," *Journal of International Affairs*, vol. 41, no. 2 (Summer 1988), pp. 325–344. Published by permission of the *Journal of International Affairs* and the Trustees of Columbia University in the City of New York. Article and notes abridged by the editors.

change of Germany's longest experiment with democracy. Yet in considering West Germany in the 1980s it is important to avoid the temptation of ahistorical historicism: constantly comparing West German democracy to the past without recognizing the extent and manner by which West German democracy has changed since 1949. I describe contemporary West Germany in this article as the "Third Republic." The term conveys a reference point dealing with the present and future, not the past. And it stresses the comparability rather than exceptionalism of West Germany. This is not to argue, however, that the past should be forgotten or that, in a different guise, the past may not repeat itself. But the essay seeks to familiarize the reader with the notion that we should study the politics of distinct political regimes not only before but also after 1945.

The precise dating of the other postwar republics is somewhat arbitrary. The First Republic lasted from 1949 to 1969 and was characterized by a conservative welfare state that "trickled down" the dividends of economic growth. The Second Republic extended from 1969 to about 1980, and was intent on a major institutional consolidation. The Third Republic was ushered in during 1980 precisely because established ways of political bargaining proved inadequate to deal with a more difficult and rapidly changing international and national environment.

Compared to such countries as France, West Germany's three republics are distinctive in their absence of dramatic changes. At the same time, West Germany in the 1980s is challenged by three different changes. The first set of changes originates in the international system; another from the system of national politics, particularly the rise of new social movements; and the third derives from the new production technologies and the organization of work in West Germany's industrial plants. Nonetheless, the major national structures of West Germany's Third Republic remain stable and tied to their predecessors by remarkable institutional and political continuities. This convergence—between experimentation and change at the grassroots and continuity and stability at the top—is the most striking political characteristic of the Third Republic. From the perspective of the 1980s, I shall examine the theme of continuity in change by characterizing three major changes in the 1980s, tracing their manifestations in West German industry and politics, comparing West Germany briefly to other states and speculating about the future pattern of change.

## THREE SETS OF CHANGES

At the international level the members of the Western Alliance continue to constitute the core for trade, monetary and investment regimes in the 1980s. Each has a major stake in the security and welfare of the others, and their interests are fundamentally compatible. Yet within that stable order there remains ample room for change. Since the 1960s, the United States has been increasingly insistent that its major allies, including West Germany, abandon their free ride and actively support a liberal international economy. For more than a decade and again on the weekend preceding the crash of 1987 the United States has urged the Federal Republic to pursue a vigorous growth policy. West Germans, cautious and fearful when it comes to the issue of inflationary growth, have either played deaf or insisted that the Americans first put their own economic house in order. Yet West Germany is vulnerable to American pressures and thus likely to keep acting as the "honest broker" mediating conflicts over macroeconomic policy, trade policies, East-West export controls and other issues. . . .

. . .The fragility of the international financial system is likely to continue as a possible source of change that could affect dramatically West Germany's economy and access to international markets. The rapid shifts in financial power during the 1980s favoring Japan and, to a lesser extent, West Germany, make plausible the assumption that any reorganization of the international debt regime, should it occur, would probably involve substantial West German financial resources. . . .

The second set of changes derives from the growth of new West German social movements. The rise of these movements has reduced the power of the Social Democratic Party (SDP), one of West Germany's main parties throughout most of the postwar era, and thus has affected the entire West German political system. The opening for these parties came in the late 1970s as major political parties and interest groups no longer occupied all the political space, and as develpments in the economy, society and politics became less tightly coupled. Ironically, this vigorous reconstitution of West Germany's civil society arguably has brought democratic participation more in line with democratic theory even though the social movements are divided on the virtues of representative democratic institutions.

The new social movements are also influenced by the introduction of new production technologies. The most important direct links are ideological as, for example, between social movements and the unions. Ecological and peace groups and the unions, for example, are constantly skirmishing over who is most entitled to press for ecological or peace issues. More typical are the indirect links. One link operates primarily through the party system. Social movements force new issues, such as ecology or nuclear power, on the political agenda. They have in fact caused the emergence of the Greens, a new party that has reflected and accelerated the process of electoral realignment.

The international system provides a second link. If new social movements are forerunners of similar movements in other countries, the pressures they exert help create growth markets for new industrial products, for example, the catalytic converter to combat pollution. But if West Germany's social movements are exceptional in their political prominence, they will burden West German producers with costs diminishing their international competitiveness. Available evidence suggests that the truth lies in the middle. West Germany's industrial profile may eventually differ from that of countries without social movements, but this does not necessarily mean the Federal Republic will be condemned to a loss of economic competiveness.

The third set of changes is the new technologies transforming the process of industrial production. The introduction of new technologies has fundamental consequences for the relative position of different groups of workers, different industries, the deployment of labor and for the way products and production are linked. Sometimes new technology can encourage the reskilling of workers and the enhancement of the power of labor in the workplace.

Alternately, they can lead to the deskilling of workers, the segmentation of the labor force and the decline of labor's power. In either case, the new technologies make the human element more, not less, important to the success of individual firms in the core sectors of the West German economy. The reduction in quantity is often accompanied by an improvement in the quality of work for at least some segments of the skilled working class. Work, in this era of transition, is growing in its quality even as the decline of mass production makes it shrink in quantity.

The reduction in the quantity of work is posing serious challenges to both the political structures and to the labor movement, with a net loss of one million jobs between 1973 and 1986 as compared to a net gain of 24 million jobs in the United States, and a sharp expansion in the number of long-term unemployed, from 14 percent in 1977 to 31 percent in 1985 as compared to a change in the United States in the same period from seven to nine percent. Early retirements and a shortening of the work week did not prevent the unemployment rate from increasing sharply to over eight percent in the 1980s.

The result has been to strain the solidarity of labor as well as weaken its political position. Growing unemployment has encouraged firms, backed by their works councils, to impose tougher criteria for recruitment. The intent is to stabilize a company's workforce and to make its disposition, both in terms of job allocation and working time, as flexible as possible. Qualification redundancies of employed workers and government policy favoring greater flexibility illustrate the growing importance of "internal" rather than "external" labor markets.

The West German labor movement in the 1980s has had an ambivalent attitude toward the introduction of new production technologies. On one hand, traditional union support is strongest among the "tolerators" or "losers" of technological change. Yet West German labor has typically welcomed rationalization and modernization. Unions have also backed a "technological offensive" to take advantage of new production technologies, although so far failing to develop a program that would receive the firm support of works councils and workers needing new skills and qualifications in the workplace.

Although the market power of labor will undoubtedly increase with the dramatic decline in the number of young workers entering the labor market for the first time in the 1990s, it will not eliminate the need for developing political concepts and strategies for strenthening worker solidarity and a broader social consensus on the role of labor in a rapidly changing economy. Short of developing such concepts and strategies, the trade-off between the quantity and the quality of work will remain a potential source for political mobilization and demands for large-scale institutional change. The structural ambivalence is also illustrated by the divergent experiences of different industries. For example, unions have intervened forcefully in the automobile industry while playing a low-key role in the chemical industry.

In sum, the analysis of the introduction of production technologies suggests something substantially new and different in West Germany in contrast to the stability of the bipolar international system and of the political continuities in the convergence of rights, redistribution and risk as the catalysts for old and new social movements. . . .

## CHANGE AND POLITICAL INSTITUTIONS

The flexibility of West German industry, both business and labor groups, to seek experimentation and adjustment to new economic conditions is to some extent paralleled in the political sphere by the programmatic debates and conflict over economic policy throughout the 1980s within and between political parties, the business community and unions. Significantly, none of these debates has led to any large-scale institutional change in national politics, and, in fact, institutional continuity is a distinctive trait of West Germany's Third Republic. . . .

. . .The institutional stability of the Third Republic is the strong legacy of para-public institutions that bridge public and private sectors and facilitate a relatively quiet process of formulating and implementing public policy. They are organized under public law in such forms as corporate bodies, foundations and institutes, including Chambers of Industry and Commerce, professional associations, public radio and television stations. Many of them date back to the nineteenth century while others were created only after 1945. The intent, however, is the same: marshal the expertise of major social and economic sectors under the auspices of state authority, thus making the exercise of state power both more technically informed and politically enlightened.

Para-public institutions, in effect, act like shock-absorbers, both directly and indirectly inducing stability. Political controversies are typically limited to the process of policy implementation, while the very presence of these institutions limits the scope of policy initiatives. They express a general German principle of organization: independent governance of society under general supervision by the state. Political conflict among different social interests finds precious little open space in the Federal Republic.

A second major reason for the stability of West German institutions is intimately linked to the first. There exist tight links between changes at the grassroots of West German industry and stable institutions in national politics. Technological, economic and social changes are thus filtered into existing institutions rather than bypassing them and pressing for a fundamental institutional change.

Industrial relations and vocational training serve as an example of one tight link between widespread grassroots change and large, stable national-level institutions. West Germany has a dual system of industrial relations in which there is a symbiotic relationship between unions and works councils. Unions are responsible for collective bargaining and participation in codetermination in the boardroom while works councils help organize working conditions at plants and workplaces. Eighty percent of the elected works councillors are union members. Modified and extended in the 1970s, the two institutions have been able to manage cooperatively the adversarial relation between labor and business.

The legal protection granted unions through codetermination has made manpower policy into a permanent objective of corporate management and maintained corporate flexibility in the face of technological change. The strong role of the works councils, conversely, has similarly encouraged a long-term approach to manpower policy conducive to accommodating technological change, since works councils handle the recruitment, dismissal and assignment of workers. In fact, the new production technologies have shifted the relative power from the unions to the works councils. The entire system of industrial relations is becoming more decentralized and based around individual enterprises. National unions, however, remain important actors. They are now offering organizational support and expertise to works councils rather than defining uniform regulations covering entire industries.

West Germany's vocational training system provides a different kind of example. The young are educated in schools and trained in firms. The system centers around West German business in providing an adequate number of vocational training positions to absorb successive generations of youngsters that enter West German labor markets each year. It involves the peak associations of business and the trade unions in cooperatively defining the school curriculum and job qualifications of a large number of occupations and trades. Finally the system requires the backing of the state to sanction as public policy the agreements hammered out by the various groups. In short, an elaborate system of organizing this important feature of West Germany's political economy links individual firms to top-level institutions.

The convergence of pervasive change in low politics with institutional continuities in high politics is distinctive of the Third Republic. Pervasive change in low politics does not lead to institutional blockages or crisis, or act as a catalyst for fundamental institutional change. Instead, pervasive change provides an opportunity for the piecemeal recalibration of institutions. Change occurs within existing institutions rather than outside of them in three ways: a new context can privilege institutions that have not been politically central; it can disempower institutions that have been central; or it can alter the relative position of existing institutions thus transforming their role in the larger political economy.

Immediately after the war, attention riveted on whether the formal institutions of West Germany's young democracy—Parliament, the executive, the judiciary, federalism and the party system—would take hold in an authoritarian society defeated in war, suffering through the trauma of national partition, bloated by a refugee population that at any moment might turn to an irredentist politics and harboring millions of former Nazis. The "economic miracle" of the 1950s promised an answer too easy for many of these troubling questions. Indeed the fear, still lingering in the 1970s, was that West German democracy might be no more than a fair weather democracy. Without the inducements of a prosperous economy the Germans would probably turn, as they had before, to nondemocratic politics.

The Second West German Republic shifted the focus. West German democracy was no longer feared to be unstable; rather it was criticized at times for being too stable. The critical components of "model Germany," such as peak associations of businesses, a centralized labor movement and centralized professional organizations often held neocorporatist politics viewed as centralized, secretive and technocratic. The Second Republic was seen as lacking in democratic participation, although its neocorporatist policies were well suited for the technical criteria of social and economic efficiency. After 1973, when the West German economy outperformed most of its competitors, political unease began to form over the evident limits of neocorporatist politics to attract political loyalties of the young and other members of oppositional social movements.

The coming of the Third West German Republic shifted attention once again to institutions such as the works councils and the vocational training system dispersed throughout West German society. New opportunities and constraints are provided to national-level institutions by changes from abroad, changes in technology and changes in civil society from new social movements. Institutional links are, however, necessary to connect grassroots changes with national-level institutions. West Germany in the 1980s includes diverse groups, such as social self-help groups often linked to the state's social service delivery agencies, and "alternative" culture and youth groups that rely on public subsidies. The institutional links existing between them and the state are a distinctive political feature of the Third Republic....

Because of their impressive stability, the national institutions are not responsive to economic and social change. The remarkable continuities between the Second and the Third Republic, furthermore, reinforce this impression. The bipolar structure of the international state system and the legacy of its semi-sovereign status hamper large-scale institutional change. National institutions, however, are open to giving expression to the more subtle changes and experiments occurring at the grassroots. Change thus occurs within rather than outside institutions, and the relative importance of these institutions shifts gradually over time. Put differently, change is not blocked, but happens in small doses to make the evolution of West Germany's political life rather predictable.

# WEST GERMANY IN COMPARATIVE PERSPECTIVE

The politics of West German industry can be compared to that of other capitalist states. West Germany resembles most closely the stable corporatist politics and flexible economic policy distinctive of the smaller European democracies.[1] This is no surprise. Germany's partition after 1945 made the country smaller and enhanced its perception of vulnerability and dependence on world markets. A consensual style of politics came to prevail over the political extremes, while centrist political parties and centralized interest groups fashioned a democratic style of politics. Over time the question of national reunification receded in importance while questions of economic productivity and social welfare assumed central importance.

In a broader perspective, West Germany's major economic rivals, the United States and Japan, typify liberal and statist political arrangements that respond differently to economic and social change. Liberal states like the United States press for international liberalization and at the same time often seek to export the costs of change to other countries. Because they lack the political means for selective intervention in their own economies, they often adopt a variety of limited protectionist policies.

Such action normally creates a temporary breathing space for producers hard-pressed by international competition but it rarely addresses long-term structural shifts in international competitiveness. Conversely, statist countries like Japan are endowed with the means and institutions to preempt the cost of change through seeking structural transformation in their economies. Because this strategy seeks to meet head-on structural changes in the world economy, it often requires protectionist policies, at least in the short- and medium-term.

Distinctive of West German politics is the relative equality in the distribution of power among different actors. No great disparities exist, by the standards of American and Japanese politics. In West Germany, business and labor are politically so well entrenched that they can accommodate themselves with relative ease to changes in government control by successive center-right or center-left coalition governments.

The organizational strength and institutional presence of both business and labor, though variable, is impressive by American and Japanese standards. In West Germany, these actors are relatively closely linked to one another, thus resembling Japan more than the United States. The relation between industry and banks also is close, based on a system of competitive bargaining rather than one of private capital markets or credits administered by the state. Government-business relations are stronger than those in the United States, and government-labor relations are more closely knit than those in Japan. Tight links between interest groups, political parties and state bureaucracies create inclusionary politics.

These broad characterizations of the political strategies and structures of "liberal democracy" in the United States, "productivity democracy" in Japan and "industrial democracy" in West Germany offer an essential reference point for understanding the distinctiveness of the West German response to change in the 1980s. In the United States and Japan industrial sectors are typically viewed as growing and declining, either autonomously through shifts in market competition or under state guidance. West Germany, with its stable industrial structure, emphasizes renewal and change within existing industrial sectors. The United States and Japan think in the categories of a "big power," either in terms of military-political domination or of economic-technological preeminence; West Germany thinks like a small state in terms of the exploitation of market niches in a favorable political environment. Finally strong segmentation tendencies in the labor force exist in the United States through deskilling and wage differentiation and in Japan through a selective solidarity that encompasses a minority of the total labor force; in West Germany these segmentation tendencies are gathering strength in the 1980s but still remain much weaker.

## CONCLUSION

If one tendency is recognizable in the bewildering array of changes found in West Germany in the 1980s, it is the trend toward decentralization. In the economic realm, for example, both public and private interventions have been decentralized in addressing crisis conditions in particular industries or of particular firms. The federal government has also studiously avoided getting itself too deeply entangled with the crises in particular sectors, such as steel and shipbuilding, and instead delegated responsibility either to individual states or to advisory councils. Similarly, the failure of West Germany's banks to rescue, in the early 1980s, West Germany's second largest electronics firm, AEG, was an important signal that the era of centralized private industrial policy was largely over.

In the area of technology policy, the growth in government programs has slowed down dramatically from 7 percent in the period from 1975 to 1979 to 2 percent in the period from 1983 to 1987. State-centered or corporatist-style technological policy is less important in the 1980s. The allocation for the largest and most centralized research program, the nuclear industry, has been slashed in half. Support for production technologies accounts for only one percent of the total federal research and development budget.

Although the federal government continues to be concerned about the international competitiveness of West German industry, it has discontinued direct funding of product development. The government has adopted instead a comprehensive plan for the development of communications technologies administered by different ministries and agencies. Thus a tendency toward decentralization is evident even though there exist strong continuities in government policy from the Second to the Third Republic.

Not all important economic sectors share in the pattern just outlined. Agriculture is an example. A powerful, centralized peak association of farmers succeeded for thirty years in extracting large subsidies to avoid adjusting to world market conditions and to stop a growing gap between agricultural and industrial incomes. The European Community's Common Agricultural Policy has given this policy sector a strong international dimension in the last two decades. The West German government, however, did not stop unilaterally subsidizing its farmers against the express opposition of its European trading partners. In this sector the political imperatives of domestic politics have clearly outweighed the demands for market competition. Agriculture is an important exception and others could be cited. Yet the core of West Germany's political economy combines widespread economic experimentation in the face of change with institutional stability.

The concept of success or failure of the Third Republic model raises the thorniest problem of all. It is easy to talk about the economic success or failure of individual firms in adapting to change. It is somewhat harder to talk about the economic and political success or failure of different segments or sectors of industry. But it is virtually impossible to talk with precision about the political success or failure of the Third Republic or for that matter of any political order. Each state distributes the benefits and costs of its policies in particular ways. There exists no metric for comparing, for example, the benefits accruing to the craft producers of machinery to the costs of unemployed Turkish steelworkers. Successful political regimes are admired because they are effective in concealing the costs of their policies, not because they are not incurring any costs. West Germany's Third Republic is no exception. Its regained industrial prowess is inextricably linked to the more difficult conditions experienced by the weakest and marginal sectors of society.

Not mentioned so far is one potential cause for large-scale change in the politics of the Third

Republic. It would be less spectacular than dramatic developments in the structure of domestic labor or international capital markets. The cumulative effect of the small changes creating pressures toward decentralization in the political institutions of the Third Republic might also at some undeterminable threshold lead to large-scale institutional change.

The structure of West German federalism is one example. Possible changes in the structure of the West German party system are another. The rise of the Greens, on the left of the political spectrum and of a small group of market advocates on the right, is evidence of a broadening spectrum of political positions in the centrist politics of the Third Republic. A gradual recalibration in the political weights eventually might have dramatic effects on the domestic balance of power that has assured export industries, the banks and the labor movement a central position in West German politics since 1949.

Pervasive small-scale change and experimentation in industry is compatible with a large measure of stability in national institutions and politics without sacrificing West Germany's international competitiveness. The national institutions of the Third Republic are stable because they accommodate many changes occurring at the microlevel. Relationships exist between new production technologies in West German plants as well as developments in the international trade and financial systems and the national political arrangements of the Federal Republic. Whether these links will weather a major crisis, should the future hold such a crisis in store, will have an important effect on how West Germany's political regime will accommodate itself to possible large-scale changes that it has to date successfully avoided.

## Notes

1. Peter J. Katzenstein, *Corporatism and Change: Austria, Switzerland and the Politics of Industry* (Ithaca, NY: Cornell University Press, 1984); Peter J. Katzenstein, *Small States in World*

*Markets: Industrial Policy in Europe* (Ithaca, NY: Cornell University Press, 1985).

## 34

# The Social Security Crisis
*Mattei Dogan*

In the most advanced and richest countries a crisis of the social-security system has developed independently, progressively and simultaneously over the last two decades.

The fact that this crisis has arisen independently in all these countries at about the same moment incites the comparatist to focus as much on the basic analogies as on the differences between them. It could be documented that certain decisions taken in a few countries on social-security matters were inspired by the legislation adopted in neighboring countries. But even if 'imitation' did play a role, the fact remains that in all of them we witness the same basic phenomenon. If the same phenomenon occurs so many times—even if we admit some political 'contamination'—it obviously cannot be by historical accident, but must arise from constant factors in each of these societies and from their combined effects.

A set of quantified indicators distinguishes these advanced countries from the rest of the 160 independent states. They include high per capita incomes, a large number of physicians and hospital beds per 1,000 inhabitants, very low infantile mortality rates, birth rates insufficient entirely to reproduce the living generation, considerable longevity, etc. The concept of post-industrialization applies closely to these countries in so far as they are undergoing a process

SOURCE: Mattei Dogan, "The Social Security Crisis in the Richest Countries," *International Social Science Journal*, vol. 37, no. 1 (1985), pp. 47–61. © Unesco 1985. Reproduced by permission of Unesco.

of de-industrialization in favour of tertiary economic activities, which is reflected in the slow but regular decline of the number of industrial workers in the overall work force.

Quite obviously, the advanced countries must face and resolve problems of a very different nature than those of the developing countries. Indeed, to those in the poorest countries the analysis of the dysfunction of social-security in the most advanced nations must resemble a topsy-turvy world. The richest countries are also pluralist democracies where a number of political forces compete at free periodic elections and conflicts are mediated through different institutions and political organizations.

These countries are further described as 'welfare states'. 'Paternal state' would be better, but terminology does not matter. Even if the definition of this concept varies from writer to writer, one may say that it fundamentally designates the political recognition of certain social rights—'rights' being opposed to charity or relief. Amongst these social rights the most important are health care, old-age pensions and unemployment benefits. We shall deal with the first two of these here, while recognizing the importance of the third, and without denying the significance which, in certain countries, attaches to child allowances or housing subsidies, for example.

The linkage between the three notions of post-industrial society, pluralist democracy and welfare state is not a haphazard one. There is only one country in the world which has been a pluralist democracy without interruption for more than a generation but which is not a post-industrial society, and that is India. There is only one which, while being post-industrial, does not possess pluralist democratic structures, and that is the German Democratic Republic. If one takes a large number of countries, let us say about one hundred, a very significant statistical correlation appears between wealth, as measured by GNP per capita, and the proportion of the GNP set aside for social security. This relationship between the economic level of a nation and the proportion of national revenue redistributed for

welfare purposes has been studied by several authors (Aharoni, 1981: Flora and Heidenheimer, 1981; Wilensky, 1975).

The fact that these countries have pursued the same direction for several decades and have adopted very similar social-security systems calls for an interdisciplinary explanation, taking into account changes in family structures and roles, changes in the nature of work resulting from technological development, cultural change, longer life-spans, low birth-rates, etc. This evolution has recently raised psychological and philosophical problems relating to attitudes to incurable diseases, senility and death.

We will here consider fifteen 'Western' countries, including the United States and Canada and thirteen Western European countries, excluding Ireland, Portugal and Greece which, although 'Western' are not yet post-industrial. Japan is a rich post-industrial society and a pluralist democracy but it is not 'Western' in the sense that it has a different historical background and is only to a limited degree a welfare state. It is unnecessary here to trace the recent development of social security in Europe and America. Suffice it to say that the social-security system, by a sort of dialectic, having resolved a number of the fundamental problems thrown up by industrial civilization is, through its extraordinary expansion, generating certain major problems at about the same time in all the most advanced countries.

My analysis is centered on fundamental similarities to such an extent that I am sometimes impelled to speak of all these countries as if they were but one. Nevertheless, one must admit that significant differences between them exist, to begin with as between Western Europe and the United States. Outlays for health, to take an example, are reimbursed from public sources at the rate of 90 per cent in the United Kingdom, 70 per cent in France but only 42 per cent in the United States. Yet it is the Americans who are best insured against health risks, even if such insurance is largely private. Wilensky (1975), underlining the fact that 'the Welfare State is at once one of the great structural uniformities of modern society', then asks 'why rich countries having adopted similar health and welfare programs diverge so sharply in their levels of spending, organization and administration of services and benefits' (p. 1).

My question is the opposite one: how did it come about that countries with such different party systems, social stratifications, ideologies current amongst leading groups as well as traditions of social-security institutions today face the same imperative: to cure the elephantiasis of social security and the perverse effects of its overdevelopment?

The social-security crisis is threefold: it concerns spending for health, old-age pensions and unemployment benefits. The gravity of the crisis arises from cumulation, for its three components do not manifest themselves in succession but add up and feed into each other. Yet their maturity is not simultaneous: spending for health has already reached a level which many observers—to the right, at the centre and to the left of the political spectrum—consider intolerable, yet which continues to rise, absorbing an increasing share of national revenue. That is the first point with which we must deal. Spending on old-age pensions has increased steadily in all the countries considered. But for demographic reasons the situation has not yet reached its most critical point. The crisis is inevitable in the medium term: that is the second point to be discussed. The third sector in trouble is unemployment which has spread in all Western countries. Such massive unemployment results in part from the recent decline in their ability to compete economically in international trade, a decline in turn linked to the social overheads of industrial production. The impact of social overheads on the ability to compete economically at the international level forms the subject of our third examination.

## CHEATING DEATH

Spending for health in the United States represented about 11 per cent of the GNP in 1983, as much as in Sweden in the same year, and it is expected to rise to 15 per cent within ten or fifteen years. In this context the dichotomy between capitalism and socialism is irrelevant. In the other Western European countries, the proportion of the GNP devoted to health expenses, both private and public, is a little lower, but it is expected to rise proportionally at a faster rate in the coming years. The social-security budget in France is larger than the national budget. For every 100 francs that a French employee received in 1984, social security gets from 43 to 47 francs, most of them for health expenses. If direct taxation is added, the French middle-class white-collar employee works from 1 January to 15 June for the state, and only for the rest of the year for himself.

There is a widespread stereotyped belief that social security is a device to redistribute national income from the rich to the poor. In reality, so far as health care is concerned, it is much more a redistribution from healthy people to sick people across all social classes. The French Minister of Social Security declared in 1983 that 70 per cent of the social-security budget is spent on 10 per cent of those insured: they belong to all social classes. Some analysts claim that, for various sociological reasons, the rich spend more than the poor. It is true that all insurance systems are based on the same principle: the more than 90 per cent of those who insure against fire or automobile accidents are paying for the 10 per cent or so who will collect. As illness is largely unpredictable, the philosophy of the social-security system is justified. But it should be recognized that it is mostly part of a transfer of resources from the healthy to the sick, rather than from the rich to the poor. . . .

If citizens are more sensitive to the benefits of social security than to its cost, this is so in part because of the lack of courage of political leaders when faced with the issue in the electoral arena. It is easier to increase taxation for social security by 1 or 2 per cent every year than in any way to limit the benefits. This is particularly clear in France, but holds true for almost all European countries. In Italy, the demagogy of politicians on the issue of social welfare has reached an intolerable level. For instance, there were in 1980 in Italy 5,419,500 disabled persons: one out of every ten citizens (including children) was considered 'unfit to work'. For this situation no epithets are more appropriate than demogogy and irresponsibility; and the proof of this is that in 1969 at least 30 per cent of former parliamentarians had been declared 'unfit for work', while by 1978 the proportion had risen to 40 per cent! (Fausto, 1983, p. 50).

The responsibility of the politicians is obvious:

> The essential problem with these welfare programs is that they occur over a vastly longer period than the relatively short time perspective of most politicians. As a result, they are extremely vulnerable to the politicians' temptation to vote short-term benefits, transferring the much longer term costs into the future—to their successors or to future taxpayers, some of them not yet even born (Lawrence Chickering and Rosa, in Rosa (ed.), 1982, p. 208).

Union leaders also push for spending on social security, but not for identical reasons on either side of the Atlantic. In Western Europe, union leaders are ideologically in favour of social redistribution in general, but they also have a second reason to favour an increase in social-security funding: they are co-managers of the funds (with higher civil servants and employers). In some countries unions obtain indirect help from the bureaucracy of the social-security system. In other countries, such as France, they have succeeded in shifting the burden of financing social security mainly to the employers. In the United States, labour unions have become financial corporations, managing enormous pension funds. If Roberto Michels were still alive, he would find in the union involvement in the social-security system a new illustration of the 'iron law of oligarchy'....

## SPIRALLING COSTS OF OLD-AGE PENSIONS

Several aspects of the problem of retirement and old-age pensions merit brief examination: longer life-spans; the increasing imbalance between the active work force and the number of retirees, the shift from capitalization to intergenerational redistribution; worsening financial imbalance through early retirement; the relatively privileged position of the majority of retired persons and the financial deficit.

In all advanced countries, longer life-spans are slow but regular features, so that one may distinguish between retired people and the really old. On the one hand, more people reach the age of retirement; on the other, elderly people tend to live longer. Thus, in the United States in 1940, 583 out of every thousand men, and 687 out of every thousand women reached the age of 65. By 1980, the proportions were, respectively, 711 and 839 per thousand. In 1950 life expectancy at the age of 65 was 13 years for men and 15 years for women. In 1980 it was 15 years for men and 20 for women (Ginzberg, 1982, pp. 55, 57)

In the Federal Republic of Germany in 1980, life expectancy at 60 was 16.2 years for men and 20.6 years for women (Tamburi, 1983, p. 322). Similar figures could be produced for nearly all the countries studied here.

Two demographic currents may be observed. The decline in the birth rate experienced over the past twenty years, and which curiously enough occurred in all the countries concerned at about the same time, will make its full impact but gradually. When the relatively few children of today join the work force they will have to subsidize the pensions of today's adults, who will meanwhile have retired. To this phenomenon over the medium term another, equally important generational one will be added, the effects of which will also arise over the medium term. The relatively large generation born after the Second World War, between 1946 and 1965, at work today, will not start to retire for another twenty years, around the year 2005, with results that can already be anticipated. If the social sciences are really scientific, that is to say, if they possess predictive capacities, the anticipation of the consequences of these twin currents should provide the soundest proof thereof.

Longer life-spans for a greater number of people will not only lead to contributions towards retirement benefits over a longer period but also to greater morbidity in old age, with what that implies by way of outlays on health. These will have to be covered by a relatively restricted working population, unless there is considerable immigration, which seems unlikely in Western Europe owing to structural unemployment. American society is nevertheless continuing to be rejuvenated by immigration, as is Canada's.

The decisive factor for old-age pensions is the relationship between the working population, which pays the contributions, and the number of retired persons. In the United States in 1945 there were fifty working people to every retired person; in 1980, but three.

'Germany is facing an extremely unfavourable ratio between pensioners and contributors to the pension scheme. Taking all pensions in payment into account, one finds that in 1979 there were 56.5 pensioners for 100 contributors. The ratio was 34.1 in 1960, and 43.9 in 1970' (Tamburi, 1983, p. 322). The ratio of workers to retirees will remain fairly constant until 1990, declining from 2.19 in 1980 to an estimated 2.11 in 1990. After then, however, the ratio will decline significantly to 1.56 in 2010 and to an incredible 1.12 in 2030 (Jüttemeier and Petersen, 1982, p. 182). This means that 112 children born in 1985 will have to underwrite the pensions of 100 young people aged 20 who will, that year, enter the work force, who will retire in 2030, at the age of 65 and most of whom will live on past the age of 85. In Italy 'in 1955 the ratio of insured workers to pensions was 3.62; in 1980 it had fallen to 1.41 and it is expected to decline further'. From 1950 to 1980 the 'much more rapid increase in the number of pensioners than in the number of workers (36.9 per cent as against 14 per cent) had led to a five-fold increase in the payroll tax rate' (Castellino, 1982, pp. 50, 55).

In France, on the basis of certain projections

the future solvency of the retirement system has been put in question, and public confidence in the system's ability to meet its commitments has been turned to mistrust.... (Kessler, 1984, p. 71)

To finance retirement nearly all the countries adopted the principle of inter-generational redistribution, also known as pay-as-you-go, abandoning capitalization on account of continuous inflation, especially during and after the Second World War. In the United States, however, retirement benefits are still partly based on the capitalization principle. Under pay-as-you-go, retirement benefits depend on contributions, which are in turn a function of the growth or shrinking of the working population in relation to the number of retired persons as well as economic boom or depression.

The imbalance between the number of contributors and the number of beneficiaries has worsened recently because of the spread of early or pre-retirement....

In Sweden, the elderly absorb an 'excessive proportion' of the GNP (Stahl, 1982, p. 118). Their situation in the Federal Republic of Germany also seems relatively advantageous since it is possible to cumulate pension benefits from different sources, so that 'net benefits for individual pensioners frequently equal more than 100 per cent of the wage, after tax' (Jüttemeier and Petersen, 1982, p. 183). In Italy, retirement benefits are so generous that one must wonder to what extent they are linked to political patronage. Civil servants who enter their career at the age of 20 can claim retirement at 40, at 60 per cent of their salaries. They then take their pension—and coverage for possible medical expenses—into the clandestine economy, which the Italians call the 'submerged' sector, referring to icebergs, a point to which we shall return later. They keep all of their pensions even if they accept new work. The same advantages are offered to women at the age of 35 if they are married and have children.

One can make the rounds of Western Europe, from Helsinki to Vienna and from Madrid to Brussels and not find a single country where the financial crisis of pension funds has not been exposed and analysed by experts and its worsening over the medium term not foreseen and calculated. But the demographers, the economists and the administrators preach in the desert most of the time: the politicians have more urgent business to settle, and 'planning French style' is, in this context, a legend for undergraduates. . . .

The same dilemma and the same song in France as in Belgium, in Austria as in Denmark, even in Canada, though it is a country of immigration. Many of those who will be paying contributions in the year 2005 are, in 1985, still children or adolescents. Will they, when they grow up, accept that three of them work several months a year in order to pay an anonymous pension to some retired person by virtue of legislation adopted by the generation of this pensioner? Will today's adults, when they have retired, manage to impose such a burden on today's children who will, by then, have grown into adults in their working prime? Since the number of the active will be too small in relation to the mass of the inactive it will be necessary—barring a currently unforeseeable technological revolution—to reduce both pensions and the number of inactive persons by postponing the age of retirement.

A further rise in social-security charges, while theoretically conceivable, would have a deleterious impact on the most advanced countries, especially on their international competitiveness, which is the next question to be examined.

## THE WELFARE STATE AND INTERNATIONAL ECONOMIC COMPETITIVENESS

If we add to the 8–11 per cent (according to country) of expenditure on health, that part of the GNP which is allocated to pensions, (10–12 per cent) and that part that goes to unemployed persons or the 'assisted poor'—the definition varies from country to country— (8–12 per cent) we reach for some countries a total one-third of the GNP and for the others more than one-quarter. This amount is taken away from creative production. This implies that only two-thirds of the national resources remain for all the other

needs of society, particularly investment in industries; extension of education for the young; higher incomes for those who are able to work; reduction of the work-load and increase of leisure time for those who are in good health.

Such a choice is politically legitimate, since it has been adopted by governments elected according to democratic rules. Socially, it is largely necessary, and corresponds to the expectations of large strata of society. It would be justified even from the economic point of view if all countries which play an important role in international economic life would spend as much for social welfare as the fifteen richest Western democracies.

The economy of each of these countries, except that of the United States, is trade-dependent for more than one-third of the GNP; in some, such as the Netherlands, for more than half of the GNP. Italy, for instance, has few natural resources except sunshine: it has to pay by exports for everything that its industry needs. The American GNP is less trade-dependent because of the continental size of the country; the United States has its own internal 'common market'.

These countries can survive at their present level of wealth as long as they are still able to trade, not only among themselves, but with the rest of the world, by exchanging finished products and services for raw materials. At the right moment, a third of a century ago, they wisely decided not to build a new 'Chinese wall' around the shores of the Atlantic to protect their scientific and technological advancement. They sold their technology to all comers, including the Soviet Union. Now it is too late. Foreign trade is vital; autarchy impossible.

If the cost of labour is much higher than in Japan and the new industrial centres of the Third World (Taiwan, the Republic of Korea, Hong Kong, Singapore, Brazil, etc.), or than in developing countries like India, the industrial products of countries where social expenditure is a high priority become non-competitive. Consequently, despite their technological advances, they experience a kind of de-industrialization.

In its turn, de-industrialization engenders unemployment, which reduces the amount of contributions to social security. The ratio between workers and retirees imbalances the social-security budget. In order to rectify the balance, more contributions are needed. Higher contributions in turn have a direct impact on the cost of labour. The higher the cost of labour, the less competitive industrial products become on the international market. It is a vicious circle, or more precisely, a mounting spiral.

The economic difficulties which the Western countries have experienced in the past decade are not temporary. In fact these countries are facing a profound and long-term structural change. The time is gone when they imported raw materials and exported finished products: they must today import what they traditionally exported. This is the reason for the crisis in certain industries (steel, textile, energy, etc.). The simultaneous growth of unemployment in so many Western countries reflects this process of de-industrialization more than it does the process of automation of industry. Moreover, the so-called 'British disease' is spreading.

The growth of the tertiary sector more or less implies this kind of de-industrialization. But part of the tertiary sector is not directly productive; it is, rather, an aspect of consumption. For instance, education, which belongs to the tertiary sector, absorbs about 20 per cent of the national budget in nearly all advanced societies. The insurance and the banking systems are not directly profitable, except in a few countries like Switzerland and Britain. The technological advances that these countries enjoy in some domains have not been important enough to compensate for the de-industrialization of the traditionally vital sectors of the economy: and even these advances are slowly or rapidly extending to the developing countries. In the near future India and China will produce their own computers. The only flourishing industrial domain for some of the major countries is the production of arms that can still be easily exported. Even in the area of high technology, optimism should be moderate. The failure of the Concorde supersonic aeroplane is a good cautionary example.

As these societies grow older and older, spend more and more on health, and are no longer able to take surplus value (in the Marxist sense) out of their industrial potential, they can invest less and less, and so they are undermining their capacity for future growth. They are already spending more than they produce.

A society which over a long period of time consumes more than it produces, cannot invest, and without investment there is no growth. Such a society lives by devouring its capital. The national debt of so many advanced countries, including the United States, France and the United Kingdom, is a measure, so to speak, of the imbalance not only between government revenue and spending but also between production and consumption, since social expenditures are partly included in the national budgets. Even if tomorrow the national debt is reduced—by deliberate inflation, for instance—this would not necessarily imply a reversal of the trend.

The ongoing slow economic decline of the advanced Western countries is a complex phenomenon involving a series of factors: levels of productivity, relations between management and employees, military expenditures, the power of organized groups to impose their will, etc. But social expenditures for health, for pensions and for unemployment also play an important role.

Society manages, to an extent, to resist the encroachment of the state. One of the most obvious symptoms of resistance to the social-security system is the rise of the underground economy everywhere, its importance varying from country to country. The underground economy, moonlighting, tax-evasion, fighting shy of ventures, the brain drain, the decline of the work ethic are so many perverse effects of excessive taxation, which finally impoverishes the community as a whole even if it does reduce inequalities. Warnings are being heard everywhere. In the United States:

> There is no doubt that too high a payroll tax can inhibit employment, creating serious problems

for the economy and society. . .Tax rate cannot be raised indefinitely without such adverse consequences as depressing workers' wages, enlarging the off-the-record economy and decreasing the total tax revenues collected (Ginzburg, 1982, p. 56).

The same diagnosis in socialist Sweden: 'Public spending at present runs at about 65 per cent of Sweden's GDP and recent budget deficits amount to almost 5 per cent of GDP. To support the level of spending, marginal tax rates have been raised to levels where they stifle industrial productivity' (Stahl, 1982, p.118).

In the Federal Republic of Germany, similar anxieties: 'We fear a growing movement into the tax-free and contributions-free underground economy. This would limit revenues more than ever, and would probably lead to a complete collapse of the social insurance system' (Jüttemeier and Petersen, 1982, p. 198).

But it is Italy, with a society which for 2,000 years has sought to resist power, which has succeeded in producing the greatest underground economy. Some estimate at a quarter, others at one-third the share of national production which escapes state control and social security. The phenomenon is well-known. The government itself tolerates this clandestine economy since it knows that without it Italy would be plunged into an economic and financial disaster. For it is the underground economy which enables Italy more or less to balance its foreign trade.

This pessimistic thesis has also been exposed by Richard Rose and Guy Peters in a book in which they showed how the mutilation of take-home pay, unacceptable psychologically, would produce 'political bankruptcy', defined as 'undermining constitutional authority by joining civic indifference to institutional ineffectiveness' (Rose and Peters, 1978, p. 32).

So the welfare state, which wanted to cushion the negative effects of the capitalist economy and the logic of the free market, produces in its turn its own dysfunctions: bureaucratic hypertrophy; overcentralization; incompetence of public servants to deal with social problems; lack of rationality in the decision-making process; and so on. It has been denied that the services which the welfare state renders compensate sufficiently for the level of taxation.

If this trend continues for many more years, what is now forseeable only by analysts will become obvious to many people, and particularly to politicians, whose myopia can be excused because they have more immediate problems to resolve.

The cumulative effect of an ageing population, increasing health costs, and de-industrialization in the fifteen most advanced Western countries, will inevitably engender relative economic decline by a kind of dialectical process. This forecast may be specified as a decline in the quality of life for most people, or, in more technical terms, a GNP per capita. It remains to be seen whether such a decline in mean income will be accompanied by higher or lower inequalities, or in technical terms, by a higher or lower standard deviation. It seems very probable that it will be accompanied by a reduction of social inequality. There will be fewer very rich people, because of the redistribution of national income, and fewer very poor people, because of the inevitable extension of social programmes under democratic regimes (except perhaps for immigrants). By decline in the quality of life we should understand, first of all, uniformization of life-styles, brought about by an impoverishment of the very rich, greater, relatively, than improvement in the condition of the very poor. It is decline, so to speak, in absolute terms of the statistical mean, a levelling down. It is also a decline in relative terms of the West as opposed to a phalanx of Third World countries. This double decline will probably be a relatively slow process, and consequently painless.

## Author's References

AHARONI, YAIR. 1981. *The No-risk Society*. Chatam, N.Y.,: Chatam House.

CASTELLINO, ONORATO. 1982. Italy. In Jean-Jacques Rosa (ed.). *The World Crisis in Social Security*, pp. 48–91. Paris: Fondation Nationale d'Economie Politique.

FAUSTO, DOMENICANTONIO. 1983. The Proliferation of Disability Pensions: An Application not
Limited to the South of Italy. *Mezzogiorno
d'Europa,* January–March.

FLORA, PETER; HEIDENHEIMER, J. ARNOLD.
1981. *The Development of Welfare States in Europe
and America.* London: Transaction Books.

GINZBERG, ELI. 1982. The Social Security System.
*Scientific American,* January, pp. 51–57.

JÜTTEMEIER, K. H.; PETERSEN, H. G. 1982. West
Germany. In Jean-Jacques Rosa (ed.), *The World
Crisis in Social Security,* pp. 181–205. Paris: Fon-
dation Nationale d'Economie Politique.

KESSLER, DENIS. 1984. Les retraités en péril? *Revue
française des affaires sociales,* June, pp.69–83.

ROSA, JEAN-JACQUES (ed.). 1982. *The World Crisis
in Social Security.* Paris: Fondation Nationale
d'Economie Politique.

ROSE, RICHARD; PETERS, GUY. 1978. *Can Government Go Bankrupt?* New York: Basic Books.

STAHL, INGEMAR. 1982. Sweden. In Jean-Jacques
Rosa (ed.), *The World Crisis in Social Security,*
pp. 93–120. Paris: Fondation Nationale d'Economie
Politique.

TAMBURI, G. 1983. Escalation of State Pension Costs:
The Reasons and the Issues. *International Labour
Review,* Vol. 122, No. 3, May–June.

WILENSKY, L. HAROLD. 1975. *The Welfare State and
Equality.* Berkeley: University of California Press.

## 35

# Socialism and Equality

*Thomas R. Dye and Harmon Zeigler*

## CAPITALISM, SOCIALISM, AND EQUALITY

It is widely asserted that socialist economies are
equalitarian. The distinguished Yale political

SOURCE: From Thomas R. Dye and Harmon Zeigler,
"Socialism and Equality in Cross-National Perspective," *PS,*
Vol. XXI, no. 1 (Winter 1988), pp. 45–56. Reprinted by permission of the American Political Science Association and
the authors. Article abridged by the editors.

scientist Charles E. Lindblom labels this proposition *undeniable:*

> It is in communist provision of...some degree
> of equality in the distribution of income and
> wealth that the communist claim to approximate
> the humanitarian vision...seems undeniable.
> On these fronts communist systems have to be
> credited with great accomplishments, on the
> whole probably greater than those of the poly-
> archies [capitalist democracies] (Lindblom, 1977,
> p. 226).

Lindblom's influential work, *Politics and
Markets: The World's Political-Economic Systems,*
expresses the conventional wisdom in academic
circles that communist regimes trade freedom
and economic prosperity for a leveling of economic benefits, and that capitalist nations opt
for freedom and economic prosperity at the
sacrifice of equality. Capitalism achieves higher
economic growth rates by providing individual
incentives for work, productivity, initiative, and
enterprise; these incentives necessarily entail
inequalities. Socialism, by eliminating private
ownership of the means of production, achieves
a leveling of wealth and income. The implication is that while capitalism is better at producing wealth, socialism is better at distributing it.

The conclusion that socialism produces
equality is usually defended on ideological
grounds. According to Lindblom:

> These equalitarian and humanitarian visions
> have been communist aspirations since the nine-
> teenth century, when the pursuit of liberty and
> equality, which had been taken up during the
> Enlightenment, went separate ways. Democrats
> went to the right, seeking liberty. Communists
> went to the left, seeking equality (Lindblom, 1977,
> p. 266).

Yet Western democratic socialists have been confounded everywhere by the repressive character
of socialist regimes and the fact that capitalism
is a necessary condition for political democracy.
Lindblom writes:

> *However poorly the market is harnessed to democratic
> purposes, only within market-oriented systems does*

*political democracy arise.* Not all market-oriented systems are democratic, but every democratic system is also a market-oriented system. Apparently, for reasons not wholly understood, political democracy has been unable to exist except when coupled with the market.

An extraordinary proposition, it has so far held without exception (Lindblom, 1977, p. 116, italics in original).

Lindblom's phrase, "for reasons not wholly understood" is puzzling. Elsewhere in his treatise he acknowledges that democracy and the market system "are historically tied together" (p. 163) and this tie "is clearly no historical accident" (p. 164). Lindblom appears to understand that individual freedom is the core value inspiring both markets and democracy. And his insightful description of "Communist Systems" (ch. 18) clearly explains why political repression is a necessary component of a centrally controlled economy.

Nonetheless, despite their misgivings about the denial of individual liberty in communist nations, western democratic socialists are unambiguous in their claims about equality in these regimes. According to Lindblom, "China and Cuba have in recent times refreshed equalitarian hopes throughout the world" (p. 266). Lindblom asserts that because wealth is privately owned in market economies and government-owned in communist nations, "on this count alone, economic equality in communist systems is significantly greater than in the market-oriented polyarchies" (p. 269). But empirical evidence of greater equality in communist regimes is weak. Lindblom acknowledges that "Statistics on earnings from wages and salaries are grandly unreliable" (p. 209), but goes on to cite Lydall (1968) and Pryor (1977) as evidence that communist systems are more equalitarian than market systems at comparable levels of economic development. The modifying phrase "at comparable levels of economic development" is significant because the studies cited by Lindblom show that a number of western democracies have achieved greater equality in income

distributions than European socialist nations. They also show that the United States is more equalitarian than the Soviet Union. Nonetheless, Lindblom concludes, "As a family of systems, however, the polyarchies [capitalist democracies] are almost certainly significantly less equalitarian than the communist family," and "communism in less developed countries. . .achieves greatly more equality than market systems achieve in comparable countries" (p. 274).

Yet there are good theoretical reasons and substantial cross-national evidence to challenge the idea that socialist systems provide greater equality than market systems. The evidence from cross-national studies indicates that:

1. Equality is primarily a result of economic development, not type of political system.
2. Capitalist systems are more successful at stimulating economic growth than socialist systems.
3. Socialist and capitalist systems at the same level of economic development pursue essentially the same welfare and educational policies.

If it is true that economic growth is the most important determinant of equality, and capitalist systems are better at stimulating growth than socialist systems, then we have a good theoretical rationale for believing that capitalism can bring about a more equitable distribution of income than socialism.

It is our argument that the prevailing view in academic circles that socialism fosters equality rests upon ideology rather than empirical observations of capitalist and socialist nations. The prevailing view ignores the overwhelming importance of economic development in achieving equality, and the importance of market incentives and individual freedom in achieving economic growth. This essay reviews some important cross-national studies of equality, presents some representative findings on the correlates of inequality, and contrasts these empirical observations with the ideological assertions in the leading academic treatise.

## ON THE STUDY OF INEQUALITY AMONG NATIONS

Economic development refers to the level of national income, while inequality alludes to the distribution of that income. It is theoretically possible for national income to increase and inequality to worsen if increases in national income are concentrated among upper income persons. It is also theoretically possible for the absolute income of the poor to increase but inequality to worsen if the income of the rich rises faster than that of the poor. In the familiar Pareto principle, general social welfare would be increased if some people are made better off and nobody is made worse off, regardless of whether or not inequality increases. However, from a political perspective, a nation may become unstable if economic growth and improvements in the absolute conditions of the poor are accompanied by greater inequality. A nation may be worse off if the poor feel relatively more deprived even though their absolute standard of living is improving. Thus, we might say that a nation's well-being depends positively on the level of national income and negatively on inequality in the distribution of that income. . . .

Almost all of the research on inequality is based on cross-sectional comparisons of nations at various points in time. Cross-sectional analyses provide us with static associations: we can observe that nations with various income distributions have various levels of GNP, capitalist or socialist systems, various levels of political participation, different levels of expenditures for defense, welfare, and education, and various indicators of the quality of life. But ideally we would wish to assess historical trends in individual nations over time. Time series analyses would allow us to observe inequality as a dynamic process: changes in measures of inequality would be associated with growth in the GNP, change from capitalist to socialist system or vice versa, increase or decrease in political participation, etc. Making inferences from cross-sectional data about dynamic processes is risky business. But it is a well-established necessity in cross-national studies where data sources are very limited.

Contemporary discussions of inequality are largely confined to market systems. The practical reason for the exclusion of communist nations from studies of inequality centers on the inability to construct comparable measures of inequality in communist and noncommunist systems. Jackman acknowledges that:

> "The decisions over which countries to include leads to the defacto exclusion of all countries with communist regimes." While some data are available on income equality for such countries, Kuznets has argued that comparisons of this data across communist and noncommunist regimes is not altogether meaningful because data are collected according to different criteria within the two categories (Jackman, 1975, p. 10).

Since communist systems do not provide convenient measures of inequality, we are unable to examine the actual distribution of economic well-being among peoples living in such systems. Yet these systems came into being largely on the promise of equality. The result is an academic equivalent of the Brezhnev doctrine: Inequality can only be studied in noncommunist countries because socialist ideology asserts that inequality has been eliminated in communist countries. And if equality has been eliminated by ideology, there is no need to collect data on inequality in communist nations or to include communist nations in studies of inequality.

The Brezhnev doctrine analogy is not so strained when we consider that the major political phenomenon for which cross-national equality measures have been employed as explanatory variables are violence, insurgency, and revolution (Nagel, 1974; Muller and Seligson, 1987). Muller and Seligson find that income inequality, as distinct from maldistribution of land, is a major determinant of political violence especially when accompanied by rising levels of economic development, ethnic separatism and repressive political regimes. They included only three socialist bloc nations in their analysis—the German Democratic

Republic, Hungary, and Poland. These nations were reported to be the most equalitarian of the nations for which these authors had data on income distributions. According to the hypothesis being tested, these three nations should have been the most stable and peaceful regimes, free of political unrest or violence! Obviously these regimes are not stable, yet the authors do not provide any explanations for these anomalies.

## WEALTH, MARKETS, AND EQUALITY

What theoretical justification might exist to challenge the conventional wisdom about the greater equality inherent in socialist economics and to assert the superiority of market economics in achieving more equalitarian distributions of economic benefits?

Simon Kuznets (1955) was among the first modern social scientists to explore fully the relationships between economic development and equality. In the early stage of economic development, Kuznets reasoned that inequality increased, because wealthier segments of the population accumulated and saved a large portion of the increased productivity. Early rapid economic growth creates inequality especially when growth is concentrated in a single sector of the economy. An accompaniment of economic development is a shift away from agriculture, "a process usually referred to as industrialization and urbanization" (p. 7), and the migration of people to urban centers where the new wealth is accumulating. This creates inequality between rural and urban populations. But as development continues, "counteracting factors" gradually reverse the early relationship between development and inequality. Over time economic development leads to greater equality, because new wealth is created by previously poor segments of the population who take advantage of new opportunities. The early wealthy stay wealthy in absolute terms, but they do not get wealthier in relative terms. The less wealthy

increase both their absolute and relative share of the nation's product, and social inequality decreases with higher levels of development. This occurs because "the very nature of a dynamic economy with relative freedom of individual opportunity" (p. 10) stimulates more and more people to strive to share in the growth. Inequality is also reduced by the spread of development from one sector of the economy to other sectors. Kuznets buttressed his argument with some of the first comparative cross-national observations of inequality. With limited data he observed that: (a) inequality is greater in the least developed nations; (b) inequality in developed nations has decreased over time; (c) inequality in less developed nations is similar to inequality in developed nations at earlier stages of their growth (Kuznets, 1963). The Kuznets inverted U-shaped hypothesis—initial increases in GNP increases inequality but continuing development greatly reduces inequality—is now a familiar staple in the developmental literature.

The positive relationship between economic development and equality suggested by Kuznets has been tested by many scholars (e.g., Cutright, 1967; Adelman and Morris, 1973; Paukert, 1973; Jackman, 1975; Ward, 1978). All of these studies report consistently strong relationships between economic development and equality. For example, Ward (1978) shows that among the nations of the world: "Inequality tends to decrease as the level of development increases. As there are *no* societies. . .which have both a low level of inequality and a low level of development, neither are there *any* with a high level of inequality and a high level of development" (p. 66). Most of the evidence derives from cross-sectional observations of nations at various levels of economic development; but a few studies (e.g., Cherney, 1974) have attempted longitudinal studies of changing income distributions over time, and they have reached essentially the same conclusion about the positive effect of economic development on equality. Other conditions found to be associated with income inequality include illiteracy and lack of education, high birth rates, a large agricultural share of the national produce, and a large rural population.

The only significant reservations to Kuznets' original set of hypotheses center on the curvilinearity and slope of the relationship between development and equality. It is argued by Field (1980) on the basis of his survey of change over time in thirteen developing nations that no initial increase in inequality is mandated by economic development. Others have observed that additional economic growth in developed countries produces only very modest declines in inequality (Paukert, 1973; Field, 1980). After a certain threshold level of economic development is achieved, further increases in development do not necessarily produce additional increases in equality. The recent experience in the United States provides an illustration of the threshold notion; continued economic growth over the past few decades has not significantly reduced the remaining inequality.

While there is substantial confirmation of the cross-sectional relationship between increasing GNP and reduced inequality, short-term time series analysis of the dynamics of this relationship (Ahluwalia, 1976; Field, 1980) has not always produced the hypothesized results. Short-term economic growth is not always accompanied by observable increases in equality. In some nations recent economic growth has been accompanied by greater equality (e.g., Taiwan, Singapore, Costa Rica, South Korea), but in other countries (Mexico, Argentina, Brazil, Philippines) growth has failed to reduce inequality (Field, 1980). Ahluwalia offers an explanation:

> There is a distinct suspicion that there are short-term forces operating independently of the long-term phenomenon which generate higher inequality as a consequence of faster growth. For example, if growth is concentrated in particular regions or sectors (as is very likely to be the case), then lags in labor mobility may create factor market disequilibria which generate significant income differentials. It is easily seen that such differentials need to be distinguished from income differentials reflecting long-term structural factors such as the scarcity of labor skills. They are

superimposed on the structurally determined income differentials and may be seen (and are often defended) as necessary lubricants to overcome some of the frictional resistance to the pursuit of high growth rates (p. 129).

## PUBLIC POLICY AND EQUALITY

What role do political factors play in the reduction of inequality? The absolute size of the economic surplus, the new opportunities for participation created by growth and sectoral diversity in economic growth, are not the only explanations for increasing equality in developed societies. Kuznets himself suggests that "legislative and political intervention" (p. 11) may also contribute to reductions in inequality. Later Lenski (1966) and Cutright (1967) elaborated on the contributions of public policy toward diminished inequality. According to Cutright:

> So long as the economy is unable to produce a large surplus, the political and economic elite can enforce inequality to ensure the existence of a surplus and their own position of privilege. Populations in industrialized societies will demand equal distribution of the society's product, and because the amount of the surplus is so vast, the elite can afford to give up some of the surplus and allow the masses to rise above the subsistence level. Societies with high levels of economic development will have an elite willing to make concessions and a population demanding equality. If economic growth is maintained, the elite can continue to take an ever increasing absolute (but not relative) share of the wealth produced by the economy (pp. 564–565).

Moreover, Cutright argues that *democratic* processes will facilitate a reduction in inequality:

> Political structures that facilitate access by the masses to the elite will decrease inequality. High levels of "constitutionalization" will decrease inequality because the power of the many to organize against the few will be guaranteed. Constitutionalization in industrial societies may be measured by the extent to which the society has extended the modern concept of "citizenship" to

all segments of the population, and thus identified human as opposed to property rights as the basis of the distributive process. To the extent that citizenship is broadly accepted, the elite will be forced to respond to the claims of the non-elite classes for a greater share of the national product. As political structures increasingly incorporate this modern concept of "citizenship," governments will enter the distributive process and counteract the self-interest of the economic elite (p. 565).

Cutright supports his theory by producing significant regression coefficients for a "political representation index" on inequality in 19 low, 13 middle, and 12 high GNP nation samples. He treats eight communist nations separately showing that economic development itself is the major influence on equality within these nations.

But income does not get redistributed by political representation itself. The crucial theoretical link between representation and redistribution is *public policy.* Ward (1978) explains:

> Public policy is one of the most important mechanisms likely to promote the translation of economic product into more equalitarian distributions of that product (p. 90).

And the most important and consistent finding in comparative cross-national policy research is that the social welfare policies of communist and capitalist nations at the same level of economic development are essentially the same (Cutright, 1965; Pryor, 1977; Wilensky, 1975). It is true that social welfare and educational policy efforts are associated with reductions in inequality (Ward, 1978, ch. 4). But these policy efforts are no greater in communist than in capitalist countries. In an interpretation of his own findings, Pryor observed:

> Such results can be interpreted in several ways. They suggest to me that the policy dilemmas facing decision makers of public consumption expenditures are quite similar in all nations, regardless of system. Such policy problems include: the desirability of financing a service through the public rather than the private sector; the proper relationship of different public consumption expenditures to the tax revenues

which must be raised; in balancing citizen's demand for particular services with the adjudged interests of the state. If the basic economic circumstances (in Marxist terminology 'productive forces') are similar and if the policy dilemmas are similar, it should not be surprising that the decisions are also roughly similar. As a study between market and centrally planned economies, one important conclusion stands out: in regard to public consumption expenditures there are few essential differences between nations of the two systems, at least on the macro-economic level on which the analysis is carried out.

Sociologist Harold L. Wilensky (1975) confirmed the findings of Cutright, Pryor, and others that nations at the same level of economic development provide roughly the same levels and types of social security and welfare services, whether these nations are socialist or capitalist. Another interesting question posed by Wilensky is whether military spending is greater among capitalist nations than socialist nations. It turns out that "military spending as a fraction of the GNP is uncorrelated with either types of political system or level of economic development."

In summary, we have good theoretical reasons and substantial evidence challenging the idea that socialist systems provide greater equality than market systems. Equality is primarily a result of economic development, not type of political or economic system. Capitalist systems are more successful in stimulating economic development than communist systems. Communist and capitalist systems at the same level of economic development make essentially the same efforts in social welfare and education policy. Thus, there is no reason to believe that socialist systems are more equalitarian than capitalist systems at the same level of economic development.

## CLASSIFYING SOCIALIST AND CAPITALIST SYSTEMS

In order to undertake any systematic observation of the real-world relationship between socialism and equality, we must first define what we mean by socialist and capitalist systems and proceed to categorize world political economies in these terms. Gastil (1986) provides a useful classification system for the world's political economies which posits a continuum from developed socialist states to developed capitalist states. . . .

Developed socialist states strive programmatically to place the entire national economy under direct government control. States such as the USSR and Cuba may allow modest private economic activity but this is by exception and rights to property may be revoked at any time. Gastil (1986) refers to these economic systems as "socialist inclusive." However, many third world nations with dual economies, that is a modern sector and a preindustrial sector, have different sets of economic policies and goals in each sector. A socialist third world state usually has nationalized all of the modern sector (except perhaps-some foreign investment) and claims government ownership of the land with perhaps only administrative assignment of it to families or cooperatives. The leadership of these states may have the same goals as the leaders of inclusive socialist states, but the traditional sectors of the economy have not yet been socialized. These "socialist noninclusive" states generally have a small socialized modern economy and a large preindustrial, traditionally-organized economy. Other "mixed socialist" states (including the People's Republic of China under the leadership of Deng Xiaoping) have nationalized their industrial sector but they have established a market system for their agricultural sector which may rely on cooperatives or even family business. They may proclaim themselves to be socialist but large portions of their economy remain in the private domain.

Developed capitalist states rely principally on markets for the production and distribution of goods and services. Taxes may be high but they are not confiscatory, and government economic activity is generally limited to subsidization, redistribution, and regulation. Third world capitalist states have a capitalist modern sector and a traditionalist agricultural sector. Gastil (1986) labels these states "capitalist

noninclusive" if more than fifty percent of the population remains in the traditional sector. This traditional sector may be family, communal, or feudal, but the direction of change as development proceeds is capitalist.

Capitalist states grade over into capitalist-statist or mixed-capitalist states. Capitalist-statist countries have very large government enterprises, as in the case of Mexico and Saudi Arabia, perhaps because of elite philosophy or major dependence on a key resource such as oil. Government plays a major role in the economy, yet the economy is organized on market principles. Mixed capitalist systems such as Israel and Sweden provide many goods and services (up to half of the GNP) through government corporations and "private ownership of property is sacrificed to egalitarian purposes."

## OBSERVING INEQUALITY IN WORLD POLITICAL ECONOMIES

We found only a single empirically based assertion that "socialist countries display markedly greater equality than others as shown by the positive and significant coefficients on dummy variables in equations" (Ahluwalia, 1976, p. 32). This conclusion is based on a dummy variable identifying six socialist countries in a study of income distributions in 62 nations. No discussion or explanation is offered, nor are the six socialist countries identified.

But if we observe inequality, as measured by Ward (1978), in capitalist and socialist nations, as described by Gastil (1986), we find no discernible relationship between socialism and equality. Rather, inequality is inextricably linked to low levels of economic development. The poorest nations of the world are the most unequal while the wealthiest are the most equal. Among the developed nations the authoritarian socialist governments of Eastern Europe do *not* provide for any more equitable distribution of income than their western counterparts. Ward concludes: "One of the most interesting characteristics of world political economies is the clustering of

European nations, all of which have low levels of inequality—irrespective of economic organization. . . . The level of inequality in market economies is roughly identical to that of nonmarket economies" (pp. 44-45). But socialist economies do sacrifice individual freedom and economic well-being. That much of the conventional academic wisdom is true. . . .

## CONCLUSIONS

These relationships are well-known among developmental economists and easily replicated from readily available sources of cross-national data. Why, then, do we confront assertions in the academic literature, notably Lindblom's influential and otherwise enlightening classic, *Politics and Markets*, that socialist regimes are equalitarian?

Socialism is not merely a way of organizing an economy; it is also a secular religion and "to the extent that socialism retains this mythic quality, it cannot be disconfirmed by empirical evidence in the minds of its adherents" (Berger, 1986). Vladimir Voinivich, a Soviet writer exiled in 1980, in his Orwellian fantasy about Moscow in the 21st century, describes a deity consisting of Christ, Marx, and Lenin; he wishes to convey the necessity of accepting socialism as a religion (Voinivich, 1986). Our evidence supports this view. There are few examples of political scientists asserting propositions with so little evidence as they do in describing the economic consequences of socialism.

### Author's References

ADELMAN, IRMA and CYNTHIA TAFT MORRIS. 1973. *Economic Growth and Social Equity in Developing Countries*. Stanford: Stanford University Press.

AHLUWALIA MONTEK. 1976. Income Distribution and Development. *American Economic Review* (May), 128-135.

BERGER, PETER L. 1986. *The Capitalist Revolution: Fifty Propositions About Capitalism*. New York: Basic Books.

CUTRIGHT, PHILLIPS. 1965. Political Structure, Economic Development, and National Social Security Programs. *American Journal of Sociology*, 70 (March), 537-550.

CUTRIGHT, PHILLIPS. 1967. Inequality: A Cross-National Analysis. *American Sociological Review*, 32 (August), 562-577.

GASTIL, RAYMOND D. 1986. *Freedom in the World*. New York: Freedom House.

HIBBS, DOUGLASS A. 1973. *Mass Political Violence*. New York: John Wiley.

JACKMAN, ROBERT W. 1975. *Politics and Social Equality: A Comparative Analysis*. New York: John Wiley.

KUZNETS, SIMON. 1955. Economic Growth and Income Inequality. *American Economic Review*, 45 (March), 1-28.

LENSKI, GERHARDT. 1966. *Power and Privilege: A Theory of Stratification*. New York: McGraw-Hill.

LINDBLOM, CHARLES E. 1977. *Politics and Markets: The World's Political-Economic Systems*. New York: Basic Books.

LYDALL, HAROLD. 1968. *The Structure of Earnings*. Landon: Oxford University Press.

MULLER, EDWARD N. and MITCHEL A. SELIGSON. 1987. Inequality and Insurgency. *American Political Science Review*, 81 (June), 425-452.

NAGEL, JACK H. 1974. Inequality and Discontent. *World Politics*, 26 (July), 453-472.

PAUKERT, F. 1973. Income Distribution at Different Levels of Development: A Survey of the Evidence. *International Labor Review* (August–September), 97-125.

PRYOR, FREDERIC R. 1977. *Property and Industrial Organization in Communist and Capitalist Nations*. Bloomington: Indiana University Press.

WARD, MICHAEL D. 1978. *The Political Economy of Distribution*. New York: Elsevier.

WILENSKY, HAROLD. 1975. *The Welfare State and Equality*. Berkeley: University of California Press.

VOINIVICH, VLADIMIR. 1986. *Moscow 2042*. New York: Harcourt Brace Jovanovich.

# PART FOUR

# Political Change

One of the most important historical developments of the twentieth century has been the achievement of independence by peoples who had been brought under the political control of European states in the course of the preceding two centuries. At least one-third of the population of the world is involved in this surge toward national independence. The Europeans were able to conquer and administer vast areas of Asia, Africa, and the Middle East because of their crushing superiority in military technology, in turn based on a vastly more developed economy. The Indonesians, Indochinese, Indians, and Africans simply were unable to resist the comparatively small but modern armed forces of the European powers intent upon expanding their influence in the world. The epoch of imperialism registered European advance and domination in all areas of human activity—economic, military, and even cultural. During the era of imperialism, political analysts confined their attention mainly to Europe and North America. Little attention was paid to other parts of the world, except by students of colonial administration.

Colonialism collapsed in the wake of the Second World War. The chief colonial powers—Great Britain, France, and Holland—were exhausted by the conflict and unable to engage in any new military ventures. Their rule over possessions in Asia and southeast Asia had been shattered by Japanese armies, which demonstrated to the world that the Europeans were not invincible. In order to gain the loyalty of India in the face of a threatened Japanese invasion, the British were compelled to promise independence. France and Holland were unable to reimpose their sovereignty in Indochina and Indonesia by force of arms. The countries of Western Europe lost their predominant position in 1945. Power shifted to two non-European states: the United States and the Soviet Union, both of whom began to court the support of former colonial peoples. The European powers were thus at a severe disadvantage in relation to their former colonies. They were not permitted by the new dominant world powers to attempt reconquest, and in any case they were no longer capable of doing so.

The new relationship among the principal areas of the world is comparable in importance to the French Revolution, the industrialization of Europe and North America, and the triumph of communism in Russia. Each of these historical events changed the social and cultural environment and led to new forms of political power and organization. The resurgence of the formerly subjugated peoples of Asia and Africa symbolizes a new kind of world crisis and requires a new focus of interest in our study of comparative politics.

But political change is not confined to the developing nations. All political systems are undergoing a rapid evolution, including those of the advanced industrial societies; change is inherent in the political process. We have already seen that in all political systems there must be institutions through which claims and demands are translated into decisions. Existing conditions are then inevitably modified. New groups assume a position of power and influence while others lose their prerogatives; new rights are proclaimed and new services provided. Throughout the nineteenth century, for example, the social groups brought into being by the industrial revolution struggled for the attainment of political rights. In the twentieth century we are witnessing a similar struggle for political emancipation in the rest of the world, as well as assumption of collective responsibility for economic development and social welfare.

The nature of change, the rate at which change takes place, and the specific correlates of change are not yet fully understood. Nor is it easy to tell in advance the direction change is likely to take. According to the Marxists, societies evolve through clearly defined stages, from feudalism through capitalism to socialism, as a result of economic pressures. Under certain conditions change is wrought by violence and revolution because the groups and classes that wield power are unwilling or unable to adapt to new conditions. Innovation may also bring about sweeping changes in social and political institutions. All societies that have undergone the technological and scientific revolutions of the past two centuries have been transformed, regardless of their particular cultures and political systems. At the present time economic, social, and political change is occurring at an accelerated rate throughout the world. Political leaders almost everywhere are now committed to a drastic overhaul of their societies. They are attempting to popularize new values and norms, and to create new attitudes in order to achieve industrialization, prosperity, and equality. There is an unparalleled urgency in this movement, which is taking place in a variety of ways and through a number of political forms. A major challenge confronting students of comparative politics is the development of analytic categories in terms of which the component elements of change can be understood and societies undergoing rapid change fruitfully compared.

## TRADITIONAL AND MODERN SOCIETIES

It will be useful for analytic purposes to distinguish between two "ideal types" or models of societies: the *traditional* and the *modern*. These terms do not imply any value judgment. A traditional society may include a large number of highly educated people whose level of culture and social grace is higher than that of the mass of inhabitants of any modern society. Furthermore, these terms refer only to abstract "constructs"; they do not describe any existing societies. For example, the United States is a predominantly modern society, but one with many traditionally oriented groups in its population.

The distinction here suggested is a familiar one in the literature of the social sciences. Similar classificatory schemes have been suggested by such eminent theoreticians as Sir Henry Maine, Ferdinand Tönnies, and especially Max Weber. Thus, Weber suggested that claims to legitimacy may be based on:

1. Rational grounds—resting on a belief in the "legality" of patterns of normative rules and the right of those elevated to authority under such rules to issue commands (legal authority);
2. Traditional grounds—resting on an established belief in the sanctity of immemorial traditions and the legitimacy of the status of those exercising authority under them (traditional authority); or finally,
3. Charismatic grounds—resting on devotion to the specific and exceptional sanctity, heroism, or exemplary character of an individual person, and of the normative patterns or order revealed or ordained by him (charismatic authority).[1]

One implication which may be drawn from Weber's scheme is that the three types correspond to historical development from simple to more complex societies. In the former, obedience is to the person of the chief, and the values of the family permeate the whole social system. A society breaks out of this stage usually under the leadership of a charismatic chief, who is obeyed because of his personal or heroic qualities. In modern societies obedience is to the legal order; it is associated with the office more than with the person who occupies it.

In both traditional and modern societies the individual participates in the political process through groups or associations, but there are fundamental differences as regards their nature and importance. Traditional societies are characterized by the predominance of the family and family-type groups (that is, primary organizations) in which the members are in a face-to-face relationship. An individual's status in the society is determined by his or her family's status. He or she is nurtured, cared for, educated, and protected by the family, which tends to be a self-sufficient economic as well as social unit. The dominant economic activity is agriculture, which requires the participation of the family as a cohesive group. Virtually the entire population (and not 1 in 10, as in modern societies) is engaged in agriculture, the hunt, or fishing in order to provide sustenance. There is little knowledge of science or technology, no opportunity to accumulate reserves of food, and no leisure class able to devote itself to the arts and culture. The people live close to nature, even as part of nature. They are almost completely at the mercy of the seasons, storms, droughts, and rains. Superstition and magic permeate the society. People seek to relate events in their own lives to external occurrences, the stars, or the seasons.

Family values—personal loyalty, authority, reverence—pervade the whole social structure. The state tends to resemble the family, with the king or chief of state in the role of father, whose paternal authority derives from a superhuman source. The various families gathered together in clans or tribes are his children, bound to obey for the same reason that each elder in the tribe is obeyed by the younger leaders. Insofar as a bureaucracy comes into existence to administer the will of the chief, it is like a huge household—with nepotism an expected practice.

There have been, historically, a wide range of types *within* the general category of "traditional societies," from the subsistence agricultural and pastoral societies of primitive tribes in Africa, to the military structure of Egypt, the land empires of Asia Minor and China, the island civilization of the Aegean, Ancient Greece, and Rome, and the feudal age. All of these societies, however, preceded the technological and industrial breakthrough of the eighteenth century.

Technical and scientific progress brought in their wake far-reaching change in social and political organization. The old agricultural subsistence economy was replaced by an industrial marketplace economy. In the model modern society, individuals gain their livelihood not within the family, but in a factory, commercial enterprise, or office. Population concentrates in the great urban centers, creating a host of administrative problems (sanitation, transportation, education, etc.). Modern societies are characterized by the predominance of *secondary organizations*—large specialized and impersonal associations like labor unions, corporations, farm cooperatives, political parties, universities, and churches. Unlike the family, the secondary organizations have large numbers of members who need not be in a face-to-face relationship, are joined by a voluntary action of the prospective members, and carry on highly specialized activities. Most of the former functions of the family are assumed by the new associations (education by the schools, charity by the state, religious instruction by the church, and exchange of produce by the banks and marketplace). The state itself tends to take on the character of these secondary organizations: It becomes large, complex, impersonal, and increasingly rational. Old ideas of divine right fall into disrepute, and more rational themes of legitimacy (for example, popular sovereignty) come into vogue. The family itself is grievously weakened and is based more and more on consent and mutual interest.

After a period of evolution, the state expands to meet the needs of an industrialized economy. The civil service, for example, cannot fulfill its obligations as the closed preserve of a single family or clan, but must recruit able people from all layers of society. As Max Weber has pointed out, a modern bureaucracy is "rational"; that is, it recruits universally and boasts a system of tenure, grade classifications, and fixed salaries. Political conflict resembles the marketplace itself: Each specialized group puts forth its offers and demands, with the state acting as a broker. Individuals express their interests primarily through the secondary organizations to which they belong.

Let us briefly summarize the differences between the two ideal types. *Traditional* societies are characterized by subsistence economies; face-to-face social structures in which the family predominates; cultural systems that emphasize heredity, devotion, and mystery; and a highly personalized political system that is virtually an extension of the joint family. *Modern* societies are the exact opposite in all these respects. They are characterized by industrial economies; complex and impersonal social structures; a culture that emphasizes the values of science, knowledge, and achievement; and a highly bureaucratized political system that is legitimized through rational processes, such as elections.

Typological analysis is only a first step in the study of modernization. In effect, it constitutes a checklist for the observer, pointing to relationships among social, economic, cultural, and political factors that might otherwise escape attention. It also makes possible an assessment of the pace and extent of modernization in any given society. But the explanatory power of typologies is limited. The complexities of world history, the rise and decline of great powers and of civilizations, and the shifting balance of international power cannot be reduced to a handful of sociological concepts. Modernization provokes crises to which there are any number of possible reactions or solutions within a political system. It is perhaps most fruitful to consider modernization as a complex process that produces a series of challenges to both modern and traditional societies. How these challenges are met is the major concern of the student of political change.

## COMPARATIVE ANALYSIS OF MODERN POLITICAL SYSTEMS

All nations on the modern side of the scale may be compared in terms of their distinctive experience of modernization. Each of these nations at one time was traditional; in each case the traditional society was undermined and eventually displaced by new forms of organization. As we have pointed out in the earlier introductory essays, the process of modernization inevitably causes a series of political crises. Whatever the nature of the traditional society and whatever the nature of the modern political institutions (whether one-, two-, or multiparty, presidential or cabinet, democratic or authoritarian), at least three political crises must be surmounted in the course of modernization: the crises of legitimacy, participation, and conflict management. The way in which these crises occur and are dealt with is of great consequence for the functioning of modern political systems.

The crisis of legitimacy is inevitable because of the close link between political values and the systems they serve to justify. The kind of values that permeate a traditional society, such as divine right or rule by a hereditary aristocracy, must undergo modification as that society is transformed. Throughout Western Europe, for example, the breakup of feudalism was accompanied by a shift in the basis of political legitimacy. Everywhere the rights of monarchs were circumscribed and the power of parliaments increased. Whether monarchy continued to exist with reduced prerogatives or was replaced by a republic, the political systems of Europe sought to justify themselves in some way as the expression of popular will and national sovereignty. The crisis of legitimacy also involved the status of the church, which was generally a bulwark of the traditional ruling classes.

A new but related crisis comes into being with the rapid growth of industry. Power continues to be wielded by a landed aristocracy, the church, and the wealthier strata. But new social groups, above all the industrial middle classes and the working class, enter upon the political scene. These classes are officially excluded from power in the traditional society; they demand entry into the political system, and they gain this entry by organizing themselves behind and through political parties. How this is accomplished—whether through slow and successful integration or with violence and grudging acceptance—makes a deep mark upon the political life of the country. In some cases the working class is never fully incorporated into the political system, and in countries like France and Italy large communist parties constitute a permanent opposition of principle. In communist systems the problem of integration is solved by eliminating the aristocracy, small peasantry, and middle classes as autonomous political forces.

Whether in stable parliamentary democracies, unstable parliamentary democracies, or authoritarian regimes, mature industrial societies pose grave problems for the political system. Specialized groups proliferate within both the middle and working classes; the scientists, managers, bureaucrats, military, and intellectuals compete with party leaders for a share of decision-making power. The state must organize itself so as to cope with these strong interest groups, integrate them into the political system, and satisfy their minimal demands. As the technology becomes more complex, the task of the political leaders requires more and more technical knowledge and competence, as well as the ability to manage the distinctive political tensions of highly industrialized societies.

Comparative analysis of modern political systems requires broad knowledge of their historical evolution. The student should compare the way in which each of the crises of modernization was handled in individual systems, and the extent of "carry-over" from one crisis to another. Many observers have suggested that the *timing* of the crises of modernization is of critical importance. Did these crises occur one by one, with a considerable period elapsing between crises? In these cases the political system has a greater opportunity to resolve them singly and thus acquire stability. Or were the crises "telescoped"? Did the political system have to confront the crises of participation and conflict management while the controversy over its basic institutions and values continued? In such cases a much greater load is placed upon the system, and an immense collective effort is required to create dynamic, effective, and stable government. Special attention should be paid to the problems of mature industrial societies. Are similar techniques being used in all modern political systems in dealing with massive technological development, urbanization, and the maintenance

of individual creativity in mass societies? Or are there significant differences between democratic and authoritarian systems? Are there differences among such parliamentary democracies as the United States and the countries of Western Europe? Between the Soviet Union on the one hand and China and Cuba on the other? Modernization theory thus provides the student a framework for inquiry; it is the starting point for the formulation of hypotheses concerning political life in all industrialized societies.

## COMPARATIVE ANALYSIS OF DEVELOPING NATIONS

Modernization theory can also be used for a study of contemporary trends in developing nations. There is a clear tendency for these societies to move from the traditional category into a *transitional period* during which they acquire many of the characteristics of modern society while retaining some traditional features. But it is impossible to foretell the exact development of any of these societies. For example, the so-called uncommitted nations are doubtless on the way to modernization. But there are two chief prototypes of advanced industrial states in the world: the Western countries (especially the United States) and the Communist nations (notably the Soviet Union). Developing countries could pattern themselves after either model of modernity.

Comparative study could usefully be focused on the decision-making or political elite: their social origin, position with respect to the masses, technical or educational qualifications for governing, relationship with the important social groups within the nation (for example, landowners, army, church, civil service, and intellectuals), and characteristic ideologies. At least four different leadership types can be distinguished in the developing nations: traditional, liberal, authoritarian, and radical.

The *traditional* leaders derive their authority from historical status and prestige and from one predominant form of property—land. They constitute a self-perpetuating group in that recruitment comes from a small circle (either royalty or landowning nobility) by virtue of birth. Their values vary from one system to another but generally reflect a family structure —the emphasis is on kinship, loyalty, devotion, duty, and courage. They are averse to changes that will endanger their economic and social position. They are apt to react unfavorably to any economic or technological innovations that might weaken the political system. They insist upon the preservation of prevailing modes of political recruitment and hence are hostile to popular participation in politics. They are opposed to industrialization and to its political and social implications.

The *liberal* leaders are in favor of "reforming out of existence" the traditionalist-oriented economy, society, and political system. They welcome industrialization and mass participation in political affairs. They accept both the goals and the methods of the Western constitutional democracies. Thus, the liberals desire political reforms, establishment of a constitutional order with guarantees of individual rights, the articulation of interests within an accepted legal order, and the gradual displacement of the traditionalist groups from positions of power. They wish to create the proper conditions within which meaningful political choices can be made by the whole people. Recruitment of the liberal elite is usually from the professional and middle classes, particularly among those who have attended European and American universities. The traditionalists and liberals tend to be allied in their respect for property rights but split over the question of democratic reforms and modernization.

*Authoritarian* leaders, like the liberals, tend to accept democracy as an ideal or goal, but they do not believe it can be achieved by indiscriminate adoption of all features of Western systems. They distinguish between "formal" or "procedural" democracy (elections, parliaments, organized opposition, etc.) and "real" or "substantive" democracy (equal opportunity, economic development, moral regeneration).

An active opposition only obstructs the efforts of the government to bring about "real" democracy and hence must be suppressed. The emphasis is therefore on national unity and the direction of the efforts of the masses by an educated, informed, morally responsible elite. Frequently the hope is held out that the people, one day in the future, after rapid economic progress has been accomplished, will be ready for representative government of the Western type. Authoritarian leaders, like the liberals, come mainly from the professional and middle classes and occasionally from the landed aristocracy.

The fourth type of leadership is *radical*. Inspired by a revolutionary ideology, the radicals are committed to drastic and rapid change of the economic and social structure. They organize their followers in a manner that will enable them to take the system by assault. The classic pattern is the single mass party led by professional revolutionaries, along lines laid down by Lenin. Radical leadership comes from the "alienated" groups, particularly the intelligentsia, and it appeals to the disaffected elements of the population—the peasants, the students, and the city workers. It is in favor of industrialization, but at the expense of the liberal values—individual rights, political freedoms, and private property. Above all it imposes collective goals upon the total society and disciplines the masses in order to achieve those goals. The main differences between the authoritarians and radicals are of degree and social origin: Radicals want more change more rapidly, with greater social control and discipline, and they tend to be drawn from less favored social classes. The radicals are also much more suspicious of the Western powers and tend to seek aid as well as ideological inspiration from the Communist camp.

The "benefits" of modernization have been felt throughout the world in the form of manufactured goods, moving pictures, radio broadcasts, and so on. All native populations have had their expectations aroused or modified as a consequence: The economic structure of traditional systems has been undermined; land ownership is no longer a secure base for a political elite; new economic activities have created new social groups and stimulated others who view the traditional elite as a stumbling block on the road to further economic development.

Industrialization, however, is viewed only as a means for the attainment of economic goals and the satisfaction of wants. Its prerequisites—the development of skills; the training of the masses; and the establishment of an orderly pattern of social intercourse, particularly discipline and regular work in the factory—are understood only by a small group of political leaders. Industrialization is often equated with a vision of plenty in the foreseeable future, and as such it becomes a potent political force. The discipline required for industrialization, however, is appreciated by very few, and perhaps only by the "radicals."

As the conflict develops over demands for industrialization, the political position of the traditional elite becomes precarious. Their legitimacy is brought into question. There follows a period of instability, overt defiance of authority, and sporadic uprisings. The new political leaders—liberal, authoritarian, and radical—vie for control. A limited number of alternatives for future political development present themselves.

One alternative is the maintenance of traditional social organization and leadership. This alternative, though always possible, is becoming anachronistic. Most of the traditional forces are fighting a losing battle for survival. The independence movement is associated with an ideology calling for social and economic reforms that are inconsistent with the interests of the traditional forces. Mobilization of the masses in the struggle for independence brings with it profound modifications in the economic and social structure. Change may be held off by a temporary alliance between the traditional and new leaderships and groups for the realization of independence, or by the inability of one particular group to impose its ideology, or by foreign intervention. But the will for change in a society generally indicates that the emerging political elite will use every means available to

eliminate the traditional leaders who are still desperately clinging to the last vestiges of their rule.

At a certain stage, the liberal elements come into sharp conflict with the authoritarian and radical elements. The liberals advocate a relatively slow pace of structural modifications and industrialization, technological improvements, a rising standard of living, the gradual training of managerial and labor groups, progressive land reforms, and involvement of the masses in politics through the extension of literacy and education. But these demands are made with little urgency, and the envisaged manner of their implementation is permissive rather than coercive. The liberal elite attempts to create the conditions within which the individual can become capable of choice, which is always considered in the best tradition of liberalism to be an individual act. The system should provide opportunities for the individual and only "hinder the hindrances."

The authoritarians and radicals, on the other hand, urge coercive and authoritarian practices in order to bring about quickly the same overall goals. Suspicious of the continuing strength of the traditionalist elements (particularly among the peasants), they insist on rapid mobilization of the masses in a manner that will wrench them from their former way of life. Distrustful of the colonial powers, they seek to industrialize rapidly by using their own human resources and by accepting aid from the Communist countries. This political leadership, therefore, uses force and not persuasion, seeks the outright organization of the masses rather than a gradual process of political education, and stresses social discipline rather than general rules, norms, and guarantees of individual freedom.

In the contest for power, the liberal leaders are at a severe disadvantage. In relatively backward economies, the application of liberal economic doctrine does not result in rapid industrialization or structural change. Development of a market economy favors the merchant class and production of consumer goods, and it fails to satisfy the pent-up demand of large social groups. Subordination of social goals to individual choice only increases the feeling of social injustice among the masses. All too often, it leads to "private wealth and public poverty." Politically, liberalism has no slogan that can activate and mobilize the masses. Most important, liberalism as a social force fails to inculcate new social incentives for the purpose of industrialization. In brief, the liberal elite is generally unable to reach the people, to capture their imagination, and to lead them into the modern era. On the other hand, the great advantage enjoyed by the authoritarian and especially the radical leaders is that they create a system of controls under which industrialization may take place.

Of course, it is impossible to predict the exact course of events in the developing nations. New forces may come to the fore, perhaps slowing down the tempo of modernization and permitting the traditional elite to rally. Industrialization may follow the Western historical experience and lead to the establishment of a legal order within which individual freedoms are guaranteed. The technician and the manager may win out over the party boss and the commissar—perhaps even in existing totalitarian systems! Indications are, however, that the new nations are departing from the norms and institutions of Western democracies. The liberal elite is finding it exceptionally difficult to attract mass support. Communism and fascism seem to be models for the most dynamic leadership groups in the new nations, even though they may follow their own paths.

Comparative study of change, revolution, and modernization obviously calls our attention to the dynamics of the political process. Are there any similarities in conditions that precede revolutions? Are the new nations in a "revolutionary" situation like that of France before 1789 or Russia before 1917? Comparative study may focus on specific social groups—the intellectuals, the working class, the peasantry—to see how they react to the traditional elite and to what extent they are influenced by revolutionary ideas. Comparison should also be made of political evolution in the developing nations. The liberal elite is more successful in gaining mass support in such nations as the Philippines and the Ivory Coast than in Ceylon and Guinea. What factors account for these similarities and differences? Analysis of political change in both industrial and traditional societies is perhaps the most serious and challenging task of contemporary political science.

## Notes

1. Max Weber, *The Theory of Social and Economic Organization* (New York: Oxford University Press, 1947), p. 328.

# CHAPTER NINE

# MODERNIZATION AND DEVELOPMENT

## 36
## The Dynamics of Modernization

*Samuel H. Beer*

### ECONOMIC MODERNIZATION

...[I have]...sought to characterize the attitudes that distinguish modern Western society from the Western societies that preceded it. I have not argued that there was a complete break. Clearly, on the contrary, there were major continuities. Indeed, I would accept Arnold J. Toynbee's argument that one of the major "intelligible fields of historical study" for the social scientist is Western Christian civilization.[1] What this means is that the continuities in European history for the past 1500 years are so fundamental as greatly to transcend the differences between the medieval and modern periods. The new attitudes, however, which with increasing prominence spread throughout Europe from the seventeenth century onward, did involve matters of very great, if not ultimate, importance.

Moreover, these ideas had consequences. The chain of effects descending from them transformed behavior and social structure, bringing into existence the distinctive traits of modern society. I wish in particular to focus

SOURCE: Samuel H. Beer, "Modern Political Development," in Samuel H. Beer, eds., *Patterns of Government: The Major Political Systems of Europe* (New York: McGraw-Hill, 1973), pp. 54-70. By permission of the author. Essay abridged by the editors.

attention upon two distinguishable, but inter-related, processes—increasing differentiation and increasing scale. Operationally, these embody the two basic orientations of modernity and by their interaction create the ever larger networks of social, economic, and political interdependence that characterize modern society. The general image of this evolution is familiar. Communities were at first small, relatively self-subsistent and similar in economy, polity, and culture—as was still the case with the village and manorial society of late medieval times. Gradually these communities were drawn together by ties of political and governmental activity, trade and industry, education and communication. This increasing interdependence introduced outside influences into the original communities, disrupting their solidarities and at the same time reshaping the fragments and binding them into vast, impersonal, highly differentiated, highly interdependent social, economic, and political wholes. Such, in brief and impressionistic terms, is the manner of creation of what Emile Durkheim called "the great society."[2]

The general formula exhibited in this process characterizes development in many different modes and different ages. Indeed, the Middle Ages displayed a process of development—we may call it "medievalization"—that also followed this general formula in the creation of its own special sort of highly developed society. My concern here is to elucidate the mechanisms of that special form of development that we call modernization—to say more precisely how the basic orientations of modernity were expressed in increasing differentiation and increasing scale and how these two processes interacted to create the large, complex networks of interdependence constituting the great society. The concepts of differentiation and scale can be used in the analysis of social, economic, or political processes. Their meaning and their manner of interaction, however, can be most readily illustrated from economic analysis, from which they originally derived. While my interest is primarily political, it will best serve the purposes of clarity to consider first the economic significance of the terms.

## The Division of Labor

In economic analysis differentiation is more commonly referred to as the *division of labor.* The eighteenth-century economist Adam Smith, who invented the term, was also the first to explore systematically its influence on productivity. On the very first page of his great work *An Inquiry into the Nature and the Causes of the Wealth of Nations* he introduces the topic, going on to illustrate it with his famous description of the pin factory in which specialization—the division of the business of making a pin into about eighteen distinct operations—increases the productive powers of labor hundreds of times over what it would be if each man worked separately, making the whole pin by himself. Smith argues that the tendency to division of labor arises from exchange, holding that it is the prospect of getting a larger return from marketing what he produces that incites the individual to raise his productivity by specialization. From this relationship it follows that "the division of labour is limited by the extent of the market." As the market is widened—for instance, by improvements in transportation—a higher degree of specialization becomes feasible, since its greater production can now be absorbed. In short, as the scale of the economy increases, so also does the division of labor within it. And as scale and differentiation increase, productivity rises.

Writing in 1776 Smith reflected—and analyzed—the experience of the first phase of economic modernization in Britain. This was the era of the "commercial revolution" when, as his analysis suggests, extension of the market (that is, increase in the scale of the economy) within Britain and abroad greatly stimulated agriculture and industry. The discovery of America, he observed,

> by opening a new and inexhaustible market to all the commodities of Europe...gave occasion to new divisions of labour and improvements of art, which, in the narrow circle of the ancient commerce, could never have taken place for want of a market to take off the greater part of their produce.

Smith was not unaware of the importance of machines and made their invention one of the principal reasons for the increase in productivity resulting from specialization. Yet he wrote before the second great phase of economic modernization in Britain, when the industrial revolution made new machinery the principal means of a vast economic advance. Writing after a hundred years of industrialization in Britain, Alfred Marshall in his *Principles of Economics* (1890) still made the division of labor central to his analysis of economic development. Like Smith he was acutely aware of the importance of scale, laying great stress on how "man's power of productive work increases with the volume of work that he does." Naturally, he was far more aware of the importance of the organization of the individual firm. But although he wrote at a time when the modern corporation was coming to be widely used and British managers were making their first large-scale experiments with industrial combinations, he still assumed that the free market controlled the firm, not vice versa.

After another long interval, which has seen "the organizational revolution" and the rise of collectivism in economics as in politics, John Kenneth Galbraith takes a very different view of the role of the market. In his *New Industrial State* (1967) he argues that the classical relation has been reversed, the great oligopolistic firms now tending to control the market rather than the market the firms. In spite of these many differences, he still finds that the division of labor is central to economic development. Writing when science has come even more prominently to the fore as the principal motor of advance, he stresses the role of technology, "the systematic application of scientific or other organized knowledge to practical tasks." Still the "most important consequence" of technology is "in forcing the division and subdivision of any such task into its component parts." The division of labor is very largely derived from specialized branches of scientific knowledge and is carried on by machines. As in the Smithian example, however, it depends upon an expansion in the scale of the economy. Only thus can its increases in productivity be used. Economies of scale resulting from such specialization are a main reason for the creation of huge business organizations and the effort to create larger trading areas such as the Common Market.

One reason these three discussions of the mechanism of economic development are interesting is that they correspond to three main periods in European economic modernization, the commercial revolution, the industrial revolution, and the organizational revolution. . . .

## Interaction of Specialization and Scale

The two processes of the mechanism of economic development are *division of labor* (or specialization) and *increase in scale*. Smith stressed the division of labor itself as the source of improvement in "the productive powers of labour." The present analysis, which finds the dynamic of economic growth in the advance of science and technology, puts the emphasis upon some step forward in scientific knowledge that, in turn, when applied to economic processes, involves their division and subdivision. Such an improvement in productivity can take place prior to an expansion of the market, as we see in the present phase of scientific advance, when

a leaping technology continually presents us with goods and services we never dreamed of, let alone demanded in the marketplace. Hence, the constant need to keep the market adjusted by the cultivation of appropriate new tastes among potential buyers.

Yet the factor of scale can also vary independently. As Smith saw it, a widening of the market stimulates further division of labor. Such an expansion of scale could be brought about by more efficient modes of transportation, as when canals and then railways opened up markets in eighteenth- and nineteenth-century Europe. It could also be brought about by political means, as when the French Revolution through an act of governmental centralization struck down local imposts and other burdens on free trade within the country. Similarly, a change in cultural standards, by producing new tastes for more consumption goods and services, could sharply stimulate economic activity.

The first proposition to derive from this analysis is that the two processes, increase in differentiation and increase in scale, can vary independently. Either type of process—for instance, a new stage of productivity resulting from greater specialization, or a new level of demand resulting from a widening of the market—can be the primary process of change. Neither theoretically nor empirically is there reason for saying that one is more important than the other. While science and technology have driven forward the productive power of the economy through new stages of specialization, so also has the growing scale of modern economies initiated new thrusts forward. The fact that each can be and has often been an independent variable should be kept in mind when we come to consider the political embodiment of these two types of social process.

The point is obvious in the case of economic development, which, depending on the situation, may be driven forward by initial changes in either specialization or scale. When these concepts are applied to other spheres, however, this dual possibility is sometimes lost sight of. In Durkheim's classic discussion, *The Division of Labor in Society,* from which I have borrowed a great deal, he makes specialization derivative. Defining "density" essentially as I have defined "scale"—that is, as the "number of social relations"—he insists that the division of labor follows from an increase in density, not vice versa.... In applying the concepts of scale and specialization to political development, it seems clear to me that we should return to the lesson of economic analysis and approach any concrete situation with an open mind, ready to find the initiation of change on either side.

The second proposition is that the two processes interact, mutually reinforcing one another. An increase in scale promotes economic specialization; an advance in specialization encourages the search for markets where the added product can be disposed of. From time to time, each has taken the lead in stimulating economic development, as when the voracious markets developed by the commercial revolution conditioned the great leaps forward in technology of the industrial revolution, and the rise in productivity in the later nineteenth century promoted the search for markets in the later stages of European imperialism. While each may vary independently, if an advance in one sphere is to be maintained, it must meet with an appropriate and concomitant response in the other. This "functional" relationship does not in itself constitute a causal connection. It is, however, readily translated into activities that do bring about effects with regard to technological advance or market expansion, as the case may be. Such a mechanism of interaction, it may also be observed, is properly called a mechanism. It is not an instance of the influence of ideas. On the contrary, it is a type of process in which "pressures," "opportunities," and "structures" are the basis for explaining the generation of change. The cultural orientations of modernity motivate distinctively new types of behavior. But once these floods of consequence have been sent forth into the world, they interact with profound effect on one another in ways that may be only dimly understood or barely perceived and not at all intended by contemporaries. The industrial revolution, the rise of the factory system, the

creation of the great manufacturing city were only in part—in small part—the intentional creations of their time.

The third proposition concerns the overall result of development. Together the increase in specialization and the increase in scale constitute a growth in interdependence. As Alfred Marshall said, drawing an analogy between economic development and organic evolution, the development of the organism, whether social or physical, involves, on the one hand, an increasing subdivision of functions between its separate parts and, on the other hand, more intimate connections between the parts, each becoming less and less self-sufficient and so more and more dependent upon the others. Economic development involves such a growth in interdependent complexity as more and more complex networks of exchange join together the increasingly differentiated parts of the growing economy.

In the conventional image of such development, the expansion of the economy is seen as involving a spread of exchange from a limited to a wider area, bringing more and more people into the system of relationships. That did often happen, as, for instance, in the expansion of the European economy to include trade with America in the seventeenth century. Yet it is crucially important to understand that economic development—and development generally—can take place and often has taken place quite apart from any increase in the number of individual units included in the expanding system. An increase in scale consists in an increase in the number of exchange relations. This can occur within an economic system and does not require physical expansion to include more people or more territory. The same number of individual units can be arranged in a simple, segmented economy or in a complex, developed economy....

## POLITICAL MODERNIZATION

The general ideas expressed in these familiar terms of economic analysis have an equally important, though less familiar, application to the study of political development. Increases in differentiation and scale have also characterized political modernization, the upshot being the great networks of interdependent complexity and centralized power that we call modern states.

In the course of political modernization, the dual orientation of modernity has been expressed in the pattern of interests and the pattern of power, respectively, of the modern polity. Scientific and technical advance has made its impact on the mobilization of power, while the thrust toward equality and democracy has been expressed in the mobilization of interests.... Most studies of the modern state have shown an overwhelming concern with the latter topic. It has long been an interest of historians and political scientists to trace the course by which political demand has broadened and deepened, involved more and more people, and been made effective in the political arena. This is the story of the rise of constitutionalism and popular government; of how over time civil, political, and social rights were made effective. Even where major defeats have taken place, as in the modern dictatorships, there has been an immense growth in political scale in the sense that the spectrum of interests imposing demands and extracting satisfactions from the state has vastly increased. The populations of the various modern polities have grown, but even more important have been the unremitting increase and variegation of demands for new and more activities and services by the state. Like the modern economy, the modern state depends upon this vast and mounting demand to maintain its activity.

Along with the mobilization of interests has gone the mobilization of power, surely no less important, although much neglected by scholars. In part driven by the demands of the groups, classes, and leaders who have constituted the effective citizenry at various times, the modern state has continually developed its potential for acting on man and nature. This story has not been told in the detail it deserves. There are histories of the "output" of the modern state—from mercantilism, through laissez faire, to the welfare state and socialism. But the mobilization of power—like the growth of productivity in the economy—consists in the increase of the capacity to produce outputs. Its history is the history of the development of the "extractive" and "repressive" functions: not only the rise of bureaucracy, but also the expansion of the tax system, the police, and especially the armed forces. It has often been remarked that the huge productive capacity developed by the modern economy is totally unprecedented when seen in a long historical perspective. The power of the modern state is no less a historical wonder, reflecting a capacity for policy outputs as vast and unprecedented as the productivity of its remarkable economic system. The centerpiece in this mobilization of power has been the growing capacity of the civilian and military bureaucracy, fed by knowledge in law, economics, engineering, and the proliferating specialties of modern science and technology.

## The Power-Interest Dynamic

In political modernization not only are the processes of increasing differentiation and increasing scale analogous to processes of economic modernization, but so also are certain mechanisms. A principal mechanism of economic development, as we have seen, is the mutual interaction of specialization with scale, of the technologically driven division of labor with growing markets, internal and external. In political development specialization and scale also interact, stimulating one another. An increase in the scale of political demand puts new requirements on the state, which often can be met only by an expansion of the state's bureaucratic capacities and possibly by further mobilization and control of the private sector. Thus, for instance, the demand for a national health service, made effective in a democratic polity by electoral victory, leads to the erection of a new ministry, to the establishment of a complex of relationships with the medical profession, and to a method of financing out of special charges and/or general taxation.

Influence also runs in the opposite direction, from the pattern of power to the pattern of interests. In this instance the advance of the instrumentalities of state power to a higher level of skill and capacity stimulates new demands upon their performance. An army, for instance, that has been mobilized and trained for a prolonged crisis may, although the crisis has passed, by its very existence give rise to proposals that it be used to defend some items of national interest that otherwise would have languished for attention. Or again, the reform of the civil service by the elimination of corruption and the institution of an effective merit system will tend to increase the efficacy of the state, and for that reason lead interested groups to see in it a means of achieving their ends. More specifically, the establishment of a special department to handle some field of policy often elicits demands for special programs adapted to the department's expertise. Whichever way the flow of influence, the politician is likely to play an important role. His more familiar role is to represent some interest in the policy-making structures of the polity. But he also often acts to communicate the new ideas and information about wider capacities to a latent public, rather like the salesman for a new product, who brings it to the attention of the consumer hitherto unaware of its availability and virtues.

A contemporary illustration of this typical mechanism of political modernization is the tendency to technocracy. . . . [M]odern government makes constantly greater demands on professional expertise, and the professional-bureaucratic complex grows in numbers, competence, and power. The advances of science and professional knowledge are often such that they can be applied directly to the formulation of governmental programs, as, for instance, new discoveries in medicine may be directly translated into action in the field of public health. Such advances continually open up new possibilities of policy. But they are produced by only a few specialists, who, moreover, are usually associated with the established bureaucracy in the relevant field. From these circles the initiative

in policy making proceeds, the politician performing the essential functions of communicating the new possibilities in layman's language to the voting public and cultivating a potential demand for them. The process of demand creation elicits the support of the voters, but the initiative is taken by the technocrats and the primary choice is theirs.

Some of the new federal programs of the United States in recent years provide illustration. The poverty programs of the mid-sixties were striking examples of what has been called "the professionalization of reform." They did not originate from the demands of pressure groups of prospective beneficiaries; on the contrary, as Patrick Moynihan has observed, in the origins of the poverty programs the poor were not only invisible, but also silent.[3] With regard to such elements as the community-action program, the basic ideas and governmental initiative came, respectively, from social scientists and reforming bureaucrats. The beneficiary groups and local and state authorities were no more prepared to understand them than the general public. This created a crucial function for politicians, from the president to congressmen; they had to explain the new programs and win consent for them. . . .

A general theme of political modernization, in short, has been this power-interest dynamic, that is, the mutual interaction and stimulation of state power and political demand. The mobilization of interests and the mobilization of power interact to promote the growth of one another. The significance of the mechanism is that it constitutes in the polity (analogously to similar mechanisms in the economy) a means by which the two main dynamic forces of modernization, so to speak, cross over and affect one another.

## Notes

1. Arnold J. Toynbee, *A Study of History,* abr. ed. (New York and London, 1947), "Introduction."

2. Emile Durkheim, *The Division of Labor in Society,* George Simpson (tr.) (New York, 1933), p. 222. The original version in French was published in 1893.

3. Daniel Patrick Moynihan, "The Professionalization of Reform," *The Public Interest,* 1 (Fall 1965), p. 8.

# 37

# The Idea of Political Development

*Harry Eckstein*

From one point of view, the study of political development is a major area of achievement in recent political inquiry; from another, which matters more, it is a conspicuous failure.

What has been achieved is great and rapid growth. The study of political development, in contemporary form, started barely two decades ago.[1] In short order, an extraordinary boom occurred in publications on the subject. By 1975, a standard overview listed over two hundred pertinent works. Accretion became especially rapid after 1964, though it seems to have "peaked out" (at a high level of production) in 1970–1971.[2]

The negative side is that the result is mostly muddle. The study of political development has all the traits of too-rapid, jerry-built growth, and of its concomitant, "decay."[3] The muddle is especially pronounced where it does the most harm: in regard to the very meaning of political development. Even scholars who were conspicuous in pushing the boom along are now viewing the matter of definition with dismay.

SOURCE: Harry Eckstein, "The Idea of Political Development: From Dignity to Efficiency," *World Politics,* July 1982, pp. 451–486. Excerpt reprinted with permission of Princeton University Press. Article and notes abridged by the editors.

Thus, Huntington and Domínguez start their review of the literature with remarks about loaded and wishful definitions—an "alarming proliferation" of them—and the consequent "superfluity" of much work on political development.[4] It stands to reason that, if a concept is encumbered with many meanings, theories using it also will vary alarmingly, because they are not about the same thing.

The study of political development thus is at a critical juncture. One can let it decay further or, not much different, choose to abandon it—Frank Lloyd Wright's prescription for what to do about Pittsburgh (and, I think, Huntington's for political development). Or one can try a project in conceptual and, through it, theoretical renewal. In this essay, I develop a basis for renovation. Abandonment might, of course, be the wiser course. But the present conceptual muddle in studies of political development seems to me due to avoidable causes; the early explorers of the subject were getting at something worth getting at—if it was attainable.

...It should be obvious that the mysteries of modernity...still are very much with us. For a long time, in contemporary political inquiry, they were shifted to the Third World. But now, again, they arise in reference to ourselves: e.g., in the concerns with the nature and future of postindustrial societies, and their governability. Developmental thought was itself developed to deal with these puzzles. Surely, it is uniquely suited to do so; thus, it is sensible to take such thought seriously—that is, to try to construct developmental theory properly. Hence this section, as groundwork for the next.

The quintessential developmental theorist, Durkheim, best summarized the spirit of the developmental mode of thought:

> Every time we explain something human, taken at a given moment in history...it is necessary to go back to its primitive and simple form, to try to account for the characterization by which it was marked at that time, and then to show how it developed and became complicated little by little, and how it became that which it is at the moment in question.[5]

I propose now to do this, in broad strokes, for the political aspect of human experience.

## SKETCH FOR A REVISED THEORY OF POLITICAL DEVELOPMENT

The passage from Durkheim succinctly describes what is needed to renovate the idea of political development. A more detailed agenda of questions to be dealt with follows from the summary of the traits of developmental thought:

1. What conception of continuous growth can plausibly describe the long passage from primal to highly advanced polities?
2. What is the essential nature of polity in its "primitive and simple" form?
3. What forces make the "advancement" of primal polities toward "higher" forms ineluctable (or at least highly probable)?
4. What distinctive stages lie along the trajectory of political time? In what ways do these stages involve both quantitative growth and change in kind?
5. What forces move polities from stage to stage?
6. What do the answers to these questions imply for polities that are at present less developed, and for "advanced," modern polities?

## 1. What Conception of Continuous Growth Describes the Passage from Simple to Highly Advanced Polities?

I have argued that contemporary theories of political development are historically myopic. Even in Georgian England—hardly remote history—the traits now most widely associated with political development were still embryonic. Democratization was certainly not far advanced. The suffrage was severely restricted; leaders (e.g., M.P.s) either were nobles and gentry or their hand-picked clients, bound to serve their patrons' interests. In regard to bureaucratization, administrative and judicial roles remained entangled, nationally and locally; recruitment was highly ascriptive; specialization and formalization were elementary. Among the more familiar conceptions of political development, only the "clarification" of societal authority was mature, for the messiness of corporate jurisdictions had certainly been cleared up by the 18th century.

How, then, can one characterize a continuum of political time on which the Georgian polity itself belongs to a rather advanced period? Recall that such a continuum must involve quantitative growth, and must be a "form" that can contain much variable content. Moreover, the dimension involved must be anchored in time by minimal and maximal poles, one corresponding substantially to rudimentary cases, the other a vision that links perceptions of modernity to its remote and nearer past and, still more important, to an approximated future.

I suggest that the most serviceable way to characterize such a continuum is also the simplest: *what grows in political development is politics as such*—the political domain of society. Through political history, political authority and competition for politically allocated values have continually increased. Using Durkheim's terminology, we might regard this as growth in "political density," perhaps as a special aspect of a growing "moral density." More and more political interactions occur, overall and in place of nonpolitical interactions.

To avoid confusion about what is being argued here, a conceptual distinction must be made. One can think of "the political" as any relations that involve, say, legitimate power, or conflict management, or the regulation of social conduct, and the like. In that case, "politics" may simply exist throughout society and not be located in any clearly defined social domain or institution. Or one can think of "politics" as the functions and activities of such a concrete domain: that of the heads of societies, the princes, chiefs, or kings (for, in its modern sense, politics is associated with government, and government and social headship are synonymous). What I argue is that, through political time, the "princely domain" has constantly grown—increasingly penetrating society. And, in conjunction, political activities and relations in the less concrete sense have also grown. Expropriation by "princes" and expansion of political activity occur in conjunction.

One pole of the dimension of political time thus might be called the *social polity*. In the social polity, as a pure type, there exists a "princely" domain: some institution of headship of society, chieftaincy, firstness. That domain, though, is little differentiated from others, in the sense of having separate organizations and administrative staffs; it is anything but a subsociety—neither a "machine" nor a "system" in itself. Above all, next to nothing is done by princes, at least as we understand political activity: there is almost no active princely management of society. The society is virtually all and the polity virtually nothing. Relations of power exist, regulations of conduct and of conflicts occur; but they do so throughout society, not in special relation to chieftaincy.

At the other pole is *political society*. In political society as a pure type, "private" relations have been wholly preempted by the "public" domain of the chiefs. The institutions of that domain are highly differentiated and separately organized; governmental officers and staffs constitute a large subsociety. That subsociety is a complex system in itself, while at the same time it permeates social life.

The passage from social polity to political society can be described summarily: The domain of princes, who at the outset do virtually nothing, has great, indeed irresistible, potential for growth: power resources. Over a long period, these power resources are gradually realized. The chiefs of society convert headship into primacy, and primacy into actual control—at first very slowly, then with gathering, ultimately runaway, momentum. The momentum results from the fact that, as power resources are converted, they are not used up, but in fact increase. As this process unfolds, growth in degree corresponds, at specifiable periods, to transmutations

of type. In our own modern period, we approach a condition in which the distinction between polity and society has again become blurred—not because the public realm is minimal, but because it has virtually eliminated all privacy. This, though, is not an end, but itself a stage in a continuing process. The political society generates its own dynamics; and we should at least be able to discern the forces likely to move it, even if not yet where it is destined to go.

This conception of political time has been anticipated by other theorists. It parallels Durkheim's view of more general social development. The minimal pole of the continuum is grounded in the anthropologists' notion of "stateless" societies.[6] The conception of political development as expropriation is in Weber: the emergence of the modern state was, for Weber, a process of continuous expropriation by princes of "autonomous and 'private' bearers of executive power," resembling the expropriation by large capitalist enterprises of small, independent economic units. In his publicist essays written shortly after the Russian Revolution, Weber envisaged the further, accelerating, and continuous expropriation by the political domain of economic life, and then also of the more intimate, and the scientific and cultural, spheres—a remarkable prevision. The idea of "total" politics now also is a recurrent theme in works on modern democratic states. Sharkansky, for example, refers to runaway governmental growth "in response to incessant demands for more services," and repeatedly alludes to the erosion of the "margins" of formal government as a consequence.[7] The vision of political society informs especially the critiques of modern governments by perspective (if also hotheaded) "libertarians": Hayek, Oakeshott, Ellul, Nisbet, and others.[8]

## 2. What Is Polity in Its "Rudimentary" Form?

To sustain the thesis that what grows and changes in political development is the political domain *per se*, one must, first of all, characterize that domain in its "primitive and simple form," from which advancement proceeds. None of the many structural or functional notions that political scientists have used to define the essence of polity seem to make sense for its very early forms. What seems distinctive and universal to the princely realm in its simplest form is that its occupants and practices represent the very fact that society exists. Chiefs, khans, liegelords "embody" society. They are figures through whom societies personify themselves or sometimes (much the same) the ideal order of things imperfectly reflected in social order. They stand for the fact that a common, thus moral, life exists, and they celebrate the common life and make it compelling.

Surely that is fundamental in society, if anything is, because societies are nothing if not collective entities with which members identify—that is, define themselves. Thus, ceremony and symbolism—what Bagehot called the dignified parts of government—are not to be regarded as mere pretty trappings of power; nor are consummatory (expressive) and instrumental politics,[9] or "sacred" and "secular" ones, distinctive types at developmental stages. At the "simple" stage (thus, perhaps, always), symbolism is the very nature of the princely, not a guise. That is why, to us, the primal political domain seems empty. Primal "symbolic politics" does not stand for "real politics." It stands for society.

The evidence suggesting that primal politics is symbolic is considerable. For instance, in Schapera's study of sub-Saharan tribes[10] the following points emerge: The chiefs, as heads of societies, do not do much at all; they are simply marked out from others (e.g., in costume), exalted (in special rituals), subjects of rejoicing and of eulogies.[11] Tribes are often defined simply by identification with chiefs, not by territoriality or even kinship. Sometimes no abstract tribal name exists, only that of the chief. Often, tribal names are the inherited names of the ancestors of chiefs, and at times chiefs are named by the tribal name. In some cases, any injury done to a member of a tribe is regarded

as an injury to the chief (as we talk about crimes against society). In short, the collective and the personal are thoroughly joined in the chief's personage. Much the same comes out in Lucy Mair's studies of primitive governments and African kingdoms.[12] Mair argues, indeed, that the substantive wielding of "power over the conduct of public affairs" generally is not so much the chief's or the court's function as that of lesser figures, for whom kings are mouthpieces. Lowie's work on North American Indian tribes makes a similar point.[13]

More important from the developmental point of view, we find this to be true also in the primitive condition of a prototypical advanced society—English society. (England may be considered as a good concrete approximation of an idealized case of continuous development: something close to an experimentally contrived universe—free of uncontrolled, deceiving contingencies—which any theory of sociopolitical development should fit closely.)

Anglo-Saxon society approaches the extreme of what I have called social polity.[14] If a "public sector" existed in that society, it could only have been that of king, *folkmoot*, and *Witan*. The king was principally a source of social identity, as were all lesser chiefs of the English tribes. His one significant activity was leadership in the common enterprise of making war, and practically no other common enterprise was engaged in. The *folkmoot* originally was not a council, but simply a local muster of warriors. By 900, local moots had pretty much been displaced by the *Witan*, a "national" council of "wise men." But the *Witan's* essential function simply was to advise the king on the nature of "unchanging custom." Here the primacy of society is especially evident: while the king embodied its consciousness of itself, the *Witan* kept him honest, as the guardian of its mores.

Much the most perceptive study of primal politics as I conceive it is Geertz's magnificent book on the 19th-century "theatre-state" in Bali, *Negara*.[15] Geertz alone seems to have grasped fully the critical significance of political ceremony and ritual: of the "poetics" of power as against its "mechanics"—as Bagehot alone discerned that the dignified parts of English government were not mere vestigial histrionics, but essential to its "efficiency." Geertz does temporize between regarding theatre as essential in polities as such and considering Bali an exotic alternative to politics as efficient power. But, at least in Bali, "power served pomp, not pomp power."

## 3. What Forces Make the Growth of Primal Polity Ineluctable?

Chieftaincy in primal polities is much indulged and rewarded, with awe and with goods. But that does not immunize chiefs (much less their retainers) against the appetite for mundane power; and, perhaps just because the chiefs are symbolic figures—awesome rather than powerful—power struggles are pervasive in primal societies. For the purpose of developmental theory, it is necessary to show next that in such struggles the princely domain has overwhelming resources for subduing rivals and enlarging its effective control over society. What, then, are its power resources?

By itself, the representation of societies is an essential resource for power—perhaps the one seed that is capable of growing into political society. Societies are requisites of personal identity, safety, the satisfaction of material needs. But, though necessary, they are highly intangible. They are complex even when they are rudimentary. Seeing them as networks, or complexes of roles, or fields of interaction, or patterns of exchange—these are major feats even for modern professionals. Even if the task of abstract understanding were less difficult, such understanding would hardly move affections, which surely are needed for identification and legitimacy. So the personal symbols of society derive potential from the fact that they perform the most necessary of societal functions: making society appear "real."

It is true that there are other ways of making societies tangible. Primal societies, in fact, are always personified in their gods, through rites and magic. Thus, priests and magicians are the logical (and actual) main rivals of the chiefs for principal power. But the chiefs themselves are generally presumed to have special links to the supernatural, magical world—for instance, as rainmakers, healers, invokers of prosperity, possessors of sacred objects (fishing spears and the like), and as wielders of curses.

These links to the supernatural not only reinforce secular symbolism (or make it sacred), but also associate chiefliness and "potency," for the magical world is a world of fateful powers. Chiefs are also considered especially potent figures in the material sense of prowess. All societies have collective business of some sort—in primal societies, for instance, moving camp and herds. The function of making decisions about societal business naturally tends to be lodged in the locus of collectiveness. The one universal collective business of rudimentary societies is warfare: in defense against predatory others, for conquest (slaves, tribute, etc.), or, often, simply as a ritual. So chiefs, though they have rivals in heroes, generally are the main loci of potency as prowess. This accounts for the strange duty of chiefs in some tribal societies to be in good health, as well as for the use of wars of succession (in which the strongest survive), and for the frequent use of the phallus as a symbol of chieftaincy.

To exist, and to carry out collective enterprises, societies must, of course, be harmonious in some degree. Conflicts must be managed, quarrels mediated, crimes avenged. There is a universal social need for adjudication, and, again, a "natural" tendency to associate that necessary function with society's embodiments. The actual management of conflicts and deviance tends, in fact, to be decentralized and dispersed in primal societies—a matter of self-help in feuds, revenge, and exacting reparations. But the chief always has at least some vague special responsibility in regard to justice. For instance, we are told by Traill that a basic function of the Anglo-Saxon kings was to go about the kingdom putting down "evil customs." Traill's catalogue of judicial duties actually is a list of things kings could *not* do; and it seems evident that kings were little more than especially prestigious "oathhelpers."[16] Still, justice and chieftaincy had special, even if largely hortatory, links.

The moral, surely, is evident. The primal princely domain is ages removed from the monopoly of legitimate power. But where could there be greater potential for eventual monopoly than in a domain standing for society itself; for potency, military, and magic; and for justice? "Dignity" and "efficiency," granted, are obverse faces of politics—but also interchangeable resources.

## 4. What Are the Stages of Political Time?

The fact remains that in primal polities, whatever the chief's potential, one can barely detect an active public core. Our own political world could hardly differ more. At "our" location in political time, as stated, it is difficult to find anything that is clearly private. I am not referring to "totalitarian" polities, or only to those, but (less categorically) to the other typically modern form of polity: popular democracies. (Modern democracies, in historical perspective, simply are the gentler twins of totalitarian rule, mitigated by open competition, free communications, and a sense of rights and liberties—which, compared to earlier times, no longer really divides the public from the private, but is a sense of political decency.)

I have described the extraordinary pervasiveness of political authority in contemporary British society elsewhere, and need not dwell much on details.[17] To convey the flavor of the matter, suffice it to say the following: (1) The national government (as in other modern democracies) now directly controls about half of GNP, and indirectly plans, guides, and channels most of the remainder. (2) Parliamentary sessions, once convened only occasionally, fill up the whole available legislative work-year, and even this at the cost of large omissions—uncontrolled "executive legislation," and a severe decline in the role of private members. (3) The

Cabinet has virtually disappeared; as I wrote in 1958:

> Cabinet functions have become dispersed to an almost unfathomably complex administrative and deliberative machinery. Decisions once made collectively in the Cabinet are now made by cabinet committees, by individual Ministers, bureaucrats, the Treasury, official committees, party machinery, and even private associations; and, most often, by interaction among all of these bodies. If power is concentrated anywhere in the British machinery of government it is concentrated not in the Cabinet but in this complex framework of decision-making.[18]

One can argue that what mainly mitigates the darker aspects of fully politicized society is the very inability to control such a concentration of functions, due to sheer diversity and overload. The gentle myths of liberal rule surely help, but perhaps not as much as the fact that monolithic authority itself is too large to manage. Privacy, in political society, is found in the interstices of authority; it is, perhaps, itself mainly a product of the structure of the public realm.

How did this transmutation to something close to "political society" come about? What lies beyond the primal polity's potential for growth? This is an enormous question, and we have not even the beginning of a plausible answer. As such a beginning, I suggest a six-stage process. The process is "logical" in that each stage manifestly is a condition for the next. The stages also make sense in the context of the English polity—our standard case for observing gradual, evolutionary "unfolding" (the literal meaning of *développer*) in politics. For this reason I will use English history—in gross summary—to exemplify the stages.

**The Politics of Primacy.** I have already treated the first stage, primal polity, using Anglo-Saxon England to illustrate its nature. The second stage involves what might be called the struggle for, and achievement of, primacy. The forces that push polities to and through that stage (and later stages) will be discussed presently. Here, it must suffice to say that nothing in political development can possibly come before the clarification of a distinct public domain that, in regard to "efficient" functions, is minimally *primus inter pares*. Without this, there is nothing that may grow. One may suppose that the establishment of a realm of substantive primacy—one that involves more than symbolic headship—will not be a tranquil process, but will involve stubborn conflicts over domination and autonomy. Aside from chiefs, there are others who have politically convertible resources: religious, economic, and military. But, as we have seen, the chiefs generally have much weightier resources for providing political goods—not least, safety, in a context of continuous struggle among social domains: Hobbes's good, and no doubt the fundamental value.

This general stage fits, in England, the period of *feudal monarchy,* say of the 12th century. The feudal monarchy certainly was quite different from the Anglo-Saxon, despite the fact, generally agreed, that the Conquest caused no sharp break. The domain of the Angevin and early Plantagenet princes, to be sure, remained mainly on the level of symbol and pomp; its practical authoritative functions were sparse. What is most conspicuous about the period is struggle for "dominion" as such. The histories portray incessant turmoil. But the tumult was not about policy, in our sense. It involved competition about spheres of autonomy and subjection; and the fundamental source of that struggle was a lack of clarification and resolution of the functions of the great and small corporations of society—all authoritative in their own domains, and constantly striving to expand or protect them.

Corporate boundaries now, though, mattered for more than symbolic reasons. They mattered because the princely domain had begun to acquire a critical function: material extraction—a condition of all effective action, and thus an obsession in feudal monarchy. The Treasury preceded all other political institutions in development. The classic account of 12th-century royal "administration" is FitzNeal's *Dialogue on the Exchequer,* the exchequer being

its one great administrative creation. It regularized the royal revenues, and the great pacification under Henry II was, at heart, a matter of reestablishing the central revenues in face of embezzlement by the barons. Extraction increased political "density," and the latter changed institutions.

Still, Henry's charter upon his coronation was little more than an assurance of liberties, grants, and customs. Petit-Dutaillis' study of feudal monarchy tells us that the King's *concilium* attended to "all sorts of business";[19] but, as to particulars, he lists only personal issues (e.g., marriages) and familiar matters of peace, war, loyalty, treason, and the administration of justice.

The last is important, however. Judicial activities now were much enlarged and wholly reorganized—equal with pomp and war as the core of royal primacy. Indeed, aside from finance and war, the whole royal establishment now looked like a sort of national judiciary. The King's "prime minister" was the Chief Justiciar; the Curia had become a "normal court" for the kingdom, not just an occasional tribunal; the judicial circuits, administering Common Law, had been established; and central justice had largely expropriated the seignorial jurisdictions, of which only "a few islets" remained.

The feudal monarchy thus achieved, gradually, a considerable legal and extractive permeation of society, as a material basis for primacy. Contestation persisted for a long time, but in an increasingly muted, one-sided way. The nascent monopoly over extraction, the increasing practical responsibility for the management of conflicts, and the emergence of specialized institutions to handle these functions, realized a potential already present in the primal polity; but, more important, all this added to the growth potential of the prince's domain.

**The "Prophylactic" Polity.** Substantive primacy, especially when added to symbolic headship, is both gratifying in itself and a supremely valuable resource for acquiring additional resources. Once it is established, struggles for its possession inevitably occur. One of the fundamental tasks of politics is to institutionalize such struggles in order to defuse them—a basic function, for instance, of competition among political parties. But institutionalization is always gradual—a sort of subtheme of development. Early on, contestation for possession of the domain of primacy must involve—in greater or lesser degree— unregulated, brutal conflicts. Lacking institutionalization (or the transformation of real and deadly conflicts into ritualized competition) damage can be limited only by prevention: prophylaxis.

In the prophylactic polity, the overriding objective of the prince is to detect and disarm usurpation, while that of others is to seize or control principality. To protect principality, it is functional to place it in a tangible physical domain and to draw potential usurpers into that domain. Hence, the identification of primacy with the prince's court. It is there that the game of trying to get and keep primacy and its perquisites is played; politics turns inward.

To a degree, however, prophylactic politics must also reach out into society, further than before. Courtly politics cannot be wholly isolated, because the discontents of society might play into the hands of usurpers. Therefore—rather than for altruistic reasons—the princely domain begins to furnish something else that is valuable to society: a degree of controlled social order, as prophylaxis in everyday life against society's *misérables*. The result is both a qualitative change in the nature of politics and the increased penetration of society by its political domain.

In England, *the era of the Tudors* illustrates the stage. The late medieval and Renaissance political struggles in England increasingly had a flavor different from those of feudalism. They were epitomized, and pretty much ended, by Tudor rule, for which "absolutism" is an egregious misnomer. Nothing really was absolute. Rather, the Tudors—especially Elizabeth—successfully coped with conspiracies *within* the realm of princely authority. If anything authoritative was absolute it was courtly absolutism, which transformed Lords into mere courtiers.

Concomitantly, political competition was courtly competition—scheming within the firm.

Nevertheless, one can discern a threshold in the permeation of society by authoritative policy. Outside of the royal palaces, authoritative regulation was still sparse; but before the Tudors (conflict management and extraction aside), authoritative space, outside its royal core, had been virtually empty. A good many histories refer to an abundance of "proclamations" by the Crown, and subservient parliaments and courts, in Tudor times. Elizabeth's parliaments did indeed pass 429 bills. The figure is often mentioned to impress. Actually, it brings out only the limitations of policy making. Elizabeth's reign lasted 45 years; nowadays, British legislative output runs to about a hundred bills a year. Much of Elizabethan "legislation" had to do with issues of diplomacy, foreign intrigues, war, and extraction. Some of the regime's authoritative activities, however, involved a novel extension of authority into society: the systematic maintenance of roads and bridges, the licensing of alehouses, controls over wages, the mobility of labor, entry into trades, dealings in commodities, interest rates, and—most familiar—a uniform law to care for the poor.

Growing political density surely is evident, especially since this reaching out into society supplemented unprecedented ceremonial activity (royal equipages and pageantry) and an even greater increase in foreign adventurism, war, and defense. The primacy of feudal monarchy clearly was now being put to use as a generalized resource. Perhaps this was a response to much-increased "social density": the manufacturing revolution in textiles, mining, iron-making, and petty trades (perfumery, barbering, etc.)—a response, in general, to a busy society of promoters, speculators, patentees, dramatists, composers, astronomers, astrologers, physicians, surgeons, alchemists, sorcerers, explorers. What Black calls "the chaos of society,"[20] however, did not engender policy as an attempt to impose any sort of rational order. Rather, the point of authoritative "outputs" seems to have been an extension of the defusing of courtly intrigues: the prevention of social discontents and marginality that were potentially threatening to the security (and isolation) of the courtly domain. The increased permeation of society under Tudor rule aimed, above all, at prophylaxis: controlling vagabonds, dealing with food riots, limiting speculators, usurers, and drunkards. The Poor Law and the relentless pursuit of religious recusants are all of a piece in this effort. A valuable resource was now being hoarded—though not yet much used for additional gain.

**The Polity of Interests.** When principality no longer needs to be preoccupied with usurpation, but has been institutionalized at least in accepted rules of succession, politics can turn outward for reasons other than prophylaxis. The primacy of a social domain above other domains and, even more, the "distancing" of courts from societies, inevitably lead to a conception of princely power and social order (not "orderliness") as being somehow unrelated. The initial extroversion of the princely domain thus can hardly be concerned with such matters as engineering social harmony or just distribution. In introverted politics, these are matters for natural order or divine ordination. When politics turns outward from the court, then, the purpose is initially not so much to manage society as to exploit primacy as a safe resource: the gainful use of primacy by privilege. In the polity of interests, competition overshadows majesty. Though it in no sense involves democratization, the arena of politics as competition becomes much enlarged and structurally altered. It still takes place in the court, but now also in institutions associated with the court (e.g., parliament) and, to a degree, in society. Through the "outputs" sought by patrons and their clients, the polity, as Durkheim would say, markedly "condenses." Royal administrative and judicial institutions become a rather complex "machinery" government.

In England, such acquisitive exploitation of established primacy—and through it the much enlarged penetration of society—is the essence

of the *Georgian period*.[21] One sees the scope of the 18th- century British polity best in the activities of its local officials. The Justices of the Peace were broadly charged with collecting and delivering revenues; assuring the proper practice and flow of trade; looking after the poor, the food supply, prices, and wages; licensing brewers and drinking-houses; supervising goals; establishing asylums and confining lunatics; seeing to the lighting of streets, their paving, policing, and cleaning. All this required at least an embryonic differentiation of political labor—though bureaucratization had hardly yet begun. There were now distinct judicial and administrative sessions, distinct highway and licensing councils, as well as individual specialists, like road surveyors and constables. Late in the century, new statutory authorities, with special duties, appeared: for instance, turnpike trusts, corporations for administering relief to the poor, and, above all, a growing number and variety of improvement commissions.

This expansion of activities, and of organizations for performing them, was not intended to manage society. The overriding trait of the Georgian polity was that it was a marketplace of influence and spoils. The central level did not really manage society, yet there was extraordinary jockeying among parliamentarians and, as a result, ministerial instability. According to Namier, men went into parliament partly out of a sort of "predestination" (men of "political families"), but even more as clients looking after patrons' interests: as placemen and as purveyors and receivers of favors (there was, says Namier, a "universal...plaguing of Ministers on behalf of friends and relations");[22] to advance themselves in the military and administrative services or reap rewards from service; to obtain contracts, jobs, subscriptions, loans, and remittances. The Enclosure Acts and what Beer calls "canal politics" epitomize this extraordinary politics of interests.

**The Politics of Incorporation and of Incumbency.** When the domain of politics is used chiefly for acquisitive purposes by privileged groups, other groups will try to become incorporated into the game as players, rather than be excluded from it as passive victims. As the stakes grow (that is, the spoils increase) so, one may suppose, does the appetite for shares. Certainly the pervasive theme of early modern (19th-century) British politics is democratization. Tilly depicts the process as one in which excluded subjects first become "challengers," and then, through challenge, incorporated "members" of the polity:[23] voters, of course, and eligible to hold office. The transformation of challenge into membership occurs because the challengers have resources of their own that can be effectively mobilized—such as strikes, violence, and the like.

As the polity's membership expands, and thus becomes more diverse in interest, the political penetration of society necessarily grows rapidly in scope; when "civic incorporation" is virtually total, so is the politicization of social life—but not just in the sense of universal citizenship. Two other processes occur that rapidly transform social into political space. One is familiar: as new members are incorporated, the volume of political demands grows, and with it, the volume of outputs; with outputs, the network of committees, agencies, departments, boards, to define and deliver them; and, with such organizations, their own demands: "withinputs," as David Easton calls them.

Perhaps this chain reaction sufficiently explains the rapid development of political society out of acquisitive politics. I would suggest, though, that a second process supplements the demand-response relation, and perhaps is more consequential. It bears at least a vague resemblance to the Tudor preoccupation with political prophylaxis. To put it starkly: political primacy in the modern polity clearly is more than ever worth possessing and keeping in possession; however great the resources of princes before, they were puny compared to the fully realized monopoly over legitimate power. The theater of political struggle, though, is no longer confined to the small stage of the court; it comprises society as such. Thus, the modern counterpart of coping with conspiracy in order to retain control

over the princely domain is either mass suppression or the search for mass support (plus the special support of the more powerful, better organized interests). Mass support is elicited, at least in part, by going *beyond* responsiveness: by "redistributive" policies that make large public groups into clients—collective placemen. The unparalleled scale both of repression in authoritarian modern polities and of the political provision of all sorts of goods in welfare states serves the maintenance of incumbency. No doubt welfare policies and other distributions of benefits result from good intentions; but surely, they also provide benefits, in the form of political support, for their providers. At any rate, here is a parsimonious explanation of the substantial consensus on social policy in the contemporary British welfare state. The politics of incorporation leads logically to that of incumbency.

"Political density" during these stages grows rapidly toward its maximal pole. The vastness of the business done by the machine of government requires, as Durkheim realized, more and more internal complexity of structure, in large part just for keeping things sorted and coordinated; it requires the development of a political "system,"[24] which is not at all the same as a machinery of government. Structures of political competition also become highly organized and institutionalized networks of organizations. In gist, the pomp of primal chiefliness virtually disappears within the systems and networks of the polity.[25]

Two important questions should be raised about the abstracted stages to determine whether they indeed constitute a general developmental sequence. First: Do the stages occur, *mutatis mutandis*, in other longitudinal political processes, and do they furnish a good typology for the "cross-sectional" classification of polities in the present? If so, we can assert (in the manner of early exponents of the "comparative method"—Ferguson, Comte, Tylor, Morgan)[26] that typological differences among polities are basically developmental: viz., that there is history, not just histories. Second: Would a schematic treatment of political functions, goals, and structures by stages indeed show qualitative distinctions in each class, along with the quantitative growth of the political domain? These questions cannot be treated briefly; they are posed here as items on an agenda to follow up this essay.

## 5. What Forces Move Polities from Stage to Stage?

In the preceding section, I have tried to show sequential connections between stages of political development: how the earlier stages are preconditions for those that follow, and how these, in turn, are latent in preceding stages. (An important, familiar issue for *praxis*—too large to be tackled here—is raised by the question whether stages can be skipped, without the occurrence of pathologies, and without regression.) This demonstration, though, says nothing about the forces that propel polities from stage to stage. We need at least a summary answer to complete our sketch for a theory of political development.

In developmental theory, one wants, ideally, to identify a general motive force that operates throughout developmental time (akin to physical inertia) and also special forces, generated in each earlier stage, which similarly lead to each later stage.

The general motive force at work in the sequence of stages I have described is surely the drive for the direct and indirect benefits of "efficient" primacy in and over society—the direct benefit of social elevation and indirect perquisites, such as material goods. That drive characterizes most directly the transformation of primal, ceremonial polity. The maintenance of primacy for getting other values follows in the polity of interests, and leads to the challenges that incorporate excluded groups in the domain of primacy. The possession of higher positions—primacy in the domain of primacy—animates political motion in the most advanced stage.

Although primacy-seeking is the essence of the initial developmental transformation of polities, it is clear that struggles for establishing

an "efficient" principal domain are only resolved when an urgent societal need for such resolution arises. In the West, that need arose from the differentiation of society into distinct but overlapping "corporations" in virtually continuous collision. One may surmise, more generally, that an initial locus of efficient primacy will emerge when it is functionally critical to social integration that this occur—that is, when the integrative force of "mechanical solidarity" no longer works. The theatrical chiefs are destined to win struggles to perform the integrative function, and to reap its benefits.

If there is such a thing as "pure" power politics, it occurs when struggles for primacy have been resolved. Pure power politics is about possessing primacy, not about establishing it. Once the domain of the prince itself is safe, a different propulsive force emerges; we might call it resource conversion.

The results of converting political into other goods now come to pose a quite different, but again functionally critical problem of integration: not of society but of the political domain itself, for the sake of its effective operation. The need for political integration has two facets. As new groups are incorporated into the polity, the plethora of interests and demands they generate must be coordinated: in Almond's terminology, a need exists to aggregate interests, so that demands may be effectively pressed and responded to. More important, as society is greatly politicized through processes of civic incorporation, the machinery of government grows into a complex system; as a result, efficient management of the system itself must increasingly become a *sine qua non* of political goals, even exploitative ones. Without efficient political management, social life itself is imperiled, precisely because the polity pervades it; and, without such management, power itself is a chimera. In this way, we can see in political development a diminution, if not a metamorphosis, of pure power politics—and still avoid the "fault" of tender-mindedness.

Thus, while struggles for primacy propel politics throughout developmental time, at each stage they take different forms and are reinforced by special forces: forces of greed and, more important, forces generated by collective functional needs. These themes of politics—primacy-seeking, power-seeking, greed, and integration—are familiar. What is not familiar is the special roles they play at different stages of political development.

The process of political development moved by these forces is monotonic in two senses. I have stressed one—the politicalization of society. The long trajectory from social polity to political society can also be considered a modulation from "dignity" to "efficiency" (the most fundamental qualitative social change conceivable), and each stage of the process can be treated as a changing balance between the two. In parallel, polities change structurally from personage to court, to machine, to system.

## CONCLUSION

The idea of political development, then, seems to me capable of renovation along the lines sketched. What I have tried to present is a design along proper "developmental" lines. The design is, and must continue to be, far from a completed theoretical structure. But if it proves to have merit, it helps to answer the final question raised above. It has important implications precisely for the issue that a developmental theory should illuminate: the puzzle of our own modernity. I will mention one such implication for a critical problem in modern political life.

We have lately heard much about a crisis of authority in highly advanced societies. The evidence is overwhelming that there is at least a malaise about authority. Strangely, that malaise seems to exist concurrently with the progressive growth of what people supposedly (and no doubt actually) want authority to be: decent, down to earth, participant, lenient, concordant, open to achievement. Might not the solution of this riddle lie in the "disenchantment" of theatrical politics (which moves affections), by

rationally effective but too-drab systems? After all, society and polity remain intangible mysteries; the social sciences are devoted to their understanding. They have become all the more mystifying as they have grown in scale, density, and differentiation. At the same time, dignity has waned in relation to efficiency. More and more, our representative figures are capable but plain, managers but not princes: Fords, Carters, Wilsons, Heaths; in our families, schools, and workplaces, authority increasingly also has derogated rank. We want this, and it seems good; but can we live with it?

Perhaps that is what Weber saw when he forecast a political "polar night of icy darkness and hardness." Perhaps, too, the tension between the needs for what Weber called matter-of-factness and devotion is the force propelling us into the future of political time.

## Notes

1. The salient exploratory works are Rupert Emerson, *From Empire to Nation* (Boston: Beacon Press, 1960), and Gabriel Almond and James S. Coleman, eds., *The Politics of the Developing Areas* (Princeton, N.J.: Princeton University Press, 1960). Among the pioneers, two others also stand out: Karl Deutsch, "Social Mobilization and Political Development," *Political Science Review* 55 (September 1961), pp. 493–514, and Lucian W. Pye, *Politics, Personality, and Nation Building* (New Haven: Yale University Press, 1962).

2. Samuel P. Huntington and Juan I. Dominguez, "Political Development," in *Handbook of Political Science*, III, ed. Fred I. Greenstein and Nelson W. Polsby (Reading, Mass: Addison-Wesley, 1975), pp. 98–114.

3. The term decay is used in Huntington's sense, as an antonym to "order." See Samuel P. Huntington, *Political Order in Changing Societies* (New Haven: Yale University Press, 1968), chap. I. Earlier, Huntington had used "decay" as an antonym to "development"; see "Political Development and Political Decay," *World Politics*, 17 (April 1965), pp. 386–430.

4. Huntington and Domínguez, "Political Development," p. 3.

5. Emile Durkheim, *The Elementary Forms of the Religious Life* (New York: Free Press, 1947), p. 3.

6. See, for instance, Lucy Mair, *Primitive Government* (Harmondsworth, Middlesex: Penguin Books, 1962), Part I—especially the chapter on "Minimal Government" (pp. 61-77).

7. Ira Sharkansky, *Whither the State?* (Chatham, N.J.: Chatham House, 1979), throughout.

8. See, for example, Kenneth S. Templeton, Jr., ed., *The Politicization of Society* (Indianapolis: Liberty Press, 1979).

9. These are Apter's terms; see David E. Apter, *The Politics of Modernization* (Chicago: University of Chicago Press, 1965), pp. 24ff.

10. I. Schapera, *Government and Politics in Tribal Societies* (London: Watts, 1956).

11. *Ibid.,* chap. 4. Varying "powers" are associated with chiefliness (102ff.). I will refer to the most common below. But simply being "chiefly" is clearly the heart of the matter.

12. Mair, *Primitive Government* (fn. 47), and *African Kingdoms* (Oxford: Clarendon Press, 1977).

13. R. H. Lowie, "Political Organization among American Aborigines," *Journal of the Royal Anthropological Institute* 78 (February 1948), pp. 1-17.

14. Dating poses difficulties here, but a sensible point in time for looking at the Anglo-Saxon polity surely is circa 900 A.D. A sense of an English society had crystallized out of the diverse identities of Teutonic tribal invaders and become personified in a single chief, Edward of Wessex. *Beowulf* remains the best primary source for understanding Anglo-Saxon life. See also J. E. A. Jolliffe, *Constitutional History of Medieval England* (New York: Norton, 1967), parts 1 and 2; Sir Frank Stenton, *Anglo-Saxon England* (Oxford: Oxford University Press, 1943); Dorothy Whitelock, *The Beginning of English Society* (Harmondsworth, Middlesex: Penguin Books, 1952).

15. Clifford Geertz, *Negara: The Theatre-State in Nineteenth Century Bali* (Princeton N.J.: Princeton University Press, 1980).

16. H. D. Traill, ed., *Social England*, I (New York: Putnam, 1894), p. 134.

17. See Samuel H. Beer and Adam Ulam, eds., *Patterns of Government*, 2d ed. (New York: Random House, 1962), chap. 10.

18. *Ibid.*, p. 235.

19. Ch. Petit-Dutaillis, *The Feudal Monarchy in England and France* (London: Adam & Charles Black, 1948), p. 128.

20. J. B. Black, *The Reign of Elizabeth: 1558-1603* (Oxford: Clarendon, 1936), p. 217.

21. The great work on the Georgian polity is Sir Lewis Namier, *The Structure of Politics at the Accession of George III* (New York: Macmillan, 1957); the standard history is J. Steven Watson, *The Reign of George III: 1750-1815* (Oxford: Clarendon, 1960); and the best concise political perspective on the period is provided by Samuel H. Beer, *British Politics in the Collectivist Age* (New York: Alfred A. Knopf, 1965).

22. Namier, *The Structure of Politics*, p. 76.

23. Charles Tilly, *From Mobilization to Revolution* (Reading, Mass.: Addison-Wesley Publishing, 1978).

24. I use "system" here in the manner of general and political systems theorists; the latter seem to me pertinent only—or anyway, chiefly—to "modern" polities. See, for instance, James G, Miller, "Living Systems: Basic Concepts," *Behavioral Science*, 10 (July 1965), pp. 193-237; David Easton, *A Systems Analysis of Political Life* (New York: John Wiley & Sons, 1965).

25. The elevation of the leader in totalitarian polities can certainly be regarded as a reaction against the fathomless sobriety of typical modern political systems. It is, of course, more satanic than sacred. And surely the "system" uses the leader, perhaps more than vice versa.

26. Robert A. Nisbet, *Social Change and History: Aspects of the Western Theory of Development* (New York: Oxford University Press, 1969).

## 38

# The Creation of Knowledge and Technique

*David Landes*

The heart of the whole process of industrialization and economic development is intellectual: it consists in the acquisition and application of a corpus of knowledge concerning technique, that is, ways of doing things. It is customary for economists to think of this corpus of knowledge as a common property of mankind, a pool into which any and all can dip at will. This assumption of general accessibility is subject, to be sure, to a significant constraint: the existence of secrets, which may or may not be protected by patent. The existence of such secrets is inherent in the character of knowledge, for knowledge is not given, it is created, and there is always a lag between the creation of knowledge or the exclusive application thereof by the creator and its communication or diffusion to others. Such secrets, however, are assumed by economists to be short-lived. Given the fact that the scientific knowledge from which technology is commonly derived is almost always published and widely disseminated, any attempt to keep a superior technique secret is bound to fail. If the technique yields a product, the object itself will almost invariably yield up its secrets to the expert eye. If the technique concerns a way of making the product (if it is what the economist calls a process innovation), imitators will either learn it (sometimes by illicit means) or find an equivalent or better substitute (there is more than one way to skin a cat).

All of these theses concerning the nature and accessibility of knowledge are based on the

SOURCE: David Landes, "The Creation of Knowledge and Technique: Today's Task and Yesterday's Experience," *Daedalus* 109, no. 1 (Winter 1980), pp. 111–120. Special issue on "Modern Technology: Problem or Opportunity?" Reprinted by permission of *Daedalus*, Journal of the American Academy of Arts and Sciences. Notes abridged by the editors.

experience of what the economist calls advanced economies. These are those few industrial nations that not only possess technologies on the frontier of human knowledge and performance, but are capable of training new scientists and technicians to work in the context of that technology and push back that frontier. Short of that happy state, however, the great majority of the people in this world are barred from access to much of this knowledge and seriously hampered in the application of such knowledge as they have. They are barred by their lack of appropriate education and training, the inadequacy of their resources, and their inability to mobilize and organize such resources as they have. Small wonder that a demand for technological parity constitutes a key plank of the platform of the so-called New Economic Order.

The advanced nations have not been unmindful of the handicap imposed on less developed countries by their ignorance of, and inability to apply, more efficient techniques. Insofar as those who possess this knowledge and enjoy the fruits thereof feel a moral obligation to reduce the gap between rich and poor, or perhaps have a prudential interest in doing so, they have been especially sympathetic to projects for the dissemination of technology. For one thing, if I may be permitted a materialist observation, knowledge is the one commodity that can be given away without impoverishing the giver. For another, it is far cheaper to teach people how to do or make things than to give them the things or, even more expensive, give them the means to make things without really showing them how.

These projects for the dissemination of knowledge have thus far had only moderate success. To the extent that advanced nations have received students from less developed countries and offered schooling and training, they have often succeeded only in adding to their own pool of scientists and technicians. American hospitals are filled with foreign interns who find the practice of medicine more remunerative and satisfying in this country than in their own poor countries. This and other examples of "brain drain" have been the subject of much moralizing and hand-wringing; but it is hard for free societies to exclude those who have in a matter of years set down roots and have acquired skills and talents that are of value not only to society at large, but to hospital administrators and laboratory directors trying to balance their budgets.

Those who return home, moreover, are as much unprepared by their experience as prepared. They know much more than when they left, but often it is the wrong knowledge—agricultural techniques, for example, that make sense in temperate climates but not in tropical. Even when they know what they need, they may lack the opportunity to apply their knowledge: equipment may be inadequate; collaborators, few and deficient; complementary services (especially governmental), wanting or maddeningly incompetent. Sometimes it may be easier to know less and try less than to know more and not be able to try or do.

As for those trained in the poor countries, they may be less surprised by the impediments to postgraduate application and achievement, but they are no less frustrated. For all the limitations of their training, they have been sorted out by it and raised beyond the knowledge, comprehension, and even sympathy of their compatriots. They, often along with those trained abroad, constitute a small elite in a sea of conservative custom, fearful self-interest, and ideological suspicion. The private sector is weak; the public, ineffective, if not corrupt and malign.

Finally, there are the foreign experts, many of them idealistic volunteers ready to accept unaccustomed hardships and difficulties in order to do something for those less fortunate. Their efforts are often rewarded by small and big successes, by the introduction of new and better crops, by a reduction in infant mortality, and by the adoption of more productive techniques. At their best, though, they are not the remedy for technological backwardness. History shows that foreign craftsmen and technicians can do wonders in teaching new ways to a less skilled population. Indeed, there is hardly an advanced country that has not benefited enormously from the migration of knowledge—the English, from the Flemish weavers of the so-called new draperies (16th century); the French, Belgians, and Germans, from British mechanics during their industrial revolution (19th century); the Americans, from a steady stream of skilled (as well as unskilled) settlers; the Japanese, from European technicians hired on during their drive to modernize under Meiji (post-1868).

The same record, however, tells us something of the conditions of effective absorption of foreign knowledge and techniques. Most of these countries kept their visitors, who constituted a permanent addition to the stock of human capital; and to the extent they did not or did not want to keep them (Japan is the best example here), made it a point to get from them whatever they had to teach before sending them on their way.

Now, this is surely the kind of task that confronts the less developed countries of our day. They will not hold their visitors, nor is it clear that they want to; and this means that they must learn these techniques and—much harder—learn to generate new techniques themselves. Outsiders may help, but unless the seeds of knowledge and invention take root, there will be a one-time increase in yield and then a return to the *status quo ante*.

This brings me to the key question: What does it take to learn and domesticate new knowledge and ways, to the point not only of doing things differently and better, but of finding new ways of one's own?

I shall not pretend to be able to answer that. (If I could, I would not be writing this article; I'd be changing the world.) But I think that history can give us clues as to what is *not* the answer. In particular, I think it shows conclusively that knowledge and skills are not disembodied things that can be propagated and received at will, like radio waves or light. Let me tell a story on that point.

In the 16th century European sailors began for the first time to undertake oceanic voyages on a continuing, regular basis.[1] They did so in spite of the fact that, once on the high seas, they could know their location only approximately, and that mistakes on this score could cost them their lives. Of the two coordinates that defined their position, they could calculate only the latitude with any precision. Longitude had to be more or less guessed at by a procedure known as dead reckoning: the officers would keep track of the ship's course and speed, and work out its presumed location at the end of each day's sailing. Since estimates of speed were made only every two hours or so, and then with gross margins of error (a floating object was thrown overboard, and the time it took to pass from one observation point to another was measured by the recital of some standard bit of prayer or verse),[2] dead reckoning could be seriously misleading. Sailors making for small targets in wide seas learned to play safe by aiming for points well to the east or west of their mark and then running the latitude to their destination. Even that was not enough, and the annals of sailing are dotted with tales of ships lost because their crews were lost.

For maritime powers of Europe, this was a costly weakness. Ocean-sailing ships were immensely valuable, in themselves, for the crew that manned them, for the cargoes they carried. Small wonder that Philip of Spain offered in 1598 a fabulous fortune to the person who would discover a way of determining longitude: a prize of 6,000 gold ducats, a life pension of 2,000, and a further gratuity of 1,000—the equivalent of millions of today's dollars. No one won the prize, though the scientific principle on which such a method might be based was well known. The rotating earth, after all, is a clock, so that differences in longitude translate into differences in time and vice versa—as Gemma Frisius had pointed out a half-century before. Since the time where one was could be determined by astronomic observation—the sun's passage of the meridian, for example—one needed only to have a clock precise enough to keep the time at another place of known longitude, and to convert the difference in time into a difference of distance.

There was no one in Spain, however, or anywhere else at the time, capable of building such a clock. The Spanish government paid smaller, but substantial, sums to numerous postulants who pretended to be well on the way to a solution, some of them cranks promising the navigational equivalent of the philosopher's stone. In the end Spain gave up: necessity may be the mother of invention, especially if backed by money, but there is no substitute for the kind of environment that generates novelty.

Over the next century and more these encouragements and enticements were imitated by the governments of Venice and Holland, in vain, and finally by those of England (Act 12 Queen Anne, 8 July 1714) and France (1716). The English prize was particularly generous: £20,000 (say $6 million today) for a method accurate to within half a degree of arc, or 30 nautical miles. By this time horology had made revolutionary advances. The invention of the pendulum clock (Huygens, 1660) had made possible time measurement to the fraction of a second, thereby enhancing enormously the effectiveness of astronomical observation. But because of the rolling motion of ships, pendulum clocks proved unusable for the determination of longitude at sea. A comparable advance in the production of smaller timepieces, the use of a coiled spring to govern the to-and-fro motion of the balance, whose beat is the heart of the timekeeping mechanism (Huygens, c. 1675), held out more promise as a controller or governor. But major sources of variation, hence imprecision, remained, so that some of the leading scientists of the time gave up hope of a horological solution. None less than Isaac Newton, commenting in 1721 on a proposal to solve the problem by "watch works of new construction," noted discouragingly: "It is not to be found at sea by any method by which it is not to be found at land. And it is not yet found at land by Watchwork."

The great pundits may have been skeptical, but some clockmakers and watchmakers were not. The challenge was accepted by a number of these in England and France, at least one of whom, Henry Sully, gave all else up to devote the rest of his life to the invention of an effective "sea clock." In the end, though, it was not a professional clockmaker who won the prize. Rather, it was an autodidact, a carpenter-son of a carpenter, John Harrison of Barrow, a tiny, isolated hamlet in north Lincolnshire, near the mouth of the Humber. Harrison, who was certainly a genius, taught himself to make clocks, using wood for plates and wheelwork, instead of the usual brass. He also so impressed one of the traveling clergymen who ministered at the local church on Sundays, that he lent him a manuscript copy of lectures on natural philosophy by Nicholas Saunderson, Lucasian Professor of Mathematics at Cambridge; and it is clear, from the careful copy Harrison made of text and diagrams, that he learned much from and was much guided by these in his further work in chronometry.

To make a long story short, Harrison succeeded over a period of some 30 years in building a timepiece accurate enough to satisfy the conditions of the prize (completed 1759, tested 1761). To do this, he had to solve a large number of difficult technical problems, which he did in the most ingenious but also the most idiosyncratic manner. His first three models were Rube Goldbergian in their size and complexity, far too cumbersome ever to serve at sea; but anyone who sees them working in the National Maritime Museum in Greenwich cannot but be awed by their craftsmanship and artistry. And then he brought out his No. 4, the clock with which he won the prize, a triumph of miniaturization, only five inches in diameter, with an entirely new array of solutions to these same problems.

Interestingly enough, these solutions never took with other makers. Harrison's devices were too difficult or costly to build, even when understood. But his contribution lay in showing that a marine chronometer was possible, that the job could be done. The most gifted horologists of both England and the Continent made it a point to examine his mechanisms and were inspired by them to undertake their own

researches and experiments. They found other answers, which proved definitive; but the honor for the great breakthrough belongs to Harrison, the self-taught nonprofessional.

One last aspect of this story deserves notice. The principle of the escapement device that is at the heart of all mechanical marine chronometers was discovered by a Frenchman, Pierre Le Roy; but its improvement and application on a production basis was largely the work of Englishmen, in particular John Arnold and Thomas Earnshaw. And although the French learned to make some of the finest chronometers to be found anywhere, it was the British who came to manufacture the great majority of these instruments. They had the largest market—the biggest navy, the biggest merchant marine. Invention may follow genius, but production follows demand.

I have told (retold) the story of John Harrison and the marine chronometer because it illustrates some of the circumstances that condition the diffusion and invention of knowledge. In particular, it emphasizes the close links among comprehension (the ability to understand and absorb), application, opportunity, and the larger cognitive and social environment. Spain, for all its priority in oceanic navigation, was in no position to experiment and invent in this sphere. It lacked the craftsmen, in part because intelligence and skill gravitated in Spain to other, more honorific occupations. It lacked a base of interest and experience in time measurement, which was far more important to merchants and manufacturers (as in England) than to conquistadores, encomenderos, and caballeros; also, for a variety of reasons, to Protestants than to Catholics.

To be sure, John Harrison was something of a sport; his achievements testify to the importance of the personal, accidental factor in history. But his career was made possible by contacts with the world of science even in his isolated Lincolnshire village; and when he went to London, he found the kind of comprehension and support that come only with sympathy and knowledge. He was fortunate enough to find in

George Graham, the leading watch- and clock-maker of the day, a man of uncommon generosity, of spirit as well as pocket. But Graham was not so exceptional that he does not convey something of the openness and mutual awareness that characterized the scientific and technological community of the time and place.

All of this, in little, exemplifies the general characteristics of European technology from the Middle Ages. Away back then, in a time that historians had long portrayed as miserably poor and backward, Europeans were quick learners and improvers of techniques from any source. Building on a long-forgotten or neglected legacy of technique from classical antiquity, with additions imported by the so-called barbarians, or acquired from more advanced cultures to the east, they succeeded in developing by the 14th century—certainly by the 15th—a corpus of knowledge and skills that not only put them far ahead of their teachers, but conferred on them a decisive superiority of power. It is on this basis that Europe changed from a hapless victim to global aggressor, from a poor backwater, obliged to make its balance of payments in slaves for want of marketable exports, to the affluent workshop of the world.

The explanation of this extraordinary turnaround and the subsequent divergence of the West from the Rest is still a matter of inquiry and debate. The economic expansion and development in themselves have usually been accounted for in Smithian terms—as the natural consequence of restored order and security. Trade was advantageous, so the Europeans traded; the rest followed.

Even if this were enough to explain what Robert Lopez calls the commercial revolution of the Middle Ages, however, it will not tell whence this inventiveness, this growing interest in novelty, this cumulative emulation in ingenuity. Other societies have known moments of commercial prosperity and economic expansion, yet they have not taken this course of sustained technological advance.

Some of the answers to this question have stressed the special character of medieval political institutions. In *The Unbound Prometheus*

I noted two of these. The first was the political fragmentation, which made for rivalry among competing units and led rulers to accept the alliance of the bourgeoisie, grant substantial autonomy to cities and towns (unknown anywhere else), and encourage and support those technicians, scientists, and artists whose work could redound to their prestige and advantage. Second, and related to the first, was the early recognition of rights of property, which afforded inventors and entrepreneurs security in the enjoyment of the fruits of their labor and wealth.[3] The contrast with other societies in this regard was striking. Listen to Sir Thomas Roe, ambassador of James I to the Mogul emperor in India (1615): "Lawes they have none written. The Kyngs judgement byndes.... His Governors of Provinces rule by his *Firmanes*.... They take life and goodes at pleasure."[4]

Yet such factors are surely only part of the story; and, indeed, one would not have to be a Marxist to turn some of this around and argue that it was the successful bourgeoisie that made the property rights and not the reverse.

Another significant element of the story was the role of the Christian church, particularly the monastic orders, which constituted highly productive agricultural and industrial communities organized not for absolute self-sufficiency but for economic autonomy. Their ranks included some of the best mechanics and architects of the time; their shops were schools for skill and technique; and their dispersion throughout Europe was a strong force for the diffusion of knowledge.

Once again, though, the existence of the institution is not in itself an explanation. The question remains: Why this behavior, which contrasts sharply with that of other religions and even with the Eastern branch of the Christian faith. Without attempting a process of endless regression, the answer to that lies in the realm of values and attitudes: the choice of activism over the contemplative life (Martha over Mary), the Benedictine equation of work to prayer (*laborare est orare*), a paradoxical concern to soften the pain of labor, the Judaic desacralization of nature, and others still to be explored.[5]

The values of the monastic orders were (became?) those of a creative minority of the population as a whole. Why this was so, I am not prepared to say: people learned from the Church; the Church learned from the people. Too many—the vast majority—of the inventors, innovators, and doers of the Middle Ages are unknown to us. But what has come down to us, largely as a result of recent research, is the sense of a growing community of savants and builders and mechanics (*homo faber*), communicating with one another, copying and improving, climbing by standing on the shoulders of those who came before, tingling with the excitement of achievement. Lynn White cites a sermon preached by the Dominican Fra Giordano of Pisa in 1306, singing the praises of invention:

> Not all the arts have been found; we shall never see an end of finding them. Every day one could discover a new art...indeed they are being found all the time. It is not 20 years since there was discovered the art of making spectacles, which help you to see well and which is one of the best and most necessary in the world. And that is such a short time ago that a new art, which never before existed, was invented.... I myself saw the man who discovered and practiced it, and I talked with him.[6]

It is this turn of mind, this excitement and pleasure, this Faustian passion even within the bosom of the Church that goes far to account for the peculiarity of European technological development. For better and worse: the same impulse that gave us eyeglasses, and added years of useful study and work to some of the best minds and most skilled hands of the age, also gave us gunpowder and firearms. (The Chinese used powder in their fireworks; the Europeans borrowed it, improved it to increase its explosive force, and used it in cannon.) And it is this turn of mind—or some approximation to it—that I would argue is a prerequisite not only for the diffusion of technology, but the ability to generate technology in preindustrial societies.

What does that mean for the education in technology of the less developed countries, with which we began? I am afraid it may seem at first sight to imply a counsel of despair: if a society does not have the kind of spirit that generates technology, it will not absorb technique or knowledge. But social scientists, no less than natural scientists or engineers, do not like counsels of despair. They prefer to think that problems have solutions, that tasks are made to be done, hence, that the diffusion of technology is everywhere feasible. If the ability to assimilate and generate knowledge is linked to the value system of the society, why then, we must find ways to inculcate and nurture the right values.

Unfortunately, it has proved easier to transfer capital, materials, and labor than values or even knowledge. It is not hard to know what to teach; the questions are: How? To whom? On what level? Should we build a broad base? Concentrate on elites? Let me attempt some first approximations to answers on the basis of the Western experience.

1.  There has been a shift from learning by doing to learning in school. The first centuries of European technological advance built on empirical experience. Apprentices learned at the bench, alongside trained workers and masters— the whole process often organized and regulated by craft guilds. Bench learning never disappeared—it is still important today—but from the 18th century on, it has been increasingly confined to skill-intensive branches of hand manufacture or to a complementary role, taking the products of school training and fitting them for the special demands of a given job.

The growing emphasis on school learning reflects, first, the changing content of technology: the newer branches of production especially (chemicals, say, or anything connected with electricity) use techniques more esoteric, less apprehensible by observation and common sense than the older branches (textiles, machine building, and so on). Second, schooling offers the possibility of training more people faster and for a wider range of activities. Bench learning tends to be job-specific; school learning can be adapted to a variety of applications. It is no wonder, then, that within Europe the so-called follower countries, those that wanted to emulate Britain in the course to industrialization, came to rely far more extensively than the British had on formal school instruction.

2. These educational programs have always been highly selective in character. They have built on a broad base of literacy and numeracy, but elementary schooling as such has been important, not for its direct contribution to economic performance, but as training in citizenship and as a device for the recruitment of talent. Other things being equal, the bigger the pool one draws from, the better the chances of finding gifted and original scientists and technicians.

3. The European achievement has always rested on a close alliance between science and technology, between theory and application. Indeed, until fairly recent times it would have made little sense to distinguish between those two modes. The scientists (that is, those whom we would call scientists) were invariably engaged in applications; indeed, derived most of their theoretical thought by reflecting on observation and experience. The technicians drew on what they knew of the corpus of scientific knowledge and added to it by study (like Harrison) and personal consultation. Even after scientific training and procedure separated themselves from application and engineering, and so-called pure science was set aside (above?) as something special, the old ties remained important. Industry in advanced countries has continued to treat faculties of science as an intellectual resource; and these same faculties have given numerous gifted students and teachers to the ranks of industry and enterprise.

4. European performance owed much to an atmosphere of competition and emulation. There have always been multiple points of initiative, of creation, imitation, improvement. This was only partly due to the political

fragmentation; it was also inextricably tied to a system of free enterprise.

5. This atmosphere of competition and emulation has been, in my opinion, a most powerful force for the sustained enthusiasm, even joy, of the European (Western, Japanese) research effort. Because of it, the pursuit of knowledge and its application have yielded great psychic as well as material rewards. We may still not be able to account for the origin of this *Neuerungsfreudigkeit*, this joy in novelty, but its persistence clearly owes much to its agonistic character.

What are the lessons in all this for the less developed countries of today? Their principal weakness lies in their inability to find the equivalents of competition and enthusiasm. The first three conditions are difficult enough, but at least one can see there the outline of an educational strategy. But the latter conditions are as much political as economic and fly in the face of all the prevailing trends and predilections. To be sure, it is not hard to postulate nonmarket (socialistic) substitutes for the stimuli and incentives of freedom and competition: loyalty to a social or national ideal (also present in a market economy such as Japan); bestowal of awards and rewards from above (the Legion of Honor or the numerous Soviet prizes and privileges); to say nothing of the power of a disinterested curiosity and creative energy.

But all of that is a promissory note without a maturity date. The historical record shows that, so far, the only nations that have generated an autonomous and creative technology have been those characterized by freedom of initiative and enterprise. The one apparent exception, the Soviet Union, was able to build on a substantial educational and industrial base inherited from the Old Regime. China may yet prove to be a second exception, though it too has had much more to work with than most of the less developed countries in Asia and Africa.[7]

These have their task cut out for them. We can help, but in the last analysis, this is one aspect of growth and development that each society has to accomplish by itself, from within.

## Notes

1. Oceanic navigation goes back earlier, of course. But these voyages were the product of accident or feats of derring-do, with the exception of the Norse leaps to Iceland and Greenland and archipelagic travel in the Pacific. It was only with the establishment of normal trading and administrative connections to Asia and America that one can speak of oceanic sailing as a continuing, regular activity.

2. Later, this technique was much improved by making use of a log and sand clock. The log was thrown astern and unwound a rope tied with knots at regular intervals. At the end of the time marked by the sand clock (far more accurate, obviously, than some verbal formula), the knots run out were counted and converted to speed, that is, distance over time. To this day the knot continues as a measure of nautical speed.

3. The latter point has since been made by Douglass North and Robert P. Thomas, the keystone of their analysis of European economic development. See *The Rise of the Western World: A New Economic History* (Cambridge: Cambridge University Press, 1973).

4. Wm. Foster, ed., *The Embassy of Sir Thomas Roe to the Court of the Great Mogul, 1615-1619,* 2 vols. (London: Hakluyt Society, 1899), vol. 1, p. 123.

5. See especially Lynn White, Jr., "Cultural Climates and Technological Advance in the Middle Ages," *Viator: Medieval and Renaissance Studies* 2 (1971), pp. 171–201.

6. *Ibid.,* p. 174.

7. In this regard, note the recent Chinese development of the technology and manufacture of optical fibers, "virtually without outside help." "Jumping a Century," *The Economist* 273 (7107) (Nov. 17, 1979), pp. 105–106.

# 39
# Modernity and Cultural Specificities
*Alain Touraine*

## THE UNITY AND DIVERSITY OF PATHS TO DEVELOPMENT
### The Widening Gap

At the present time, nobody seems to be concerned with development, if that term is taken to mean the idea of a social, economic and cultural transformation of what may be called society. On the one hand, in most of the world society does not hold the centre of the stage, nor is it even a focal point of interest in public life. All authority, all command, is vested in the state, a state which by definition is responsible for repulsing enemies without and countering threats from the outside world, and for the difficult task of integration in the case of countries which are segmented or loosely integrated economically or ethnically.

On the other hand, it is the individual and the seductions of consumption which prevail. On both sides, the major casualties are social problems and social trends. The contemporary world does not seem capable of producing collective protagonists, unless they are directly controlled by a central authority or else reduced to the extremely vague entity of a fashion or a trend of opinion. The nineteenth century in Europe was dominated by social entities: financial and industrial capitalism, the working class, the major political parties, and even the newspapers, which were associated with the defence of economic or social causes. Today, neither social movements or political parties, as such, seem to wield any great influence. The centre

SOURCE: *International Social Science Journal* (November 1988), pp. 443–458. © Unesco 1988. Reproduced by permission of Unesco. Article abridged by the editors.

of the stage, which was teeming with activity a century ago, has been vacated and activity seems to have shifted to either side, towards the state on the one hand and to society on the other. Who talks of labour and property? There is much talk of war, of threats of nuclear or ecological catastrophes, human rights and the protection of minorities; others speak of autonomy, individualism, equality of opportunity, freedom of movement and freedom to rise in the social scale. The weakness, almost the disappearance, of social movements and major political mobilizations is tied in with the crisis of the idea of development. For the strength of the social movements of the previous century lay in the fact that their action embraced both the internal problems of a given type of society and problems linked with a process of social transformation, whether institutionalized or revolutionary. The weakening of the collective protagonists is explained primarily by the separation of internal, structural problems specific to a given type of society and problems linked with development, industrialization or national liberation. For we know today that the principal protagonist in historical transformations is not a social group (because any social group is linked with a type of society and so cannot create another type of society) but rather the state, associated with either a ruling class or nationalist forces, or even revolutionary groups which, however, maintains the unity and continuity of a political collectivity through economic, social and cultural transformations. On the other hand, we no longer believe that economic and social transformations solve the problems of either individual happiness or collective freedoms. The ideology of progress, the idea that economic development and personal and collective happiness go hand in hand, is but a dream of the past. Between the problems of the state on the one hand and those of individuals on the other, there is a void, filled only superficially by the mass media, putting over either the political razzmatazz or the cult of personality.

Thus is defined the purpose of our reflections and their accompanying investigations: is it possible for what societies do to themselves in order to manage and transform themselves

to become meaningful once more? Or must we recognize that this definition of public life belongs to the past and that all the problems of the present and of the future will be more radical than in the past, because they will be dominated by the confrontation, almost without mediation, of an ever more powerful state and ever more demanding individuals?

But how can one go along with this desocialization of history when we are at present faced with two fundamental threats: nuclear war on the one hand, and famine on the other? The former reminds us that the triumph of science and technology can cause nations to be subordinated to superpowers and welfare to be subordinated to war. And similarly, does not the existence of hunger in large areas of the world, along with chronic poverty and even in many cases increasing marginality and exclusion, remind us of the derisory nature of a consumer-oriented individualism which creates far-distant destructive shock-waves? The same applies to the urge to escape and to self-destruction through drugs, which gives rise to a wildcat economy elsewhere in the world and generates violence and destruction. If the theme of development were to be abandoned in favour of a neo-classical conception of social peace, we would willingly agree, even if we were not entirely convinced; but the abandonment of the theme of development would mean that some would sink deeper into poverty and others would regress into military and political confrontations absorbing a large share of the world's resources.

It is clear that this bi-polarization of the world between Third World hunger and the risk of nuclear war is no more than the extreme practical form of the growing split between a triumphant reason charged with authority and avid for power, and cultural and social groups increasingly on the defensive and often imprisoned in their own decomposition.

The destiny of the world is not in the hands of the leaders of one camp or the other; nor is it in the hands of international assemblies. It depends first and foremost on the ability of all concerned to bridge the gap between reason and cultures, between development as a universal and quantitative goal, with cultures defined as value choices, and specific paths of economic development and social changes. Have we not reached the extreme limit of dualization between over-armed superpowers and societies in crisis or even in the process of decomposition? On what conditions can we retrace our steps, bridge the gap between the quantitative and qualitative, between the universal and the particular, between economic interest and passion, or to revert to conventional language, between society and the community?

## Modernity and Modernization

The first condition for such a rapprochement is to separate what has been fused together. . . . The Western model fell into error in identifying itself with reason, in believing that its own modernization was entirely endogenous. The anti-Western models fell into equally serious error in believing that an absolute authority could by its will alone and its force of compulsion achieve modernity at the cost of sacrificing one or several generations. The whole picture changes when we recognize the fact that nowhere in the world is it possible to live either solely at the level of the internal problems of a given society or at the level of permanent historical change; or to put it more simply, the problems of the state and those of social life cannot be unified; in all forms of development, in one way or another reason must go along with violence and rationalism with voluntarism.

So let us define modernity in itself as a set of attributes of social organization, without confusing it with modernization, which is a movement, something willed, a mobilization at the head of which is in any case the state, whatever the social forces on which it depends.

It is naturally in the Western model that we find the best analysis of modernity, provided we have recourse to the latest and most liberated finalism of the former evolutionary views. What characterizes these new representations is that they no longer define modernity in terms of rationalization, of the triumph of the general rule, but more in terms of the capacity to respond to a changing environment and to manage complex systems, and this places the themes of complexity and uncertainty at the centre of the analysis.

But these general characteristics of modernity are not sufficient to define it. They are only a first level of analysis, the most descriptive and the most quantitative level, which must be followed by two others in order that the notion of development may have a meaning that can be put to some use.

In the first place, development is not a continuous evolution, a gradual passage from the particular to the universal. It is the transition from one type of society to another, defined more structurally, by cultural factors and social relationships. It is the transition from seeing things in terms of continuity to seeing them in terms of discontinuity which marks the principal break between present-day thought and the thought of the previous century. A set of cultural orientations, that is to say the management of resources, cannot be defined purely quantitatively, but primarily in terms of the level at which a society transforms itself. This is a central assertion, since instead of associating the idea of modernity with that of an impersonal and rational way of running things, it leads us to define it in terms of the self-transformation of society. Thus we must reintroduce the traditional notion of types of society and forms of production. A mercantile economy is one whose activity is commanded by investments which transform the conditions of trade: land and sea routes, monetary techniques, weights and measures, laws and regulations, the protection of transport, and so on. An industrial society is one which transforms manufacturing conditions and the division of labour, replacing hand crafts and home-made products by the co-ordinated labour of workers in factories and workshops. We are currently seeing the emergence of societies beyond the limits of industrial societies, which I call programmed societies and whose major investments relate to the mass production and dissemination of symbolic goods: goods of a cultural nature, information, representation knowledge, affecting not solely the organization of labour but the goals of the activity involved, and hence culture itself.

So societies can be said to progress from the capacity to organize trade to the capacity to produce industrial goods and subsequently 'cultural goods'. Each type of society must be defined in terms not only of a specific type of investment, but also a form of representation of the world and a definition of the subject. It is no exaggeration to say that looking at things from this angle, rationalization, and hence the naturalization of human activity, is not the most advanced form of modernity, but one of its most primitive forms. The cosmogonies which put man back into his place in nature were profoundly rationalist, as are all attempts to identify man with a natural order of things, with the principles laid down by a logos. The mercantile world is a profoundly rationalist world, and that is what Max Weber had in mind in referring to rationalization and bureaucratization. On the other hand, the central themes of an industrialized society are less purely rationalist, since they place the notions of labour, enterprise and profit at the centre of economic analysis. Man is seen not so much as a rational being imposing his laws on nature as a worker, admittedly rational but also a suffering being engaged in a productive effort. This establishes a link between the rationalist tradition deriving from the Enlightenment and the Judeo-Christian tradition attaching merit to hard work and redemption through suffering. It is evident that what have been termed post-industrial societies have an even more integrated and complex view of the subject, and define their investments not by the application of general rules but in terms of the capacity to meet requirements, to respond to demands, which are not expressed at the level of reason alone but which mobilize all levels of personality and culture.

These cultural patterns do not sit enthroned at the centre of society; they are the subject of discussions and conflicts between social forces which attempt to appropriate them and give them a social form. The theme of industrialization is common to entrepreneurs (in both the public and private sectors) and workers, but each party interprets it so differently that social conflicts of central importance arise as a result. Consequently the complete interdependence between the nature of cultural models and the nature of social conflicts leads us to believe that the most modern societies are not those furthest from rationalist models, but those which most fully incorporate in the theme of rationalization other dimensions of action, social organization and the protagonists themselves. The image presented by conventional thinkers and the founders of sociology seems to be very far from present-day reality. And here the social sciences can take the evolution of the natural sciences as an example. In the days of Descartes, Leibnitz and Laplace, the world was regarded as a mechanism whose general laws scientists tried to discover. The contemporary science which seems to be the most fecund and which has the greatest influence on the way we think and behave is biology, one of whose main branches, genetics, seeks to understand individuality; naturally this does not lead to any sort of irrationalist approach, but on the contrary it leads to the idea that the principal purpose of scientific analysis is to gain a knowledge of individual differences. Hence came about a profound modification in what may be called Western ideology, the key word of which was rationalization. Only thus does it become possible to resolve the apparently insurmountable contradiction between the reign of universal reason and the resistance of particular cultures, since modernity cannot be identified with the impersonal supremacy of reason; on the contrary it must be seen as an increasingly expanding action exerted by society on itself.

A brief reference to a definition of modernity suffices to make it clear that the notion must be completely separated from that of modernization. But is it not much easier today than previously? It seems obvious that a century ago the most modern countries were those that modernized most, and the historical experience of the United States for long reinforced this mistaken assessment, for the United States were at one and the same time modern, rationalist and strongly modernizing, attracting as they did men and capital to populate and organize the wide open spaces. Today this is no longer the case, and we have become accustomed, in actual fact since the late nineteenth century and the rapid industrial expansion of Germany and Japan, to recognizing that non-modern countries can be more modernizing than countries that have advanced furthest into modernity. It has become commonplace nowadays to compare Japanese management with American management, and rightly so, for to do so makes the opposition between modernity and modernization immediately clear. American management, taught in the best business schools is an application of the principles of the philosophy of the Enlightenment and of rational thought to the running of a business. Good management is that which defines functions, differentiates activities, and enables everything to be calculated; and even if we criticize this conception and in particular reject the pseudo-scientific aspects of the methods applied to the work of men and women, the fact remains that this conception of modernity has enjoyed spectacular success. But nowadays we are less impressed by this success than by that, apparently greater, of Japanese management, which has recourse not to rationalism but to mobilization; it is not concerned with universal principles of action but with strengthening the capacity for change of large organizations or small groups, relying on cultural and social as well as economic parameters. Here, as in the army, the objective to be attained is defined in specific terms: the conquest of a market, the mastery of a technique. And efficiency is measured in terms of how a complex organization succeeds in adapting to new forms of operation. American-style management can be defined as more modern, and Japanese management as more modernizing or more mobilizing. And to the Japanese example many others could be added

when we consider the quite large number of countries, such as Mexico and India, which have undergone an accelerated economic development in the course of the last 50 years.

Is it possible to formulate a theory of modernization completely separate from a theory of modernity? Can it be said that the conditions of industrialization are different from those of the functioning of an industrial society? The question is a long-standing one and was already posed by Marx, for example, when he referred to primitive accumulation, distinguishing it from the operational elements of capitalist industry. And indeed it appears essential to analyse development, the transition from one type of society to another, and in particular industrialization, in different terms from those of the internal functioning of one type of society or another. And when we consider the analyses of industrialization, or more broadly of development, that are proposed, what strikes us is that internal and external factors, economic and social factors, are always presented as interdependent, so that development can never be reduced to the analysis of the endogenous factors of economic growth. A given type of society does not change without an initial break with the previous systems of social and cultural reproduction or control. In many cases this has found expression in revolution, ranging from the English revolution of Cromwell and the role of the Puritans to the twentieth-century revolutions in Third World countries. But in addition to this internal crisis there must also be a break-through from external sources, such as the great discoveries and the role of the merchant venturers of the seventeenth century or, in our own day the role of rapidly-developing technology as well as that of international competition. Similarly, economic and social transformation supposes not only an accumulation of capital and of means of production, but also a response to social demands, otherwise investment may simply be wasted or merely strengthen military production. And internal and external demand must always be considered an external factor in a system of economic organization.

Instead of setting endogenous development against exogenous development, as though the two extreme types existed in the pure state it might be preferable to assert that all processes of successful development combine internal and external factors and economic and socio-cultural factors.

## Social Movements and Historical Movements

The separation of problems of modernity from those of modernization must extend to a knowledge of the protagonists themselves. Here again, long-standing traditions have required us to merge the two types of action. The Western model held that workers' trade union action was at one and the same time an instrument of economic redistribution and a factor of improvement in production, by forcing employers to have recourse to technologies which step up productivity and therefore enable higher wages to be paid. Conversely, the voluntaristic models of the Second and Third Worlds imagined that those who took part in social and national liberation were directly transformed into the protagonists of a new type of society. But what we have to realize is that the two kinds of approach are widely separated. Let us state them in their plainest terms: the functioning of a society mobilizes protagonists who in all cases are directly or indirectly defined in terms of social classes, that is to say they are defined by their role in an economic and social system of production; while those who participate in the process of historical transformation are—because they are defined more directly in relation to the state rather than in relation to a dominant elite—primarily national protagonists. This is evidenced not only by the central importance of the national liberation movements of the twentieth century, but also by the importance of the national components in the revolutionary movements of countries on the periphery of the capitalist development of the nineteenth century. Yet the most powerful ideologies are those that have asserted the existence of full-bodied social movements, that is to say capable of being both class movements and national liberation movements—in particular post-Leninist movements whose importance in developing countries has been and still is considerable. Nevertheless it can be said today that there has never been a synthesis of class movements and national liberation movements. On the eve of the First World War in the Austro–Hungarian Empire, where Austro–Marxist theoreticians were trying to define the relationships between nationalism and the worker's movement, Czech and other workers asserted the primacy of their national struggles over their social struggles. In other cases, the contrary occurred, in particular in countries which were the first to become industrialized. But the point is that the gap between movements of national and cultural defence and movements of economic modernization has constantly widened to the point where the most dramatic line of cleavage in the present-day world is between the demise of militant revolutionary nationalists who are rejected by cultural nationalist movements which repudiate the revolutionary theme of the class struggle and also by workers' organizations which wield major influence in the functioning of modern societies, whether democratic or not. From the Middle East to Latin America, and even in post-war Japan, we have seen and we are still seeing the desperate action, which in some cases overflows into pure violence, of groups which have attempted to combine objectives that are if not contradictory, at least fundamentally different.

This does not mean that social objectives and national objectives may not be combined in movements which, as a result, have the most mobilizing effect of all; but they may combine only insofar as they make a distinction between the two objectives and have recourse to democratic procedures, that is to say differentiating between different themes and different areas of conflict and negotiation.

## Intellectuals Divided Between Revolution and Democracy

Nowadays, intellectuals are among the most influential agents of the dissociation of a world in process of change. Some of them espouse the cause of national, political or cultural assertion, while others analyse the economic phenomena of production supposedly governed by the rational quest for economic advantage. Even within the Western world itself, the social sciences seem to have divided into two main trends: a critical school of thought which denounces all social life as a mechanism of domination, manipulation and exclusion, and a methodological individualism which rejects any kind of view of the social system and reduces the social protagonist to a seeker after economic advantage or at least a strategist of its defence. This duality of orientation is catastrophic, and to a large extent contributes to the destruction of the social field and its analysis and to the dualizing of the world, one part of which seems to be inhabited by rational consumers and the other to be entirely governed by centralized mechanisms of order and mobilization.

This ideological division of intellectuals is open to challenge; we must abandon the illusion of homogeneous societies on the one hand, and on the other hand the no less illusory idea of a society reduced to a market in which consumers are able to discern their long-term advantages and organize their social and political conduct in consequence. The development of the social sciences in many countries has already made it possible, and should make it increasingly possible, to replace these extreme views by a more integrated study of the various ways in which different regions or countries of the world have taken different roads to modernization and achieved modernity by a combination of different processes.

It is by renouncing the extreme and simplified forms of rationalism and culturalism, or to revert to nineteenth-century terminology, English-style evolutionism and German-style historicism, that we can arrive, in theory and in practice, at a comparison between historical processes all of which have their specificity but all of which are component parts of one and the same historical mainstream, because their unity lies in the fact that they all relate to the same modernity, while the plurality of historical processes lies in the extreme diversity of mechanisms of modernization corresponding to very different historical situations. We must therefore constantly combine two complementary intellectual operations. One consists of separating what may be called synchronistic analysis and diachronistic analysis—the study of the functioning of social systems and the study of the transition from one type of society to another. The other is the recognition of the combination, in any concrete historical situation, of structural mechanisms and mechanisms of change; of synchronistic and diachronistic analysis. What has to be avoided is monism, be it the assertion of the almost natural triumph of reason or almost evident need to defend a cultural specificity. All ideologies which have been identified with any single principle have been transformed into ideological and political instruments for justifying a ruling elite, be it economic or political, civil or military. Before raising the classic problem of the relationships between investment and participation, between the creation of new products and the development of consumption, we have to recognize the interdependece, the complementarity, but consequently also the separation, of modernity and modernization. It is by rejecting the Western world's claim to identification with modernity, and the claim of many other countries elsewhere in the world to identification with modernization, that we can begin to reconstruct a picture and a programme of historical transformations avoiding all the risks of absolutism and of the ideological deformation of reality.

Such a task must necessarily be undertaken in all parts of the world at once. No country, no continent, can present itself as a model to be imitated by the rest of the world, if it is not to diminish or disintegrate. To put it very simply, what are needed today more than ever before are comparative studies, but in the best sense of the term, for comparative studies can cover the two deviations to which I have just referred. The comparative approach may confine us to the study of differences and specificities, but if different countries or cultures have nothing in common, how can they establish relationships between one another other than those of conflict, or at least estrangement? Conversely, if a comparative study leads simply to placing different historical situations on a quantitative scale, does it not clash with reality, whose cultural patterns, political regimes and collective social projects cannot be ignored? A comparative study has little meaning unless it interrelates very many studies covering different fields, all of them related more or less directly to the same set of problems. It seems to me that the time has come to contribute to the gradual elaboration, step by step and in concrete terms, of such an analysis; that is to say to give thought to the interrelations between the unity of modernity and plurality of ways and means of modernization. We must realize that the complete opposition between the universalism of reason and the specificity of cultural identities threatens to split the world apart; it is perhaps not as dramatic a threat as that of war, but it is one which is bound to cause the rot to set in and to give rise to a sort of latent civil war in most countries, from the richest to the poorest, from North to South and from East to West. To rely on the unity of reflection is the contrary of relying on the supremacy of a hegemonic model of thought and action. What has to be done is to work as actively and effectively as possible for peace, which itself supposes the recognition of differences and at the same time a common destiny and common projects.

At the close of the present century, we do not yet know whether the world will be divided ever more dramatically between superpowers and communities, between the safeguarding of identities and the manipulation of the most advanced techniques; but we ought at least to express clearly our determination to combat this growing dualization by re-establishing the links between the histories of different parts of the world. It may be convenient to speak of a First, Second and Third World, provided they are not set one against the other as units between which there is no communication. The time has come to give priority to reflection, study and discussion directed, towards the theoretical and practical reintegration of objectives of universal scope and of measures taking account in all cases of the specificity of historical situations, social projects and forms of political action....

# 40

# The Ethnocentrism of Social Science

*Howard J. Wiarda*

The proposition advanced here is that the vast bulk of our social science findings, models, and literature, which purport to be universal, are in fact biased, ethnocentric, and not universal at all. They are based on the narrow and rather particular experiences of Western Europe (actually a much smaller nucleus of countries in central and northwest Europe) and the United States, and they may have little or no relevance to the rest of the world. A growing number of scholars, particularly those who have had long research experience in the so-called developing nations, have now come to recognize this fact; and among others new efforts are being made to reexamine the very "Western" experience on which so many of our social science "truths" and models have been based. Because these verities

SOURCE: Howard J. Wiarda, "The Ethnocentrism of the Social Science Implications for Research and Policy," *The Review of Politics*, April 1981, pp. 163–197. With permission of *The Review of Politics*, University of Notre Dame. Article and notes abridged by the editors.

are still widely believed, however, by many scholars and policymakers alike, the ethnocentric biases and assumptions undergirding them need to be examined and their implications for research and policy explored.[1]

\* \* \*

## THE NATURE OF THE WESTERN BIASES

To most of us a liberal arts education is something familiar, comfortable, an integral part of our intellectual upbringing. It shapes our thinking, our attitudes and our intellectual preconceptions. However much our liberal arts heritage is celebrated, nonetheless, we must also recognize the biases inherent in that approach. Indeed, it may be that it is the very nature of our liberal arts focus that lies at the heart of our present dilemma and of our incomprehension of Third World nations. For as presently structured liberal arts education is essentially *Western* education, the Greco-Roman and Judaeo-Christian traditions and European history, from which derive a set of concepts, ethics, and governing norms and experiences that have their bases in the Western background and that may have little reference to or applicability in other global areas. Although it is understandable that those who inhabit the West should structure their educational system as an appreciation of their own history and culture, we must also recognize such training for what it is: traditional liberal arts education is essentially the first "area study" program.

Our concepts of "justice," "fair play," "good government," "progress," and "development" are similarly Western concepts. The latter two terms imply a certain unilinearism and inevitability in the evolution of man's social and political institutions. The former three imply some shared expectations as to the social and political institutions and concomitants that are supposed to follow from industrialization and economic development. So long as we could

divide the world into two parts, Western and non-Western, and so long as we assumed, à la Hegel, Marx, or W. W. Rostow, that the non-western world would inevitably follow the same developmental path as the West ("the developed world shows to the less developed the mirror of its own future"), our social science assumptions rested easily and comfortably. By this point, however, it is abundantly clear that these conditions no longer, if they ever did, apply. The world cannot be so simply divided, and it seems obvious that the developmental experience of today's emerging nations cannot repeat or mirror the experience of Western Europe. Our social science assumptions, based so heavily on the European experience, therefore require close reexamination as well....

It is one of the contentions of this essay that such concepts as "development" or "modernization" must be re-recognized for what they are: metaphors, poetic devices, shorthand tools, abstractions that have some importance in defining, outlining, or describing reality but that should not be mistaken for reality itself. Not only are they metaphorical devices with all the limitations for describing reality that implies, but they are *Western* metaphors which may or may not (most likely the latter) have relevance to the non-Western world. Let us examine these propositions in terms of three major disciplinary areas of particular importance, both to the study of development and to our understanding of the Western biases therein: political theory, political sociology, and political economy....

### Political Theory

...To assert that the great tradition of political thought with which we are familiar is of less than universal applicability and that there are major geographic and culture areas, including within the West, that are entirely neglected in our political and social theory courses is to imply that there *is* something worth studying in these other areas and traditions. That is a difficult proposition to demonstrate to those who have always thought in Eurocentric terms, and it helps explain why so many of those studying other areas spend much of their professional careers defensively seeking to justify to their colleagues why their areas may be just as profound and complex, with as many important research implications, as Britain, France, Germany, or the United States. It is a long, uphill battle which is still only partially won but seems to be gaining added momentum due to the relative decline of these core areas in recent years and the corresponding increase in importance of such previously neglected nations as Brazil, China, India, Iran, Mexico, Nigeria, and Tanzania. In my own research and writing I have tried to show the continued importance of Iberian and Latin American organic-corporatist thought and sociopolitical organization, to present this as a viable alternative to the usual liberal-pluralist models with which we look at these areas, to understand Latin America, in the words of novelist Carlos Fuentes, as a distinct *civilization* and not as a series of agreements about tomatoes (or coffee, sugar, or bananas). In other quite distinct cultural and national settings, comparable studies are now appearing or being rediscovered of traditions of thought, law, and social and political organization that were previously ignored and remain largely unknown but which are probably at least as important as the European ones for analyzing these nations' unique developmental processes. It is not our purpose here to describe these alternative traditions in any detail but merely to note that they exist and to point readers toward some of the literature.[2]

## Political Sociology

Political sociology demonstrates many of the same biases as does political theory, and is probably more dangerous because sociology is taken more seriously than political theory. Indeed an entire generation and more grew up on the development sociology literature of the last three decades, a body of literature that is as narrow,

particularistic, ethnocentric, and Western-biased as the theory just analyzed....

I wish to suggest that the empirical evidence does not support the claims to universalism and inevitability put forth by the major Western theories of sociopolitical development concerning the impact of industrialization on the broader social system.[3] The transition from agraria to industria and such factors as increased population, urbanization, the separation of place of residence from place of work, coupled with rising occupational differentiation and specialization have tended *in the West* to have brought specific kinds of changes in familial, religious, political, and all other major areas of social organization. It is for this reason, and because at that time the sociologists and political economists who analyzed these changes were themselves exclusively from that area, that the specifically Western social and political concomitants of industrialization came to be incorporated into theoretical conceptualizations of the change process per se. Given the historical context (the mid-to-late 19th century), the fact that northwest Europe experienced these mammoth changes first, and particularly at that time the lack of any non-Western experience with the transition to an industrial society, one might well say that the Western social adaptations occurring then almost *had* to be closely associated with a more general and presumptively universal theory of development and modernization.

The Western bias pervades the work of the great figures in sociology. For example, Weber's and Tawney's work on the mutual influence of religion and economics in the growth of rational capitalism, Toennies's *Gemeinschaft and Gesellschaft*, Durkheim's mechanical and organic solidarity, and the mass society concept developed by MacIver are major examples of analyses concerned with particular aspects of a particular *Western* cultural history. The development literature was largely grounded on this same set of concepts and understandings, generalizing unduly from what was a narrow and limited historical and cultural experience. There is no reason to assume that in other culture areas the same sociopolitical concomitants of industrialization must necessarily follow. Students of non-western or partly Western areas, whose development is taking place in a quite different context, must face the more difficult task of distinguishing between the processes and dynamics of industrialization *and* the social and political changes accompanying these which may take quite different and varied directions from those of "the West."

Not only are the timing, sequences, and international context of development different, but non-Western societies have generally been quite selective in accepting what is useful from Western modernization while often rejecting the rest. Of course this is a mixed situation, for while some elements associated with Western modernization are kept out, other aspects enter regardless of the barriers erected. But the process itself is one of filtering and not simply of imitating and inevitably following. For example, Japanese modernization under the Meiji came about through the cooperation of government and powerful family groups. The tenacity of such traditional family elements and their persistence were not the result merely of nostalgic attachment to the past or to some vague tradition; rather there were valid economic reasons— Japan's abundance of manpower as opposed to capital, her traditional family handicraft industry which could be used to generate the needed capital—for their retention. The result has been that the Japanese pattern of modernization indicates significant differences from that of the West (and it obviously continues to do so). The social and political concomitants that in the West followed from industrialization have not necessarily followed.

The Japanese evidence and parallel findings from other regions of the world suggest that the forms of Western social and political organization are not the inevitable consequence of the replacement of feudalism, traditionalism, and agriculturalism by a modern industrial technology. Instead the capitalistic individualism, secularism, the particular role of the middle classes and middle classness, the growth of liberalism and interest group pluralism, and a host of other features that are so much a part of the northwest European and United States religious, familial, social, and political system and order should be seen as only one of numerous possible alternatives in the urban-industrial transition, and not necessarily a more developed or ethically or morally superior one. Other, *alternative* routes to modernization also command our attention....

In sociology as in political theory the models and metaphors used derived exclusively from the Euro-American experience. It is not necessary here to go into non-Western concepts of time and space, cyclical theories of history as opposed to the predominantly evolutionary ones of the West, notions of permanence and continuity as opposed to Western belief in perpetual change. Suffice it to say that the images, perceptions, and understandings used to depict development were all Western in origin, that we had no comprehension of societies based on presumptions other than that of constant progress. How arrogant that no consideration was given to non-western concepts, except as these constituted traditional, dysfunctional "problems to be overcome." It is small wonder that theories purporting to be universal but actually quite particularistic should run up against major barriers or produce unexpected results when they were applied to societies where their major assumptions had no bases in local history, tradition, or understandings.

Especially presumptuous was the expectation of a single, unilinear path to development. There was only one acceptable route along with certain common signposts—all derived from the Western experience—along the path. "Traditional society" was seldom further differentiated, leaving the impression that all Third World nations had a common background, began at the same starting point, and, once started, embarked on a single path that led them to shed their traditional features and proceed irreversibly to modernization. Almost no thought was given to the fact that not only were the starting points, the nature of traditional societies, immensely different, but that the paths (plural!) to development and the end products were certain to be vastly dissimilar as well. The image that should have been used was not that of a single path or route to development but that of a much more complex *lattice,* with numerous, diverse beginnings and multiple, crisscrossing channels.[4]

A key reason developmental sociology went astray—and a major cause of its attractiveness— is that a close identification was made between development as a process and development as a moral and ethical good. Not only could we as social scientists analyze development but we could also identify with it, like apple pie and motherhood, as a desirable normative goal toward which all "right-thinking" people should surely work. Particularly as development was closely identified with the values that social scientists hold—secularism, rationalism, pluralism, and the like—and as it implied the destruction or replacement of the values and institutions social scientists tend not to like (authoritarian and traditional structures; religious beliefs and institutions; familial, tribal, or clan ties), it carried enormous appeal.

There is certainly something we can analyze as *change:* development and modernization are probably too Western, too loaded, to be of much use. But change should be regarded as a neutral process and not involve the intrusion of ethical, political, or moral judgments—unless we are willing to abandon all pretense to objectivity and assume that our private values are or ought to be everyone's values. How conceited and pretentious that is! Certainly it is difficult to be against development and modernization. The mistake was in social science presuming to *know* what a developed society looked like (liberal, pluralist, democratic: our idealized image of ourselves) and in assuming that the values of Western civilization were or had to become everyone's values. Hence, if traditional societies or institutions—African tribalism, Indian caste associations, a host of others—failed to develop in terms of prevailing social science theory, they had of necessity to be uprooted and obliterated

in favor of new modernizing ones; and if in the process the modernizing institutions such as political parties and trade unions failed to develop, it was again the societies that were dysfunctional rather than the theory that needed reexamination....

There are, certainly, universals in the development process and perhaps Western Europe and the United States provide us with a model of how this occurs. Economic development and industrialization are occurring in virtually all areas of the globe; class transformations are under way: people are being uprooted and mobilized; urbanization is accelerating; traditional institutions are changing and new ones are being created; specialization and differentiation are going forward. The mistake of the development literature was in ascribing specific social and political concomitants to these changes based on a model that was not universalistic, as it claimed, but particularistic and narrowly Euro-American. All economic and class transformations are, after all, filtered through and shaped by distinct, indigenous cultural, social, and political institutions, no less so in the Third World than in Western Europe; and the timing, sequences, and context of these changes are also quite varied. What the social sciences did, however, was to generalize inappropriately from the sociopolitical institutional concomitants of modernization in Western Europe, which they knew best and assumed to be desirable, to other nations which they knew less well and with whose traditional institutions they felt uncomfortable. Generalization from a single unique case to the rest of the world is not unusual among social scientists; in the case of the development literature, however, the assumptions were widely shared, and the results for developing nations have been particularly unfortunate. The costs of this myopia we must now begin to pay.

## Political Economy

...Non-Marxian developmental economics is as Eurocentric as is the classical Marxian variety. The famous aeronautical stages in the "non-Communist manifesto" of W. W. Rostow ("drive to take off," "take off," etc.), which so strongly shaped—as did Parsons and Lipset in sociology and the Almond and Coleman volume on "The Politics of the Developing Areas" in political science—whole generations of development-minded economists, were based almost exclusively on the Western European and United States experiences. The logic of the Rostow analysis (and of the Alliance for Progress and U.S. foreign assistance, since as National Security Adviser Rostow was also the chief influence in shaping these programs) was that if only the United States could pour in sufficient economic aid, "take off" would occur and the following social and political effects would be felt: organized labor would become less extremist and revolutionary; more professional, and hence less political, armies and bureaucracies would grow; a large middle class would emerge that would be a bulwark of stable, middle-of-road rule; the peasants would become yeomen, middle-class family farmers; and radical ideologies such as communism—a "disease of the transition," Rostow called it—would diminish in attractiveness....

By this point it should be abundantly clear that the Rostowian stages do not necessarily follow one another, that there is no unilinear and inevitable path to development, that with the oil crisis, the internationalization of capital, and other features, the condition of the Third World nations today is fundamentally different from those prevailing a century or more ago, that the development process in these nations hence will not and cannot be a mirror of the European experience, that there are numerous culturally conditioned routes to modernization and not just the European one, and therefore that the social and political concomitants which, based on the European experience, are supposed to follow from modernization may not, in these quite different temporal and spatial contexts, follow at all.[5] Rather, development will take directions that reflect indigenous traditions and institutions: and it is time that we recognize this fact rather than continue to dismiss these processes

and institutions as dysfunctional or try to interpret them through a Western social science framework that has only limited relevance in non-Western areas. As David Apter reminded us some time ago, industrialization in the West is only one form of industrialization.[6] The dilemma for most developing nations is hence not westernization or even modernization but how to gain and employ Western capital and technology while preserving what they see as valuable in their own cultures and traditions.

## CONSEQUENCES OF THE WESTERN BIASES

The theory and assumptions we have applied to the developing nations have often led us to expect certain trends to occur and institutions to develop that have, in fact, not consistently developed. We have expected, and perhaps hoped, that modernization would produce more pluralist and secular societies when, in fact, in Iran and elsewhere powerful religious revivals are taking place that are monistic and theocratic, that proclaim a single right-and-wrong way to do everything which seems appallingly oppressive to most Westerners. We celebrate democracy and pluralism in our theories in the political sphere as well, when the real question in virtually all developing nations is which form authoritarianism will take.[7] We have expected more universalist (our own?) criteria to take hold when in fact particularism seems everywhere on the rise. We applaud merit and have elevated it to a universal norm of modernity when the fact is ascriptive criteria seem ascendant, perhaps increasingly so even in our own society. Obviously, differentiation of labor, specialization of function, and rationalization and bureaucratization have occurred throughout the developing world, but rather than producing much democratization in countries where a strong imperious central state has been either the norm or the aspiration, these trends have chiefly produced more efficient and centralized forms of statism and even terror.[8]

Our social science assumptions have also led us to look for the growth of an increasingly more prosperous working class and hence a more apolitical trade unionism when in fact, in Italy, Argentina, and elsewhere the latter does not seem necessarily to follow from the former; for an increasingly professional and thus apolitical military when in fact increased professionalism leads many militaries (Brazil, Chile, Peru, Portugal) to become more political rather than less; for stronger local government when in fact the dominant tendency even of our "community development" programs, has been toward greater concentration of state power; for mass-based political parties that perform the interest aggregation and articulation functions when actually most "parties" in the developing nations are that only in name and may not at all be inclined to perform the functions Western political science assigns to them; for a middle class that is moderate, democratic, and inclined to assist the less favored elements in the society, when in fact the divided middle sectors in most Third World nations are inclined to ape upper-class ways and use the instruments of the state (armies, labor ministries, and the like) to keep their own lower classes subservient; for elites and businessmen who recognize their social responsibilities to the poor in a more pluralist setting when the real situation is that the elites are intent not on sharing but on getting more wealth and monopolizing it; for greater respect for civil liberties and democracy rather than the increased statism, authoritarianism, and corporatism that seems to be the real life situation virtually everywhere in the Third World. The list of misapplied theories and programs goes on and on. In short, few of the social and political concomitants of modernization that our Western experience would lead us to expect to see developing are in fact developing. The problem lies not in the developing areas since they are often merely continuing preferred and traditional practices; rather, the problem lies in the Western-based concepts and ofttimes wishful social science with which we have sought to interpret these nations.

At the same time that too much attention has been devoted to those institutions that, based on the Western experience, social scientists expected or hoped to develop, too little has been afforded those not in accord with these preferences. It seems obvious, for example, that in the Islamic world and elsewhere religious beliefs and institutions cannot simply be relegated to the ashcans of history under the "inevitable" onslaught of "secularism," nor can the former be dismissed as part of traditional society certain to be superseded. The same applies to tribal and caste associations: these are not just traditional institutions certain to give way under modernization's impact. Behind much of the ideological skirmishing in Africa, for instance, is a tribal context, one that should not be denied or wished away as much social science does but taken as a given and perhaps as a base for other kinds of social and political associations than the preferred Western ones. Similarly, India's caste associations, once consigned to the realm of the traditional, are now viewed as adaptable institutions capable of serving as modernizing agencies.[9] There is a refreshing degree of realism now on the part of political leaders and intellectuals in the Third World to take such institutions as givens and potential developmental building blocks rather than as symbols of "backwardness" that had to be destroyed. The functioning and changes in such institutions during epochs of transition ought also to be a primary focus of social scientists, rather than the easy dismissal of them.

With the strong social-democratic bias that undergirds much of the development literature, social scientists have disregarded a variety of other institutions either because we do not like them politically or because they do not fit our preferred models. Most social scientists, for instance, are uncomfortable with, and often quite hostile toward, the Catholic, elitist, and authoritarian assumptions of traditional Latin society. Because we do not like elite-structured societies, we have seldom studied the dynamics of elite strategies and elite networks, preferring to dismiss these out of hand or apply the familiar traditional label, which seemingly helps make the problem go away. There is abundant literature on labor and peasant movements but very little on elites, both because of practical research problems and because social scientists, like most Americans, are ill at ease with elitist assumptions. We do not like theocratic societies either and especially despise the Islamic mullahs for seeking to resurrect one, but our understanding of events in Iran and other nations will not be advanced by complete hostility or the dismissal of such popular movements as irrational.

Military coups provide another illustration of the familiar biases. Most Western social science, with its favoritism toward democratic and civilian government, treats coups as aberrations, irregular, dysfunctional, and unconstitutional, thus ignoring their normalcy, regularity, functionality, and often times legal-constitutional basis, the reasons for them, their functional similarity to elections and the fact the former may be no more comic opera than the latter. Our antimilitary bias, however, often prevents us from seeing these events neutrally and scientifically.

The examples of such ethnocentrism are numerous in the areas of both public policy and institutions. In President Carter's human rights campaign, for example, it was consistently the United States model and understanding that was imposed abroad; no consideration was given to the fact that other societies define terms like *rights, democracy,* or *justice* in different ways, that they see these differently or assign them a different priority. One pales also at the thought of how many countries and how many women and men in them have been called irrational because they desire larger families rather than smaller, a decision that in their circumstances may well be perfectly rational. Or, in another tradition, one wonders at the easy and widespread use of the term "false consciousness" to describe peasants and workers who may be uncomfortable with or suspicious toward revolutionary movements organized, so they claim, on the lower classes' behalf. The number of policy areas and institutions in which labels and

slogans substitute for close examination, dismissal or relegance to the dustbins of history or to the ranks of traditionalism or dysfunctionality for hard analysis, seems almost endless. Even whole continents and regions, such as Latin America and Africa are often dismissed by social scientists as constituting areas without political culture and therefore unworthy of study. Such attitudes reflect not the true importance of these areas but the biases of the social sciences, the fact these areas seldom fit our favored models and because we are often vaguely antipathetic toward their underlying premises.

If these errors of both commission and omission by social scientists and policymakers were merely benignly neutral, there would be little to worry about; unfortunately, such errors and oversights are neither benign, neutral, nor harmless. The subject merits much fuller attention; here let it simply be said that: (1) based on the ethnocentric developmental assumptions of the social sciences, enormous amounts of money and effort have been wasted on a variety of misguided and misdirected programs; (2) confirmed in the modernity and hence superiority of our own institutions, we have continued patronizingly to dismiss or disparage as traditional or primitive a large number of beliefs, practices, and institutions in the Third World; (3) because our models and perspectives are so narrow and Eurocentric, our comprehension of the real dynamics of change and continuity in these nations remains woefully inadequate, based more on prejudice and/or romance than actuality; (4) grounded on this same particularistic and ethnocentric northwest European and United States experience, the policy measures we have sought to implement have produced hosts of backfires, unanticipated consequences, and sheer disasters; and (5) in the name of advancing modernity, we have helped undermine a great variety of quite viable traditional and transitional institutions, thus contributing by our policies to the breakdown, chaos, and ruination of many developing nations that we had ostensibly sought to avoid.

All these charges are serious but the last one may have the gravest long-term consequences.

By helping destroy their traditional institutions and by erecting ephemeral modern ones cast in our own image to replace them but often entirely inappropriate in the societies where we have sought to locate them, we have left many developing nations with neither the traditional and indigenous institutions which might have helped them bridge the wrenching transition to modernity, nor with viable new ones that have any bases or hope of functioning effectively in the native soil. By forcing some wrong and falsely dichotomous choices on the developing nations ("traditional" *or* "modern," "democracy" *or* "dictatorship"), social scientists and policymakers have contributed strongly to the institutional vacuum that plagues these countries and to the "basket cases" that, in the absence of genuinely homegrown institutions, they are certain to become.[10]

## CONCLUSIONS AND IMPLICATIONS

The development literature, whether in political science, sociology, or economics, assumes that the path to modernization in the Third World can be explained by reference to the past or present of the already industrialized nations. Development in Africa, Asia, Latin America, and the Middle East is seen in Glaucio Ary Dillon Soares's words, as specific instances of a general course of events already studied and fully comprehended in the experience of the Western European countries and the United States.[11] Such an approach assumes quite distinct culture areas and historical epochs can be understood using the same terms and concepts as in the West. It assumes a single unilinear path to development and also the universality of what is a far narrower and particular European or Western experience and set of institutions. The ethnocentrism of this interpretation and the absurdity of reducing a great variety of histories and sociopolitical formations to the single matrix of the Western European-United States experience are patent. This approach has stultified the creation of new concepts, prevented us from understanding the realities of the developing nations, wreaked positive harm upon them, and cast the

developing nations and those who study them in an inferior position vis-à-vis both the developed countries and those who study them. . . .

The universals in the modernization process include economic growth and industrialization, class and societal changes, division of labor and increased specialization of functions, rationalization and bureaucratization of society and polity, and the impact of what Lucian Pye once called the "world culture" (not just jeans, Coke, and rock but also outside political ideologies and forces).[12] The difficulty is that the presumed more specific social and political concomitants of these changes—modern political parties, armies, etc.—have not in fact developed concomitantly. The problem is not just "lag" or "uneven development" but that we have failed to appreciate sufficiently the present era's changed circumstances and also the strength and functionality of many traditional institutions and how these may shape, mold, even determine the impact of these larger, more universal changes. We have dismissed as traditional the role of tribes, caste associations, mullahs, religious and fundamentalist movements, elites and family structures, patron-client systems transferred to the national level, and a host of other local and particularistic institutions, rather than seeing them as persistent, flexible, perhaps viable structures on which an indigenous process of development might be based. By now it is clear such institutions will not necessarily disappear or be superseded as modernization proceeds, nor should they be easily dismissed, as our social science literature is wont to do, as dysfunctional. We must recognize the diversity of societies and developmental experiences.

Social scientists must begin with a renewed awareness of their biases, societal likes and dislikes, the Eurocentric bases of so many of their theories, their particularistic rather than universalistic nature. This will require a fundamental reexamination of most of the truths social scientists, especially [North] American social scientists, hold to be self-evident. It will also require a new and stronger dose of cultural relativism. Cultural relativism need not be carried so far as to accept or remain neutral toward a Hitler or a Bokassa. But it does imply a much more empathetic than previously understanding of foreign cultures and institutions, an understanding of them in terms of their own cultural traditions and even language, rather than through the distorting, blinding prism of Western social science.[13] The social sciences have been guilty of over- and too-hasty generalization; hence, we require more modesty than before concerning the universal applicability of our social science notions, greater uncertainty in our assertions of global social science wisdom, more reluctance to apply the social science findings (apples) of our culture to the realities (oranges) of another, where they neither fit nor add up.[14]

To say that much social science theory we took as universal is somewhat less than that implies that future theory ought probably to be formulated at a lower, culture-area level. We shall probably have to develop an African social science, an Islamic social science, a Latin American social science, and so on. It may be that such middle-range theory at the culture-area level will eventually yield again some more general, even universal findings about the development process, but this will be a long-term process and we may well find few universals on which to hang our social science hats. Many social scientists will be uncomfortable with this fact; a more useful approach may be to take the absence of such universals as a given and proceed from there. Some prominent social scientists are already saying that theory and research at the culture-area level, the examination of more particularistic, culturally unique, perhaps regionally specific institutions and processes, will probably be the focus of future comparative development studies. The necessity of analyzing indigenous institutions on their own terms and in their own cultural contexts rather than through Western social science frameworks seems particularly appropriate in the present circumstances, given both the assertion of indigenous ideologies and movements in many developing nations, and the corresponding rejection of European, American,

and Western ones. In my own particular areas of special research interest, for example, Latin America and southern Europe, I have been fascinated both by the new literature on corporatism, dependency, patron-client relations, center-periphery relations, organic-statism, and the like, which have helped form the bases for a new Latin American, or perhaps Iberic-Latin, social science, *and* the way these concepts have now found their way into interpretations of other areas and into the general literature. It may be that the flow of ideas and concepts, historically from Europe and European studies out to the periphery, may be in the process of being reversed. It may be that Western social scientists will now have to learn from Africa, Asia, Latin America, and the Middle East instead of their always learning from us.[15]

The emergence and articulation of such distinctive Latin American, African, Islamic, and so forth sociologies and political sciences of development raise a host of intriguing issues for scholarship. Implied is that we now take the developing nations and their alternative civilizations seriously for the first time, and on their own terms rather than through the condescension and superiority of United States or Western European perspectives. It means that the rising sense of nationalism and independence throughout the Third World is likely also to be reflected in a new insistence on indigenous models and institutions of development. It requires the formulation or reformulation of a host of new concepts and interpretations. It also implies that if the West, particularly the United States, is no longer to be the world's policeman, it must also cease being its philosopher-king, in terms of its assertion of the universality of its particular developmental experience.

This essay has been something of a broadside. Its claims and criticisms are sweeping. Essentially it says the social sciences of development must start all over. Of course one purposely overstates the case in order more forcefully to make it. We have seen there are universals in the development process, and we need to sort out more carefully what non-Western developing societies allow in and what gets winnowed out. We need sharper distinctions between cultural definitions of concepts as implicitly influencing social science theory construction, ethnocentrism as a distortion of perception, lack of research in specific culture areas, simple analogy to the Western development experience instead of analysis of the respective dynamics of given cases, political shortsightedness and interest politics. We require qualification and refinement of other arguments. Nonetheless the criticisms leveled here are fundamental and far-reaching.

The policy implications of these comments are also major. They mean the reexamination and likely scrapping of most of our aid and foreign assistance programs directed toward developing nations. They imply the shortsightedness and impropriety of seeking to apply European and North American strategies and institutional paraphernalia to societies and cultures where they simply do not fit; hence, they mean also a drastic curtailing of the travel and consulting fees that all those presumably developmentalism experts have been enjoying. They imply that United States and international agency decision makers be much more circumspect in their assertion that they know best for the developing nations. Even more fundamental, these comments imply a virtually complete reeducation, in nonethnocentric understandings, of at least two generations of social scientists, policymakers, and the informed public, indeed of our educational focus, national ethos, and career system. One should not be optimistic.

## Notes

1. The themes treated here complement those developed in Reinhard Bendix, "Tradition and Modernity Reconsidered," *Comparative Studies in Society and History* 9 (April 1967), pp. 292–346; reprinted in Bendix, *Embattled Reason* (New York, 1970). The present essay goes considerably beyond Bendix's argument, however, develops some distinctive propositions, and elaborates more far-reaching conclusions.

2. For starters see Paul E. Sigmund, ed., *The Ideologies of the Developing Nations* (New York:

Praeger Publishers, 1972); W. A. Beling and G. O. Totten, eds., *Developing Nations: Quest for a Model* (New York: Van Nostrand Reinhold, 1970); Howard J. Wiarda, *Politics and Social Change in Latin America: The Distinct Tradition* (Amherst, Mass.: University of Massachusetts Press, 1974).

3. The analysis here and in the next three paragraphs derives in large measure from Thomas O. Wilkinson, "Family Structure and Industrialization in Japan," *American Sociological Review* 28 (October 1962), pp. 678–682; and his *The Urbanization of Japanese Labor* (Amherst, Mass.: University of Massachusetts Press, 1965).

4. The image is that of Philippe C. Schmitter, "Paths to Political Development in Latin America," in *Changing Latin America* (New York: Academy of Political Science, 1972), pp. 83–105.

5. These considerations of "historical space-time," a concept that has often confused U.S. observers, lay behind the efforts of Haya de la Torre and the Peruvian *Apristas* to develop an indigenous ideology for Latin America.

6. D. Apter, *The Politics of Modernization* (Chicago: University of Chicago Press, 1965).

7. Anthony, James Joes, *Fascism in the Contemporary World* (Boulder, Colo.: Westview, 1978); James Malloy, ed., *Authoritarianism and Corporatism in Latin America* (Pittsburgh: University of Pittsburgh Press, 1977).

8. Claudio Veliz, *The Centralist Tradition of Latin America* (Princeton, N.J.: Princeton University Press, 1979); A. James Gregor, *Italian Fascism and Developmental Dictatorship* (Princeton, N.J.: Princeton University Press, 1979); David Collier, ed., *The New Authoritarianism in Latin America* (Princeton, N.J.: Princeton University Press, 1979).

9. Lloyd I. Rudolph and Susanne Hoeber Rudolph, *The Modernity of Tradition: Political Development in India* (Chicago: University of Chicago Press, 1967); Randall Stokes and Anthony Harris, "South African Development and the Paradox of Racial Particularism: Toward a Theory of Modernization from the Center," *Economic Development and Cultural Change* 26 (January 1978), pp. 245–269.

10. For one such example see Howard J. Wiarda, *Dictatorship, Development, and Disintegration: Politics and Social Change in the Dominican Republic* (Ann Arbor: Xerox University Microfilms Monograph Series, 1975).

11. Dillon Soares, "Latin American Studies in the United States: A Critique and a Proposal," *Latin American Research Review* 2 (1976), pp. 51–69.

12. In Lucian Pye and Sidney Verba, eds., *Political Culture and Political Development* (Princeton, N.J.: Princeton University Press, 1965).

13. For such a *verstahen* approach and its effect both on the region studied and the researchers, see Jean Duvignaud, *Change at Shebika: Report from a North African Village* (New York, 1970).

14. Peter Winch, *The Idea of a Social Science and Its Relations to Philosophy* (London: Routledge & Kegan Paul, 1960).

15. Howard J. Wiarda, "Toward a Framework for the Study of Political Change in the Iberic-Latin Tradition," *World Politics* 25 (1973); *Politics and Social Change*, "The Latin Americanization of the United States," *The New Scholar* 7 (1977), pp. 51–85; and *Corporatism and National Development in Latin America* (Boulder: Westview Press, 1981).

# CHAPTER TEN

# Dependency

41

## British Rule in India

*Karl Marx*

...There cannot...remain any doubt but that the misery inflicted by the British on Hindostan is of an essentially different and infinitely more intensive kind than all of Hindostan had to suffer before....

All the civil wars, invasions, revolutions, conquests, famines, strangely complex, rapid and destructive as the successive action in Hindostan may appear, did not go deeper than its surface. England has broken down the entire framework of Indian society, without any symptoms of reconstruction yet appearing. This loss of his old world, with no gain of a new one, imparts a particular kind of melancholy to the present misery of the Hindoo, and separates Hindostan, ruled by Britain, from all its ancient traditions, and from the whole of its past history.

There have been in Asia, generally, from immemorial times, but three departments of Government: that of Finance, or the plunder of the interior; that of War, or the plunder of the exterior; and, finally, the department of Public Works. Climate and territorial conditions, especially the vast tracts of desert, extending from the Sahara, through Arabia, Persia, India and Tartary, to the most elevated Asiatic highlands, constituted artificial irrigation by canals and waterworks the basis of Oriental agriculture. As in Egypt and India, inundations

SOURCE: Published in the New York *Daily Tribune*, 25 June 1853.

are used for fertilising the soil of Mesopotamia, Persia, etc.: advantage is taken of a high level for feeding irrigative canals. This prime necessity of an economical and common use of water, which, in the Occident, drove private enterprise to voluntary association, as in Flanders and Italy, necessitated, in the Orient where civilisation was too low and the territorial extent too vast to call into life voluntary association, the interference of the centralising power of Government. Hence an economical function devolved upon all Asiatic Governments the function of providing public works. This artificial fertilisation of the soil, dependent on a Central Government, and immediately decaying with the neglect of irrigation and drainage, explains the otherwise strange fact that we now find whole territories barren and desert that were once brilliantly cultivated, as Palmyra, Petra, the ruins in Yemen, and large provinces of Egypt, Persia and Hindostan: it also explains how a single war of devastation has been able to depopulate a country for centuries, and to strip it of all its civilisation....

...However changing the political aspect of India's past must appear, its social condition has remained unaltered since its remotest antiquity, until the first decennium of the 19th century. The hand-loom and the spinning-wheel, producing their regular myriads of spinners and weavers, were the pivots of the structure of that society. From immemorial times, Europe received the admirable textures of Indian labour, sending in return for them her precious metals, and furnishing thereby his material to the goldsmith, that indispensable member of Indian society, whose love of finery is so great that even the lowest class, those who go about nearly naked, have commonly a pair of golden ear-rings and a gold ornament of some kind hung round their necks. Rings on the fingers and toes have also been common. Women as well as children frequently wore massive bracelets and anklets of gold or silver, and statuettes of divinities in gold and silver were met with in the households. It was the British intruder who broke up the Indian hand-loom and destroyed the spinning wheel. England began with driving the Indian cottons from the European market; it then introduced twist into Hindostan and in the end inundated the very mother country of cotton with cottons. . . .

These two circumstances—the Hindoo, on the one hand, leaving, like all Oriental peoples, to the central government the care of the great public works, the prime condition of his agriculture and commerce, dispersed, on the other hand over the surface of the country, and agglomerated in small centres by the domestic union of agricultural and manufacturing pursuits—these two circumstances had brought about, since the remotest times, a social system of particular features—the so-called *village system,* which gave to each of these small unions their independent organisation and distinct life. . . .

These small stereotype forms of social organism have been to the greater part dissolved, and are disappearing, not so much through the brutal interference of the British tax-gatherer and the British soldier, as to the working of English steam and English free trade. Those family-communities were based on domestic industry, in that peculiar combination of hand-weaving, hand-spinning and hand-tilling agriculture which gave them self-supporting power. English interference having placed the spinner in Lancashire and the weaver in Bengal, or sweeping away both Hindoo spinner and weaver, dissolved these small semi-barbarian, semi-civilised communities, by blowing up their economical basis, and thus produced the greatest, and to speak the truth, the only *social* revolution ever heard of in Asia.

Now, sickening as it must be to human feeling to witness those myriads of industrious patriarchal and inoffensive social organisations disorganised and dissolved into their units, thrown into a sea of woes, and their individual members losing at the same time their ancient form of civilisation, and their hereditary means of subsistence, we must not forget that these idyllic village communities, inoffensive though they may appear, had always been the solid foundation of Oriental despotism, that they restrained the human mind within the smallest possible compass, making it the unresisting tool of superstition, enslaving it beneath traditional rules, depriving it of all grandeur and historical energies. We must not forget the barbarian egotism which, concentrating on some miserable patch of land, had quietly witnessed the ruin of empires, the perpetration of unspeakable cruelties, the massacre of the population of large towns, with no other consideration bestowed upon them than on natural events, itself the helpless prey of any aggressor who deigned to notice it at all. We must not forget that this undignified, stagnatory, and vegetative life, that this passive sort of existence evoked on the other part, in contradistinction, wild, aimless, unbounded forces of destruction and rendered murder itself a religious rite in Hindostan. We must not forget that these little communities were contaminated by distinctions of caste and by slavery, that they subjugated man to external circumstances instead of elevating man to be the sovereign of circumstances, that they transformed a self-developing social state into never changing natural destiny, and thus brought about a brutalising worship of nature, exhibiting its degradation in the fact that man, the sovereign of nature, fell down on his knees in adoration of *Hanuman,* the monkey, and *Sabbala,* the cow.

England, it is true, in causing a social revolution in Hindostan, was actuated only by the vilest interests, and was stupid in her manner of enforcing them. But that is not the question. The question is, can mankind fulfill its destiny without a fundamental revolution in the social state of Asia? If not, whatever may have been the crimes of England she was the unconscious tool of history in bringing about that revolution. . . .

# 42

# The Capitalist World-Economy

*Immanuel Wallerstein*

Words can be the enemy of understanding and analysis. We seek to capture a moving reality in our terminology. We thereby tend to forget that the reality changes as we encapsulate it, and by virtue of that fact. And we are even more likely to forget that others freeze reality in different ways, using however the very same words to do it. And still we cannot speak without words; indeed we cannot think without words.

Where then do we find the *via media*, the working compromise, the operational expression of a dialectical methodology? It seems to me it is most likely to be found by conceiving of provisional long-term, large-scale wholes within which concepts have meanings. These wholes must have some claim to relative space-time autonomy and integrity. They must be long enough and large enough to enable us to escape the Scylla of conceptual nominalism, but short enough and small enough to enable us to escape the Charybdis of ahistorical, universalizing abstraction. I would call such wholes "historical systems"—a name which captures their two essential qualities. It is a whole which is integrated, that is, composed of interrelated parts, therefore in some sense systematic and with comprehensible patterns. It is a system which has a history, that is, it has a genesis, an historical development, a close (a destruction, a disintegration, a transformation, an *Aufhebung*).

I contrast this concept of "historical system" with that of the more usual term of "society" (or of "social formation," which I believe is used more or less synonymously). Of course, one may use the term "society" in the same sense I am using "historical system," and then the

issue is simply the choice of formal symbol. But in fact the standard use of "society" is one which is applied indiscriminately to refer to modern states (and quasi-states), to ancient empires, to supposedly autonomous "tribes," and to all manner of other *political* (or cultural-aspiring-to-be-political) structures. And this lumping together presumes what is to be demonstrated —that the political dimension is the one that unifies and delineates social action.

If boundaries drawn in every conceivable way—integrated production processes, exchange patterns, political jurisdiction, cultural coherence, ecology—were in fact always (or even usually) synonymous (or even highly overlapping), there would be little problem. But, as a matter of empirical fact, taking the last 10,000 years of human history, this is not at all the case. We must therefore choose among alternate criteria of defining our arenas of social action, our units of analysis. One can debate this in terms of philosophical *a priori* statements, and if so my own bias is a materialist one. But one can also approach this heuristically: which criterion will account for the largest percentage of social action, in the sense that changing its parameters will most immediately and most profoundly affect the operation of other parts of the whole?

I believe one can argue the case for integrated production processes as constituting this heuristic criterion, and I shall use it to draw the boundaries which circumscribe a concrete "historical system," by which I mean an empirical set of such production processes integrated according to some particular set of rules, the human agents of which interact in some "organic" way, such that changes in the functions of any group or changes in the boundaries of the historical system must follow certain rules if the entity's survival is not to be threatened. This is what we mean by such other terms as a social economy, or a specific social division of labour. To suggest that a historical system is organic is not to suggest that it is a frictionless machine. Quite the contrary: historical systems are beset by contradictions, and contain

SOURCE: Immanuel Wallerstein, "The States in the Institutional Vortex of the Capitalist World-Economy," *International Social Science Journal* vol. 32, no. 4 (1980), pp. 743-751. © Unesco 1980. Reproduced by permission of Unesco.

within them the seeds of processes that eventually destroy the system. But this, too, is very consonant with the "organic" metaphor.

This is a long preface to a coherent analysis of the role of states in the modern world. I think much of our collective discussion has been a prisoner of the word "state," which we have used transhistorically to mean any political structure which had some authority network (a leading person or group or groups, with intermediate cadres enforcing the will of this leading entity). Not only do we assume that what we are designating as "states" in the 20th century are in the same universe of discourse as what we designate as "states" in, say, the 10th century, but even more fantastically, we frequently attempt to draw lines of historical continuity between two such "states"—of the same name, or found in the same general location in terms of longitude and latitude—said to be continuous because scholars can argue affinities of the languages that are spoken, or the cosmologies that are professed, or the genes that are pooled.

The capitalist world-economy constitutes one such historical system. It came into existence, in my view, in Europe in the 16th century. The capitalist world-economy is a system based on the drive to accumulate capital, the political conditioning of price levels (of capital, commodities and labour), and the steady polarization of classes and regions (core/periphery) over time. This system has developed and expanded to englobe the whole earth in the subsequent centuries. It has today reached a point where, as a result of its contradictory developments, the system is a long crisis.[1]

The development of the capitalist world-economy has involved the creation of all the major institutions of the modern world: classes, ethnic/national groups, households—and the "states." All of these structures postdate, not antedate capitalism; all are consequence, not cause. Furthermore, these various institutions, in fact, create each other. Classes, ethnic/national groups, and households are defined by the state, through the state, in relation to the state, and in turn create the state, shape the state, and

transform the state. It is a structured maelstrom of constant movement, whose parameters are measurable through the repetitive regularities, while the detailed constellations are always unique.

What does it mean to say that a state comes into existence? Within a capitalist world-economy, the state is an institution whose existence is defined by its relation to other "states." Its boundaries are more or less clearly defined. Its degree of juridical sovereignty ranges from total to nil. Its real power to control the flows of capital, commodities, and labour across its frontiers is greater or less. The real ability of the central authorities to enforce decisions on groups operating within state frontiers is greater or less. The ability of the state authorities to impose their will in zones outside state frontiers is greater or less.

Various groups located inside, outside, and across any given state's frontiers are constantly seeking to increase, maintain, or decrease the "power" of the state, in all the ways referred to above. These groups are seeking to change these power constellations because of some sense that such changes will improve the particular group's ability to profit, directly or indirectly, from the operations of the world market. The state is the most convenient institutional intermediary in the establishment of market constraints (quasi-monopolies, in the broadest sense of the term) in favour of particular groups.

The historical development of the capitalist world-economy is that, beginning with relatively amorphous entities, more and more "states" operating within the interstate system have been created. Their boundaries and the definitions of their formal rights have been defined with increasing clarity (culminating in the contemporary United Nations structure of international law). The modalities and limits of group pressures in state structures have also been increasingly defined (in the sense both of the legal limits placed on such pressures, and of the rational organization by groups to transcend these limits). None the less, despite what might be called the "honing" of this institutional network, it is probably safe to say that the relative power continuum of stronger and weaker states has remained relatively unchanged over 400-odd years. That is not to say that the same "states" have remained "strong" and "weak". Rather, there has been at all moments a power hierarchy of such states, but also at no moment has there been any one state whose hegemony was totally unchallenged (although relative hegemony has occurred for limited periods).

Various objections have been made to such a view of the modern state, its genesis and its mode of functioning. There are four criticisms which seem to be the most frequent and worthy of discussion.

First, it is argued that this view is too instrumental a view of the state, that it makes the states into a mere conscious instrument of acting groups with no life and integrity of their own, with no base of social support in and for themselves.

It seems to me this counter-argument is based on a confusion about social institutions in general. Once created, all social institutions, including the states, have lives of their own in the sense that many different groups will use them, support them, exploit them for various (and even contradictory) motives. Furthermore, institutions large and structured enough to have permanent staffs thereby generate a group of persons—the bureaucracies of these institutions —who have a direct socio-economic stake in the persistence and flourishing of the institution as such, quite independent of the ideological premises on which the institution was created and the interests of the major social forces that sustain it.

None the less, the issue is not who has some say in the ongoing decisions of a state-machinery but who has decisive or critical say, and what are the key issues that are fought about in terms of state policy. We believe that these key issues are: (1) the rules governing the social relations of production, which critically affect the allocation of surplus-value; and (2) the rules governing the flow within and across frontiers of the factors of production—capital,

commodities and labour—which critically affect the price structures of markets. If one changes the allocation of surplus-value and the price structures of markets, one is changing the relative competitivity of particular producers, and therefore their profit-levels.

It is the states that make these rules, and it is primarily the states that intervene in the process of other (weaker) states when the latter attempt to make the rules as they prefer them.

The second objection to this mode of analysis is that it ignores the reality of traditional continuities, as ensconsed in the operative consciousnesses of groups. Such consciousnesses do indeed exist and are very powerful, but are the consciousnesses themselves continuous? I think not, and believe the merest glance at the empirical reality will confirm that. The history of nationalisms, which are one of the salient forms of such consciousnesses, shows that everywhere that nationalist movements emerge, they create consciousness, they revive (even partially invent) languages, they coin names and emphasize customary practices that come to distinguish their group from other groups. They do this in the name of what is claimed to have always been there, but frequently (if not usually) they must stretch the interpretation of the historical evidence in ways that disinterested observers would consider partisan. This is true not only of the so-called "new" nations of the 20th century[2] but of the "old" nations as well.[3]

It is also clear that the successive ideological statements about a given name—what it encompasses, what constitutes its "tradition"—are discontinuous and different. Each successive version can be explained in terms of the politics of its time, but the fact that these versions vary so widely is itself a piece of evidence against taking the assertion of continuity as more than a claim of an interested group. It surely is shifting sand on which to base an analysis of the political functioning of states.

The third argument against this form of analysis is that it is said to ignore the underlying centrality of the class struggle, which is implicitly asserted to exist within some fixed entity called a society or a social formation, and which in turn accounts for the structure of the state.

If, however, classes is the term we use for groups deriving from positions in relation to the mode of production, then it is to the realities of the set of integrated production processes that we must look to determine who constitute our classes. The boundaries of these integrated production processes are in fact, of course, far wider than the individual states, and even sub-sets of production processes do not correlate very often with state boundaries. There is consequently no a priori reason to assume that classes are in some objective sense circumscribed by state boundaries.

Now, it may fairly be argued that class consciousnesses have tended historically to be national in form. This is so, for good reasons we shall discuss below. But the fact that this is so is no evidence that the analytic perception is correct. On the contrary, this fact of the national form of consciousness for trans-state classes becomes itself a major explicandum of the modern world.

Finally, it is said that this mode of analysis ignores the fact that the wealthiest states are not the strongest states, but tend indeed to be relatively weak. But this is to misperceive what constitutes the strength of state machineries. It is once again to take ideology for analytic reality.

Some state machineries preach the line of a strong state. They seek to limit opposition; they seek to impose decisions on internal groups; they are bellicose vis-à-vis external groups. But what is important is the success of the assertion of power, not its loudness. Oppositions only need to be suppressed where they seriously exist. States that encompass relatively more homogeneous strata (because of the unevenness of allocation of class forces in the world economy) may achieve via consensus what others strive (and perhaps fail) to achieve via the iron hand. Entrepreneurs who are economically strong in the market do not need state assistance to create monopoly privileges, though they may need state aid to oppose the creation by others, in other states, of monopoly

privileges which would hurt these market-strong entrepreneurs.

The states are thus, we are arguing, created institutions reflecting the needs of class forces operating in the world economy. They are not however created in a void, but within the framework of an interstate system. This interstate system is, in fact, the framework within which the states are defined. It is the fact that the states of the capitalist world economy exist within the framework of an interstate system that is the *differentia specifica* of the modern state, distinguishing it from other bureaucratic polities. This interstate system constitutes a set of constraints which limit the abilities of individual state machineries, even the strongest among them, to make decisions. The ideology of this system is sovereign equality, but the states are in fact neither sovereign nor equal. In particular, the states impose on each other—not only the strong on the weak, but the strong on the strong—limitations on their modes of political (and therefore military), behaviour, and even more strikingly limitations on their abilities to affect the law of value underlying capitalism. We are so used to observing all the things states do that constitute a defiance of other states that we do not stop to recognize how few these things are, rather than how many. We are so used to thinking of the interstate system as verging on anarchy that we fail to appreciate how rule-ridden it is. Of course, the "rules" are broken all the time, but we should look at the consequences—the mechanisms that come into play to force changes in the policies of the offending states. Again, we should look less at the obvious arena of political behaviour, and more at the less observed arena of economic behaviour. The story of states with communist parties in power in the 20th-century interstate system is striking evidence of the efficacities of such pressures.

The production processes of the capitalist world-economy are built on a central relationship or antinomy: that of capital and labour. The ongoing operations of the system have the effect of increasingly circumscribing individuals (or rather households), forcing them to participate in the work process in one capacity or the other, as contributors of surplus-value or as receivers.

The states have played a central role in the polarization of the population into those living off appropriated surplus, the bourgeoisie, and those whose surplus-value is appropriated from them, the proletariat. For one thing, the states created the legal mechanisms which not merely permitted or even facilitated the appropriation of surplus-value, but protected the results of the appropriation by enacting property rights. They created institutions which ensured the socialization of children into the appropriate roles.

As the classes came into objective existence, in relation to each other, they sought to alter (or to maintain) the unequal bargaining power between them. To do this, they had to create appropriate institutions to affect state decisions, which largely turned out to be over-time institutions created within the boundaries of the state, adding thereby to the world-wide definiteness of state structures.

This has led to deep ambivalences in their self-perception and consequently contradictory political behaviour. Both the bourgeoisie and the proletariat are classes formed in a world economy, and when we speak of objective class position, it is necessarily classes of this world economy to which we refer. As, however, the bourgeoisie first began to become class-conscious and only later the proletariat, both classes found disadvantages as well as advantages to defining themselves as world classes.

The bourgeoisie, in pursuit of its class interest, the maximization of profit in order to accumulate capital, sought to engage in its economic activities as it saw fit without constraints on geographic location or political considerations. Thus, for example, in the 16th or 17th centuries, it was frequent for Dutch, English or French entrepreneurs to "trade with the enemy" in wartime, even in armaments. And it was frequent for entrepreneurs to change place of domicile and citizenship in pursuit of optimizing gain. The bourgeoisie then (as now) reflected this self-perception in tendencies towards a "world" cultural style—in consumption, in language, etc. However, it was also true then, and now, that, however much the bourgeoisie chafed under limitations placed by particular state authorities for particular reasons at one or another moment, the bourgeoisies also needed to utilize state machineries to strengthen their position in the market vis-à-vis competitors and to protect them vis-à-vis the working classes. And this meant that the many fractions of the world bourgeoisie had an interest in defining themselves as "national" bourgeoisies.

The same pattern held for the proletariat. On the one hand, as it became class-conscious, it recognized that a prime organizational objective has to be the unity of proletarians in their struggle. It is no accident that the *Communist Manifesto* proclaimed: "Workers of the world, unite!" It was clear that precisely the fact that the bourgeoisie operated in the arena of a world-economy, and could (and would) transfer sites of production whenever it was to its advantage, meant that proletarian unity, if it were to be truly efficacious, could only be at the world level. And yet we know that world proletarian unity has never really been efficacious (most dramatically in the failure of the Second International to maintain an anti-nationalist stance during the First World War). This is so for a very simple reason. The mechanisms most readily available to improve the relative conditions of segments of the working classes are the state machineries, and the political organization of the proletariat has almost always taken the form of state-based organizations. Furthermore, this tendency has been reinforced, not weakened, by whatever successes these organizations have had in attaining partial or total state power.

We arrive thus at a curious anomaly: both the bourgeoisie and the proletariat express their consciousness at a level which does not reflect their objective economic role. Their interests are a function of the operations of a world-economy, and they seek to enhance their interests by affecting individual state machineries, which in fact have only limited power (albeit real power, none the less) to affect the operations of this world economy.

It is this anomaly that constantly presses bourgeoisies and proletariats to define their interests in status-group terms. The most efficacious status-group in the modern world is the nation, since the nation lays claim to the moral right to control a particular state structure. To the extent that a nation is not a state, we find the potential for a nationalist movement to arise and flourish. Of course, there is no essence that is a nation and that occasionally breeds a nationalist movement. Quite the contrary. It is a nationalist movement that creates an entity called a nation, or seeks to create it. Under the multiple circumstances in which nationalism is not available to serve class interests, status-group solidarities may crystallize around substitute poles: religion, race, language, or other particular cultural patterns.

Status-group solidarities remove the anomaly of national class organization or consciousness from the forefront of visibility and hence relax the strains inherent in contradictory structures. But, of course, they may also obfuscate the class struggle. To the extent that particular ethnic consciousnesses therefore lead to consequences which key groups find intolerable, we see re-emergence of overt class organizations, or if this creates too much strain, of redefined status-group solidarities (drawing the boundaries differently). That particular segments of the world bourgeoisie or world proletariat might flit from, say, pan-Turkic to pan-Islamic to national to class-based movements over a period of decades reflects not the inconsistency of the struggle but the difficulties of navigating a course that can bridge the antinomy: objective classes of the world economy/subjective classes of a state structure.

Finally the atoms of the classes (and of the status-groups), the income-pooling households, are shaped and constantly reshaped not only by the objective economic pressures of the ongoing dynamic of the world-economy but they also are regularly and deliberately manipulated by the states that seek to determine (to alter) their boundaries in terms of the needs of the labour-market, as well as to determine the flows and forms of income that may in fact be pooled. The households in turn may assert their own solidarities and priorities and resist the pressures, less effectively by passive means, more effectively, when possible, by creating the class and status-group solidarities we have just mentioned.

All these institutions together—the states, the classes, the ethnic/national/status-groups, the households—form an institutional vortex which is both the product and the moral life of the capitalist world-economy. Far from being primordial and pre-existing essences, they are dependent and coterminous existences. Far from being segregated and separable, they are indissociably intertwined in complex and contradictory ways. Far from one determining the other, they are in a sense avatars of each other.

## Notes

1. I have developed these theses at length in *The Modern World-System*, 2 vols. (New York: Academic Press, 1974 and 1980); and *The Capitalist World-Economy* (Cambridge: Cambridge University Press, 1979).

2. In 1956, Thomas Hodgkin wrote in a "Letter" to Saburi Biobaku (*Odu*, No. 4, 1957, p. 42): "I was struck by your statement that the use of the term 'Yoruba' to refer to the whole range of peoples who would nowadays describe themselves as Yoruba (as contrasted with the Oyo peoples simply) was due largely to the influence of the Anglican Mission at Abeokuta, and its work in evolving a standard 'Yoruba' language, based on Oyo speech. This seems to me an extremely interesting example of the way in which Western influences have helped to stimulate a new kind of national sentiment. Everyone recognizes that the notion of 'being a Nigerian' is a new kind of conception. But it would seem that the notion of 'being a Yoruba' is not very much older. I take it from what you say that there is no evidence that those who owed allegiance to the kingdom of Oyo—or to the earlier State system based upon Ife?—used any common name to describe themselves, although it is possible that they may have done so?"

3. George Bernard Shaw has the Nobleman in *Saint Joan* exclaim: "A Frenchman! Where did you pick up that expression? Are these Burgundians and Bretons and Picards and Gascons beginning to call themselves Frenchmen, just as our fellows are beginning to call themselves Englishmen? They actually talk of France and England as their countries. Theirs, if you please! What is to become of me and you if that way of thinking comes into fashion?"

# 43
# Modernization and Dependency

*J. Samuel Valenzuela and Arturo Valenzuela*

The end of World War II marked the beginning of fundamental transformations in world affairs. The defeat of the Axis powers and the devastating toll which the war had exacted on Britain and the European allies propelled the United States into a position of economic and military preeminence. However, the United States' power did not go unchallenged. The Soviet Union was able to influence the accession of power of socialist regimes throughout Eastern Europe and Chinese Communists defeated their Western-backed adversaries to gain control of the most populous nation on earth. These events called for an urgent strategy to revitalize the economies of the Western nations. With massive U.S. public and private economic investment, Western Europe and Japan soon recovered from the ravages of war.

But World War II ushered in another important change whose global implications would not be felt for some years to come. The weakening

SOURCE: J. Samuel Valenzuela and Arturo Valenzuela, "Modernization and Dependency: Alternative Perspectives in the Study of Latin American Underdevelopment," *Comparative Politics* 10 (July 1978), pp. 535–537. Permission to reprint by *Comparative Politics*, © The City University of New York. Article and notes abridged by the editors.

of the European powers and the logic of a war effort aimed at preserving self-determination, marked the final collapse of the vast colonial empires of the 19th century and the establishment of a multiplicity of states each claiming sovereign and independent status. The "new nations" soon drew the attention of U.S. policymakers concerned with the claim that Marxism presented the best and most logical road to full incorporation into the modern world. They also captured the attention and imagination of U.S. scholars who in the pursuit of knowledge, as well as the desire to influence government policy, began to produce a vast literature on the "developing" nations. For many economists the solution was another Marshall plan designed for the Third World. But other social scientists argued that fundamental differences between the developmental experience of Europe and the less-developed countries mitigated against the success of such a strategy. It was not simply a matter of reconstruction but one of development and, as such, a fundamental question needed answering before policy recommendations could be advanced: Why was there such a stark contrast in the developmental experience of a few Western countries and most of the rest of the world?

The answer to this question led to the development of the "modernization perspective." Elaborated by a few economists and by anthropologists, sociologists, and political scientists, this perspective argued that it was essential to consider the cultural characteristics of "new" nations in determining their potential for development. These "noneconomic" factors became the cornerstone of a conceptual framework which would influence the U.S. response to the Third World. Though "Latin Americanists" did not write the major theoretical or conceptual works of the modernization literature, that perspective soon became the dominant approach influencing the methodology and conclusions of the most important and trendsetting studies.

U.S. scholars, however, were not the only ones preoccupied with the difficulties of applying neoclassical economic assumptions to the developmental problems of Latin America. In international agencies, notably the United Nations Economic Commission for Latin America, and university research centers, Latin American social scientists tried to come to grips with the widespread economic stagnation which affected the region in the postwar period. Working separately, often with little communication, scholars in various disciplines soon turned to the broader and more basic question of the roots of Latin American underdevelopment. Many intellectual strands came together in the 1960s with the elaboration of a more general and comprehensive conceptual framework. The "dependency perspective" became the dominant approach in most Latin American intellectual circles by the mid to late 1960s.

* * *

Modernization and dependency are two sharply different perspectives seeking to explain the same reality. They originated in different areas, with different evaluative judgments, different assumptions, different methodologies, and different explanations. The purpose of this review essay is not to describe the origins of the two perspectives, their "extra scientific" elements, but to compare their conceptual approaches to the study of Latin America. As such, it will be necessary to consider the two perspectives as "ideal types," accentuating important characteristics of each framework in a manner not found in any particular author. There is a good deal of variety and several polemics (particularly in the dependency literature) stemming from disagreements over the emphasis given to key elements of the conceptual framework, the operationalization of concepts, and the way in which certain processes occur empirically. Though the essay will mention some of the controversies within each perspective, its purpose is to draw broad comparisons and to provide some judgment as to the relative utility of these competing frameworks in explaining Latin American underdevelopment.

## THE MODERNIZATION PERSPECTIVE

**Assumptions.** The basic building blocks of the modernization perspective are parallel tradition-modernity ideal types of social organization and value systems, distinctions borrowed from 19th-century sociology.[1] Since societies are understood to move from tradition to modernity, the ideal typical dichotomy constitutes the polar ends of an evolutionary continuum, though at some point incremental changes give way to the qualitative jump into modernity. The location of this point is unclear; and yet, Third World countries, including those of Latin America, are perceived to be below the threshold of modernity, with a preponderance of traditional features.

The specific elements included in the two polarities vary substantially in the literature. The traditional society is variously understood as having a predominance of ascriptive, particularistic, diffuse, and affective patterns of action, an extended kinship structure with a multiplicity of functions, little spatial and social mobility, a deferential stratification system, mostly primary economic activities, a tendency toward autarchy of social units, an undifferentiated political structure, with traditional elitist and hierarchical sources of authority, etc. By contrast, the modern society is characterized by a predominance of achievement; universalistic, specific, and neutral orientations and patterns of action; a nuclear family structure serving limited functions; a complex and highly differentiated occupational system; high rates of spatial and social mobility; a predominance of secondary economic activities and production for exchange; the institutionalization of change and self-sustained growth; highly differentiated political structures with rational legal sources of authority; and so on.

The literature assumes that the values, institutions, and patterns of action of traditional society are both an expression and a cause of underdevelopment and constitute the main obstacles in the way of modernization. To enter the modern world, underdeveloped societies have to overcome traditional norms and structures opening the way for social, economic, and political transformations. For some authors modernization derives from a greater differentiation of societal functions, institutions, and roles and the development of new sources of integration. For others, modernization is based more on the actual transformation of individuals through their assimilation of modern values. But in general, the primary source of change is discussed in terms of innovations, that is, the rejection of procedures related to traditional institutions, together with the adoption of new ideas, techniques, values, and organizations. Innovations are pursued by innovators and the group that assumes this role inevitably clashes with defenders of the old order. The struggle is over two different ways of life.[2]

In describing the assumptions of the modernization literature, it is important to note that the modern pole of the parallel ideal types is the pivotal conceptual and analytical point because it best approximates the characteristics that societies must attain in order to develop. The traditional end of the dichotomy is largely a residual category, established by logical opposition to the modern end. In turn, the basic features of the modern pole are derived from characteristics attributed to those countries already considered modern. Moreover, since in the process of modernization all societies will undergo by and large similar changes, the history of the presently modern nations is taken as the source of universally useful conceptualization. Thus, as historian C. Black notes, "Although the problems raised by generalizations from a rather narrow base (the now modern countries) must be acknowledged, the definition of modernity takes the form of a set of characteristics believed to be applicable to all societies. This conception of modernity, when thought of as a model or ideal type, may be used as a yardstick with which to measure any society."[3] G. Almond adds that to study modernization in the non-Western areas the political

scientist needs to "master the model of the modern, which in turn can only be derived from the most careful empirical and formal analysis of the functions of the modern Western polities."[4]

These assumptions are logically consistent with the view that the impetus to modernize in the now developed countries was the result of endogenous cultural and institutional transformations, while change in the late developers results primarily from exogenous stimuli, that is, the diffusion of modern values and institutions from the early modernizers. Modernizing Third World elites are understood to be guided by the Western model adopting and adapting its technology; assimilating its values and patterns of action; importing its financial, industrial, and educational institutions; and so on. Western colonialism, foreign aid, foreign educational opportunities, overseas business investments, the mass media, etc., are all important channels for the transmission of modernity. For some writers this means that the world is converging toward a uniform and standardized culture resembling that of the United States and Western Europe.

Though, as will be noted below, there is disagreement on the extent to which traditional features will disappear, there is broad agreement on the notion that individual developing countries must in some way replicate the path followed by the early modernizers. The principal difference between already developed countries and developing ones is not in the nature of the process, but in the speed and intensity making it possible for the late modernizers to "skip stages" or "telescope time."[5] Despite the fact that the modernization perspective stresses the importance of the worldwide context in its analysis of social change, the basic historical setting for modernization is the nation state. As Black notes, "Societies in the process of modernization must . . . be considered both as *independent* entities, the traditional institutions of which are being adapted to modern functions, and also as societies under the influence of many *outside* forces."[6] The world is fragmented, and yet bound by intersocietal communication. It is, in the words of Dankwart Rustow, a "world of nations."[7]

Finally, it is clear that the stress on the differences in values from one context to another has some important implications for the modernization perspective's concept of human nature. The characteristic of developed societies which has received the most attention in the literature is the presumed "rationality" of both leaders and followers. Indeed, W. Moore has recently argued that modernization is best understood as "the process of rationalization of social behavior and social organization." Rationalization, or the "institutionalization of rationality," is defined as the "normative expectation that objective information and rational calculus of procedures will be applied in pursuit or achievement of any utilitarian goal.... It is exemplified but not exhausted in the use of sophisticated technology in construction and production."[8] As such, modernization theorists agree with the assumption of economic rationality implicit in the economic growth models of traditional economic theory. But as Moore noted in a 1950s article, where they differ with traditional economics is in the assumption that rational behavior is a universal human characteristic. By contrast with the developed countries, attitudes and values in developing nations are such that individuals "behave in ways that are 'irrational' or 'non-rational' as judged on economic grounds."[9] This explains why Bolivian businessmen will not take risks with their capital, preferring to put money in Swiss banks. Or why Ecuadorians will study law rather than enter a more lucrative career in business or technology.

In concluding this section, it is necessary to note that from the very outset certain elements of the modernization perspective came into criticism from scholars who shared its basic assumptions. It is revealing that much of the criticism came from researchers who were experts in many of the features of individual "traditional" societies. They were uncomfortable with the arbitrary designation of a wide variety of phenomena as "traditional," with little concern for the rich, complex, and often strikingly different characteristics subsumed under that vague concept. They argued that many belief systems and institutional arrangements with no common referent in the United States or Western Europe could indeed have modernizing functions. J. Gusfield has summarized many of the relevant arguments adding that even in modern societies certain traditional characteristics may survive or gain renewed importance.[10] These arguments do not, however, constitute a rejection of the assumptions of the modernization perspective but an illustration of their use. Despite the title of his article, Gusfield does not argue that tradition and modernity are "misplaced polarities." Gusfield simply points to a confusion in the use of terms and their misapplication in concrete situations. He continues to accept the assumptions that tradition and modernity are valid theoretical polarities and that tradition in its many ramifications is the basic obstacle to modernization. If a particular society or region experiences significant economic growth, what was thought to be an other-worldly religion undermining rational economic behavior may in fact be a creed capable of promoting instrumental values conducive to modernization. There can be a "modernity of tradition."[11]

Recent amendments to the modernization perspective are extensions of the same internal critique. Reflecting the sobering reality of the 1970s with many studies pointing to an ever increasing gap between rich and poor nations, several modernization writers have questioned the earlier belief in an inevitable and uniform process leading to the convergence of societies on economic as well as social and political grounds.[12] Others, while not questioning the inevitability of the process, point more forcefully than before to its disruptive and negative effects which affect the "latecomers" much more seriously than the "survivors."[13] It still remains the case that to modernize, however good or inevitable that process may be, it is by definition necessary to overcome traditional values and institutions and substitute them for more modern ones.

**Latin America and the Modernization Perspective.** Mainstream U.S. scholarship on Latin America has implicitly or explicitly drawn on the modernization perspective to explain Latin American underdevelopment. Often contrasting the Latin American experience to that of the United States or Western Europe, it has argued that traditional attitudes and institutions stemming from the colonial past have proven to be serious, if not fatal, stumbling blocks to any indigenous effort to develop economically, socially, or politically. The values of Catholicism, of large Indian populations, or of aristocratic rural elites have contributed to "irrational" patterns of behavior highly detrimental to modernization.

One of the most influential statements is S. M. Lipset's "Values, Education and Entrepreneurship," the introductory essay to the bestselling text *Elites in Latin America*. Lipset draws directly from T. Parsons and D. McClelland in arguing that:

> The relative failure of Latin American countries to develop on a scale comparable to those of North America or Australasia has been seen as, in some part, a consequence of variations in value systems dominating these two areas. The overseas offspring of Great Britain seemingly had the advantage of values derivative in part from the Protestant Ethic and from the formation of "New Societies" in which feudal ascriptive elements were missing. Since Latin America, on the other hand is Catholic, it has been dominated for centuries by ruling elites who created a social structure congruent with feudal social values.[14]

In his article Lipset concentrates primarily on explaining economic underdevelopment as a function of the lack of adequate entrepreneurial activity. The lack of instrumental behavior, weak achievement orientations, and the disdain for the pragmatic and material have prevented the rise of a risk-taking business sector oriented toward rational competitive and bureaucratic enterprise. The educational system has only served to perpetuate the problem by continuing to socialize the population with inappropriate attitudes. "Even [in Argentina] the second most

developed Latin American country. . .the traditional landed, aristocratic disdain for manual work, industry, and trading, continues to affect the educational orientations of many students."[15] Lipset cites a whole host of studies, many of which were based on survey research in Latin America, to conclude that "the comparative evidence from the various nations of the Americas sustains the generalization that cultural values are among the major factors which affect the potentiality for economic development."[16] Recent textbooks on Latin America have clearly been influenced by such observations. Thus, R. Adie and G.E. Poitras note that "there is in Latin America a social climate in which the very rewards which have spurred on the entrepreneurs in, for example, North America, are consistently deemphasized. . .socioeconomic change dependent on business activities. . .cannot necessarily be expected to follow the same path as it has elsewhere."[17]

\* \* \*

## THE DEPENDENCY PERSPECTIVE

Like the modernization perspective, the dependency perspective resulted from the work of many different scholars in different branches of the social sciences. . . .

In its emphasis on the expansive nature of capitalism and in its structural analysis of society, the dependency literature draws on Marxist insights and is related to the Marxist theory of imperialism. However, its examination of processes in Latin America imply important revisions in classical Leninist formulations, both historically and in light of recent trends. The focus is on explaining Latin American underdevelopment, and not on the functioning of capitalism, though some authors argue that their efforts will contribute to an understanding of capitalism and its contradictions.

**Assumptions.** The dependency perspective rejects the assumption made by modernization writers that the unit of analysis in studying underdevelopment is the national society. The domestic cultural and institutional features of Latin America are in themselves simply not the key variables accounting for the relative backwardness of the area, though, as will be seen below, domestic structures are certainly critical intervening factors. The relative presence of traditional and modern features may, or may not, help to differentiate societies; but it does not in itself explain the origins of modernity in some contexts and the lack of modernity in others. As such, the tradition-modernity polarity is of little value as a fundamental working concept. The dependency perspective assumes that the development of a national or regional unit can only be understood in connection with its historical insertion into the worldwide political-economic system which emerged with the wave of European colonizations of the world. This global system is thought to be characterized by the unequal but combined development of its different components. As Sunkel and Paz put it:

> Both underdevelopment and development are aspects of the same phenomenon, both are historically simultaneous, both are linked functionally and, therefore, interact and condition each other mutually. This results. . .in the division of the world between industrial, advanced or "central" countries, and underdeveloped, backward or "peripheral" countries.[18]

The center is viewed as capable of dynamic development responsive to internal needs, and as the main beneficiary of the global links. On the other hand, the periphery is seen as having a reflex type of development; one which is both constrained by its incorporation into the global system and which results from its adaptation to the requirements of the expansion of the center. As Theotônio dos Santos indicates:

> Dependency is a situation in which a certain number of countries have their economy conditioned by the development and expansion of another . . .placing the dependent countries in a backward position exploited by the dominant countries.[19]

It is important to stress that the process can be understood only by reference to its historical dimension and by focusing on the total network of social relations as they evolve in different contexts over time. For this reason dependence is characterized as "structural, historical and totalizing" or an "integral analysis of development."[20] It is meaningless to develop, as some social scientists have, a series of synchronic statistical indicators to establish relative levels of dependence or independence among different national units to test the "validity" of the model.[21] The unequal development of the world goes back to the 16th century with the formation of a capitalist world economy in which some countries in the center were able to specialize in industrial production of manufactured goods because the peripheral areas of the world which they colonized provided the necessary primary goods, agricultural and mineral, for consumption in the center. Contrary to some assumptions in economic theory the international division of labor did not lead to parallel development through comparative advantage. The center states gained at the expense of the periphery. But, just as significantly, the different functions of center and peripheral societies had a profound effect on the evolution of internal social and political structures. Those which evolved in the periphery reinforced economies with a narrow range of primary exports. The interdependent nature of the world capitalist system and the qualitative transformations in that system over time make it inconceivable to think that individual nations on the periphery could somehow replicate the evolutionary experience of the now developed nations.[22]

It follows from an emphasis on global structural processes and variations in internal structural arrangements that contextual variables, at least in the long run, shape and guide the behavior of groups and individuals. It is not inappropriate attitudes which contribute to the absence of entrepreneurial behavior or to institutional arrangements reinforcing underdevelopment. Dependent, peripheral development produces an opportunity structure such that personal gain for dominant groups and entrepreneurial elements is not conducive to the collective gain of balanced development. This is a fundamental difference with much of the modernization literature. It implies that dependence analysts, though they do not articulate the point explicitly, share the classical economic theorists' view of human nature. They assume that individuals in widely different societies are capable of pursuing rational patterns of behavior; able to assess information objectively in the pursuit of utilitarian goals. What varies is not the degree of rationality, but the structural foundations of the incentive systems which, in turn, produce different forms of behavior given the same process of rational calculus. It was not attitudinal transformations which generated the rapid industrialization which developed after the Great Depression, but the need to replace imports with domestic products. Or, as Cardoso points out in his studies of entrepreneurs, it is not values which condition their behavior as much as technological dependence, state intervention in the economy, and their political weakness vis-à-vis domestic and foreign actors.[23] What appear as anomalies in the modernization literature can be accounted for by a focus on contextual processes in the dependence literature.

It is necessary to underscore the fact that dependency writers stress the importance of the "way internal and external structural components are connected" in elaborating the structural context of underdevelopment. As such, underdevelopment is not simply the result of "external constraints" on peripheral societies, nor can dependency be operationalized solely with reference to clusters of external variables.[24] Dependency in any given society is a complex set of associations in which the external dimensions are determinative in varying degrees and, indeed, internal variables may very well reinforce the pattern of external linkages. Historically it has been rare for local interests to develop on the periphery which are capable of charting a successful policy of self-sustained development. Dominant local interests, given the nature of

class arrangements emerging from the characteristics of peripheral economies, have tended to favor the preservation of rearticulation of patterns of dependency in their interests.

It is also important to note that while relations of dependency viewed historically help to explain underdevelopment, it does not follow that dependent relations today necessarily perpetuate across the board underdevelopment. With the evolution of the world system, the impact of dependent relations can change in particular contexts. This is why Cardoso, in studying contemporary Brazil, stresses the possibility of "associated-dependent development," and Sunkel and Fuenzalida are able to envision sharp economic growth among countries most tied into the contemporary transnational system.[25] Because external-internal relations are complex, and because changes in the world system over time introduce new realities, it is indispensable to study comparatively concrete national and historical situations. As Anibal Quijano says, "The relationships of dependency. . .take on many forms. The national societies in Latin America are dependent, as is the case with the majority of the Asian, African and some European countries. However, each case does not present identical dependency relations."[26] The dependency perspective has thus concentrated on a careful historical evaluation of the similarities and differences in the "situations of dependency" of the various Latin American countries over time implying careful attention to "preexisting conditions" in different contexts.

The description of various phases in the world system and differing configurations of external-internal linkages, follow from this insistence on diachronic analysis and its application to concrete cases. The dependency perspective is primarily a historical model with no claim to "universal validity." This is why it has paid less attention to the formulation of precise theoretical constructs, such as those found in the modernization literature, and more attention to the specification of historical phases which are an integral part of the framework.

The dependency literature distinguishes between the "mercantilistic" colonial period (1500–1750), the period of "outward growth" dependent on primary exports (1750–1914), the period of the crisis of the "liberal model" (1914–1950), and the current period of "transnational capitalism."

As already noted, because of the need for raw materials and foodstuffs for the growing industrialization of England, Germany, the United States, and France, Latin American productive structures were aimed from the outset at the export market. During the colonial period, the economic specialization was imposed by the Iberian monarchies. As Bagú notes in his classic study, "Colonial production was not directed by the needs of national consumers, and not even by the interests of local producers. The lines of production were structured and transformed to conform to an order determined by the imperial metropolis. The colonial economy was consequently shaped by its complementary character. The products that did not compete with those of Spain or Portugal in the metropolitan, international or colonial markets, found tolerance or stimulus." [27] During the 19th century, exports were actively pursued by the politically dominant groups. The independence movement did not attempt to transform internal productive structures; it was aimed at eliminating Iberian interference in the commercialization of products to and from England and northern Europe. The logic of the productive system in this period of "outwardly directed development," in ECLA's terms, was not conducive to the creation of a large industrial sector. Economic rationality, not only of individual entrepreneurs but also of the system, dictated payments in kind and/or extremely low wages and/or the use of slavery, thus markedly limiting the internal market. At the same time, the accumulation of foreign exchange made relatively easy the acquisition of imported industrial products. Any expansion of exports was due more to political than economic factors and depended on a saleable export commodity, and plenty of land and labor, for its success.

There were, however, important differences between regions and countries. During the colonial period these are attributable to differences in colonial administrations, natural resources, and types of production. During the 19th century a key difference was the degree of local elite control over productive activities for export. Though in all countries elites controlled export production initially (external commercialization was mainly under foreign control), towards the end of the century in some countries control was largely relinquished to foreign exploitation. Where this occurred, the economic role of local elites was reduced considerably, though the importance of this reduction varied depending both on the degree to which the foreign enclave displaced the local elite from the export sector and the extent to which its economic activities were diversified. Concurrently, the state bureaucracy expanded and acquired increasing importance through regulations and taxation of the enclave sector. The state thus became the principal intermediary between the local economy and the enclave, which generally had little *direct* internal secondary impact. Other differences, especially at the turn of the century, are the varying importance of incipient industrialization, the size and importance of middle- and working-class groups, variations in export products, natural resources, and so on.

The world wars and the depression produced a crisis in the export-oriented economies through the collapse of external demand, and therefore of the capacity to import. The adoption of fiscal and monetary policies aimed at supporting the internal market and avoiding the negative effects of the external disequilibrium produced a favorable climate for the growth of an industrial sector under national auspices. The available foreign exchange was employed to acquire capital goods to substitute imports of consumer articles. The early successes of the transition to what ECLA calls "inwardly directed development" depended to a large extent on the different political alliances which emerged in the various national settings, and on the characteristics of the social and political structures inherited from the precrisis period.

Thus, in the enclave situations the earliest developments were attained in Mexico and Chile, where middle- and lower-class groups allied in supporting state development policies, ultimately strengthening the urban bourgeoisie. The alliance was successful in Chile because of the importance of middle-class parties which emerged during the final period of export-oriented development, and the early consolidation of a trade union movement. The antecedents of the Mexican situation are to be found in the destruction of agricultural elites during the revolution. Such structural conditions were absent in other enclave situations (Bolivia, Peru, Venezuela, and Central America) where the internal development phase began later under new conditions of dependence, though in some cases with similar political alliances (Bolivia, Venezuela, Guatemala, Costa Rica). Throughout the crisis period agrarian-based and largely nonexporting groups were able to remain in power, appealing in some cases to military governments, and preserving the political scheme that characterized the export-oriented period.

In the nonenclave situations, considerable industrial growth was attained in Argentina and Brazil. In the former, export-oriented agrarian entrepreneurs had invested considerably in production for the internal market and the contraction of the export sector only accentuated this trend. In Brazil the export-oriented agrarian groups collapsed with the crisis and the state, as in Chile and Mexico, assumed a major developmental role with the support of a complex alliance of urban entrepreneurs, nonexport agrarian elites, popular sectors, and middle-class groups. In Colombia the export-oriented agrarian elites remained in power and did not foster significant internal industrialization until the fifties.

The import substituting industrialization attained greatest growth in Argentina, Brazil, and Mexico. It soon, however, reached its limits, given the parameters under which it was realized. Since capital goods for the establishment

of industrial parks were acquired in the central nations, the success of the policy ultimately depended on adequate foreign exchange supplies. After reaching maximum growth through the accumulation of foreign exchange during the Second World War, the industrialization programs could only continue—given the available political options—on the basis of an increased external debt and further reliance on foreign investments. This accumulation of foreign reserves permitted the success of the national-populist alliances in Argentina and Brazil which gave the workers greater welfare while maintaining investments. The downfall of Perón and the suicide of Vargas symbolized the end of this easy period of import substitution.

But the final blow to "import substitution" industrialization came not from difficulties in the periphery but further transformations in the center which have led, in Sunkel's term, to the creation of a new "transnational" system. With rapid economic recovery the growing multinational corporations sought new markets and cheaper production sites for their increasingly technological manufacturing process. Dependency consequently acquired a "new character" as Dos Santos noted, which would have a profound effect on Latin America. Several processes were involved resulting in (1) the investment of centrally based corporations in manufactures within the periphery for sales in its internal market or, as Cardoso and Faletto note, the "internalization of the internal market"; (2) a new international division of labor in which the periphery acquires capital goods, technology, and raw materials from the central nations, and export profits, along with its traditional raw materials and a few manufactured items produced by multinational subsidiaries; and (3) a denationalization of the older import substituting industries established originally.[28] Although the "new dependence" is in evidence throughout the continent, the process has asserted itself more clearly in the largest internal markets such as Brazil, where the weakness of the trade-union movement (the comparison with Argentina in this respect is instructive) coupled with authoritarian political structures has created a singularly favorable investment climate.

In subsequent and more recent works writers in the dependency framework have pursued different strategies of research. Generally speaking, the early phases of the historical process have received less attention, though the contribution of I. Wallerstein to an understanding of the origins of the world system is a major addition to the literature. Most writers have preferred to focus on the current "new situation" of dependence. Some have devoted more attention to an effort at elaborating the place of dependent capitalism as a contribution to the Marxist analysis of capitalist society. Scholars in this vein tend to argue more forcefully than others that dependent capitalism is impossible and that socialism provides the only historically viable alternative. Others have focused more on the analysis of concrete cases of dependence, elaborating in some detail the various interconnections between domestic and foreign forces, and noting the possibility of different kinds of dependent development.[29] Still others have turned their attention to characterizing the nature of the new capitalist system, with particular emphasis on the emergence of a "transnational system" which is rendering more complex and problematic the old distinctions of center and periphery. Particularly for the last two tendencies, the emphasis is on the design of new empirical studies while attempting to systematize further some of the propositions implicit in the conceptual framework.

## SUMMARY AND CONCLUSIONS

Modernization and dependency are two different perspectives each claiming to provide conceptual and analytical tools capable of explaining the relative underdevelopment of Latin America. The object of inquiry is practically the only thing that these two competing "visions" have in common, as they differ substantially not only on fundamental assumptions, but also on

methodological implications and strategies for research.

Though there are variations in the literature, the *level of analysis* of a substantial tradition in the modernization perspective, and the one which informs most reflections on Latin America, is behavioral or microsociological. The primary focus is on individuals or aggregates of individuals, their values, attitudes, and beliefs. The dependency perspective, by contrast, is structural or macrosociological. Its focus is on the mode of production, patterns of international trade, political and economic linkages between elites in peripheral and central countries, group and class alliances and conflicts, and so on. Both perspectives are concerned with the process of development in national societies. However, for the modernization writer the national society is the basic *unit of analysis,* while the writer in a dependence framework considers the global system and its various forms of interaction with national societies as the primary object of inquiry.

For the dependency perspective, the *time dimension* is a crucial aspect of what is fundamentally a historical model. Individual societies cannot be presumed to be able to replicate the evolution of other societies because the very transformation of an interrelated world system may preclude such an option. The modernization potential of individual societies must be seen in light of changes over time in the interactions between external and internal variables. The modernization perspective is obviously concerned about the origins of traditional and modern values; but, the time dimension is not fundamental to the explanatory pretensions of a model which claims "universal validity." Without knowing the source of modernity inhibiting characteristics, it is still possible to identify them by reference to their counterparts in developing contexts.

At the root of the differences between the two perspectives is a fundamentally different *perception of human nature.* Dependency assumes that human behavior in economic matters is a "constant." Individuals will behave differently in different contexts not because they are different but because the contexts are different. The insistence on structures and, in the final analysis, on the broadest structural category of all, the world system, follows logically from the view that opportunity structures condition human behavior. Modernizationists, on the other hand, attribute the lack of certain behavioral patterns to the "relativity" of human behavior; to the fact that cultural values and beliefs, regardless of opportunity structures, underlie the patterns of economic action. Thus, the *conception of change* in the modernization perspective is a product of innovations which result from the adoption of modern attitudes among elites, and eventually followers. Though some modernization theorists are now more pessimistic about the development potential of such changes, modernizing beliefs are a prerequisite for development. For dependency analysts the conception of change is different. Change results from the realignment of dependency relations over time. Whether or not development occurs and how it occurs is subject to controversy. Given the rapid evolution of the world system, dependent development is possible in certain contexts, not in others. Autonomy, through a break in relations of dependency, may not lead to development of the kind already arrived at in the developed countries because of the inability to recreate the same historical conditions, but it might lead to a different kind of development stressing different values. Thus, the *prescription for change* varies substantially in the dependency perspective depending on the ideological outlook of particular authors. It is not a logical consequence of the historical model. In the modernization perspective the prescription for change follows more automatically from the assumptions of the model, implying greater consensus.

From a methodological point of view the modernization perspective is much more parsimonious than its counterpart. And the focus of much of the literature on the microsociological level makes it amenable to the elaboration of precise explanatory propositions such as those of D. McClelland or E. Hagen. Dependency, by

contrast, is more descriptive and its macrosociological formulations are much less subject to translation into a simple set of explanatory propositions. Many aspects of dependency, and particularly the linkages between external phenomena and internal class and power relations are unclear and need to be studied with more precision and care. For this reason the dependency perspective is an "approach" to the study of underdevelopment rather than a "theory." And yet, precisely because modernization theory relies on a simple conceptual framework and a reductionist approach, it is far less useful for the study of a complex phenomenon such as development or underdevelopment.

But the strengths of the dependency perspective lie not only in its consideration of a richer body of evidence and a broader range of phenomena, it is also more promising from a methodological point of view. The modernization perspective has fundamental flaws which make it difficult to provide for a fair test of its own assumptions. It will be recalled that the modernization perspective draws on a model with "universal validity" which assumes that traditional values are not conducive to modern behavioral patterns of action. Given that underdevelopment, on the basis of various economic and social indicators, is an objective datum, the research task becomes one of identifying modernizing values and searching for their opposites in underdeveloped contexts.

In actual research efforts, the modernity inhibiting characteristics are often "deduced" from impressionistic observation. This is the case with much of the political science literature on Latin America. However, more "rigorous" methods, such as survey research, have also been employed, particularly in studies of entrepreneurial activity. Invariably, whether through deduction or survey research, less appropriate values for modernization such as "arielismo" (a concern for transcendental as opposed to material values) or "low-achievement" (lack of risk-taking attitudes) have been identified thus "confirming" the hypothesis that traditional values contribute to underdevelopment. If by chance the use of control groups should establish little or no difference in attitudes in a developed and underdeveloped context, the research instrument can be considered to be either faulty or the characteristics tapped not the appropriate ones for identifying traditional attitudes. The latter alternative might lead to the "discovery" of a new "modernity of tradition" literature or of greater flexibility than anticipated in traditional norms or of traditional residuals in the developed country.

The problem with the model and its behavioral level of analysis is that the explanation for underdevelopment is part of the preestablished conceptual framework. It is already "known" that in backward areas the modernity inhibiting characteristics play the dominant role, otherwise the areas would not be backward. As such, the test of the hypothesis involves a priori acceptance of the very hypothesis up for verification, with empirical evidence gathered solely in an illustrative manner. The focus on individuals simply does not permit consideration of a broader range of contextual variables which might lead to invalidating the assumptions. Indeed, the modernity of tradition literature, which has pointed to anomalies in the use of the tradition modernity "polarities," is evidence of how such a perspective can fall victim to the "and so" fallacy. Discrepancies are accounted for not by a reformulation, but by adding a new definition or a new corollary to the preexisting conceptual framework.

Much work needs to be done within a dependency perspective to clarify its concepts and causal interrelationships, as well as to assess its capacity to explain social processes in various parts of peripheral societies. And yet the dependency approach appears to have a fundamental advantage over the modernization perspective: It is open to historically grounded conceptualization in underdeveloped contexts, while modernization is locked into an illustrative methodological style by virtue of its very assumptions.

## Notes

1. For antecedents of the modernization literature, see the work of scholars such as Maine, Tonnies, Durkheim, Weber, and Redfield.

2. See Cyril Black, *The Dynamics of Modernization* (New York, 1966), pp. 68–75.

3. Ibid., pp. 53–54.

4. Gabriel Almond, "Introduction: A Functional Approach to Comparative Politics," in Almond and James S. Coleman, *The Politics of the Developing Areas* (Princeton, 1960) p. 64. Statements such as these have led to the criticism that modernization is an ethnocentric approach. But rather than pointing out their ethnocentricity, it is more important to indicate that they reflect an assumption which becomes a key methodological option, ethnocentric or otherwise.

5. See Kalman H. Silvert, *The Conflict Society: Reaction and Revolution in Latin America* (New York, 1966), p. 261.

6. Black, *The Dynamics of Modernization*, p. 50 (emphasis added).

7. Dankwart A. Rustow, *A World of Nations: Problems of Political Modernization* (Washington: The Brookings Institution, 1967).

8. Wilbert Moore "Modernization and Rationalization: Processes and Restraints," *Economic Development and Cultural Change*, 35 (1977, supplement), pp. 34–35.

9. Moore, "Motivational Aspects of Development," in *Social Change*. Amitai and Eva Etzioni, (New York, 1964), p. 292. See also his "Social Change" in the *International Encyclopedia of the Social Sciences* (1968).

10. J. Gusfield, "Tradition and Modernity: Misplaced Polarities in the Study of Social Change," *American Journal of Sociology* 72 (January 1967).

11. Lloyd I. and Susanne H. Rudolph, *The Modernity of Traditional Development in India* (Chicago, 1967). Another work in this vein is Robert Wand and Rustow, eds, *Political Modernization in Japan and Turkey* (Princeton, 1964).

12. S. N. Eisenstadt, *Tradition, Change and Modernity* (New York, 1973) and Moore, "Modernization and Rationalization."

13. Marion Levy, Jr., *Modernization: Latecomers and Survivors* (New York, 1972).

14. Seymour Martin Lipset, "Values, Education and Entrepreneurship," in *Elites in Latin America,* ed. Lipset and Aldo Solari, (New York, 1963). For another study in which Lipset expresses similar views about Latin America, while extolling the opposite values in the United States, see his *The First New Nation* (New York, 1963).

15. Lipset, "Values, Education and Entrepreneurship," p. 19.

16. Ibid., p. 30. Some of the studies cited include T. C. Cohran, "Cultural Factors in Economic Growth," *Journal of Economic History* 20 (1974); T. R. Fillol, *Social Factors in Economic Development: The Argentine Case* (Cambridge, Mass., 1961); B. J. Siegel, "Social Structure and Economic Change in Brazil," in *Economic Growth: Brazil, India, Japan,* ed. Simon Kuznets et al., (Durham, N.C., 1955); and W. P. Strassman, "The Industrialist," in *Continuity and Change in Latin America,* ed. John J. Johnson, (Stanford, 1964).

17. R. Adie and G. E. Poitras, *Latin America: The Politics of Immobility* (Englewood Cliffs, N.J., 1974), pp. 73, 75. For similar views see pp. 252–253 and W. R. Duncan, *Latin American Politics: A Developmental Approach* (New York, 1976), p. 240.

18. Osvaldo Sunkel and Pedro Paz, *El subdesarrollo latinoamericano y la teoria del desarrollo* (Mexico, 1970), p. 6.

19. Theotônio dos Santos, "La crisis del desarrollo y las relaciones de dependencia en América Latina," in *La dependencia politico-económica de América Latina,* ed. H. Jaguaribe et al, (Mexico, 1970), p. 180. See also his *Dependencia y cambio social* (Santiago, 1970) and *Socialismo o Fascismo: El nuevo carácter de la dependencia y el dilema latinoamericano* (Buenos Aires, 1972).

20. Sunkel and Paz, *El subdesarrollo latinoamericano,* p. 39; Fernando Henrique Cardoso and Enzo Faletto, *Dependencia y desarrollo en América Latina* (Mexico, 1969), chap 2.

21. This is the problem with the studies by Robert Kaufman et al., "A Preliminary Test of the Theory of Dependency," *Comparative Politics* 7 (April 1975), pp. 303–330, and C. Chase-Dunn, "The Effects of International Economic Dependence on Development and Inequality: A Cross National Study," *American Sociological Review* 40 (December 1975). It is interesting to note that Marxist scholars make the same mistake. They point to features in the dependency literature such as unemployment, marginalization etc., noting that they are not peculiar to peripheral countries but characterize capitalist countries in general. Thus "dependence" is said to have no explanatory value beyond a Marxist theory of capitalist society. See Sanyaya Lall, "Is Dependence a Useful Concept in Analyzing Underdevelopment?" *World Development* 3 (November 1975) and Theodore Weisscopf, "Dependence as an Explanation of Underdevelopment: A Critique." (Paper presented at the Sixth Annual Latin American Studies Association Meeting, Atlanta, Georgia, 1976). The point of dependency analysis is not the relative mix at one point in time of certain identifiable factors but the evolution over time of structural relations which help to explain the differential development of capitalism in different parts of the world. As a historical model it cannot be tested with cross national data. For an attempt to differentiate conceptually contemporary capitalism, see Samir Amin, *Accumulation on a World Scale* (New York, 1974).

22. Some authors have criticized the focus of the literature on the evolution of the world capitalist system. David Ray, for example, has argued that "soviet satellites" are also in a dependent and unequal relationship vis-à-vis the Soviet Union and that the key variable should not be capitalism but "political power." Robert Packenham has also argued that the most important critique of the dependency literature is that it does not consider the implications of "power." See Ray, "The Dependency Model of Latin American Underdevelopment: Three Basic Fallacies," *Journal of Interamerican Studies and*

*World Affairs* 15 (February 1973) and Packenham, "Latin American Dependency Theories: Strengths and Weaknesses." (Paper presented to the Harvard-MIT Joint Seminar on Political Development, February, 1974), especially pp. 16–17, 54. This criticism misses the point completely. It is not power relations today which cause underdevelopment, but the historical evolution of a world economic system which led to economic specialization more favorable to some than others. It is precisely this concern with the evolution of world capitalism which has led to the preoccupation in the dependency literature with rejecting interpretations stressing the "feudal" rather than "capitalist" nature of colonial and post colonial Latin American agriculture. On this point see Sergio Bagú, *Economía de la Sociedad Colonial* (Buenos Aires, 1949); Luis Vitale; "America Latina: Feudal o Capitalista?" *Revista Estrategia*, 3 (1966) and *Interpretación Marxista de la historia de Chile* (Santiago, 1967); and E. Laclau, "Feudalism and Capitalism in Latin America," *New Left Review* 67 (May–July 1971). A brilliant recent exposition of the importance of studying the evolution of the capitalist world system in order to understand underdevelopment which focuses more on the center states than on the periphery is Immanuel Wallerstein, *The Modern World System: Capitalist Agriculture and the Origins of the European World Economy in the Sixteenth Century* (New York, 1974).

23. Cardoso, *Empresário industrial e desenvolvimento economico no Brazil* (São Paulo, 1964) and *Ideologías de la burguesia industrial en sociedades dependientes (Mexico, 1971).*

24. *Cardoso and Faletto, Dependencia y desarrollo, p. 20.* Indeed Cardoso argues that the distinction between external and internal is "metaphysical." See his "Teoria de la dependencia o análisis de situaciones concretas de dependencia?" *Revista Latinoamericana de Ciencia Politica* (December 1970), p. 404. The ontology implicit in such an analysis is the one of "internal relations." See Bertell Ollman, *Alienation: Marx's Conception of Man in Capitalist Society* (London, 1971). This point is important because both Frank and the early ECLA literature was criticized for their almost mechanistic relationship between external and internal variable. Frank acknowledges this problem and tries to answer his critics in *Lumpenbourgeoisie and Lumpen-development* (New York, 1967). "Tests" of dependency theory also attribute an excessively mechanical dimension to the relationship. See Kaufman et al., "A Preliminary Test."

25. Cardoso, "Associated Dependent Development: Theoretical Implications," in *Authoritarian Brazil,* ed. Alfred Stepan (New Haven, 1973). For fallacies in the dependency literature see Cardoso "Las contradicciones del desarrollo asociado," *Desarrollo Económico* 4 (April–June 1974).

26. Anibal Quijano, "Dependencia, Cambio Social y Urbanización en América Latina," in *América Latina: Ensayos de interpretación sociológico politico,* ed. Cardoso and F. Weffort (Santiago, 1970).

27. Bagú, *Economía de la sociedad colonial,* pp. 122–123.

28. Sunkel "Capitalismo transnacional y desintegración nacional en América Latina," *Estudios Internacionales* 4 (January–March 1971) an "Big Business and Dependencia: A Latin American View," *Foreign Affairs* 50 (April 1972); Cardoso and Faletto, *Dependencia y desarrollo;* Dos Santos, El nuevo carácter de la dependencia (Santiago, 1966).

29. Cardoso, "Teoria de la dependencia." A recent trend in dependency writings attempts to explain the current wave of authoritarianism in Latin America as a result of economic difficulties created by the exhaustion of the easy import substituting industrialization. The new situation leads to a process of development led by the state and the multinational corporations, which concentrates income toward the top, increases the levels of capital accumulation and expands heavy industry; the old populist alliances can therefore no longer be maintained. See Dos Santos, *Socialismo o fascismo: el nuevo carácter de la dependencia y el dilema latinoamericano* (Buenos Aires, 1972): Guillermo O'Donnell, *Modernization and Bureaucratic-Authoritarianism:*

*Studies in Latin American Politics* (Berkeley: University of California, 1973); Atilio Borón, "El fascismo como categoría histórica: en torno al problema de las dictaduras en América Latina," *Revista Mexicana de Sociología* 34 (April–June 1977); the effects of this situation on labor are explored in Kenneth P. Erickson and Patrick Peppe, "Dependent Capitalist Development, U.S. Foreign Policy, and Repression of the Working Class in Chile and Brazil," *Latin American Perspectives* 3 (Winter 1976). However, in the postscript to their 1968 book, Cardoso and Faletto caution against adopting an excessively mechanistic view on this point, against letting "economism kill history": Cardoso and Faletto. "Estado y proceso político en América Latina," *Revista Mexicana de Sociología* 34 (April–June 1977), p. 383. Articles with dependency perspective appear frequently in the *Revista Mexicana de Sociología* as well as in *Latin American Perspectives*.

# CHAPTER ELEVEN

# Revolution

## 44

## The Anatomy of Revolution

*Crane Brinton*

### SOME TENTATIVE UNIFORMITIES

When all necessary concessions are made to those who insist that events in history are unique, it remains true that the four revolutions we have studied (English, American, French, and Russian) do display some striking uniformities. Our conceptual scheme of the fever can be worked out so as to bring these uniformities clearly to mind. We shall find it worth while, in attempting to summarize the work of these revolutions, to recapitulate briefly the main points of comparison on which our uniformities are based.

We must be very tentative about the prodromal symptoms of revolution. Even retrospectively, diagnosis of the four societies we studied was very difficult, and there is little ground for belief that anyone today has enough knowledge and skill to apply formal methods of diagnosis to a contemporary society and say, in this case revolution will or will not occur shortly. But some uniformities do emerge from a study of the old regimes in England, America, France, and Russia.

First, these were all societies on the whole on the upgrade economically before the revolution came, and the revolutionary movements

SOURCE: Crane Brinton, *The Anatomy of Revolution* (Englewood Cliffs, N.J.: Prentice-Hall, 1952). Reprinted with Permission of Prentice-Hall, Inc., © 1938, 1952 by Prentice-Hall, Inc., renewed by Cecilia Bogner. Published by Prentice-Hall, Inc., Englewood Cliffs, NJ 07632.

seem to originate in the discontents of not unprosperous people who feel restraint, cramp, annoyance, rather than downright crushing oppression. Certainly these revolutions are not started by down-and-outers, by starving, miserable people. These revolutionists are not worms turning, not children of despair. These revolutions are born of hope, and their philosophies are formally optimistic.

Second, we find in our prerevolutionary society definite and indeed very bitter class antagonisms, though these antagonisms seem rather more complicated than the cruder Marxists will allow. It is not a case of feudal nobility against bourgeoisie in 1640, 1776, and 1789, or of bourgeoisie against proletariat in 1917. The strongest feelings seem generated in the bosoms of men—and women—who have made money, or at least who have enough to live on, and who contemplate bitterly the imperfections of a socially privileged aristocracy. Revolutions seem more likely when social classes are fairly close together than when they are far apart. "Untouchables" very rarely revolt against a God-given aristocracy, and Haiti gives one of the few examples of successful slave revolutions. But rich merchants whose daughters can marry aristocrats are likely to feel that God is at least as interested in merchants as in aristocrats. It is difficult to say why the bitterness of feeling between classes *almost* equal socially seems so much stronger in some societies than others—why, for instance, a Marie Antoinette should be so much more hated in 18th century France than a rich, idle, much publicized heiress in contemporary America; but at any rate the existence of such bitterness can be observed in our prerevolutionary societies, which is, clinically speaking, enough for the moment.

Third, there is what we have called the desertion of the intellectuals. This is in some respects the most reliable of the symptoms we are likely to meet. Here again we need not try to explain all the hows and whys, need not try to tie up the desertion of the intellectuals with a grand and complete sociology of revolutions. We need state simply that it can be observed in all four of our societies.

Fourth, the governmental machinery is clearly inefficient, partly through neglect, through a failure to make changes in old institutions, partly because new conditions—in the societies we have studied, pretty specifically conditions attendant on economic expansion and the growth of new monied classes, new ways of transportation, new business methods— these new conditions laid an intolerable strain on governmental machinery adapted to simpler, more primitive, conditions.

Fifth, the old ruling class—or rather, many individuals of the old ruling class—come to distrust themselves, or lose faith in the traditions and habits of their class, grow intellectual, humanitarian, or go over to the attacking groups. Perhaps a larger number of them than usual lead lives we shall have to call immoral, dissolute, though one cannot by any means be as sure about this as a symptom as about the loss of habits and traditions of command effective among a ruling class. At any rate, the ruling class becomes politically inept.

The dramatic events that start things moving, that bring on the fever of revolution, are in three of our four revolutions intimately connected with the financial administration of the state. In the fourth, Russia, the breakdown of administration under the burdens of an unsuccessful war is only in part financial. But in all our societies the inefficiency and inadequacy of the governmental structure of the society come out clearly in the very first stages of the revolution. There is a time—the first few weeks or months—when it looks as if a determined use of force on the part of the government might prevent the mounting excitement from culminating in an overthrow of the government. These governments attempted such a use of force in all four instances, and in all four their attempt was a failure. This failure indeed proved a turning point during the first stages, and set up the revolutionists in power.

Yet one is impressed in all four instances more with the ineptitude of the governments' use of force than with the skill of their opponents' use of force. We are here speaking of the situation wholly from a military and police point of view. It may be that the majority of the people are discontented, loathe the existing government, wish it overthrown. Nobody knows. They don't take plebiscites *before* revolutions. In the actual clash—even Bastille Day, Concord, or the February Days in Petrograd—only a minority of the people is actively engaged. But the government hold over its own troops is poor, its troops fight halfheartedly or desert, its commanders are stupid, its enemies acquire a nucleus of the deserting troops or of a previous militia, and the old gives place to the new. Yet, such is the conservative and routine-loving nature of the bulk of human beings, so strong are habits of obedience in most of them, that it is almost safe to say that no government is likely to be overthrown until it loses the ability to make adequate use of its military and police powers. That loss of ability may show itself in the actual desertion of soldiers and police to the revolutionists, or in the stupidity with which the government manages its soldiers and police, or in both ways.

The events we have grouped under the names of first stages do not of course unroll themselves in exactly the same order in time, or with exactly the same content, in all four of our revolutions. But we have listed the major elements—and they fall into a pattern of uniformities—financial breakdown, organization of the discontented to remedy this breakdown (or threatened breakdown), revolutionary demands on the part of these organized discontented, demands which if granted would mean the virtual abdication of those governing, attempted use of force by the government, its failure, and the attainment of power by the revolutionists. These revolutionists have hitherto been acting as an organized and nearly unanimous group, but with the attainment of power it is clear that they are not united. The group which dominates these first stages we call the moderates. They are not always in a numerical majority in this stage—indeed it is pretty clear that if you limit the moderates to the Kadets they were not in a majority in Russia in February, 1917. But they seem the natural heirs of the old government, and they have their chance. In three of our revolutions they are sooner or later driven from office to death or exile. Certainly there is to be seen in England, France, and Russia a process in which a series of crises—some involving violence, street fighting, and the like—deposes one set of men and puts in power another and more radical set. In these revolutions power passes by violent or at least extralegal methods from Right to Left, until at the crisis period the extreme radicals, the complete revolutionists, are in power. There are, as a matter of fact, usually a few even wilder and more lunatic fringes of the triumphant extremists—but these are not numerous or strong and are usually suppressed or otherwise made harmless by the dominant radicals. It is therefore approximately true to say that power passes on from Right to Left until it reaches the extreme Left.

The rule of the extremists we have called the crisis period. This period was not reached in the American Revolution, though in the treatment of Loyalists, in the pressure to support the army, in some of the phases of social life, you can discern in America many of the phenomena of the Terror as it is seen in our three other societies. We cannot here attempt to go into the complicated question as to why the American Revolution stopped short of a true crisis period, why the moderates were never ousted in this country. We must repeat that we are simply trying to establish certain uniformities of description, and are not attempting a complete sociology of revolutions.

The extremists are helped to power no doubt by the existence of a powerful pressure toward centralized strong government, something which in general the moderates are not capable of providing, while the extremists, with their discipline, their contempt for half measures, their willingness to make firm decisions, their freedom from libertarian qualms, are quite able and willing to centralize. Especially in France and Russia, where powerful foreign enemies threatened the very existence of the nation, the machinery of government during the crisis period was in part constructed to serve as a government of national defense. Yet though modern wars, as we know in this country, demand a centralization of authority, war alone does not seem to account for all that happened in the crisis period in those countries.

What does happen may be a bit oversimply summarized as follows: emergency centralization of power in an administration, usually a council or commission, and more or less dominated by a "strong man"—Cromwell, Robespierre, Lenin; government without any effective protection for the normal civil rights of the individual—or if this sounds unrealistic, especially for Russia, let us say the normal private life of the individual; setting up of extraordinary courts and a special revolutionary police to carry out the decrees of the government and to suppress all dissenting individuals or groups; all this machinery ultimately built up from a relatively small group—Independents, Jacobins, Bolsheviks—which has a monopoly on all governmental action. Finally, governmental action becomes a much greater part of all human action than in these societies in their normal condition: this apparatus of government is set to work indifferently on the mountains and molehills of human life—it is used to pry into and poke about corners normally reserved for priest or physician, or friend, and it is used to regulate, control, plan, the production and distribution of economic wealth on a national scale.

This pervasiveness of the Reign of Terror in the crisis period is partly explicable in terms of the pressure of war necessities and of economic struggles as well as of other variables: but it must probably also be explained as in part the manifestation of an effort to achieve intensely religious ends here on earth. The little band of violent revolutionists who form the nucleus of all action during the Terror behave as men have been observed to behave before when under the influence of active religious faith. Independents, Jacobins, Bolsheviks, all sought to make all human activity here on earth conform to an ideal pattern, which, like all such patterns, seems deeply rooted in their sentiments. A striking uniformity in all these patterns is their asceticism, or if you prefer, their condemnation of what we may call the minor as well as the major vices. Essentially, however, these patterns are a good deal alike, and all resemble closely what we may call conventional Christian ethics. Independents, Jacobins, and Bolsheviks, at least during the crisis period, really make an effort to enforce behavior in literal conformity with these codes or patterns. Such an effort means stern repression of much that many men have been used to regarding as normal; it means a kind of universal tension in which the ordinary individual can never feel protected by the humble routines to which he has been formed: it means that the intricate network of inter-actions among individuals—a network which is still to the few men devoted to its intelligent study almost a complete mystery—this network is temporarily all torn apart. John Jones, the man in the street, the ordinary man, is left floundering.

We are almost at the point of being carried away into the belief that our conceptual scheme is something more than a mere convenience, that it does somehow describe "reality." At the crisis, the collective patient does seem helpless, thrashing his way through a delirium. But we must try to avoid the emotional, metaphorical appeal, and concentrate on making clear what seems to be the really important point here. Most of us are familiar with the favorite old Tory metaphor: the violent revolutionist tears down the noble edifice society lives in, or burns it down, and then fails to build up another, and poor human beings are left naked to the skies. That is not a good metaphor, save perhaps for purposes of Tory propaganda. Even at the height of a revolutionary crisis period, more of the old

building is left standing than is destroyed. But the whole metaphor of the building is bad. We may take instead an analogy from the human nervous system, or think of an immensely complicated gridwork of electrical communications. Society then appears as a kind of a network of interactions among individuals, interactions for the most part fixed by habit, hardened and perhaps adorned as ritual, dignified into meaning and beauty by the elaborately interwoven strands of interaction we know as law, theology, metaphysics, and similar noble beliefs. Now sometimes many of these interwoven strands of noble beliefs, some even of those of habit and tradition, can be cut out, and others inserted. During the crisis period of our revolutions some such process seems to have taken place; but the whole network itself seems so far never to have been altered suddenly and radically, and even the noble beliefs tend to fit into the network in the same places. If you kill off *all* the people who live within the network, you don't so much change the network of course as destroy it. And in spite of our prophets of doom, this type of destruction is rare in human history. Certainly in none of our revolutions was there even a very close approach to it.

What did happen, under the pressure of class struggle, war, religious idealism, and a lot more, was that the hidden and obscure courses which many of the interactions in the network follow were suddenly exposed, and passage along them made difficult in the unusual publicity and, so to speak, self-consciousness. The courses of other interactions were blocked, and the interactions went on with the greatest of difficulties by all sorts of detours. The courses of still other interactions were confused, short-circuited, paired off in strange ways. Finally, the pretensions of the fanatical leaders of the revolution involved the attempted creation of a vast number of new interactions. Now though for the most part these new interactions affected chiefly those strands we have called the noble beliefs— law, theology, metaphysics, mythology, folklore, high-power abstractions in general—still some of them did penetrate at an experimental level into the obscurer and less dignified part of the network of interactions among human beings and put a further strain on it. Surely it is no wonder that under these conditions men and women in the crisis period should behave as they would not normally behave, that in the crisis period nothing should seem as it used to seem. . . .

Certainly none of our revolutions quite ended in the death of civilization and culture. The network was stronger than the forces trying to destroy or alter it, and in all of our societies the crisis period was followed by a convalescence, by a return to most of the simpler and more fundamental courses taken by interactions in the old network. More especially, the religious lust for perfection, the crusade for the Republic of Virtue, died out, save among a tiny minority whose actions could no longer take place directly in politics. An active, proselyting, intolerant, ascetic, chiliastic faith became fairly rapidly an inactive, indifferent, worldly ritualistic faith.

The equilibrium has been restored and the revolution is over. But this does not mean that nothing has been changed. Some new and useful tracks or courses in the network of interactions that makes society have been established, some old and inconvenient ones—you may call them unjust if you like—have been eliminated. There is something heartless in saying that it took the French Revolution to produce the metric system and to destroy *lods et ventes* and similar feudal inconveniences, or the Russian Revolution to bring Russia to use the modern calendar and to eliminate a few useless letters in the Russian alphabet. These tangible and useful results look rather petty as measured by the brotherhood of man and the achievement of justice on this earth. The blood of the martyrs seems hardly necessary to establish decimal coinage.

Yet those who feel that revolution is heroic need not despair. The revolutionary tradition is an heroic one, and the noble beliefs which seem necessary to all societies are in our Western democracies in part a product of the revolutions we have been studying. Our revolutions made tremendous and valuable additions to those

strands in the network of human interactions which can be isolated as law, theology, metaphysics and, in the abstract sense, ethics. Had these revolutions never occurred, you and I might still beat our wives or cheat at cards or avoid walking under ladders, but we might not be able to rejoice in our possession of certain inalienable rights to life, liberty, and the pursuit of happiness, or in the comforting assurance that one more push will bring the classless society.

When one compares the whole course of these revolutions, certain tentative uniformities suggest themselves. If the Russian Revolution at the end of our series is compared with the English at its beginning, there seems to be a development of conscious revolutionary technique. This is of course especially clear since Marx made the history of revolutionary movements of the past a necessary preparation for revolutionists of the present. Lenin and his collaborators had a training in the technique of insurrection which Independents and Jacobins lacked. Robespierre seems almost a political innocent when his revolutionary training is compared with that of any good Bolshevik leaders. Sam Adams, it must be admitted, seems a good deal less innocent. All in all, it is probable that this difference in the explicitness of self-conscious preparation for revolution, this growth of a copious literature of revolution, this increasing familiarity of revolutionary ideas, is not one of the very important uniformities we have to record. It is a conspicuous uniformity, but not an important one. Revolutions are still not a form of logical action. The Bolsheviks do not seem to have guided their actions by the "scientific" study of revolutions to an appreciably greater degree than the Independents or the Jacobins. They simply adapted an old technique to the days of the telegraph and railroad trains.

This last suggests another conspicuous but not very important tendency in our four revolutions. They took place in societies increasingly influenced by the "Industrial Revolution," increasingly subject to those changes in scale which our modern conquests of time and space have brought to societies. Thus the Russian Revolution directly affected more people and more square miles of territory than any previous revolution; its sequence of events compresses into a few months what in England in the 17th century had taken years to achieve; in its use of the printing press, telegraph, radio, airplanes and the rest it seems, as compared with our other revolutions, definitely a streamlined affair. But again we may well doubt whether such changes of scale are in themselves really important factors. Men's desires are the same, whether they ride toward their achievement in airplanes or on horseback. Revolutions may be bigger nowadays, but surely not better. Our prophets of doom to the contrary notwithstanding, the loudspeaker does not change the words.

Finally, at the risk of being tedious, we must come back to some of the problems of methods in the social sciences which were suggested in our first chapter. We must admit that the theorems, the uniformities, which we have been able to put forward in terms of our conceptual scheme, are vague and undramatic. They are by no means as interesting or as alarming as the ideas of revolution held by the late George Orwell, who really believed that totalitarian revolutionary leaders have learned how to change human beings into something wholly different from their immediate predecessors. They cannot be stated in quantitative terms, cannot be used for purposes of prediction or control. But at the very outset we warned the reader not to expect too much. Even such vague theorems as that of the desertion of the intellectuals, that of the role of force in the first stages of revolution, that of the part played by "religious" enthusiasm in the period of crisis, that of the pursuit of pleasure during Thermidor, are, one hopes, not without value for the study of men in society. In themselves they amount to little, but they suggest certain possibilities in further work.

In the first place, by their very inadequacies they point to the necessity for a more rigorous treatment of the problems involved, challenging those who find them incomplete and unsatisfactory to do a better job. In the second place,

they will serve the purpose of all first approximations in scientific work—they will suggest further study of the *facts,* especially in those fields where the attempt to make first approximations has uncovered an insufficient supply of the necessary facts. Notably here the facts for a study of class antagonisms are woefully inadequate. So, too, are the facts for a study of the circulation of the elite in prerevolutionary societies. But there are a hundred such holes, some of which can surely be filled. Our first approximations will then lead the way to another's second approximations. No scientist should ask more, even though the public does.

## A PARADOX OF REVOLUTION

Wider uniformities will, to judge by the past of science, someday emerge from more complete studies of the sociology of revolutions. Here we dare not hazard much that we have not already brought out in the course of our analysis of four specific revolutions. After all, these are but four revolutions of what seems to be the same type, revolutions in what may be not too uncritically called the democratic tradition. So precious a word is "revolution" to many in that tradition, and especially to Marxists, that they indignantly refuse to apply it to such movements as the relatively bloodless but certainly violent and illegal assumption of power by Mussolini or Hitler. These movements, we are told, were not revolutions because they did not take power from one class and give it to another. Obviously with a word in some ways as imprecise as "revolution" you can play all sorts of tricks like this. But for the scientific study of social change it seems wise to apply the word revolution to the overthrow of an established and legal parliamentary government by Fascists. If this is so, then our four revolutions are but one kind of revolution, and we must not attempt to make them bear the strain of generalizations meant to apply to all revolutions.

It is even more tempting to try to fit these revolutions into something like a philosophy of history. But the philosophy of history is almost bound to lead into the kind of prophetic activity we have already firmly forsworn. It may be that mankind is now in the midst of a universal "time of troubles" from which it will emerge into some kind of universal authoritarian order. It may be that the democratic revolutionary tradition is no longer a living and effective one. It may be that the revolutions we have studied could only have taken place in societies in which "progress" was made a concrete thing by opportunities for economic expansion which cannot recur in our contemporary world, with no more frontiers and no more big families. It may even be that the Marxists are right, and that imperialistic capitalism is now digging its own grave, preparing the inevitable if long-delayed world revolution of the proletariat. There are many possibilities, as to which it is almost true that one man's guess is as good as another's. Certainly a conscientious effort to study four great revolutions in the modern world as a scientist might cannot end in anything as ambitious and as unscientific as social prognosis.

We need not, however, end on a note of blank skepticism. It would seem that there are, from the study of these revolutions, three major conclusions to be drawn: first, that, in spite of their undeniable and dramatic differences, they do present certain simple uniformities of the kind we have tried to bring together under our conceptual scheme of the fever; second, that they point sharply to the necessity of studying men's deeds and men's words without assuming that there is always a simple and logical connection between the two, since throughout their courses, and especially at their crises, they frequently exhibit men saying one thing and doing another; third, that they indicate that in general many things men do, many human habits, sentiments, dispositions, cannot be changed at all rapidly, that the attempt made by the extremists to change them by law, terror, and exhortation fails, that the convalescence brings them back not greatly altered.

Yet one hesitant major generalization binding all four of these revolutions together may here be made from many anticipations earlier in this book.

These four revolutions exhibit an increasing scale of promises to the "common man"—promises as vague as that of complete "happiness" and as concrete as that of full satisfaction of all material wants, with all sorts of pleasant revenges on the way. Communism is but the present limit of this increasing set of promises. It is not for us here to rail or protest, but simply to record. So far, these promises in their extreme form have been fulfilled nowhere. That they are made at all offends the traditional Christian, the humanist, perhaps even the man of common sense. But they are made, more vigorously perhaps today in China, in Southeast Asia, in the Near East, wherever Communism is still a young, fresh, and active faith. It is not enough for us Americans to repeat that the promises are impossible of fulfillment, and ought not to be made. It would be folly for us to tell the world that we Americans can fill these promises, especially since we have not filled them at home. Revolution is not a fever that will yield to such innocent and deceptive remedies. For a time, at least, we must accept it as being as incurable as cancer.

As to what the experience of a great revolution does to the society that experiences it, we cannot conclude here too widely without trespassing on wider fields of history and sociology. Yet it does seem that the patient emerges stronger in some respects from the conquered fever, immunized in this way and that from attacks that might be more serious. It is an observable fact that in all our societies there was a flourishing, a peak of varied cultural achievements, after the revolutions. Certainly we may not moralize too much about the stupidities and cruelties of revolutions, may not lift up our hands in horror. It is quite possible that wider study would show that feeble and decadent societies do not undergo revolutions, that revolutions are, perversely, a sign of strength and youth in societies.

One quiet person emerges from his study, not indeed untouched by a good deal of horror and disgust, but moved also with admiration for a deep and unfathomable strength in men which, because of the softer connotations of the word, he is reluctant to call spiritual. Montaigne saw and felt it long ago:

I see not one action, or three, or a hundred, but a commonly accepted state of morality so unnatural, especially as regards inhumanity and treachery, which are to me the worst of all sins, that I have not the heart to think of them without horror; and they excite my wonder almost as much as my detestation. *The practice of these egregious villainies has as much the mark of strength and vigor of soul as of error and disorder.*

Berkman the anarchist, who loathed the Russian Revolution, tells a story which may represent merely his own bias, but which may nonetheless serve as a brief symbolical epilogue to this study. Berkman says he asked a good Bolshevik acquaintance during the period of attempted complete communization under Lenin why the famous Moscow cabmen, the *izvoschiks*, who continued in diminished numbers to flit about Moscow and to get enormous sums in paper roubles for their services, were not nationalized like practically everything else. The Bolshevik replied, "We found that if you don't feed human beings they continue to live somehow. But if you don't feed the horses, the stupid beasts die. That's why we don't nationalize the cabmen." That is not an altogether cheerful story, and in some ways one may regret the human capacity to live without eating. But clearly if we were as stupid—or as sensible—as horses we should have no revolutions.

# 45

# Social Revolutions and Mobilization

*Theda Skocpol*

"The changes in the state order which a revolution produces are no less important than the

SOURCE: Theda Skocpol, "Social Revolutions and Mass Military Mobilization," *World Politics*, vol. 40, no. 2 (January 1988), pp. 147-168. © 1988 by Princeton University Press. Excerpts reprinted with permission of Princeton University Press.

changes in the social order."[1] Franz Borkenau's insight, published in 1937, has become the central theme of more recent comparative studies. "A complete revolution," writes Samuel P. Huntington in *Political Order in Changing Societies*, "involves...the creation and institutionalization of a new political order," into which an "explosion" of popular participation in national affairs is channeled.[2] Similarly, in my *States and Social Revolutions: A Comparative Analysis of France, Russia, and China*, I argue that in "each New Regime, there was much greater popular incorporation into the state-run affairs of the nation. And the new state organizations forged during the Revolutions were more centralized and rationalized than those of the Old Regime."[3]

Huntington has developed his arguments about revolutionary accomplishments in critical dialogue with liberal-minded modernization theorists, while I have developed mine in critical dialogue with Marxian class analysts. Modernization theorists and Marxians both analyze revolutionary transformations primarily in relation to long-term socioeconomic change. These scholars also highlight the contributions of certain revolutions to liberalism or to democratic socialism—that is, to "democracy" understood *in opposition to* authoritarian state power.

The classical Marxist vision on revolutionary accomplishments was unblinkingly optimistic. According to this view, "bourgeois revolutions" clear away obstacles to capitalist economic development and lay the basis for historically progressive but socially limited forms of liberal democracy. "Proletarian revolutions," in turn, create the conditions for classless economies and for universal social and political democracy, accompanied by the progressive "withering away of the state." The first modern social revolution to be accomplished in the name of Marxism, the Russian Revolution of 1917, obviously belied this vision, however, for it established a communist dictatorship that ruled in the name of the proletariat while actually exploiting workers for purposes of crash industrialization, and imposing a brutal "internal colonialism" on the peasant majority.[4]

Reacting to the Stalinist denouement of the Russian Revolution, liberal-minded theorists operating within the broad framework of modernization theory have offered their own view of the accomplishments of revolutions. Theorists as disparate as S. N. Eisenstadt and Michael Walzer agree that the only salutary revolutions have been the mildest ones—the least violent and the least suddenly transformative of preexisting social and political relations.[5] In contrast to such supposedly liberal revolutions as the French and the English, the more severe and thoroughgoing revolutions boomeranged to produce totalitarian dictatorships—more penetrating authoritarian regimes—rather than democratization as these modernization theorists understand it.

Modernization theorists, moreover, tend to view the political aspects of the revolutions as inefficient and probably temporary aberrations in the course of socioeconomic development. An ideologically committed vanguard may rise to central-state power—and perhaps stay there—through the mobilization and manipulation of grass roots political organizations such as militias, workplace councils, or neighborhood surveillance committees. From the perspective of modernization theorists, however, this kind of revolutionary political mobilization—known either as "the terror" or as totalitarianism, depending on whether it is a phrase or an institutionalized outcome in any given revolution—is both morally reprehensible and technically inefficient for dealing with the practical tasks that modern governments must face.

Converging on what might be called a realist perspective, analysts like Huntington and myself have reached different conclusions about the political accomplishments of revolutions. In the realist view, a special sort of democratization—understood not as an extension of political liberalism or the realization of democratic socialism, but as an enhancement of popular involvement in national political life—*accompanies* the revolutionary strengthening of centralized national states directed by authoritarian executives or political parties.

Briefly put, this happens because during revolutionary interregnums competition among elites for coercive and authoritative control spurs certain leadership groups to mobilize previously politically excluded popular forces by means of both material and ideological incentives. Popular participation is especially sought in the forging of organizations that can be used to subdue less "radical" contenders. New state organizations—armies, administrations, committees of surveillance, and so forth—are at once authoritarian and unprecedentedly mass-mobilizing. In some revolutions, especially those involving prolonged guerrilla wars, this process works itself out prior to the formal seizure of national-state power; in others, especially those in which inter-elite struggles are fought out in urban street battles, tends to occur during and after that seizure. Either way, the logic of state-building through which social revolutions are successfully accomplished promotes both authoritarianism and popular mobilization.

In the realist view, moreover, the strengthened political and state orders that emerge from social-revolutionary transformations may perform some kinds of tasks very effectively—certainly more effectively than did the old regimes they displaced. But which tasks? Perhaps because we have argued with the modernization and Marxian theorists, Huntington and I tend to explore the accomplishments of revolutionary regimes in such areas as maintaining political order during the course of socioeconomic transformation, enforcing individual or collective property rights, and promoting state-led industrialization. Yet I would argue that the task which revolutionized regimes in the modern world have performed best is the mobilization of citizen support across class lines for protracted international warfare.

There is a straightforward reason why this should be true: the types of organizations formed and the political ties forged between revolutionary vanguards and supporters (in the course of defeating other elites and consolidating the new regime's state controls) can readily be converted to the tasks of mobilizing resources, including dedicated officers and soldiers, for international warfare. Guerrilla armies and their support systems are an obvious case in point. So are urban militias and committees of surveillance, which seem to have served as splendid agencies for military recruitment from the French Revolution to the Iranian. Moreover, if revolutionary leaders can find ways to link a war against foreigners to domestic power struggles, they may be able to tap into broad nationalist feelings—as well as exploit class and political divisions—in order to motivate supporters to fight and die on behalf of the new regime. Talented members of families that supported the old regime can often be recruited to the revolutionary-nationalist cause, along with enthusiasts from among those who had previously been excluded from national politics.

Whether we in the liberal-democratic West like to acknowledge it or not, the authoritarian regimes brought to power through revolutionary transformations—from the French Revolution of the late 18th century to the Iranian Revolution of the present—have been democratizing in the mass-mobilizing sense. The best evidence of this has been the enhanced ability of such revolutionized regimes to conduct humanly costly wars with a special fusion of popular zeal, meritocratic professionalism, and central coordination. Whatever the capacities of revolutionary regimes to cope with tasks of economic development (and the historical record suggests that those capacities are questionable), they seem to excel at motivating their populations to make supreme sacrifices for the nation in war. That is no mean accomplishment in view of the fact that the prerevolutionary polities in question excluded most of the people from symbolic or practical participation in national politics.

In the remainder of this brief essay, I will illustrate the plausibility of these arguments by surveying two groups of social revolutions in modern world history. First, I will examine the classic social revolutions that transformed the imperial-monarchical states of Bourbon France, Romanov Russia, and Manchu China, probing their accomplishments in relation to the expectations of the liberal, Marxian, and realist

perspectives just outlined. Then I will discuss a number of the nation-building social revolutions that have transformed postcolonial and neocolonial countries in the 20th century. I shall pay special attention to the ways in which the geopolitical contexts of particular revolutions have facilitated or discouraged the channeling of popular political participation into defensive and aggressive wars. Whether "communist" or not, I argue, revolutionary elites have been able to build the strongest states in those countries whose geopolitical circumstances allowed or required the emerging new regimes to become engaged in protracted and labor-intensive international warfare.

Can one make rigorous statements about the geopolitical circumstances that affect revolutions in progress, and that are in turn affected by them? Revolutionary outbreaks do seem to make wars more likely because domestic conflicts tend to spill over to involve foreign partners, and because revolutions create perceived threats and opportunities for other states. Beyond this, however, no glib generalizations are possible; for example, more sweeping revolutions do not automatically generate greater wars or stronger efforts at foreign intervention. As we are about to see, the geopolitical contexts of social revolutions in the modern world have varied greatly; so have the intersections of domestic state-building struggles with international threats or conflicts. At this point in the development of knowledge about these matters, the best way to proceed is through exploratory analyses and comparisons of a wide range of historical cases.

## SOCIAL REVOLUTIONS AND WAR-MAKING IN FRANCE, RUSSIA, AND CHINA

The word "revolution" did not take on its modern connotation of a fundamental sociopolitical change accompanied by violent upheavals from below until the French Revolution of the late 18th century.[6] This etymological fact appropriately signals the reality that the French Revolution (unlike the English, Dutch, and American) was a *social* revolution, in which class-based revolts from below, especially peasant revolts against landlords, propelled sudden transformations in the class structure along with permanently centralizing changes in the structures of state power. In *States and Social Revolutions,* I group the French Revolution for comparative analysis with the Russian Revolution from 1917 to the 1930s and with the Chinese Revolution from 1911 to the 1960s. The French Revolution, I argue, was neither primarily "bourgeois" in the Marxist sense nor "liberal" in the modernization sense. Nor was the Russian Revolution "proletarian" in the Marxist sense. Rather, the French, Russian, and Chinese revolutions, despite important variations, displayed striking similarities of context, cause, process, and outcomes.

All three classic social revolutions occurred in large, previously independent, predominantly agrarian monarchical states that found themselves pressured militarily by economically more developed competitors on the international scene. Social revolutions were sufficiently caused when (a) the centralized, semi-bureaucratic administrative and military organizations of the old regimes disintegrated due to combinations of international pressures and disputes between monarchs and landed commercial upper classes, and (b) widespread peasant revolts took place against landlords. After more or less protracted struggles by political forces trying to consolidate new state organizations, all three revolutions resulted in more centralized and mass-mobilizing national states, more powerful in relation to all domestic social groups, and also more powerful than the prerevolutionary regimes had been in relation to foreign competitors. In particular, all three social revolutions markedly raised their nations' capacities to wage humanly costly wars.[7]

The differences in the outcomes and accomplishments of the French, Russian, and Chinese revolutions are not well explained by referring, as a Marxist analyst would do, to the greater role of bourgeois class forces in the French case or to the unique contributions of proletarian revolts to the urban struggles of 1917 in Russia. Nor can one explain the different outcomes, as the modernization theorists do, by suggesting that the milder, less violent, and less thoroughgoing the revolutionary conflicts and changes, and the briefer the rule of an ideological vanguard, the more efficient and liberal-democratic the revolutionary outcome. None of these revolutions had a liberal-democratic outcome, and none of them resulted in a socialist democracy. Instead, the differences in the essentially mass-mobilizing and authoritarian outcomes and accomplishments of the French, Russian, and Chinese revolutions are in large part attributable to the international geopolitical contexts in which the conflicts of these revolutions played themselves out. They are also attributable to the political relationships established, during and immediately after the revolutionary interregnums, between state-building leaderships and rebellious lower classes. One feature that these three social revolutions have in common is that all of them enhanced national capacities to wage humanly costly foreign wars.

The French Revolution has typically been characterized as a modernizing liberal-democratic revolution or as a bourgeois, capitalist revolution. In terms of economics, it is difficult if not impossible to show that the French Revolution was necessary for the "economic modernization" or "capitalist development" of France: the absolutist old regime had been facilitating commercialization and petty industry just as much as post-revolutionary regimes did. Politically, moreover, analysts tend to forget that the end result of the French Revolution was not any form of liberalism, but Napoleon's nationalist dictatorship, which left the enduring legacy of a highly centralized and bureaucratic French state with a recurrent tendency to seek national glory through military exploits.

The political phases of the French Revolution from 1789 through 1800 certainly included attempts to institutionalize civil liberties and electoral democracy, as well as the important legalization of undivided private property rights for peasants and bourgeois alike. Moreover, the fact that the French Revolution created a private-propertied society rather than a party-state that aspired to manage the national economy directly left open space for the eventual emergence of liberal-democratic political arrangements in France. At the time of the Revolution itself, however, democratization was more emphatically and enduringly furthered through "careers open to talent" in the military officer corps, through mass military conscription, and through the more efficient pressing of the state's fiscal demands on all citizens.

From a European continental perspective, the most striking and consequential accomplishment of the French Revolution was its ability to launch highly mobile armies of motivated citizen-soldiers, coordinated with enhanced deployment of artillery forces. The Jacobins from 1792 to 1794 began the process of amalgamating political commissioners and *sans-culotte* militias with the remnants of the royal standing armies. Even though they did not find a way to stabilize their "Republic of Virtue," the Montagnard Jacobins fended off the most pressing domestic and international counterrevolutionary threats. Yet their fall was not the end of military mass-mobilization in France. Napoleon consolidated a conservative bureaucratic regime and came to terms with private property holders (including the peasant smallholders) and with the Church (including the local priests so influential with the peasantry). Then he expanded the process of French military mobilization, deploying citizen armies of an unprecedented size and a capacity for rapid maneuver. The enhanced popular political participation and the messianic sense of French nationalism and democratic mission unleashed by the Revolution were thus directed outward. Before their eventual exhaustion in the unconquerable vastness of Russia, French citizen armies redrew the political map of modern Europe in irreversible ways and inspired the emergence of other European nationalisms in response.

Russia and China both experienced thorough-going social revolutionary transformations that resulted in the rule of communist-directed party-states. These social revolutions occurred under Leninist party leaderships in the modern industrial era, when the model of a state-managed economy was available; and both occurred in countries more hard-pressed geopolitically than late 18th-century France had been. The authoritarian and mass-mobilizing energies of the immediate postrevolutionary regimes, both in Soviet Russia and Communist China, were mainly directed not to *imperial* military conquests as in France, but to the promotion of national economic development, which was deemed to be the key to national independence in a world dominated by major industrial powers. Even so, in due course both of the new regimes demonstrated greatly enhanced capacities (compared to the prerevolutionary era) for successfully waging international war.

From the modernization perspective, the Russian and the Chinese revolutions were tyrannical and antidemocratic: they were more violent and transformative than the French Revolution, and ideological vanguards stayed in power both in Russia and in China. (By contrast, the Montagnard perpetrators of the Terror fell from power in France.) The Soviet regime, however, through the Stalinist "revolution from above," became more coercive and inegalitarian than did the Chinese Communist regime after 1949. Modernization theory cannot explain the contrasts between the Russian and Chinese new regimes. The civil war interregnum of the Chinese Revolution, stretching from 1911 to 1949, was much more protracted than the brief Russian revolutionary civil war of 1917–1921; and in practice, the Soviet regime probably built directly upon more structures and policies from Russia's tsarist past than the Chinese Communist regime did on China's Confucian-imperial past. Nor do the contrasting revolutionary outcomes make sense from a Marxian perspective: the Russian Revolution was politically based on the urban industrial proletariat, and thus should have resulted in practices closer to socialist ideals than the peasant-based Chinese Revolution.

The somewhat less murderous and less authoritarian features of the Chinese Communist state after 1949—at least from the point of view of local peasant communities—can be attributed to the guerrilla mode by which the Chinese Communist Party came to power. The party could not achieve national state power directly in the cities; instead, it found itself faced with the necessity of waging rural guerrilla warfare against both the Japanese invaders and its Kuomintang competitors for domestic political control. Nationalist appeals helped the Chinese communists in the early 1940s to attract educated middle-class citizens to their cause. Attention to the pressing material and self-defense needs of the peasantry in North China also allowed the communists to gain sufficient access to the villages to reorganize poor and middle-class peasants into associations that would support the Red Armies economically and militarily.

After 1949, the Chinese communists were able, by building upon their preexisting political relations with much of the peasantry, to carry out agricultural collectivization with less brutality than the Bolsheviks. Simultaneously, the relatively favorable geopolitical context of postrevolutionary China, situated in a world of nuclear superpower balance between the Soviet Union and the United States, allowed the Chinese communists to place less emphasis upon creating a heavy industrial capacity for mechanized military forces than they might otherwise have done. Their limited resources sufficed, however, to establish an independent Chinese nuclear capacity, symbol of major-power status in the post-World War II era.

Communist China was able to pursue economic development policies that stressed light industries and rural development as well as some heavy industries. Meanwhile, the party could also infuse peasant-based, guerrilla-style military practices inherited from the revolutionary civil war into standing forces that could intervene effectively in the Korean War and make limited forays against India and Vietnam. As Jonathan Adelman has argued, performance of the People's Liberation Army in the Korean War battles of 1950–51 was "simply outstanding" compared to the "disastrous" Kuomintang military

performance against the Japanese in the 1930s and 1940s. The Revolution, Adelman concludes, had "created a whole new Chinese army."[8]

By contrast, the Soviet regime consolidated under Stalin's auspices took a much more brutal stance toward the peasant majority. Essentially, it substituted an autocratic dictatorship for a mass-mobilizing revolutionary regime. The Bolsheviks originally claimed state power in 1917 through political and very limited military maneuverings in the cities and towns of Russia, and they initially abstained from efforts at nationalist military mobilization. Most of the Russian populace acquiesced in their rule simply because of the exhaustion brought by Imperial Russia's defeat in World War I. The Russian revolutionary civil war of 1917 to 1921 was won by the deployment of urban guards and conventionally structured standing armies. Peasants were involved only as reluctantly coerced conscripts. The one major foreign adventure of the fledgling Bolshevik regime, the invasion of Poland in 1920, ended in military defeat. In fact, the new Russian regime was fortunate that World War I had defeated or exhausted its major foreign opponents. For new-born Soviet Russia did not conform to the pattern of most other social revolutions: its central authorities were not in a good position to channel mass political participation into international warfare. Instead, they turned toward deepening internal warfare— against the peasantry and among elites.

After 1921, the Bolshevik regime lacked organized political ties to the peasant villages, which had made their own autonomous local revolutions against landlords in 1917 and 1918. Stalin rose to power in the 1920s and 1930s by convincing many cadres in the Soviet party-state that Russian "socialism" would have to be built "in one country" that was isolated and threatened economically and militarily by Western industrial powers. The crash program of heavy industrialization was alleged to be necessary not only to build Marxian socialism, but also to prepare Russia for land-based military warfare. The peasantry became a domestic obstacle to Stalinist policies when it refused to provide economic surpluses at exploitative rates. Stalin's subsequent bureaucratic and terroristic drive to force peasant communities into centrally controlled agricultural collectives succeeded only at a terrible cost in human lives and agricultural productivity; the political reverberations in urban and official Russia helped to spur his purges of the Soviet elite in the 1930s. The Stalinist consolidation of the new regime was thus initially a product of conflicts between an urban-based party-state and the peasantry, played out in a geopolitically threatening environment—though *not* in an environment in which direct national mobilization for international war was either necessary or possible.

It is significant that Stalinism evolved into a *popular* mass-mobilizing regime as a result of the travails of World War II. When the invading Nazis conducted themselves with great brutality against the Slav populations they conquered, Stalinist Russia finally had to mobilize for a total international war. Despite the setbacks of the first few months, the Soviet Union met the military challenges of World War II much more effectively than tsarist Russia had met the exigencies of World War I. The Soviet people and armed forces fought back with considerable efficiency and amazing zeal in the face of terrible casualties. For the first time since 1917, Soviet rulers were able to use Russian nationalism to bolster their leadership. Stalin did not hesitate to revive many symbols of Russian national identity from prerevolutionary times, and he also restored prerogatives of rank and expertise in the military. It is therefore not surprising that, when World War II ended in victory for the U.S.S.R. and the Allies, the Soviet rulers' domestic legitimacy—as well as the country's global great-power status—had been enhanced significantly.

## SOCIAL REVOLUTIONS IN DEPENDENT COUNTRIES: GEOPOLITICAL CONTEXTS AND THE POSSIBILITIES FOR MILITARIZATION

In the classic social revolutions of France, Russia, and China, long-established monarchical states were transformed into mass-mobilizing national regimes; most other social revolutions in the modern era, however, have occurred in smaller, dependent countries.[9] In some, such as Vietnam and the Portuguese colonies of Africa, which had been colonized by foreign imperial powers, social-revolutionary transformations were part of the process of national liberation from colonialism. In others, such as Cuba, Mexico, Iran, and Nicaragua, neopatrimonial dictatorships were caught in webs of great-power rivalries within the capitalist world economy and the global geopolitical system. Social revolutions in these countries have forged stronger states that are markedly more nationalist and mass-incorporating than the previous regimes and other countries in their respective regions. Still, the new regimes have remained minor powers on the world scene.

With the exception of the Iranian Revolution of 1977–1979, which was primarily carried out through urban demonstrations and strikes, all third-world social revolutions have depended on at least a modicum of peasant support for their success. In most instances, both peasants and city dwellers were mobilized for guerrilla warfare by nationalist revolutionary elites; only in the Mexican and Bolivian revolutions were peasant communities able to rebel on their own as did the French and Russian peasant communities. Most third-world social revolutions have been played out as military struggles among leaderships contending to create or redefine the missions of national states. And these revolutions have happened in settings so penetrated by foreign influences—economic, military, and cultural—that social-revolutionary transformations have been as much about the definition of autonomous identities on the international scene as they have been about the forging of new political ties between indigenous revolutionaries and their mass constituents.

Consequently, the various international contexts in which third-world revolutions have occurred become crucial in conditioning the new regimes that have emerged from them. One basic aspect of the international situation is the relationship between a country undergoing revolution and the great powers, whatever they may be in a given phase of world history. Military, economic, and cultural aspects of such relations all need to be considered in our analysis. The regional context of each revolution also matters: What have been the possibilities for military conflicts with immediate neighbors? Have revolutionized third-world nations faced invasions by third-world neighbors, or have they been able to invade their neighbors without automatically involving great powers in the conflict? As I will illustrate in the remainder of this section, attention to international contexts can help us to explain at least as much about the structures and orientations of social-revolutionary new regimes in the third world as analyses of their class basis or propositions about the inherent logic of modernization and the violence and disruptiveness of various revolutions....

## Social Revolutions in the Shadow of a Great Power

...[A] major social revolution right on America's doorstep, the Cuban Revolution of 1959, culminated in a new regime remarkably adept at mobilizing human resources for military adventures across the globe. The failure of the United States to prevent or overthrow Fidel Castro's triumph over the Batista dictatorship helped to account for this outcome. But the global superpower rivalry of the United States and the Soviet Union was also a crucial ingredient, for Soviet willingness to protect and bankroll the new regime gave Cuban "anti-imperialists" a leverage against the United States that would have been unimaginable to the earlier Mexican revolutionaries.

Once established in power, Castro could assert Cuban national autonomy against the overwhelming U.S. economic and cultural presence. Having done so, he could then protect his rule from U.S.-sponsored overthrow only by allying himself domestically with the Cuban Communist Party and internationally with the Soviet Union. Subsequently, Cuba has become economically and militarily so dependent on

Moscow that it finds itself serving Soviet interests throughout the third world.[10] Cubans are trained and mobilized for foreign service both as military advisors and as educated civilian technicians, which is a way in which Castro can partially repay the Soviets. In addition, it is an opportunity for a small, dependent revolutionary nation to create enhanced mobility for trained citizens.[11] It also allows Cuba to exert considerable military and ideological influence on the world scene—an amazing feat for such a tiny country located only ninety miles from a hostile superpower.

The weakest and poorest southern neighbors of the United States to experience social revolutions have been Bolivia in 1952–1964 and Nicaragua since 1979. These two cases demonstrate opposite effects of U.S. determination to counter radical change in contexts where the Soviet Union could not or would not do as much as it did for Castro's Cuba.

In Bolivia, spontaneous popular revolts by peasant communities and tin miners initially expropriated major owners, both domestic and foreign, and threatened to create a nationalist new regime that was not under the influence of the United States. After international tin prices collapsed, however, the new Bolivian authorities accepted international aid, including help from the United States, to rebuild a professional military apparatus. In due course, the refurbished military took over, establishing Bolivian governments which, while not attempting to reverse the peasant land expropriations of 1952, have followed both domestic-economic and foreign policies that are amenable to American interests. In essence, the United States used a combination of benign neglect and cleverly targeted foreign aid to deradicalize the Bolivian Revolution. A number of circumstances facilitated American containment policies. Bolivian revolutionaries in 1952 had no foreign wars to fight, and popular radicalism (led by Trotskyist cadres) remained focused on internal class struggles. What is more, Bolivian revolutionaries were not reacting to—or capitalizing upon—a bitter prior history of direct Yankee military interventions, which was the case in Cuba and Nicaragua.

In Nicaragua as in Cuba, U.S. authorities initially acquiesced in the overthrow of a corrupt and domestically weakened patrimonial dictator even though he had originally been installed under U.S. sponsorship. Then, again as in Cuba, a dialectic got underway between a revolutionary radicalization couched in anti-American rhetoric and increasing efforts by U.S. authorities to roll back or overthrow the revolution.[12] American counterrevolutionary efforts became more determined and sustained after Ronald Reagan was elected President in 1980. At first, they seemed to make some headway when economic shortages and domestic unrest in the face of an unpopular military draft tended to undercut the Sandinistas' legitimacy as leaders of a popular guerrilla movement against the Somoza regime. Because of domestic political constraints, however, the United States has been unable to invade Sandinista Nicaragua, having to rely instead on economic pressures and the financing of Nicaraguan counterrevolutionary fighters; but the latter have proved to be neither militarily efficient nor politically adept.

Predictably—in the light of the history of foreign efforts to subvert emerging revolutionary regimes in such ways—these U.S. measures have simply provided the Sandinistas with excuses for economic shortages. More importantly, the U.S. efforts have nourished sustained but not overwhelming counterrevolutionary military threats, which have actually helped the Sandinistas to consolidate a mass-mobilizing authoritarian regime through nationalist appeals and an unprecedented military buildup. In short, U.S. policies since 1980, declaredly aimed at "democratizing" Nicaragua, have had the opposite effect; they have undermined elements of pluralism in a postrevolutionary regime and enhanced the nationalist credentials of the more authoritarian Nicaraguan Leninists. Still, as of this writing in 1987, it remains possible that shifts in American policy may stop this process of militarization short of full-scale war in Central America.

## Militarized Third-World Revolutions under Communism and Islam

Far removed from the areas of the New World that are close to the United States, the Vietnamese and Iranian revolutions are two instances in which great-power rivalries, along with geographical distance, have made it possible for revolutionary regimes to take a stand against "American imperialism" without being overthrown by U.S. military intervention. What is more, Vietnam and Iran in the mid-20th century, like France in the late 18th, are examples of the awesome power of social-revolutionary regimes to wage humanly costly wars and to transform regional political patterns and international balances of power. Both revolutions demonstrate this, even though one is a "communist" revolution and the other "Islamic" and thus militantly anticommunist.

Analysts of agrarian class struggles have stressed that the Vietnamese Revolution was grounded in peasant support in both the northern and southern parts of the country. But attempts to explain the overall logic of this revolution in terms of the social conditions of either the northern or the southern peasantry have inevitably missed the other main ingredient in the revolution's success. From the French colonial period on, educated Vietnamese found the Communist Party of Vietnam and the various movements associated with it to be the most effective and persistent instruments of resistance to foreign domination—first by the French colonialists, then by the Japanese occupiers during World War II, then by the returning French, and finally by the United States. The Vietnamese communists were their country's most uncompromising nationalists; they were willing, when conditions required or allowed, to wage guerrilla warfare through peasant mobilization. By contrast, foreign occupiers and their Vietnamese collaborators worked from the cities outward, especially in the south, which had been the center of French colonial control.

Geopolitically, the Vietnamese communists benefited from the distance the French and

American forces had to traverse to confront them, from the availability of sanctuaries in Laos and Cambodia, and (after the partial victory in the north) from their ability to receive supplies through China from both China and the Soviet Union. Had the United States been able or willing to use nuclear weapons in the Southeast Asian theatre, or had the Soviet Union and China not temporarily cooperated to help the Vietnamese, it seems doubtful that the Vietnamese Revolution could have reunified the country, notwithstanding the extraordinary willingness of northern and many southern Vietnamese to die fighting the U.S. forces.

Since the defeat of the United States in southern Vietnam, the Hanoi regime has faced difficult economic conditions; it seems to tackle such problems with much less efficiency and zeal than it tackled the anti-imperialist wars from the 1940s to the 1970s. As the unquestionably dominant military power in its region, the Vietnamese state has invaded and occupied Cambodia and engaged in occasional battles with a now-hostile China. Vietnam continues to rely on Soviet help to counterbalance U.S. hostility and the armed power of China. But, what is perhaps more important now that Vietnam is indeed "the Prussia of Southeast Asia," the Vietnamese communists still find it possible to legitimate their leadership through never-ending mobilization of their people for national military efforts. The Chinese threat, Cambodian resistance, and American opposition to the normalization of Vietnam's gains have provided just the kind of internationally threatening context that the Vietnamese communists, after so many years of warfare, find most congenial to their domestic political style.

The militant Shi'a clerics of Iran, who seem to be so different from the Vietnamese communists, are another mass-mobilizing and state-building revolutionary elite that has been helped immensely by a facilitating geopolitical context and protracted international warfare.[13] The Iranian Revolution is still in progress, and it is therefore too early to characterize its outcome in any definitive way. Nevertheless, the process

of this remarkable upheaval has already dramatized the appropriateness of viewing contemporary social revolutions as promoting ideologically reconstructed national identities involving the sudden incorporation of formerly excluded popular groups into state-directed projects. Moreover, this revolution shows that mass mobilization for war, aggressive as well as defensive, is an especially congenial state-directed project for revolutionary leaders.

From both Marxian and modernization perspectives, the Iranian Revolution, especially the consolidation of state power by the Ayatollah Khomeini and the Islamic Republican Party since the overthrow of the Shah in 1979, has been a puzzle. Marxist analysts have been reluctant to call this a "social revolution" because class conflicts and transformations of economic property rights have not defined the main terms of struggle or the patterns of sociopolitical change. Modernization theorists, meanwhile, have been surprised at the capacity of the untrained and traditionist Islamic clerics to consolidate their rule; these theorists expected that, after a brief "terror," such noncommunist and ideologically fanatical leaders would give way to technically trained bureaucrats if not to liberal-democratic politicians.

In fact, from 1979 through 1982, the Islamic Republican Party in Iran systematically reconstructed state organizations to embody direct controls by Shi'a clerics. Step by step, all other leading political forces—liberal Westernizers, the Mujhahedeen, the Tudeh Party, and technocrats and professional military officers loyal to Abolhassan Bani-Sadr—were eliminated from what had once been the all-encompassing revolutionary alliance. The party did this by deploying and combining the classic ingredients for successful revolutionary state building.

For one thing, the Islamic Republican clerics shared a commitment to a political ideology that gave them unlimited warrant to rule exclusively in the name of all the Shi'a believers. Khomeini had developed a militant-traditionalist reading of Shi'a beliefs, calling on the clerics themselves to govern in place of secular Iranian rulers corrupted by Western cultural imperialism. The Islamic Republican Constitution for Iran officially enshrined such clerical supervision over all affairs of state; concrete political organizations, including the Islamic Republican Party that dominated the Majlis (parliament), also embodied this orientation.

Moreover, the Islamic Republican clerics and their devout nonclerical associates did not hesitate to organize, mobilize, and manipulate mass popular support, including the unemployed as well as workers and lower-middle-class people in Teheran and other cities. Islamic judges supervised neighborhood surveillance bodies; Islamic militants organized revolutionary guards for police and military duties; and consumer rations and welfare benefits for the needy were dispensed through neighborhood mosques. Iranians never before involved in national political life became directly energized through such organization; those with doubts were subjected to peer controls as well as to elite supervision. With these means of mass-based power at their disposal, the Islamic Republican Party had little trouble eliminating liberal and leftist competitors from public political life.

Right after the Shah's overthrow ideologically committed Islamic cadres, backed by mass organizations, reconstructed major public institutions in Iranian national life. Not only special committees of revolutionary justice, but also traditionally educated clerical judges took over the criminal and civil legal system, reorienting it to procedural and substantive norms in line with their understanding of the Koran. The next targets were Western-oriented cultural institutions, particularly schools and universities. These were first closed and then purged, turned into bastions of Islamic education and revolutionary propaganda. Civil state bureaucracies were similarly purged and transformed; and so, in due course, were the remnants of the Shah's military forces, particularly the army.

The kinds of transformations I have just summarized took place not automatically but through hard-fought political, bureaucratic,

and street struggles that pitted other elites—alternative would-be consolidators of the Iranian Revolution—against the militant clerics and their supporters. As these struggles within Iran unfolded, the emerging clerical authoritarianism repeatedly benefited from international conditions and happenings that allowed them to deploy their ideological and organizational resources to maximum advantage.

Overall, the version of the Iranian Revolution that the clerics sought to institutionalize has been virulently anti-Western, and defined especially in opposition to "U.S. imperialism." Opposition to Soviet imperialism has also been a consistent theme. Fortunately for the clerics, the fiscal basis of the Iranian state after as well as before the revolution lies in the export of oil, for which an international market has continued to exist. A geopolitical given is coterminous with this economic given: neither the Soviet Union nor the United States has been in a position to intervene militarily against the Iranian Revolution, in part because Iran lies between their two spheres of direct control. It is also fortunate for Iran's radical clerics that the United States has acted in ways that were symbolically provocative while not being materially or militarily powerful enough to control events in Iran. The admission of the deposed Shah to the United States, the subsequent seizure of the American embassy by pro-Khomeini youths, and the ensuing unsuccessful efforts of the U.S. authorities to free the American hostages, all created an excellent political matrix within Iran for the clerics to discredit as pro-American a whole series of their secular competitors for state power.

Then, in the autumn of 1980, the secularist-Islamic regime of Saddam Hussein in neighboring Iraq attacked revolutionary Iran; since the Iraqis perceived Khomeini's regime as weak and internally disorganized, they expected it to fall. What happened with the Jacobins in 18th-century revolutionary France then repeated itself in revolutionary Iran. At first, the foreign invaders made headway, for the remnants of the Shah's military, particularly the army, were indeed disorganized at the command level. But revolutionary Islamic guards poured out to the fronts, and the Iraqi offensives began to come up against fanatically dogged resistance. Islamic fundamentalists and Iranian secular nationalists pulled together, however grudgingly, to resist the common enemy.

Domestic Iranian power struggles have not stopped during the war with Iraq. During the final months of his attempt to survive within the Khomeini regime, President Bani-Sadr tried to use the newly essential regular army to build up secular-technocratic leverage against clerical rule. But he and his followers, along with many army officers, were defeated and removed. Thereafter, during 1981 and into 1982, despite setbacks in the war due to the initial lack of coordination between revolutionary guards and regular army forces, a new Islamic military loyal to the clerical regime was gradually synthesized for Iran. It was able to combine regular strategic planning for battles with the use of such unconventional tactics as human waves of martyrs willing to clear Iraqi mine fields with their bodies. By early 1982, the Iranians had succeeded in driving the Iraqis out of their country; the latter have been on the defensive ever since, as the consolidated clerical regime in Iran has doggedly pursued the war in the name of its transnationalist ideological vision.

In the end, the Iranian Revolution will probably settle down into some sort of Islamic-nationalist authoritarianism that coexists, however uneasily, with its neighbors. The Iranian armies are unlikely to overrun the Middle East the way the French revolutionary armies temporarily overran much of continental Europe. Iran is still a third-world nation; on the global scene, it faces superpowers who can inhibit its wildest aspirations. Nevertheless, Iran's military accomplishments have already disproved the expectation of modernization theorists that a regime run by anti-Western Shi'a clerics would not be viable in the contemporary world. By consolidating and reconstructing state power through ideologically coordinated mass mobilization, and by directing popular zeal against a faraway superpower and channeling it into a war against a less populous neighboring state, the Islamic Republicans of Iran have proven once again that social revolutions are less about class struggles or "modernization" than about state building and the forging of newly assertive national identities in a modern world that remains culturally pluralistic even as it inexorably becomes economically more interdependent.

## CONCLUSION

If, as Franz Borkenau argued, students of revolutions must attend to "changes in the state order," much remains to be understood about the kinds of political transformation that revolutions have accomplished and the activities to which their enhanced state capacities have been directed with varying degrees of success. In this essay, which is suggestive rather than conclusive, I have speculated that many social-revolutionary regimes have excelled at channeling enhanced popular participation into protracted international warfare. Because of the ways revolutionary leaders mobilize popular support in the course of struggles for state power, the emerging regimes can tackle mobilization for war better than any other task, including the promotion of national economic development. The full realization of this revolutionary potential for building strong states depends on threatening but not overwhelming geopolitical circumstances.

The full exploration of these notions will require more precise theorizing and more systematic comparative research, going well beyond the historical illustrations offered here. Yet further investigations of war-making as a proclivity of social-revolutionary regimes could hardly be more timely. The image of teen-age Iranians blowing themselves up on Iraqi land mines as a way to heaven should remind us that the passions of 16th- to 18th-century Europe have yet to play themselves out fully in the third world of the 20th century. These passions will not often embody themselves in social-revolutionary transformations, but when they do—and when geopolitical circumstances unleash international conflicts and do not proscribe the outbreak of war—we can expect aspirations for equality and dignity, both within nations and on the international stage, to flow again and again into military mass mobilization. Arguably, this is the mission that revolutionized regimes perform best. In the face of serious (but not overwhelming) foreign threats, they excel at motivating the formerly excluded to die for the glory of their national states.

## Notes

1. Borkenau, "State and Revolution in the Paris Commune, the Russian Revolution, and the Spanish Civil War," *Sociological Review* 29 (January 1937), 41–75, at 41.

2. Huntington, *Political Order in Changing Societies* (New Haven: Yale University Press, 1968), 266. Chapter 5 is also relevant.

3. See Theda Skocpol, *States and Social Revolutions: A Comparative Analysis of France, Russia, and China* (New York and Cambridge: Cambridge University Press, 1979), 161.

4. This characterization comes from Alvin Gouldner, "Stalinism: A Study of Internal Colonialism," in *Political Power and Social Theory* (research annual edited by Maurice Zeitlin) I (1980) (Greenwich, CT.: JAI Press), 209–259.

5. Eisenstadt, *Revolution and Transformation of Societies* (New York: Free Press, 1978); Walzer, "A Theory of Revolution," *Marxist Perspectives*, No. 5 (Spring 1979), 30–44.

6. Karl Griewank, "The Emergence of the Concept of Revolution," in Bruce Mazlish, Arthur D. Kaledin, and David B. Ralston, eds., *Revolution: A Reader* (New York: Macmillan, 1971), 13–17.

7. Thorough elaboration and documentation of this conclusion appears in Jonathan R. Adelman, *Revolution, Armies, and War: A Political History* (Boulder, CO: Lynne Rienner Publishers, 1985), chaps. 3–11.

8. Adelman (see note 7), 144.

9. For useful overviews, see Eric R. Wolf, *Peasant Wars of the Twentieth Century* (New York:

Harper & Row, 1969), chaps. 1, 4–6; John Dunn, *Modern Revolutions* (Cambridge: Cambridge University Press, 1972), chps. 2, 4–8.

10. Kosmos Tsokhas, "The Political Economy of Cuban Dependence on the Soviet Union," *Theory and Society* 9 (March 1980), 319–362.

11. Susan Eckstein, "Structural and Ideological Bases of Cuba's Overseas Programs," *Politics and Society* 11 (No. 1, 1982), 95–121.

12. My account of Nicaragua draws upon Walter LaFeber, *Inevitable Revolutions: The United States in Central America* (New York: W. W. Norton, 1983); Shirley Christian, *Nicaragua: Revolution in the Family* (New York: Vintage Books, 1986); and Lawrence Shaefer, "Nicaraguan-United States Bilateral Relations: The Problems within Revolution and Reconstruction" (Senior honors thesis, University of Chicago, 1984).

13. The following discussion draws on Theda Skocpol, "Rentier State and Shi'a Islam in the Iranian Revolution," *Theory and Society* 11 (No. 3, 1982), 265–284. It also relies heavily on R. K. Ramazani, *Revolutionary Iran: Challenge and Response in the Middle East* (Baltimore: The Johns Hopkins University Press, 1986), and Shaul Bakhash, *The Reign of the Ayatollahs: Iran and the Islamic Revolution* (New York: Basic Books), 1984.

## 46

# Radicalism or Reformism

*Seymour Martin Lipset*

From my work on my doctoral dissertation down to the present, I have been interested in the

SOURCE: Seymour Martin Lipset, "Radicalism or Reformism: The Sources of Working-Class Politics," *The American Political Science Review* 77, No. 1 (March 1983), pp. 1–18. By permission. From a presidential address to the American Political Science Association, Denver, Colo., 1982. Article and references abridged by the editors.

problem of "American exceptionalism." That curious phrase emerged from the debate in the international Communist movement in the 1920s concerning the sources of the weakness of left-wing radical movements in the United States. The key question repeatedly raised in this context has been, is America qualitatively different from other industrial capitalist countries? Or, to use Sombart's words, "Why is there no Socialism in the United States?"

In a forthcoming book, I evaluate the hypotheses advanced by various writers from Karl Marx onward to explain the absence of an effective socialist party on the American political scene. (For a preliminary formulation, see Lipset 1977b, pp. 31–149, 346–363.) If any of the hypotheses are valid, they should also help to account for the variation among working-class movements in other parts of the world. In this article, therefore, I shall reverse the emphasis from that in my book and look at socialist and working-class movements comparatively, applying elsewhere some of the propositions that have been advanced to explain the American situation.

A comparative analysis of working-class movements in western society is limited by an obvious methodological problem: too many variables and too few cases. The causal factors that have been cited as relevant literally approach two dozen. Among them are economic variables, such as the timing of industrialization, the pace of economic growth, the concentration of industry, the occupational structure, the nature of the division of labor, and the wealth of the country; sociological factors, such as the value system (collectivist versus individualist orientations), the status systems (open or rigid), social mobility, religious differences, ethnic variations, rates of immigration, and urbanization; and political variables, such as the timing of universal suffrage, of political rights, and of freedom of organization, the electoral systems, the extent of centralization, the size of the country, orientations of conservative parties, and the nature of the welfare systems in the country concerned.

Obviously, it would be well nigh hopeless to compare systematically western countries on all of the relevant variables. To limit the task to manageable proportions, I will concentrate on variations in national environments that determined what Stein Rokkan called "the structure of political alternatives" for the working class in different western countries before the First World War. Although much has changed since then, the nature of working-class politics has been profoundly influenced by the variations in the historic conditions under which the proletariat entered the political arena. Experiences antedating the First World War affected whether workers formed class-based parties and, where such parties developed, whether they were revolutionary or reformist.

Of the factors that shaped the character of working-class movements, two are particularly important: first, the nature of the social-class system before industrialization; second, the way in which the economic and political elites responded to the demands of workers for the right to participate in the polity and the economy.

With respect to the first, the following general proposition is advanced: the more rigid the status demarcation lines in a country, the more likely the emergence of radical working-class-based parties. Where industrial capitalism emerged from a feudal society, with its emphasis on strong status lines and barriers, the growing working class was viewed as a *Stand*, a recognizable social entity. As Max Weber emphasized, *Staende*, or "*status groups* are normally communities" defined by particular lifestyles, claims to social honor, and social intercourse among their members; as such they provide the direct basis for collective activity. In this respect, they differ from economic classes whose members share a common market situation, for "'classes' are not communities, they merely represent possible, and frequent, bases for communal action." Nations characterized by an elaborate, highly institutionalized status structure, *combined* with the economic class tensions usually found in industrial societies, were more likely to exhibit class-conscious politics than those in which status lines were imprecise and not formally recognized. In contrast, in nations that were "born modern" and lacked a feudal and aristocratic past, class position was less likely to confer a sense of shared corporate identity.

The second proposition maintains that the ways in which the dominant strata reacted to the nascent working-class movements conditioned their orientations. Where the working class was denied full political and economic citizenship, strong revolutionary movements developed. Conversely, the more readily working-class organizations were accepted into the economic and political order, the less radical their initial and subsequent ideologies.

This proposition subsumes a number of subpropositions: (1) The denial of political rights in a situation in which a social stratum is led to claim such rights will increase its feelings of deprivation and increase the likelihood of a favorable response to revolutionary and extremist doctrines. (2) The existence of political rights will tend to lead governments and conservative political forces to conciliate the lower classes, thus enhancing the latter's sense of self-respect, status, and efficacy. (3) The development of political parties, trade unions, and other workers' organizations permits the most politically active members of the working class to increase their income, status, and power and in the process to become a privileged group within society and a force for political moderation. (4) A capable lower-class stratum that has been allowed to develop legitimate economic and political organizations, through which it can achieve some share of power in the society and improve its social situation, is potentially less radical in a crisis situation than a comparable stratum that has been unable to develop institutionalized mechanisms for accommodating political demands.

In the remainder of this article, I will present the evidence that substantiates these generalizations, beginning with variations in social status.

## STATUS SYSTEMS

The proposition that rigid status systems are conducive to the emergence of radical working-class movements may be illustrated by contrasting the development of workers' parties in North America and Europe. In countries such as the United States and Canada, which did not inherit a fixed pattern of distinct status groups from feudalism, the development of working-class political consciousness, the notion of belonging to a common "class" with unique interests, required an act of intellectual imagination. In Europe, however, workers were placed in a common class by the stratification system. In a sense, workers absorbed a "consciousness of kind" from their ascribed position in the social structure. As Val Lorwin notes: "Social inequality was as provoking as economic injustice. Citizens of a country that has not passed through a feudal age cannot easily imagine how long its heritage conditions social attitudes" (Lorwin 1954, p. 37; Sturmthal 1953, p. 18).

The early socialists were aware of the problem that the lack of a feudal tradition in the United States posed for them. In 1890, Friedrich Engels argued that Americans are "born conservatives—just because America is so purely bourgeois, so entirely without a feudal past" (Engels 1936, p. 467, see also p. 501). The Austrian-born American socialist leader, Victor Berger, also accounted for the weakness of socialism as a result of the fact that "the feeling of class distinction in America...has not the same historic foundation that it has in Germany, France, or England. There the people were accustomed for over a thousand years to have distinct classes and castes fixed by law" (quoted in Friedberg 1974, p. 351). In 1906, H. G. Wells, then a Fabian, explained the absence in America of two English parties, Conservative and Labour, in terms of the absence of a "medieval heritage" of socially dominant and inferior strata (Wells 1906, pp. 72–76; Hartz 1955, pp. 50–64).

The absence of feudalism in the United States and Canada, as well as in Australia and

New Zealand, sharply differentiated the working-class movements in these countries from those on the European continent. In North America, socialist parties were either very weak (the United States) or emerged late and remained small (Canada), while in Australia and New Zealand, working-class labor parties have always been much less radical than most of the socialist parties of continental Europe.

Still, the early existence of a powerful Labor party in Australia may seem to challenge the hypothesis that the absence of feudalism and aristocracy undermines class-conscious politics on the part of workers. The pattern of politics in Australia, however, was profoundly influenced by the fact that it was largely settled by 19th-century working-class immigrants from industrial Britain, who brought the strong class awareness of the mother country with them.

Many Australian immigrants had been involved in Chartist and similar working-class movements in Britain. Hence, Australia imported the class values of the working class of the mother country. The emergence of class politics in Australia, in contrast with the North American pattern, also reflects the fact that the rural frontier in the Antipodes was highly stratified with sharp divisions between the owners of large farms and a numerous farm labor population. But despite strong class feelings, which facilitated the emergence of a powerful labor party, it was not Marxist, and hardly socialist or otherwise radical.

The case of New Zealand was somewhat different. Less urbanized than Australia, with a larger proportion of small, family-owned farms, its early British-derived two-party system of Liberals and Conservatives resembled that of the United States. The Liberals appealed to the small holders and the workers. The Labour party was weak until the post-World War I period. As in Britain, anti-union legislation induced the unions to try to elect Labour candidates. After having achieved the position of a strong third party in the 1920s, the New Zealand Labour party won power in 1935,

capitalizing on the discontents of the Depression. Its electoral program in that year was characterized "by the omission of socialism and the substitution of measures which revived the old Liberal tradition" (Lipson 1948, p. 230).

In Europe, on the other hand, as Friedrich Engels noted, throughout the 19th century "the political order remained feudal." Writing in 1892, he emphasized: "It seems a law of historical development that the bourgeoisie can in no European country get hold of political power—at least for any length of time. . . . A durable reign of the bourgeoisie has been possible only in countries, like America, where feudalism was unknown" (Engels 1968a, p. 394).

As Joseph Schumpeter pointed out, in much of Europe, the nobility "functioned as a *classe dirigeante*. . . . The aristocratic element continued to rule the roost *right to the end of the period of intact and vital capitalism*" (Schumpeter 1950, pp. 136–137, emphasis in original). More recently, Arno Mayer has brilliantly detailed the ways in which "the feudal elements retained a formidable place in Europe's authority systems," down to World War II (Mayer 1981, p. 135; Bell 1973, pp. 371–372).

Although from the perspective of this article, the sharpest contrast in the political impact of varying status systems lies in the differences between the working-class movements of the English-speaking settler societies and those of continental Europe, there was great variation in the political behavior of the working classes within Europe that also may be related to differences in status systems.

Germany, whose socialist party was the largest in Europe before World War I, has frequently been cited as the prime example of an industrial society deeply influenced by the continuation of feudal and aristocratic values. Writing in the late 1880s, Engels stressed that Germany was "still haunted by the ghosts of the feudal Junker" and that it was "to late in Germany for a secure and firmly founded domination of the bourgeoisie" (Engels 1968b, p. 97). Max Weber pointed to the continued emphasis on "feudal prestige" in Imperial

Germany in explaining the behavior of its social classes (Dahrendorf 1967, p. 50). As Dahrendorf has noted: "If one wants to give the social structure of Imperial Germany a name, it would be a paradoxical one of an industrial feudal society" (Dahrendorf 1967, p. 58; Parsons 1969, p. 71).

Many historians and social analysts have placed considerable emphasis on status differentiation in explaining the existence in Germany of numerous parties, each representing a particular status group and having a distinct ideology. Skilled German workers and socialist leaders exhibited a stronger hostility to the lowest segments of the population than occurred in other western countries. For most European socialist parties, all depressed workers, whether urban or rural, were a latent source of support. But for the German socialists, the lowest stratum was a potential enemy. Writing in 1892, in a major theoretical work, Karl Kautsky, the leading Social Democratic theorist, described the "slum proletariat" as "cowardly and unprincipled, . . . ready to fish in troubled waters . . . exploiting every revolution that has broken out, only to betray it at the earliest opportunity" (Kautsky 1910, p. 196).

The Austrian part of the Hapsburg Empire also retained major postfeudal elements into the 20th century, as reflected in its electoral system, similar to that of Hohenzollern Prussia. Until 1895, the Austrian electorate was divided into separate entities—the aristocracy, chambers of commerce, cities, and rural districts, with the latter two being limited by property franchise. In 1895, a fifth class, all others, was added to give the poorer strata some limited form of representation. And, as in Germany, the socialist movement was radical and Marxist.

The strong support obtained by the Social Democrats in Sweden, culminating in the formation of the most durable majority socialist government in Europe, was deeply influenced by the strength of *Staendestaat* elements in the most status-bound society of northern Europe. Comparing the three Scandinavian countries at the end of the 19th century, Herbert Tingsten

noted that "the Swedish nobility. . . still enjoyed considerable social prestige and acted partly as a rural aristocracy, partly as a factor in the bureaucratic machinery and officers' corps, [and] was far more numerous than the Danish. . . . [while] in Norway there was no indigenous nobility" (Tingsten 1973, p. 11; Rokken 1981, pp. 60–61). The social structure of Sweden in this respect resembled that of Wilhelmine Germany. Class position has correlated more strongly with party choice in Sweden than in any other European country, a phenomenon that helped generate majority support for the Social Democrats.

The strength of the Finnish Socialists, who in 1916 formed the first majority labor-based government in Europe, also can be linked to the character of the class system. The Finns were exposed to the strong emphasis on status and aristocracy that characterized both Russian and Swedish culture. Finland was a Grand Duchy under the Czar from 1809 on, and a small Swedish minority was predominant within the social and economic upper classes. Before 1905, the Finnish Parliament was divided "into Four Estates or Houses: the Nobility, the Clergy, the Burghers, and the Peasantry. . . . Major cleavages formed along these status dimensions and tended to co-align and reinforce each other" (Martin and Hopkins 1980, p. 186).

The political history of Great Britain, however, would seem to contradict the hypothesis that radical class consciousness was encouraged by sharp status differentiation derived from a feudal past and the continued influence of aristocracy. Marxists, such as Friedrich Engels, emphasized the importance of status factors in accounting for the fact that in England, the major capitalist nation of the 19th century, "the bourgeoisie never held undivided sway." As he noted, the "English bourgeoisie are, up to the present day [1892] . . . deeply penetrated by a sense of their social inferiority . . .; and they consider themselves highly honoured whenever one of themselves is found worthy of admission into this select and privileged body" of the titled nobility (Engels 1968a, pp. 394–395).

The emphasis on status clearly has had an impact on British working-class politics from the outset of the Industrial Revolution down to the post-World War II period. E. P. Thompson has stressed that in the early 19th century, "there was a consciousness of the identity of interests of the working class or 'productive classes,' as against those of other classes; and within this was maturing the claim for an alternative *system*" (Thompson 1968, pp. 887–888). Such consciousness presumably facilitated the emergence of Chartism, the strongest working-class movement in the first half of the 19th century, which mobilized workers in a militant class-conscious struggle for the suffrage and ultimately may have helped to create the strong correlation between class position and electoral choice that has characterized British politics since World War I. As Peter Pulzer put it: "Class is the basis of British party politics; all else is embellishment and detail" (Pulzer 1967, p. 98).

But socialist movements were much weaker in Britain than in most Continental countries in the late 19th and early 20th centuries. The Labour Party, allied to the Liberals, did not become a factor in British politics until 1906, when it elected 30 members to Parliament, and it only secured major-party status after the First World War. This seeming anomaly is explained by analysts of British politics by the strength of *noblesse oblige* norms among the aristocracy, who consciously served as a "protective stratum" for workers by enacting factory reforms and welfare-state legislation, activities that won the support of the workers (to be discussed in more detail below).

In Latin countries such as France, Italy, and Spain, the strength of revolutionary labor movements (anarchist, syndicalist, left socialist, and later communist) on the one hand, and ultra-reactionary political tendencies among the middle and upper classes, on the other, has been related to the failure of these societies to develop a full-grown industrial system until after the Second World War. The aristocracies in these countries had declined in power by the late 19th century and did little to foster noblesse-oblige

welfare policies for the workers. At the same time, their business classes in the late 19th and early 20th centuries were weakly developed and resembled a semifeudal stratum whose position was tied to family property. Not withstanding the Revolution of 1789, the French social structure reflected, in Stanley Hoffman's words, a "feudal hangover...traditional Catholic doctrines (notably concerning the evils of capitalist accumulation) left their mark...; the bourgeoisie in many ways imitated the aristocracy" (Hoffman 1963, p. 5). As Val Lorwin emphasizes, writing about the bourgeoisie of France and Italy, "they flaunted inequalities by their style of living. Their class consciousness helped shape the class consciousness of workers" (Lorwin 1958, pp. 342–343). This orientation, with its emphasis on family and its concern for the maintenance of explicit status lines, was associated with a profound antagonism to collective bargaining, labor legislation, and social security.

Strikingly, efforts to account for the moderate multiclass "people's party" orientations of the Belgian, Dutch, Swiss, and Danish labor and socialist movements have pointed to the weakness of feudal elements in these societies. Carl Landauer notes that Belgium had been much less of a *Staendestaat* than its neighbors.

> Belgium is a business country, with a weak feudal tradition—much weaker than in Germany, France, or Britain.... In Belgium, fewer upper-class people than elsewhere think that they owe it to their pride to resist the aspiration of the under-privileged.... [E]ven less than in Britain or France and certainly less than in Germany was exploitation motivated by the idea that the humble must be kept in their places (Landauer 1959, p. 479).

A similar thesis has been advanced by Hans Daalder for two other small European countries, the Netherlands and Switzerland. As he notes (1966b, p. 55), in both, "the position of the nobility against that of burghers and independent peasants tended always to be weak and to grow weaker as capitalism expanded." And writing of his native country, the Netherlands,

Daalder points out that the historic "political, social, and economic prestige" of the Dutch bourgeoisie, which dates back to preindustrial times, fostered conditions which "dampened working class militancy, and eased the integration of the working class into the national political community" (Daalder 1966a, p. 197).

Preindustrial Switzerland "was one of small farms, with no considerable estates or landed aristocracy." Erich Gruner cites a comment by a Swiss writer in the late 1860s that "the poor man felt himself less oppressed, since he had the satisfaction of having his freedom in the community *(Gemeinde)* and province *(Landsgemeinde)* and the pride that, he, himself, counted for as much as the richest factory owner, which gave him self-respect and let him raise his head high" (Gruner 1968, p. 156). Factory and welfare legislation was enacted before 1900. Unlike the large German and Austrian Social Democratic parties, the small Swiss "Socialist movement . . .was on the extreme right wing of the Second International" before World War I (Cole 1956, p. 611).

The labor and socialist movements of Denmark have been the most moderate in Europe. One recent analyst of the Danish case notes that although the Social Democratic Party has been "the dominant force in Danish politics for the past half century," its pragmatic reformist orientation poses the same question as that raised for the United States, "why there is no socialism in Denmark," a question that can only be answered by reference to its past (Cornell, n.d.). While the explanation for Denmark, as for the United States, must be multivariate, part of it would appear to be, as Herbert Tingsten has noted, that feudalism and the nobility were much less important in Denmark than in Germany and Sweden. And in Britain, "moral responses to the miseries that existed. . .[were] sufficient to preclude any revolutionary movement" (Cornell, n.d., p. 19).

The clearest discrepancy in the relationship between status systems and working-class politics outlined here occurred in Norway. There is consensus among students of Scandinavian society that Norway was less affected by feudalism and aristocratic status norms than the other northern countries. Nevertheless, the major socialist movement in Norway decided in 1919 to join the Communist International and remained affiliated until 1923.

Analysts of Norwegian politics agree, however, that this development was an historic anomaly, an event response that was out of character with the behavior of Norwegian workers, as evidenced by the fact that the link with the Third International lasted only a few years. Norway appears to be "the exception that proves the rule." The Norwegian labor and socialist movements were weak and moderate until World War I. But the war, in conjunction with the development of cheap hydro-electric power, resulted in a period of sudden and very rapid industrialization and social dislocation, which created a large segment of workers without political traditions or loyalties who were prone to support of labor militancy and radicalism. The bulk of Norwegian workers were first organized at the time of the Russian Revolution and, as in many other countries, were swept up in the enthusiasm for the Revolution. But Norwegian socialism and trade unionism soon returned to the characteristic pattern of social democratic moderation. Thus, Norway fits the "pattern" up to 1914 and from the mid-twenties on. Even during the Great Depression of the 1930s, the Communists remained a weak party, securing less than 2 percent of the vote.

## THE RIGHT TO PARTICIPATE

As emphasized at the outset, cross-national variations in working-class political activity were also affected by differences in the extent to which the proletariat was legally free to form class-based organizations and participate in the economic and political life of their societies. The greater the duration and intensity of state repression of working-class economic and political rights, the more likely workers were to respond favorably to revolutionary doctrines.

As Max Weber concluded in his essay on the suffrage and democracy in Germany, "All the might of the masses is directed *against* a state in which they are only objects and not participants" (Weber 1958, p. 279).

The effect of participation may best be illustrated by examining the two principal paths by which the members of the working classes were accepted into the fabric of societies as political and economic citizens. The first involves their right to vote and to organize political parties that could play a constructive role in the polity; the second refers to the way working-class economic combinations, in the form of labor unions, were accepted as formally legitimate by the state and substantively legitimate by employers.

The absence of these rights throughout Europe for much of the 19th century emphasized the inferior status of the workers and peasants. The political organization of much of premodern Europe was based on functional representation by Estate or *Stand*. The lower classes, including the emerging proletariat, were not accepted as an Estate worthy of representation. And the parliaments of many European countries—Austria, Finland, Prussia, and Sweden, among others—were composed of members elected by the more privileged *Staende*. Some eventually created a new Estate for the outcaste groups. Thus their Constitutions legitimated the fixed hierarchical status orders. The contradiction between such patterns of hierarchical representation and the universalistic norms of capitalism and liberalism fostered efforts to secure plebiscitarian electoral systems, one man, one vote, as well as struggles for the right of free association, particularly for trade unions. The fight for the vote and the right to organize were perceived in terms of opposition to hierarchical class role, as part of a broad struggle for equality.

The importance of the early granting of democratic rights for political activity has been emphasized by social analysts and historians in numerous contexts. T. H. Marshall, for one, noted that extreme ideologies initially emerged among new strata, in particular the bourgeoisie

and working class, as they fought for the political and social rights of citizenship. Along these lines, many writers concerned with the question of "why no socialism in America?" have pointed to the early enfranchisement of the white working class as an important causal factor. Selig Perlman made this argument in *The Theory of the Labor Movement* when he suggested that a major cause of the lack of class consciousness among American workers

> was the free gift of the ballot which came to labor at an early date as a by-product of the Jeffersonian democratic movement. In other countries where the labor movement started while workingmen were still denied the franchise, there was in the last analysis no need for a theory of "surplus value" to convince them that they were a class apart and should therefore be "class conscious." There ran a line like a red thread between the laboring class and the other classes. Not so, where the line is only an economic one (Perlman 1928, p. 167).

This view was shared by Lenin, who maintained that the weakness of socialism in America and Britain before World War I stemmed from "the absence of any at all big, nation-wide *democratic* tasks facing the proletariat" (Lenin, n.d., p. 51). Other countries, in which manhood suffrage and full democratic rights were secured in the 19th century, such as Australia, Canada, Denmark, and Switzerland, were also resistant to efforts to create strong socialist parties.

Conversely, the denial of the suffrage proved to be a strong motive for class political organization in many European nations. The first major British labor movement, Chartism, was centered on the struggle for the vote. In some countries, general strikes were called by workers to force through a change in the electoral laws (Austria, 1896 and 1905; Finland, 1905; Belgium, 1902 and 1913; and Sweden, 1902). The struggle for suffrage often had a quasi-religious fervor and was viewed by its advocates as the key to a new and more egalitarian society, since the poor outnumbered the rich and would presumably secure a radical redistribution of income and opportunity if they had the necessary political rights. The existence of a limited franchise based on property made it clear to workers that political power and economic privilege were closely related. The withholding of the franchise often became a symbol of the position of workers as a deprived and pariah group. A restricted franchise encouraged the ideologists of both unfranchised and privileged groups to analyze politics in terms of class power.

The exclusion of workers from the fundamental political rights of citizenship effectively fused the struggle for political and economic equality and cast that struggle in a radical mold. Thus, a large number of European socialist movements grew strong and adopted a radical Marxist ideology while the working class was still unfranchised or was discriminated against by an electoral system that was explicitly class or property biased. Such was the history of Austria, Germany, Finland, and Sweden, among others.

The variations in legal rights that influenced the character of working-class politics also helped to determine the relationship of trade unions to labor parties in different nations. Where both trade union rights and male suffrage existed at an early date, the unions and the workers as a social force were able to press for political objectives by working with one or more of the non-socialist parties. And even when labor parties emerged, they did not adopt radical objectives.

As Gary Marks has noted in his study of trade-union political activity:

> Where trade unions were firmly established before party-political mobilization was underway, the resulting party had to adapt itself to an already "formed" working class with its cultural ties and institutional loyalties. Unlike the parties that were established before the rise of trade unions, these parties could not integrate the working classes into a singular, inclusive, and politically oriented sub-culture of radical or revolutionary resistance against capitalism. In this important respect, then, the Social Democratic Party, the early guardian and shaper of trade unionism in Germany, stands opposite the British

Labour Party, which, in Ernest Bevin's telling phrase, "has grown out of the bowels of the T.U.C." (Marks 1982, p. 89; Sturmthal 1953, pp. 37–62; Derfler 1973, p. 73)

Labor unions in the English-speaking countries became legitimate pressure groups oriented to pragmatic and immediate economic goals. They were involved in many of the nonideological issues of the day, such as protection versus free trade, and immigration policies. Some of the more left or liberal nonsocialist bourgeois parties supported social legislation desired by labor unions.

In those countries in which the trade union movement created a labor party, such as Australia and Britain, the original radical socialist promotion groups had comparatively little influence. The dominant working-class parties were controlled by trade unions and followed a pragmatic non-Marxian ideology. Socialists remained a comparatively small pressure group within these organizations or sought to build their own parties outside the labor parties.

In nations where the state repressed economic combination, unions were faced with a common and overriding task, that of changing the rules of the game. The more intensive and longer lasting the state repression, the more drastic the consequences. Where the right to combine in the labor market was severely restricted, as it was in Germany, Austria, Russia, France, Spain, and Italy, the decision to act in politics was forced on trade unions. Whether they liked it or not, unions became political institutions; they had first to change the distribution of political power within the state before they could effectively exert power in the market. At the same time, extreme state repression or employer opposition minimized the ability of privileged groups of skilled workers to improve their working conditions in a sectional fashion. In this important respect, then, repression fostered socialist or anarchist ideologies that emphasized the common interests of all workers.

Where fundamental economic rights were denied to workers, strong radical organizations were established before unions were well developed. This meant that the parties formulated their ideologies in the absence of pressures for pragmatic policies from trade unions.

Where the working class was deprived of both economic and political rights, those who favored social change were necessarily revolutionary. The identification of state repression with privileged and powerful groups reinforced political ideologies that conceived of politics in demonological terms. Perhaps the most important example of this pattern was Czarist Russia. There, every effort to form legal trade unions or establish a democratic parliamentary regime was forcibly suppressed. This situation provided the ground for revolutionary lower-class political movements under the leadership of intellectuals or others of middle- or upper-class origin.

Although the goals of party and union tend to differ when both are tolerated by the state, under repression there is much less space for diversity. Both share the task of changing the political status quo. As Lenin observed in the context of Czarist Russia:

> the yoke of the autocracy appears...to obliterate all distinctions between a Social-Democratic organization and trade unions, because *all* workers' associations and *all* circles are prohibited, and because the principal manifestation and weapon of the workers' economic struggle—the strike—is regarded as a criminal (and sometimes even as a political) offense (Lenin 1973, p. 139).

The Leninist concept of the "combat party," with its reliance on secrecy and authoritarian discipline and its emphasis on the "conquest of power," developed as a reaction to the political situation of the time.

* * *

In Germany, to be discussed in more detail below, the continued domination of the Reichstag by traditional conservative forces, the absence of a democratic franchise in Prussia, and the strong repressive measures taken by Bismarck against the socialists in the 1870s and 1880s, bound the socialists and the trade unions formed by them into a distinct subculture having

an explicitly revolutionary ideology. In practice, of course, as Robert Michels and many other contemporary observers argued, the bureaucracy of the party gradually became conservative and opposed any measures that threatened its organizational stability. Nevertheless, the position of the labor movement as a semi-legitimate opposition group helped to perpetuate its use of radical terminology.

In Austria, as in Germany, the intransigence of the upper class had a decisive influence on the character and ideology of the working-class movement. Anti-Socialist laws were in effect from 1866 to 1881, and a special law repressed the workers' party in many regions from 1881 to 1891. The party and the unions, which cooperated closely in the struggle for the suffrage, adhered to a radical class-conscious ideology. Manhood suffrage for parliamentary elections was only attained in 1907.

The achievement of this political goal, followed by a sharp increase in parliamentary representation, however, served to undermine the cohesion and radicalism of the workers' movement. As G. D. H. Cole notes, "the very success of the Austrians in winning the vote necessarily weakened their sense of the need for close unity. The main plank in their common programme having been withdrawn, it was none too easy to find another to take its place. Now that they had become an important parliamentary party the emphasis tended to shift to the struggle for social and economic reforms, especially for improved labour laws regulating conditions of employment and the development of social services on the German model. But these were poor substitutes because they tended to change the Socialist Party into a reformist party" (Cole 1956, p. 538).

The Socialist party and the trade unions continued to make significant progress after the defeat and breakup of the Hapsburg monarchy in World War I. Such a situation should have resulted in the development of working-class political and labor movements integrated into the body politic, and a further moderation of their ideology in the direction of the British and

Scandinavian patterns. In fact, this did not occur. But the responsibility did not lie with the Austrian labor movement. Rather, the Austrian conservatives, whose support was based on the rural population and business elements, and who were tied closely to the Catholic church, aristocracy, and monarchism, refused to accept the rising status of labor. Faced with rebuffs from the conservatives, the church, and the business strata, the socialists responded by adhering to Marxian class-war principles. Within the Socialist International, the Austrian party was considered to be on the far left, before it was suppressed in 1934.

\* \* \*

In analyzing the relationship between economic and political rights and working-class political behavior, I have thus far dealt primarily with formal rights, that is, whether adult suffrage existed, and whether trade unions could function without serious legal difficulties. In fact, however, legal rights were only partial indicators of the will and capacity of the upper and business classes to resist the emergence of the working class as a political force. The right to vote or organize unions did not necessarily mean that labor had acquired a legitimate place in society, or that the pressures toward radicalism flowing from the position of the worker as political outcast had disappeared.

It is possible to distinguish among three situations: total repression, legal existence but constant conflict (i.e., *de jure* but not *de facto* recognition), and *de jure* and *de facto* recognition. The existence of the first two conditions usually indicates that the business classes still desire to destroy the organized expression of the labor movement. Under such conditions, labor may be expected to react strongly against capitalism and, perhaps, the existing political system as well.

France before World War II, Spain before 1975, and pre-fascist Italy are examples of nations where unions were weak because the business and conservative classes refused to grant *de facto* recognition to them. The consequences

of this for union strategy have been recognized by Fred Ridley:

> There is a close relationship between weak, unorganized labour movements and the outbreak of revolutionary or anarchist activity in Russia, Spain and Italy, as well as in France. The unions had little bargaining power when it came to across-the-table negotiations with employers; they had neither the membership nor the organization with which to impress. Lack of funds, inability to pay strike benefits, meant that they could not hope to achieve their ends by ordinary peaceful strikes. They were thus forced to play for quick results: violence, intimidation and sabotage were the obvious weapons to choose (Ridley 1970, p. 18).

In much of Latin Europe, both the state and employers denied legitimacy to trade unions, i.e., their right to become the institutionalized representatives of workers, although in France manhood suffrage existed in the 1870s and in Spain from 1889. In France the Socialist party was able to gain electoral strength before unions were well developed. The party, however, had little success in fostering social legislation or trade-union organizations, given "the ferocity of bourgeois response to it" (Derfler 1973, p. 78; Sturmthal 1953, pp. 55–56). In countries where a wide franchise failed to provide "an effective lever in the hands of the masses, such 'democratic' reforms could paradoxically develop into a measure of plebiscitary control over them. This could result in an enduring alienation of sizable sections of the population rather than in their permanent integration in an effectively responsive political system" (Daalder 1966b, p. 54).

The French trade-union movement continued to face strong resistance from the state and the business class, both of which refused to grant unions a legitimate role as bargaining agents in the economy. The unions required a revolutionary ideology to motivate membership and leadership participation and thus sustain their organization. They found this ideology in syndicalism. As a number of historians have suggested, syndicalism, with its faith in violence and in worker spontaneity, was not merely an impractical flight of idealism, but a response to constraints that served to limit the alternatives facing unions. Ridley has noted:

> The law forced workers into opposition to the state; in a measure, indeed, it persuaded them to reject the state altogether. Its provisions, biased heavily in favour of the employer, excluded the worker from its benefits—left him to all interests an outcast—*hors du pays légal*. The syndicalist doctrine of autonomy, the insistence that the labour movement must develop outside the state, create its own institutions to reinforce it, can be understood in the light of its experience (Ridley 1970, p. 23; see also Stearns 1971, p. 13).

Distrust of parliamentary government and a strong emphasis on syndicalist and revolutionary class organization developed in Spain and Italy as well. As noted, Spain introduced universal male suffrage relatively early. But the government "continued to manage elections as it pleased, to the extent of deciding centrally who were to be elected, not only for its own party, but also to represent the recognized opposition groups." In the big cities, it counted the ballots; in small towns and rural areas, the "caciques," local bosses, controlled. In Italy, the Liberals, who dominated the government in the late 19th and early 20th centuries, rigged the election results among a more restricted electorate by a variety of corrupt practices, comparable to those used in Spain. "These practices...left a heritage of cynicism, highly politicized administrative machinery, corruption, and the absence of civic pride and of vital local government" (Barnes 1966, pp. 306–308). The expansion of the suffrage in 1912 was followed by an election in which the governing Liberals added to corrupt practices a heavy "dose of violence to ensure success" (Gaetano Salvemini, quoted in Barnes 1966, p. 308).

In both countries, trade union organizations were harassed by state institutions that claimed to represent the electorate democratically. Because unions were weak, the conditions for the emergence of a genuine working-class leadership were absent. Consequently, intellectuals

or other upper-class radicals came to dominate the labor movement. The weakness and instability of trade unions also resulted in few achievements that could legitimate gradualist and pragmatic goals. As Juan Linz notes with respect to Spain:

> The bitterness of class conflict that ultimately led to semirevolutionary general strikes, local or regional insurrections...should not hide the fact that the labor movement was weak by comparison with other countries. Spanish labor lacked numbers, organizational and economic resources for strikes, success at the polls, and capacity for nationwide activities (Linz 1981, p. 368).

In Italy and Spain, as in France, the business classes continually resisted coming to terms with the trade union movement. Although unions had *de jure* recognition, the history of labor in these countries was characterized by constant warfare. Revolutionary syndicalism was strong in each country (Malefakis 1973, p. 5). In Italy, syndicalism gained strength as a reaction to the repeated suppression of local strikes and popular protest movements that often involved the use of violence. In Spain, anarchism grew in response to "alternate periods of legal toleration and savage repression." This pattern culminated in the triumph of authoritarianism in both Italy and Spain and the establishment of regimes that were primarily oriented toward maintaining the economic and class status quo. And as in France, the working class and its leaders responded by supporting extremist doctrines. Thus, in Spain, moderate socialism was relatively weak, whereas doctrines such as revolutionary socialism, anarchism, and even Trotskyism were strong. In Italy, anarchism and left socialism were influential before Mussolini, and moderate socialism, even today, remains relatively weak; the bulk of the working class supports the Communist party.

It is also worth noting that both Spain and Italy were industrially backward societies in the late 19th century when radical working-class movements emerged. Like fascism itself, anarchism has been viewed as an antimodern doctrine, a reaction against the strains of modernity. In this context, it should be noted that in France, too, syndicalism was strongest among craft workers in small-scale industries that were most threatened by industrialization and mass production.

The adoption of an anarchist or syndicalist political ideology had specific and identifiable consequences for trade-union movements. Syndicalism committed them to a loose, unstable, and relatively unbureaucratic organization. This structure, in turn, required the unions and their leaders to stress ideology at the expense of building loyalty on the basis of concrete gains achieved through collective bargaining. It also reduced those inhibitions on militant action that result from the need to protect an established structure.

In discussing the denial of legitimacy to socialists and trade unions, I have focused primarily on the influence this had on their activities and ideologies. But, obviously, the relationship is not a simple cause-and-effect one. The behavior of the left had its effect on the right. In particular, one should not ignore that France, Italy, Spain, and Austria are Catholic, which meant that the traditional struggle between the left and right was not solely, or even primarily, an economic class struggle but also was a confrontation between Catholicism and atheism or secularism. Many of the Catholic conservative leaders viewed the battle against Marxism and working-class institutions as part of the fight for their religion. To accept the legitimacy of a working-class movement that was Marxist and irreligious involved a much greater modification in their value systems than was necessary in situations where religious values were not involved, as in Britain and Australia.

In the Catholic societies of Western Europe, the church, in alliance with landed interests, attempted to establish trade unions and political organizations to counter the influence of socialism among the lower classes. The result was the "pillarization" of the working class into mutually antagonistic Catholic and socialist tendencies. In France, Italy, Spain, and Austria, socialist parties not only were rejected by the ruling

powers, they were also opposed by a major segment of the working class. Both of these factors furthered the development of radical movements. Reformism tended to be more typical of working-class politics and unions in countries where labor was powerfully represented by unitary organizations that were accepted into the political and economic mainstream.[1]

## EFFORTS AT INTEGRATION: BRITAIN AND GERMANY

The previous discussion indicates that radical ideologies were strongest where social and political groups attempted to reduce or destroy the influence of leftist or working-class movements by refusing them legitimacy and continually fighting them. In countries in which the working class was incorporated into the body politic at an early date, the chances that workers would come to support extremist or revolutionary doctrines were considerably reduced.

The American experience clearly illustrates the consequences for working-class movements of integration into society. There the absorption occurred as a result of social structures, values, and events that predated industrial society. The European experience offers insights into the effects of deliberate efforts to win the allegiance of the working class. An examination of Great Britain and Germany is particularly informative because in both countries, sections of the ruling strata consciously sought to reduce the class antagonism of the workers by accommodating their demands; yet the attempt succeeded in Britain and failed in Germany.

The conventional explanation of why Marxism is weak in Britain suggests that the landed aristocracy and their party, the Tories, who retained considerable power in 19th-century Britain, sought to stem the growing power and ideology of the rising industrial business class by winning the allegiance of the "lower orders." In their opposition to the new capitalist society and in a desire to preserve past institutions and values, Conservatives, led by Disraeli, often took the same position as the spokesmen of the working classes. As Hearnshaw points out:

> The "young England" Tories [which Disraeli joined]...with their curious affection for an idealized feudalism and chivalry, had much in common with the Chartists and other proletarian reformers of the early Victorian days. With them they deplored and resented the operation of the new poor law of 1834; they opposed the principles of laissez-faire; they hated the new machinery and the hideous mills in which it was housed; they protested the repeal of the usury laws and the corn laws; they distrusted the new stock-jobbers and the joint-stock bankers... [their] principles flowed naturally from the mainstream of the conservative tradition (Hearnshaw 1933, pp. 219–220).

The Tories, however, maintained a traditional view of the relationship between rich and poor, one that was based on an idealization of class relations as they existed in pre-industrial society. They assumed that the lower classes should remain "dependent" on the upper class and that the latter, in turn, should be responsible for the welfare of the lower strata.

Some of the leaders of the aristocratic upper classes were able to perceive the extent to which the new industrial workers—despite occasional violent protest actions and increasing class consciousness—shared their view of "the good old days and the bad new days," and, more important, desired recognition and status within the existing order. Disraeli believed in the traditionalism of the lower classes. He was able to secure the passage of the Electoral Reform Act of 1867 as well as some social legislation. To this must be added the relative freedom that British trade unions attained in the last quarter of the 19th century, especially through the labor laws of 1875. The facts of political life, plus the steadily rising standard of living, demonstrated to workers and their leaders that it was possible to improve their position within British society. Both the Tories and Liberals formed working-men's associations.

The reformist policies of British politicians in the late 19th and early 20th centuries helped to integrate workers into the national community, to reduce their hostility to existing political institutions (the state, the throne, and the major parties), and to adopt gradualist rather than revolutionary methods. Friedrich Engels noted that the absence of "a separate political working-class party" was to be expected "in a country where the ruling classes have set themselves the task of carrying out, parallel with other concessions, one point of the Chartists' programme, the People's Charter, after another" (Engels 1953, p. 466). Although a labor party gained strength in Britain in the early 1900s, following the Taff-Vale court decision that threatened the power of the trade unions, the leaders of the new movement did not view the other parties as class enemies who had to be eliminated. Rather, they conceived of a separate labor party as an electoral tactic, which would place labor in a better position to bargain with the older parties. The development of a stable, legitimate, labor movement created a stratum of working-class leaders who had secured position and power within the existing social system and consequently had close ties to it. The emergence of Fabianism as a political force in Britain is in large measure explicable by the fact that the Fabians, with their initial hope that the upper class could be converted to socialism, reflected the actual British historical experience of aristocratic intervention on behalf of the workers.

In Germany, a situation similar in certain important respects to that in Britain led to a comparable effort to integrate the lower classes into the society. The aristocracy, crown, and state bureaucracy sought to inhibit the influence of the rising liberal bourgeoisie. Bismarck, who was the chief exponent of this policy, established universal suffrage in the federal empire after 1867 so that he could use the votes of the rural lower classes, and to a certain extent of the workers themselves, against the urban middle classes, who, he realized, would dominate in a restricted property-based suffrage.

Unlike Disraeli and the British Tories, however, Bismarck had little confidence that the workers' organizations would become incorporated into the social order. This led him to outlaw the socialist movement in 1878 and to hope that by enacting social welfare measures advocated by the socialists he could win the loyalty of workers to the regime. The conservative *Sozialpolitik*, however, came too late. The workers had already begun to support the socialist movement; efforts to suppress it only served to undermine moderate representatives of the working class. This act of repression is generally recognized to be one of the chief sources of the difference in the political development of the German and British working classes.

Bismarck attempted to incorporate the proletariat by winning its loyalty to society without permitting workers to have their own organizations and leaders. By the time working-class political organization was legalized in 1890, the Social Democrats had acquired a revolutionary ideology that was difficult to discard even after the party had become a strong and stable movement, capable of antagonizing and frightening the middle and upper classes.

The Bismarckian policies deeply affected the outlook and strategy of German workers. First, and most important, they placed Social Democracy in a paradoxical position. On the one hand, the party was successful: it grew steadily from one election to the next, attracted hundreds of thousands of members and employed a large bureaucracy. It gradually adapted itself to the role of a parliamentary opposition, which anticipated coming to power through democratic means. On the other hand, however, the ideology developed during and immediately following the period of repression gave it the appearance of being devoted to purely revolutionary ends and legitimized the agitation of extreme leftists within its ranks. (The party rewrote its program in 1891, after 12 years of overt repression, to emphasize its intransigence.) Until World War I, the SPD refused to repudiate its formal belief in class warfare. In large part, the subsequent strength of left-wing socialists and Communists may be explained by the legitimacy the ideology of the Social Democratic

party gave to such groups within the working class.

Second, Bismarck's policies, and the socialists' ideological reactions to them, prevented the SPD from becoming a legitimate national party in the eyes of other political movements. The socialist revolutionary rhetoric may have prevented many of the middle-class, white-collar strata from supporting the Party, while at the same time strengthening the potential for an alliance between the middle class and industrialists and large landowners.

Third, Bismarck's "social revolution from above" included a number of welfare programs that in other countries had been the responsibility of the unions themselves and had helped to stabilize conservative unions. August Bebel, the leader of the Social Democratic party, pointed this out in a speech in 1893:

> In Germany, the state system of workingmen's insurance took away from the trade unions that branch of activity, and has in effect cut a vital nerve, as it were. For benefit systems had meant enormously in the furthering of unionism in Britain and among the German printers. Labor legislation has likewise preempted many other lines of activity which properly belong to the trade unions (Bebel, quoted in Perlman 1928, pp. 77–78).

The fact that the state, rather than the unions, controlled welfare funds and dictated policies, which elsewhere were handled through collective bargaining, served to increase the awareness of workers and their leaders of the need to influence state policy. The potential for a syndicalist antistatist doctrine was reduced, since conservative state intervention stimulated the belief that workers should take over and use the state system. The trade unions, far from becoming antistatist, became more statist in their orientation. But at the same time, the elimination of various trade-union functions weakened the loyalty of workers to the labor movement and reduced the stability of the unions, which denied them the role in maintaining political stability that unions in various other countries, particularly Britain, assumed.

The effect of varying upper-class policies on the behavior of working-class movements can be illustrated within Germany as well as through international comparisons. As a number of political commentators have noted, the socialist movement in Prussia was quite different from that in southern Germany, especially Bavaria. In Prussia, which contained over half the population of the country, Bismarck pursued the same combination of repression and paternalism that he adopted for the federal empire. Prussia, a highly industrialized part of Germany, retained legal limits on the potential power of the workers even after the anti-Socialist laws were repealed. These restrictions were in the form of an electoral system based on three estates, which gave the middle classes and the landed nobility effective control over the Prussian legislature. The restrictions were, in large part, motivated by the fact that a purely democratic franchise would give a majority to the Socialists and the Catholic Zentrum, both antigovernment parties. And as Kautsky noted in 1911, the working-class movement in Prussia gave much more emphasis to class-struggle doctrines.

In the South, where governments were much less autocratic than in Prussia, in part because the old landed aristocracy was relatively unimportant and the rural and urban petty bourgeoisie proportionately stronger, the degree of political freedom was much greater. In Southern Germany, the Social Democrats cooperated with nonsocialist parties, in the process reducing their original emphasis on class struggle. The Revisionist doctrines of Eduard Bernstein were given their earliest and strongest support in the South. The Bavarian socialists, for example, broke with the tradition of the party and voted for the state budget.

Bismarck failed in his effort to destroy German socialism through force. His refusal to incorporate the socialist political movement in a democratic parliamentary system helped to perpetuate revolutionary rhetoric. But the fact remains that the Social Democrats eventually became a stable, moderate, opposition party. Its commitment to Marxism was largely aimed against the militarist imperial state.

The failure of Bismarckian policy is evident in the rise of large movements on the left of the Social Democrats after World War I. The momentum for such movements emerged from the prewar contradiction between Social Democratic party behavior and ideology. Although support for the Communists declined in the late 20s, they made considerable headway in the early 1930s. In Britain, on the other hand, communism and fascism were weak and found no social roots.

The identification of varying British and German policies with Disraeli and Bismarck is not intended to suggest that the sharply divergent histories of the two countries may be credited to the wisdom of one and the stupidity of the other. Rather, as Barrington Moore has emphasized, the structural histories of the British and German aristocracies differed greatly. A combination of factors led the British upper classes to collaborate economically with the rising bourgeoisie and to set their peasants free. The landed aristocracy developed "bourgeois economic habits" and accepted parts of liberal political doctrine. In Germany, on the other hand, the aristocracy continued to preside over a "labor-repressive agrarian system" and to work with the monarchy and the "royal bureaucracy" rather than the business classes. This relationship produced, or rather reinforced, an emphasis on obedience and control from the top. Thus, the divergent policies of British and German upper-class conservatives reflected basic variations in their nations' social structures (Moore 1967, pp. 413–450).

## CONCLUSION

In this article I have analyzed some of the ways in which the character of working-class movements has been influenced by the varying status systems of different societies and by the degree to which workers and their organizations were able to participate legitimately in the economic and political decision-making processes. In the United States, and to a lesser extent in Canada, the absence of an aristocratic or feudal past, combined with a history of political democracy prior to industrialization, served to reduce the salience of class-conscious politics and proposals for major structural change. As Walter Dean Burnham has emphasized: "No feudalism, no socialism: with these four words one can summarize the basic sociocultural realities that underlie American electoral politics in the industrial era" (Burnham 1974, p. 718).

Conversely, in much of Europe, a "post-feudal" background was critical in shaping the political consciousness of the working class. As William Sewell, Jr. notes, "one of the most important roots of European class consciousness may have been the corporate cultural tradition of the pre-industrial European working class. This tradition made workingmen feel that their destiny was linked to that of their fellow workers, and predisposed them to collective, rather than individualistic, ideologies and modes of social and political action" (Sewell 1976, pp. 232–233).

The proletarian movements, born as *Staende*, adopted Marxism as their ideological cement and sought to achieve legitimation within the bourgeois order through constitutional reforms, the acquisition of citizenship. The emergence of radical politics originated as a consequence of the meshing of the hierarchical *Staende* with the inequalities of an emerging capitalist society differentiated into economic classes. Ironically, in trying to change the perception of the social hierarchy from *Stand* to class, radical working-class movements drew on and revitalized the sense of *Stand*-consciousness that they inherited. Many of the pre-World War I Social Democratic parties, as well as postwar Communist parties, also sustained corporative forms of group solidarity by creating a socially encapsulated working-class culture, in which their followers were involved in a plethora of party and union-related organizations.

Where the corporate tradition broke down or never existed, what developed were interest-group organizations and ideologies. As Lenin and Perlman argued from contrary political perspectives, the orientation that stems from the class position of the proletariat is pure and simple trade unionism, or "economism," not revolutionary class consciousness. Against the background of Marxist theory, the outcome is paradoxical. For Marx and Engels maintained that the "logic of capitalism" would give rise to revolutionary movements, and that, to the degree that remnants of feudalism were removed and the victorious bourgeoisie established civic and political rights, class disparities would become the politically decisive facts engendering working-class consciousness and leading to proletarian revolution. The historical experience suggests that, with respect to the legacy of feudalism and political rights, the reasons for working-class radicalism were quite the opposite.

The impact of these variables is formalized in Table 1, which links the relationship between the social-class system and the rights to political and economic citizenship to the way in which workers responded in the decades before World War I. Table 1 illustrates both the weakness and strength of the type of comparative analysis undertaken here. The attempt to specify the kind of working-class movements that emerged under varying status systems and citizenship rights does not express the complexity of the phenomenon. Obviously, a static classification based on the dichotomization of three continuous variables cannot be expected to produce categories into which each national case fits through time. (For example, the United States and Denmark may both be classified as nonrigid status systems, although that of Denmark clearly has a greater continuity with a preindustrial corporate *Stand* tradition than the United States.)

The behavior of workers in western societies before and after World War I was, of course, deeply affected by other variables, including the pace, extent, and shape of industrial development within their societies or how closely the objective social and economic situation "fit" the Marxist two-class model of an oppressive society. It is also important to recognize that these three factors are not independent of each other, although they may be distinguished

**TABLE 1** Outcomes of different combinations of social-class patterns and citizenship rights before World War I

| Economic citizenship | Political citizenship | Nonrigid | Rigid |
|---|---|---|---|
| Early | Early | Low political consciousness, weak interest-group unions (U.S.) | Low political consciousness, strong reformist unions (Britain) |
| Early | Late | Strong reformist parties and unions (Low countries) | Radical parties, strong pragmatic unions (Germany) |
| Late | Early | Weak reformist parties, radical unions (Switzerland) | Strong reformist parties, radical unions (France) |
| Late | Late | | Revolutionary movements (Russia, Finland) |

analytically. Britain apart, the extension of post-feudal aristocratic power or values into the industrial era was associated with repressive political or economic patterns. And the British case may be explained by the fact that the aristocracy developed closer links to business than elsewhere. The emergence of democratic rights was in large measure tied to bourgeois hegemony. As Barrington Moore phrased it: "No bourgeois, no democracy" (Moore 1967, p. 418).

While the stress on the relationship between fundamental economic and political rights and the ideology of the labor movements is not meant to suggest that the character of contemporary movements is determined simply by their early history, the formative experiences did initiate certain trends or institutional patterns that took on a self-perpetuating character and hence affected ideology, structure, and political outcomes in later years. Most of the countries in which workers found it difficult to attain economic or political citizenship before World War I were the ones in which fascist and communist movements were strong in the interwar period: Austria, Finland, France, Germany, Italy, and Spain. Currently, commitment to democratic institutions appears strong in Austria and Germany, but, as Dahl notes, "it is untested by adversity" (Dahl 1966, p. 360). Although declining

in electoral strength, communist movements are still very influential among workers in Finland, France, and Italy. Spain, democratic since 1975, remains problematic.

Although formative experiences continue to have an impact on the contemporary body politic, particularly in distinguishing the European from the overseas settler societies, it is obvious that many of the differences discussed here no longer hold for present-day Europe. Apart from Britain, postfeudal elements have declined greatly or have disappeared in the industrialized countries. The economic miracle of prosperity and growth that followed World War II changed occupational structures, status systems, levels of income, and the distribution of educational attainments in ways that reduced many of the social strains characteristic of prewar industrial societies. Logically, in terms of the analysis presented here, which derives from the approaches of Max Weber and Joseph Schumpeter, the amount of class-related political conflict should be reduced as the dynamics of an industrial society undermine the status mechanisms inherited from the feudal precapitalist order. The imposition on the stratification system of capitalism's or industrial society's stress on achievement and universalism should weaken rather than increase class-linked consciousness of kind. And significantly, the correlations between class and party voting have been declining steadily.

These changes, however, have given rise to new tensions reflective of an emerging post-industrial society. The new divisions can be understood as the most recent examples of the basic cleavages that structure comparative mass politics, systematically analyzed by Stein Rokkan (1970). I have discussed the character of these conflicts elsewhere and will not elaborate on them here (Lipset 1981, pp. 503–521).But it is important to note that the prominence of so-called postmaterialist issues, such as quality of life, ecology, sexual equality, international relations, and ethnic rights, have changed the divisions between the left and right and have affected their bases of support. These new issues are linked to an increase in middleclass political radicalism and working-class social conservatism.

The working classes in western society no longer have to undergo repression. They have acquired economic and political citizenship. It is still possible, however, to relate the forms of present-day politics, particularly party labels and formal ideologies, to the emergence of new social strata in the formative period of modern politics. Should the western world experience a major crisis, it is likely that national politics will vary along lines that stem from the past, much as they did during the 1930s. Political scientists of the future, who seek to explain events in the last quarter of this century, will undoubtedly find important explanatory variables in earlier variations in the behavior of the major political actors.

## Notes

1. It should also be noted that the involvement of workers in religious parties also helped move such groups to the left in social policies, once democratic institutions were stabilized. In the Low countries, in particular, the recognition of workers' rights by the religious groups helped to moderate the behavior of the socialists (Daalder 1981, pp. 207–208).

## Author's References

AUBERT, V. 1974. Stratification. In *Norwegian society.* ed. N. R. Ramsoy, New York. Humanities Press.

BARNES,S. H. 1966. Italy: oppositions on left, right, and center. *In Political oppositions in western democracies.* ed. R. A. Dahl, New Haven: Yale University Press.

BELL, D. 1973. *The coming of post-industrial society.* New York: Basic Books.

BURNHAM, W. D. 1974. The United States: the politics of heterogeneity. *In Electoral behavior; a comparative handbook.* ed. R. Rose, New York: Free Press.

COLE, G. D. H. 1956. *A history of socialist thought,* Vol. III, *The second internatioal, 1889–1914.* London: Macmillan.

CORNELL, R. (n.d.). Culture, values, and the development of socialism in Denmark. Unpublished paper, Department of Political Science, York University, Toronto, Canada.

DAALDER, H. 1981. Consociationalism, center and periphery in the Netherlands. In *Mobilization, center-periphery structures and nation-building.* ed. Per Torsvik, Bergen: Universitetsforlaget.

———. 1966a. The Netherlands: opposition in a segmented society. In *Political oppositions in western democracies.* ed. R. A. Dahl, New Haven: Yale University Press.

———. 1966b. Parties, elites, and political developments in Western Europe. In *Political parties and political development.* ed. J. La Palombara and M. Weiner, Princeton, N.J.: Princeton University Press.

DAHL, R. A. 1966. Some explanations. In *Political oppositions in western democracies.* ed. R. A. Dahl, New Haven: Yale University Press.

DAHRENDORF, R. 1967. *Society and democracy in Germany.* Garden City, N.Y.: Doubleday/Anchor.

DERFLER, L. 1973. *Socialism since Marx.* New York: St. Martin's Press.

DEUTSCH, K. 1953. *Nationalism and social communication.* New York: John Wiley.

DRAPER, T. 1960. *American communism and Soviet Russia.* New York: Viking.

ECKSTEIN, H. 1966. *Division and cohesion in democracy. A study of Norway.* Princeton, N.J.: Princeton University Press.

ENGELS, F. 1936. Engels to Sorge, February 8, 1890 and December 31, 1982. In K. Marx and F. Engels, *Selected correspondence, 1846–1895.* New York: International Publishers.

_____. 1953 The English elections. In K. Marx and F. Engels, *On Britain*. Moscow: Foreign Languages Publishing House.

_____. 1968a. Introduction to *Socialism: Utopian and Scientific*. In K. Marx and F. Engels, *Selected works*. New York: International Publishers.

_____. 1968b. *The role of force in history*. London: Lawrence and Wishart.

EPSTEIN, L. D. 1980. *Political parties in western democracies*. New Brunswick, N.J.: Transaction.

FRIEDBERG, G. 1974. Comment. *In Failure of a dream?* ed. J. H. M. Laslett and S. M. Lipset, Garden City, N.Y.: Anchor Press/Doubleday.

GRUNER, E. 1968. *Die Arbeiter in der Schweiz im 19. Jahrhundert*. Bern: Francke Verlag.

GULICK, C. A. 1948. *Austria from Hapsburg to Hitler*, Vol. I, *Labor's workshop of democracy*. Berkeley: University of California Press.

HARTZ, L. 1955. *The liberal tradition in America*. New York: Harcourt, Brace and World.

HEARNSHAW, F. J. O. 1933. *Conservatism in England, an analytical, historical and political survey*. London: Macmillan.

HOFFMANN, S. 1963. Paradoxes of the French political community. In S. Hoffman et al., *In search of France*, Cambridge, Mass.: Harvard University Press.

KAUTSKY, K. 1910. *The class struggle (The Erfurt Program)*. Chicago: Charles H. Kerr.

KNOELLINGER, C. E. 1960. *Labor in Finland*. Cambridge, Mass.: Harvard University Press.

LAIDLER, H. 1927. *Socialism in thought and action*. New York: Macmillan.

LANDAUER, C. 1959. *European socialism*, Vol. I. Berkeley: University of California Press.

LENIN, V. I. (n.d.). Preface to the Russian translation of "Letters by J. Ph. Becker, J. Dietzgen, F. Engels, K. Marx and others to F. A. Sorge and others." In *On Britain*. ed. V. I. Lenin, Moscow: Foreign Languages Publishing House.

_____. 1973. *What is to be done?* Peking: Foreign Languages Press.

LIDTKE, V.L. 1966. *The outlawed party: social democracy in Germany 1878–1890*. Princeton, N.J.: Princeton University Press.

LINZ, J. 1981. A century of politics and interests in Spain. In *Organizing interests in Western Europe*. ed. S. Berger, New York: Cambridge University Press.

_____. 1977b. Why no socialism in the United States? In *Sources of contemporary radicalism*, ed. S. Bialer And S. Sluzar, Boulder, Colo.: Westview.

_____. 1981. *Political man: the social bases of politics*. Baltimore: Johns Hopkins University Press (expanded edition of original, published in 1960).

LIPSON, L. 1948. *The politics of equality. New Zealand's adventures in democracy*. Chicago: University of Chicago Press.

LORWIN, V. 1954. *The French labor movement*. Cambridge, Mass.: Harvard University Press.

_____. 1958. Working-class politics and economic development: Western Europe. *The American Historical Review* 63:338–351.

MANNHEIM, K. 1936. *Ideology and utopia*. New York: Harcourt, Brace.

MARKS, G. W. 1982. Trade unions in politics. Ph.D. dissertation, Department of Political Science, Stanford University.

MARSHALL, T. H. 1964. Class, citizenship and social development. Garden City: Doubleday.

MARTIN, W. C., and Hopkins, K. 1980. Cleavage crystallization and party linkages in Finland, 1900–1918. In *Political parties and linkages, a comparative perspective*. ed. K. Lawson, New Haven: Yale University Press.

MAYER, A. J. 1981. *The persistence of the old regime: Europe to the great war*. New York: Pantheon.

MOORE, B. Jr. 1967. *Social origins of dictatorship and democracy*. Boston: Beacon Press.

PARSONS, T. 1969. *Politics and social structure*. New York: Free Press.

PAYNE, S. G. 1970. *The Spanish revolution*. New York: W. W. Norton.

PERLMAN, S. 1928. *A theory of the labor movement*. New York: Macmillan.

PIERSON, S. 1979. *British socialists: the journey from fantasy to politics*. Cambridge, Mass.: Harvard University Press.

PULZER, P. 1967. *Political representation and elections in Britain*. New York: Praeger.

RIDLEY, F. F. 1970. *Revolutionary syndicalism in France*. Cambridge: Cambridge University Press.

ROKKAN, S. 1970. *Citizens, elections, parties*. New York: David McKay.

_____. 1981. The growth and structuring of mass politics. In *Nordic democracy*, ed. E. Allardt et al. Copenhagen: Det Danske Selskab.

ROSECRANCE, R. N. 1960. The radical tradition in Australia: an interpretation. *The Review of Politics* 22:115–132.

SCHUMPETER, J. 1950. *Capitalism, socialism and democracy*. New York: Harper & Row.

SEWELL, W. H., Jr. 1976. Social mobility in a nine-teenth-century European city: some findings and implications. *Journal of Interdisciplinary History* 7:217–233.

STEARNS, P. N. 1971. *Revolutionary syndicalism and French labor.* New Brunswick, N.J.: Rutgers University Press.

STURMTHAL, A. 1953. *Unity and diversity in European labor.* Glencoe, Ill.: Free Press.

_____. 1972. *Comparative labor movements.* Belmont, Calif: Wadsworth.

THOMPSON, E. P. 1968. *The making of the English working class.* London: Penguin.

TINGSTEN, H. 1973. *The Swedish social democrats: their ideological development.* Totowa, N.J.: Bedminster Press.

WEBER, M. 1946. *Essays in sociology.* ed. H. H. Gerth and C. Wright Mills. New York: Oxford University Press.

_____. 1958. *Gesammelte politische Schriften.* Tuebingen: J. C. B. Mohr.

# 47

# Revolution and Anomie

*Bernard E. Brown*

## THE CRISES OF MODERNIZATION

One fruitful way of studying the complex process of modernization is to view it as a series of crises or challenges, to which a number of different responses are possible. A distinction can be made among the crises of legitimacy, participation, and tension-management (occurring roughly in that chronological order). As European societies went through the experience of modernization they necessarily had to cope with each of these crises. Feudal societies could not survive the Enlightenment, and the concept

SOURCE: Bernard E. Brown, *Protest in Paris: Anatomy of a Revolt* (Morristown, N.J.: General Learning Press, 1974), pp. 212–222. By permission.

of divine right gave way to more rational theories of political legitimacy. With industrialization new groups emerged (an energetic entrepreneurial class, a managerial and clerical class, and a massive working class), and the existing political elites somehow had to deal with the demands of these new groups and integrate them into the political system. As the European economy became more complex each national society had to devise a system of controls, enabling it to coordinate the activities of increasingly specialized associations.

Nothing is fated to work out in favor of modernization in any of these crises. Revolt against the monarchy may be crushed; reactionary forces may overthrow a republic and reestablish monarchy; new or greatly expanded social groups, in particular the working class, may not be effectively integrated into the political system; and a society may be unable to cope with the problems of coordination. But punishment for failure is severe. A country that falls behind is likely to come under the influence or even the rule of those who have been more successful in meeting these challenges.

Each of the crises of modernization has posed serious problems for the French. Take, for example, the crisis of legitimacy. One of the basic assumptions of modernization theory is that as a society becomes more complex, the values serving to legitimize political authority become more rational. Or, rather than imply any causal relationship, rationalization of authority proceeds along with industrialization and increasing complexity of social structure. This assumption is borne out in a striking manner by the French experience, because of the great divide of the Revolution of 1789. The Tennis Court Oath, the August decrees abolishing feudalism, and the Declaration of the Rights of Man and Citizen marked an irrevocable break with absolutism and feudalism, and signaled the emergence of more rational principles of political legitimacy. Although France was converted almost overnight into a modern state as regards its official pattern of legitimacy, it did not thereby achieve a large popular consensus on its basic institutions. The revolution was repudiated by conservatives, and the revolutionaries were themselves divided. The result was a long period of constitutional instability. The transformation of French society continued. But the way in which the French tackled the successive crises of modernization was drastically affected by inability to agree on political structures. In the first great crisis of modernization in France, bursting forth in the Revolution of 1789 but continuing to this day, intransigence rather than compromise became characteristic of the political process.

Dissensus carried over from one historical phase to another. When the French turned to the problem of integrating the working class into the political system a pattern of rejection, opposition, and violence had already taken hold and made it more difficult (though not impossible) to formulate policy. The French working and business classes, from the outset, have been reluctant to bargain with each other—although compelled to do so by circumstances. The heritage of class distrust and conflict continues to interfere with the smooth functioning of the political system. That 20 to 25 percent of the electorate votes fairly consistently for the Communist Party, and that the Communist-led CGT is the most powerful of the French trade unions, are indications of profound dissatisfaction within the French working class. In turn, exclusion of the Communist Party from governing coalitions drives the political balance to the right, placing the working class at a disadvantage in the political process and further intensifying feelings of class consciousness and alienation from the political system. Without having completely resolved the crises of legitimacy and participation, the French have plunged into the later phase of modernization, for the alternative is national decline. But the carryover of dissensus creates friction and grievances throughout the society. Much of the May Revolt—in particular the readiness of masses of students, workers, and even professionals to defect—can be explained by the relative failure of the French, compared with other industrial nations, to cope with the successive crises of modernization.

However, revolutionary dissent combined with an intensive destructive urge is a general trend among students and middle class intellectuals in all liberal-industrial societies today. The May Revolt never could have begun in a stagnant or traditional society. It came about in the first place only because, despite all the difficulties in their way, the French managed to create an advanced industrial nation by 1968. We are led to the paradoxical conclusion that not only the failures, but also the very *success* of a society in meeting the challenges of modernization may lead to its own downfall.

## ANOMIE

Accompanying modernization in France, and everywhere else, is the phenomenon of *anomie* —a term popularized almost a century ago by Emile Durkheim. We have already encountered explanations of the May Revolt along the lines of Durkheim's theory, for example in Raymond Aron's *La révolution introuvable,* and the remarks of Georges Pompidou (before the National Assembly on May 14, 1968) and of General de Gaulle (during the television interview with Michel Droit on June 7, 1968). Durkheim asserted that the appetites and desires of men are infinite and that every society must impose a discipline or "regulator" in order to survive. In traditional society the family and religion constitute the regulator. Every person knows his role in family and religious activities; his desires are limited by his own perception of social status. But when a traditional society breaks up, the family structure and the church are brought into question. New values and new social structures arise (science, the republic, the corporation, the university, and so on); but frequently the individual in transition cannot accept them. Caught between the traditional and modern forms, his reactions may be those of resignation (ranging from apathy to suicide) or of rage against established authority. It is Durkheim's great insight that every modern society carries within itself the seeds of its own destruction. The more the individual is encouraged by society to realize his individuality, the greater is the risk that he will reject discipline and become perpetually discontent.[1]

The "anomic" reaction to social change in France has taken the form of violent opposition to the modern state and to urban industrial life. Hostility to industrial life has been especially vigorous in France among artists and writers, who have drawn a sharp contrast between bucolic nature and the polluted inhumanity of cities. As we have seen, under the influence of Proudhon and Bakunin, French anarchists have traditionally celebrated the glories of village and farm society. Such literary movements as Dada and surrealism have questioned science, rationality, and modern society, exulting instead in the gesture of the child, the unpredictable happening, and the immediate gratification of desires. The anarchist, dadaist, and surrealist traditions resurfaced in the May Revolt with astonishing force.

The anomic opposition to modernization is only one form of protest against poverty and exploitation. The dominant wing of the global revolutionary movement fully accepts modernization, though not through capitalism. The goal is to eliminate the capitalist, not science and technology—to base socialism on a modern, not a primitive economy. The question of whether to fight against exploitation by recapturing the spirit of traditional societies, or by transcending that spirit altogether has been a running controversy among revolutionaries ever since the Industrial Revolution started, and was especially pressing in May 1968.

Anomie is an unexpected consequence of the ability of modern societies to triumph over obstacles that seemed insurmountable a century ago. The development of science and technology has resulted in extraordinary increases in economic production and national wealth, in France and elsewhere; and though income differentials persist, it would require an excessive devotion to 19th-century Marxist texts to believe that workers in France, Britain, the United States, or any other industrial society have become increasingly miserable and impoverished in the

past hundred years. There are always enough grave instances of social injustice, no matter how productive an economy, to inspire any number of protest movements—but this cannot account for the astonishing spurt of revolutionary activity in all modern societies today.

It is not only poverty that causes protest and revolt in a modern society, but also prosperity—a fatal defect in societies whose very rationale is to create more wealth. Poverty, however lamentable may be its consequences for individuals, is a school for discipline. A man fearful of losing his job because he will cease to eat is remarkably receptive to commands from his superiors. He may rebel from time to time but even in revolt he continues to carry out orders. In contrast, prosperity gives people the illusion that they are totally independent of others, that any obstacles can be overcome by an effort of individual will. When life is easy there is no reason to obey commands and no penalty for insubordination or indiscipline. When an individual successfully defies one authority he is tempted to defy another, and another, until finally the very notion of authority becomes unbearable. Prosperity unaccompanied by a strong sense of social responsibility undermines collective effort and may undo a society.[2]

The possibility of the dissolution of social discipline is especially great when wealth increases suddenly or when opportunities open up for a previously depressed class of people. It was precisely this kind of change in the condition of life that fascinated Durkheim from the time he first noticed that suicide rates increase sharply along with the progress of civilization. It is the dream of the poor that sudden wealth (winning first prize in the national lottery, an unexpected inheritance, a fabulous marriage) will open wide the gates of paradise—and in some cases it may. But the struggle to be successful may be more satisfying than success itself, in all walks of life. It is classic that the writer or artist who finally gains recognition after many years of effort goes through a crisis of confidence, fearing that he cannot repeat his success or, worse, so disappointed with the fruits of success that going on seems pointless. Similarly, the active businessman thrives on his work, telling himself that his goal is to retire young and enjoy life, only to discover later that he is incapable of savoring an existence without the challenge of work.

When the moorings of a society give way, everything goes—social discipline, political authority, the incentive to produce, and sometimes the incentive to live. As Durkheim perceptively remarked, "one cannot remain in contemplation before a vacuum without being progressively drawn in to it."[3] He had in mind primarily suicide; lesser variations on the same theme are to "drop out" of normal society or to escape the real world through the use of drugs. This form of anomic behavior is especially noticeable among the children of parents who themselves had to work hard to succeed. The corroding effect of prosperity is most evident at one remove.

Once in a condition of anomie, the individual may react in altogether unforeseeable ways. One tendency, we have noted, is toward renunciation, withdrawal, loss of zest for life, or suicide. But, as is stressed by Durkheim in a less well-known part of his analysis, anomie gives birth to a state of exasperation and irritated lassitude, "which can, depending upon circumstances, turn the individual against himself or against others."[4] He was referring not only to the extreme cases of suicide and homicide, but also to alternating political attitudes of apathy and violent attacks upon authority, the attempt either to escape from reality or to destroy it. Apathy and terrorism are related aspects of the same continuing reaction to modernization.

The May Revolt displayed many of the characteristics of the instability characterized by Durkheim as anomie. It took place in a society that had just experienced 20 years of unprecedented economic growth and was more prosperous than at any other time of its history. Poverty and injustice had hardly been eliminated, but the workers scraping along on the minimum wage, and other unfavored groups, took no initiatives and even throughout the general strike remained primarily concerned with improvement of material conditions rather than with revolution. Those who were in the forefront of the revolutionary movement were precisely those labeled by Durkheim as prime candidates for anomie—the children of the newly prosperous middle classes. It is significant that the most raucous and undisciplined campus in the entire French university system was Nanterre, whose students are drawn from the comfortable sections of the west of Paris. It was striking that students from modest backgrounds were more interested in their own social mobility than in abstract revolution in May.[5] Also noteworthy was the interaction and in many cases interchangeability between the two related anomic tendencies of apathy and rage. Once they had lost their ties to French society, many students and others glided back and forth between a diffuse counterculture of dropouts and organized revolutionary groups. Extreme individualism blossomed into extreme collectivism only to disintegrate again upon meeting the slightest resistance. Those who wanted to escape all authority and those who wanted to impose iron discipline upon everyone else were the two marching wings of the revolutionary coalition; the ease with which many people switched from one to the other called attention to anomie as the common element of the diverse revolutionary groups.[6]

The May Revolt highlights in dramatic fashion the existence of a new dimension in the continuing crisis of participation or "entry into politics" of important social groups. Anomie was Durkheim's formulation of the problem of integrating the middle and working classes into political systems that had previously been dominated by a landed aristocracy. He saw that the working class was becoming increasingly isolated from the owning class. The life style of the capitalists was more and more remote from the reality of workday experience. A point is reached where it is beyond the capacity of workers and capitalists even to understand each other. He later broadened the meaning of anomie to include the lack of purpose in life under capitalism where individuals are engaged in the single minded pursuit of wealth.[7]

In later stages of industrialization the social force undergoing the greatest rate of expansion is the intellectual class—the scientists, engineers, technicians, administrators, and so on—who receive their training in scientific institutes and universities. This newly massive intellectual class follows in the tradition of its predecessors by making demands upon the political system. Just as hereditary monarchy was repudiated by the bourgeoisie, and parliamentary democracy questioned by the revolutionary wing of the working class, so many intellectuals find the dominant liberal synthesis inadequate. Liberalism seems to many to be a cover for the supremacy of money or numbers. Intellectuals are uncomfortable with political values that give an advantage to the wealthy and to demagogues. The life style of the intellectuals is also distinctive. In Durkheim's sense, many intellectuals are in a condition of anomie because they are increasingly isolated from the rest of society.

In addition, a certain amount of alienation is generated simply because there is a confrontation between an existing elite and a rising social group. At every stage of the modernizing process there is an anomic reaction due to the weakening of traditional values and the failure of the new values to replace them. The conflict between old and new norms must affect the intellectuals in the scientific civilization, as it affected workers in the industrial civilization. Just as the assembly line provoked irritation and revolt among workers, so the organization of social activity on the basis of scientific and rational criteria creates a feeling of "dehumanization" in many intellectuals. It is to be expected that a certain number of individuals will be left, at least during a transitional period, in a state of normlessness, or "deregulation." Those who repudiate the old and fear or disdain to accept the new display the symptoms of anomie.

That there should be an anomic reaction to modernization among intellectuals is not unusual; but the depth and intensity of this reaction—expressing itself in withdrawal and rage, political apathy and political terrorism—is startling. Why should the mass of anomie increase so sharply? At least three reasons may be suggested.

First, a large number of people break under the greater strain. In a scientific civilization there necessarily are rigorous standards of education and performance. There is no short cut to acquisition of scientific knowledge. Those who are not capable of acquiring this knowledge, or are not sufficiently motivated, fall by the wayside. Furthermore, the amount of knowledge to be mastered is increasing at an enormous rate, and with it the pressure on students. While examinations and student anxiety have always existed, in the past there have also been many ways of getting ahead on the basis of a modest education. When the major avenue to success is the university, those who cannot meet its demands are at a greater disadvantage than ever before.

Secondly, the productivity of the scientific civilization makes it possible to carry a marginal element within the society. Technically, it is feasible for any advanced industrial society to support a large class of dropouts and drones—provided that this class remains within manageable bounds and does not deprive the productive classes of their motivation to work. Many young people are able to enjoy—or endure—a life of anomie with the bemused support of their parents. Poverty is a highly effective social technique for imposing limits on anomie; prosperity, however, creates the conditions for the existence of a large alienated group.

Freedom itself may be a major cause of anomie in the intellectual class. Modernization makes possible a great expansion of individual freedom. As Durkheim points out, primitive man is merely an extension of the group, hemmed in by custom and taboo. He has no mind of his own. Modern man enjoys greater autonomy and is free to think as he pleases.[8] But the heavy responsibility of making a free choice can be utterly demoralizing, leading either to a desire to escape or to revolt. In authoritarian regimes the masses and the intellectuals can be conditioned, mobilized, and commanded. Problems may not actually be solved, but the over-pressured individual is relieved of the burden of choice.

The disorder inherent in liberalism and the scientific civilization is eliminated. Anomic groups serve as pile drivers, splitting the foundations of the liberal state. Authoritarian elites pick up the pieces and impose the discipline that so many desperately crave.

In the scientific civilization what Durkheim called the "regulator" is more essential than ever. The intellectual must be imaginative, creative, and even enthusiastic if the collective scientific enterprise is to flourish. Doubts, hesitation, and withdrawal will block the system. The political integration of the intellectual class may well prove to be inherently more difficult than was the case for the capitalist and working classes. The landed aristocrats and capitalists were numerically weak in relation to the rest of the society and could be outmaneuvered in politics. But while the working class had the advantage of numbers, its function within the economy was to carry out orders rather than to give them, to obey rather than to innovate. As a class the workers were unable to direct themselves, let alone the rest of society. The intellectual class is not subject to the same handicaps. Unlike the old aristocrats or the capitalists, intellectuals are a large social force. Unlike the workers, they have ability, inculcated by their social function, to direct and command.

The question may be raised whether parliamentary democracies like France can cope with the entry of the intellectuals as a massive social force into the political system. Wherever freedom of criticism is permitted, opportunities for exploiting tensions are almost unlimited. In a climate of freedom the intellectuals are even more likely to rebel than the old working class, and more likely to withdraw their cooperation from the establishment. The parliamentary democracies that experienced great difficulty in securing the integration of the working class probably will continue to be unstable as they move into the scientific civilization and deal with the intellectual class. Even relatively consensual parliamentary democracies may have difficulty in adjusting to these new circumstances. It may well be that integration of the intellectuals into the political system can be accomplished only by an authoritarian elite (whether of the left or right) in order to eliminate that anarchy which is incompatible with the continued functioning and further development of a scientific civilization.

We are living through an era of reversal of values and of social relationships perhaps best comprehended through Hegel's parable of the master and the servant in which the servant, compelled to live by his work, becomes self-reliant, while the master comes to depend completely on the servant. Thus, capitalists may be overturned by proletarians, any dominant group may be subverted by any dominated group, the most contradictory and unforeseen developments may occur in the unfolding of history.

Most social scientists postulate that science is sweeping all before it, thrusting aside magic, superstition, and religion, bringing about the rationalization of social behavior, laying the basis for modern industry, unprecedented prosperity, and the full flowering of human freedom. In the model modern society it is assumed that the ideological conflict of early industrialization will be transcended and replaced by pragmatic negotiation among claimant groups for larger shares of ever increasing national revenues. The long-term trend would thus be toward stability, prosperity, and freedom. But, through an irony of history, mastery can be converted into dependence, political trends can be reversed. A complex economy can be paralyzed by the determined opposition of relatively few people in key positions. An abundance of material wealth can lead to dissipation of individual motivation and disintegration of social ties. The privilege of exercising a free choice can turn into an agony. From stability may come instability, from prosperity may come misery, and out of freedom may come a new and fearful discipline.

## Notes

1. For Durkheim's views on anomie: *De la division du travail social* (P.U.F.,1967, 8th ed.), pp. 343–365; and *Le suicide* (P.U.F., 1960), pp. 264–311. An excellent contemporary interpretation is in

Robert M. MacIver, *The Ramparts We Guard* (New York: Macmillan, 1950).

2. On the connection between poverty-wealth and discipline-anomie, see the suggestive comments of Durkheim in *Le suicide*, p. 282. Note also Raoul Vaneigem's call for a revolt against prosperity, in *Traité de savoir-vivre à l'usage des jeunes générations* (Gallimard, 1967), pp. 73, 88–91.

3. E. Durkheim, *Le suicide*, p. 316.

4. Durkheim quote on the link between suicide and homicide, *Le suicide*, p. 322. See also, ibid., p. 408, and on the correspondence between suicide-homicide and apathy-terrorism, ibid., p. 424.

5. That revolutionary students came in large proportion from "comfortable" situations is remarked by R. Boudon, "Quelques causes de la révolte estudiantine," *La Table Ronde* (Dec. 1968–Jan. 1969), p. 180. Also generously represented are Jews—corresponding to Durkheim's category of previously depressed groups suddenly enjoying new opportunities for advancement. Alain Krivine has publicly charged that the French police are now using Vichy records because so many Jews are in the New Left.

6. We have previously commented on the way in which surrealists suddenly became Communists or Trotskyists, and just as suddenly returned to anarchism. Note the recent overnight conversion of a leading American activist to an Eastern religion. In a press conference reported by the *New York Times* (May 6, 1973) one of the "Chicago 7" defendants, Rennie Davis, relates that during a flight to Paris on his way to meet Vietcong negotiators in January 1973 he heard about a 15-year-old guru in India called Maharaj Ji. His immediate reaction was skepticism and even hostility. But he went to India and after eight days "received knowledge" from a disciple of the guru, whom he now calls "the one perfect master" on earth at this time. Although at first uncomfortable with the boy (who was about 10 years old at the time of the Chicago riots), Mr. Davis told the press conference that he now loved him. "I would cross the planet on my hands and knees," he said, "to touch his toe." The guru has been under investigation by the government of India on the charge of smuggling money, jewels and watches (all gifts from devoted followers) into the country.

7. For general treatments of the "entry into politics" problem, see T. H. Marshall, *Citizenship and Social Class* (Cambridge: Cambridge University Press, 1950); S. M. Lipset, *Political Man* (Garden City, N.Y.: Doubleday Publishing, 1960); Reinhard Bendix, *Nation-Building and Citizenship* (New York: John Wiley & Sons, 1964); Barrington Moore, Jr., *Social Origins of Dictatorship and Democracy* (Boston: Beacon Press, 1967); and J. G. LaPalombara and M. Weiner, ed., *Political Parties and Political Development* (Princeton: Princeton University Press, 1966).

8. For Durkheim's views on freedom in primitive and modern societies, Cf. *De la division du travail social*, pp. 35–102. See also Alvin Toffler, *Future Shock* (New York: Bantam Books, 1971), pp. 98, 319–322.

# SELECTED BIBLIOGRAPHY

## Part One Comparative Analysis: Method and Concepts

### Comparing Political Systems

ALMOND, GABRIEL A., and POWELL, BINGHAM G. *Comparative Politics: System, Process, and Policy.* 2d ed. Boston: Little, Brown, 1978.

———, eds. *Comparative Politics Today: A World View.* 4th ed. Glenview, IL: Scott, Foresman, 1988.

BILL, JAMES, and HARDGRAVE, ROBERT. *Comparative Politics: The Quest for Theory.* Columbus, OH: Merrill, 1973.

BROWN, BERNARD E. *New Directions in Comparative Politics.* London: Asia Publishers, 1962.

CHILCOTE, RONALD H. *Theories of Comparative Politics: The Search for a Paradigm.* Boulder, CO: Westview, 1981.

EASTON, DAVID. *A Framework for Political Analysis.* Englewood Cliffs, NJ: Prentice-Hall, 1965.

ECKSTEIN, HARRY, and APTER, DAVID E. eds. *Comparative Politics: A Reader.* New York: Free Press, 1963.

FRIEDRICH, CARL J. *Man and His Government: An Empirical Theory of Politics.* New York: McGraw-Hill, 1963.

HEMPEL, CARL G. *Aspects of Scientific Explanation.* New York: Free Press, 1970.

HOLT, ROBERT T., and TURNER, JOHN E. eds. *The Methodology of Comparative Research.* New York: Free Press, 1970.

KUHN, THOMAS S. *The Structure of Scientific Revolutions.* 2d ed. Chicago: University of Chicago Press, 1970.

LANDAU, MARTIN. *Political Theory and Political Science.* Atlantic Highlands, NJ: Humanities Press, 1972.

LAPALOMBARA, JOSEPH. *Politics Within Nations.* Englewood Cliffs, NJ: Prentice-Hall, 1974.

MACRIDIS, ROY C. *The Study of Comparative Government.* New York: Random House, 1955.

———. *Modern Political Regimes: Patterns and Institutions.* Boston: Little, Brown, 1986.

MERKL, PETER H. *Modern Comparative Politics.* 2d ed. New York: Holt, Rinehart & Winston, 1977.

MERRITT, RICHARD L. *Systematic Approaches to Comparative Politics.* Skokie, IL: Rand McNally, 1970.

NAGEL, ERNEST. *The Structure of Science.* New York: Harcourt Brace Jovanovich, 1961.

POPPER, KARL R. *Conjectures and Refutations: The Growth of Scientific Knowledge.* New York: Harper & Row, 1968.

PRZEWORSKI, ADAM, and TEUNE, HENRY. *The Logic of Comparative Social Inquiry.* New York: Wiley, 1970.

SARTORI, GIOVANNI. *Social Science Concepts.* Newbury Park, CA: Sage, 1985.

WEBER, MAX. "Politics as a Vocation" and "Science as a Vocation," in *From Max Weber,* ed. H. H. Gerth and C. W. Mills. New York: Oxford University Press, 1958, pp. 77–156.

WIARDA, HOWARD J., ed. *New Directions in Comparative Politics.* Boulder, CO: Westview, 1985.

### The State and Its Context

ALMOND, GABRIEL A. "The Return to the State," *American Political Science Review,* vol. 82, no. 3 (September 1988): 853–874.

BENDIX, REINHARD. *Nation-Building and Citizenship.* New York: Wiley, 1964.

CARNOY, MARTIN. *The State and Political Theory.* Princeton, NJ: Princeton University Press, 1984.

EASTON, DAVID. "The Political System Besieged by the State," *Political Theory,* vol. 9, no. 3 (August 1981): 303–325.

EVANS, PETER, and SKOCPOL, THEDA. eds. *Bringing the State Back In.* New York: Cambridge University Press, 1985.

KRASNER, STEPHEN. "Approaches to the State," *Comparative Politics,* vol. 16, no. 2 (January 1984): 223–246.

MACIVER, ROBERT M. *The Web of Government.* New York: Macmillan, 1947.

MANN, MICHAEL. *The Sources of Social Power: A History of Power.* New York: Cambridge University Press, 1986.

MIGDAL, JOEL S. *Strong Societies and Weak States: State-Society Relations and State Capabilities in the Third World.* Princeton, NJ: Princeton University Press, 1988.

MILIBAND, RALPH. *Class Power and State Structure.* London: Verso Editions, 1978.

NORDLINGER, ERIC A. *On the Autonomy of the Democratic State.* Cambridge, MA: Harvard University Press, 1981.

POULANTZAS, NICOS. *State, Power, Socialism.* London: Verso Editions, 1980.

TILLY, CHARLES, ed. *The Formation of National States in Europe.* Princeton, NJ: Princeton University Press, 1975.

# Part Two Contemporary Political Regimes

## Democracies

ALMOND, GABRIEL A., and VERBA, SIDNEY. *The Civic Culture.* Boston: Little, Brown, 1963.

_____, eds. *The Civic Culture Revisited.* Boston: Little, Brown, 1980.

ARON, RAYMOND. *Democracy and Totalitarianism.* New York: Praeger, 1968.

BENJAMIN, ROGER, and ELKIN, STEPHEN L. eds. *The Democratic State.* Lawrence, KA: University Press of Kansas, 1985.

CROZIER, MICHEL, HUNTINGTON, S. P., and WATANUKI, JOJU. *The Crisis of Democracy.* New York: New York University Press, 1975.

DAHL, ROBERT A. *Polyarchy: Participation and Opposition.* New Haven, CT: Yale University Press, 1971.

_____. *A Preface to Democratic Theory.* Chicago: University of Chicago Press, 1956.

_____. *A Preface to Economic Democracy.* Berkeley: University of California Press, 1985.

DIAMOND, LARRY et al. *Democracy in Developing Countries.* 4 vols. Boulder, CO: Lynne Rienner, 1988.

DOGAN, MATTEI. *Comparing Pluralist Democracies: Strains on Legitimacy.* Boulder, CO: Westview, 1988.

DOWNS, ANTHONY. *An Economic Theory of Democracy.* New York: Harper & Row, 1957.

ECKSTEIN, HARRY. *Division and Cohesion in a Democracy: A Study of Norway.* Princeton, NJ: Princeton University Press, 1966.

FRIEDRICH, CARL J. *Constitutional Government and Democracy.* 4th ed. Waltham, MA: Blaisdell, 1968.

LIJPHART, AREND. *Democracies: Patterns of Majoritarian and Consensus Government in Twenty-One Countries.* New Haven, CT: Yale University Press, 1984.

LINZ, JUAN, and STEPAN, ALFRED. eds. *The Breakdown of Democratic Regimes.* 2 vols. Baltimore: The Johns Hopkins University Press, 1978.

MOORE, BARRINGTON, Jr. *Social Origins of Dictatorship and Democracy: Lord and Peasant in the Making of the Modern World.* Boston: Beacon Press, 1966.

POPPER, KARL R. *The Open Society and Its Enemies.* 2 vols., 5th ed. London: Routledge & Kegan Paul, 1945.

POWELL, G. BINGHAM. *Comparing Democracies: Power, Stability and Violence.* Cambridge, MA: Harvard University Press, 1982.

PRZEWORSKI, ADAM. *Capitalism and Social Democracy.* New York: Cambridge University Press, 1985.

RAWLS, JOHN. *A Theory of Justice.* Cambridge, MA: Harvard University Press, 1971.

SARTORI, GIOVANNI. *Theory of Democracy Revisited.* 2 vols. Chatham, NJ: Chatham, 1987.

SCHUMPETER, JOSEPH A. *Capitalism, Socialism, and Democracy.* 3rd ed. New York: Harper & Row, 1950.

## Authoritarianism: Old, New, Transitional

ALLEN, WILLIAM S. *The Nazi Seizure of Power: The Experience of a Single German Town, 1930–35.* 2d ed. New York: F. Watts, 1984.

ARENDT, HANNAH. *The Origins of Totalitarianism,* 2d ed. New York: Harcourt Brace Jovanovich, 1973.

BRACHER, KARL D. *The German Dictatorship: The Origin, Structure and Effects of National Socialism.* New York: Praeger, 1970.

COLLIER, DAVID, ed. *The New Authoritarianism in Latin America.* Princeton, NJ: Princeton University Press, 1979.

FRIEDRICH, CARL J., and BRZEZINSKI, ZBIGNIEW. *Totalitarian Dictatorship and Autocracy.* 2d ed. New York: Praeger, 1969.

FRIEDRICH, CARL J., CURTIS, MICHAEL, and BARBER, BENJAMIN R. *Totalitarianism in Perspective: Three Views.* New York: Praeger, 1969.

GREGOR, JAMES A. *Italian Fascism and Developmental Dictatorship.* Princeton, NJ: Princeton University Press, 1979.

HUNTINGTON, SAMUEL P., and MOORE, CLEMENT H. *Authoritarian Politics in Modern Society.* New York: Basic Books, 1970.

JACKSON, ROBERT H., and ROSBERG, CARL. *Personal Rule in Black Africa: Prince, Autocrat, Prophet, Tyrant.* Berkeley: University of California Press, 1981.

KIRKPATRICK, JEANE. *Dictatorship and Double Standards.* New York: Simon & Schuster, 1982.

LAQUEUR, WALTER, ed. *Fascism: A Reader's Guide.* Berkeley: University of California Press, 1977.

NEUMANN, FRANZ L. *Behemoth: The Structure and Practice of National Socialism.* New York: Octagon, 1963.

_____. *The Democratic and the Authoritarian State.* New York: Free Press, 1957.

O'DONNELL, GUILLERMO, SCHMITTER, PHILIPPE, and WHITEHEAD, LAURENCE. eds. *Transitions from Authoritarian Rule.* 4 vols. Baltimore: The Johns Hopkins University Press, 1986.

PERLMUTTER, AMOS. *Modern Authoritarianism: A Comparative Institutional Analysis.* New Haven, CT: Yale University Press, 1981.

STRAUSS, LEO. *On Tyranny.* Rev. ed. Ithaca, NY: Cornell University Press, 1968.

WIARDA, HOWARD J. *Dictatorship and Development: The Methods of Control in Trujillo's Dominican Republic.* Gainesville: University of Florida Press, 1968.

## Communist Regimes

BIALER, SERWYN. *Stalin's Successors: Leadership, Stability and Change in the Soviet Union.* New York: Cambridge University Press, 1980.

_____. *The Soviet Paradox: External Expansion, Internal Decline.* New York: Random House, 1987.

BRZEZINSKI, ZBIGNIEW. *The Grand Failure: Communism's Terminal Crisis.* New York: Scribner, 1989.

CARRÈRE D'ENCAUSSE, HELÈNE. *Confiscated Power: How Soviet Russia Really Works.* New York: Harper & Row, 1982.

CONQUEST, ROBERT. *The Harvest of Sorrow: Soviet Collectivization and the Terror-Famine.* New York: Oxford University Press, 1986.

DOMINGUEZ, JORGE I. *Cuba: Order and Revolution.* Cambridge, MA: Harvard University Press, 1978.

HAZARD, JOHN. *The Soviet System of Government.* 5th ed. Chicago: University of Chicago Press, 1980.

HILL, RONALD, and FRANK, PETER. *The Soviet Communist Party.* 3d ed. Winchester, MA: Unwin Hyman, 1986.

HOUGH, JERRY F. *Russia and the West: Gorbachev and the Politics of Reform.* New York: Simon & Schuster, 1988.

HOUGH, JERRY F., and FAINSOD, MERLE. *How the Soviet Union is Governed.* Cambridge, MA: Harvard University Press, 1979.

PYE, LUCIAN W. *The Dynamics of Chinese Politics.* Cambridge, MA: Oelgeschlager, Gunn & Hain, 1981.

SCHAPIRO, LEONARD. *Totalitarianism.* London: Macmillan, 1983.

SKILLING, H. GORDON, and GRIFFITHS, FRANKLIN. eds. *Interest Groups in Soviet Politics.* Princeton, NJ: Princeton University Press, 1971.

SMITH, TONY. *Thinking Like a Communist: The State and Legitimacy in the Soviet Union, China, and Cuba.* New York: Norton, 1987.

TUCKER, ROBERT C. *Political Culture and Leadership in Soviet Russia.* New York: Norton, 1987.

ULAM, ADAM. *The Bolsheviks: The Intellectual and Political History of the Triumph of Communism in Russia.* New York: Macmillan, 1965.

_____. *Stalin: The Man and His Era.* New York: Viking Press, 1973.

WALLER, DEREK J. *The Government and Politics of the People's Republic of China.* 3d ed. New York: New York University Press, 1981.

WHITE, STEPHEN. *Political Culture and Soviet Politics.* New York: Macmillan, 1979.

WHITE, STEPHEN, and NELSON, DANIEL. *Communist Legislatures in Comparative Perspective.* Albany: State University of New York Press, 1982.

# Part Three Political Dynamics and Processes

## Political Authority

BERLE, ADOLF A. *Power.* New York: Harcourt Brace Jovanovich, 1969.

BUCHANAN, JAMES M., and TULLOCK, G. *The Calculus of Consent: Logical Foundations of Constitutional Democracy.* Ann Arbor: University of Michigan Press, 1962.

DAHL, ROBERT A., ed. *Regimes and Oppositions.* New Haven, CT: Yale University Press, 1973.

DEUTSCH, KARL W. *The Nerves of Government.* New York: Free Press, 1963.

INGLEHART, RONALD. *The Silent Revolution: Changing Values and Political Styles Among Western Publics.* Princeton, NJ: Princeton University Press, 1977.

KIRKPATRICK, JEANE J. *Legitimacy and Force.* New Brunswick, NJ: Transaction Books, 1988.

MACRIDIS, ROY C. *Contemporary Political Ideologies.* 4th ed. Glenview, IL: Scott, Foresman, 1989.

MOSCA, GAETANO. *The Ruling Class.* New York: McGraw-Hill, 1939.

PYE, LUCIAN, and VERBA, SIDNEY. eds. *Political Culture and Political Development.* Princeton, NJ: Princeton University Press, 1965.

LIPSET, SEYMOUR M. *Political Man: The Social Bases of Politics.* Rev. ed. Baltimore: The Johns Hopkins University Press, 1981.

MACRIDIS, ROY C., ed. *Political Parties: Contemporary Trends and Ideas.* New York: Harper & Row, 1967.

MICHELS, ROBERTO. *Political Parties: A Sociological Study of the Oligarchic Tendencies of Modern Democracy.* New York: Free Press, 1958.

NEUMANN, SIGMUND, ed. *Modern Political Parties.* Chicago: University of Chicago Press, 1954.

OSTROGORSKI, MOISEI. *Democracy and the Organization of Political Parties.* 2 vols. Garden City, NY: Doubleday, 1964.

RAE, DOUGLAS W. *The Political Consequences of Electoral Laws.* New Haven, CT: Yale University Press, 1967.

ROSE, RICHARD. *Do Parties Make a Difference?* 2d ed. Chatham, NJ: Chatham House, 1984.

SARTORI, GIOVANNI. *Parties and Party Systems.* New York: Cambridge University Press, 1976.

TRUMAN, DAVID. *The Governmental Process.* New York: Knopf, 1951.

## Groups, Parties, and Elections

BERGER, SUZANNE, ed. *Organized Interests in Western Europe.* New York: Cambridge University Press, 1983.

BROWN, BERNARD E., ed. *Eurocommunism and Eurosocialism: The Left Confronts Modernity.* New York: Irvington, 1978.

BUTLER, DAVID et al. *Democracy at the Polls.* Washington, DC: American Enterprise Institute, 1981.

DUVERGER, MAURICE. *Political Parties.* 3rd ed. London: Methuen, 1969.

EHRMANN, HENRY W., ed. *Interest Groups on Four Continents.* Pittsburgh: University of Pittsburgh Press, 1958.

EPSTEIN, LEON. *Political Parties in Western Democracies.* New Brunswick, NJ: Transaction Books, 1980.

HIRSCHMAN, ALBERT O. *Exit, Voice, and Loyalty.* Cambridge, MA: Harvard University Press, 1970.

LAPALOMBARA, JOSEPH, and WEINER, MYRON. eds. *Political Parties and Political Development.* Princeton, NJ: Princeton University Press, 1966.

LEISERSON, AVERY. *Parties and Politics: An Institutional and Behavioral Approach.* New York: Knopf, 1958.

## Political Institutions

ABERBACH, JOEL D., PUTNAM, ROBERT D., and ROCKMAN, BERT A. *Bureaucrats and Politicians in Western Democracies.* Cambridge, MA: Harvard University Press, 1981.

ARMSTRONG, JOHN A. *The European Administrative Elite.* Princeton, NJ: Princeton University Press, 1973.

BARNARD, CHESTER I. *The Functions of the Executive.* Cambridge, MA: Harvard University Press, 1968.

BLONDEL, JEAN. *The Organization of Governments: A Comparative Study of Governmental Structures.* Newbury Park, CA: Sage, 1982.

_____. *Government Ministers in the Contemporary World.* Newbury Park, CA: Sage, 1985.

_____. *Political Leadership: Towards a General Analysis.* Newbury Park, CA: Sage, 1987.

CROZIER, MICHEL. *The Bureaucratic Phenomenon.* Chicago: University of Chicago Press, 1964.

DOGAN, MATTEI, ed. *The Mandarins of Western Europe: The Political Role of Top Civil Servants.* New York: Wiley, 1975.

HIRSCH, HERBERT, and HANCOCK, M. DONALD. eds. *Comparative Legislative Systems: A Reader in Theory and Research.* New York: Free Press, 1971.

KORNBERG, ALLAN, ed. *Legislatures in Comparative Perspective.* New York: McKay, 1973.

LAPALOMBARA, JOSEPH, ed. *Bureaucracy and Political Development.* Princeton, NJ: Princeton University Press, 1963.

LOEWENBERG, GERHARD, ed. *Modern Parliaments: Change or Decline?* Chicago: University of Chicago Press, 1971.

LOEWENBERG, GERHARD, and PATTERSON, SAMUEL C. *Comparing Legislatures.* Boston: Little, Brown, 1979.

PRESTHUS, ROBERT V. *Elites in the Policy Process.* New York: Cambridge University Press, 1974.

ROSE, RICHARD, and SULEIMAN, EZRA. eds. *Presidents and Prime Ministers.* Washington, DC: American Enterprise Institute, 1980.

SIFFIN, WILLIAM J., ed. *Towards the Comparative Study of Public Administration.* Bloomington: Indiana University Press, 1957.

WHEARE, K. C. *Legislatures.* London: Oxford University Press, 1963.

WILNER, RUTH ANN. *The Spellbinders: Charismatic Political Leadership.* New Haven, CT: Yale University Press, 1984.

## Political Performance

ASHFORD, DOUGLAS. *Emergence of the Welfare State.* Oxford: Blackwell, 1986.

BATES, ROBERT H. *Markets and States in Tropical Africa.* Berkeley: University of California Press, 1981.

BENJAMIN, ROGER W. *The Limits of Political Collective Goods and Political Change in Postindustrial Societies.* Chicago: University of Chicago Press, 1980.

ECKSTEIN, HARRY. *The Evaluation of Political Performance.* Newbury Park, CA: Sage, 1971.

EISENSTADT, SAMUEL N., and AHLMEIR, ORA. *Welfare State and Its Aftermath.* London: Croom Helm, 1985.

ENLOE, CYNTHIA. *The Politics of Pollution in a Comparative Perspective.* New York: McKay, 1975.

GROTH, ALEXANDER J. *Public Policy Across Nations: Social Welfare in Industrial Settings.* Greenwich, CT: JAI Press, 1985.

HECLO, HUGH. *Modern Social Politics in Britain and Sweden.* New Haven, CT: Yale University Press, 1974.

HEIDENHEIMER, ARNOLD J., HECLO, HUGH, and ADAMS, CAROLYN TEICH. *Comparative Public Policy: The Politics of Social Choice in Europe and America.* 2d ed. New York: St. Martin's Press, 1983.

HIRSCHMAN, ALBERT O. *Shifting Involvements: Private Interest and Public Action.* Princeton, NJ: Princeton University Press, 1982.

JACKMAN, ROBERT W. *Politics and Social Equality: A Comparative Analysis.* New York: Wiley, 1975.

KATZENSTEIN, PETER. *Corporatism and Change: Austria, Switzerland, and the Politics of Industry.* Ithaca, NY: Cornell University Press, 1984.

_____. *Small States in World Markets: Industrial Policy in Europe.* Ithaca, NY: Cornell University Press, 1985.

KEOHANE, ROBERT. *After Hegemony: Cooperation and Discord in the World Political Economy.* Princeton, NJ: Princeton University Press, 1984.

LINDBLOM, CHARLES. *Politics and Markets.* New York: Basic Books, 1977.

WILENSKY, HAROLD. *The Welfare State and Equality.* Berkeley: University of California Press, 1975.

# Part Four Political Change

# Modernization and Development

ALMOND, GABRIEL A., and COLEMAN, JAMES S. eds. *The Politics of the Developing Areas.* Princeton, NJ: Princeton University Press, 1960.

APTER, DAVID E. *The Politics of Modernization.* Chicago: University of Chicago Press, 1965.

_____. *Rethinking Development: Modernization, Dependency and Postmodern Politics.* Newbury Park, CA: Sage, 1987.

BEER, SAMUEL H. *Modern Political Development.* New York: Random House, 1974.

BELL, DANIEL. *The Coming of Post-Industrial Society.* New York: Basic Books, 1973.

BINDER, LEONARD et al. *Crises and Sequences in Political Development.* Princeton, NJ: Princeton University Press, 1971.

BLACK, CYRIL E. *The Dynamics of Modernization: A Study in Comparative History.* New York: Harper & Row, 1966.

_____, ed. *Comparative Modernization: A Reader.* New York: Free Press, 1976.

EISENSTADT, SAMUEL N. *Modernization: Protest and Change.* Englewood Cliffs, NJ: Prentice-Hall, 1966.

FINKLE, JASON L., and GABLE, RICHARD W. eds. *Political Development and Social Change.* 2d ed. New York: Wiley, 1971.

HOROWITZ, IRVING L. *Beyond Empire and Revolution: Militarization and Consolidation in the Third World.* Princeton, NJ: Princeton University Press, 1972.

HUNTINGTON, SAMUEL P. *Political Order in Changing Societies.* New Haven, CT: Yale University Press, 1972.

HUNTINGTON, SAMUEL P., and NELSON, JOAN M. *No Easy Choice: Political Participation in Developing Countries.* Cambridge, MA: Harvard University Press, 1976.

LIPSET, SEYMOUR M. *The First New Nation: The United States in Historical and Comparative Perspective.* New York: Basic Books, 1963.

OLSON, MANCUR. *Rise and Decline of Nations: Economic Growth, Stagflation, and Social Rigidities.* New Haven, CT: Yale University Press, 1982.

ORGANSKI, A. F. K. *The Stages of Political Development.* New York: Knopf, 1965.

RUSTOW, DANKWART A. *A World of Nations: Problems of Political Modernization.* Washington, DC: The Brookings Institution, 1967.

WEINER, MYRON, and HUNTINGTON, SAMUEL P. eds. *Understanding Political Development: An Analytic Study.* Boston: Little, Brown, 1987.

WIARDA, HOWARD J. *Corporatism and National Development in Latin America.* Boulder, CO: Westview, 1981.

YOUNG, CRAWFORD. *Ideology and Development.* New Haven, CT: Yale University Press, 1982.

## Dependency

AMIN, SAMIR. *Accumulation on a World Scale.* New York: Monthly Review Press, 1974.

COCKCROFT, JAMES D., ed. *Dependence and Underdevelopment.* New York: Anchor Books, 1972.

EVANS, PETER. *Dependent Development: The Alliance of Multinational, State, and Local Capital in Brazil.* Princeton, NJ: Princeton University Press, 1979.

FANON, FRANTZ. *The Wretched of the Earth.* New York: Grove Press, 1966.

FRANK, ANDRÉ GUNDAR. *Crisis in the World Economy.* New York: Holmes & Meier, 1981.

_____. *Dependent Accumulation and Underdevelopment.* New York: Monthly Review Press, 1979.

_____. *Lumpenbourgeoisie, Lumpendevelopment: Dependence, Class, and Politics in Latin America.* New York: Monthly Review Press, 1972.

O'DONNELL, GUILLERMO. *Modernization and Bureaucratic Authoritarianism: Studies in South American Politics.* Berkeley: University of California Press, 1973.

WALLERSTEIN, IMMANUEL. *The Capitalist World-Economy.* New York: Cambridge University Press, 1979.

_____. *The Modern World-System.* 2 vols. New York: Academic Press, 1974 and 1980.

_____. *The Politics of the World Economy.* New York: Cambridge University Press, 1984.

## Revolution

APTER, DAVID. *Against the State: Politics and Social Protest in Japan.* Cambridge, MA: Harvard University Press, 1984.

ARENDT, HANNAH. *On Revolution.* New York: Viking Press, 1963.

BRINTON, CRANE. *The Anatomy of Revolution.* Rev. ed. Englewood Cliffs, NJ: Prentice-Hall, 1952.

DUNN, JOHN. *Modern Revolutions.* New York: Cambridge University Press, 1972.

GURR, TED ROBERT. *Why Men Rebel.* Princeton, NJ: Princeton University Press, 1970.

JOHNSON, CHALMERS. *Revolutionary Change.* 2d ed. Stanford, CA: Stanford University Press, 1982.

MIGDAL, JOEL. *Peasants, Politics, and Revolutions: Pressures Toward Political and Social Change in the Third World.* Princeton, NJ: Princeton University Press, 1974.

SCOTT, JAMES. *Weapons of the Weak: Everyday Forms of Peasant Rebellion.* New Haven, CT: Yale University Press, 1985.

SKOCPOL, THEDA. *States and Social Revolution.* New York: Cambridge University Press, 1979.

DE TOCQUEVILLE, ALEXIS. *The Old Regime and the French Revolution.* Garden City, NY: Anchor, 1955.